JOHN CONSTANTINE, HELLBLAZER: THE FEAR MACHINE

JAMIE DELANO WRITER

MARK BUCKINGHAM RICHARD PIERS RAYNER
MIKE HOFFMAN ALFREDO ALCALA ARTISTS

LOVERN KINDZIERSKI COLORIST

ELITTA FELL TODD KLEIN LETTERERS

DAVID FINCH COVER ART

DAVE MCKEAN KENT WILLIAMS ORIGINAL SERIES COVERS

Karen Berger Editor – Original Series
Art Young Associate Editor – Original Series
Scott Nybakken Editor
Robbin Brosterman Design Director – Books
Robbie Biederman Publication Design

Shelly Bond Executive Editor – Vertigo
Hank Kanalz Senior VP – Vertigo & Integrated Publishing

Diane Nelson President
Dan DiDio and Jim Lee Co-Publishers
Geoff Johns Chief Creative Officer
Amit Desai Senior VP – Marketing & Franchise Management
Amy Genkins Senior VP – Business & Legal Affairs
Nairi Gardiner Senior VP – Finance
Jeff Boison VP – Publishing Planning
Mark Chiarello VP – Art Direction & Design
John Cunningham VP – Marketing
Terri Cunningham VP – Editorial Administration
Larry Ganem VP – Talent Relations & Services
Alison Gill Senior VP – Manufacturing & Operations
Jay Kogan VP – Business & Legal Affairs, Publishing
Jack Mahan VP – Business Affairs, Talent
Nick Napolitano VP – Manufacturing Administration
Sue Pohja VP – Book Sales
Fred Ruiz VP – Manufacturing Operations
Courtney Simmons Senior VP – Publicity
Bob Wayne Senior VP – Sales

Cover color by Jeromy Cox

JOHN CONSTANTINE, HELLBLAZER: THE FEAR MACHINE

Published by DC Comics. Cover and compilation

DC Comics, 1700 Broadway, New York, NY 10019
A Warner Bros. Entertainment Company
Printed in the USA. Third Printing.
ISBN: 978-1-4012-3519-2

Library of Congress Cataloging-in-Publication Data

Delano, Jamie.
Hellblazer. Vol. 3, The fear machine / Jamie Delano, Mark Buckingham, Richard Piers Rayner, Mike Hoffman, Alfredo Alcala.
pages cm
"Originally published in single magazine form as Hellblazer 14-22."
ISBN 978-1-4012-3519-2
1. Constantine, John (Fictitious character)—Comic books, strips, etc. 2. Graphic novels. I. Buckingham, Mark. II. Rayner, Richard Piers. III. Hoffman, Mike. IV. Alcala, Alfredo P. V. Title. VI. Title: Fear machine.
PN6728.H383D36 2013
741.5'973—dc23

2013012656

Sustainable Forestry Initiative
Certified Sourcing
www.sfiprogram.org
SFI-01042
APPLIES TO TEXT STOCK ONLY

THE FEAR MACHINE

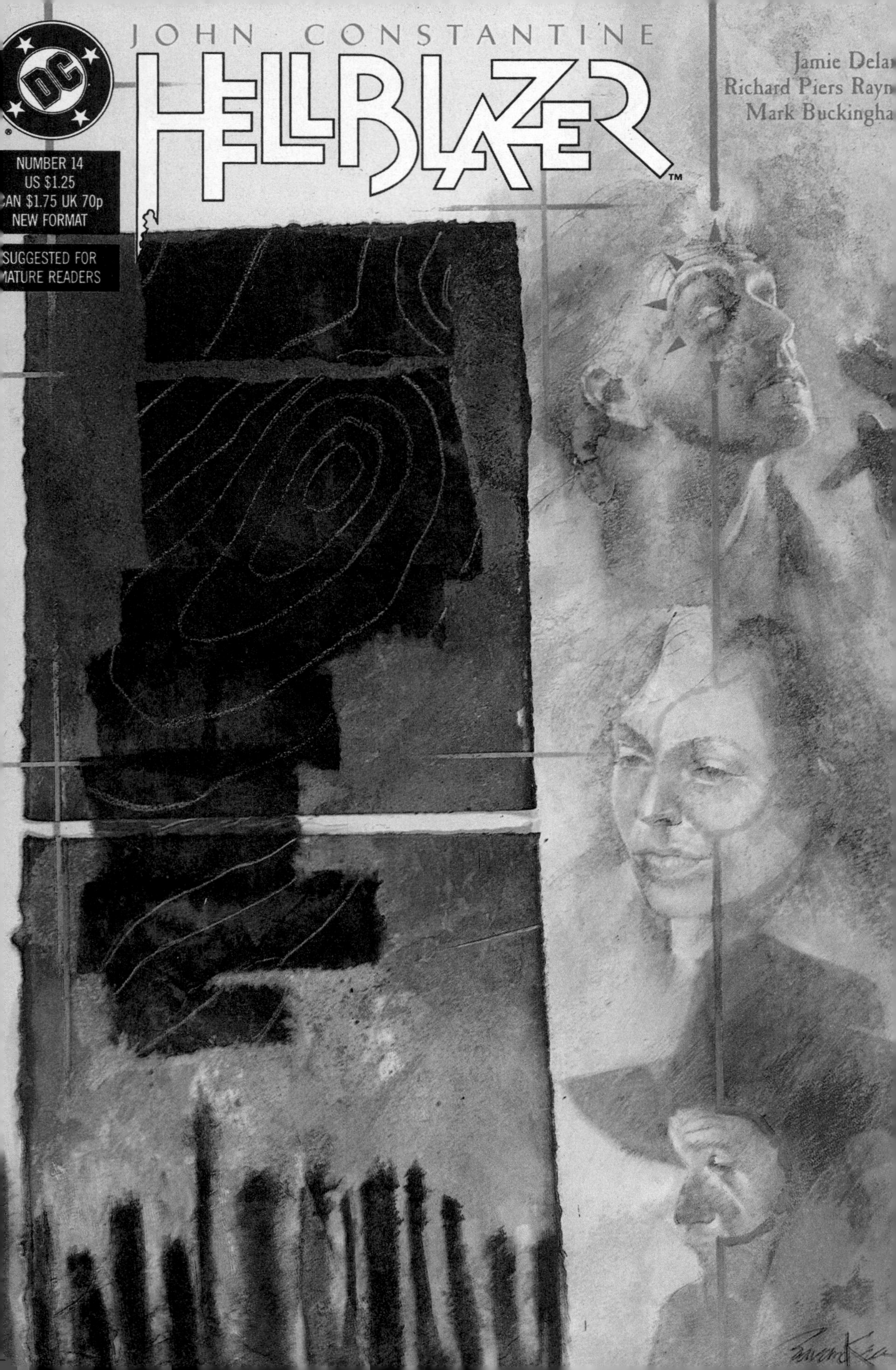
DC
JOHN CONSTANTINE
HELLBLAZER™
NUMBER 14
US $1.25
AN $1.75 UK 70p
NEW FORMAT
SUGGESTED FOR
ATURE READERS
Jamie Dela
Richard Piers Rayn
Mark Buckingha

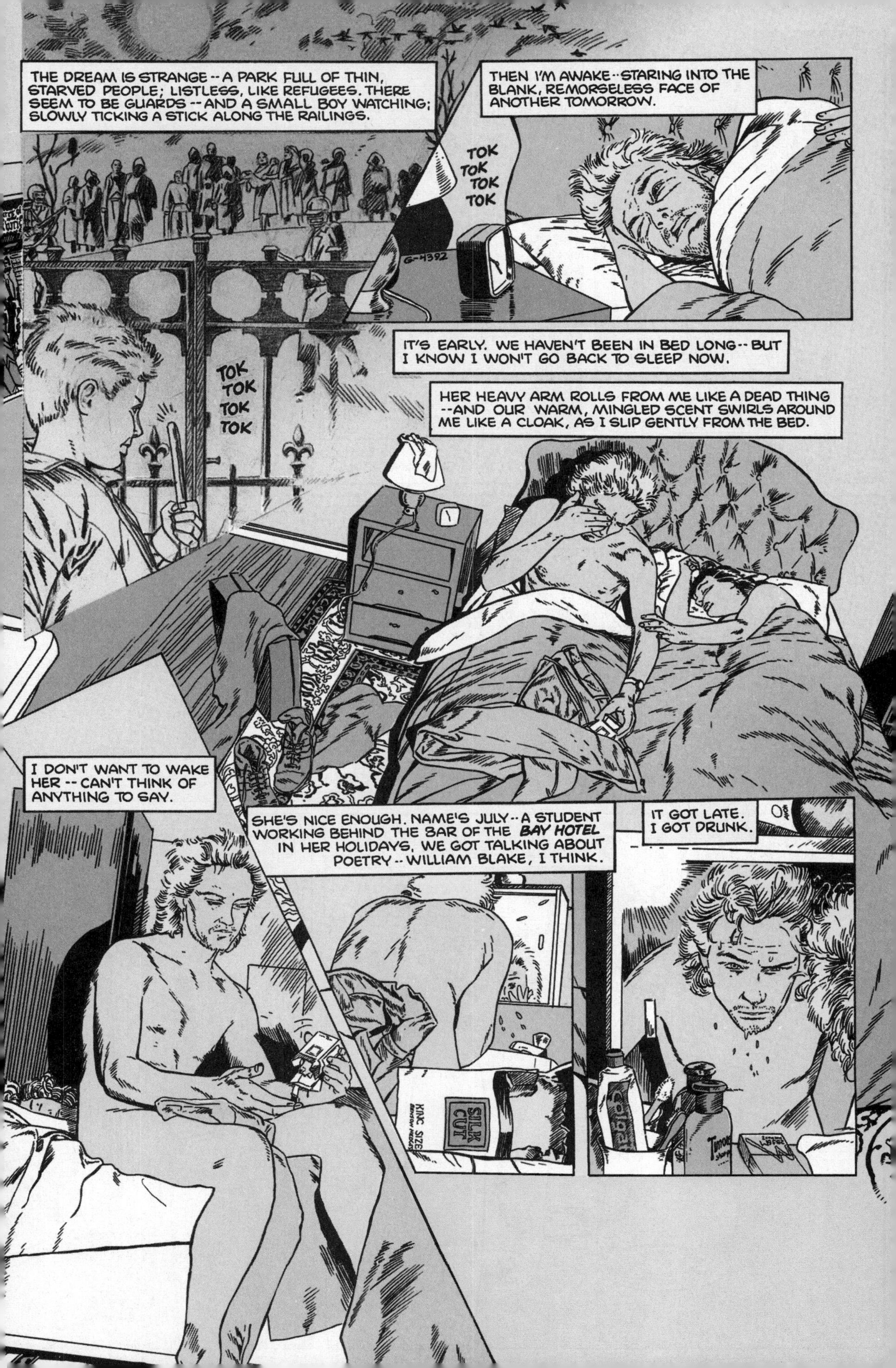
THE DREAM IS STRANGE -- A PARK FULL OF THIN, STARVED PEOPLE; LISTLESS, LIKE REFUGEES. THERE SEEM TO BE GUARDS -- AND A SMALL BOY WATCHING; SLOWLY TICKING A STICK ALONG THE RAILINGS.
TOK TOK TOK TOK
THEN I'M AWAKE -- STARING INTO THE BLANK, REMORSELESS FACE OF ANOTHER TOMORROW.
TOK TOK TOK TOK
G-4392
IT'S EARLY. WE HAVEN'T BEEN IN BED LONG -- BUT I KNOW I WON'T GO BACK TO SLEEP NOW.
HER HEAVY ARM ROLLS FROM ME LIKE A DEAD THING -- AND OUR WARM, MINGLED SCENT SWIRLS AROUND ME LIKE A CLOAK, AS I SLIP GENTLY FROM THE BED.
I DON'T WANT TO WAKE HER -- CAN'T THINK OF ANYTHING TO SAY.
SHE'S NICE ENOUGH. NAME'S JULY -- A STUDENT WORKING BEHIND THE BAR OF THE *BAY HOTEL* IN HER HOLIDAYS. WE GOT TALKING ABOUT POETRY -- WILLIAM BLAKE, I THINK.
IT GOT LATE. I GOT DRUNK.
SILK CUT
KING SIZE

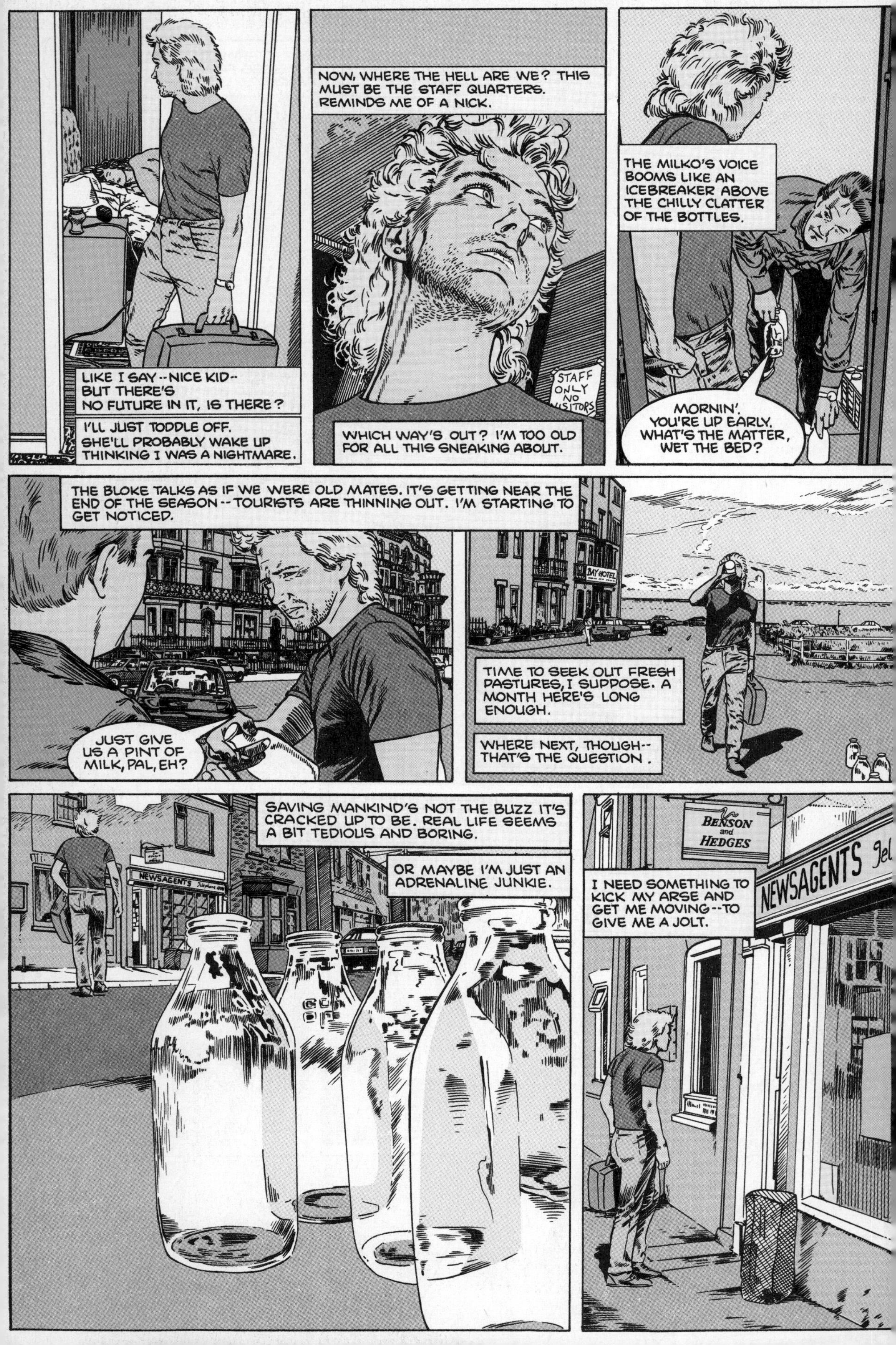
LIKE I SAY--NICE KID--
BUT THERE'S
NO FUTURE IN IT, IS THERE?
I'LL JUST TODDLE OFF.
SHE'LL PROBABLY WAKE UP
THINKING I WAS A NIGHTMARE.
NOW, WHERE THE HELL ARE WE? THIS
MUST BE THE STAFF QUARTERS.
REMINDS ME OF A NICK.
STAFF ONLY NO VISITORS
WHICH WAY'S OUT? I'M TOO OLD
FOR ALL THIS SNEAKING ABOUT.
THE MILKO'S VOICE
BOOMS LIKE AN
ICEBREAKER ABOVE
THE CHILLY CLATTER
OF THE BOTTLES.
MORNIN'.
YOU'RE UP EARLY.
WHAT'S THE MATTER,
WET THE BED?
THE BLOKE TALKS AS IF WE WERE OLD MATES. IT'S GETTING NEAR THE
END OF THE SEASON--TOURISTS ARE THINNING OUT. I'M STARTING TO
GET NOTICED.
JUST GIVE
US A PINT OF
MILK, PAL, EH?
BAY HOTEL
TIME TO SEEK OUT FRESH
PASTURES, I SUPPOSE. A
MONTH HERE'S LONG
ENOUGH.
WHERE NEXT, THOUGH--
THAT'S THE QUESTION.
SAVING MANKIND'S NOT THE BUZZ IT'S
CRACKED UP TO BE. REAL LIFE SEEMS
A BIT TEDIOUS AND BORING.
OR MAYBE I'M JUST AN
ADRENALINE JUNKIE.
NEWSAGENTS
BENSON and HEDGES
I NEED SOMETHING TO
KICK MY ARSE AND
GET ME MOVING--TO
GIVE ME A JOLT.
NEWSAGENTS

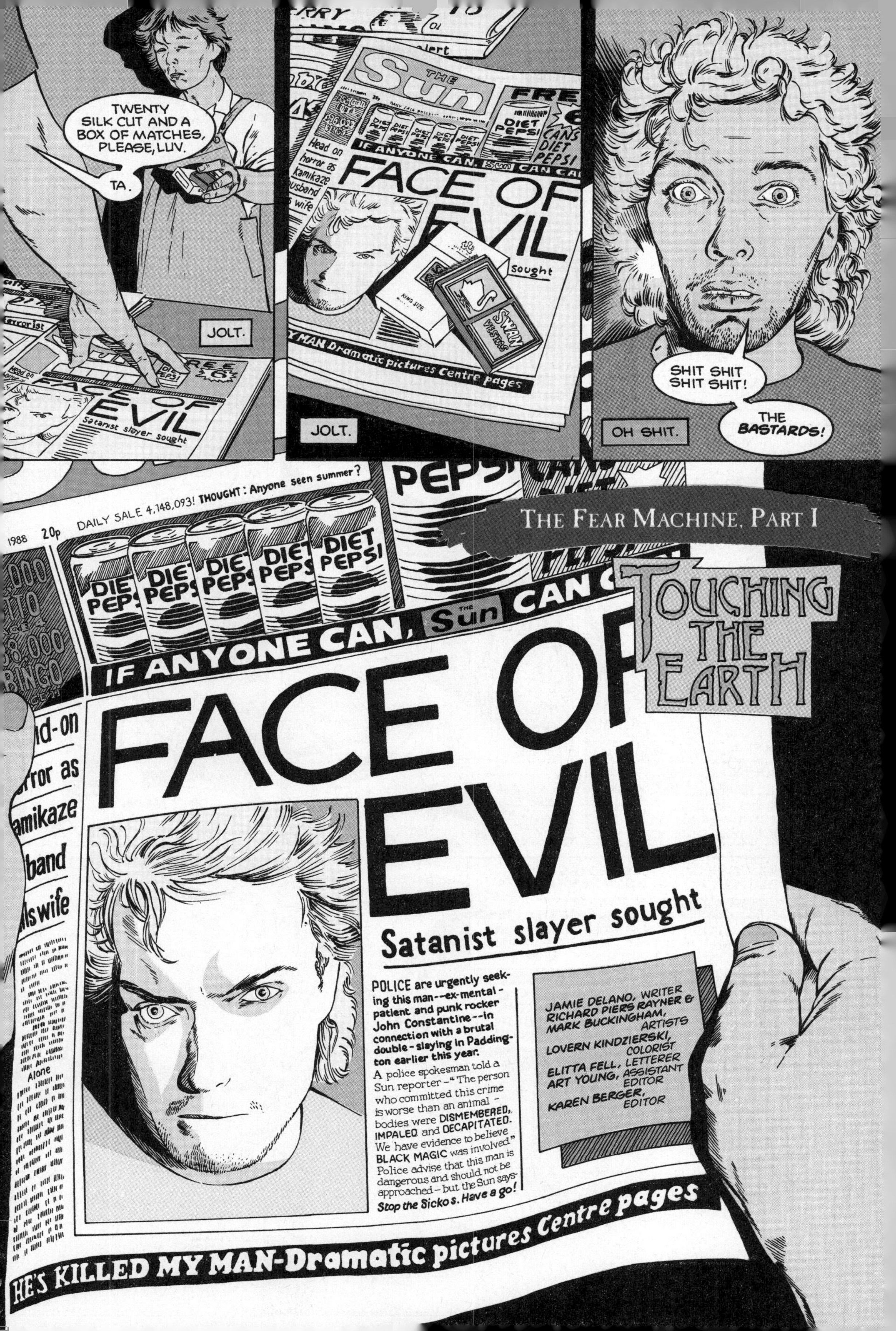
TWENTY SILK CUT AND A BOX OF MATCHES, PLEASE, LUV.
TA.
JOLT.
JOLT.
SHIT SHIT SHIT SHIT!
THE BASTARDS!
OH SHIT.
THE FEAR MACHINE, PART I
TOUCHING THE EARTH
1988 20p DAILY SALE 4,148,093! THOUGHT: Anyone seen summer?
DIET PEPSI
IF ANYONE CAN, THE Sun CAN
FACE OF EVIL
Satanist slayer sought
POLICE are urgently seeking this man--ex-mental-patient and punk rocker John Constantine--in connection with a brutal double-slaying in Paddington earlier this year.
A police spokesman told a Sun reporter -"The person who committed this crime is worse than an animal - bodies were DISMEMBERED, IMPALED and DECAPITATED. We have evidence to believe BLACK MAGIC was involved."
Police advise that this man is dangerous and should not be approached - but the Sun says-
Stop the Sickos. Have a go!
JAMIE DELANO, WRITER
RICHARD PIERS RAYNER & MARK BUCKINGHAM, ARTISTS
LOVERN KINDZIERSKI, COLORIST
ELITTA FELL, LETTERER
ART YOUNG, ASSISTANT EDITOR
KAREN BERGER, EDITOR
HE'S KILLED MY MAN-Dramatic pictures Centre pages

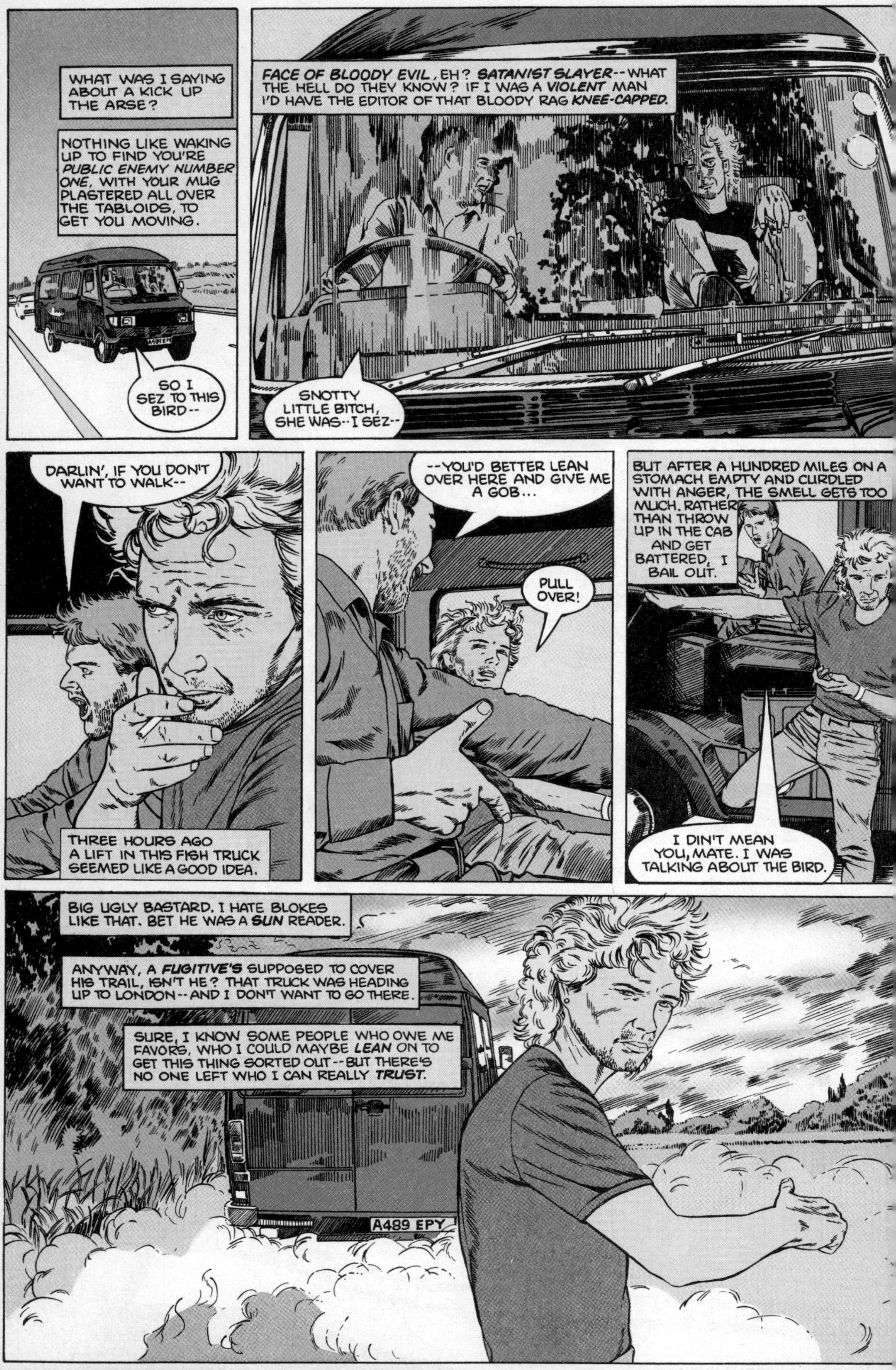
WHAT WAS I SAYING ABOUT A KICK UP THE ARSE?
NOTHING LIKE WAKING UP TO FIND YOU'RE PUBLIC ENEMY NUMBER ONE, WITH YOUR MUG PLASTERED ALL OVER THE TABLOIDS, TO GET YOU MOVING.
SO I SEZ TO THIS BIRD--
FACE OF BLOODY EVIL, EH? SATANIST SLAYER-- WHAT THE HELL DO THEY KNOW? IF I WAS A VIOLENT MAN I'D HAVE THE EDITOR OF THAT BLOODY RAG KNEE-CAPPED.
SNOTTY LITTLE BITCH, SHE WAS-- I SEZ--
DARLIN', IF YOU DON'T WANT TO WALK--
THREE HOURS AGO A LIFT IN THIS FISH TRUCK SEEMED LIKE A GOOD IDEA.
--YOU'D BETTER LEAN OVER HERE AND GIVE ME A GOB...
PULL OVER!
BUT AFTER A HUNDRED MILES ON A STOMACH EMPTY AND CURDLED WITH ANGER, THE SMELL GETS TOO MUCH. RATHER THAN THROW UP IN THE CAB AND GET BATTERED, I BAIL OUT.
I DIN'T MEAN YOU, MATE. I WAS TALKING ABOUT THE BIRD.
BIG UGLY BASTARD. I HATE BLOKES LIKE THAT. BET HE WAS A SUN READER.
ANYWAY, A FUGITIVE'S SUPPOSED TO COVER HIS TRAIL, ISN'T HE? THAT TRUCK WAS HEADING UP TO LONDON--AND I DON'T WANT TO GO THERE.
SURE, I KNOW SOME PEOPLE WHO OWE ME FAVORS, WHO I COULD MAYBE LEAN ON TO GET THIS THING SORTED OUT--BUT THERE'S NO ONE LEFT WHO I CAN REALLY TRUST.
A489 EPY

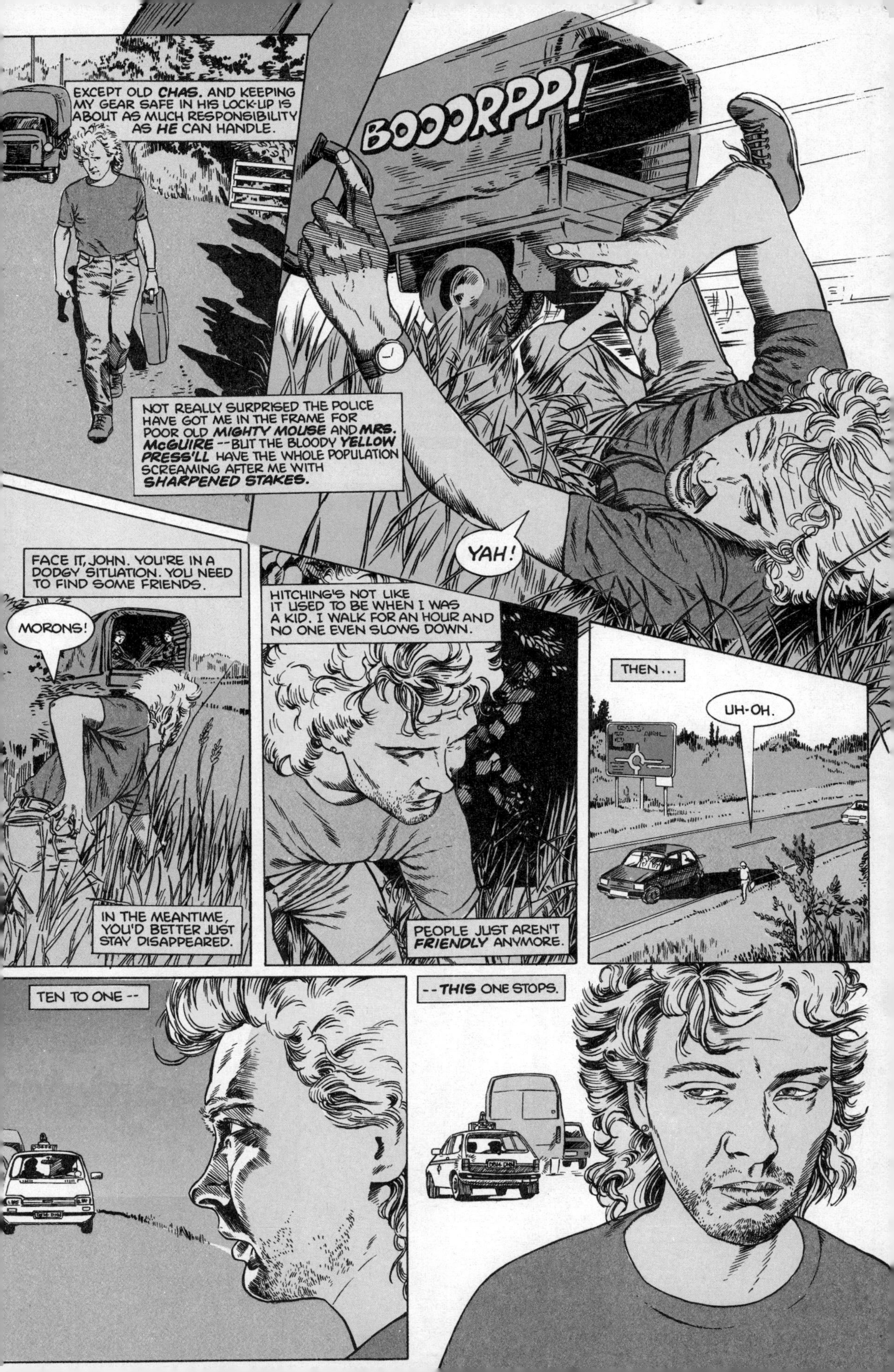
EXCEPT OLD CHAS. AND KEEPING MY GEAR SAFE IN HIS LOCK-UP IS ABOUT AS MUCH RESPONSIBILITY AS HE CAN HANDLE.
NOT REALLY SURPRISED THE POLICE HAVE GOT ME IN THE FRAME FOR POOR OLD MIGHTY MOUSE AND MRS. McGUIRE -- BUT THE BLOODY YELLOW PRESS'LL HAVE THE WHOLE POPULATION SCREAMING AFTER ME WITH SHARPENED STAKES.
BOOORPPP!
YAH!
FACE IT, JOHN. YOU'RE IN A DODGY SITUATION. YOU NEED TO FIND SOME FRIENDS.
MORONS!
IN THE MEANTIME, YOU'D BETTER JUST STAY DISAPPEARED.
HITCHING'S NOT LIKE IT USED TO BE WHEN I WAS A KID. I WALK FOR AN HOUR AND NO ONE EVEN SLOWS DOWN.
PEOPLE JUST AREN'T FRIENDLY ANYMORE.
THEN...
UH-OH.
TEN TO ONE --
-- THIS ONE STOPS.

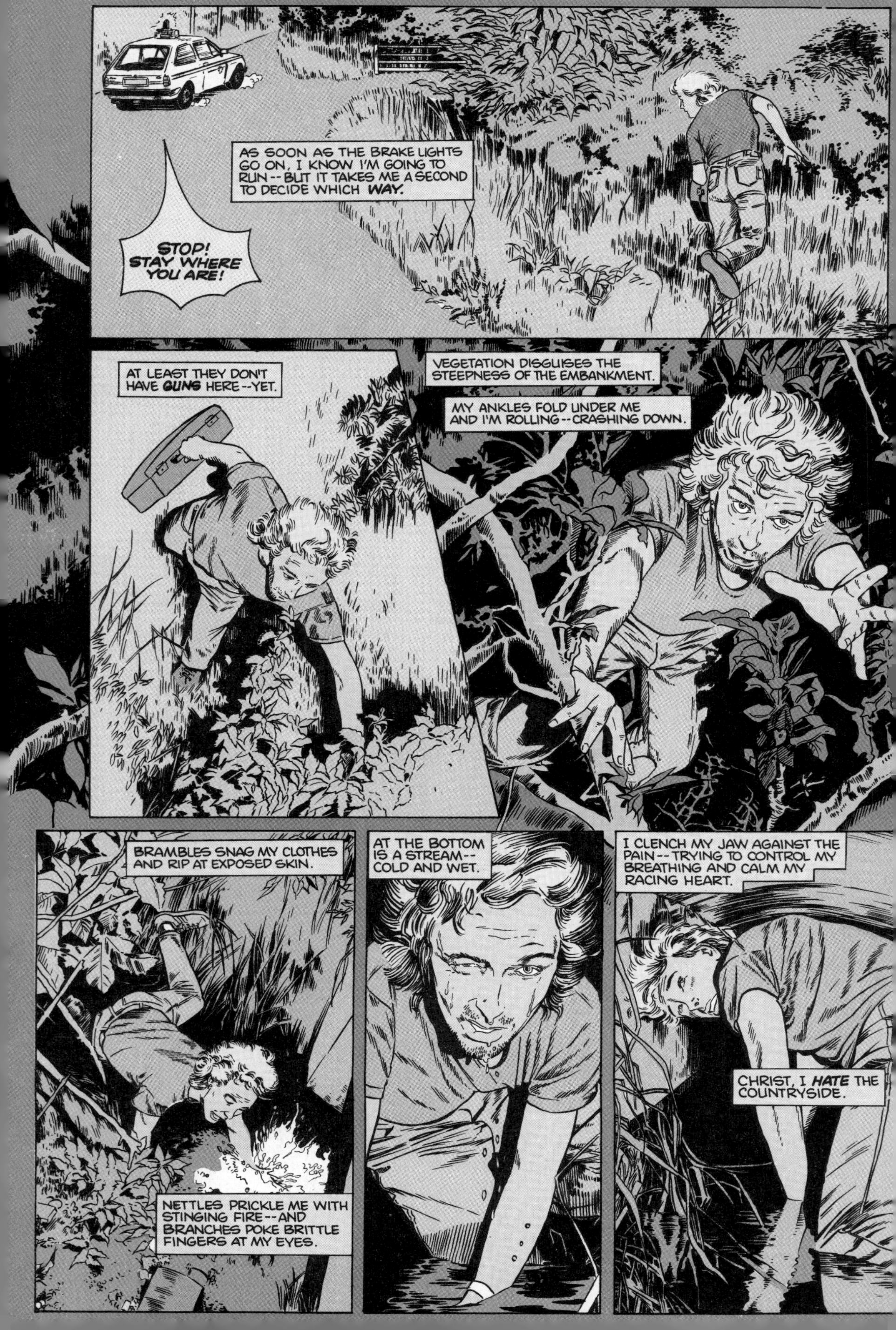
AS SOON AS THE BRAKE LIGHTS GO ON, I KNOW I'M GOING TO RUN--BUT IT TAKES ME A SECOND TO DECIDE WHICH WAY.
STOP! STAY WHERE YOU ARE!
AT LEAST THEY DON'T HAVE GUNS HERE--YET.
VEGETATION DISGUISES THE STEEPNESS OF THE EMBANKMENT.
MY ANKLES FOLD UNDER ME AND I'M ROLLING--CRASHING DOWN.
BRAMBLES SNAG MY CLOTHES AND RIP AT EXPOSED SKIN.
NETTLES PRICKLE ME WITH STINGING FIRE--AND BRANCHES POKE BRITTLE FINGERS AT MY EYES.
AT THE BOTTOM IS A STREAM--COLD AND WET.
I CLENCH MY JAW AGAINST THE PAIN--TRYING TO CONTROL MY BREATHING AND CALM MY RACING HEART.
CHRIST, I HATE THE COUNTRYSIDE.

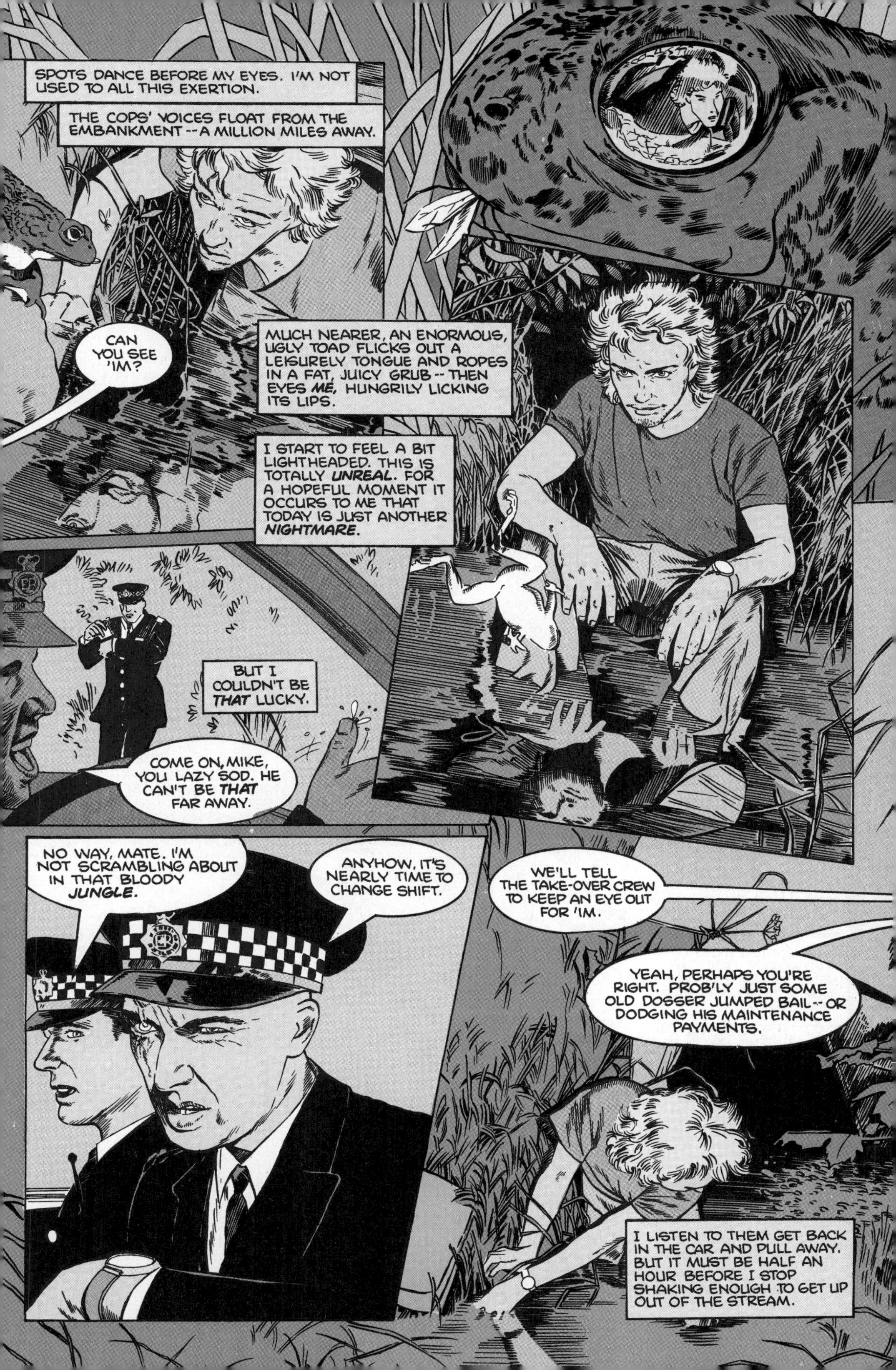
SPOTS DANCE BEFORE MY EYES. I'M NOT USED TO ALL THIS EXERTION.
THE COPS' VOICES FLOAT FROM THE EMBANKMENT --A MILLION MILES AWAY.
CAN YOU SEE 'IM?
MUCH NEARER, AN ENORMOUS, UGLY TOAD FLICKS OUT A LEISURELY TONGUE AND ROPES IN A FAT, JUICY GRUB -- THEN EYES *ME,* HUNGRILY LICKING ITS LIPS.
I START TO FEEL A BIT LIGHTHEADED. THIS IS TOTALLY ***UNREAL***. FOR A HOPEFUL MOMENT IT OCCURS TO ME THAT TODAY IS JUST ANOTHER ***NIGHTMARE***.
BUT I COULDN'T BE ***THAT*** LUCKY.
COME ON, MIKE, YOU LAZY SOD. HE CAN'T BE ***THAT*** FAR AWAY.
NO WAY, MATE. I'M NOT SCRAMBLING ABOUT IN THAT BLOODY ***JUNGLE***.
ANYHOW, IT'S NEARLY TIME TO CHANGE SHIFT.
WE'LL TELL THE TAKE-OVER CREW TO KEEP AN EYE OUT FOR 'IM.
YEAH, PERHAPS YOU'RE RIGHT. PROB'LY JUST SOME OLD DOSSER JUMPED BAIL -- OR DODGING HIS MAINTENANCE PAYMENTS.
I LISTEN TO THEM GET BACK IN THE CAR AND PULL AWAY. BUT IT MUST BE HALF AN HOUR BEFORE I STOP SHAKING ENOUGH TO GET UP OUT OF THE STREAM.

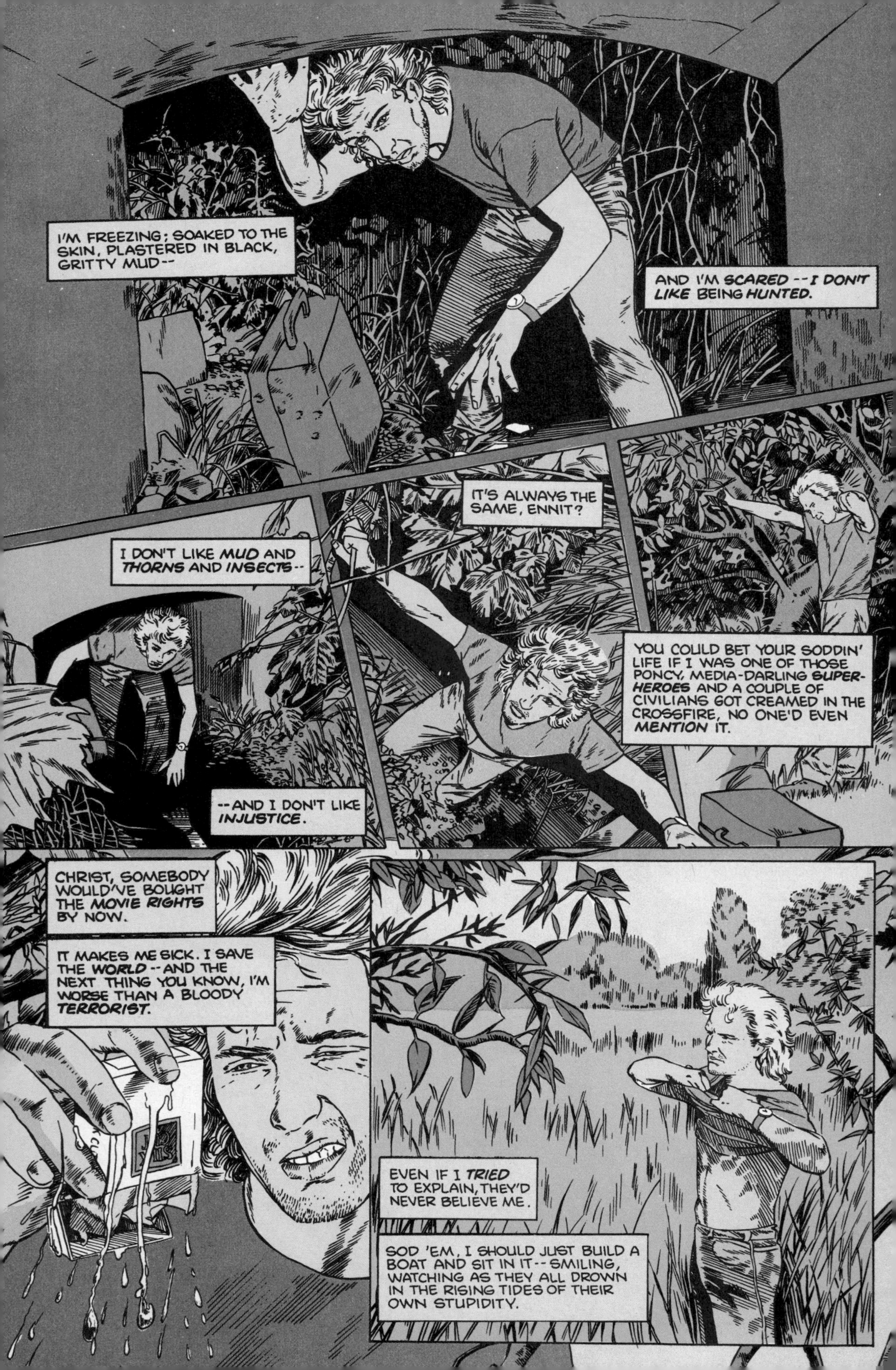
I'M FREEZING; SOAKED TO THE SKIN, PLASTERED IN BLACK, GRITTY MUD--
AND I'M SCARED --I DON'T LIKE BEING HUNTED.
I DON'T LIKE MUD AND THORNS AND INSECTS--
--AND I DON'T LIKE INJUSTICE.
IT'S ALWAYS THE SAME, ENNIT?
YOU COULD BET YOUR SODDIN' LIFE IF I WAS ONE OF THOSE PONCY, MEDIA-DARLING SUPER-HEROES AND A COUPLE OF CIVILIANS GOT CREAMED IN THE CROSSFIRE, NO ONE'D EVEN MENTION IT.
CHRIST, SOMEBODY WOULD'VE BOUGHT THE MOVIE RIGHTS BY NOW.
IT MAKES ME SICK. I SAVE THE WORLD--AND THE NEXT THING YOU KNOW, I'M WORSE THAN A BLOODY TERRORIST.
EVEN IF I TRIED TO EXPLAIN, THEY'D NEVER BELIEVE ME.
SOD 'EM, I SHOULD JUST BUILD A BOAT AND SIT IN IT--SMILING, WATCHING AS THEY ALL DROWN IN THE RISING TIDES OF THEIR OWN STUPIDITY.

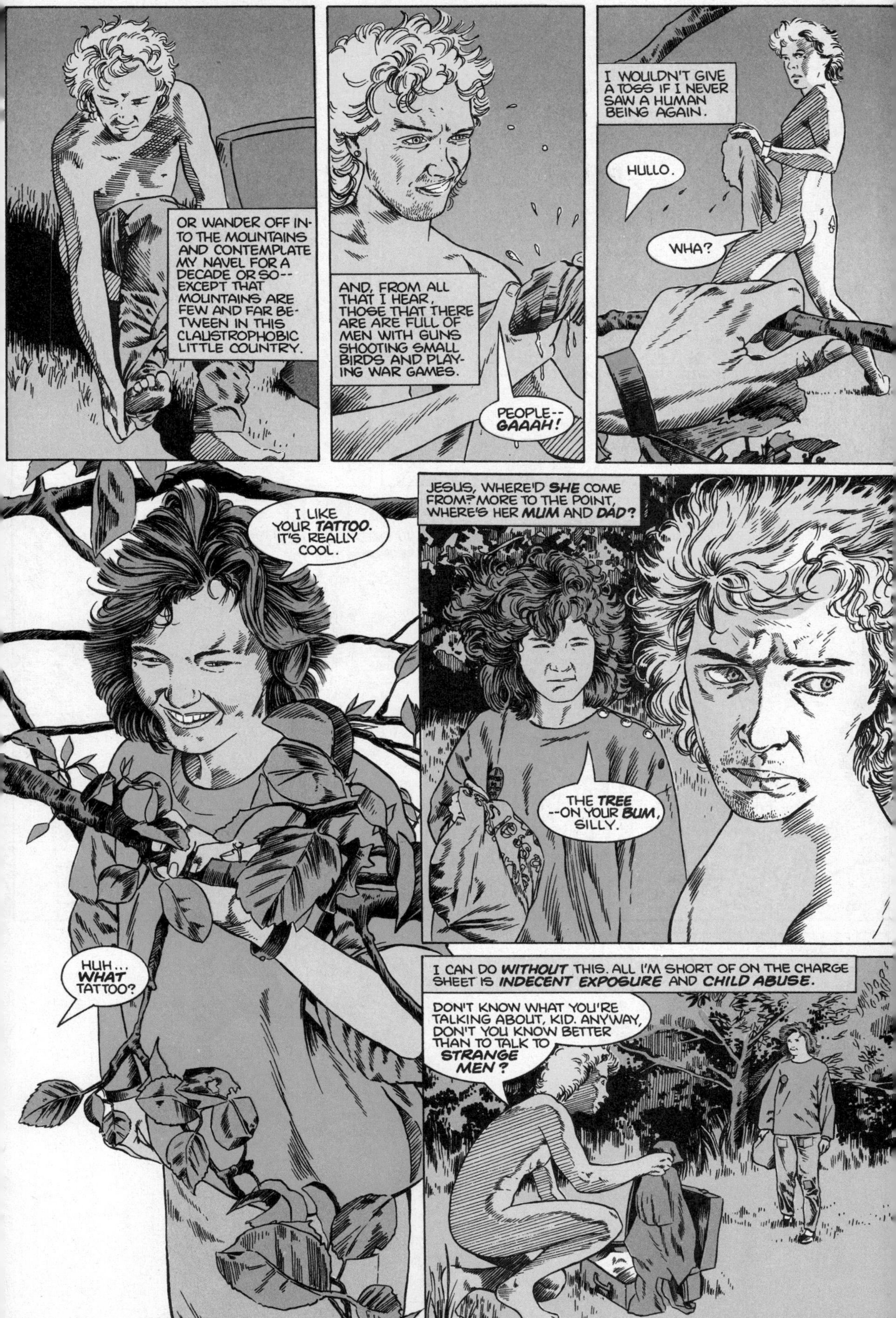
OR WANDER OFF INTO THE MOUNTAINS AND CONTEMPLATE MY NAVEL FOR A DECADE OR SO--EXCEPT THAT MOUNTAINS ARE FEW AND FAR BETWEEN IN THIS CLAUSTROPHOBIC LITTLE COUNTRY.
AND, FROM ALL THAT I HEAR, THOSE THAT THERE ARE ARE FULL OF MEN WITH GUNS SHOOTING SMALL BIRDS AND PLAYING WAR GAMES.
PEOPLE-- GAAAH!
I WOULDN'T GIVE A TOSS IF I NEVER SAW A HUMAN BEING AGAIN.
HULLO.
WHA?
I LIKE YOUR TATTOO. IT'S REALLY COOL.
HUH... WHAT TATTOO?
JESUS, WHERE'D SHE COME FROM? MORE TO THE POINT, WHERE'S HER MUM AND DAD?
THE TREE --ON YOUR BUM, SILLY.
I CAN DO WITHOUT THIS. ALL I'M SHORT OF ON THE CHARGE SHEET IS INDECENT EXPOSURE AND CHILD ABUSE.
DON'T KNOW WHAT YOU'RE TALKING ABOUT, KID. ANYWAY, DON'T YOU KNOW BETTER THAN TO TALK TO STRANGE MEN?

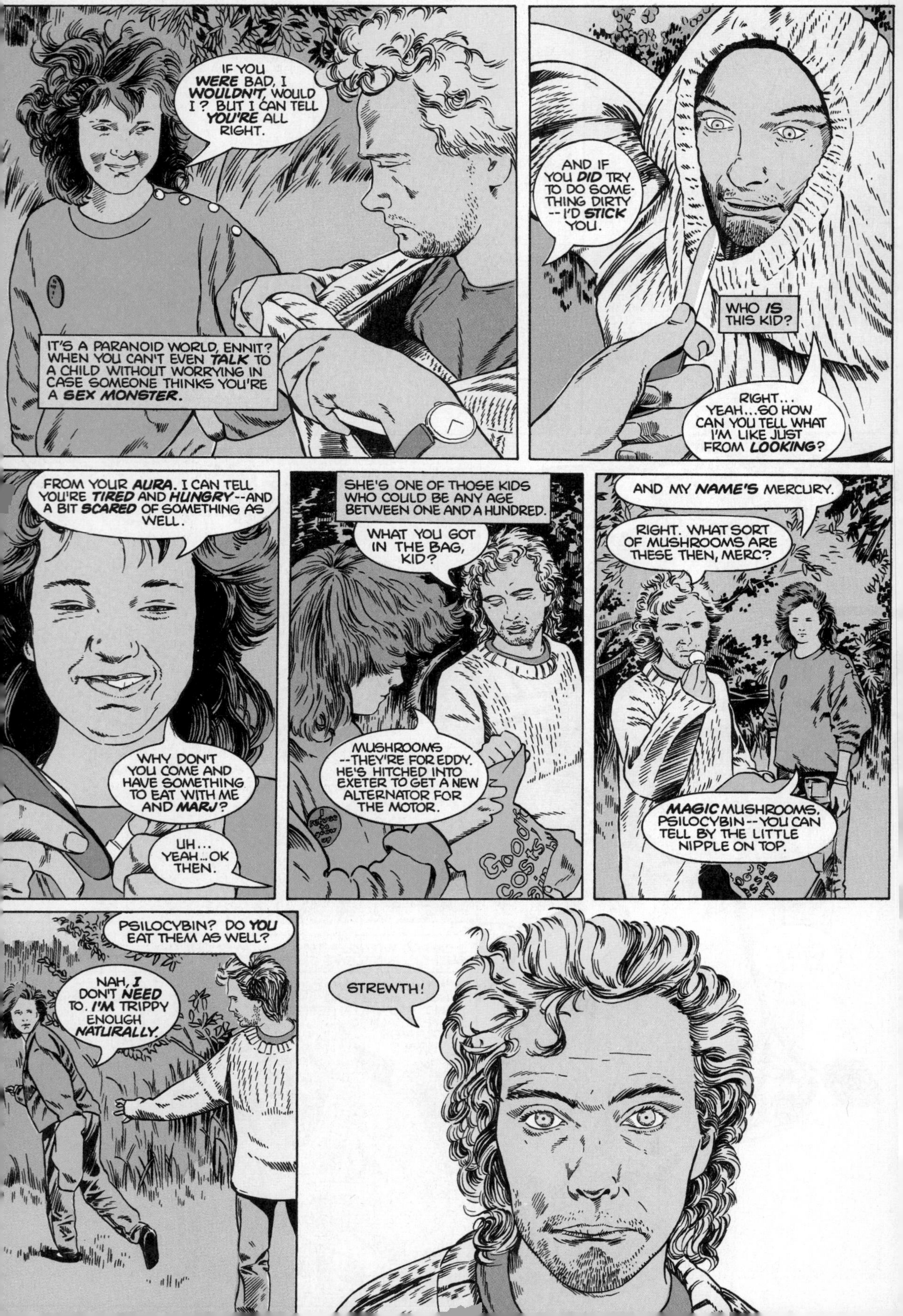

IF YOU WERE BAD, I WOULDN'T, WOULD I? BUT I CAN TELL YOU'RE ALL RIGHT.
IT'S A PARANOID WORLD, ENNIT? WHEN YOU CAN'T EVEN TALK TO A CHILD WITHOUT WORRYING IN CASE SOMEONE THINKS YOU'RE A SEX MONSTER.
AND IF YOU DID TRY TO DO SOME-THING DIRTY --I'D STICK YOU.
WHO IS THIS KID?
RIGHT... YEAH...SO HOW CAN YOU TELL WHAT I'M LIKE JUST FROM LOOKING?
FROM YOUR AURA. I CAN TELL YOU'RE TIRED AND HUNGRY--AND A BIT SCARED OF SOMETHING AS WELL.
WHY DON'T YOU COME AND HAVE SOMETHING TO EAT WITH ME AND MARJ?
UH... YEAH...OK THEN.
SHE'S ONE OF THOSE KIDS WHO COULD BE ANY AGE BETWEEN ONE AND A HUNDRED.
WHAT YOU GOT IN THE BAG, KID?
MUSHROOMS --THEY'RE FOR EDDY. HE'S HITCHED INTO EXETER TO GET A NEW ALTERNATOR FOR THE MOTOR.
AND MY NAME'S MERCURY.
RIGHT. WHAT SORT OF MUSHROOMS ARE THESE THEN, MERC?
MAGIC MUSHROOMS. PSILOCYBIN--YOU CAN TELL BY THE LITTLE NIPPLE ON TOP.
PSILOCYBIN? DO YOU EAT THEM AS WELL?
NAH, I DON'T NEED TO. I'M TRIPPY ENOUGH NATURALLY.
STREWTH!

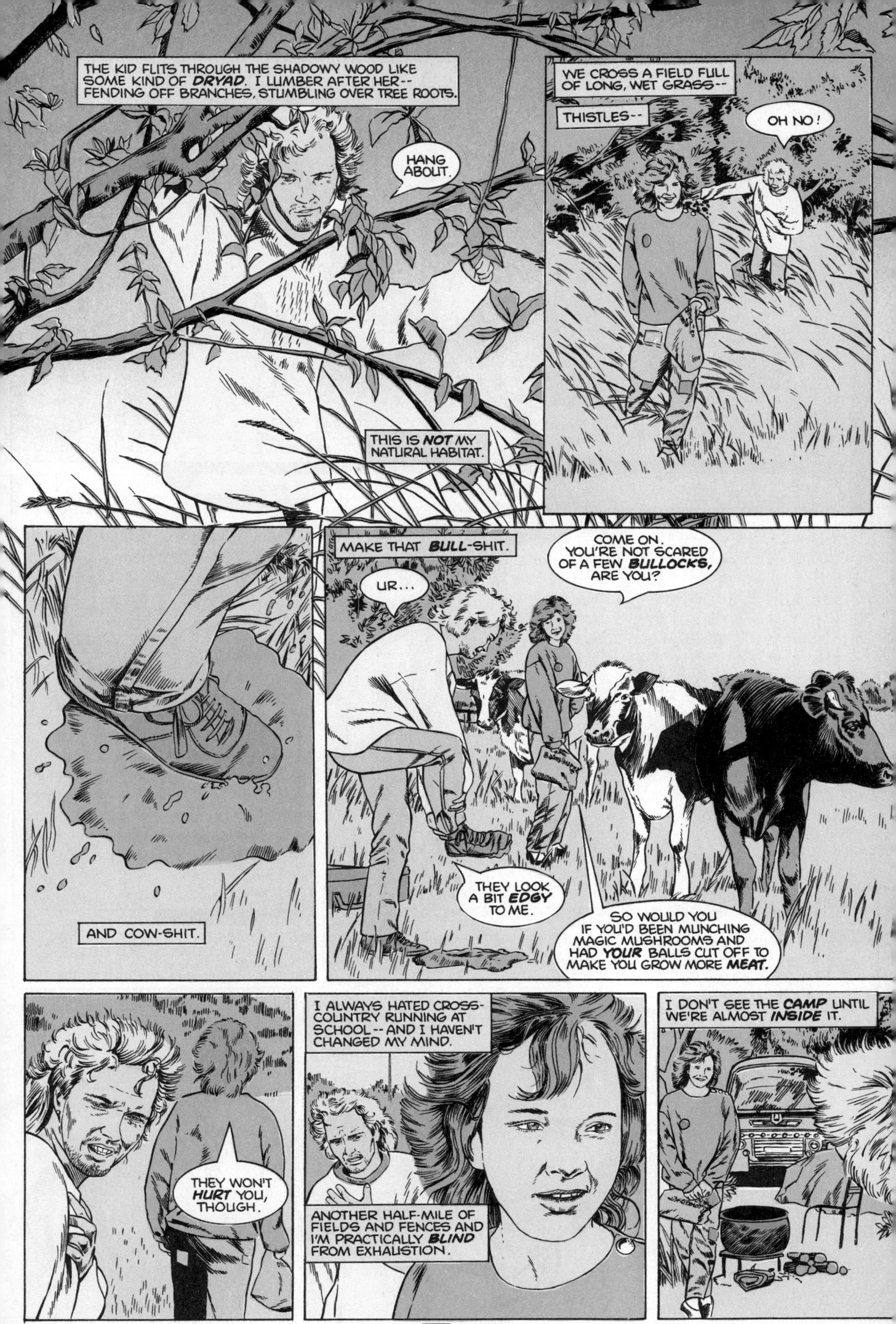
THE KID FLITS THROUGH THE SHADOWY WOOD LIKE SOME KIND OF **DRYAD**. I LUMBER AFTER HER-- FENDING OFF BRANCHES, STUMBLING OVER TREE ROOTS.
HANG ABOUT.
THIS IS **NOT** MY NATURAL HABITAT.
WE CROSS A FIELD FULL OF LONG, WET GRASS--
THISTLES--
OH NO!
AND COW-SHIT.
MAKE THAT **BULL**-SHIT.
UR...
COME ON. YOU'RE NOT SCARED OF A FEW **BULLOCKS,** ARE YOU?
THEY LOOK A BIT **EDGY** TO ME.
SO WOULD YOU IF YOU'D BEEN MUNCHING MAGIC MUSHROOMS AND HAD **YOUR** BALLS CUT OFF TO MAKE YOU GROW MORE **MEAT.**
THEY WON'T **HURT** YOU, THOUGH.
I ALWAYS HATED CROSS-COUNTRY RUNNING AT SCHOOL -- AND I HAVEN'T CHANGED MY MIND.
ANOTHER HALF-MILE OF FIELDS AND FENCES AND I'M PRACTICALLY **BLIND** FROM EXHAUSTION.
I DON'T SEE THE **CAMP** UNTIL WE'RE ALMOST **INSIDE** IT.

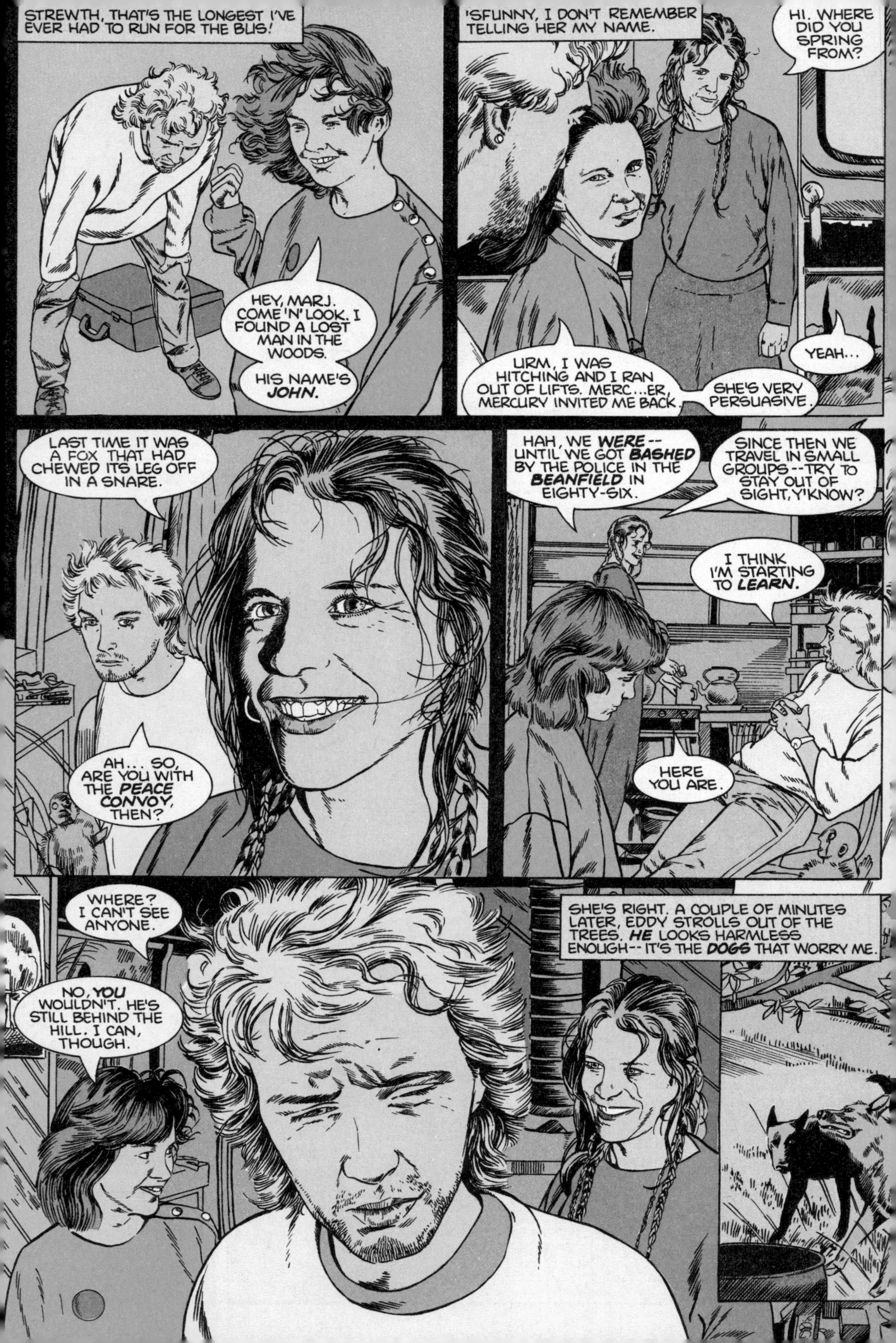
STREWTH, THAT'S THE LONGEST I'VE EVER HAD TO RUN FOR THE BUS!
HEY, MARJ. COME 'N' LOOK. I FOUND A LOST MAN IN THE WOODS.
HIS NAME'S **JOHN.**
'SFUNNY, I DON'T REMEMBER TELLING HER MY NAME.
HI. WHERE DID YOU SPRING FROM?
URM, I WAS HITCHING AND I RAN OUT OF LIFTS. MERC...ER, MERCURY INVITED ME BACK.
YEAH...
SHE'S VERY PERSUASIVE.
LAST TIME IT WAS A FOX THAT HAD CHEWED ITS LEG OFF IN A SNARE.
AH... SO, ARE YOU WITH THE ***PEACE CONVOY***, THEN?
HAH, WE ***WERE***-- UNTIL WE GOT ***BASHED*** BY THE POLICE IN THE ***BEANFIELD*** IN EIGHTY-SIX.
SINCE THEN WE TRAVEL IN SMALL GROUPS--TRY TO STAY OUT OF SIGHT, Y'KNOW?
I THINK I'M STARTING TO ***LEARN.***
HERE YOU ARE.
WHERE? I CAN'T SEE ANYONE.
NO, ***YOU*** WOULDN'T. HE'S STILL BEHIND THE HILL. I CAN, THOUGH.
SHE'S RIGHT. A COUPLE OF MINUTES LATER, EDDY STROLLS OUT OF THE TREES. ***HE*** LOOKS HARMLESS ENOUGH-- IT'S THE ***DOGS*** THAT WORRY ME.

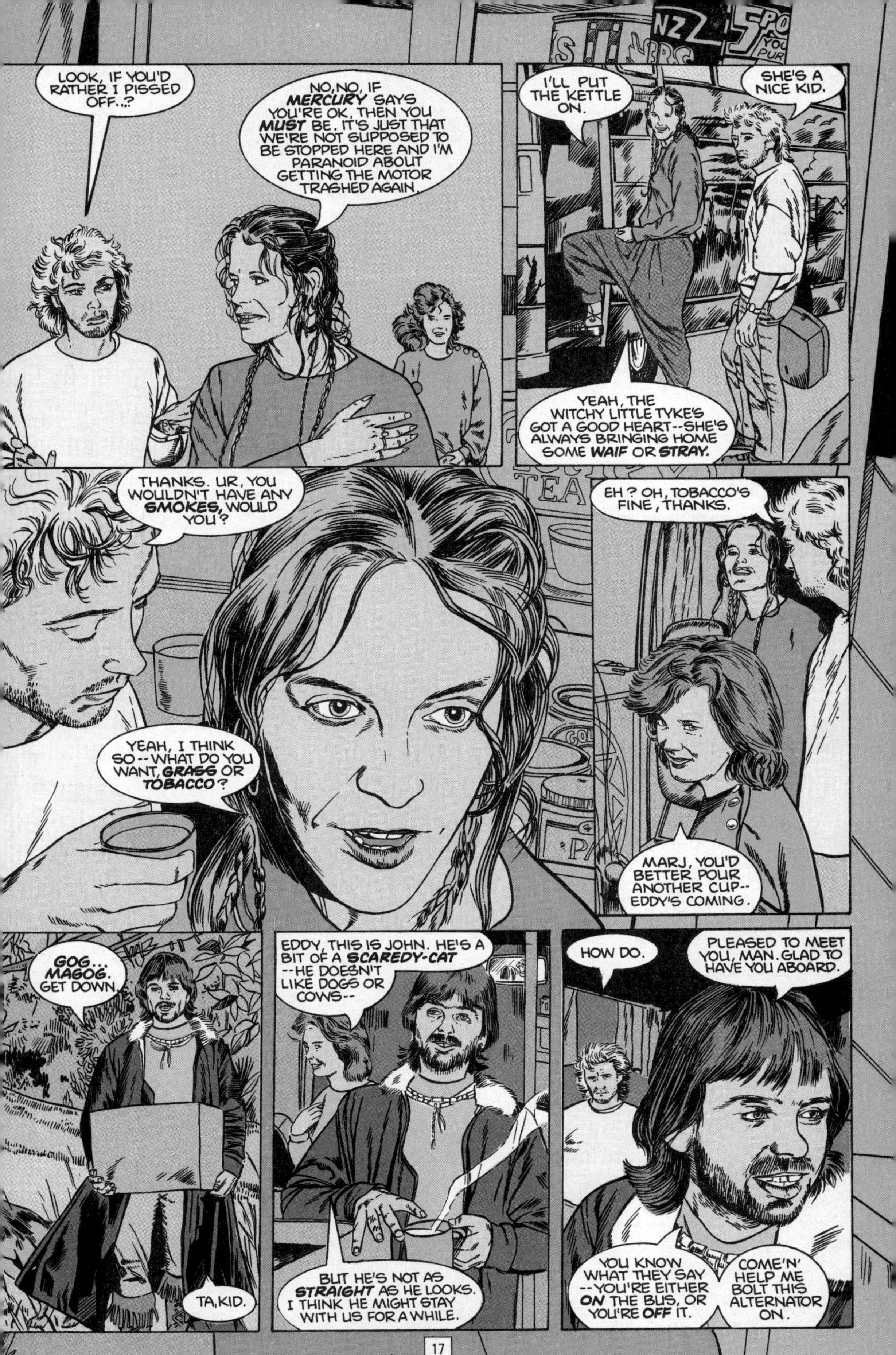
LOOK, IF YOU'D RATHER I PISSED OFF..?
NO, NO, IF MERCURY SAYS YOU'RE OK, THEN YOU MUST BE. IT'S JUST THAT WE'RE NOT SUPPOSED TO BE STOPPED HERE AND I'M PARANOID ABOUT GETTING THE MOTOR TRASHED AGAIN.
I'LL PUT THE KETTLE ON.
SHE'S A NICE KID.
YEAH, THE WITCHY LITTLE TYKE'S GOT A GOOD HEART--SHE'S ALWAYS BRINGING HOME SOME WAIF OR STRAY.
THANKS. UR, YOU WOULDN'T HAVE ANY SMOKES, WOULD YOU?
YEAH, I THINK SO--WHAT DO YOU WANT, GRASS OR TOBACCO?
EH? OH, TOBACCO'S FINE, THANKS.
MARJ, YOU'D BETTER POUR ANOTHER CUP--EDDY'S COMING.
GOG... MAGOG. GET DOWN.
TA, KID.
EDDY, THIS IS JOHN. HE'S A BIT OF A SCAREDY-CAT --HE DOESN'T LIKE DOGS OR COWS--
BUT HE'S NOT AS STRAIGHT AS HE LOOKS. I THINK HE MIGHT STAY WITH US FOR A WHILE.
HOW DO.
PLEASED TO MEET YOU, MAN. GLAD TO HAVE YOU ABOARD.
YOU KNOW WHAT THEY SAY --YOU'RE EITHER ON THE BUS, OR YOU'RE OFF IT.
COME'N' HELP ME BOLT THIS ALTERNATOR ON.

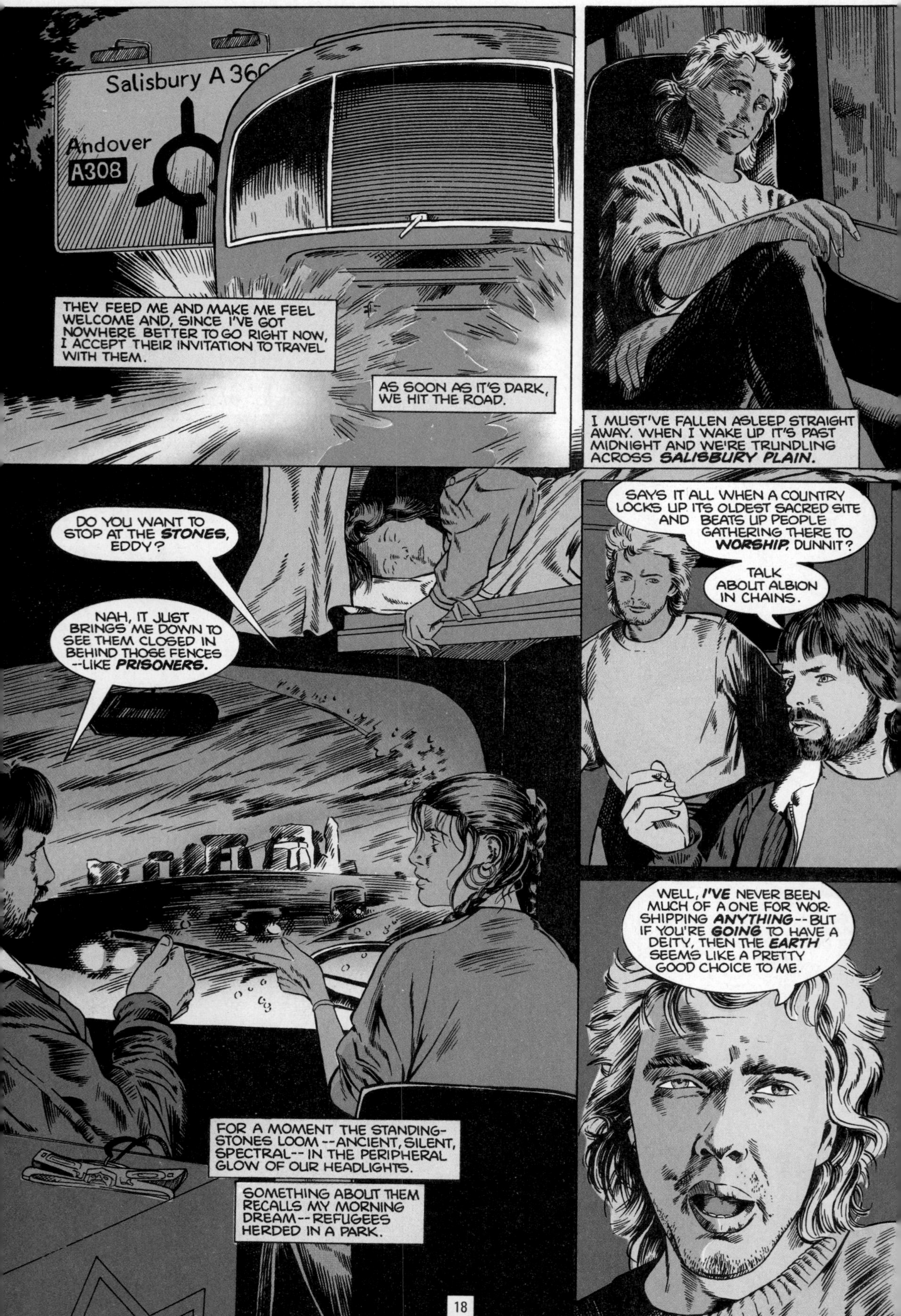
Salisbury A 36
Andover
A308
THEY FEED ME AND MAKE ME FEEL WELCOME AND, SINCE I'VE GOT NOWHERE BETTER TO GO RIGHT NOW, I ACCEPT THEIR INVITATION TO TRAVEL WITH THEM.
AS SOON AS IT'S DARK, WE HIT THE ROAD.
I MUST'VE FALLEN ASLEEP STRAIGHT AWAY. WHEN I WAKE UP IT'S PAST MIDNIGHT AND WE'RE TRUNDLING ACROSS SALISBURY PLAIN.
DO YOU WANT TO STOP AT THE STONES, EDDY?
NAH, IT JUST BRINGS ME DOWN TO SEE THEM CLOSED IN BEHIND THOSE FENCES --LIKE PRISONERS.
SAYS IT ALL WHEN A COUNTRY LOCKS UP ITS OLDEST SACRED SITE AND BEATS UP PEOPLE GATHERING THERE TO WORSHIP, DUNNIT?
TALK ABOUT ALBION IN CHAINS.
FOR A MOMENT THE STANDING-STONES LOOM --ANCIENT, SILENT, SPECTRAL-- IN THE PERIPHERAL GLOW OF OUR HEADLIGHTS.
SOMETHING ABOUT THEM RECALLS MY MORNING DREAM--REFUGEES HERDED IN A PARK.
WELL, I'VE NEVER BEEN MUCH OF A ONE FOR WOR-SHIPPING ANYTHING-- BUT IF YOU'RE GOING TO HAVE A DEITY, THEN THE EARTH SEEMS LIKE A PRETTY GOOD CHOICE TO ME.

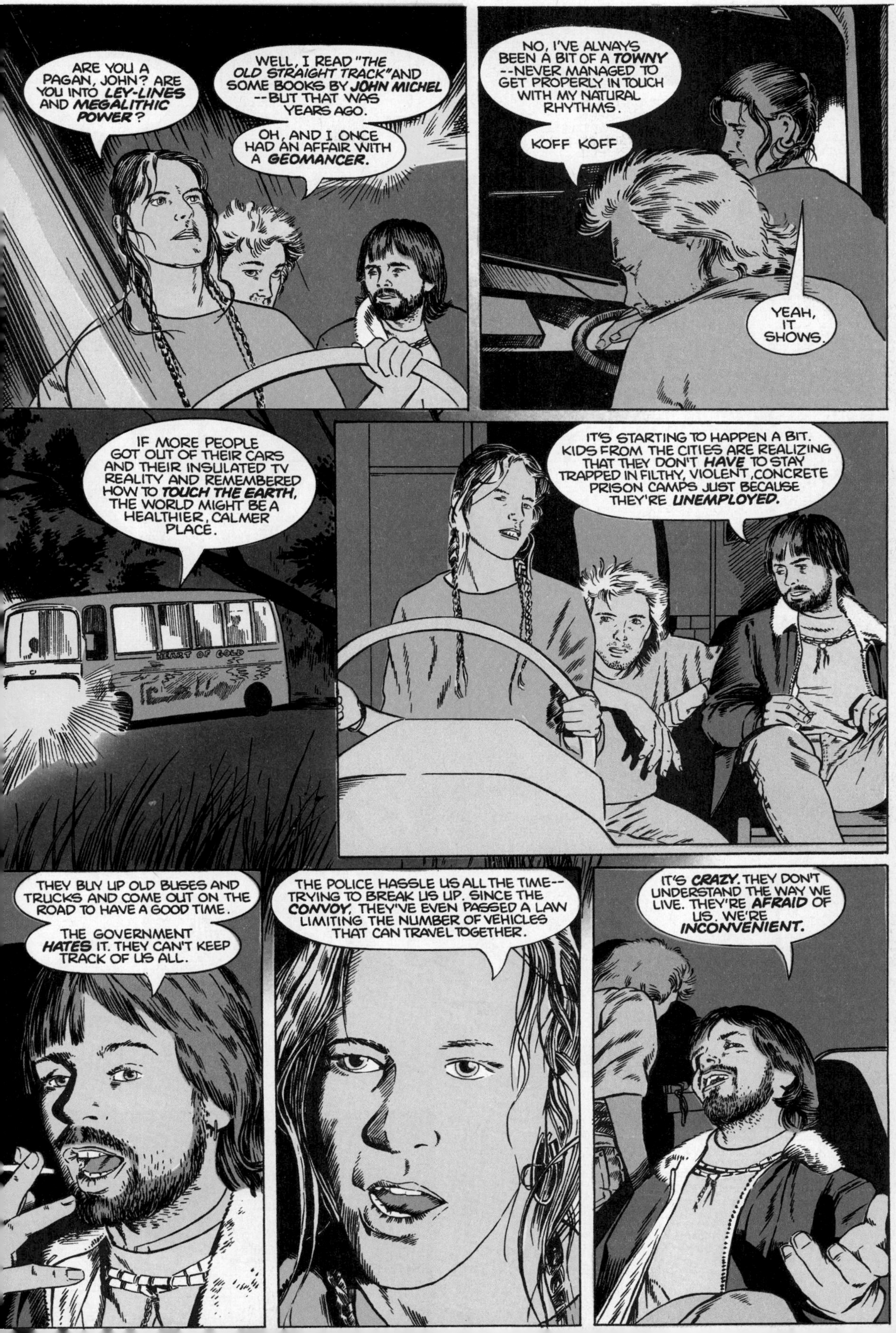
ARE YOU A PAGAN, JOHN? ARE YOU INTO LEY-LINES AND MEGALITHIC POWER?
WELL, I READ "THE OLD STRAIGHT TRACK" AND SOME BOOKS BY JOHN MICHEL --BUT THAT WAS YEARS AGO.
OH, AND I ONCE HAD AN AFFAIR WITH A GEOMANCER.
NO, I'VE ALWAYS BEEN A BIT OF A TOWNY --NEVER MANAGED TO GET PROPERLY IN TOUCH WITH MY NATURAL RHYTHMS.
KOFF KOFF
YEAH, IT SHOWS.
IF MORE PEOPLE GOT OUT OF THEIR CARS AND THEIR INSULATED TV REALITY AND REMEMBERED HOW TO TOUCH THE EARTH, THE WORLD MIGHT BE A HEALTHIER, CALMER PLACE.
HEART OF GOLD
IT'S STARTING TO HAPPEN A BIT. KIDS FROM THE CITIES ARE REALIZING THAT THEY DON'T HAVE TO STAY TRAPPED IN FILTHY, VIOLENT, CONCRETE PRISON CAMPS JUST BECAUSE THEY'RE UNEMPLOYED.
THEY BUY UP OLD BUSES AND TRUCKS AND COME OUT ON THE ROAD TO HAVE A GOOD TIME.
THE GOVERNMENT HATES IT. THEY CAN'T KEEP TRACK OF US ALL.
THE POLICE HASSLE US ALL THE TIME-- TRYING TO BREAK US UP. SINCE THE CONVOY, THEY'VE EVEN PASSED A LAW LIMITING THE NUMBER OF VEHICLES THAT CAN TRAVEL TOGETHER.
IT'S CRAZY. THEY DON'T UNDERSTAND THE WAY WE LIVE. THEY'RE AFRAID OF US. WE'RE INCONVENIENT.

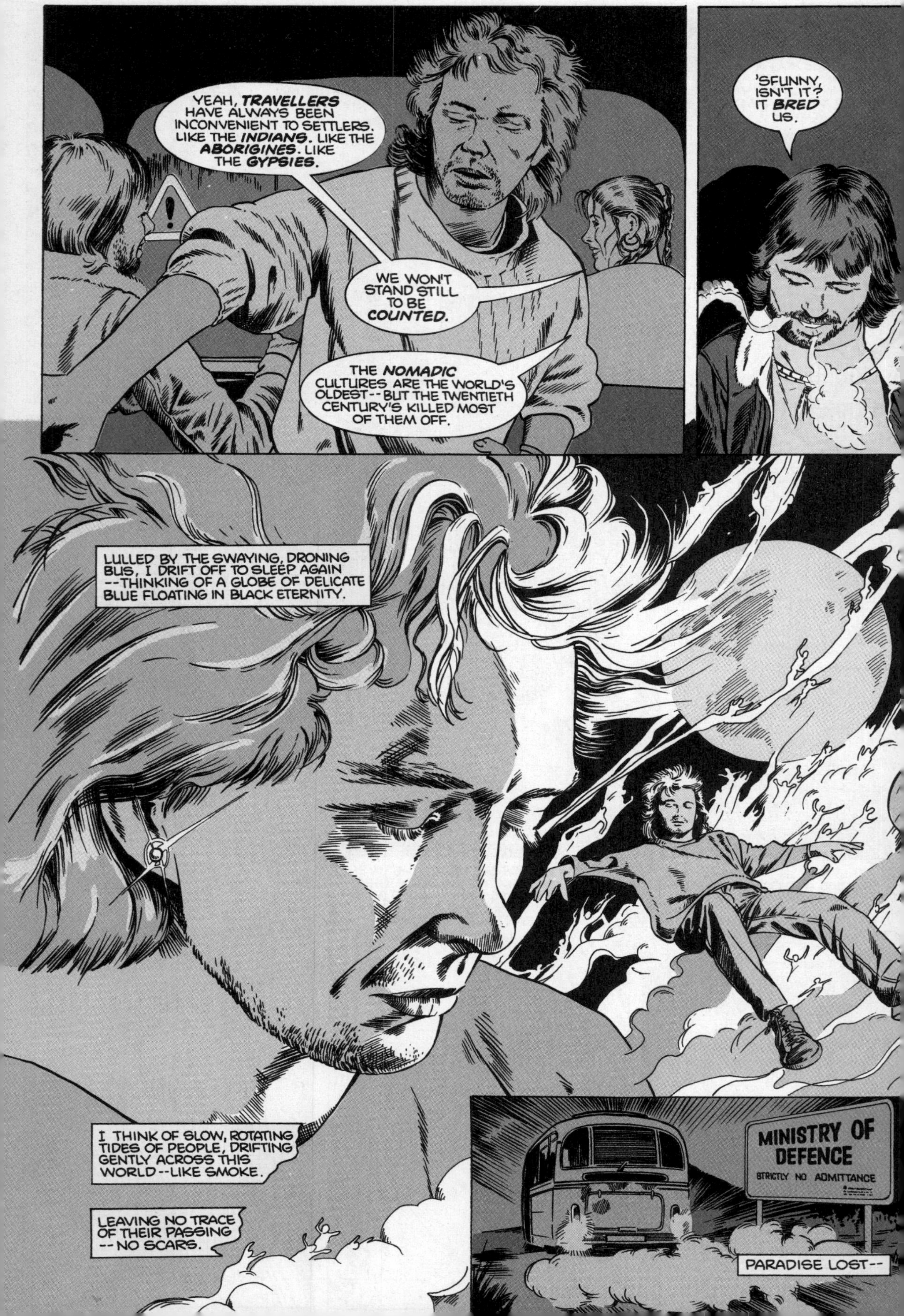
YEAH, TRAVELLERS HAVE ALWAYS BEEN INCONVENIENT TO SETTLERS. LIKE THE INDIANS. LIKE THE ABORIGINES. LIKE THE GYPSIES.
WE WON'T STAND STILL TO BE COUNTED.
THE NOMADIC CULTURES ARE THE WORLD'S OLDEST--BUT THE TWENTIETH CENTURY'S KILLED MOST OF THEM OFF.
'SFUNNY, ISN'T IT? IT BRED US.
LULLED BY THE SWAYING, DRONING BUS, I DRIFT OFF TO SLEEP AGAIN --THINKING OF A GLOBE OF DELICATE BLUE FLOATING IN BLACK ETERNITY.
I THINK OF SLOW, ROTATING TIDES OF PEOPLE, DRIFTING GENTLY ACROSS THIS WORLD--LIKE SMOKE.
LEAVING NO TRACE OF THEIR PASSING --NO SCARS.
MINISTRY OF DEFENCE
STRICTLY NO ADMITTANCE
PARADISE LOST--

--OR FOUND?

HEART OF GOLD

SUNLIT, MISTY WITH PASTORAL SOFTNESS -- IN A HIDDEN VALLEY, SOMEWHERE IN THE WELSH BORDERS -- THIS IS THE *WYKES VALLEY* PARK-UP.

PARK-UPS, MARJ HAD EXPLAINED, WERE A NETWORK OF STOPPING PLACES, SET UP AND MAINTAINED ACROSS THE COUNTRY -- USUALLY ON LAND OWNED BY SYMPATHETIC SMALL-FARMERS.

GOOD, THERE'S PLENTY OF ROOM.

THE TRAVELLERS COULD COME AND GO BETWEEN THESE -- MOVING ON WHEN THEY GOT TOO CROWDED. THEY WERE USEFUL TO THE FARMERS AS A MOBILE WORK-FORCE WITH ITS OWN ACCOMMODATIONS.

GREAT! THE *FREEDOM MOB'S* HERE!

PEACE CONVOY
RISEN FROM THE ASHES

THEY COULD EARN CASH PICKING CROPS OR ECOLOGICALLY MANAGING WOODLANDS.

IT ALL SEEMS A BIT IDEALISTIC, PRIMITIVE, AND *MUDDY* TO ME. PLEASANT ENOUGH FOR A HOLIDAY, MAYBE -- BUT WHAT HAPPENS IN *WINTER*?

MY ONLY EXPERIENCE OF COMMUNAL LIVING WAS IN A BRIXTON *SQUAT* IN THE EARLY SEVENTIES -- ROTTEN CARPETS AND BOARDED WINDOWS -- NEEDLESS TO SAY, IT ENDED IN TEARS.

JO AND SAM ARE HERE.

YEAH, AND ERROL "THE BOLLOCKS."

THE *IDEA* ALWAYS SOUNDS GOOD, BUT THE *PEOPLE* USUALLY SCREW IT UP.

STILL, PLAYING INJUN IN TEPEES MIGHT BE A GOOD WAY TO STAY OUT OF SIGHT FOR A FEW MONTHS.

GOOD, THEY'VE GOT THE SWEAT-LODGE UP.

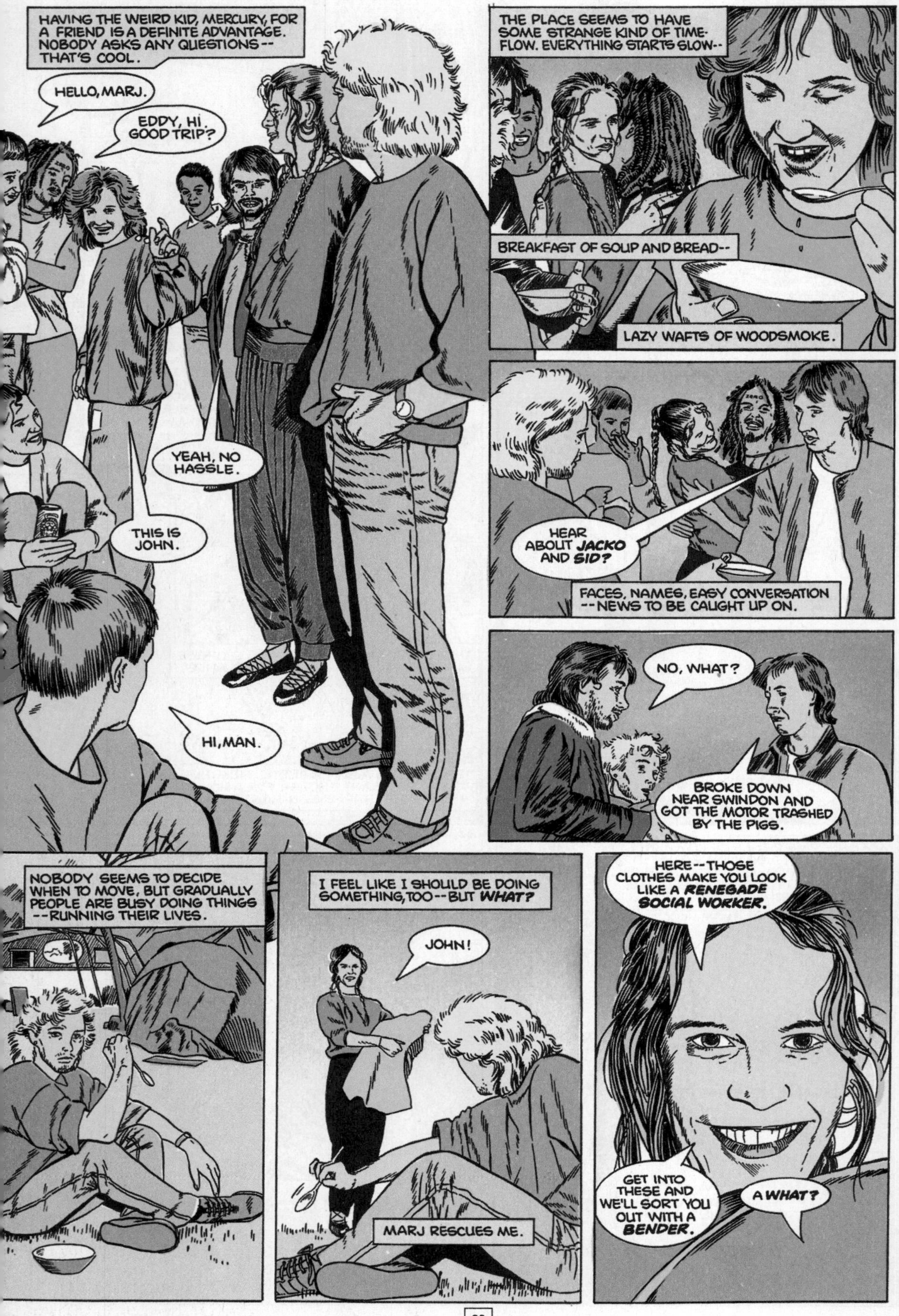

HAVING THE WEIRD KID, MERCURY, FOR A FRIEND IS A DEFINITE ADVANTAGE. NOBODY ASKS ANY QUESTIONS -- THAT'S COOL.
HELLO, MARJ.
EDDY, HI. GOOD TRIP?
YEAH, NO HASSLE.
THIS IS JOHN.
HI, MAN.
THE PLACE SEEMS TO HAVE SOME STRANGE KIND OF TIME-FLOW. EVERYTHING STARTS SLOW--
BREAKFAST OF SOUP AND BREAD--
LAZY WAFTS OF WOODSMOKE.
HEAR ABOUT JACKO AND SID?
FACES, NAMES, EASY CONVERSATION --NEWS TO BE CAUGHT UP ON.
NO, WHAT?
BROKE DOWN NEAR SWINDON AND GOT THE MOTOR TRASHED BY THE PIGS.
NOBODY SEEMS TO DECIDE WHEN TO MOVE, BUT GRADUALLY PEOPLE ARE BUSY DOING THINGS --RUNNING THEIR LIVES.
I FEEL LIKE I SHOULD BE DOING SOMETHING, TOO -- BUT WHAT?
JOHN!
MARJ RESCUES ME.
HERE -- THOSE CLOTHES MAKE YOU LOOK LIKE A RENEGADE SOCIAL WORKER.
GET INTO THESE AND WE'LL SORT YOU OUT WITH A BENDER.
A WHAT?

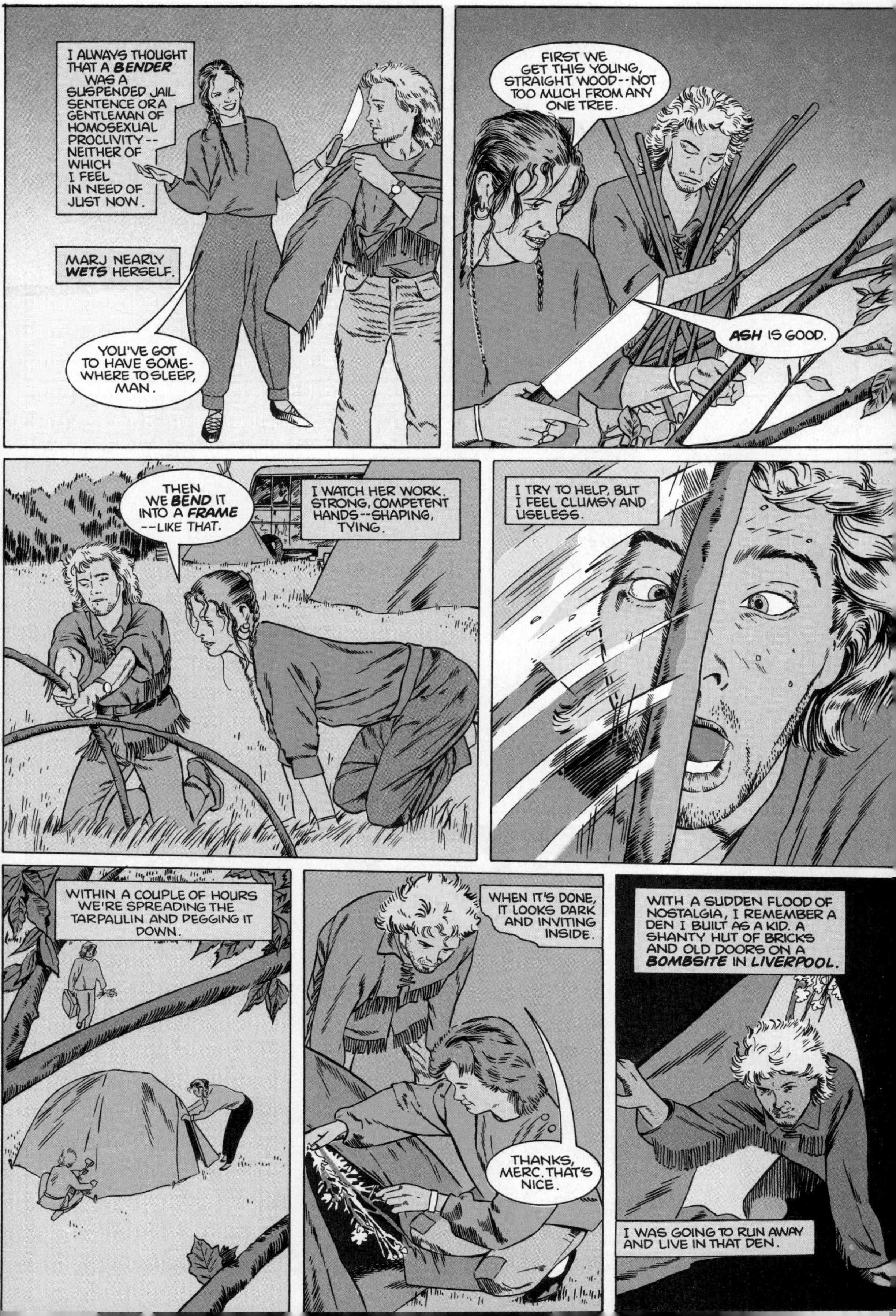
I ALWAYS THOUGHT THAT A BENDER WAS A SUSPENDED JAIL SENTENCE OR A GENTLEMAN OF HOMOSEXUAL PROCLIVITY -- NEITHER OF WHICH I FEEL IN NEED OF JUST NOW.
MARJ NEARLY WETS HERSELF.
YOU'VE GOT TO HAVE SOMEWHERE TO SLEEP, MAN.
FIRST WE GET THIS YOUNG, STRAIGHT WOOD -- NOT TOO MUCH FROM ANY ONE TREE.
ASH IS GOOD.
THEN WE BEND IT INTO A FRAME -- LIKE THAT.
I WATCH HER WORK. STRONG, COMPETENT HANDS -- SHAPING, TYING.
I TRY TO HELP, BUT I FEEL CLUMSY AND USELESS.
WITHIN A COUPLE OF HOURS WE'RE SPREADING THE TARPAULIN AND PEGGING IT DOWN.
WHEN IT'S DONE, IT LOOKS DARK AND INVITING INSIDE.
THANKS, MERC. THAT'S NICE.
WITH A SUDDEN FLOOD OF NOSTALGIA, I REMEMBER A DEN I BUILT AS A KID. A SHANTY HUT OF BRICKS AND OLD DOORS ON A BOMBSITE IN LIVERPOOL.
I WAS GOING TO RUN AWAY AND LIVE IN THAT DEN.

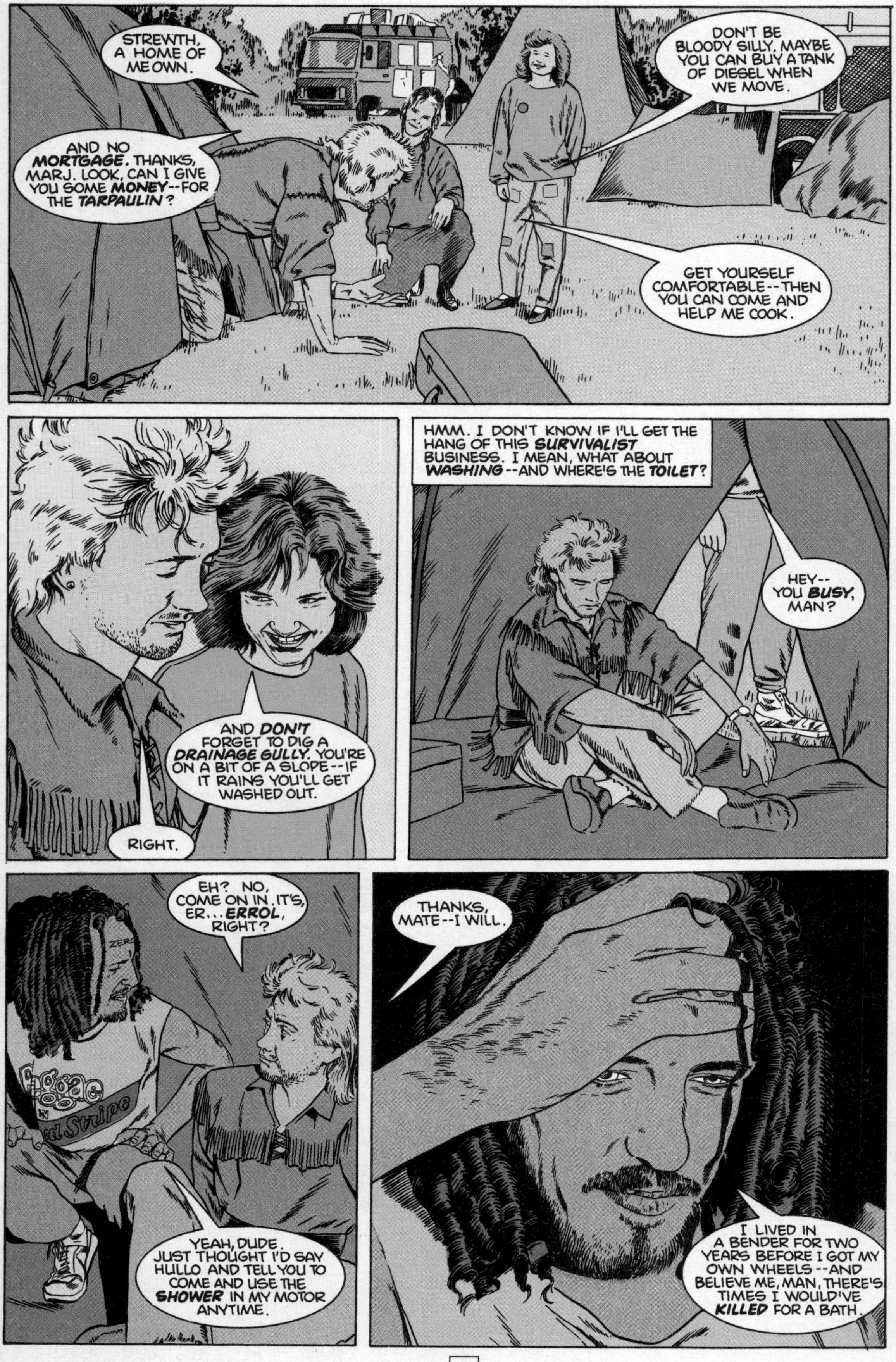
STREWTH, A HOME OF ME OWN.
DON'T BE BLOODY SILLY. MAYBE YOU CAN BUY A TANK OF DIESEL WHEN WE MOVE.
AND NO MORTGAGE. THANKS, MARJ. LOOK, CAN I GIVE YOU SOME MONEY--FOR THE TARPAULIN?
GET YOURSELF COMFORTABLE--THEN YOU CAN COME AND HELP ME COOK.
AND DON'T FORGET TO DIG A DRAINAGE GULLY. YOU'RE ON A BIT OF A SLOPE--IF IT RAINS YOU'LL GET WASHED OUT.
RIGHT.
HMM. I DON'T KNOW IF I'LL GET THE HANG OF THIS SURVIVALIST BUSINESS. I MEAN, WHAT ABOUT WASHING--AND WHERE'S THE TOILET?
HEY--YOU BUSY, MAN?
EH? NO, COME ON IN. IT'S, ER...ERROL, RIGHT?
YEAH, DUDE. JUST THOUGHT I'D SAY HULLO AND TELL YOU TO COME AND USE THE SHOWER IN MY MOTOR ANYTIME.
THANKS, MATE--I WILL.
I LIVED IN A BENDER FOR TWO YEARS BEFORE I GOT MY OWN WHEELS--AND BELIEVE ME, MAN, THERE'S TIMES I WOULD'VE KILLED FOR A BATH.

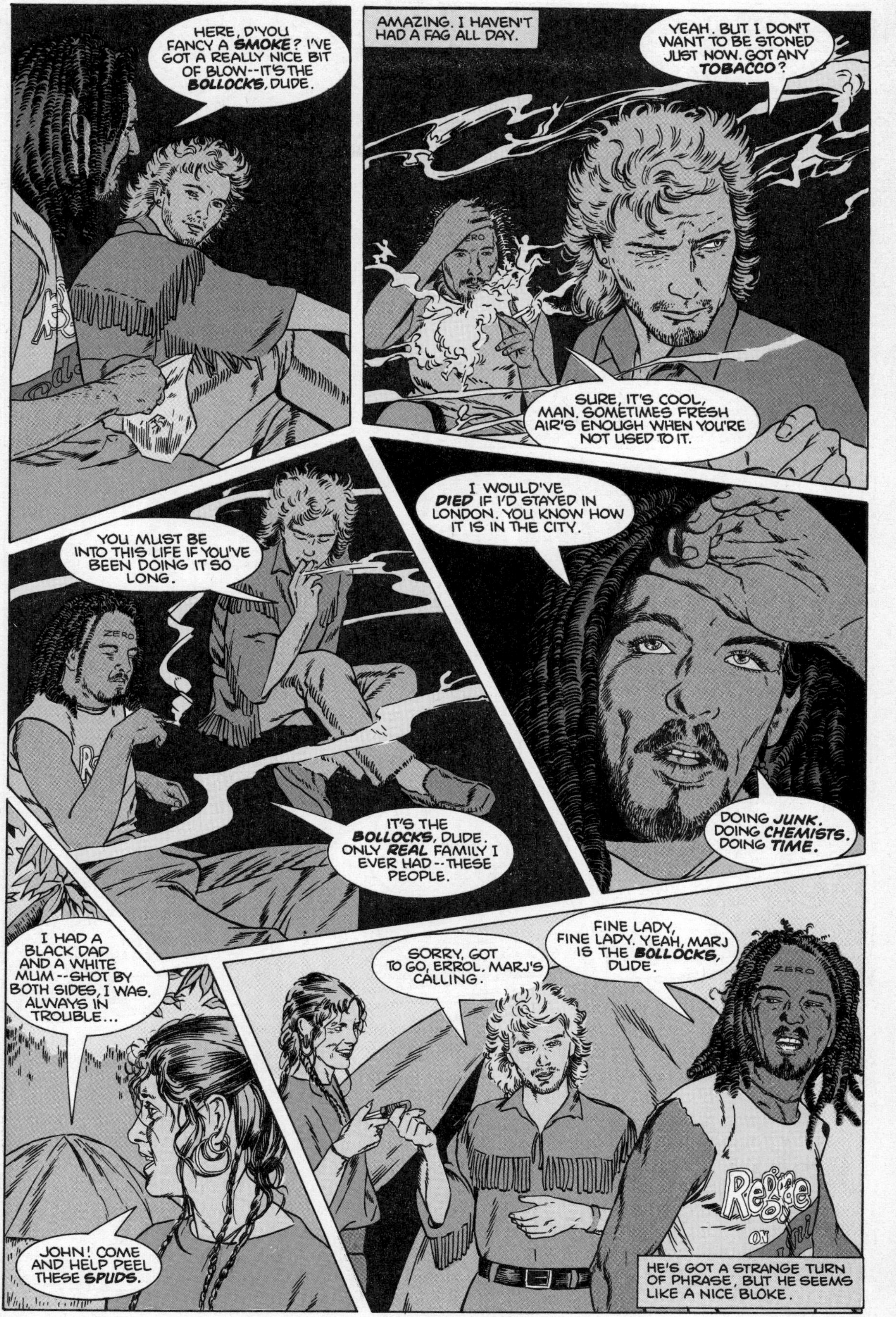
HERE, D'YOU FANCY A SMOKE? I'VE GOT A REALLY NICE BIT OF BLOW--IT'S THE BOLLOCKS, DUDE.
AMAZING. I HAVEN'T HAD A FAG ALL DAY.
YEAH. BUT I DON'T WANT TO BE STONED JUST NOW. GOT ANY TOBACCO?
ZERO
SURE, IT'S COOL, MAN. SOMETIMES FRESH AIR'S ENOUGH WHEN YOU'RE NOT USED TO IT.
YOU MUST BE INTO THIS LIFE IF YOU'VE BEEN DOING IT SO LONG.
ZERO
IT'S THE BOLLOCKS, DUDE. ONLY REAL FAMILY I EVER HAD--THESE PEOPLE.
I WOULD'VE DIED IF I'D STAYED IN LONDON. YOU KNOW HOW IT IS IN THE CITY.
DOING JUNK. DOING CHEMISTS. DOING TIME.
I HAD A BLACK DAD AND A WHITE MUM--SHOT BY BOTH SIDES, I WAS. ALWAYS IN TROUBLE...
JOHN! COME AND HELP PEEL THESE SPUDS.
SORRY, GOT TO GO, ERROL. MARJ'S CALLING.
FINE LADY, FINE LADY. YEAH, MARJ IS THE BOLLOCKS, DUDE.
ZERO
HE'S GOT A STRANGE TURN OF PHRASE, BUT HE SEEMS LIKE A NICE BLOKE.

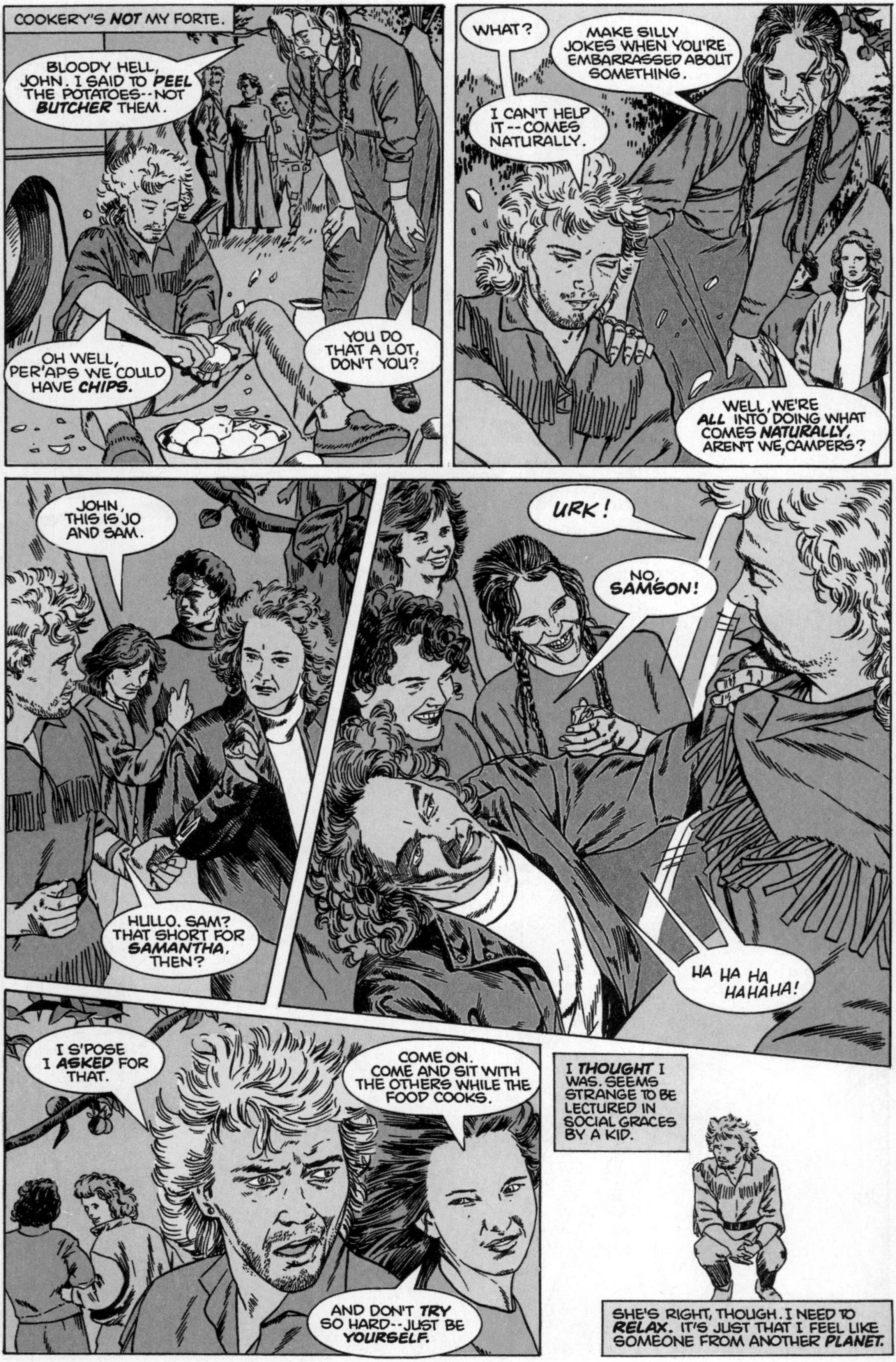

COOKERY'S **NOT** MY FORTE.
BLOODY HELL, JOHN. I SAID TO **PEEL** THE POTATOES--NOT **BUTCHER** THEM.
OH WELL, PER'APS WE COULD HAVE **CHIPS.**
YOU DO THAT A LOT, DON'T YOU?
WHAT?
MAKE SILLY JOKES WHEN YOU'RE EMBARRASSED ABOUT SOMETHING.
I CAN'T HELP IT--COMES NATURALLY.
WELL, WE'RE **ALL** INTO DOING WHAT COMES **NATURALLY,** AREN'T WE, CAMPERS?
JOHN, THIS IS JO AND SAM.
HULLO. SAM? THAT SHORT FOR **SAMANTHA,** THEN?
URK!
NO, **SAMSON!**
HA HA HA HAHAHA!
I S'POSE I **ASKED** FOR THAT.
COME ON. COME AND SIT WITH THE OTHERS WHILE THE FOOD COOKS.
AND DON'T **TRY** SO HARD--JUST BE **YOURSELF.**
I **THOUGHT** I WAS. SEEMS STRANGE TO BE LECTURED IN SOCIAL GRACES BY A KID.
SHE'S RIGHT, THOUGH. I NEED TO **RELAX.** IT'S JUST THAT I FEEL LIKE SOMEONE FROM ANOTHER **PLANET.**

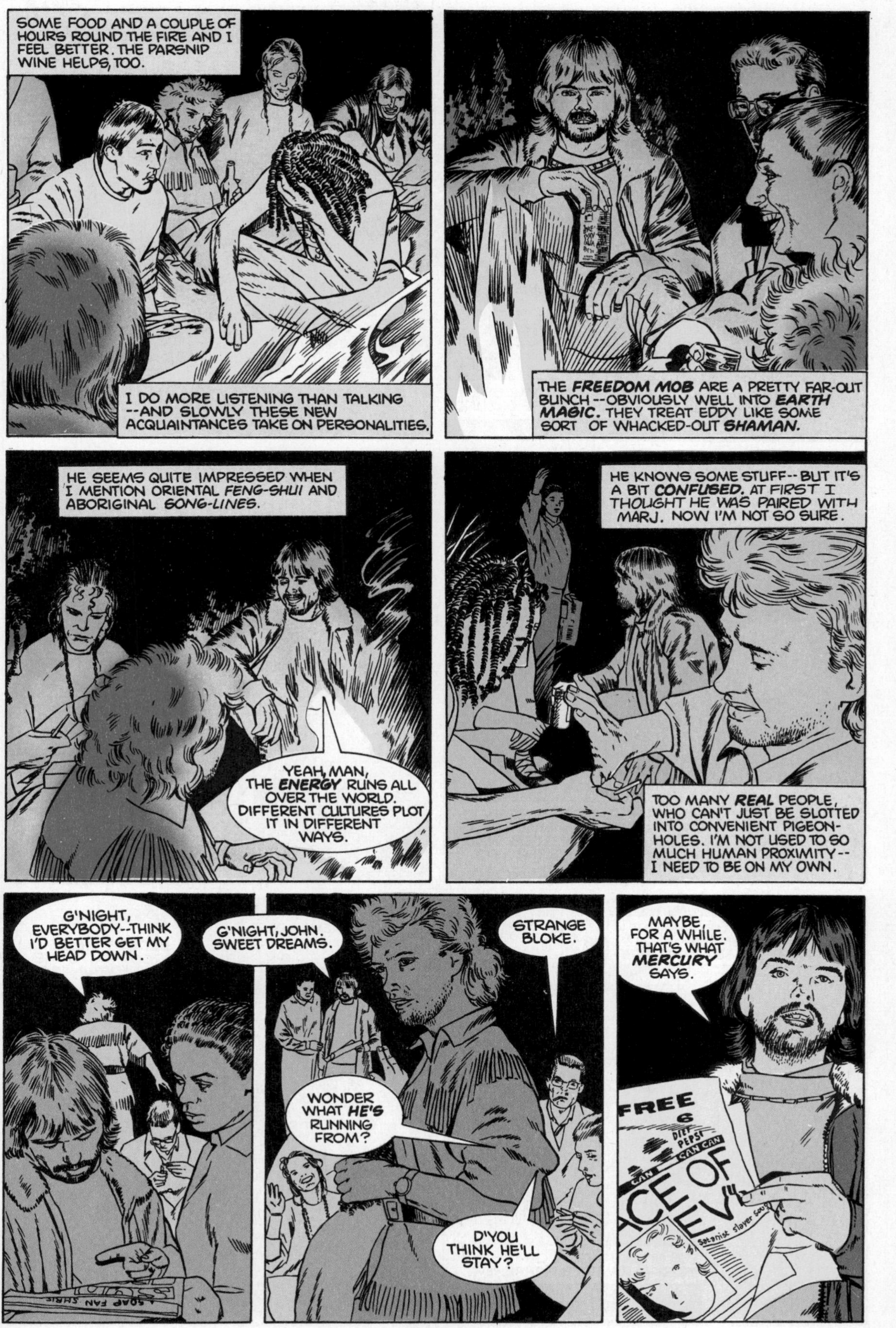
SOME FOOD AND A COUPLE OF HOURS ROUND THE FIRE AND I FEEL BETTER. THE PARSNIP WINE HELPS, TOO.
I DO MORE LISTENING THAN TALKING --AND SLOWLY THESE NEW ACQUAINTANCES TAKE ON PERSONALITIES.
THE FREEDOM MOB ARE A PRETTY FAR-OUT BUNCH --OBVIOUSLY WELL INTO EARTH MAGIC. THEY TREAT EDDY LIKE SOME SORT OF WHACKED-OUT SHAMAN.
HE SEEMS QUITE IMPRESSED WHEN I MENTION ORIENTAL FENG-SHUI AND ABORIGINAL SONG-LINES.
YEAH, MAN, THE ENERGY RUNS ALL OVER THE WORLD. DIFFERENT CULTURES PLOT IT IN DIFFERENT WAYS.
HE KNOWS SOME STUFF-- BUT IT'S A BIT CONFUSED. AT FIRST I THOUGHT HE WAS PAIRED WITH MARJ. NOW I'M NOT SO SURE.
TOO MANY REAL PEOPLE, WHO CAN'T JUST BE SLOTTED INTO CONVENIENT PIGEON-HOLES. I'M NOT USED TO SO MUCH HUMAN PROXIMITY-- I NEED TO BE ON MY OWN.
G'NIGHT, EVERYBODY--THINK I'D BETTER GET MY HEAD DOWN.
G'NIGHT, JOHN. SWEET DREAMS.
STRANGE BLOKE.
WONDER WHAT HE'S RUNNING FROM?
D'YOU THINK HE'LL STAY?
MAYBE, FOR A WHILE. THAT'S WHAT MERCURY SAYS.
FREE

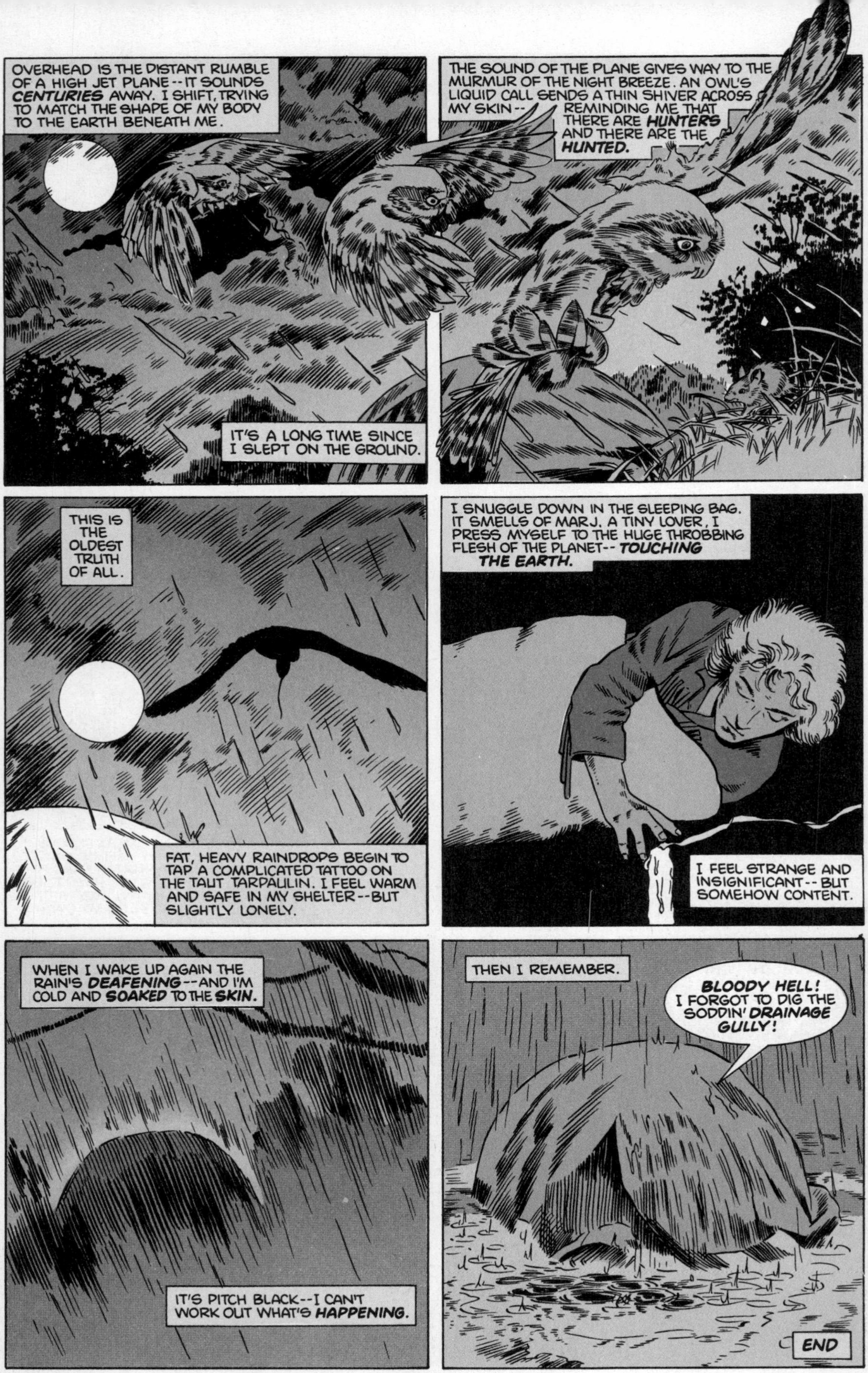
OVERHEAD IS THE DISTANT RUMBLE OF A HIGH JET PLANE--IT SOUNDS CENTURIES AWAY. I SHIFT, TRYING TO MATCH THE SHAPE OF MY BODY TO THE EARTH BENEATH ME.
IT'S A LONG TIME SINCE I SLEPT ON THE GROUND.
THE SOUND OF THE PLANE GIVES WAY TO THE MURMUR OF THE NIGHT BREEZE. AN OWL'S LIQUID CALL SENDS A THIN SHIVER ACROSS MY SKIN--
REMINDING ME THAT THERE ARE HUNTERS AND THERE ARE THE HUNTED.
THIS IS THE OLDEST TRUTH OF ALL.
FAT, HEAVY RAINDROPS BEGIN TO TAP A COMPLICATED TATTOO ON THE TAUT TARPAULIN. I FEEL WARM AND SAFE IN MY SHELTER--BUT SLIGHTLY LONELY.
I SNUGGLE DOWN IN THE SLEEPING BAG. IT SMELLS OF MARJ. A TINY LOVER, I PRESS MYSELF TO THE HUGE THROBBING FLESH OF THE PLANET--TOUCHING THE EARTH.
I FEEL STRANGE AND INSIGNIFICANT--BUT SOMEHOW CONTENT.
WHEN I WAKE UP AGAIN THE RAIN'S DEAFENING--AND I'M COLD AND SOAKED TO THE SKIN.
IT'S PITCH BLACK--I CAN'T WORK OUT WHAT'S HAPPENING.
THEN I REMEMBER.
BLOODY HELL! I FORGOT TO DIG THE SODDIN' DRAINAGE GULLY!
END

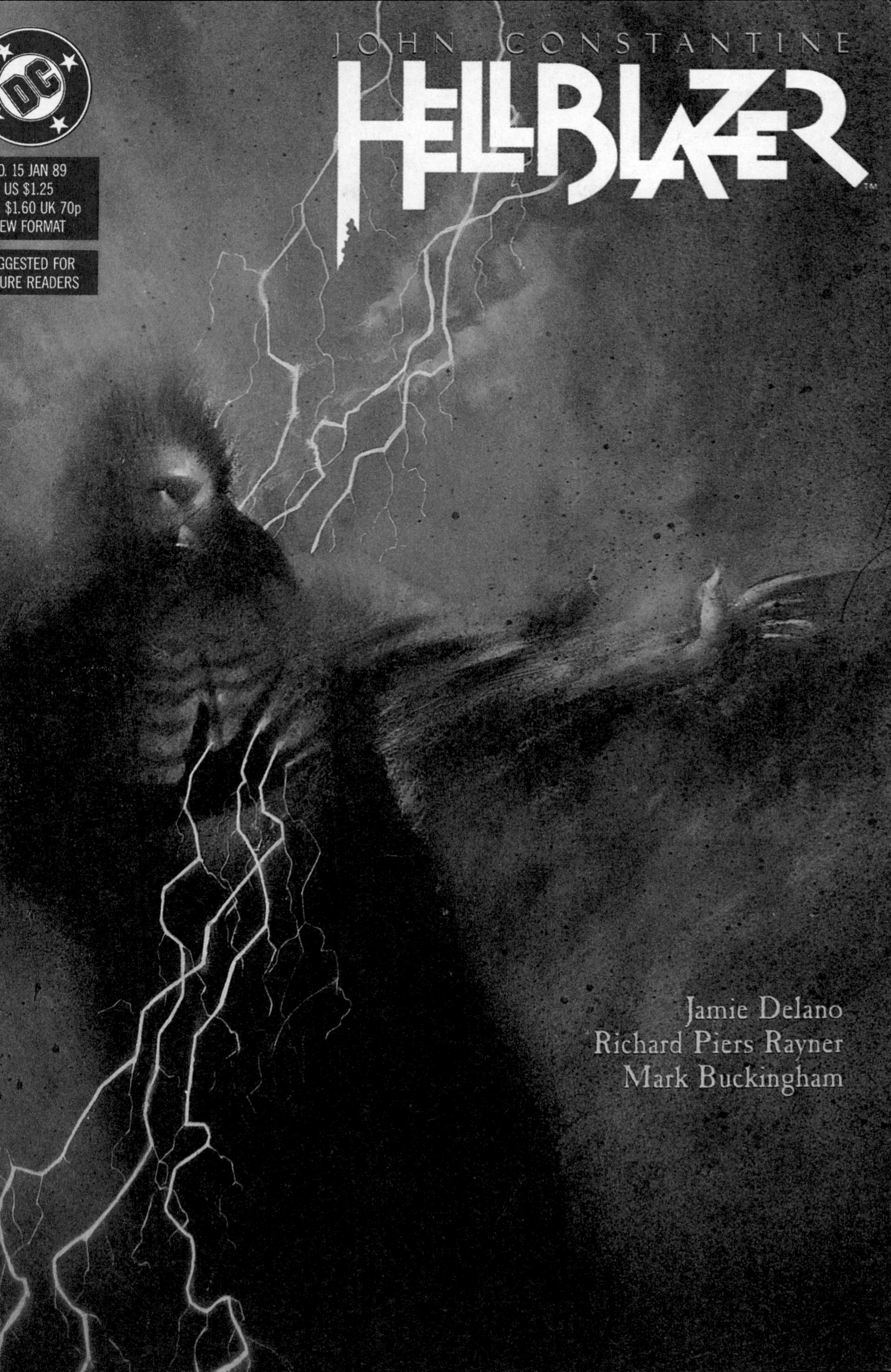
JOHN CONSTANTINE
HELLBLAZER
TM
O. 15 JAN 89
US $1.25
$1.60 UK 70p
EW FORMAT
GGESTED FOR
URE READERS
Jamie Delano
Richard Piers Rayner
Mark Buckingham

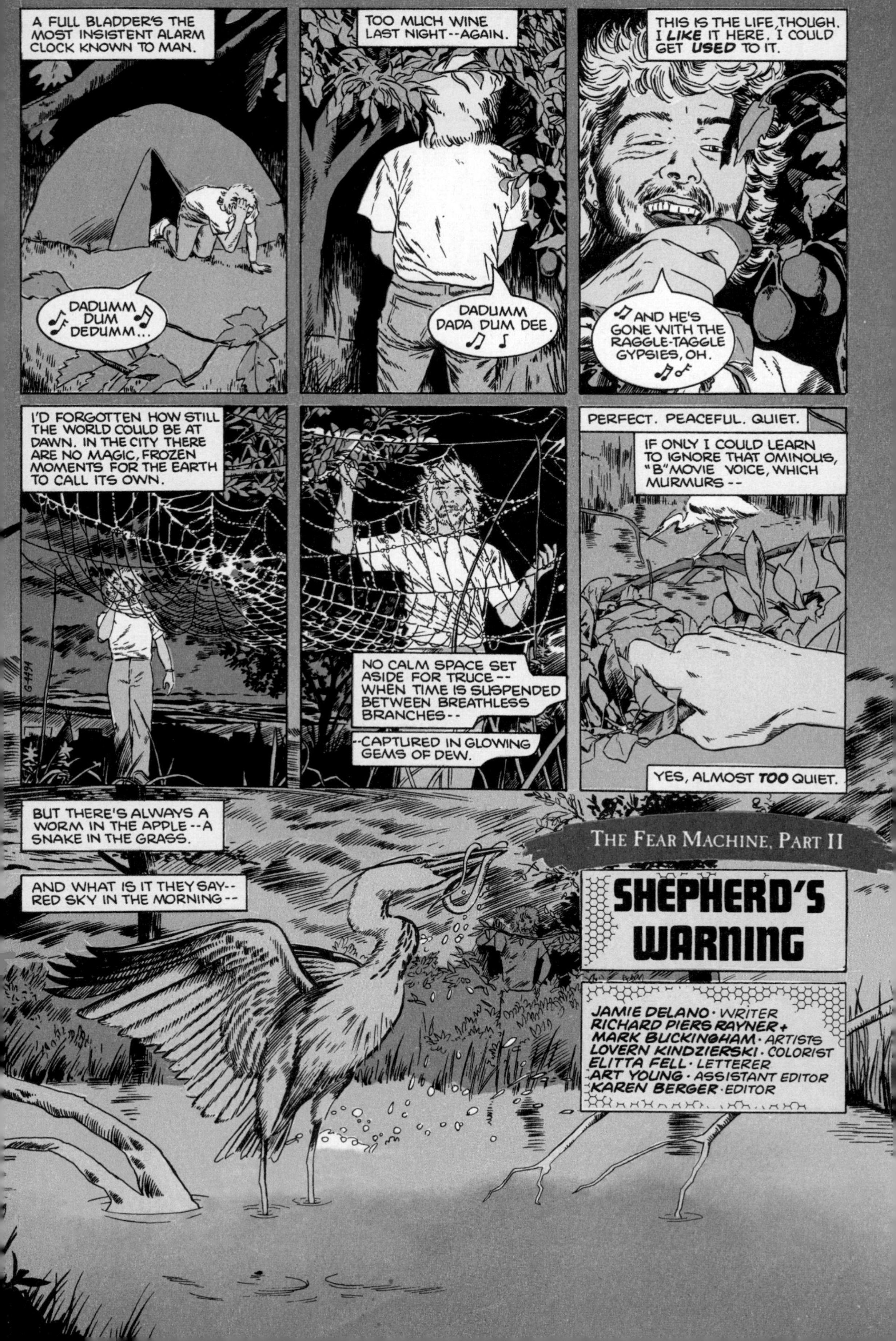
A FULL BLADDER'S THE MOST INSISTENT ALARM CLOCK KNOWN TO MAN.
DADUMM DUM DEDUMM...
TOO MUCH WINE LAST NIGHT--AGAIN.
DADUMM DADA DUM DEE.
THIS IS THE LIFE, THOUGH. I LIKE IT HERE. I COULD GET USED TO IT.
AND HE'S GONE WITH THE RAGGLE-TAGGLE GYPSIES, OH.
I'D FORGOTTEN HOW STILL THE WORLD COULD BE AT DAWN. IN THE CITY THERE ARE NO MAGIC, FROZEN MOMENTS FOR THE EARTH TO CALL ITS OWN.
NO CALM SPACE SET ASIDE FOR TRUCE-- WHEN TIME IS SUSPENDED BETWEEN BREATHLESS BRANCHES--
--CAPTURED IN GLOWING GEMS OF DEW.
PERFECT. PEACEFUL. QUIET.
IF ONLY I COULD LEARN TO IGNORE THAT OMINOUS, "B" MOVIE VOICE, WHICH MURMURS--
YES, ALMOST TOO QUIET.
BUT THERE'S ALWAYS A WORM IN THE APPLE--A SNAKE IN THE GRASS.
AND WHAT IS IT THEY SAY-- RED SKY IN THE MORNING--
THE FEAR MACHINE, PART II
SHEPHERD'S WARNING
JAMIE DELANO · WRITER
RICHARD PIERS RAYNER + MARK BUCKINGHAM · ARTISTS
LOVERN KINDZIERSKI · COLORIST
ELITTA FELL · LETTERER
ART YOUNG · ASSISTANT EDITOR
KAREN BERGER · EDITOR

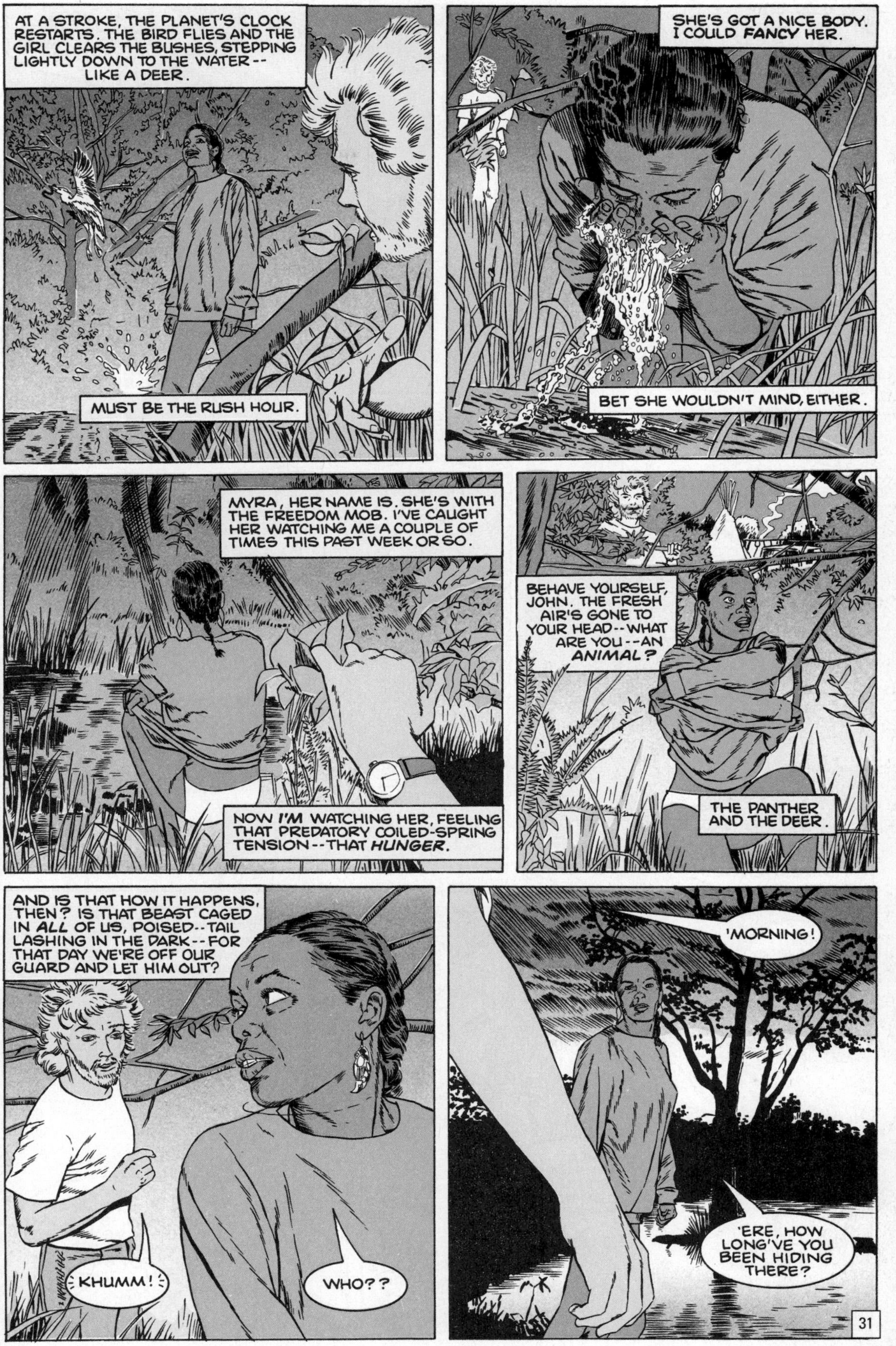
AT A STROKE, THE PLANET'S CLOCK RESTARTS. THE BIRD FLIES AND THE GIRL CLEARS THE BUSHES, STEPPING LIGHTLY DOWN TO THE WATER -- LIKE A DEER.
MUST BE THE RUSH HOUR.
SHE'S GOT A NICE BODY. I COULD FANCY HER.
BET SHE WOULDN'T MIND, EITHER.
MYRA, HER NAME IS. SHE'S WITH THE FREEDOM MOB. I'VE CAUGHT HER WATCHING ME A COUPLE OF TIMES THIS PAST WEEK OR SO.
NOW I'M WATCHING HER, FEELING THAT PREDATORY COILED-SPRING TENSION -- THAT HUNGER.
BEHAVE YOURSELF, JOHN. THE FRESH AIR'S GONE TO YOUR HEAD -- WHAT ARE YOU -- AN ANIMAL?
THE PANTHER AND THE DEER.
AND IS THAT HOW IT HAPPENS, THEN? IS THAT BEAST CAGED IN ALL OF US, POISED -- TAIL LASHING IN THE DARK -- FOR THAT DAY WE'RE OFF OUR GUARD AND LET HIM OUT?
KHUMM!
WHO??
'MORNING!
'ERE, HOW LONG'VE YOU BEEN HIDING THERE?

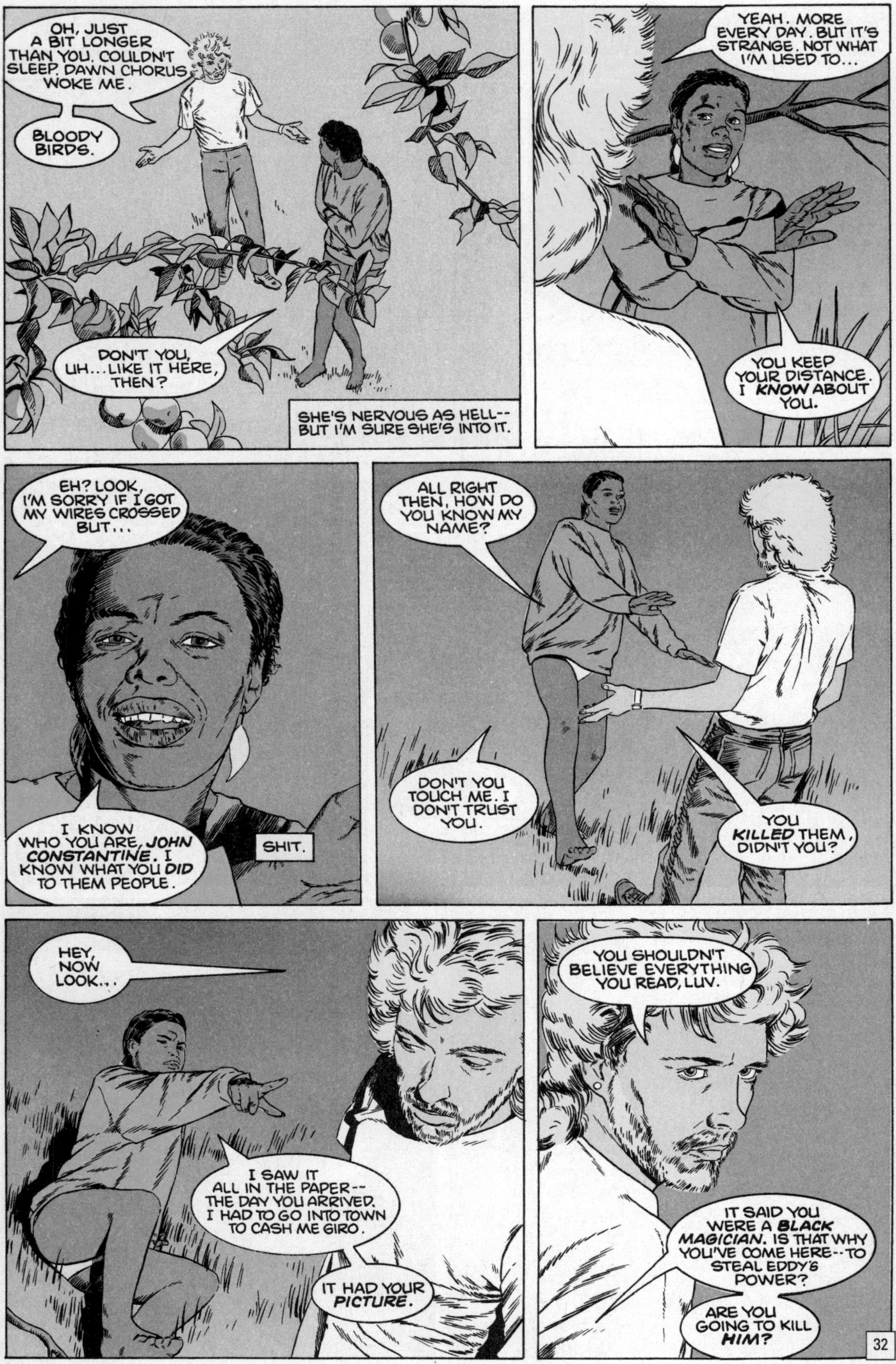
OH, JUST A BIT LONGER THAN YOU. COULDN'T SLEEP. DAWN CHORUS WOKE ME.
BLOODY BIRDS.
DON'T YOU, UH... LIKE IT HERE, THEN?
SHE'S NERVOUS AS HELL-- BUT I'M SURE SHE'S INTO IT.
YEAH. MORE EVERY DAY. BUT IT'S STRANGE. NOT WHAT I'M USED TO...
YOU KEEP YOUR DISTANCE. I KNOW ABOUT YOU.
EH? LOOK, I'M SORRY IF I GOT MY WIRES CROSSED BUT...
I KNOW WHO YOU ARE, JOHN CONSTANTINE. I KNOW WHAT YOU DID TO THEM PEOPLE.
SHIT.
ALL RIGHT THEN, HOW DO YOU KNOW MY NAME?
DON'T YOU TOUCH ME. I DON'T TRUST YOU.
YOU KILLED THEM, DIDN'T YOU?
HEY, NOW LOOK...
I SAW IT ALL IN THE PAPER-- THE DAY YOU ARRIVED. I HAD TO GO INTO TOWN TO CASH ME GIRO.
IT HAD YOUR PICTURE.
YOU SHOULDN'T BELIEVE EVERYTHING YOU READ, LUV.
IT SAID YOU WERE A BLACK MAGICIAN. IS THAT WHY YOU'VE COME HERE--TO STEAL EDDY'S POWER?
ARE YOU GOING TO KILL HIM?

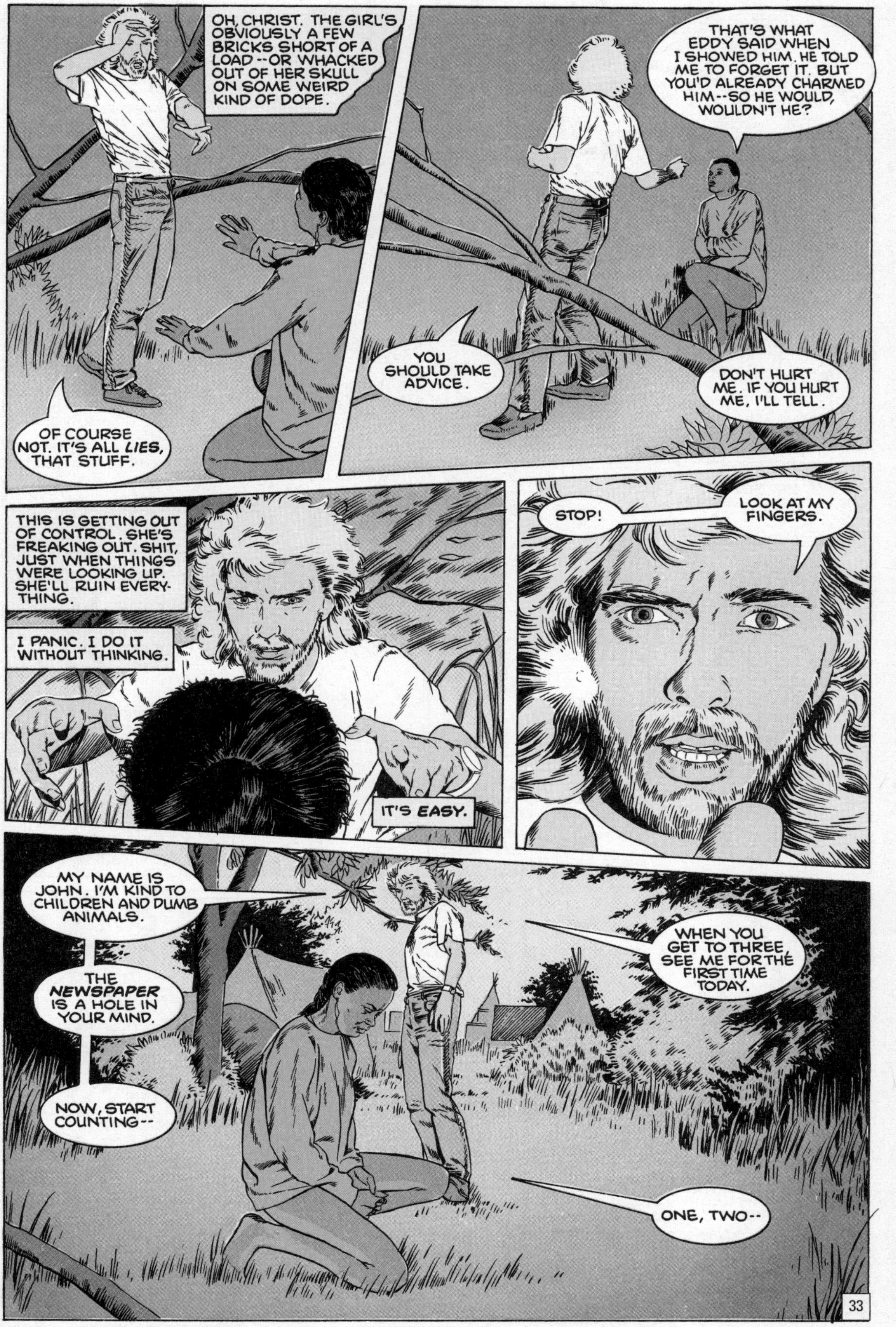
OH, CHRIST. THE GIRL'S OBVIOUSLY A FEW BRICKS SHORT OF A LOAD--OR WHACKED OUT OF HER SKULL ON SOME WEIRD KIND OF DOPE.
OF COURSE NOT. IT'S ALL *LIES*, THAT STUFF.
THAT'S WHAT EDDY SAID WHEN I SHOWED HIM. HE TOLD ME TO FORGET IT. BUT YOU'D ALREADY CHARMED HIM--SO HE WOULD, WOULDN'T HE?
YOU SHOULD TAKE ADVICE.
DON'T HURT ME. IF YOU HURT ME, I'LL TELL.
THIS IS GETTING OUT OF CONTROL. SHE'S FREAKING OUT. SHIT, JUST WHEN THINGS WERE LOOKING UP. SHE'LL RUIN EVERY-THING.
I PANIC. I DO IT WITHOUT THINKING.
IT'S *EASY*.
STOP!
LOOK AT MY FINGERS.
MY NAME IS JOHN. I'M KIND TO CHILDREN AND DUMB ANIMALS.
THE *NEWSPAPER* IS A HOLE IN YOUR MIND.
NOW, START COUNTING--
WHEN YOU GET TO THREE, SEE ME FOR THE FIRST TIME TODAY.
ONE, TWO--

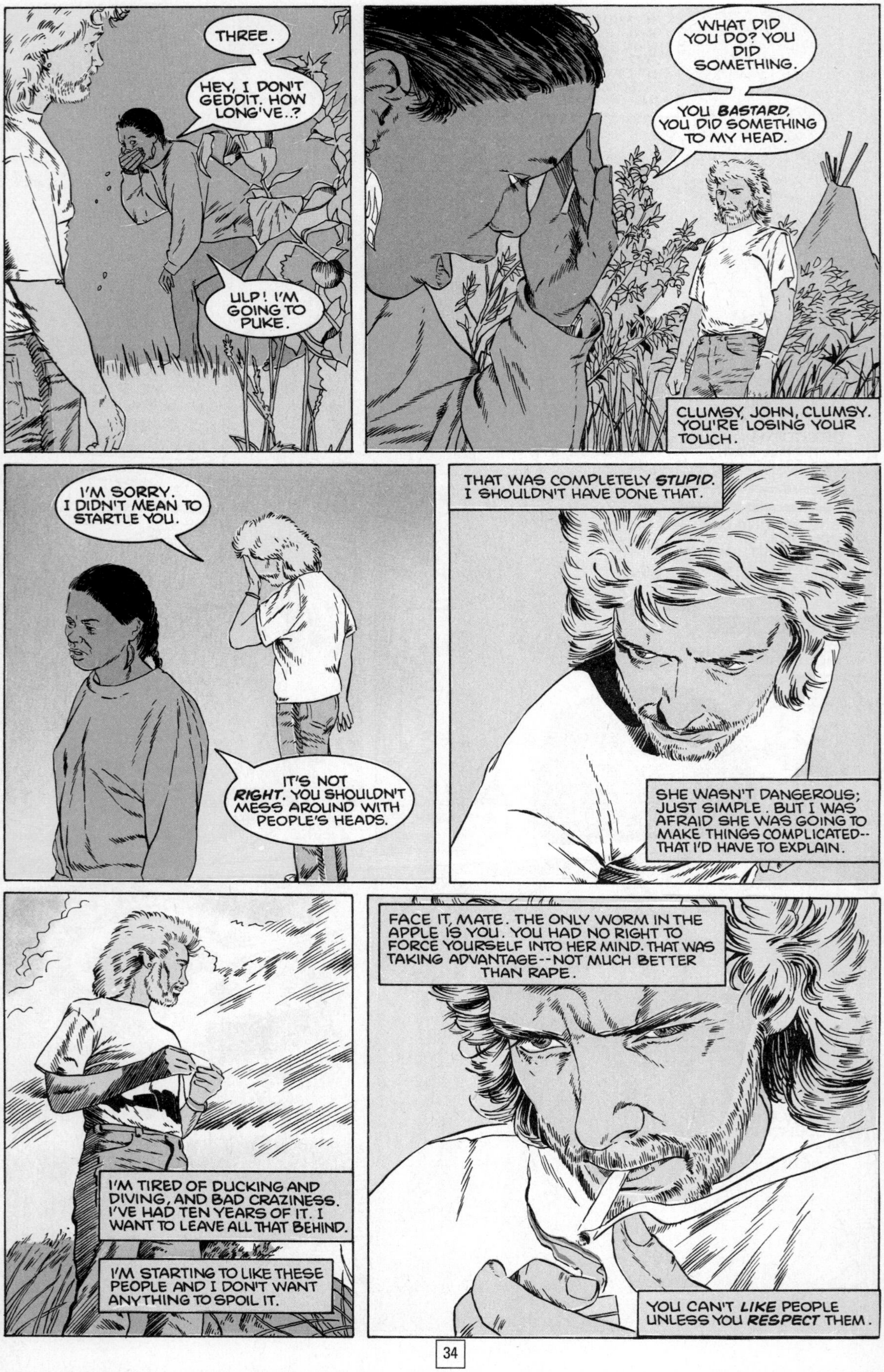
THREE.
HEY, I DON'T GEDDIT. HOW LONG'VE..?
ULP! I'M GOING TO PUKE.
WHAT DID YOU DO? YOU DID SOMETHING.
YOU BASTARD, YOU DID SOMETHING TO MY HEAD.
CLUMSY, JOHN, CLUMSY. YOU'RE LOSING YOUR TOUCH.
I'M SORRY. I DIDN'T MEAN TO STARTLE YOU.
IT'S NOT RIGHT. YOU SHOULDN'T MESS AROUND WITH PEOPLE'S HEADS.
THAT WAS COMPLETELY STUPID. I SHOULDN'T HAVE DONE THAT.
SHE WASN'T DANGEROUS; JUST SIMPLE. BUT I WAS AFRAID SHE WAS GOING TO MAKE THINGS COMPLICATED--THAT I'D HAVE TO EXPLAIN.
I'M TIRED OF DUCKING AND DIVING, AND BAD CRAZINESS. I'VE HAD TEN YEARS OF IT. I WANT TO LEAVE ALL THAT BEHIND.
I'M STARTING TO LIKE THESE PEOPLE AND I DON'T WANT ANYTHING TO SPOIL IT.
FACE IT, MATE. THE ONLY WORM IN THE APPLE IS YOU. YOU HAD NO RIGHT TO FORCE YOURSELF INTO HER MIND. THAT WAS TAKING ADVANTAGE--NOT MUCH BETTER THAN RAPE.
YOU CAN'T LIKE PEOPLE UNLESS YOU RESPECT THEM.

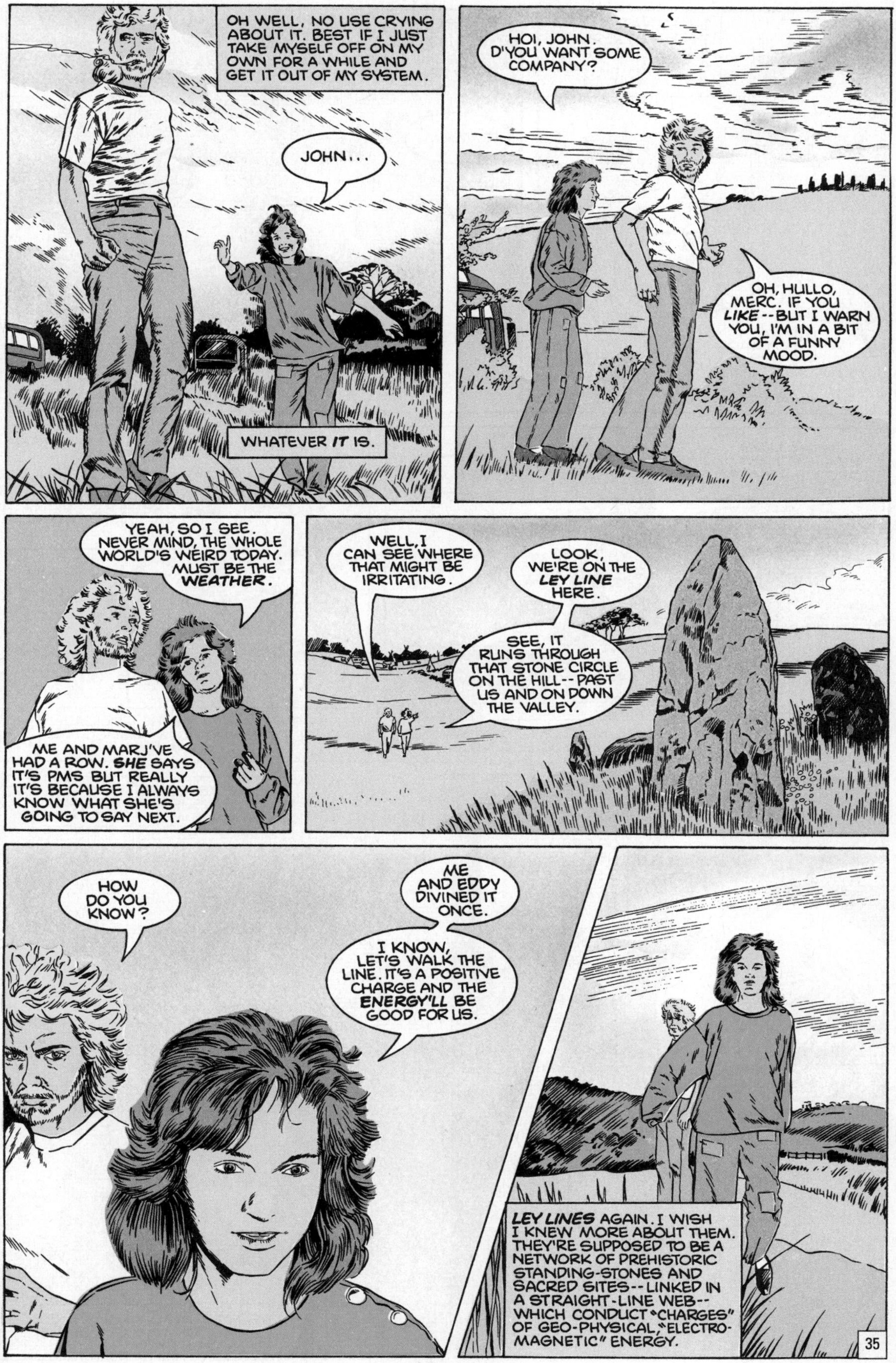
OH WELL, NO USE CRYING ABOUT IT. BEST IF I JUST TAKE MYSELF OFF ON MY OWN FOR A WHILE AND GET IT OUT OF MY SYSTEM.
JOHN...
WHATEVER IT IS.
HOI, JOHN. D'YOU WANT SOME COMPANY?
OH, HULLO, MERC. IF YOU LIKE--BUT I WARN YOU, I'M IN A BIT OF A FUNNY MOOD.
YEAH, SO I SEE. NEVER MIND, THE WHOLE WORLD'S WEIRD TODAY. MUST BE THE WEATHER.
ME AND MARJ'VE HAD A ROW. SHE SAYS IT'S PMS BUT REALLY IT'S BECAUSE I ALWAYS KNOW WHAT SHE'S GOING TO SAY NEXT.
WELL, I CAN SEE WHERE THAT MIGHT BE IRRITATING.
LOOK, WE'RE ON THE LEY LINE HERE.
SEE, IT RUNS THROUGH THAT STONE CIRCLE ON THE HILL--PAST US AND ON DOWN THE VALLEY.
HOW DO YOU KNOW?
ME AND EDDY DIVINED IT ONCE.
I KNOW, LET'S WALK THE LINE. IT'S A POSITIVE CHARGE AND THE ENERGY'LL BE GOOD FOR US.
LEY LINES AGAIN. I WISH I KNEW MORE ABOUT THEM. THEY'RE SUPPOSED TO BE A NETWORK OF PREHISTORIC STANDING-STONES AND SACRED SITES--LINKED IN A STRAIGHT-LINE WEB--WHICH CONDUCT "CHARGES" OF GEO-PHYSICAL, "ELECTRO-MAGNETIC" ENERGY.

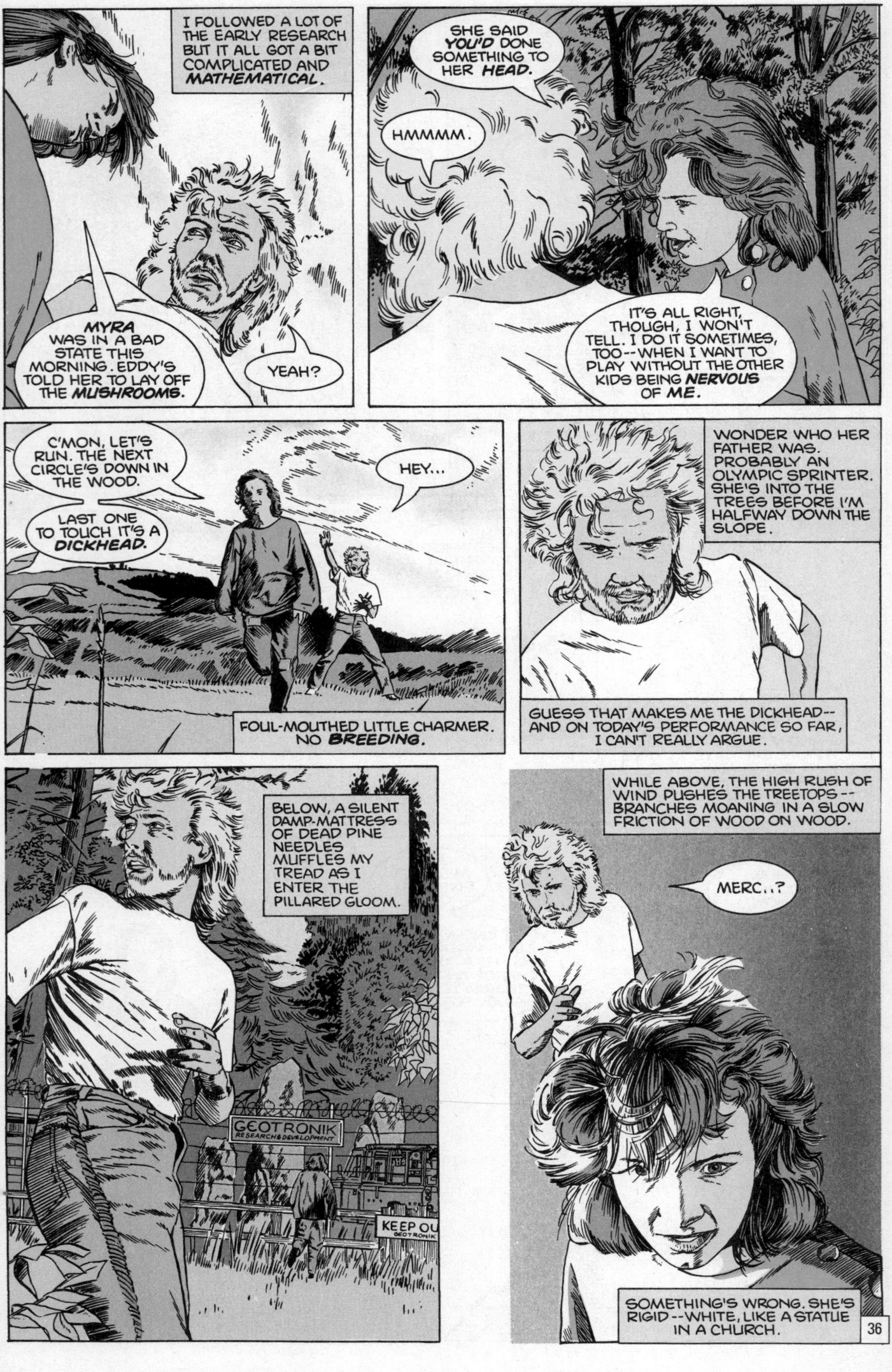

I FOLLOWED A LOT OF THE EARLY RESEARCH BUT IT ALL GOT A BIT COMPLICATED AND MATHEMATICAL.
MYRA WAS IN A BAD STATE THIS MORNING. EDDY'S TOLD HER TO LAY OFF THE MUSHROOMS.
YEAH?
SHE SAID YOU'D DONE SOMETHING TO HER HEAD.
HMMMM.
IT'S ALL RIGHT, THOUGH, I WON'T TELL. I DO IT SOMETIMES, TOO--WHEN I WANT TO PLAY WITHOUT THE OTHER KIDS BEING NERVOUS OF ME.
C'MON, LET'S RUN. THE NEXT CIRCLE'S DOWN IN THE WOOD.
LAST ONE TO TOUCH IT'S A DICKHEAD.
HEY...
FOUL-MOUTHED LITTLE CHARMER. NO BREEDING.
WONDER WHO HER FATHER WAS. PROBABLY AN OLYMPIC SPRINTER. SHE'S INTO THE TREES BEFORE I'M HALFWAY DOWN THE SLOPE.
GUESS THAT MAKES ME THE DICKHEAD-- AND ON TODAY'S PERFORMANCE SO FAR, I CAN'T REALLY ARGUE.
BELOW, A SILENT DAMP-MATTRESS OF DEAD PINE NEEDLES MUFFLES MY TREAD AS I ENTER THE PILLARED GLOOM.
GEOTRONIK
RESEARCH & DEVELOPMENT
KEEP OU
GEOTRONIK
WHILE ABOVE, THE HIGH RUSH OF WIND PUSHES THE TREETOPS -- BRANCHES MOANING IN A SLOW FRICTION OF WOOD ON WOOD.
MERC..?
SOMETHING'S WRONG. SHE'S RIGID--WHITE, LIKE A STATUE IN A CHURCH.

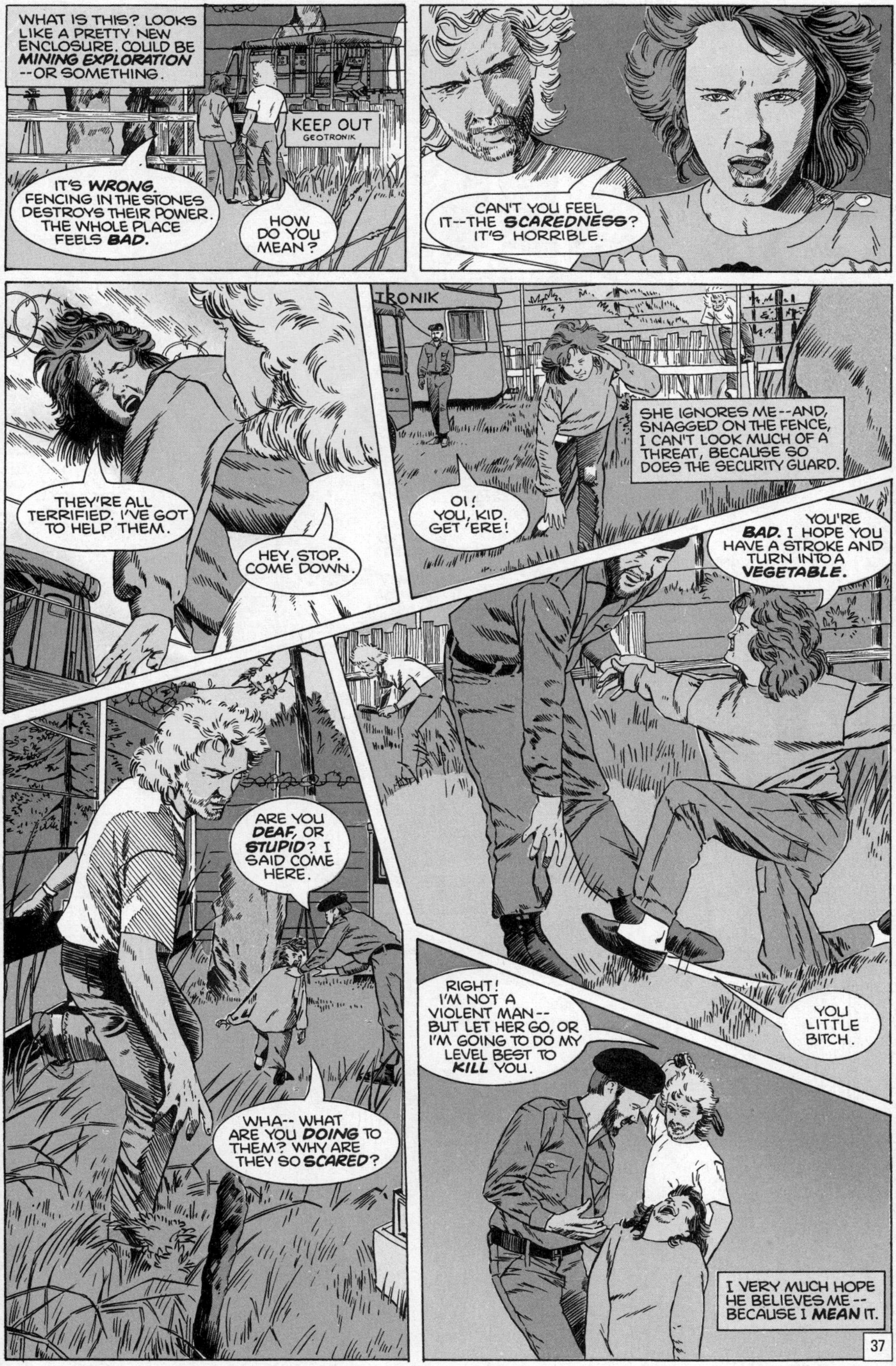
WHAT IS THIS? LOOKS LIKE A PRETTY NEW ENCLOSURE. COULD BE MINING EXPLORATION --OR SOMETHING.
KEEP OUT GEOTRONIK
IT'S WRONG. FENCING IN THE STONES DESTROYS THEIR POWER. THE WHOLE PLACE FEELS BAD.
HOW DO YOU MEAN?
CAN'T YOU FEEL IT--THE SCAREDNESS? IT'S HORRIBLE.
THEY'RE ALL TERRIFIED. I'VE GOT TO HELP THEM.
HEY, STOP. COME DOWN.
TRONIK
SHE IGNORES ME--AND, SNAGGED ON THE FENCE, I CAN'T LOOK MUCH OF A THREAT, BECAUSE SO DOES THE SECURITY GUARD.
OI! YOU, KID. GET 'ERE!
ARE YOU DEAF, OR STUPID? I SAID COME HERE.
WHA-- WHAT ARE YOU DOING TO THEM? WHY ARE THEY SO SCARED?
YOU'RE BAD. I HOPE YOU HAVE A STROKE AND TURN INTO A VEGETABLE.
YOU LITTLE BITCH.
RIGHT! I'M NOT A VIOLENT MAN-- BUT LET HER GO, OR I'M GOING TO DO MY LEVEL BEST TO KILL YOU.
I VERY MUCH HOPE HE BELIEVES ME-- BECAUSE I MEAN IT.

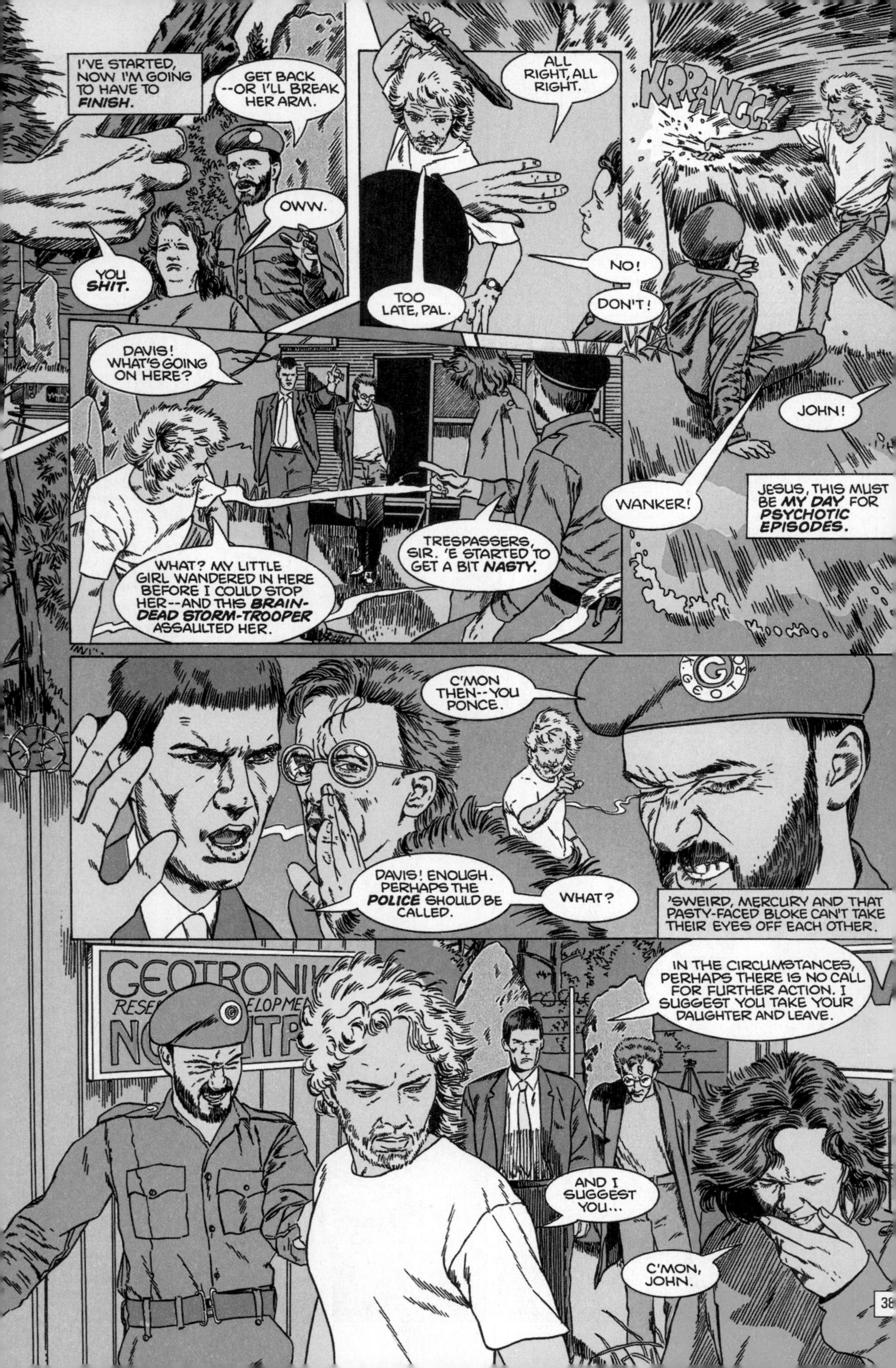
I'VE STARTED, NOW I'M GOING TO HAVE TO FINISH.
GET BACK --OR I'LL BREAK HER ARM.
OWW.
YOU SHIT.
ALL RIGHT, ALL RIGHT.
TOO LATE, PAL.
NO!
DON'T!
KRRANCC!
JOHN!
DAVIS! WHAT'S GOING ON HERE?
TRESPASSERS, SIR. 'E STARTED TO GET A BIT NASTY.
WHAT? MY LITTLE GIRL WANDERED IN HERE BEFORE I COULD STOP HER--AND THIS BRAIN-DEAD STORM-TROOPER ASSAULTED HER.
WANKER!
JESUS, THIS MUST BE MY DAY FOR PSYCHOTIC EPISODES.
C'MON THEN--YOU PONCE.
GEOTRO
DAVIS! ENOUGH. PERHAPS THE POLICE SHOULD BE CALLED.
WHAT?
'SWEIRD, MERCURY AND THAT PASTY-FACED BLOKE CAN'T TAKE THEIR EYES OFF EACH OTHER.
GEOTRONI
RESE ELOPME
NO TR
IN THE CIRCUMSTANCES, PERHAPS THERE IS NO CALL FOR FURTHER ACTION. I SUGGEST YOU TAKE YOUR DAUGHTER AND LEAVE.
AND I SUGGEST YOU...
C'MON, JOHN.

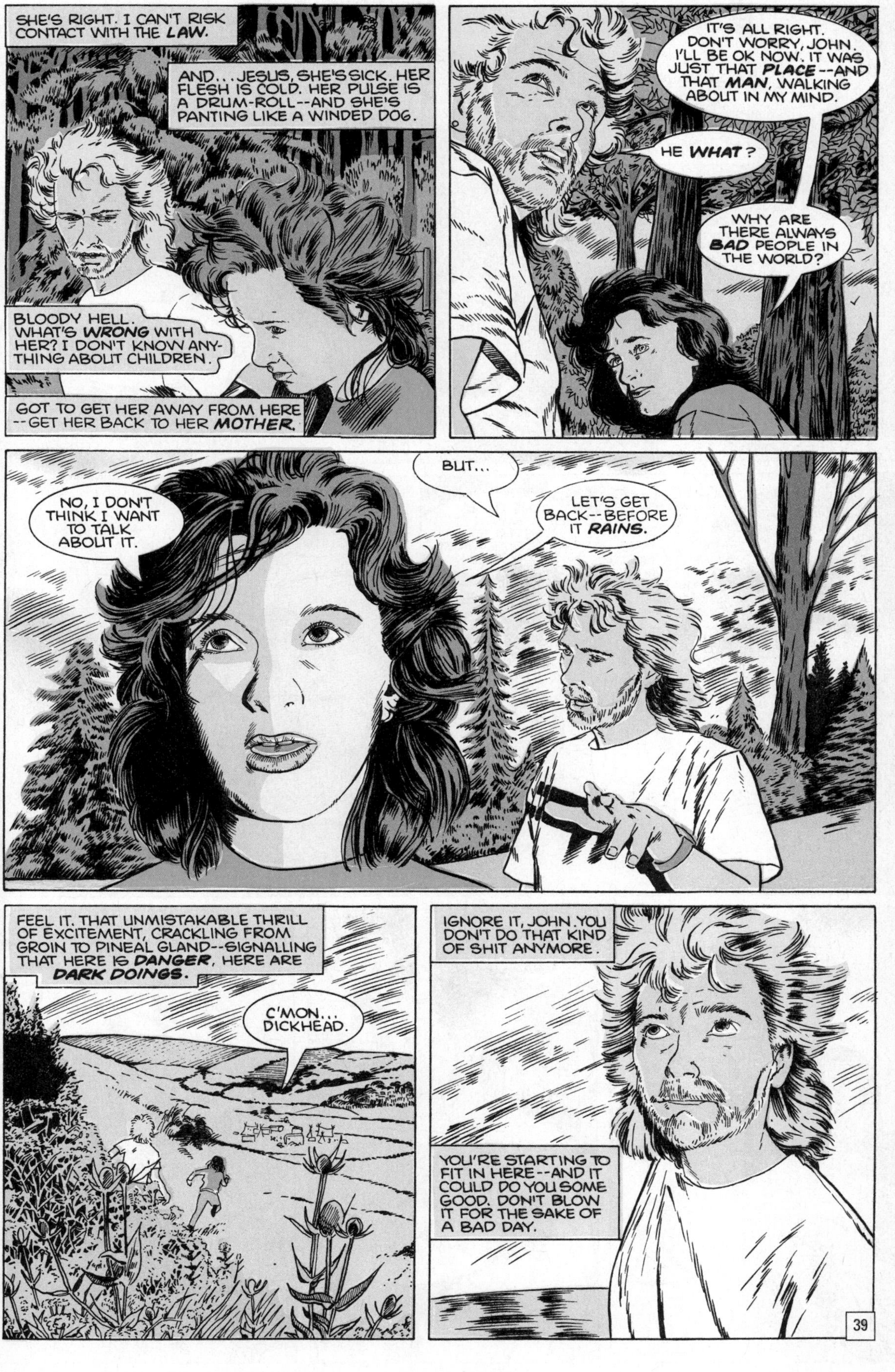
SHE'S RIGHT. I CAN'T RISK CONTACT WITH THE LAW.
AND... JESUS, SHE'S SICK. HER FLESH IS COLD. HER PULSE IS A DRUM-ROLL--AND SHE'S PANTING LIKE A WINDED DOG.
BLOODY HELL. WHAT'S WRONG WITH HER? I DON'T KNOW ANYTHING ABOUT CHILDREN.
GOT TO GET HER AWAY FROM HERE --GET HER BACK TO HER MOTHER.
IT'S ALL RIGHT. DON'T WORRY, JOHN. I'LL BE OK NOW. IT WAS JUST THAT PLACE--AND THAT MAN, WALKING ABOUT IN MY MIND.
HE WHAT?
WHY ARE THERE ALWAYS BAD PEOPLE IN THE WORLD?
NO, I DON'T THINK I WANT TO TALK ABOUT IT.
BUT...
LET'S GET BACK--BEFORE IT RAINS.
FEEL IT. THAT UNMISTAKABLE THRILL OF EXCITEMENT, CRACKLING FROM GROIN TO PINEAL GLAND--SIGNALLING THAT HERE IS DANGER, HERE ARE DARK DOINGS.
C'MON... DICKHEAD.
IGNORE IT, JOHN. YOU DON'T DO THAT KIND OF SHIT ANYMORE.
YOU'RE STARTING TO FIT IN HERE--AND IT COULD DO YOU SOME GOOD. DON'T BLOW IT FOR THE SAKE OF A BAD DAY.

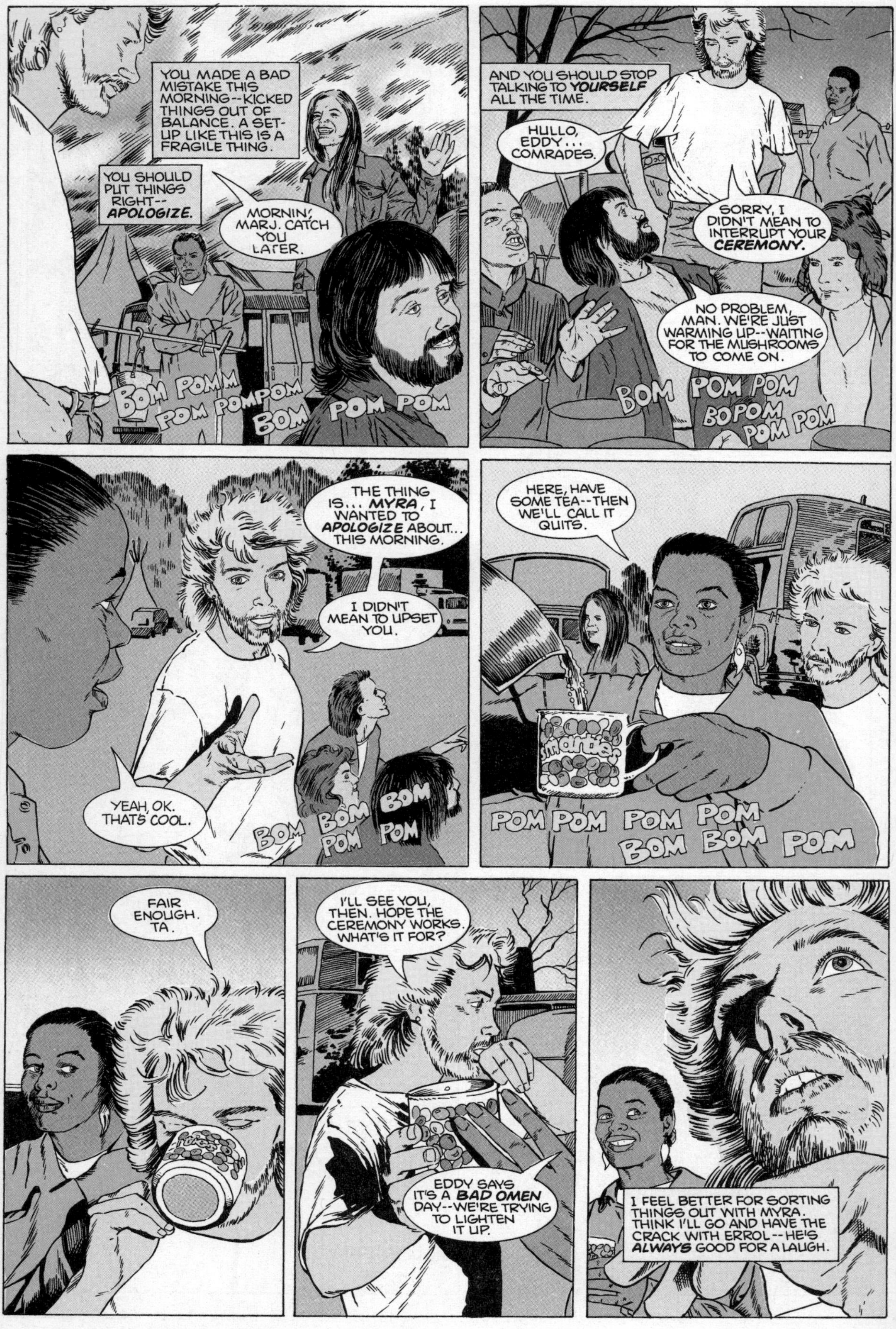
YOU MADE A BAD MISTAKE THIS MORNING--KICKED THINGS OUT OF BALANCE. A SET-UP LIKE THIS IS A FRAGILE THING.
YOU SHOULD PUT THINGS RIGHT--*APOLOGIZE.*
MORNIN', MARJ. CATCH YOU LATER.
BOM POMM POM POMPOM BOM POM POM
AND YOU SHOULD STOP TALKING TO *YOURSELF* ALL THE TIME.
HULLO, EDDY... COMRADES.
SORRY, I DIDN'T MEAN TO INTERRUPT YOUR *CEREMONY.*
NO PROBLEM, MAN. WE'RE JUST WARMING UP--WAITING FOR THE MUSHROOMS TO COME ON.
BOM POM POM BOPOM POM POM
THE THING IS... *MYRA*, I WANTED TO *APOLOGIZE* ABOUT... THIS MORNING.
I DIDN'T MEAN TO UPSET YOU.
YEAH, OK. THAT'S COOL.
BOM BOM BOM POM POM
HERE, HAVE SOME TEA--THEN WE'LL CALL IT QUITS.
POM POM POM POM BOM BOM POM
FAIR ENOUGH. TA.
I'LL SEE YOU, THEN. HOPE THE CEREMONY WORKS. WHAT'S IT FOR?
EDDY SAYS IT'S A *BAD OMEN* DAY--WE'RE TRYING TO LIGHTEN IT UP.
I FEEL BETTER FOR SORTING THINGS OUT WITH MYRA. THINK I'LL GO AND HAVE THE CRACK WITH ERROL--HE'S *ALWAYS* GOOD FOR A LAUGH.

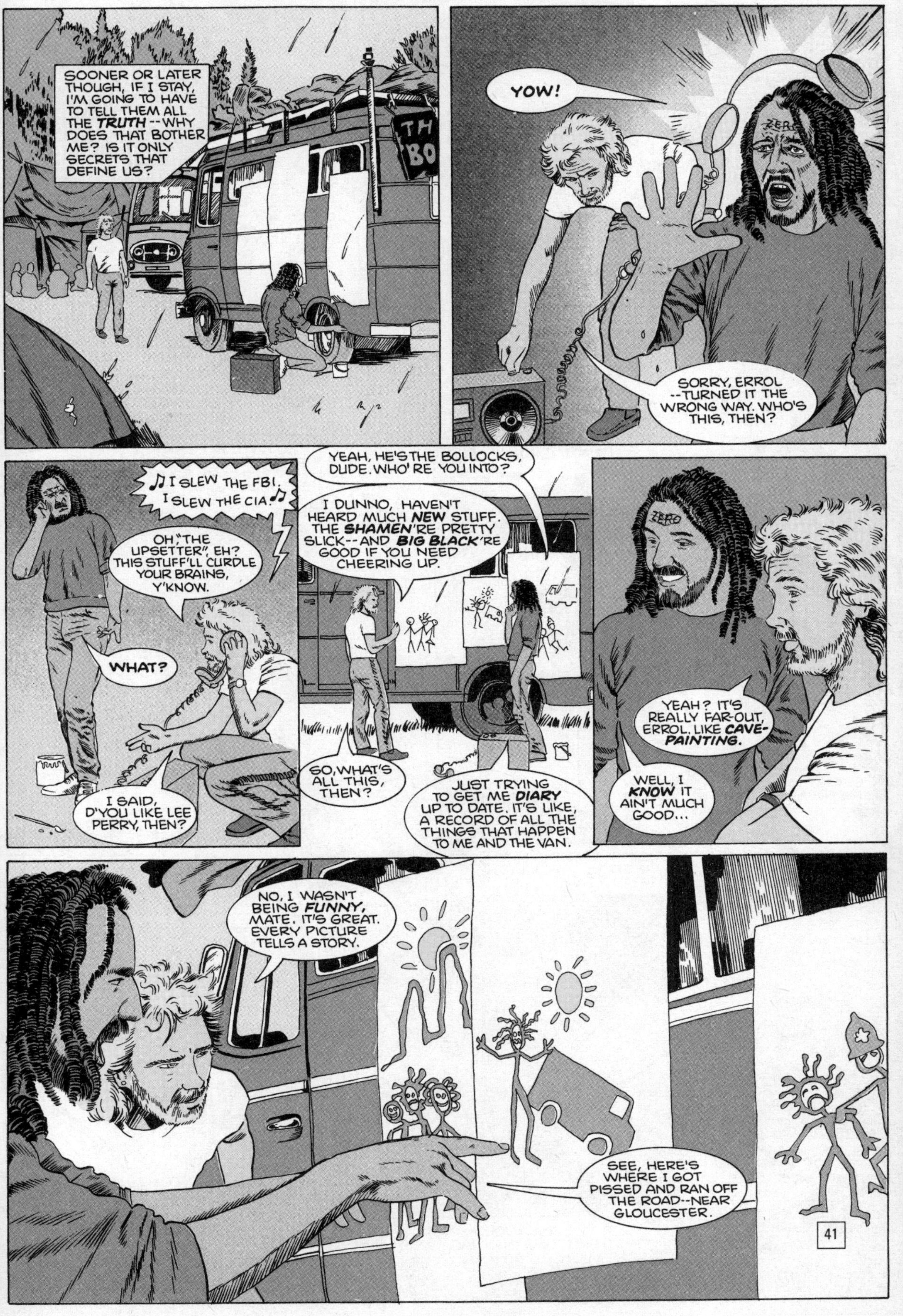

SOONER OR LATER THOUGH, IF I STAY, I'M GOING TO HAVE TO TELL THEM ALL THE **TRUTH**--WHY DOES THAT BOTHER ME? IS IT ONLY SECRETS THAT DEFINE US?
YOW!
SORRY, ERROL --TURNED IT THE WRONG WAY. WHO'S THIS, THEN?
♫ I SLEW THE FBI. I SLEW THE CIA. ♫
OH, "THE UPSETTER", EH? THIS STUFF'LL CURDLE YOUR BRAINS, Y'KNOW.
WHAT?
I SAID, D'YOU LIKE LEE PERRY, THEN?
YEAH, HE'S THE BOLLOCKS, DUDE. WHO'RE YOU INTO?
I DUNNO, HAVEN'T HEARD MUCH **NEW** STUFF. THE **SHAMEN**'RE PRETTY SLICK--AND **BIG BLACK**'RE GOOD IF YOU NEED CHEERING UP.
SO, WHAT'S ALL THIS, THEN?
JUST TRYING TO GET ME **DIARY** UP TO DATE. IT'S LIKE, A RECORD OF ALL THE THINGS THAT HAPPEN TO ME AND THE VAN.
YEAH? IT'S REALLY FAR-OUT, ERROL. LIKE **CAVE-PAINTING.**
WELL, I **KNOW** IT AIN'T MUCH GOOD...
NO, I WASN'T BEING **FUNNY,** MATE. IT'S GREAT. EVERY PICTURE TELLS A STORY.
SEE, HERE'S WHERE I GOT PISSED AND RAN OFF THE ROAD--NEAR GLOUCESTER.

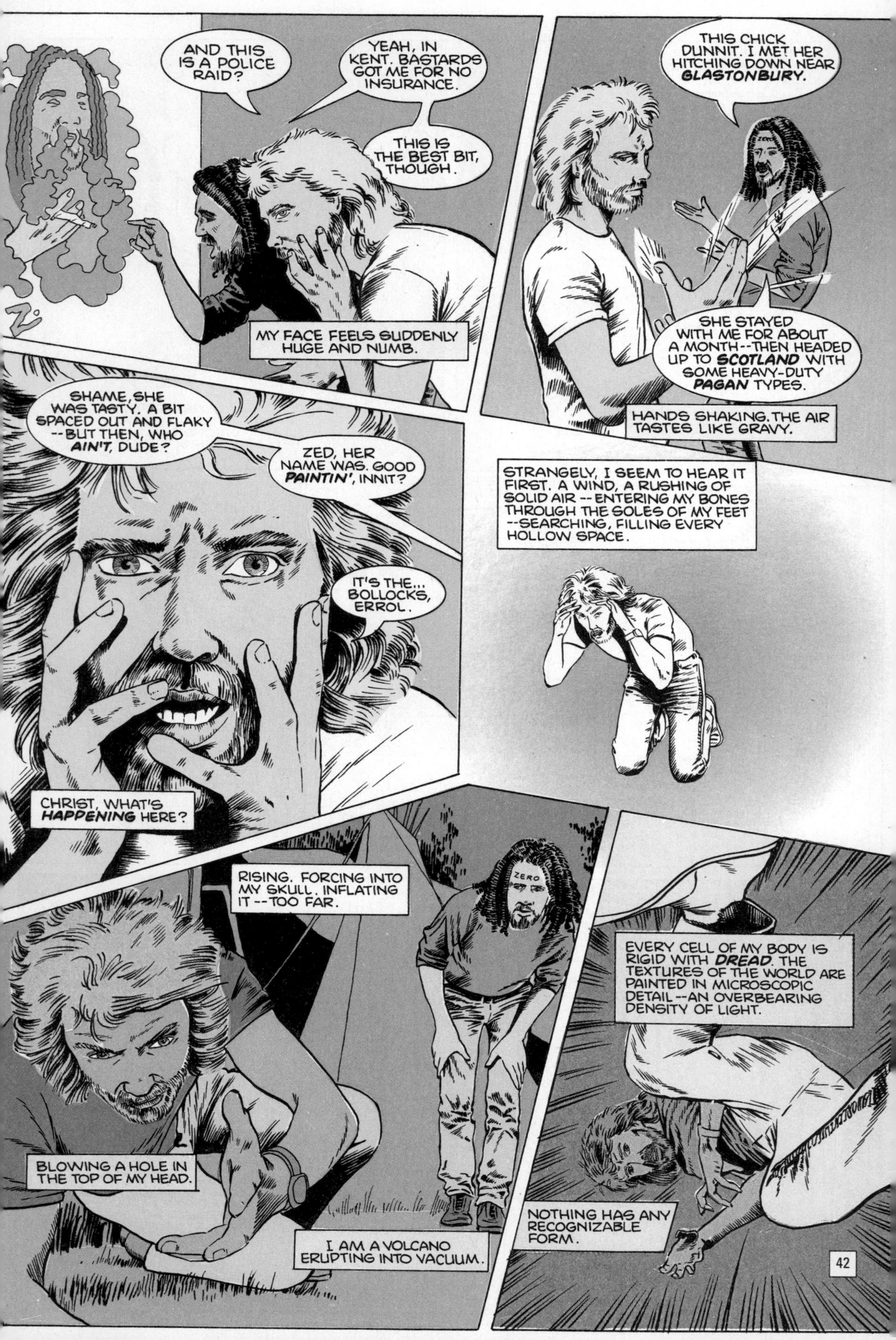
AND THIS IS A POLICE RAID?
YEAH, IN KENT. BASTARDS GOT ME FOR NO INSURANCE.
THIS IS THE BEST BIT, THOUGH.
MY FACE FEELS SUDDENLY HUGE AND NUMB.
THIS CHICK DUNNIT. I MET HER HITCHING DOWN NEAR GLASTONBURY.
SHE STAYED WITH ME FOR ABOUT A MONTH--THEN HEADED UP TO SCOTLAND WITH SOME HEAVY-DUTY PAGAN TYPES.
HANDS SHAKING. THE AIR TASTES LIKE GRAVY.
SHAME, SHE WAS TASTY. A BIT SPACED OUT AND FLAKY --BUT THEN, WHO AIN'T, DUDE?
ZED, HER NAME WAS. GOOD PAINTIN', INNIT?
IT'S THE... BOLLOCKS, ERROL.
CHRIST, WHAT'S HAPPENING HERE?
STRANGELY, I SEEM TO HEAR IT FIRST. A WIND, A RUSHING OF SOLID AIR -- ENTERING MY BONES THROUGH THE SOLES OF MY FEET --SEARCHING, FILLING EVERY HOLLOW SPACE.
RISING. FORCING INTO MY SKULL. INFLATING IT -- TOO FAR.
ZERO
BLOWING A HOLE IN THE TOP OF MY HEAD.
I AM A VOLCANO ERUPTING INTO VACUUM.
EVERY CELL OF MY BODY IS RIGID WITH DREAD. THE TEXTURES OF THE WORLD ARE PAINTED IN MICROSCOPIC DETAIL--AN OVERBEARING DENSITY OF LIGHT.
NOTHING HAS ANY RECOGNIZABLE FORM.

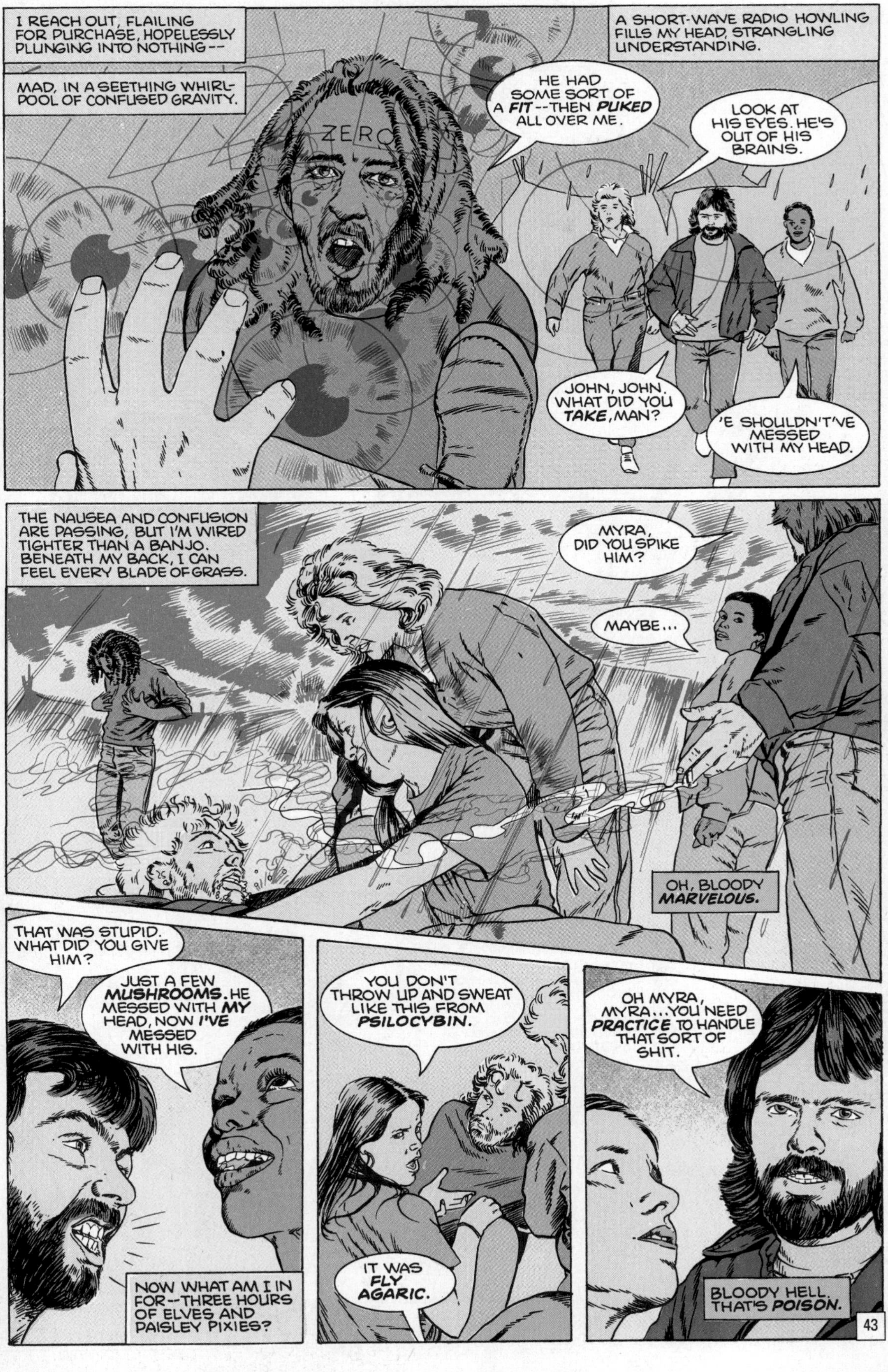
I REACH OUT, FLAILING FOR PURCHASE, HOPELESSLY PLUNGING INTO NOTHING--
A SHORT-WAVE RADIO HOWLING FILLS MY HEAD, STRANGLING UNDERSTANDING.
MAD, IN A SEETHING WHIRLPOOL OF CONFUSED GRAVITY.
ZERO
HE HAD SOME SORT OF A FIT--THEN PUKED ALL OVER ME.
LOOK AT HIS EYES. HE'S OUT OF HIS BRAINS.
JOHN, JOHN. WHAT DID YOU TAKE, MAN?
'E SHOULDN'T'VE MESSED WITH MY HEAD.
THE NAUSEA AND CONFUSION ARE PASSING, BUT I'M WIRED TIGHTER THAN A BANJO. BENEATH MY BACK, I CAN FEEL EVERY BLADE OF GRASS.
MYRA, DID YOU SPIKE HIM?
MAYBE...
OH, BLOODY MARVELOUS.
THAT WAS STUPID. WHAT DID YOU GIVE HIM?
JUST A FEW MUSHROOMS. HE MESSED WITH MY HEAD, NOW I'VE MESSED WITH HIS.
NOW WHAT AM I IN FOR--THREE HOURS OF ELVES AND PAISLEY PIXIES?
YOU DON'T THROW UP AND SWEAT LIKE THIS FROM PSILOCYBIN.
IT WAS FLY AGARIC.
OH MYRA, MYRA...YOU NEED PRACTICE TO HANDLE THAT SORT OF SHIT.
BLOODY HELL. THAT'S POISON.

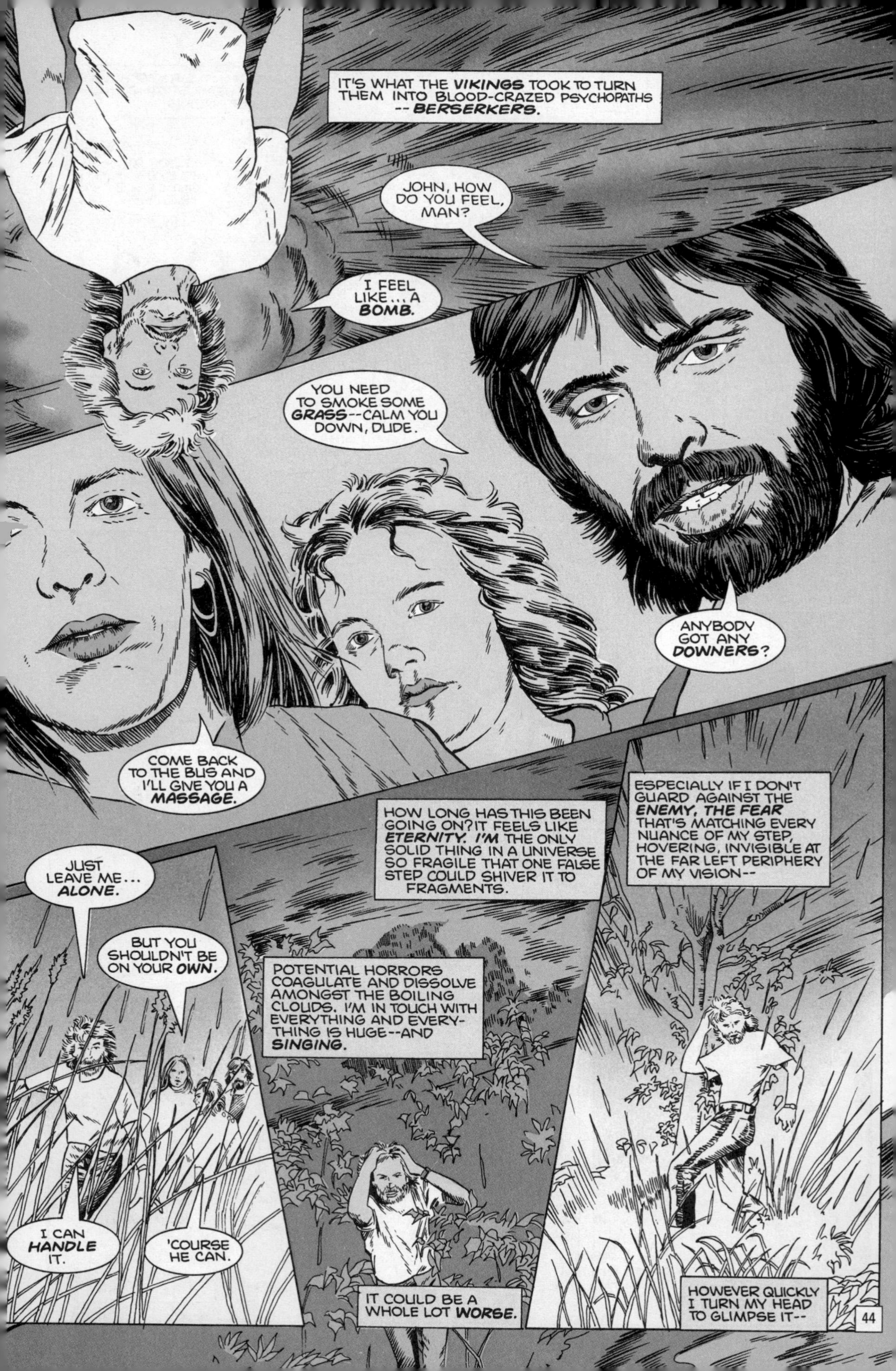
IT'S WHAT THE VIKINGS TOOK TO TURN THEM INTO BLOOD-CRAZED PSYCHOPATHS --BERSERKERS.
JOHN, HOW DO YOU FEEL, MAN?
I FEEL LIKE... A BOMB.
YOU NEED TO SMOKE SOME GRASS--CALM YOU DOWN, DUDE.
ANYBODY GOT ANY DOWNERS?
COME BACK TO THE BUS AND I'LL GIVE YOU A MASSAGE.
JUST LEAVE ME... ALONE.
BUT YOU SHOULDN'T BE ON YOUR OWN.
I CAN HANDLE IT.
'COURSE HE CAN.
HOW LONG HAS THIS BEEN GOING ON? IT FEELS LIKE ETERNITY. I'M THE ONLY SOLID THING IN A UNIVERSE SO FRAGILE THAT ONE FALSE STEP COULD SHIVER IT TO FRAGMENTS.
POTENTIAL HORRORS COAGULATE AND DISSOLVE AMONGST THE BOILING CLOUDS. I'M IN TOUCH WITH EVERYTHING AND EVERYTHING IS HUGE--AND SINGING.
IT COULD BE A WHOLE LOT WORSE.
ESPECIALLY IF I DON'T GUARD AGAINST THE ENEMY, THE FEAR THAT'S MATCHING EVERY NUANCE OF MY STEP, HOVERING, INVISIBLE AT THE FAR LEFT PERIPHERY OF MY VISION--
HOWEVER QUICKLY I TURN MY HEAD TO GLIMPSE IT--

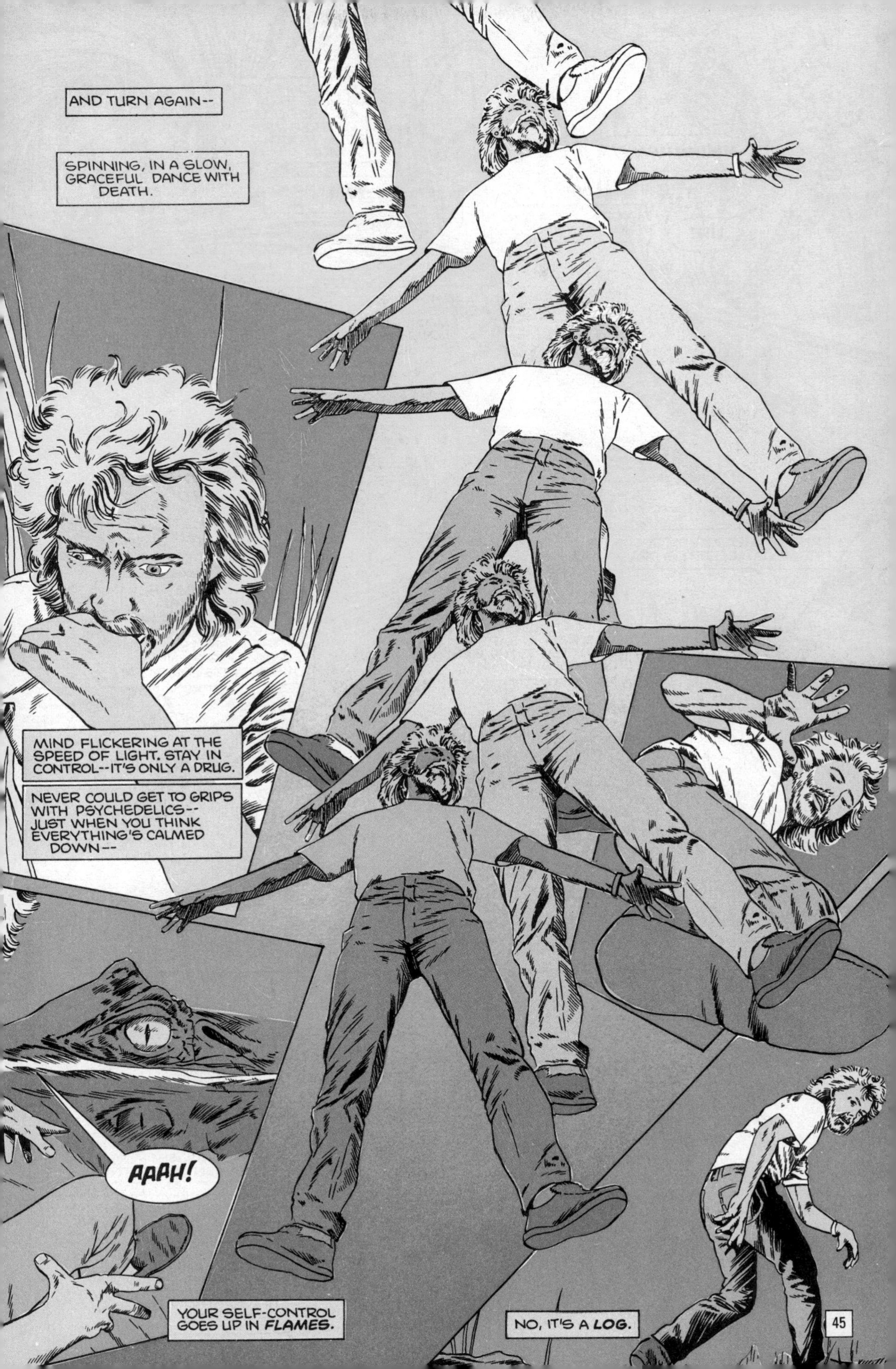
AND TURN AGAIN--
SPINNING, IN A SLOW, GRACEFUL DANCE WITH DEATH.
MIND FLICKERING AT THE SPEED OF LIGHT. STAY IN CONTROL--IT'S ONLY A DRUG.
NEVER COULD GET TO GRIPS WITH PSYCHEDELICS-- JUST WHEN YOU THINK EVERYTHING'S CALMED DOWN--
AAAH!
YOUR SELF-CONTROL GOES UP IN *FLAMES*.
NO, IT'S A *LOG*.

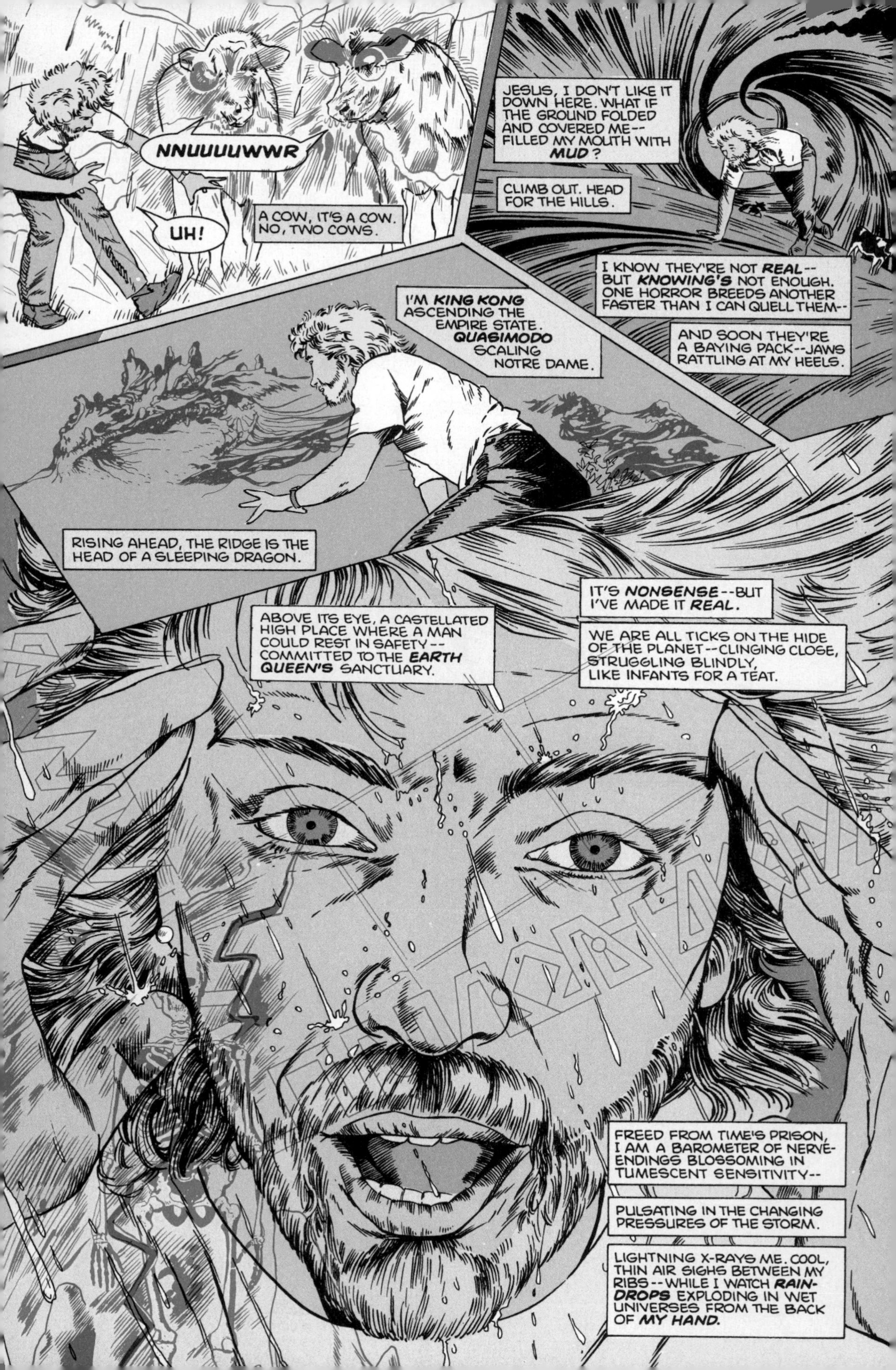
NNUUUUWWR
UH!
A COW, IT'S A COW. NO, TWO COWS.
JESUS, I DON'T LIKE IT DOWN HERE. WHAT IF THE GROUND FOLDED AND COVERED ME-- FILLED MY MOUTH WITH MUD?
CLIMB OUT. HEAD FOR THE HILLS.
I KNOW THEY'RE NOT REAL-- BUT KNOWING'S NOT ENOUGH. ONE HORROR BREEDS ANOTHER FASTER THAN I CAN QUELL THEM--
AND SOON THEY'RE A BAYING PACK--JAWS RATTLING AT MY HEELS.
I'M KING KONG ASCENDING THE EMPIRE STATE. QUASIMODO SCALING NOTRE DAME.
RISING AHEAD, THE RIDGE IS THE HEAD OF A SLEEPING DRAGON.
ABOVE ITS EYE, A CASTELLATED HIGH PLACE WHERE A MAN COULD REST IN SAFETY-- COMMITTED TO THE EARTH QUEEN'S SANCTUARY.
IT'S NONSENSE--BUT I'VE MADE IT REAL.
WE ARE ALL TICKS ON THE HIDE OF THE PLANET--CLINGING CLOSE, STRUGGLING BLINDLY, LIKE INFANTS FOR A TEAT.
FREED FROM TIME'S PRISON, I AM A BAROMETER OF NERVE-ENDINGS BLOSSOMING IN TUMESCENT SENSITIVITY--
PULSATING IN THE CHANGING PRESSURES OF THE STORM.
LIGHTNING X-RAYS ME. COOL, THIN AIR SIGHS BETWEEN MY RIBS--WHILE I WATCH RAIN-DROPS EXPLODING IN WET UNIVERSES FROM THE BACK OF MY HAND.

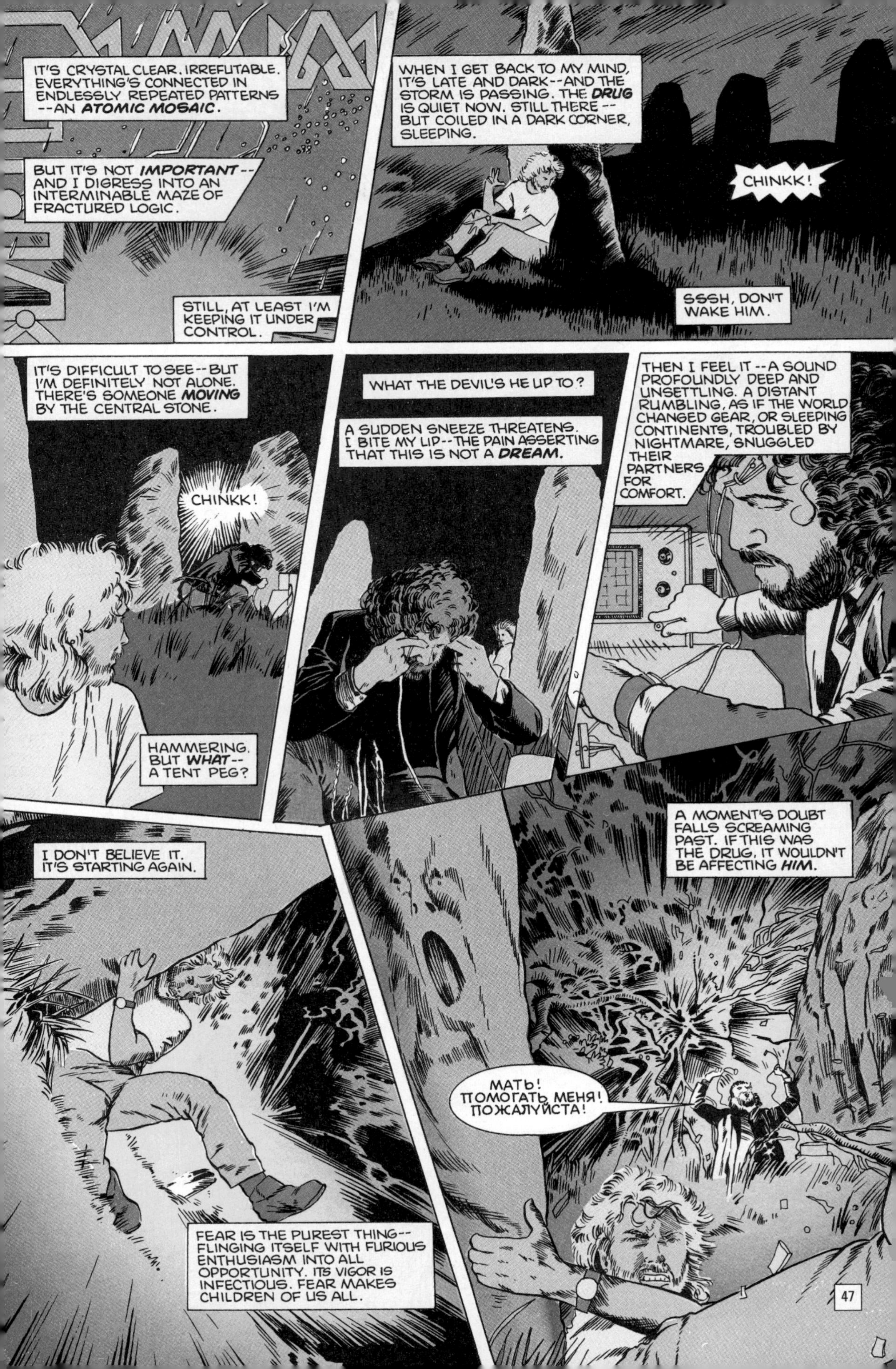

IT'S CRYSTAL CLEAR. IRREFUTABLE. EVERYTHING'S CONNECTED IN ENDLESSLY REPEATED PATTERNS --AN ATOMIC MOSAIC.
BUT IT'S NOT IMPORTANT -- AND I DIGRESS INTO AN INTERMINABLE MAZE OF FRACTURED LOGIC.
STILL, AT LEAST I'M KEEPING IT UNDER CONTROL.
WHEN I GET BACK TO MY MIND, IT'S LATE AND DARK--AND THE STORM IS PASSING. THE DRUG IS QUIET NOW. STILL THERE -- BUT COILED IN A DARK CORNER, SLEEPING.
CHINKK!
SSSH, DON'T WAKE HIM.
IT'S DIFFICULT TO SEE-- BUT I'M DEFINITELY NOT ALONE. THERE'S SOMEONE MOVING BY THE CENTRAL STONE.
CHINKK!
HAMMERING. BUT WHAT-- A TENT PEG?
WHAT THE DEVIL'S HE UP TO?
A SUDDEN SNEEZE THREATENS. I BITE MY LIP-- THE PAIN ASSERTING THAT THIS IS NOT A DREAM.
THEN I FEEL IT --A SOUND PROFOUNDLY DEEP AND UNSETTLING. A DISTANT RUMBLING, AS IF THE WORLD CHANGED GEAR, OR SLEEPING CONTINENTS, TROUBLED BY NIGHTMARE, SNUGGLED THEIR PARTNERS FOR COMFORT.
I DON'T BELIEVE IT. IT'S STARTING AGAIN.
FEAR IS THE PUREST THING-- FLINGING ITSELF WITH FURIOUS ENTHUSIASM INTO ALL OPPORTUNITY. ITS VIGOR IS INFECTIOUS. FEAR MAKES CHILDREN OF US ALL.
A MOMENT'S DOUBT FALLS SCREAMING PAST. IF THIS WAS THE DRUG, IT WOULDN'T BE AFFECTING HIM.
МАТЬ! ПОМОГАТЬ МЕНЯ! ПОЖАЛУЙСТА!

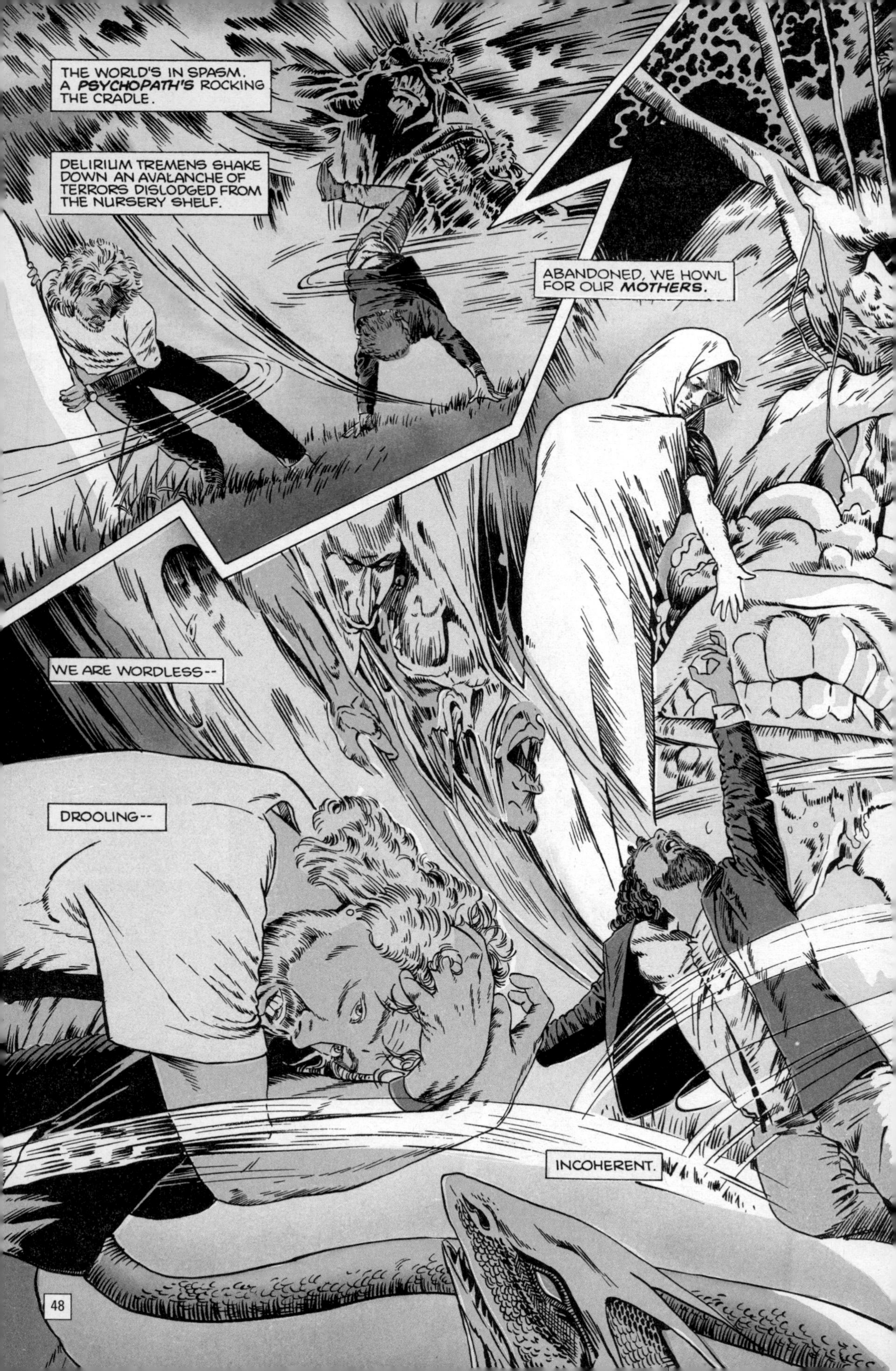
THE WORLD'S IN SPASM. A PSYCHOPATH'S ROCKING THE CRADLE.
DELIRIUM TREMENS SHAKE DOWN AN AVALANCHE OF TERRORS DISLODGED FROM THE NURSERY SHELF.
ABANDONED, WE HOWL FOR OUR MOTHERS.
WE ARE WORDLESS--
DROOLING--
INCOHERENT.

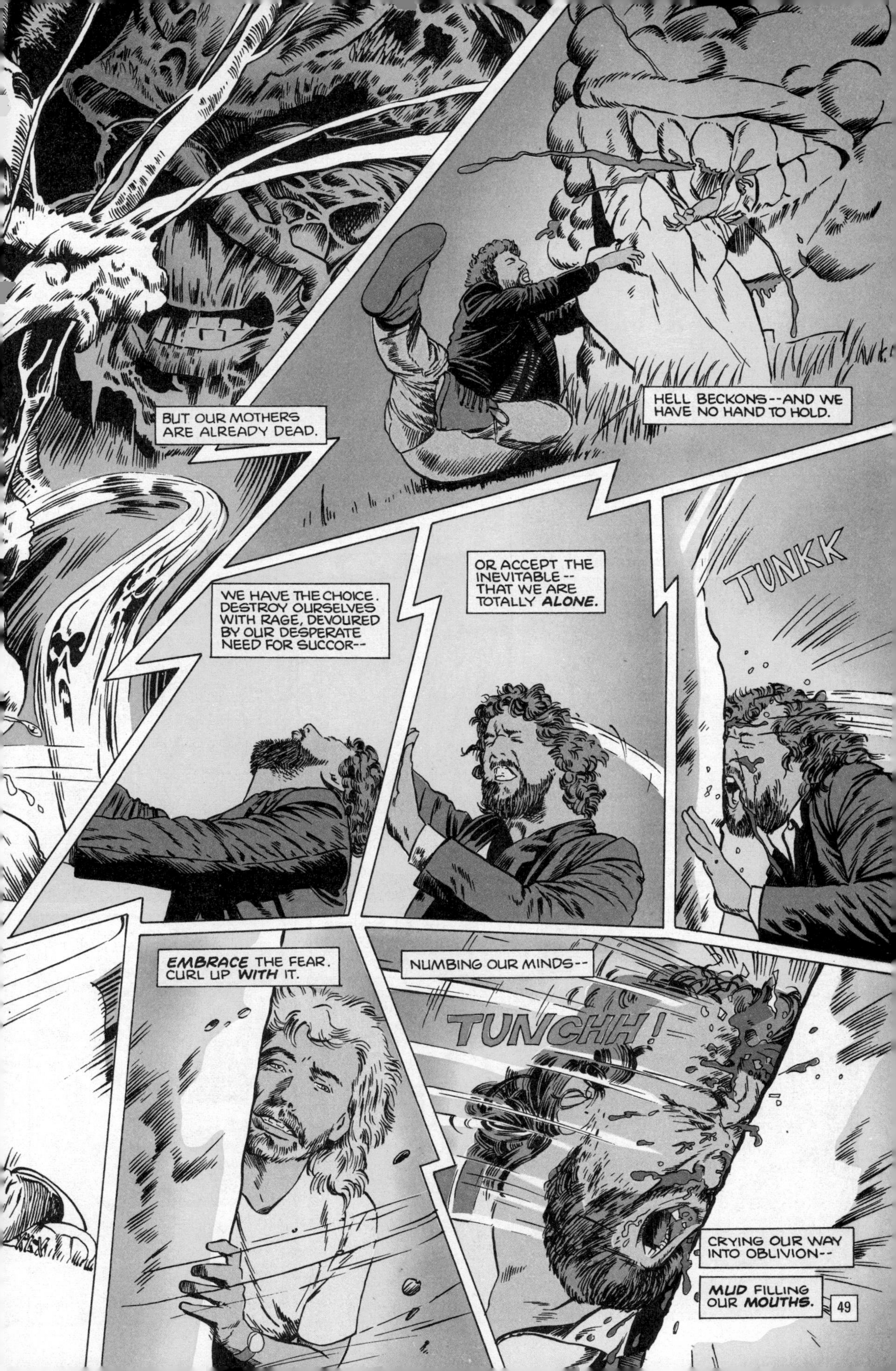

BUT OUR MOTHERS ARE ALREADY DEAD.
HELL BECKONS--AND WE HAVE NO HAND TO HOLD.
WE HAVE THE CHOICE. DESTROY OURSELVES WITH RAGE, DEVOURED BY OUR DESPERATE NEED FOR SUCCOR--
OR ACCEPT THE INEVITABLE--THAT WE ARE TOTALLY ALONE.
TUNKK
EMBRACE THE FEAR. CURL UP WITH IT.
NUMBING OUR MINDS--
TUNCHH!
CRYING OUR WAY INTO OBLIVION--
MUD FILLING OUR MOUTHS.

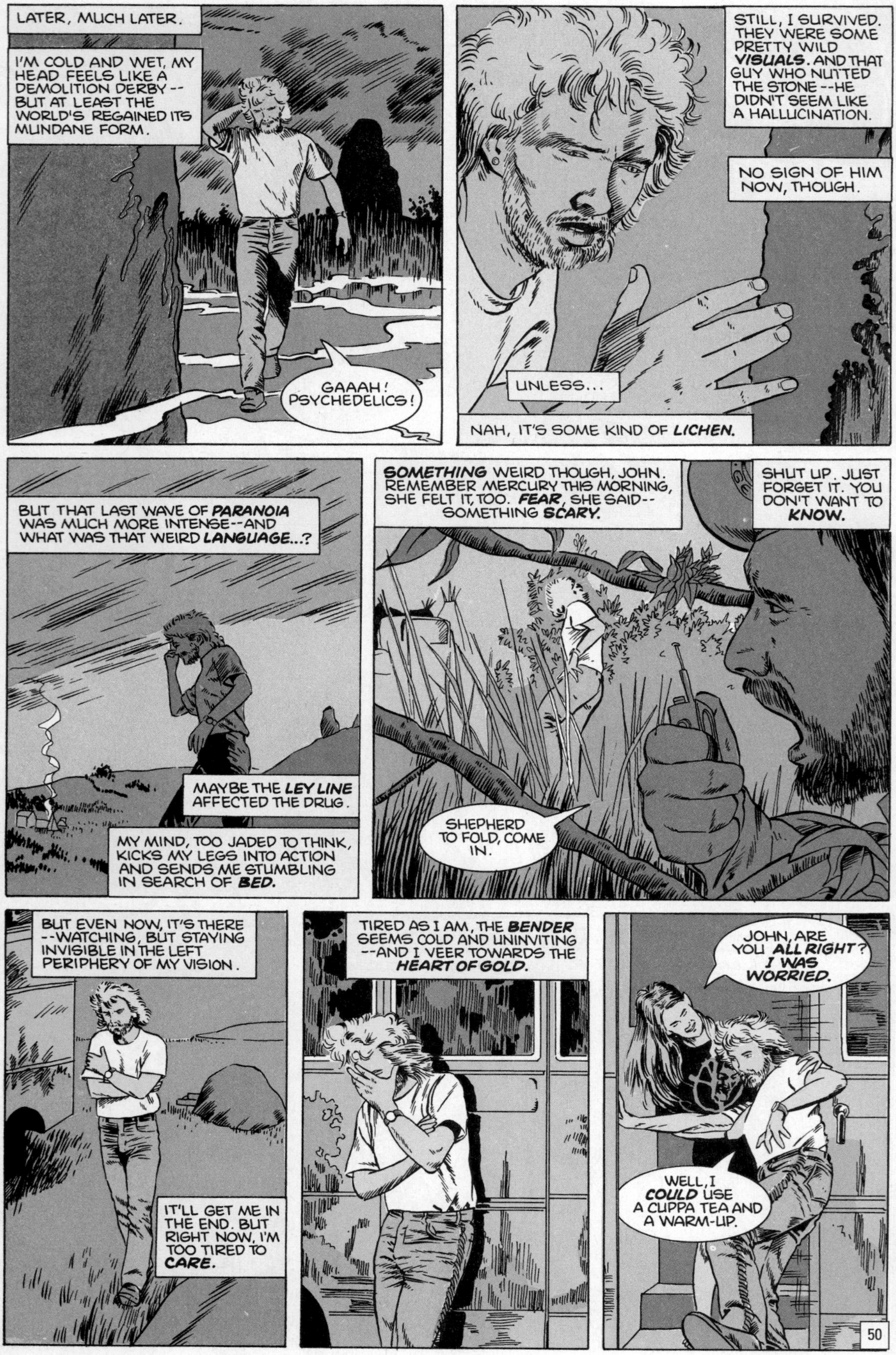
LATER, MUCH LATER.
I'M COLD AND WET, MY HEAD FEELS LIKE A DEMOLITION DERBY -- BUT AT LEAST THE WORLD'S REGAINED ITS MUNDANE FORM.
GAAAH! PSYCHEDELICS!
STILL, I SURVIVED. THEY WERE SOME PRETTY WILD VISUALS. AND THAT GUY WHO NUTTED THE STONE --HE DIDN'T SEEM LIKE A HALLUCINATION.
NO SIGN OF HIM NOW, THOUGH.
UNLESS...
NAH, IT'S SOME KIND OF LICHEN.
BUT THAT LAST WAVE OF PARANOIA WAS MUCH MORE INTENSE--AND WHAT WAS THAT WEIRD LANGUAGE...?
MAYBE THE LEY LINE AFFECTED THE DRUG.
MY MIND, TOO JADED TO THINK, KICKS MY LEGS INTO ACTION AND SENDS ME STUMBLING IN SEARCH OF BED.
SOMETHING WEIRD THOUGH, JOHN. REMEMBER MERCURY THIS MORNING, SHE FELT IT, TOO. FEAR, SHE SAID-- SOMETHING SCARY.
SHUT UP. JUST FORGET IT. YOU DON'T WANT TO KNOW.
SHEPHERD TO FOLD, COME IN.
BUT EVEN NOW, IT'S THERE --WATCHING, BUT STAYING INVISIBLE IN THE LEFT PERIPHERY OF MY VISION.
IT'LL GET ME IN THE END. BUT RIGHT NOW, I'M TOO TIRED TO CARE.
TIRED AS I AM, THE BENDER SEEMS COLD AND UNINVITING --AND I VEER TOWARDS THE HEART OF GOLD.
JOHN, ARE YOU ALL RIGHT? I WAS WORRIED.
WELL, I COULD USE A CUPPA TEA AND A WARM-UP.
50

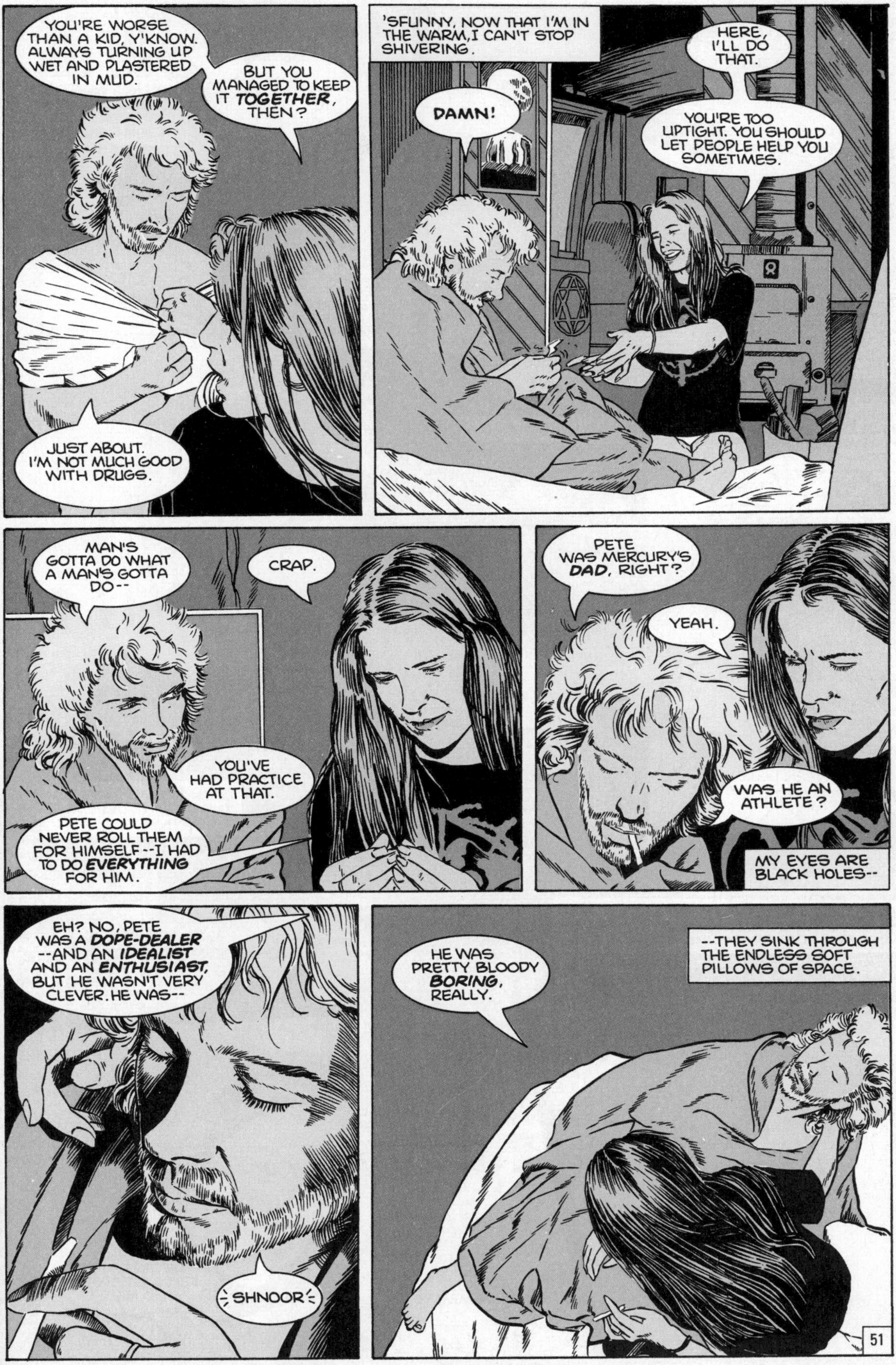

YOU'RE WORSE THAN A KID, Y'KNOW. ALWAYS TURNING UP WET AND PLASTERED IN MUD.
BUT YOU MANAGED TO KEEP IT *TOGETHER*, THEN?
JUST ABOUT. I'M NOT MUCH GOOD WITH DRUGS.
'SFUNNY, NOW THAT I'M IN THE WARM, I CAN'T STOP SHIVERING.
DAMN!
HERE, I'LL DO THAT.
YOU'RE TOO UPTIGHT. YOU SHOULD LET PEOPLE HELP YOU SOMETIMES.
MAN'S GOTTA DO WHAT A MAN'S GOTTA DO--
CRAP.
YOU'VE HAD PRACTICE AT THAT.
PETE COULD NEVER ROLL THEM FOR HIMSELF--I HAD TO DO *EVERYTHING* FOR HIM.
PETE WAS MERCURY'S *DAD*, RIGHT?
YEAH.
WAS HE AN ATHLETE?
MY EYES ARE BLACK HOLES--
EH? NO, PETE WAS A *DOPE-DEALER* --AND AN *IDEALIST* AND AN *ENTHUSIAST*, BUT HE WASN'T VERY CLEVER. HE WAS--
SHNOOR
HE WAS PRETTY BLOODY *BORING*, REALLY.
--THEY SINK THROUGH THE ENDLESS SOFT PILLOWS OF SPACE.

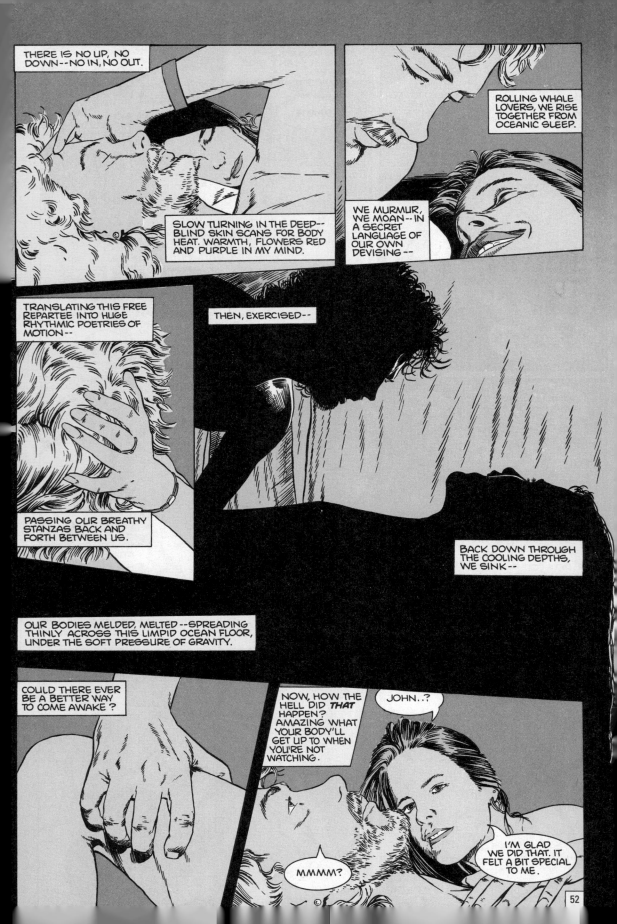

THERE IS NO UP, NO DOWN--NO IN, NO OUT.

ROLLING WHALE LOVERS, WE RISE TOGETHER FROM OCEANIC SLEEP.

SLOW TURNING IN THE DEEP-- BLIND SKIN SCANS FOR BODY HEAT. WARMTH, FLOWERS RED AND PURPLE IN MY MIND.

WE MURMUR, WE MOAN--IN A SECRET LANGUAGE OF OUR OWN DEVISING--

TRANSLATING THIS FREE REPARTEE INTO HUGE RHYTHMIC POETRIES OF MOTION--

THEN, EXERCISED--

PASSING OUR BREATHY STANZAS BACK AND FORTH BETWEEN US.

BACK DOWN THROUGH THE COOLING DEPTHS, WE SINK--

OUR BODIES MELDED, MELTED --SPREADING THINLY ACROSS THIS LIMPID OCEAN FLOOR, UNDER THE SOFT PRESSURE OF GRAVITY.

COULD THERE EVER BE A BETTER WAY TO COME AWAKE ?

NOW, HOW THE HELL DID *THAT* HAPPEN? AMAZING WHAT YOUR BODY'LL GET UP TO WHEN YOU'RE NOT WATCHING.

JOHN..?

MMMM?

I'M GLAD WE DID THAT. IT FELT A BIT SPECIAL TO ME.

52

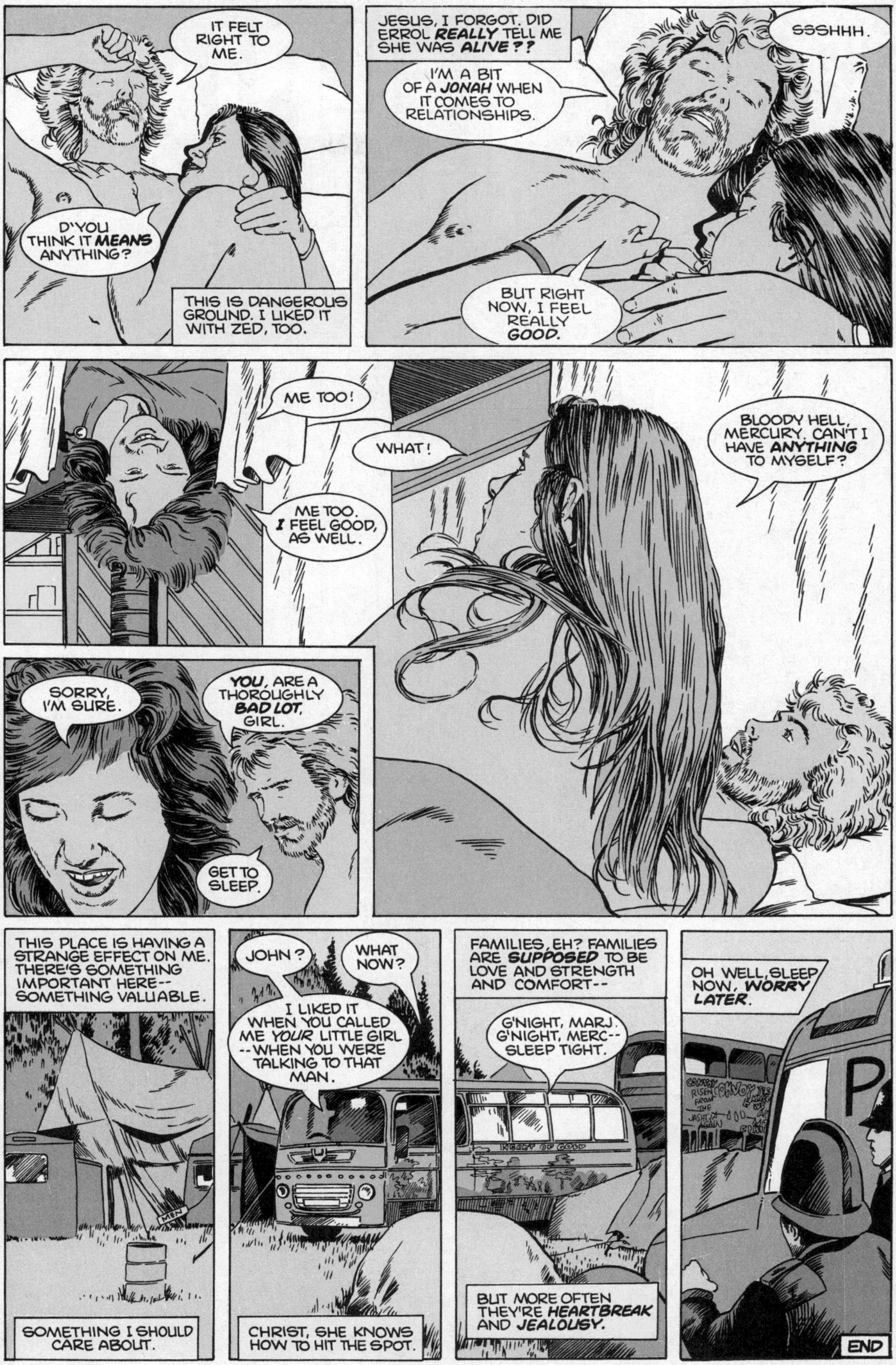
IT FELT RIGHT TO ME.
D'YOU THINK IT MEANS ANYTHING?
THIS IS DANGEROUS GROUND. I LIKED IT WITH ZED, TOO.
JESUS, I FORGOT. DID ERROL REALLY TELL ME SHE WAS ALIVE??
I'M A BIT OF A JONAH WHEN IT COMES TO RELATIONSHIPS.
SSSHHH.
BUT RIGHT NOW, I FEEL REALLY GOOD.
ME TOO!
ME TOO. I FEEL GOOD, AS WELL.
WHAT!
BLOODY HELL, MERCURY. CAN'T I HAVE ANYTHING TO MYSELF?
SORRY, I'M SURE.
YOU, ARE A THOROUGHLY BAD LOT, GIRL.
GET TO SLEEP.
THIS PLACE IS HAVING A STRANGE EFFECT ON ME. THERE'S SOMETHING IMPORTANT HERE--SOMETHING VALUABLE.
MEN
SOMETHING I SHOULD CARE ABOUT.
JOHN?
WHAT NOW?
I LIKED IT WHEN YOU CALLED ME YOUR LITTLE GIRL--WHEN YOU WERE TALKING TO THAT MAN.
CHRIST, SHE KNOWS HOW TO HIT THE SPOT.
FAMILIES, EH? FAMILIES ARE SUPPOSED TO BE LOVE AND STRENGTH AND COMFORT--
G'NIGHT, MARJ. G'NIGHT, MERC--SLEEP TIGHT.
BUT MORE OFTEN THEY'RE HEARTBREAK AND JEALOUSY.
OH WELL, SLEEP NOW, WORRY LATER.
CONVOY
P
END

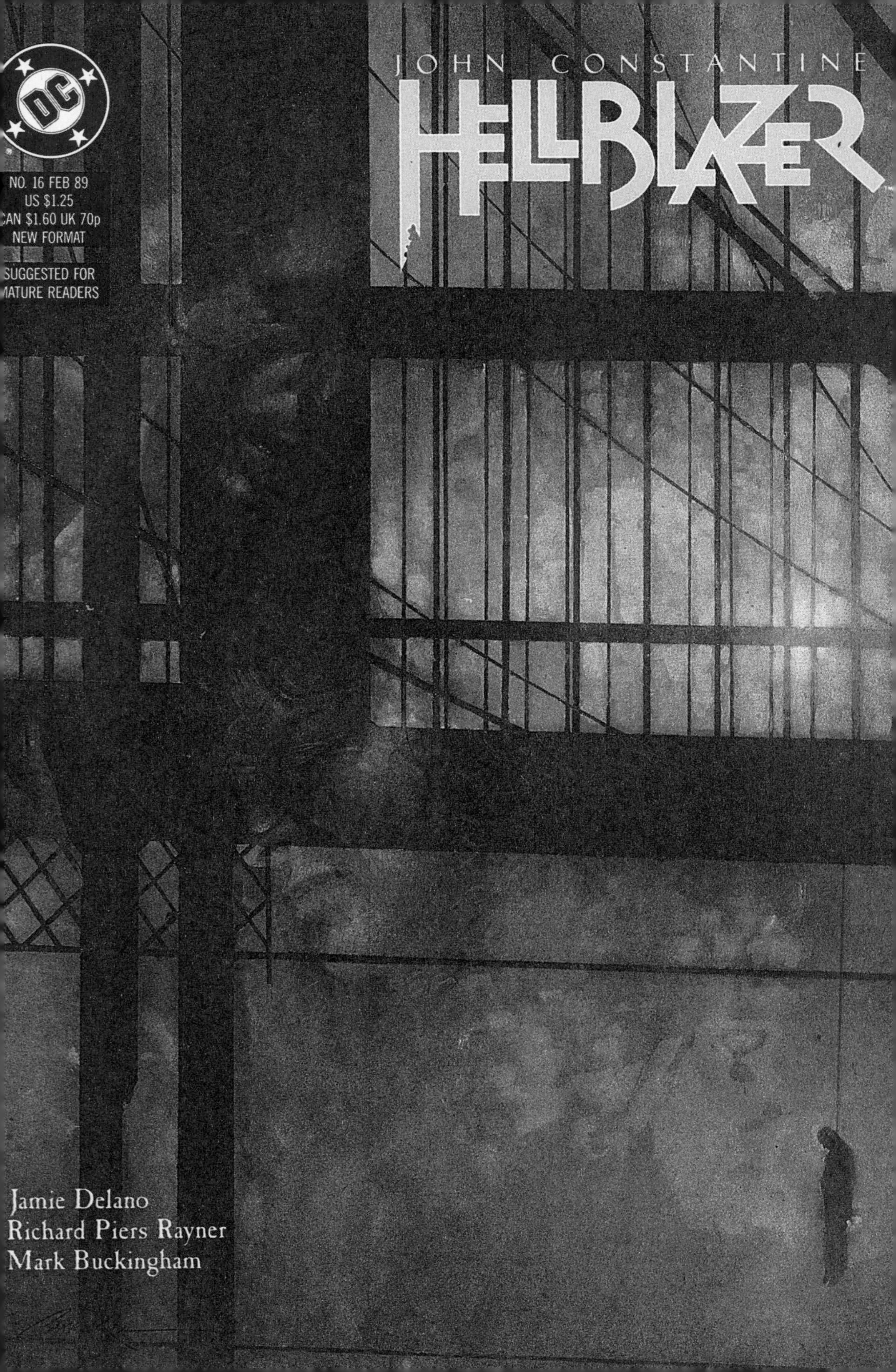
DC
JOHN CONSTANTINE
HELLBLAZER
NO. 16 FEB 89
US $1.25
CAN $1.60 UK 70p
NEW FORMAT
SUGGESTED FOR
MATURE READERS
Jamie Delano
Richard Piers Rayner
Mark Buckingham

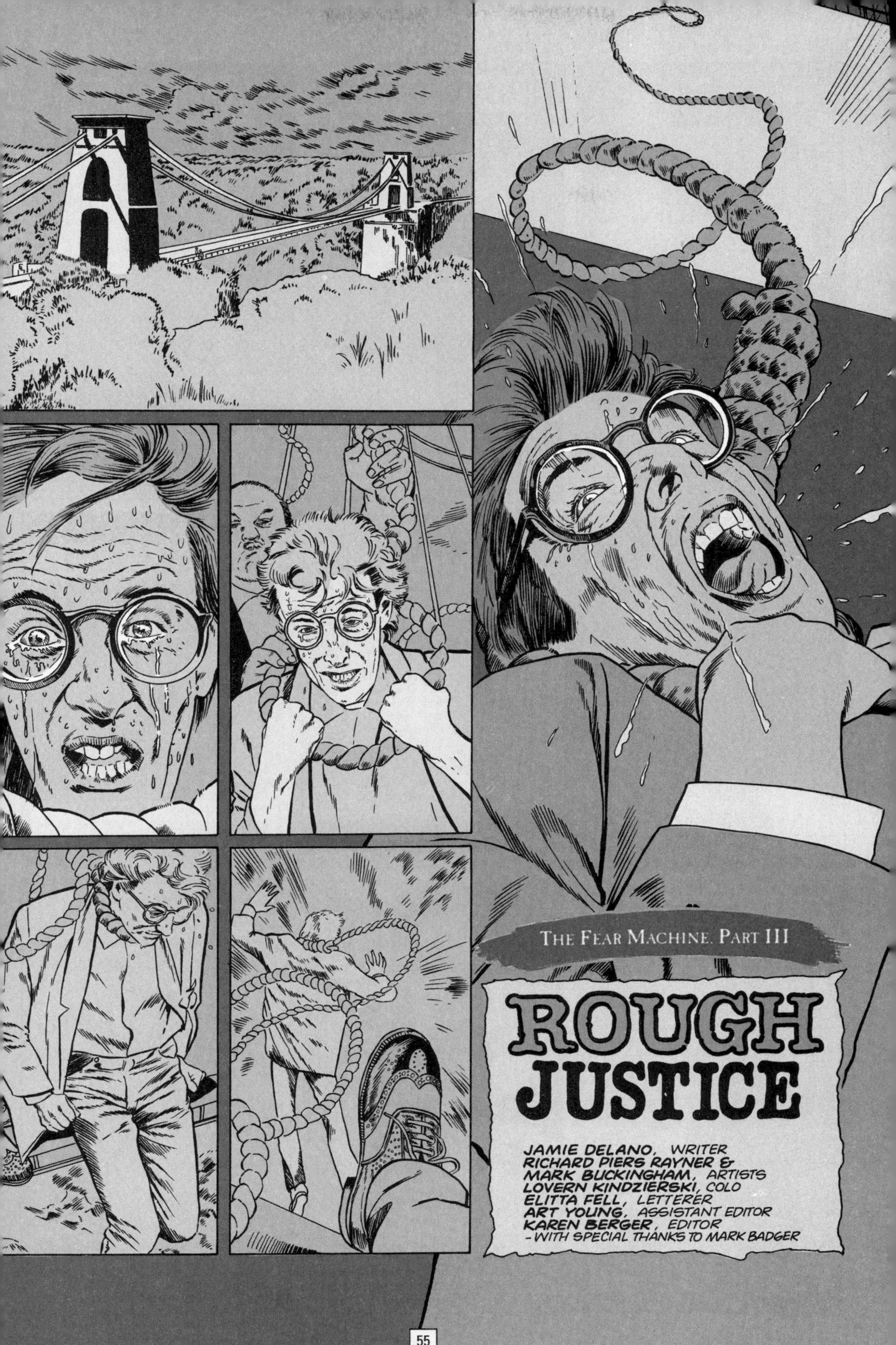
THE FEAR MACHINE, PART III
ROUGH JUSTICE
JAMIE DELANO, WRITER
RICHARD PIERS RAYNER &
MARK BUCKINGHAM, ARTISTS
LOVERN KINDZIERSKI, COLO
ELITTA FELL, LETTERER
ART YOUNG, ASSISTANT EDITOR
KAREN BERGER, EDITOR
-WITH SPECIAL THANKS TO MARK BADGER

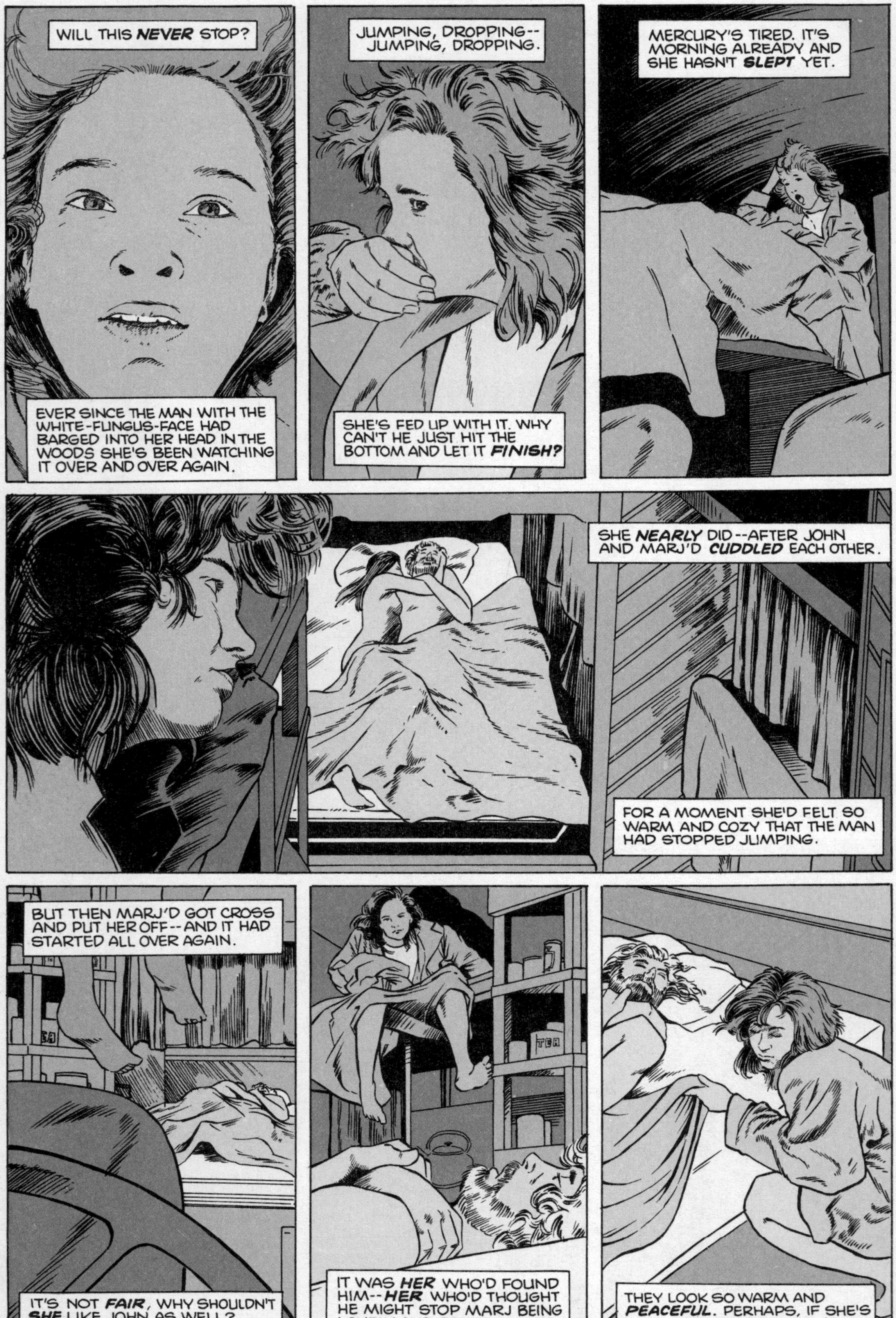
WILL THIS NEVER STOP?
EVER SINCE THE MAN WITH THE WHITE-FUNGUS-FACE HAD BARGED INTO HER HEAD IN THE WOODS SHE'S BEEN WATCHING IT OVER AND OVER AGAIN.
JUMPING, DROPPING-- JUMPING, DROPPING.
SHE'S FED UP WITH IT. WHY CAN'T HE JUST HIT THE BOTTOM AND LET IT FINISH?
MERCURY'S TIRED. IT'S MORNING ALREADY AND SHE HASN'T SLEPT YET.
SHE NEARLY DID--AFTER JOHN AND MARJ'D CUDDLED EACH OTHER.
FOR A MOMENT SHE'D FELT SO WARM AND COZY THAT THE MAN HAD STOPPED JUMPING.
BUT THEN MARJ'D GOT CROSS AND PUT HER OFF--AND IT HAD STARTED ALL OVER AGAIN.
IT'S NOT FAIR, WHY SHOULDN'T SHE LIKE JOHN AS WELL?
TEA
IT WAS HER WHO'D FOUND HIM--HER WHO'D THOUGHT HE MIGHT STOP MARJ BEING LONELY AND BAD TEMPERED ALL THE TIME.
THEY LOOK SO WARM AND PEACEFUL. PERHAPS, IF SHE'S VERY CAREFUL, THEY WON'T NOTICE HER CREEPING IN.

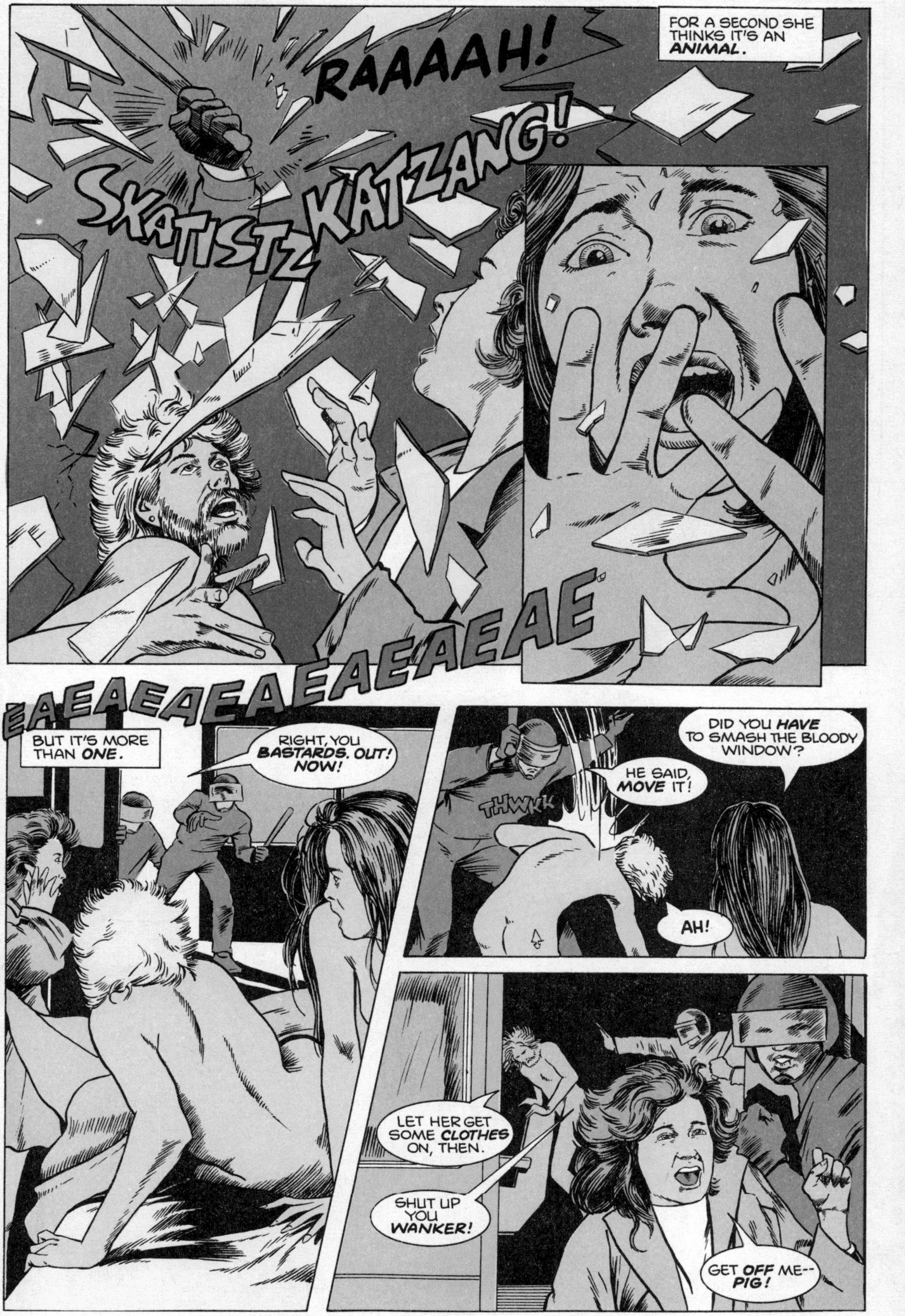
FOR A SECOND SHE THINKS IT'S AN **ANIMAL**.
RAAAAH!
SKATISTZ KATZANG!
EAEAEAEAEAEAEAEAE
BUT IT'S MORE THAN **ONE**.
RIGHT, YOU **BASTARDS. OUT! NOW!**
THWKK
HE SAID, **MOVE** IT!
DID YOU **HAVE** TO SMASH THE BLOODY WINDOW?
AH!
LET HER GET SOME **CLOTHES** ON, THEN.
SHUT UP YOU **WANKER!**
GET **OFF** ME-- **PIG!**

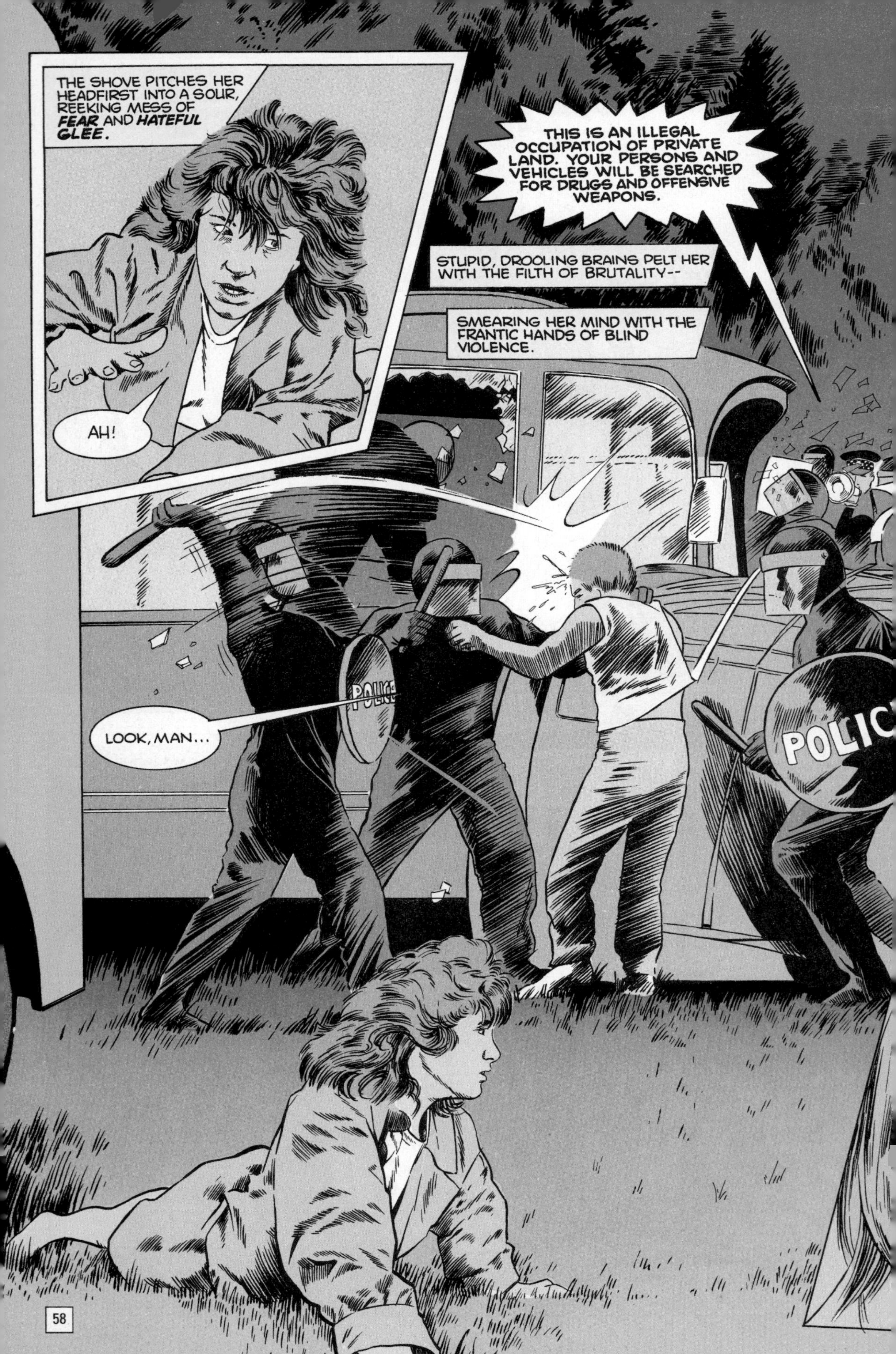
THE SHOVE PITCHES HER HEADFIRST INTO A SOUR, REEKING MESS OF FEAR AND HATEFUL GLEE.
AH!
THIS IS AN ILLEGAL OCCUPATION OF PRIVATE LAND. YOUR PERSONS AND VEHICLES WILL BE SEARCHED FOR DRUGS AND OFFENSIVE WEAPONS.
STUPID, DROOLING BRAINS PELT HER WITH THE FILTH OF BRUTALITY--
SMEARING HER MIND WITH THE FRANTIC HANDS OF BLIND VIOLENCE.
POLICE
LOOK, MAN...
POLIC

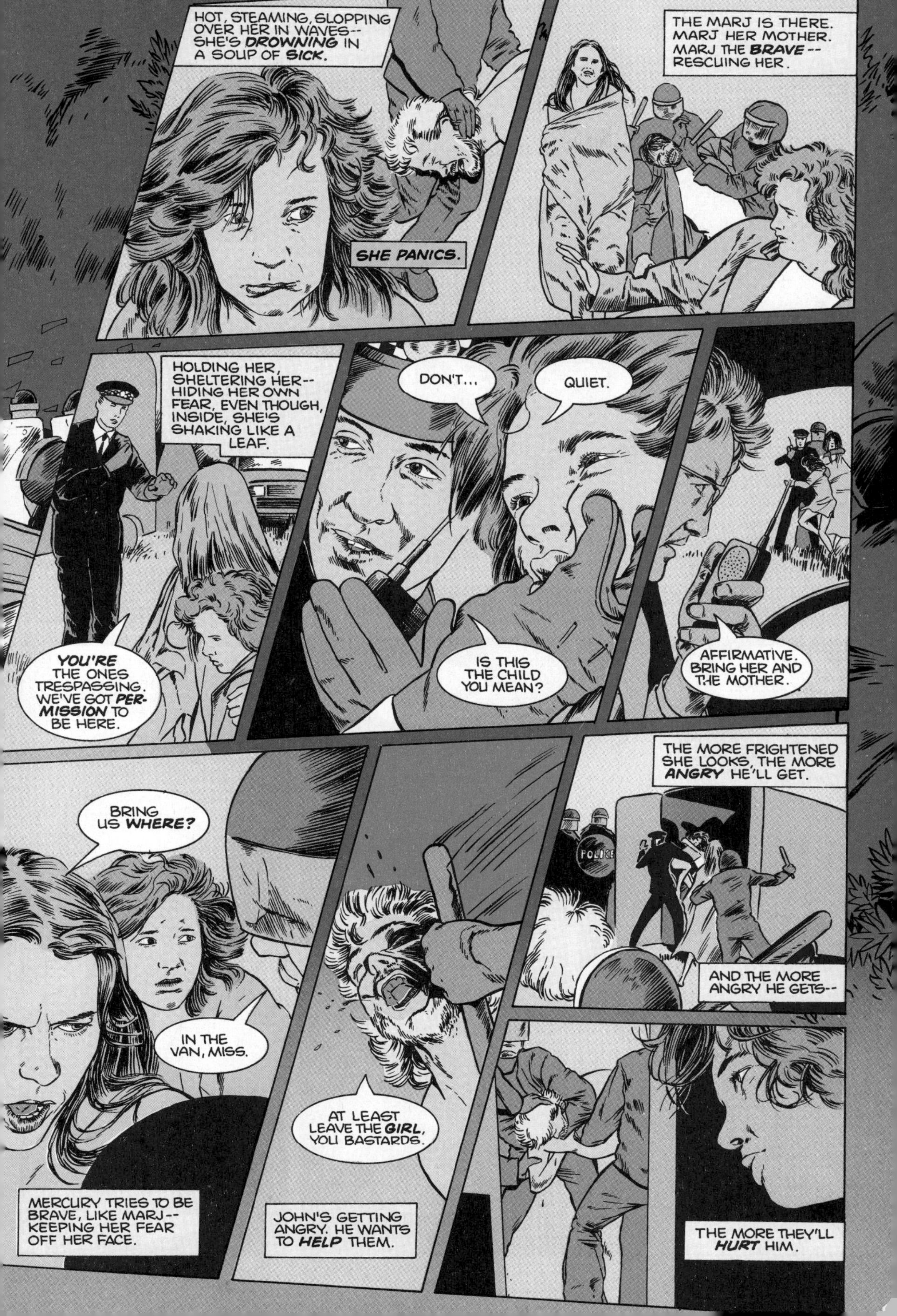
HOT, STEAMING, SLOPPING OVER HER IN WAVES-- SHE'S DROWNING IN A SOUP OF SICK.
SHE PANICS.
THE MARJ IS THERE. MARJ HER MOTHER. MARJ THE BRAVE -- RESCUING HER.
HOLDING HER, SHELTERING HER-- HIDING HER OWN FEAR, EVEN THOUGH, INSIDE, SHE'S SHAKING LIKE A LEAF.
YOU'RE THE ONES TRESPASSING. WE'VE GOT PERMISSION TO BE HERE.
DON'T...
QUIET.
IS THIS THE CHILD YOU MEAN?
AFFIRMATIVE. BRING HER AND THE MOTHER.
BRING US WHERE?
IN THE VAN, MISS.
MERCURY TRIES TO BE BRAVE, LIKE MARJ-- KEEPING HER FEAR OFF HER FACE.
AT LEAST LEAVE THE GIRL, YOU BASTARDS.
JOHN'S GETTING ANGRY. HE WANTS TO HELP THEM.
THE MORE FRIGHTENED SHE LOOKS, THE MORE ANGRY HE'LL GET.
POLICE
AND THE MORE ANGRY HE GETS--
THE MORE THEY'LL HURT HIM.

BOUNCED AND JOGGLED IN THE BACK OF THE VAN, HER HEAD SCREAMS.

IT'S NEARLY DARK, BUT MERCURY CAN **SMELL** THEM--SWEAT AND LEATHER.

DO THEY HAVE **EYES** BEHIND THOSE VISORS --ARE THEY **HUMAN**?

THEY MUST BE. SHE CAN **FEEL** THEM. THEIR THOUGHTS ARE THICK AND NASTY--BITTER. LIKE THE SMOKE FROM RUBBISH SMOLDERING ON A DUMP.

THEY'RE THINKING ABOUT MARJ--ABOUT HER **MOTHER**, THINKING WHAT THEY'D LIKE TO DO WITH HER.

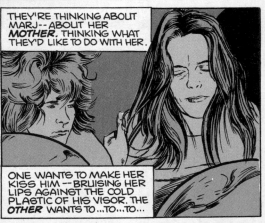

ONE WANTS TO MAKE HER KISS HIM -- BRUISING HER LIPS AGAINST THE COLD PLASTIC OF HIS VISOR. THE **OTHER** WANTS TO ...TO ...TO...

NO! **STOP** IT! LEAVE HER **ALONE**.

MERCURY, DON'T...

YOU'RE **FILTHY** --**DISGUSTING**...

LET GO OF HER, YOU BASTARD.

BASTARD.

FOR A SECOND HE LOOKS **GUILTY**, LIKE A BOY CAUGHT AT MISCHIEF. THEN HE GRABS HER WRIST AND SQUEEZES--**HARD**.

RIGHT.

BASTARD.

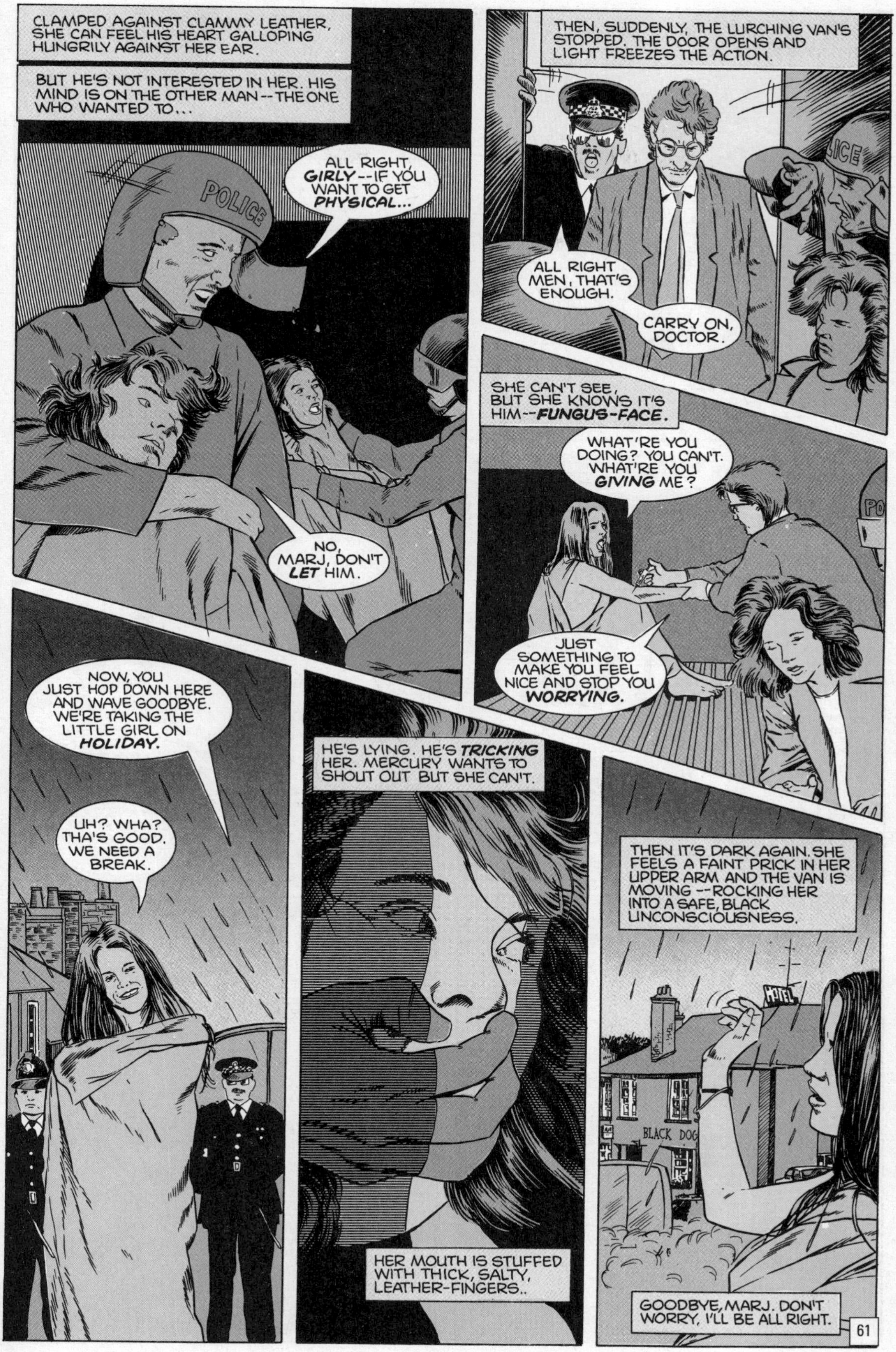
CLAMPED AGAINST CLAMMY LEATHER, SHE CAN FEEL HIS HEART GALLOPING HUNGRILY AGAINST HER EAR.
BUT HE'S NOT INTERESTED IN HER. HIS MIND IS ON THE OTHER MAN--THE ONE WHO WANTED TO...
POLICE
ALL RIGHT, GIRLY--IF YOU WANT TO GET PHYSICAL...
NO, MARJ, DON'T LET HIM.
THEN, SUDDENLY, THE LURCHING VAN'S STOPPED. THE DOOR OPENS AND LIGHT FREEZES THE ACTION.
ALL RIGHT MEN, THAT'S ENOUGH.
CARRY ON, DOCTOR.
SHE CAN'T SEE, BUT SHE KNOWS IT'S HIM--FUNGUS-FACE.
WHAT'RE YOU DOING? YOU CAN'T. WHAT'RE YOU GIVING ME?
JUST SOMETHING TO MAKE YOU FEEL NICE AND STOP YOU WORRYING.
NOW, YOU JUST HOP DOWN HERE AND WAVE GOODBYE. WE'RE TAKING THE LITTLE GIRL ON HOLIDAY.
UH? WHA? THA'S GOOD. WE NEED A BREAK.
HE'S LYING. HE'S TRICKING HER. MERCURY WANTS TO SHOUT OUT BUT SHE CAN'T.
HER MOUTH IS STUFFED WITH THICK, SALTY, LEATHER-FINGERS..
THEN IT'S DARK AGAIN. SHE FEELS A FAINT PRICK IN HER UPPER ARM AND THE VAN IS MOVING--ROCKING HER INTO A SAFE, BLACK UNCONSCIOUSNESS.
HOTEL
BLACK DOG
GOODBYE, MARJ. DON'T WORRY, I'LL BE ALL RIGHT.

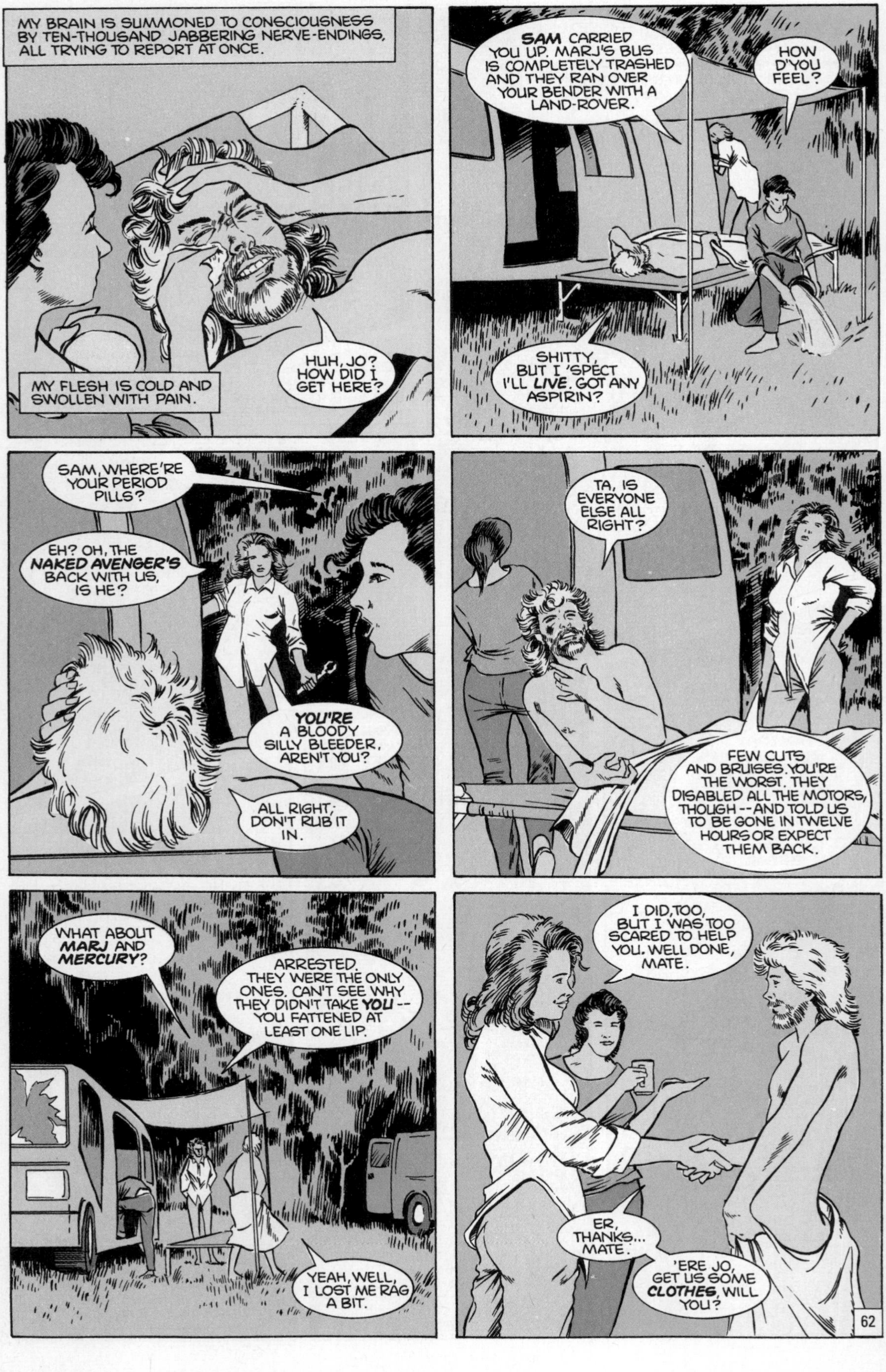
MY BRAIN IS SUMMONED TO CONSCIOUSNESS BY TEN-THOUSAND JABBERING NERVE-ENDINGS, ALL TRYING TO REPORT AT ONCE.
MY FLESH IS COLD AND SWOLLEN WITH PAIN.
HUH, JO? HOW DID I GET HERE?
SAM CARRIED YOU UP. MARJ'S BUS IS COMPLETELY TRASHED AND THEY RAN OVER YOUR BENDER WITH A LAND-ROVER.
HOW D'YOU FEEL?
SHITTY, BUT I 'SPECT I'LL LIVE. GOT ANY ASPIRIN?
SAM, WHERE'RE YOUR PERIOD PILLS?
EH? OH, THE NAKED AVENGER'S BACK WITH US, IS HE?
YOU'RE A BLOODY SILLY BLEEDER, AREN'T YOU?
ALL RIGHT,- DON'T RUB IT IN.
TA, IS EVERYONE ELSE ALL RIGHT?
FEW CUTS AND BRUISES. YOU'RE THE WORST. THEY DISABLED ALL THE MOTORS, THOUGH -- AND TOLD US TO BE GONE IN TWELVE HOURS OR EXPECT THEM BACK.
WHAT ABOUT MARJ AND MERCURY?
ARRESTED. THEY WERE THE ONLY ONES. CAN'T SEE WHY THEY DIDN'T TAKE YOU -- YOU FATTENED AT LEAST ONE LIP.
YEAH, WELL, I LOST ME RAG A BIT.
I DID, TOO, BUT I WAS TOO SCARED TO HELP YOU. WELL DONE, MATE.
ER, THANKS... MATE.
'ERE JO, GET US SOME CLOTHES, WILL YOU?

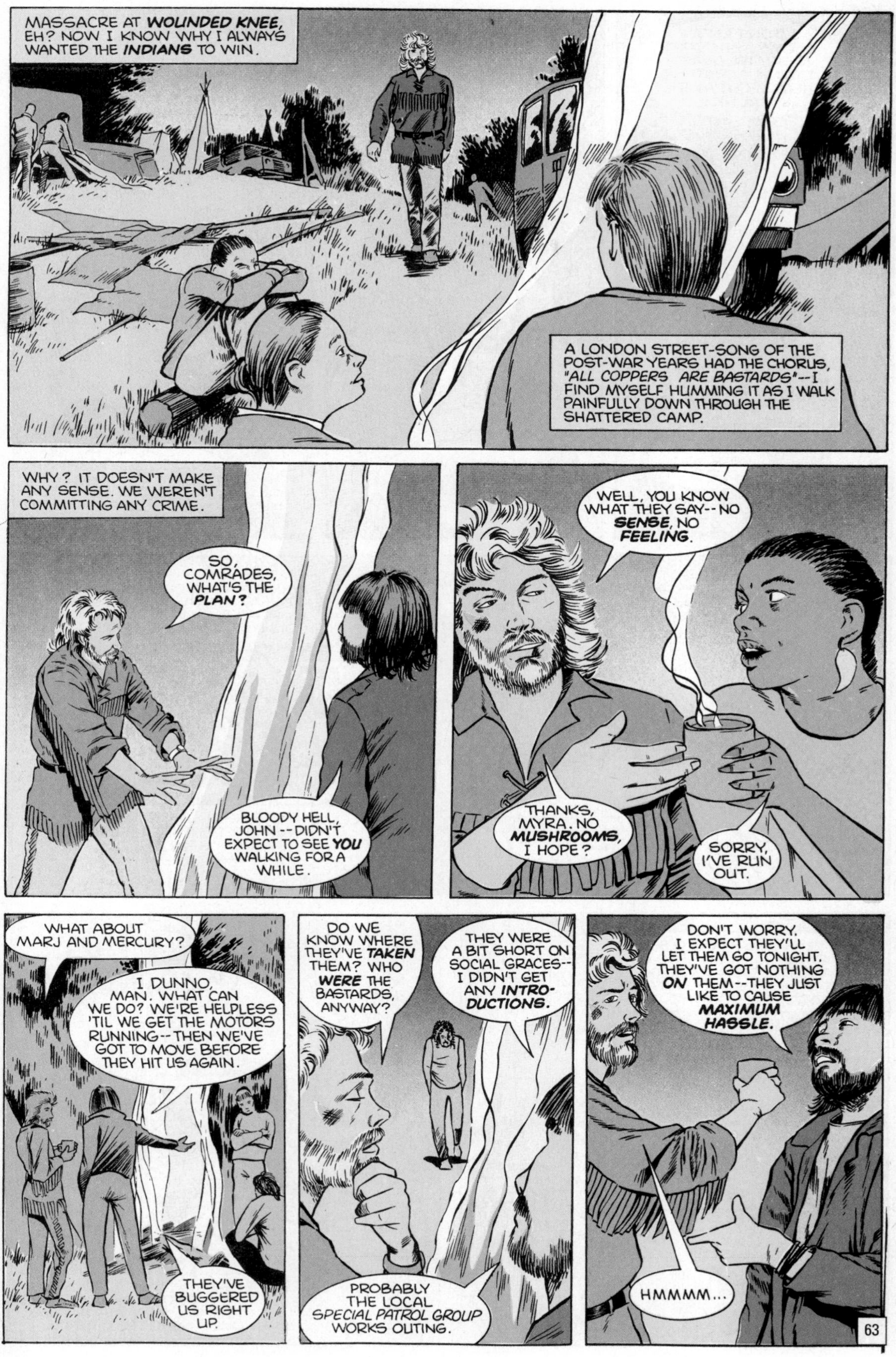

MASSACRE AT **WOUNDED KNEE**, EH? NOW I KNOW WHY I ALWAYS WANTED THE **INDIANS** TO WIN.
A LONDON STREET-SONG OF THE POST-WAR YEARS HAD THE CHORUS, *"ALL COPPERS ARE BASTARDS"*--I FIND MYSELF HUMMING IT AS I WALK PAINFULLY DOWN THROUGH THE SHATTERED CAMP.
WHY? IT DOESN'T MAKE ANY SENSE. WE WEREN'T COMMITTING ANY CRIME.
SO, COMRADES, WHAT'S THE ***PLAN?***
BLOODY HELL, JOHN --DIDN'T EXPECT TO SEE **YOU** WALKING FOR A WHILE.
WELL, YOU KNOW WHAT THEY SAY-- NO **SENSE**, NO **FEELING**.
THANKS, MYRA. NO **MUSHROOMS**, I HOPE?
SORRY, I'VE RUN OUT.
WHAT ABOUT MARJ AND MERCURY?
I DUNNO, MAN. WHAT CAN WE DO? WE'RE HELPLESS 'TIL WE GET THE MOTORS RUNNING--THEN WE'VE GOT TO MOVE BEFORE THEY HIT US AGAIN.
THEY'VE BUGGERED US RIGHT UP.
DO WE KNOW WHERE THEY'VE **TAKEN** THEM? WHO **WERE** THE BASTARDS, ANYWAY?
THEY WERE A BIT SHORT ON SOCIAL GRACES-- I DIDN'T GET ANY **INTRO-DUCTIONS**.
PROBABLY THE LOCAL *SPECIAL PATROL GROUP* WORKS OUTING.
DON'T WORRY. I EXPECT THEY'LL LET THEM GO TONIGHT. THEY'VE GOT NOTHING **ON** THEM--THEY JUST LIKE TO CAUSE **MAXIMUM HASSLE**.
HMMMM...

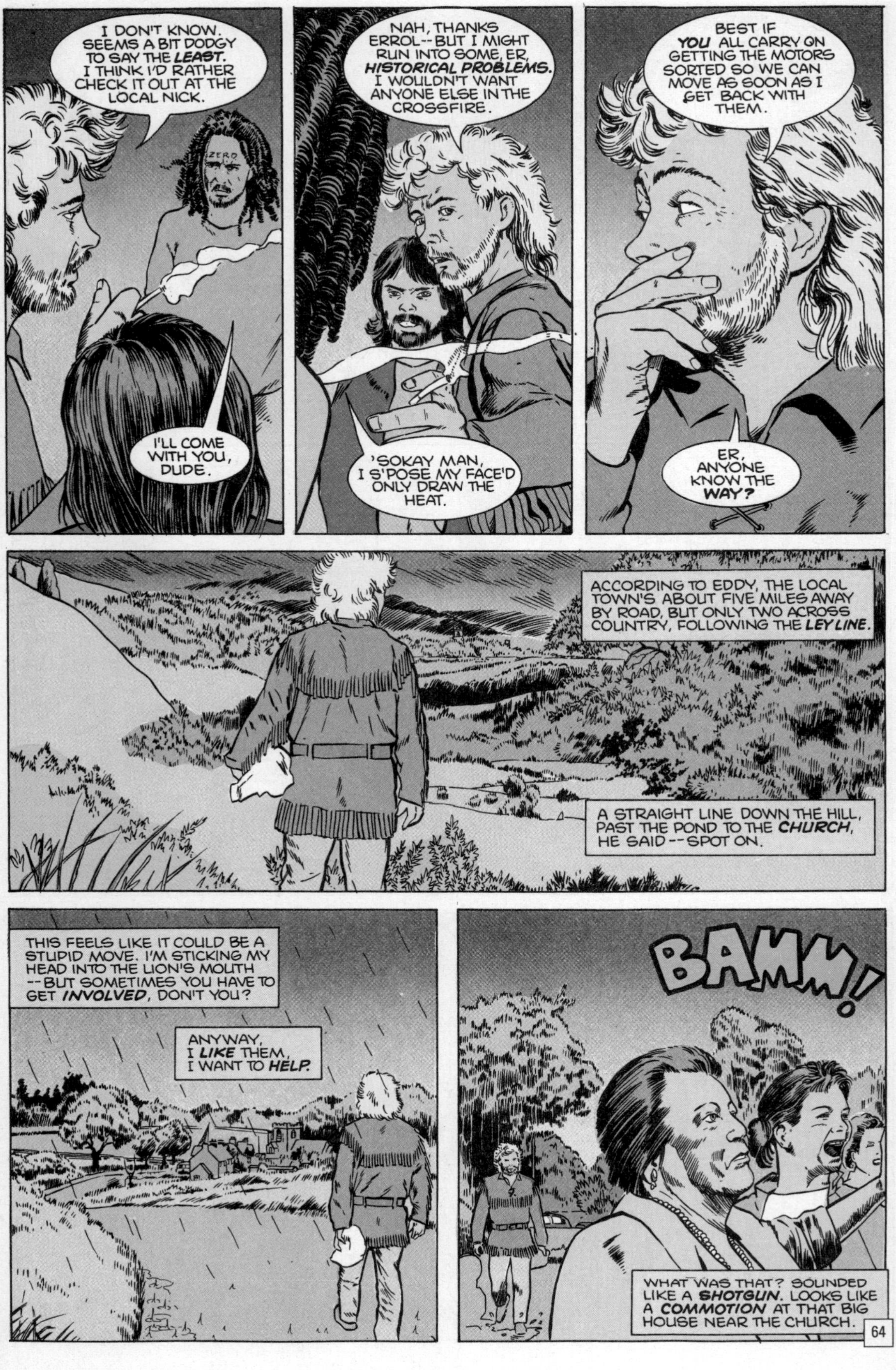
I DON'T KNOW. SEEMS A BIT DODGY TO SAY THE LEAST. I THINK I'D RATHER CHECK IT OUT AT THE LOCAL NICK.
I'LL COME WITH YOU, DUDE.
ZERO
NAH, THANKS ERROL-- BUT I MIGHT RUN INTO SOME, ER, HISTORICAL PROBLEMS. I WOULDN'T WANT ANYONE ELSE IN THE CROSSFIRE.
'SOKAY MAN, I S'POSE MY FACE'D ONLY DRAW THE HEAT.
BEST IF YOU ALL CARRY ON GETTING THE MOTORS SORTED SO WE CAN MOVE AS SOON AS I GET BACK WITH THEM.
ER, ANYONE KNOW THE WAY?
ACCORDING TO EDDY, THE LOCAL TOWN'S ABOUT FIVE MILES AWAY BY ROAD, BUT ONLY TWO ACROSS COUNTRY, FOLLOWING THE LEY LINE.
A STRAIGHT LINE DOWN THE HILL, PAST THE POND TO THE CHURCH, HE SAID--SPOT ON.
THIS FEELS LIKE IT COULD BE A STUPID MOVE. I'M STICKING MY HEAD INTO THE LION'S MOUTH --BUT SOMETIMES YOU HAVE TO GET INVOLVED, DON'T YOU?
ANYWAY, I LIKE THEM, I WANT TO HELP.
BAMM!
WHAT WAS THAT? SOUNDED LIKE A SHOTGUN. LOOKS LIKE A COMMOTION AT THAT BIG HOUSE NEAR THE CHURCH.

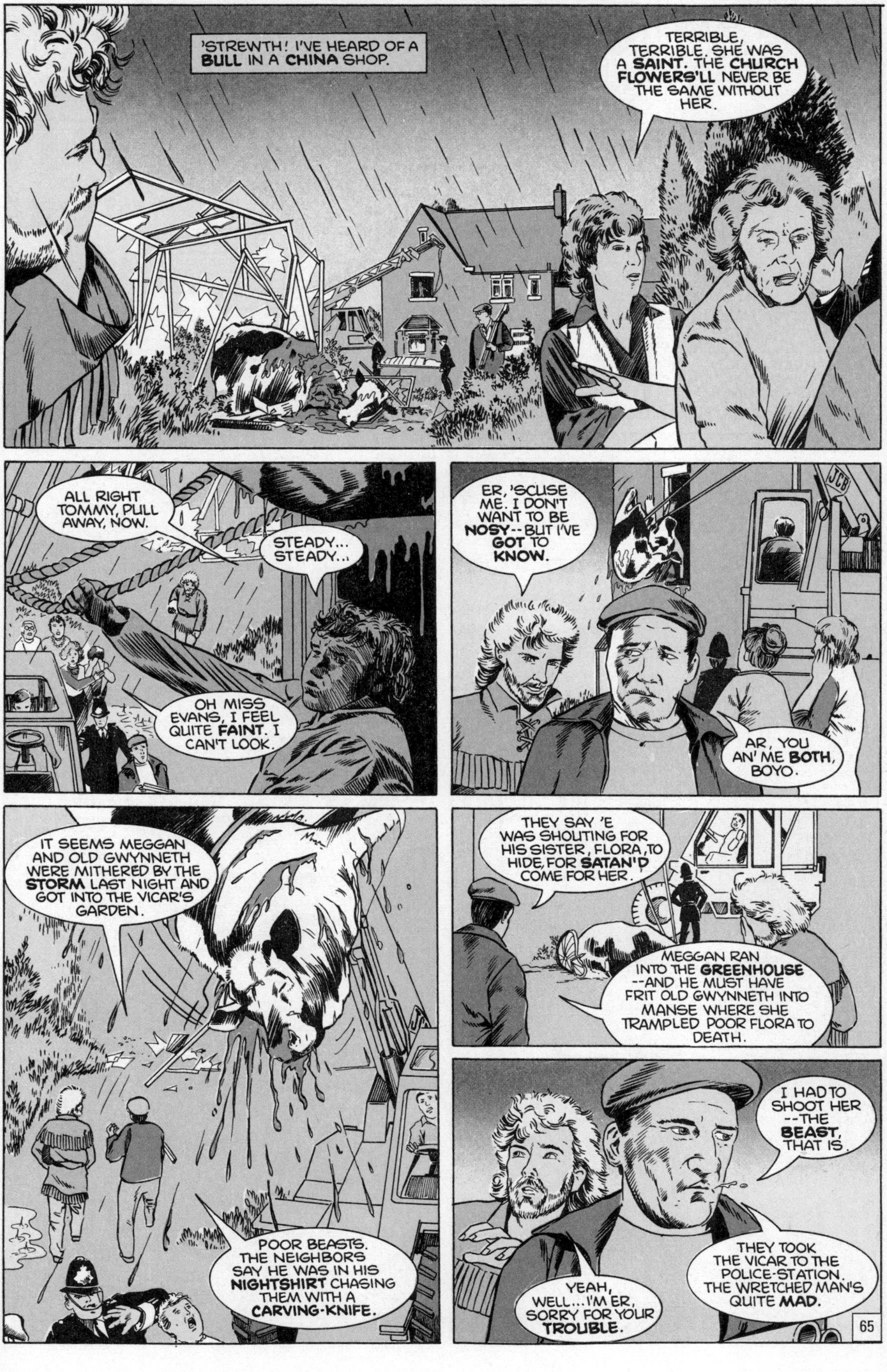
'STREWTH! I'VE HEARD OF A BULL IN A CHINA SHOP.
TERRIBLE, TERRIBLE. SHE WAS A SAINT. THE CHURCH FLOWERS'LL NEVER BE THE SAME WITHOUT HER.
ALL RIGHT TOMMY, PULL AWAY, NOW.
STEADY... STEADY...
OH MISS EVANS, I FEEL QUITE FAINT. I CAN'T LOOK.
ER, 'SCUSE ME. I DON'T WANT TO BE NOSY--BUT I'VE GOT TO KNOW.
AR, YOU AN' ME BOTH, BOYO.
IT SEEMS MEGGAN AND OLD GWYNNETH WERE MITHERED BY THE STORM LAST NIGHT AND GOT INTO THE VICAR'S GARDEN.
POOR BEASTS. THE NEIGHBORS SAY HE WAS IN HIS NIGHTSHIRT CHASING THEM WITH A CARVING-KNIFE.
THEY SAY 'E WAS SHOUTING FOR HIS SISTER, FLORA, TO HIDE, FOR SATAN'D COME FOR HER.
MEGGAN RAN INTO THE GREENHOUSE --AND HE MUST HAVE FRIT OLD GWYNNETH INTO MANSE WHERE SHE TRAMPLED POOR FLORA TO DEATH.
I HAD TO SHOOT HER --THE BEAST, THAT IS.
THEY TOOK THE VICAR TO THE POLICE-STATION. THE WRETCHED MAN'S QUITE MAD.
YEAH, WELL... I'M ER, SORRY FOR YOUR TROUBLE.

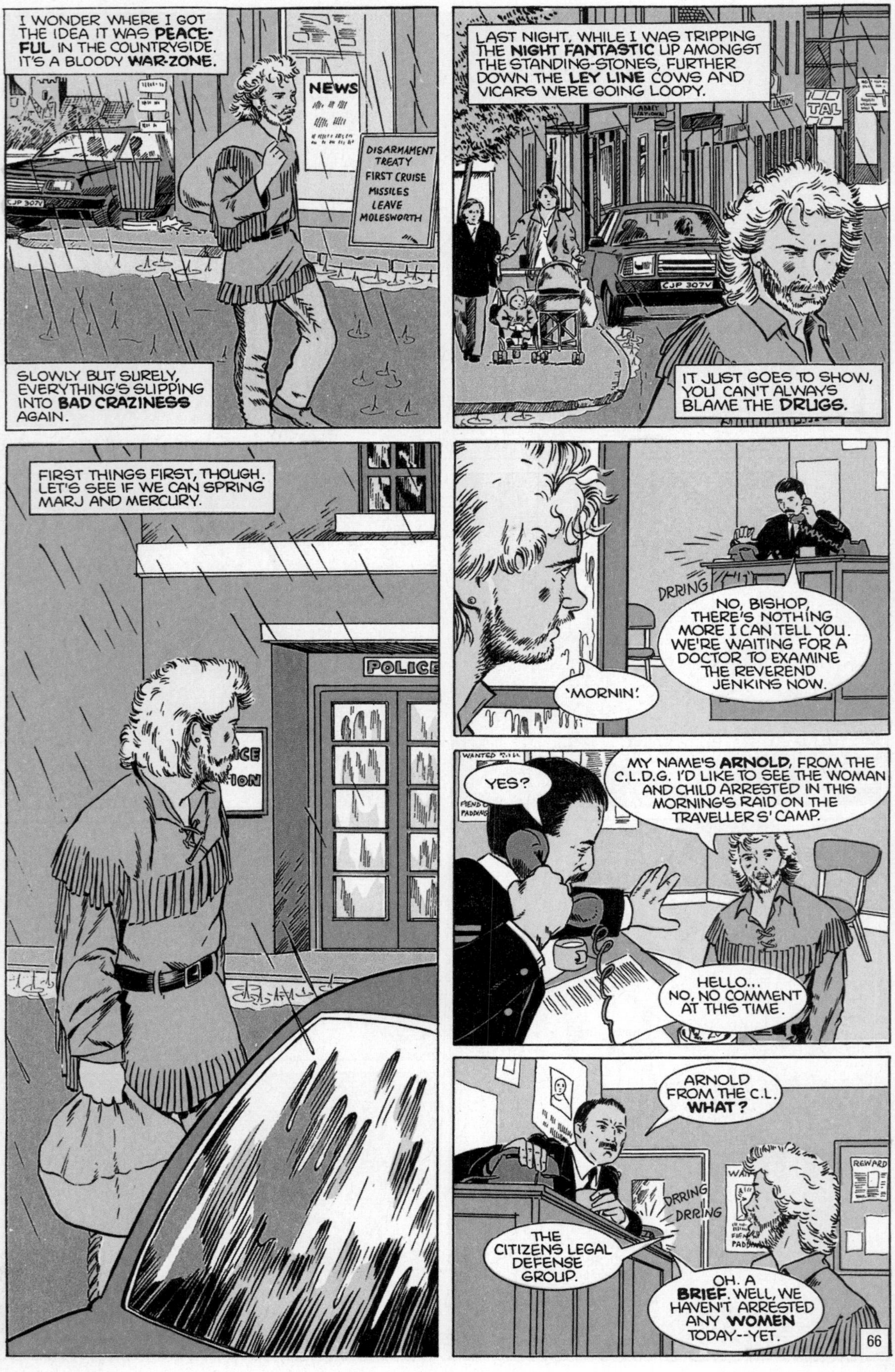

I WONDER WHERE I GOT THE IDEA IT WAS **PEACEFUL** IN THE COUNTRYSIDE. IT'S A BLOODY **WAR-ZONE**.
NEWS
DISARMAMENT TREATY FIRST CRUISE MISSILES LEAVE MOLESWORTH
CJP 307V
SLOWLY BUT SURELY, EVERYTHING'S SLIPPING INTO **BAD CRAZINESS** AGAIN.
LAST NIGHT, WHILE I WAS TRIPPING THE **NIGHT FANTASTIC** UP AMONGST THE STANDING-STONES, FURTHER DOWN THE **LEY LINE** COWS AND VICARS WERE GOING LOOPY.
ABBEY NATIONAL
LLOYDS
TAL
CJP 307V
IT JUST GOES TO SHOW, YOU CAN'T ALWAYS BLAME THE **DRUGS**.
FIRST THINGS FIRST, THOUGH. LET'S SEE IF WE CAN SPRING MARJ AND MERCURY.
POLICE
DRRING
NO, BISHOP, THERE'S NOTHING MORE I CAN TELL YOU. WE'RE WAITING FOR A DOCTOR TO EXAMINE THE REVEREND JENKINS NOW.
'MORNIN'.
YES?
MY NAME'S **ARNOLD**, FROM THE C.L.D.G. I'D LIKE TO SEE THE WOMAN AND CHILD ARRESTED IN THIS MORNING'S RAID ON THE TRAVELLER'S' CAMP.
HELLO... NO, NO COMMENT AT THIS TIME.
ARNOLD FROM THE C.L. **WHAT**?
REWARD
DRRING
DRRING
THE CITIZENS LEGAL DEFENSE GROUP.
OH. A **BRIEF**. WELL, WE HAVEN'T ARRESTED ANY **WOMEN** TODAY--YET.

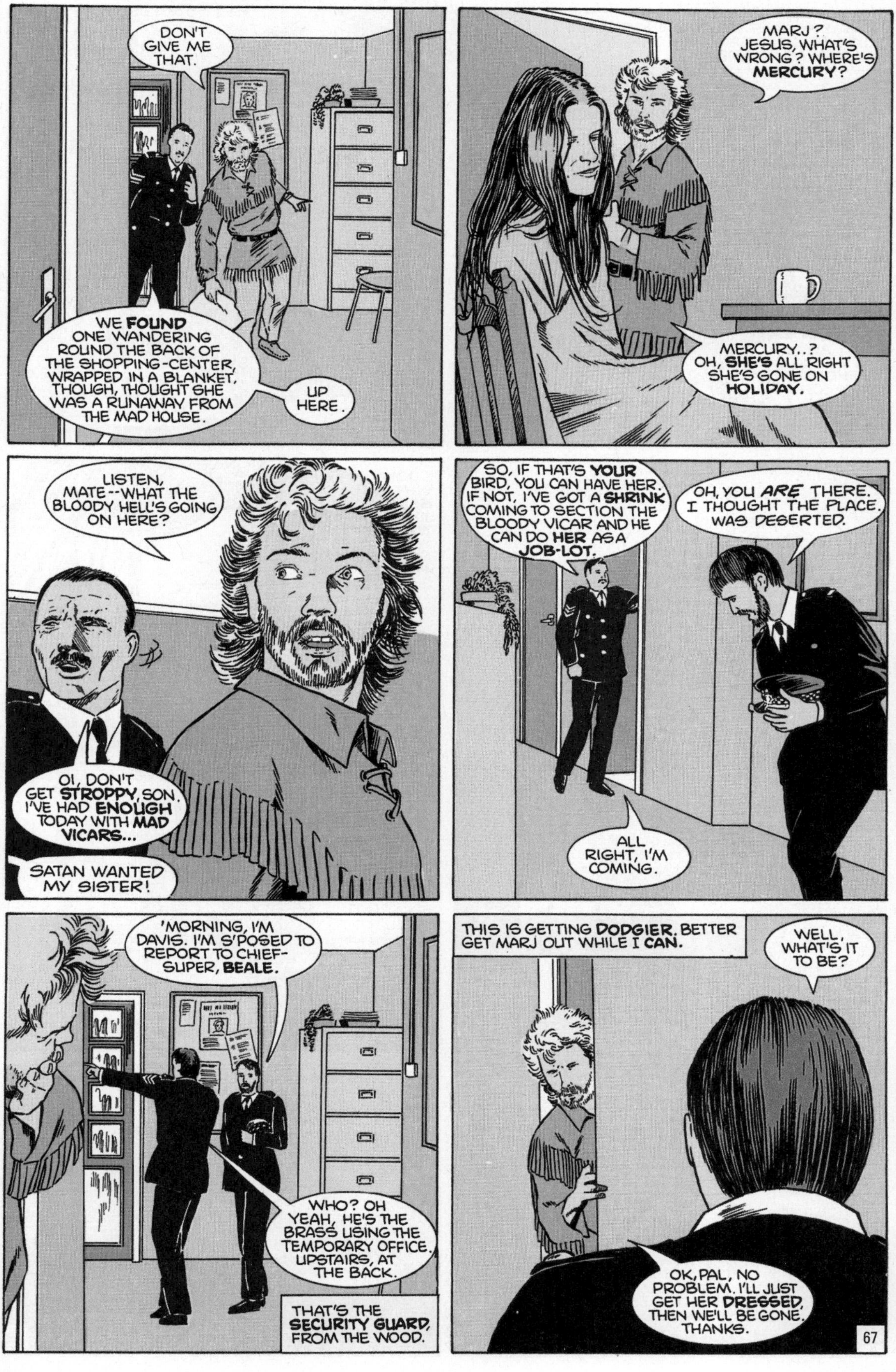
DON'T GIVE ME THAT.
WE FOUND ONE WANDERING ROUND THE BACK OF THE SHOPPING-CENTER, WRAPPED IN A BLANKET. THOUGHT, THOUGHT SHE WAS A RUNAWAY FROM THE MAD HOUSE.
UP HERE.
MARJ? JESUS, WHAT'S WRONG? WHERE'S MERCURY?
MERCURY..? OH, SHE'S ALL RIGHT SHE'S GONE ON HOLIDAY.
LISTEN, MATE--WHAT THE BLOODY HELL'S GOING ON HERE?
OI, DON'T GET STROPPY, SON. I'VE HAD ENOUGH TODAY WITH MAD VICARS...
SATAN WANTED MY SISTER!
SO, IF THAT'S YOUR BIRD, YOU CAN HAVE HER. IF NOT, I'VE GOT A SHRINK COMING TO SECTION THE BLOODY VICAR AND HE CAN DO HER AS A JOB-LOT.
OH, YOU ARE THERE. I THOUGHT THE PLACE WAS DESERTED.
ALL RIGHT, I'M COMING.
'MORNING, I'M DAVIS. I'M S'POSED TO REPORT TO CHIEF-SUPER, BEALE.
WHO? OH YEAH, HE'S THE BRASS USING THE TEMPORARY OFFICE. UPSTAIRS, AT THE BACK.
THAT'S THE SECURITY GUARD, FROM THE WOOD.
THIS IS GETTING DODGIER. BETTER GET MARJ OUT WHILE I CAN.
WELL, WHAT'S IT TO BE?
OK, PAL, NO PROBLEM. I'LL JUST GET HER DRESSED, THEN WE'LL BE GONE. THANKS.

IT WAS *MYRA'S* IDEA TO BRING THE CLOTHES. I GET MARJ INTO THEM AS QUICKLY AS POSSIBLE.

IT ISN'T EASY--SHE'S ON ANOTHER *PLANET.*

ARE WE GOING ON *HOLIDAY* TOO, JOHN?

SURE, MARJ --WHEREVER YOU LIKE.

ISN'T HE *NICE*--LOOKING AFTER ME.

JUST GET HER *OUT* OF HERE, WILL YOU?

THANKS, MATE --LOOK, ARE YOU *SURE* YOU DON'T KNOW ANYTHING ABOUT THE RAID AND THE LITTLE GIRL?

DON'T MAKE your pier a thief take-on

Lock it

DON'T PUSH YOUR LUCK.

NO, RIGHT, OK.

I DON'T KNOW WHY, BUT I *BELIEVE* HIM. HE'S JUST A SMALL-TOWN COPPER. THOSE GUYS THIS MORNING WERE *PROFESSIONAL* BASTARDS.

JOHN, I DON'T FEEL VERY WELL.

YEAH, I KNOW, LUV, ME NEITHER.

DON'T WORRY, THOUGH. I'LL SORT IT OUT.

BUT FIRST I'VE GOT TO SORT MYSELF OUT. I'M *KNACKERED.*

POLICE

STILL, IT'S NOT A TOTAL COCK-UP. AT LEAST I'VE GOT *MARJ* BACK --AND TWO NAMES WITH A CONNECTION, *DAVIS* AND *BEALE.*

TAXI!

I THINK I'VE EARNED A CAB RIDE, AT LEAST.

68

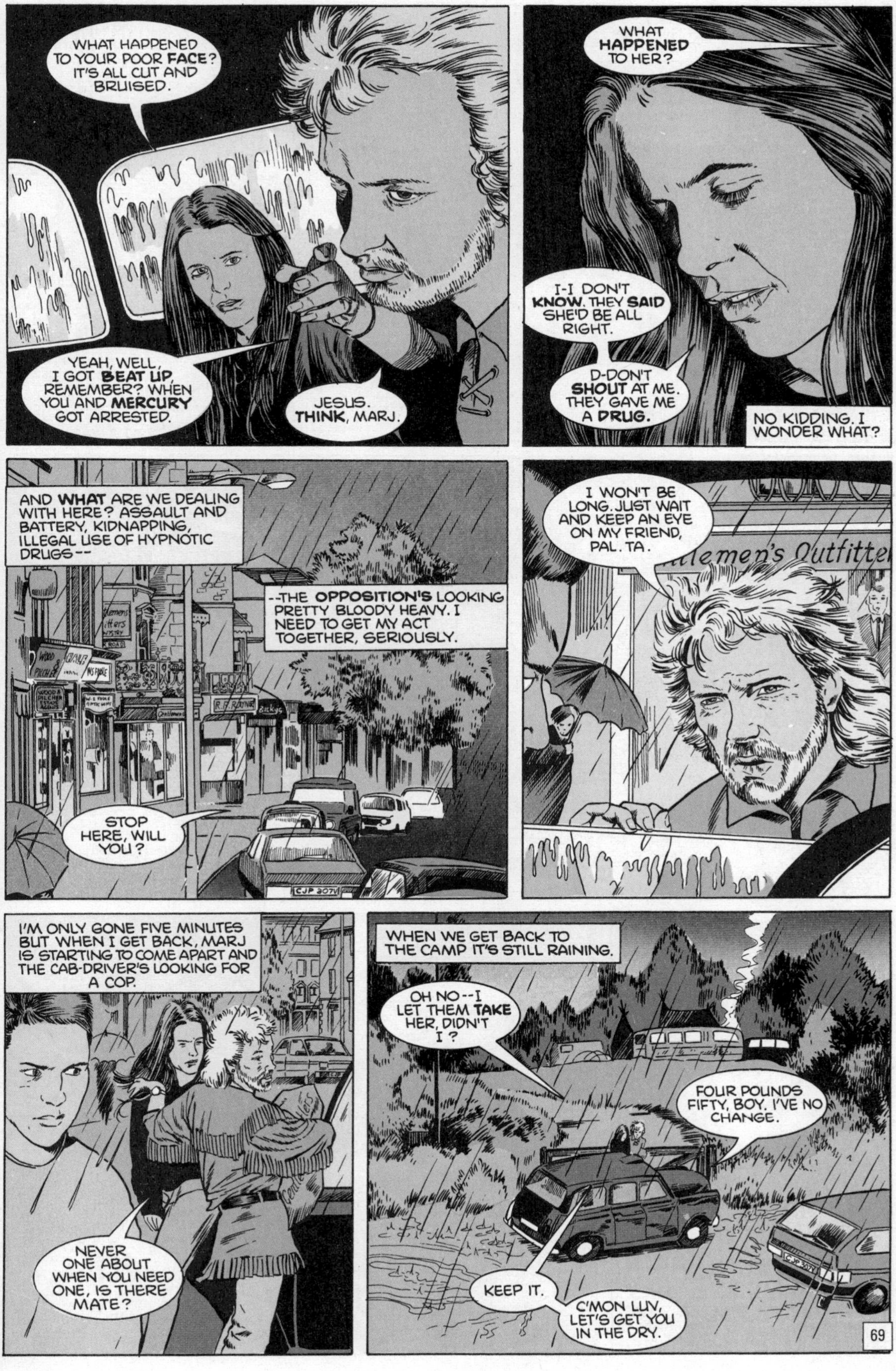

WHAT HAPPENED TO YOUR POOR **FACE**? IT'S ALL CUT AND BRUISED.
YEAH, WELL, I GOT **BEAT UP**, REMEMBER? WHEN YOU AND **MERCURY** GOT ARRESTED.
JESUS. **THINK**, MARJ.
WHAT **HAPPENED** TO HER?
I-I DON'T **KNOW**. THEY **SAID** SHE'D BE ALL RIGHT.
D-DON'T **SHOUT** AT ME. THEY GAVE ME A **DRUG.**
NO KIDDING. I WONDER WHAT?
AND **WHAT** ARE WE DEALING WITH HERE? ASSAULT AND BATTERY, KIDNAPPING, ILLEGAL USE OF HYPNOTIC DRUGS--
--THE **OPPOSITION'S** LOOKING PRETTY BLOODY HEAVY. I NEED TO GET MY ACT TOGETHER, SERIOUSLY.
STOP HERE, WILL YOU?
CJP 307V
I WON'T BE LONG. JUST WAIT AND KEEP AN EYE ON MY FRIEND, PAL. TA.
I'M ONLY GONE FIVE MINUTES BUT WHEN I GET BACK, MARJ IS STARTING TO COME APART AND THE CAB-DRIVER'S LOOKING FOR A COP.
NEVER ONE ABOUT WHEN YOU NEED ONE, IS THERE MATE?
WHEN WE GET BACK TO THE CAMP IT'S STILL RAINING.
OH NO--I LET THEM **TAKE** HER, DIDN'T I?
FOUR POUNDS FIFTY, BOY. I'VE NO CHANGE.
KEEP IT.
C'MON LUV, LET'S GET YOU IN THE DRY.

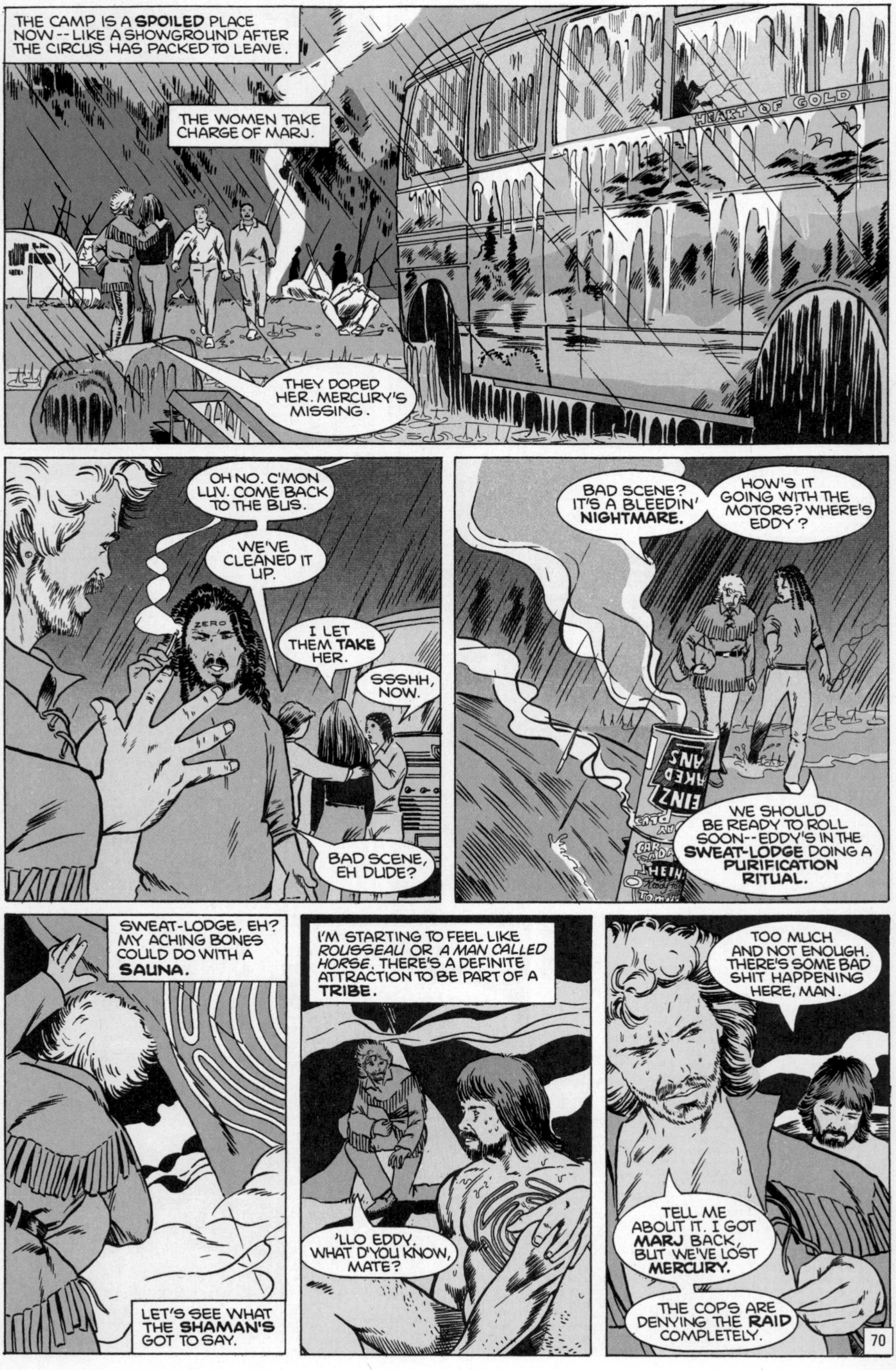
THE CAMP IS A SPOILED PLACE NOW -- LIKE A SHOWGROUND AFTER THE CIRCUS HAS PACKED TO LEAVE.
THE WOMEN TAKE CHARGE OF MARJ.
HEART OF GOLD
THEY DOPED HER. MERCURY'S MISSING.
OH NO. C'MON LUV. COME BACK TO THE BUS.
WE'VE CLEANED IT UP.
I LET THEM TAKE HER.
SSSHH, NOW.
BAD SCENE, EH DUDE?
BAD SCENE? IT'S A BLEEDIN' NIGHTMARE.
HOW'S IT GOING WITH THE MOTORS? WHERE'S EDDY?
WE SHOULD BE READY TO ROLL SOON-- EDDY'S IN THE SWEAT-LODGE DOING A PURIFICATION RITUAL.
SWEAT-LODGE, EH? MY ACHING BONES COULD DO WITH A SAUNA.
LET'S SEE WHAT THE SHAMAN'S GOT TO SAY.
I'M STARTING TO FEEL LIKE ROUSSEAU OR A MAN CALLED HORSE. THERE'S A DEFINITE ATTRACTION TO BE PART OF A TRIBE.
'LLO EDDY. WHAT D'YOU KNOW, MATE?
TOO MUCH AND NOT ENOUGH. THERE'S SOME BAD SHIT HAPPENING HERE, MAN.
TELL ME ABOUT IT. I GOT MARJ BACK, BUT WE'VE LOST MERCURY.
THE COPS ARE DENYING THE RAID COMPLETELY.

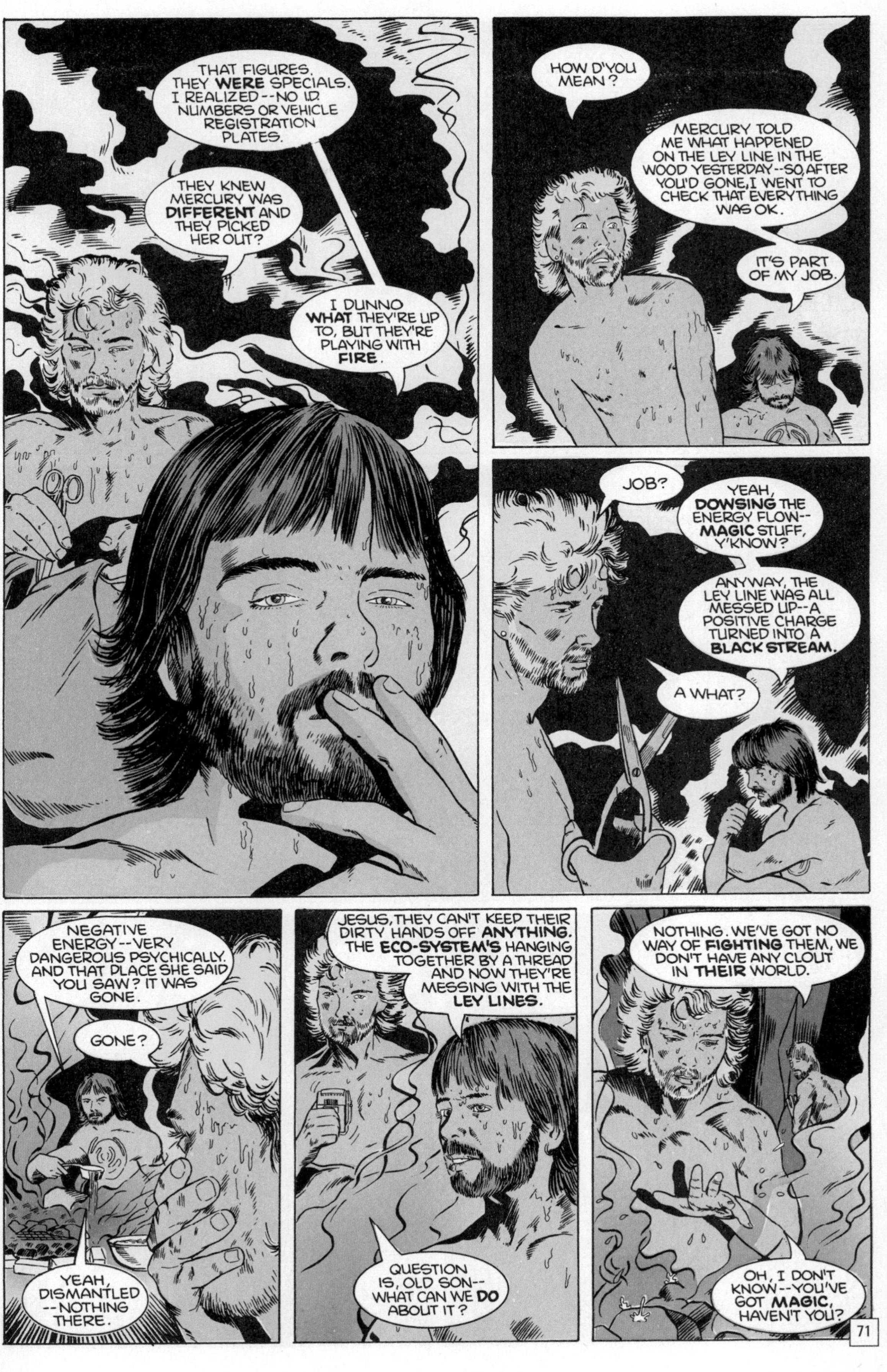

THAT FIGURES. THEY **WERE** SPECIALS. I REALIZED--NO I.D. NUMBERS OR VEHICLE REGISTRATION PLATES.
THEY KNEW MERCURY WAS **DIFFERENT** AND THEY PICKED HER OUT?
I DUNNO **WHAT** THEY'RE UP TO, BUT THEY'RE PLAYING WITH **FIRE**.
HOW D'YOU MEAN?
MERCURY TOLD ME WHAT HAPPENED ON THE LEY LINE IN THE WOOD YESTERDAY--SO, AFTER YOU'D GONE, I WENT TO CHECK THAT EVERYTHING WAS OK.
IT'S PART OF MY JOB.
JOB?
YEAH, **DOWSING** THE ENERGY FLOW--**MAGIC** STUFF, Y'KNOW?
ANYWAY, THE LEY LINE WAS ALL MESSED UP--A POSITIVE CHARGE TURNED INTO A **BLACK STREAM**.
A WHAT?
NEGATIVE ENERGY--VERY DANGEROUS PSYCHICALLY. AND THAT PLACE SHE SAID YOU SAW? IT WAS GONE.
GONE?
YEAH, DISMANTLED--NOTHING THERE.
JESUS, THEY CAN'T KEEP THEIR DIRTY HANDS OFF **ANYTHING**. THE **ECO-SYSTEM'S** HANGING TOGETHER BY A THREAD AND NOW THEY'RE MESSING WITH THE **LEY LINES**.
QUESTION IS, OLD SON--WHAT CAN WE **DO** ABOUT IT?
NOTHING. WE'VE GOT NO WAY OF **FIGHTING** THEM, WE DON'T HAVE ANY CLOUT IN **THEIR** WORLD.
OH, I DON'T KNOW--YOU'VE GOT **MAGIC**, HAVEN'T YOU?

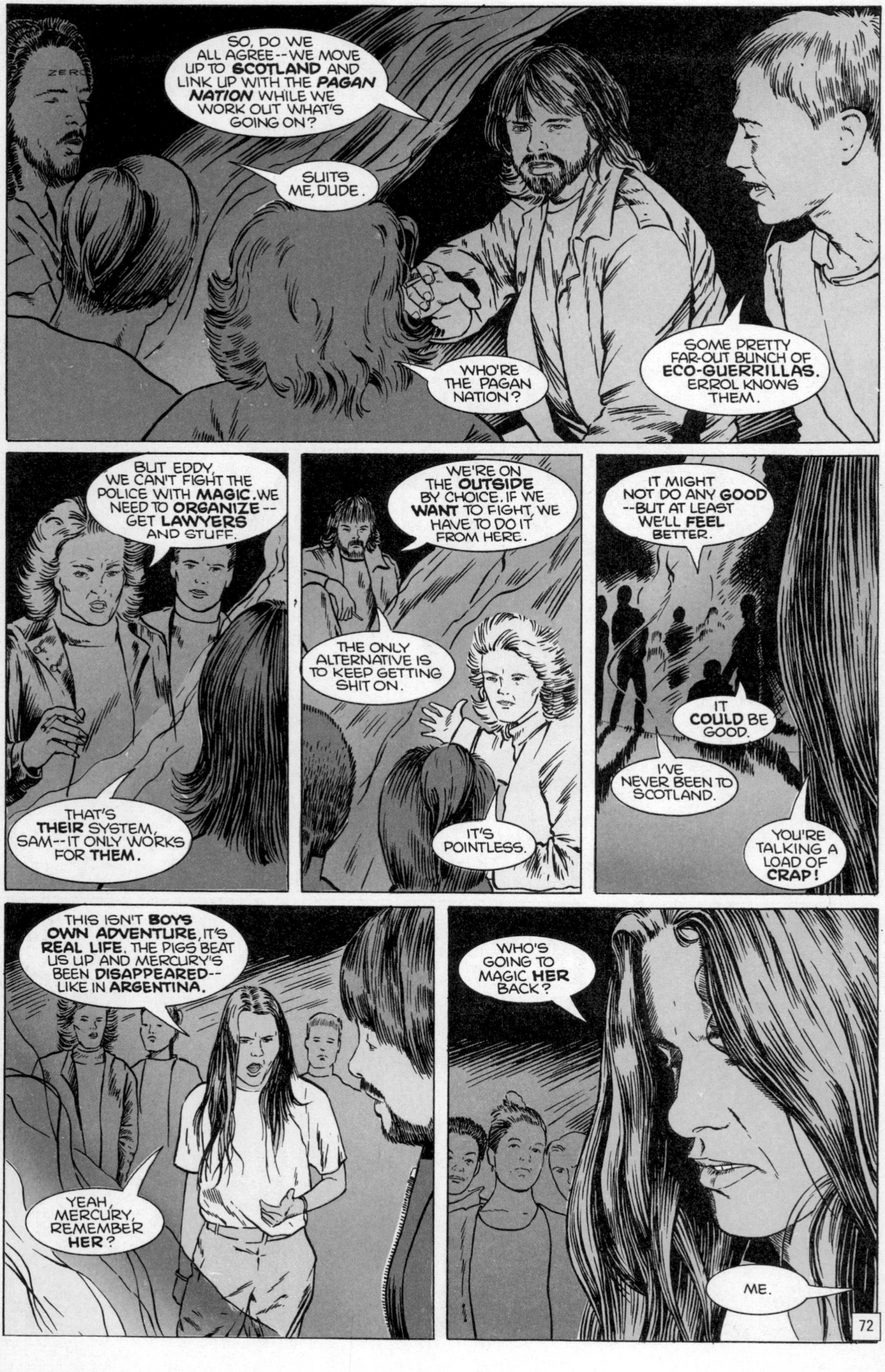
ZERO
SO, DO WE ALL AGREE--WE MOVE UP TO SCOTLAND AND LINK UP WITH THE PAGAN NATION WHILE WE WORK OUT WHAT'S GOING ON?
SUITS ME, DUDE.
WHO'RE THE PAGAN NATION?
SOME PRETTY FAR-OUT BUNCH OF ECO-GUERRILLAS. ERROL KNOWS THEM.
BUT EDDY, WE CAN'T FIGHT THE POLICE WITH MAGIC. WE NEED TO ORGANIZE--GET LAWYERS AND STUFF.
THAT'S THEIR SYSTEM, SAM--IT ONLY WORKS FOR THEM.
WE'RE ON THE OUTSIDE BY CHOICE. IF WE WANT TO FIGHT, WE HAVE TO DO IT FROM HERE.
THE ONLY ALTERNATIVE IS TO KEEP GETTING SHIT ON.
IT'S POINTLESS.
IT MIGHT NOT DO ANY GOOD--BUT AT LEAST WE'LL FEEL BETTER.
IT COULD BE GOOD.
I'VE NEVER BEEN TO SCOTLAND.
YOU'RE TALKING A LOAD OF CRAP!
THIS ISN'T BOYS OWN ADVENTURE, IT'S REAL LIFE. THE PIGS BEAT US UP AND MERCURY'S BEEN DISAPPEARED--LIKE IN ARGENTINA.
YEAH, MERCURY, REMEMBER HER?
WHO'S GOING TO MAGIC HER BACK?
ME.

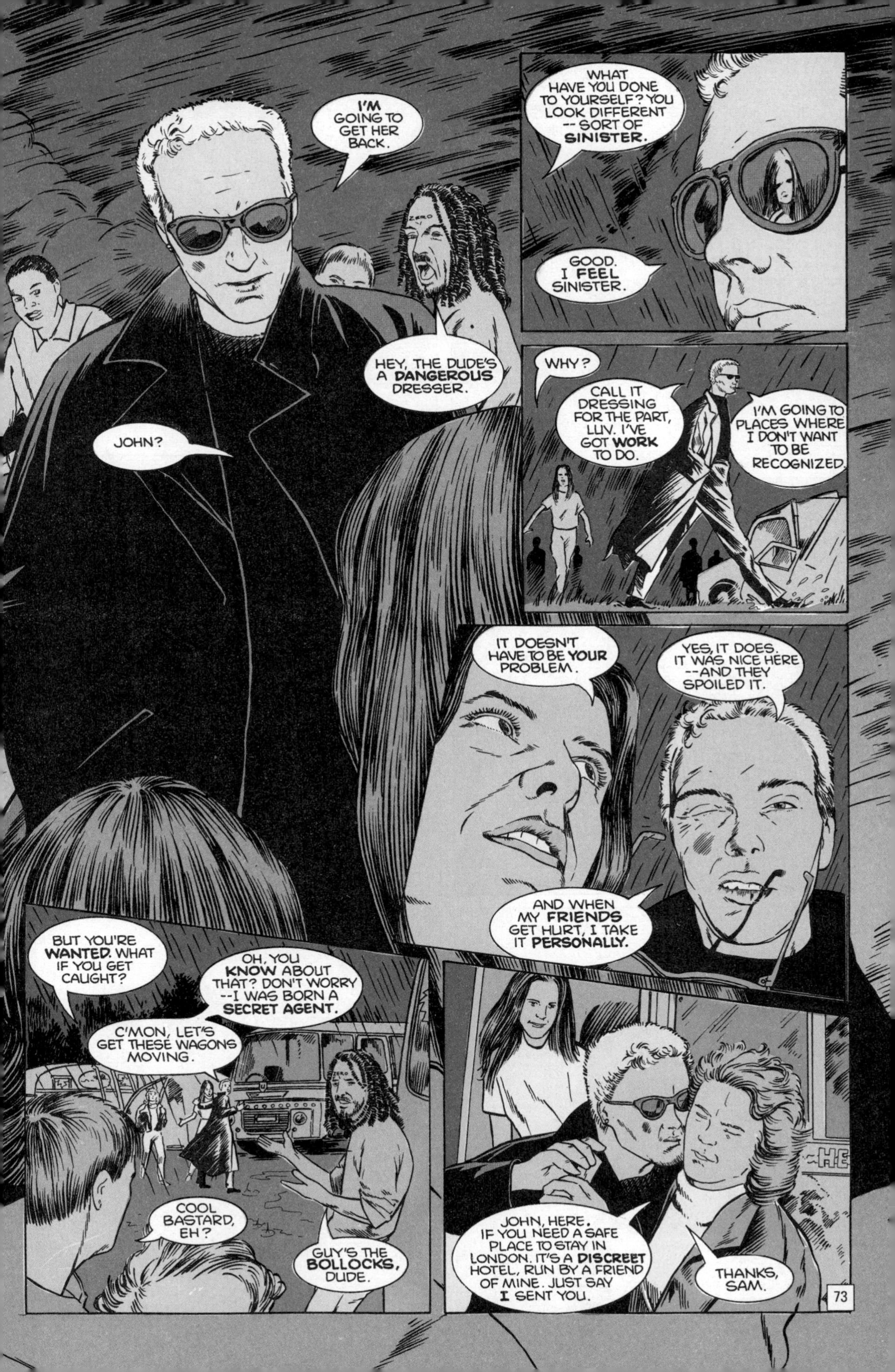
I'M GOING TO GET HER BACK.
HEY, THE DUDE'S A DANGEROUS DRESSER.
JOHN?
WHAT HAVE YOU DONE TO YOURSELF? YOU LOOK DIFFERENT -- SORT OF SINISTER.
GOOD. I FEEL SINISTER.
WHY?
CALL IT DRESSING FOR THE PART, LUV. I'VE GOT WORK TO DO.
I'M GOING TO PLACES WHERE I DON'T WANT TO BE RECOGNIZED.
IT DOESN'T HAVE TO BE YOUR PROBLEM.
YES, IT DOES. IT WAS NICE HERE --AND THEY SPOILED IT.
AND WHEN MY FRIENDS GET HURT, I TAKE IT PERSONALLY.
BUT YOU'RE WANTED. WHAT IF YOU GET CAUGHT?
OH, YOU KNOW ABOUT THAT? DON'T WORRY --I WAS BORN A SECRET AGENT.
C'MON, LET'S GET THESE WAGONS MOVING.
COOL BASTARD, EH?
GUY'S THE BOLLOCKS, DUDE.
JOHN, HERE. IF YOU NEED A SAFE PLACE TO STAY IN LONDON. IT'S A DISCREET HOTEL, RUN BY A FRIEND OF MINE. JUST SAY I SENT YOU.
THANKS, SAM.

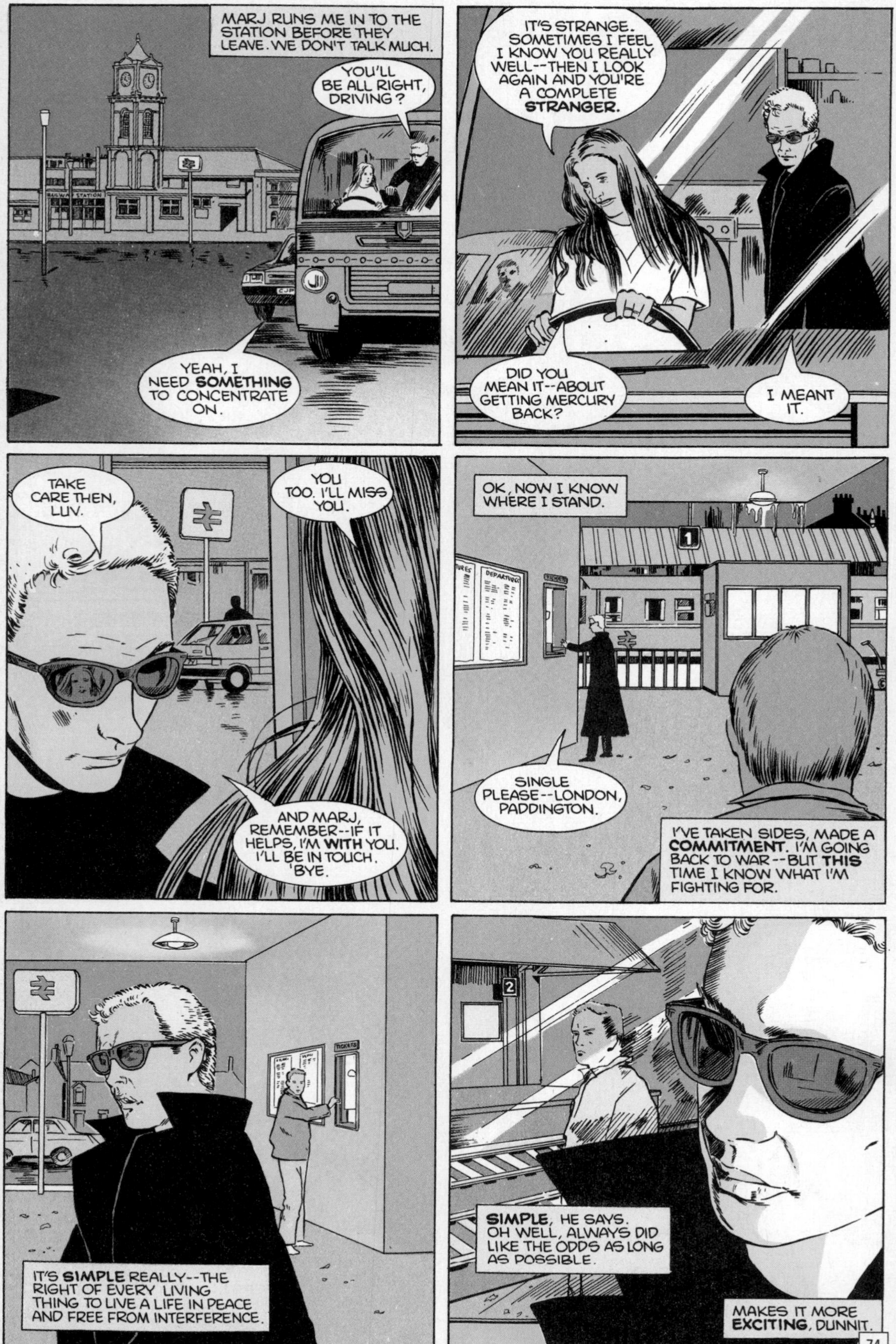
MARJ RUNS ME IN TO THE STATION BEFORE THEY LEAVE. WE DON'T TALK MUCH.
YOU'LL BE ALL RIGHT, DRIVING?
YEAH, I NEED **SOMETHING** TO CONCENTRATE ON.
IT'S STRANGE. SOMETIMES I FEEL I KNOW YOU REALLY WELL--THEN I LOOK AGAIN AND YOU'RE A COMPLETE **STRANGER.**
DID YOU MEAN IT--ABOUT GETTING MERCURY BACK?
I MEANT IT.
TAKE CARE THEN, LUV.
YOU TOO. I'LL MISS YOU.
AND MARJ, REMEMBER--IF IT HELPS, I'M **WITH** YOU. I'LL BE IN TOUCH. 'BYE.
OK, NOW I KNOW WHERE I STAND.
SINGLE PLEASE--LONDON, PADDINGTON.
I'VE TAKEN SIDES, MADE A **COMMITMENT**. I'M GOING BACK TO WAR--BUT **THIS** TIME I KNOW WHAT I'M FIGHTING FOR.
IT'S **SIMPLE** REALLY--THE RIGHT OF EVERY LIVING THING TO LIVE A LIFE IN PEACE AND FREE FROM INTERFERENCE.
SIMPLE, HE SAYS. OH WELL, ALWAYS DID LIKE THE ODDS AS LONG AS POSSIBLE.
MAKES IT MORE **EXCITING**, DUNNIT.

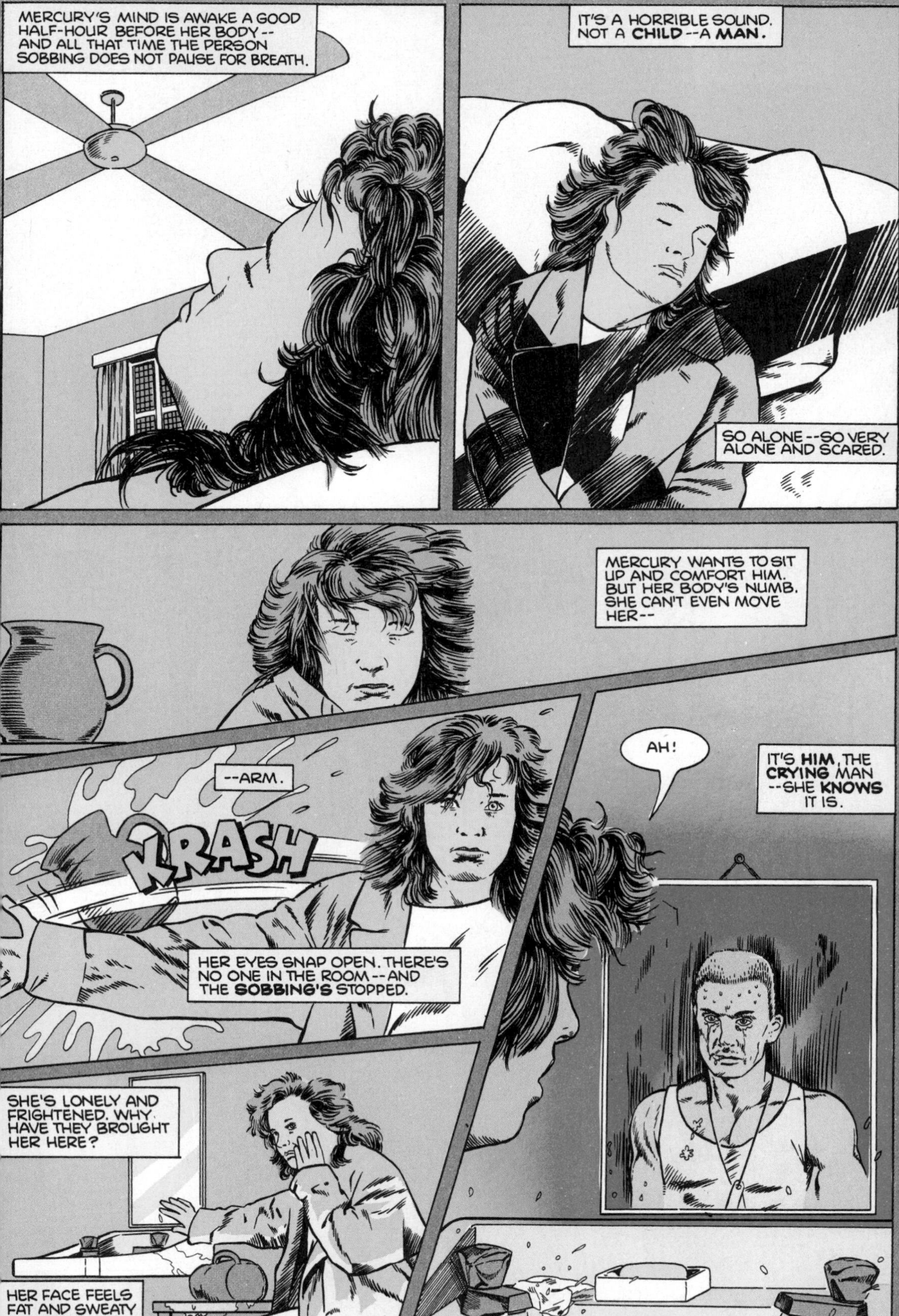
MERCURY'S MIND IS AWAKE A GOOD HALF-HOUR BEFORE HER BODY-- AND ALL THAT TIME THE PERSON SOBBING DOES NOT PAUSE FOR BREATH.
IT'S A HORRIBLE SOUND. NOT A CHILD--A MAN.
SO ALONE--SO VERY ALONE AND SCARED.
MERCURY WANTS TO SIT UP AND COMFORT HIM. BUT HER BODY'S NUMB. SHE CAN'T EVEN MOVE HER--
--ARM.
KRASH
HER EYES SNAP OPEN. THERE'S NO ONE IN THE ROOM--AND THE SOBBING'S STOPPED.
AH!
IT'S HIM, THE CRYING MAN --SHE KNOWS IT IS.
SHE'S LONELY AND FRIGHTENED. WHY HAVE THEY BROUGHT HER HERE?
HER FACE FEELS FAT AND SWEATY --SHE WANTS TO WASH.

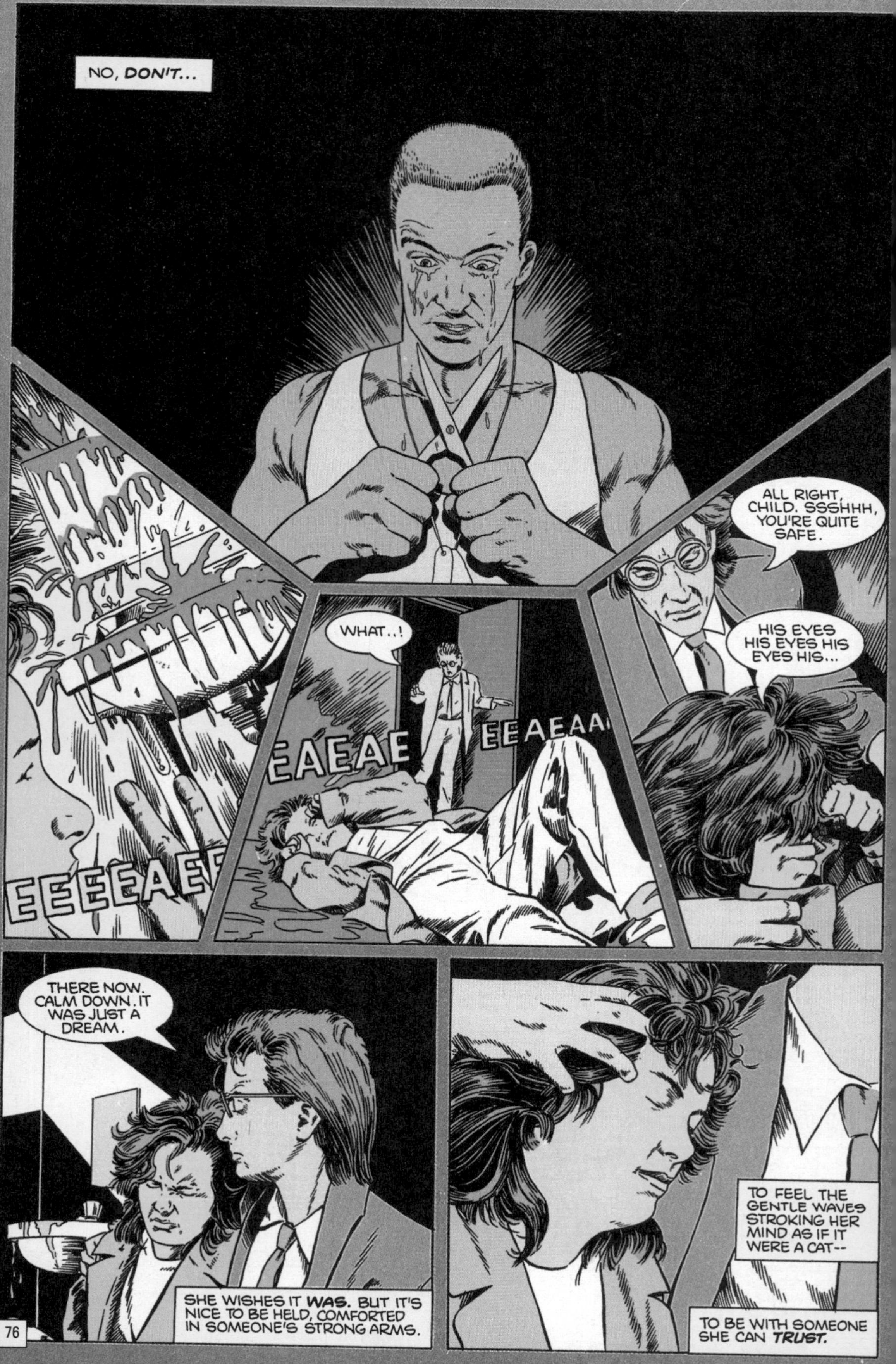

NO, DON'T...
EEEEAEE
WHAT..!
EAEAE
EEAEAA
ALL RIGHT, CHILD. SSSHHH, YOU'RE QUITE SAFE.
HIS EYES HIS EYES HIS EYES HIS...
THERE NOW. CALM DOWN. IT WAS JUST A DREAM.
SHE WISHES IT WAS. BUT IT'S NICE TO BE HELD, COMFORTED IN SOMEONE'S STRONG ARMS.
TO FEEL THE GENTLE WAVES STROKING HER MIND AS IF IT WERE A CAT--
TO BE WITH SOMEONE SHE CAN TRUST.

BUT NOT *HIM*, NOT *FUNGUS-FACE*.

NO! STOP IT. YOU'RE A *LIAR!*

NOW, DON'T GET *FRIGHTENED* AGAIN.

I'M NOT FRIGHTENED --BUT *YOU* SHOULD BE.

BECAUSE *I* KNOW WHAT *HAPPENS* TO YOU.

SHALL I *SHOW* YOU?

WHY?

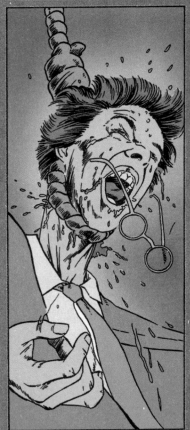

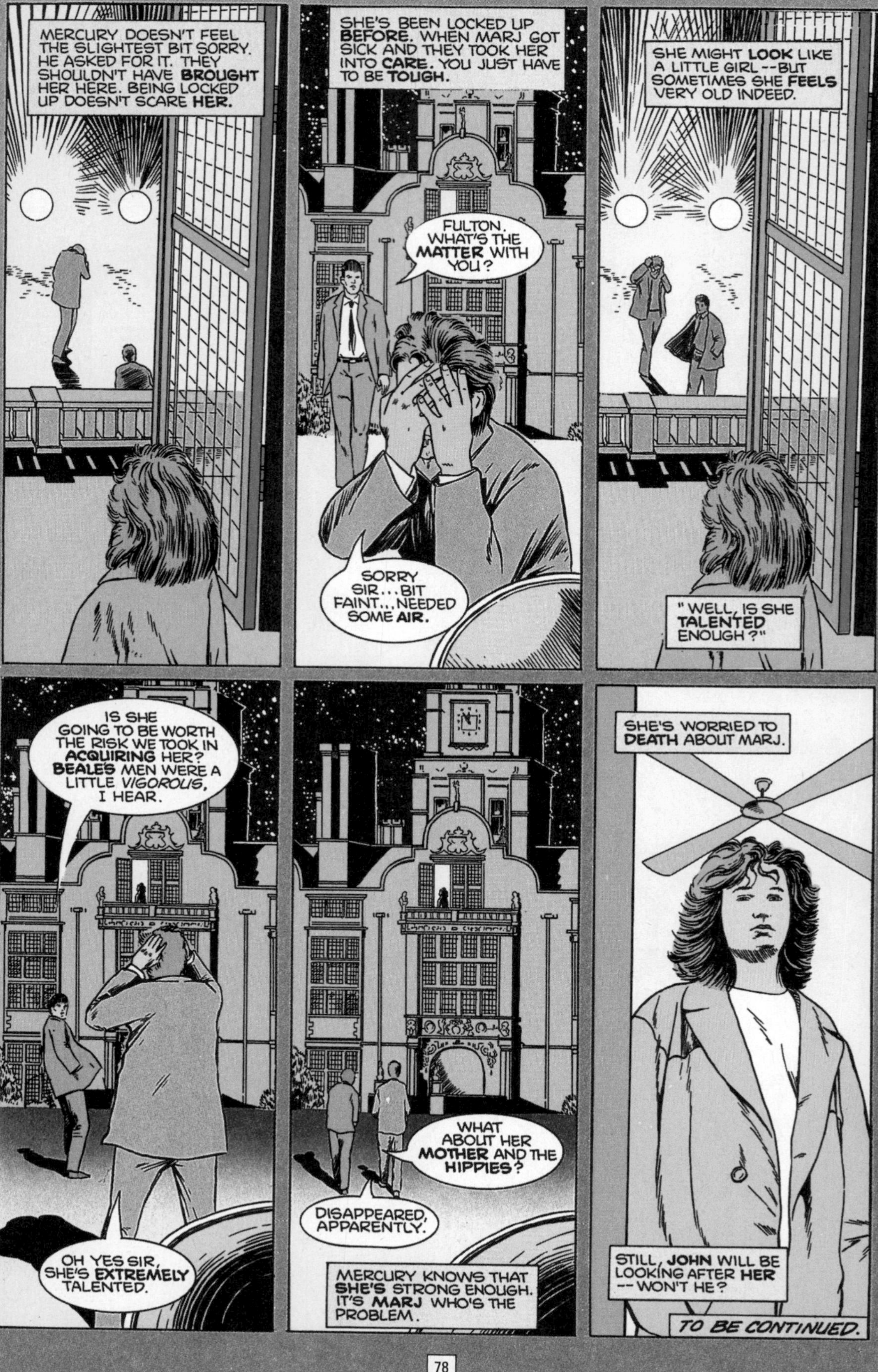
MERCURY DOESN'T FEEL THE SLIGHTEST BIT SORRY. HE ASKED FOR IT. THEY SHOULDN'T HAVE BROUGHT HER HERE. BEING LOCKED UP DOESN'T SCARE HER.
SHE'S BEEN LOCKED UP BEFORE. WHEN MARJ GOT SICK AND THEY TOOK HER INTO CARE. YOU JUST HAVE TO BE TOUGH.
FULTON. WHAT'S THE MATTER WITH YOU?
SORRY SIR... BIT FAINT... NEEDED SOME AIR.
SHE MIGHT LOOK LIKE A LITTLE GIRL --BUT SOMETIMES SHE FEELS VERY OLD INDEED.
"WELL, IS SHE TALENTED ENOUGH?"
IS SHE GOING TO BE WORTH THE RISK WE TOOK IN ACQUIRING HER? BEALE'S MEN WERE A LITTLE VIGOROUS, I HEAR.
OH YES SIR, SHE'S EXTREMELY TALENTED.
WHAT ABOUT HER MOTHER AND THE HIPPIES?
DISAPPEARED, APPARENTLY.
MERCURY KNOWS THAT SHE'S STRONG ENOUGH. IT'S MARJ WHO'S THE PROBLEM.
SHE'S WORRIED TO DEATH ABOUT MARJ.
STILL, JOHN WILL BE LOOKING AFTER HER --WON'T HE?
TO BE CONTINUED.

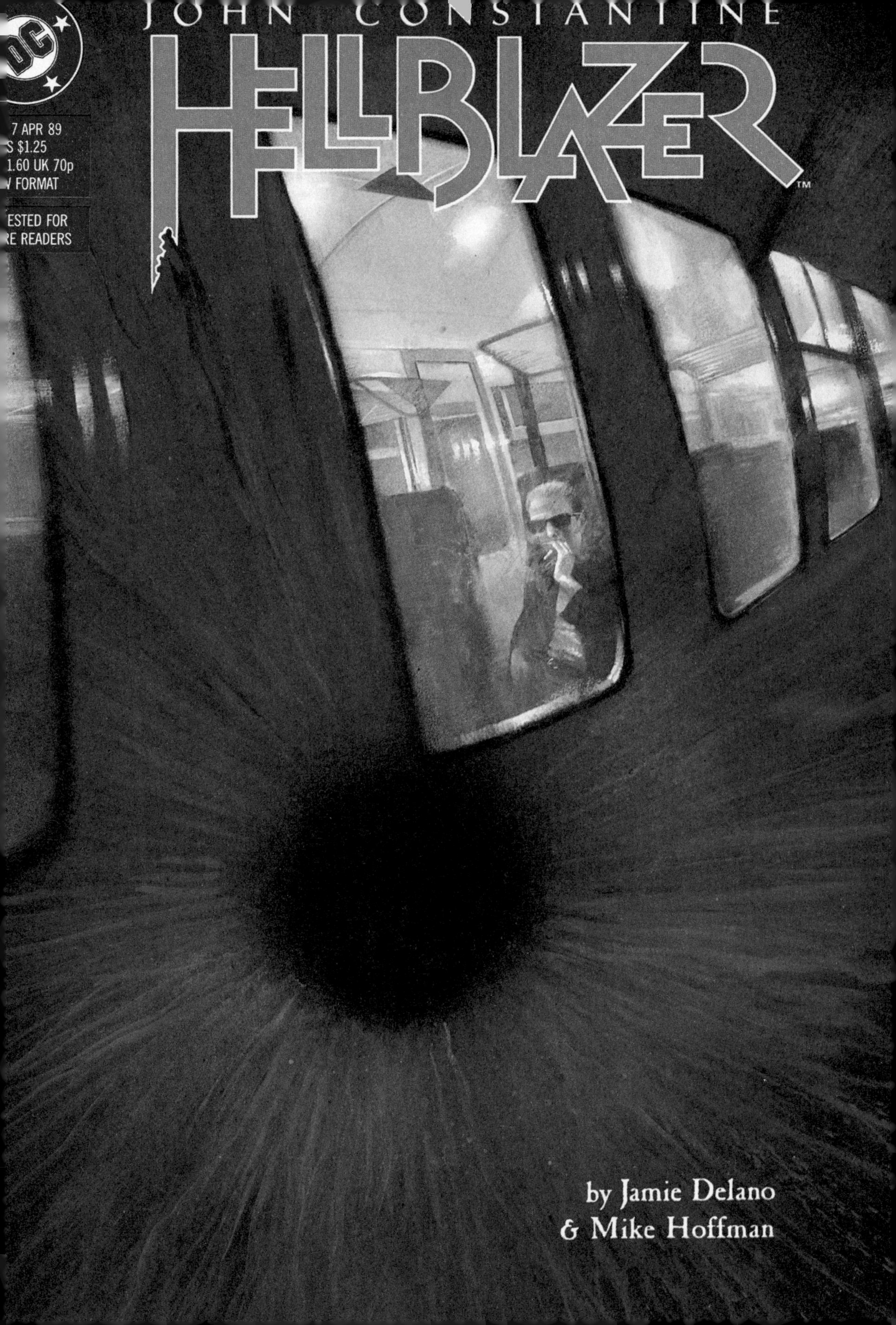
JOHN CONSTANTINE
HELLBLAZER
7 APR 89
S $1.25
1.60 UK 70p
V FORMAT
ESTED FOR
E READERS
by Jamie Delano
& Mike Hoffman

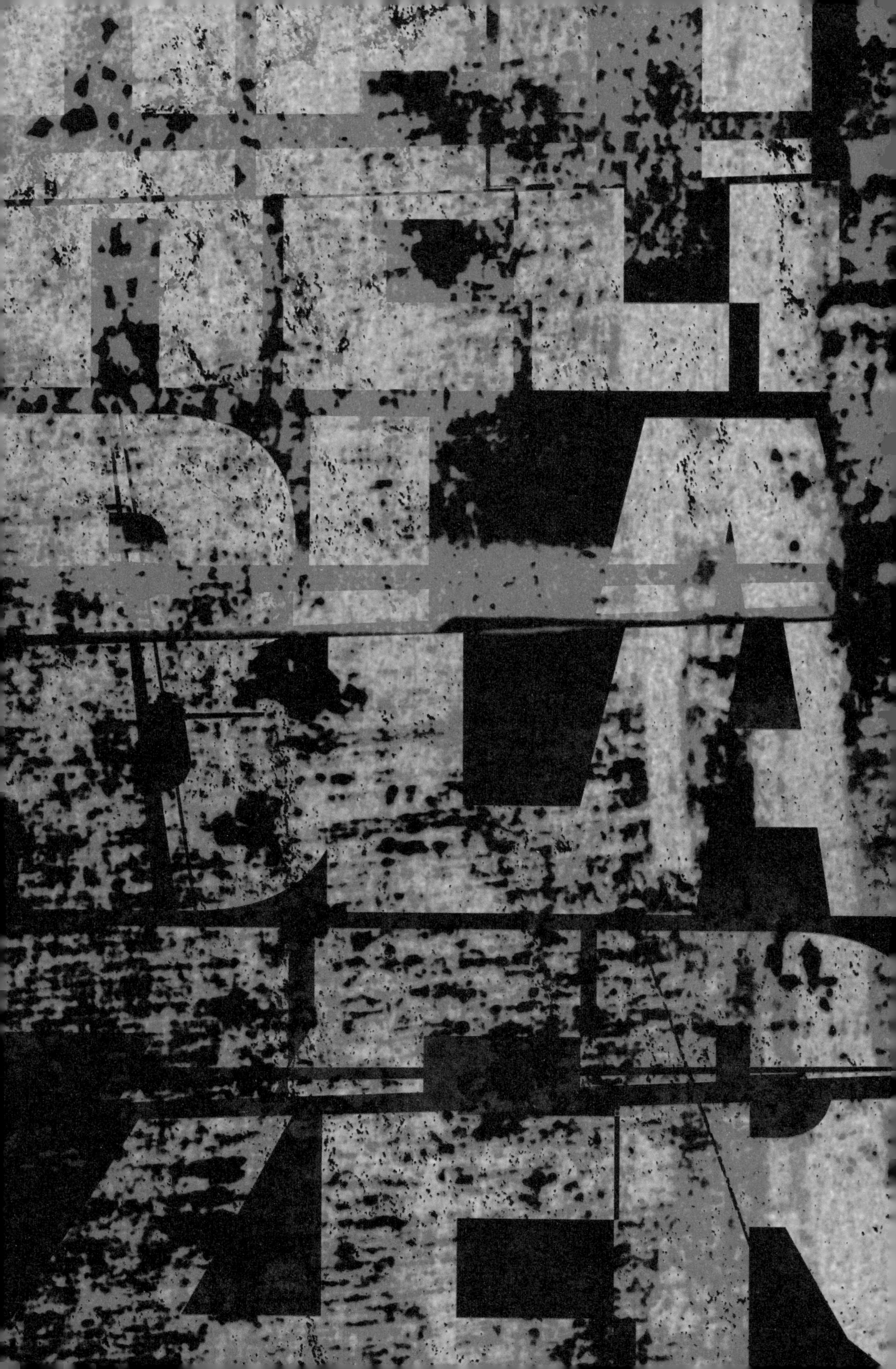

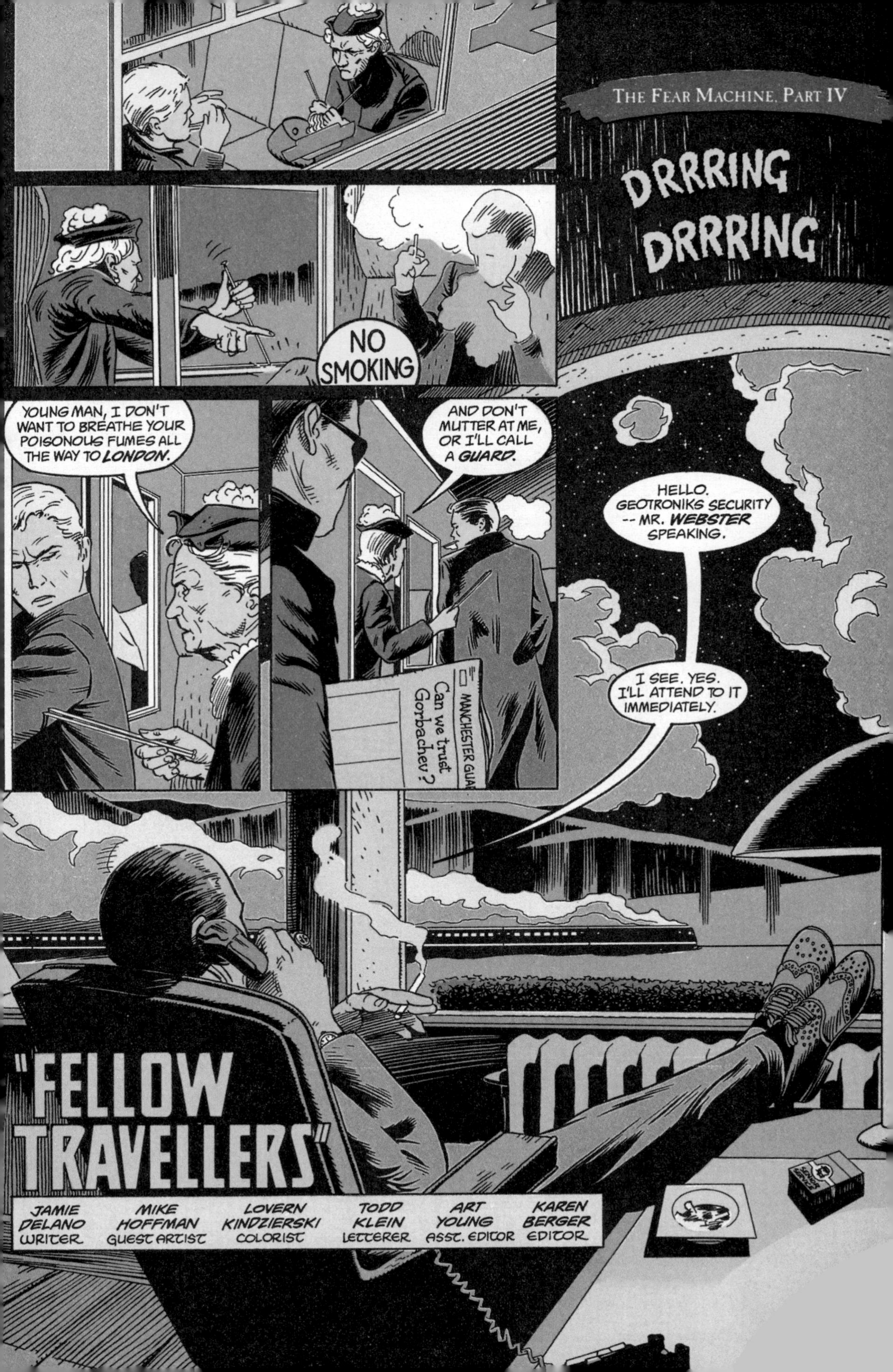
THE FEAR MACHINE, PART IV
DRRRING
DRRRING
NO SMOKING
YOUNG MAN, I DON'T WANT TO BREATHE YOUR POISONOUS FUMES ALL THE WAY TO LONDON.
AND DON'T MUTTER AT ME, OR I'LL CALL A GUARD.
MANCHESTER GUAR
Can we trust Gorbachev?
HELLO. GEOTRONIKS SECURITY -- MR. WEBSTER SPEAKING.
I SEE. YES. I'LL ATTEND TO IT IMMEDIATELY.
"FELLOW TRAVELLERS"
JAMIE DELANO WRITER
MIKE HOFFMAN GUEST ARTIST
LOVERN KINDZIERSKI COLORIST
TODD KLEIN LETTERER
ART YOUNG ASST. EDITOR
KAREN BERGER EDITOR

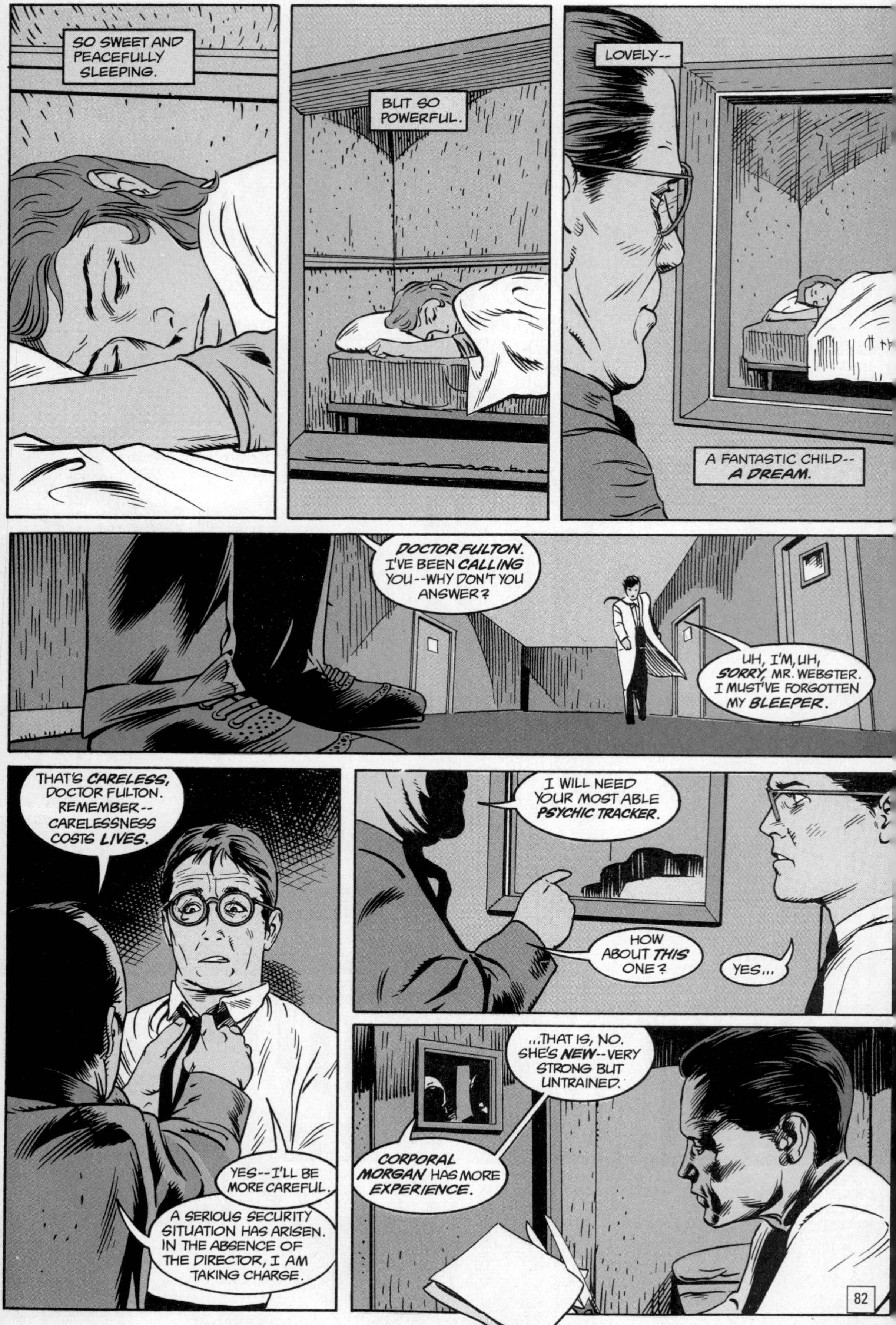
SO SWEET AND PEACEFULLY SLEEPING.
BUT SO POWERFUL.
LOVELY--
A FANTASTIC CHILD-- A DREAM.
DOCTOR FULTON. I'VE BEEN CALLING YOU--WHY DON'T YOU ANSWER?
UH, I'M, UH, SORRY, MR. WEBSTER. I MUST'VE FORGOTTEN MY BLEEPER.
THAT'S CARELESS, DOCTOR FULTON. REMEMBER-- CARELESSNESS COSTS LIVES.
YES--I'LL BE MORE CAREFUL.
A SERIOUS SECURITY SITUATION HAS ARISEN. IN THE ABSENCE OF THE DIRECTOR, I AM TAKING CHARGE.
I WILL NEED YOUR MOST ABLE PSYCHIC TRACKER.
HOW ABOUT THIS ONE?
YES...
...THAT IS, NO. SHE'S NEW--VERY STRONG BUT UNTRAINED.
CORPORAL MORGAN HAS MORE EXPERIENCE.

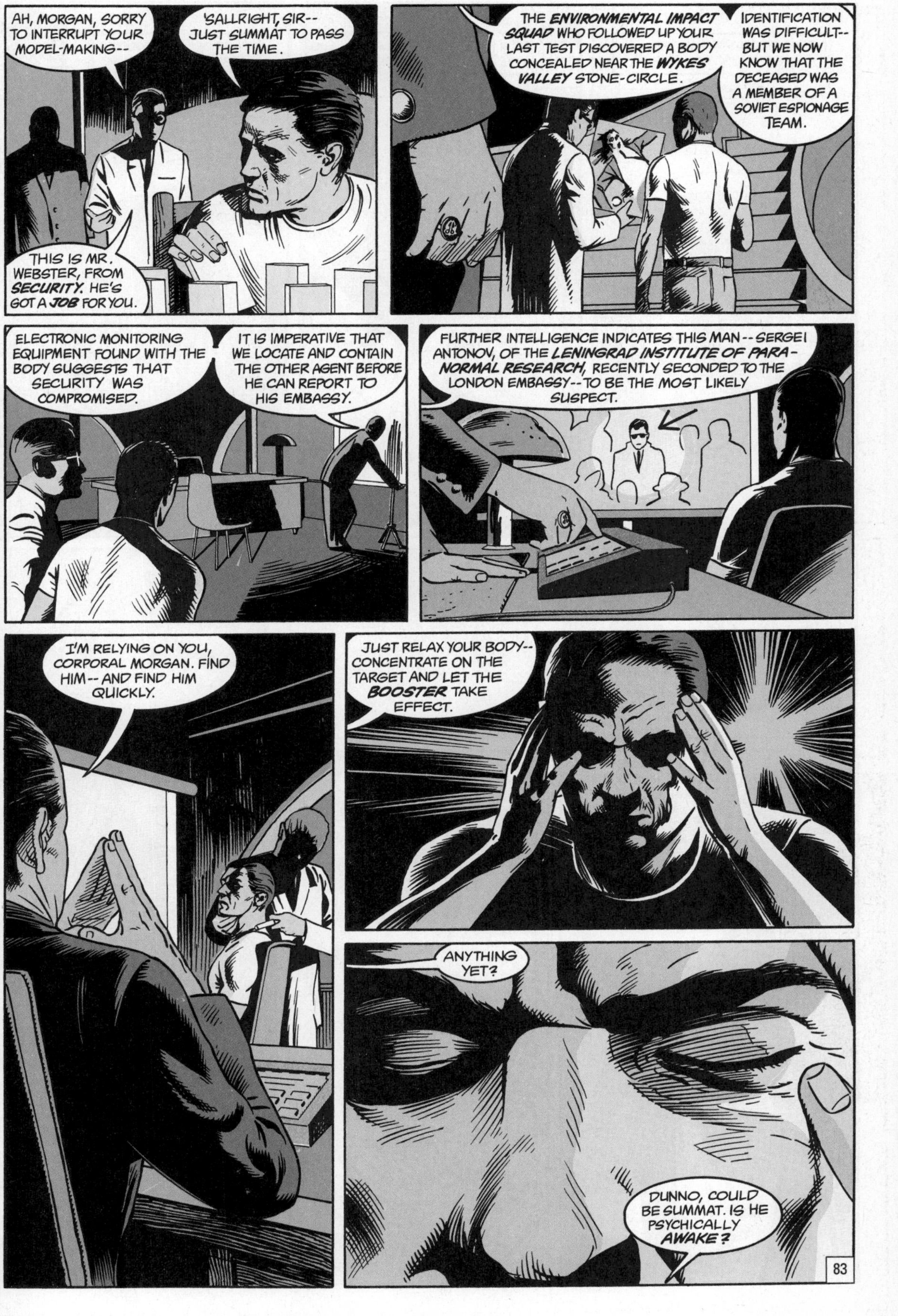
AH, MORGAN, SORRY TO INTERRUPT YOUR MODEL-MAKING--
'SALLRIGHT, SIR-- JUST SUMMAT TO PASS THE TIME.
THIS IS MR. WEBSTER, FROM SECURITY. HE'S GOT A JOB FOR YOU.
THE ENVIRONMENTAL IMPACT SQUAD WHO FOLLOWED UP YOUR LAST TEST DISCOVERED A BODY CONCEALED NEAR THE WYKES VALLEY STONE-CIRCLE.
IDENTIFICATION WAS DIFFICULT-- BUT WE NOW KNOW THAT THE DECEASED WAS A MEMBER OF A SOVIET ESPIONAGE TEAM.
ELECTRONIC MONITORING EQUIPMENT FOUND WITH THE BODY SUGGESTS THAT SECURITY WAS COMPROMISED.
IT IS IMPERATIVE THAT WE LOCATE AND CONTAIN THE OTHER AGENT BEFORE HE CAN REPORT TO HIS EMBASSY.
FURTHER INTELLIGENCE INDICATES THIS MAN--SERGEI ANTONOV, OF THE LENINGRAD INSTITUTE OF PARA-NORMAL RESEARCH, RECENTLY SECONDED TO THE LONDON EMBASSY--TO BE THE MOST LIKELY SUSPECT.
I'M RELYING ON YOU, CORPORAL MORGAN. FIND HIM--AND FIND HIM QUICKLY.
JUST RELAX YOUR BODY-- CONCENTRATE ON THE TARGET AND LET THE BOOSTER TAKE EFFECT.
ANYTHING YET?
DUNNO, COULD BE SUMMAT. IS HE PSYCHICALLY AWAKE?

"YES, PROBABLY. WHERE IS HE? THINK MAN, *THINK*."

"IT'S HARD TO SEE, 'SALL MIXED UP--HE'S *MOVING*."

"HARDER, TRY *HARDER*. *HOW* IS HE MOVING? IS HE WALKING, RUNNING, *FLYING...*?"

BUFFET

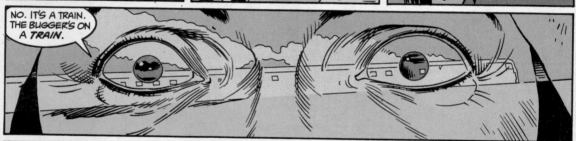

NO. IT'S A TRAIN. THE BUGGER'S ON A *TRAIN*.

NOT *ENOUGH*. I MUST KNOW *WHAT* TRAIN. WHERE'S IT *GOING*?

UH... UH... UH...

IT'S...IT'S...THE *TEN-FORTY-FOUR* -- FROM BRISTOL TO LONDON PADDINGTON.

GOOD, REST NOW--BUT KEEP IN TOUCH WITH HIM.

TIMETABLE SOUTH-WEST REGION

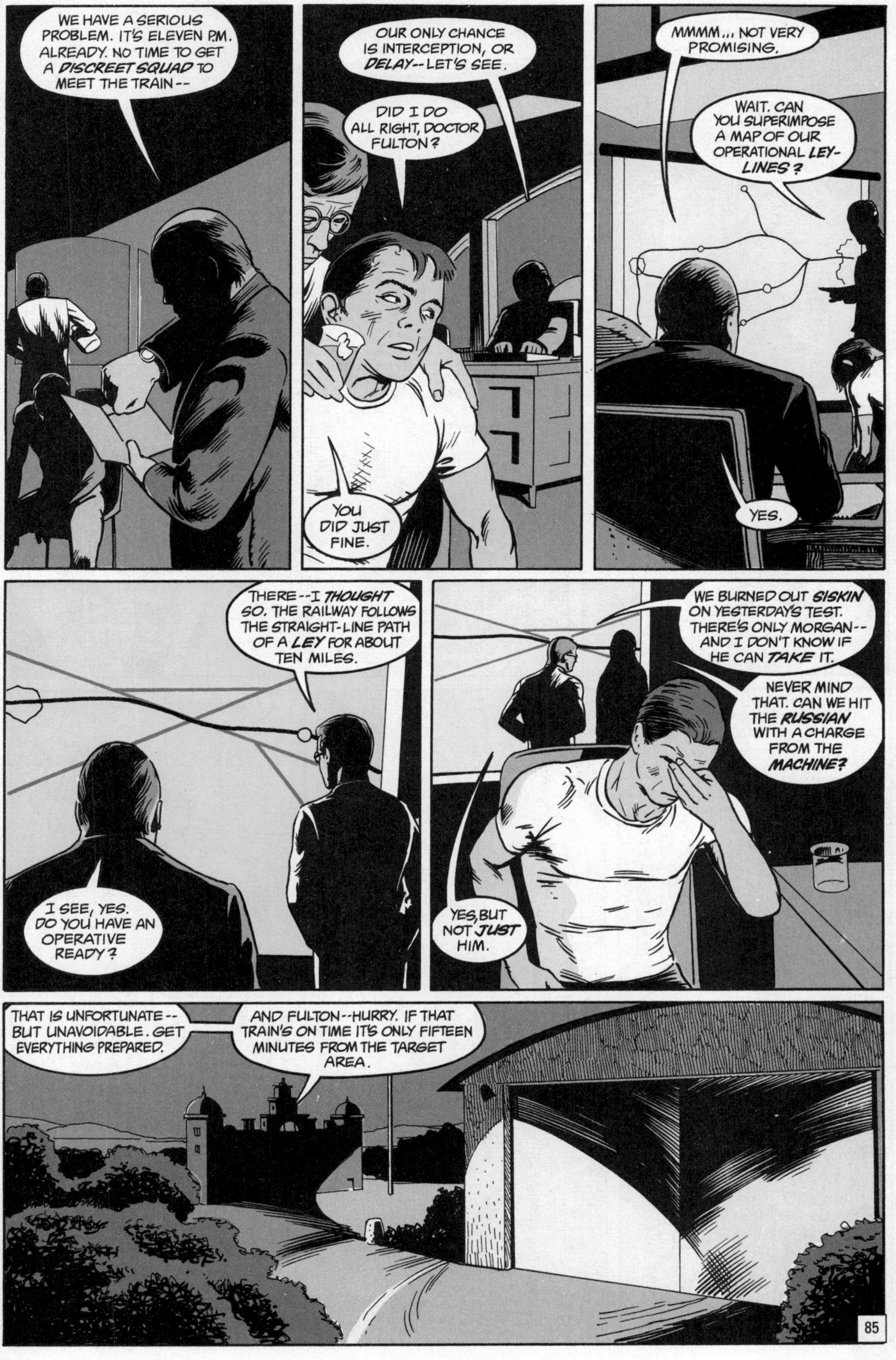
WE HAVE A SERIOUS PROBLEM. IT'S ELEVEN P.M. ALREADY. NO TIME TO GET A DISCREET SQUAD TO MEET THE TRAIN --
OUR ONLY CHANCE IS INTERCEPTION, OR DELAY-- LET'S SEE.
DID I DO ALL RIGHT, DOCTOR FULTON?
YOU DID JUST FINE.
MMMM... NOT VERY PROMISING.
WAIT. CAN YOU SUPERIMPOSE A MAP OF OUR OPERATIONAL LEY-LINES?
YES.
THERE--I THOUGHT SO. THE RAILWAY FOLLOWS THE STRAIGHT-LINE PATH OF A LEY FOR ABOUT TEN MILES.
I SEE, YES. DO YOU HAVE AN OPERATIVE READY?
WE BURNED OUT SISKIN ON YESTERDAY'S TEST. THERE'S ONLY MORGAN-- AND I DON'T KNOW IF HE CAN TAKE IT.
NEVER MIND THAT. CAN WE HIT THE RUSSIAN WITH A CHARGE FROM THE MACHINE?
YES, BUT NOT JUST HIM.
THAT IS UNFORTUNATE -- BUT UNAVOIDABLE. GET EVERYTHING PREPARED.
AND FULTON--HURRY. IF THAT TRAIN'S ON TIME IT'S ONLY FIFTEEN MINUTES FROM THE TARGET AREA.

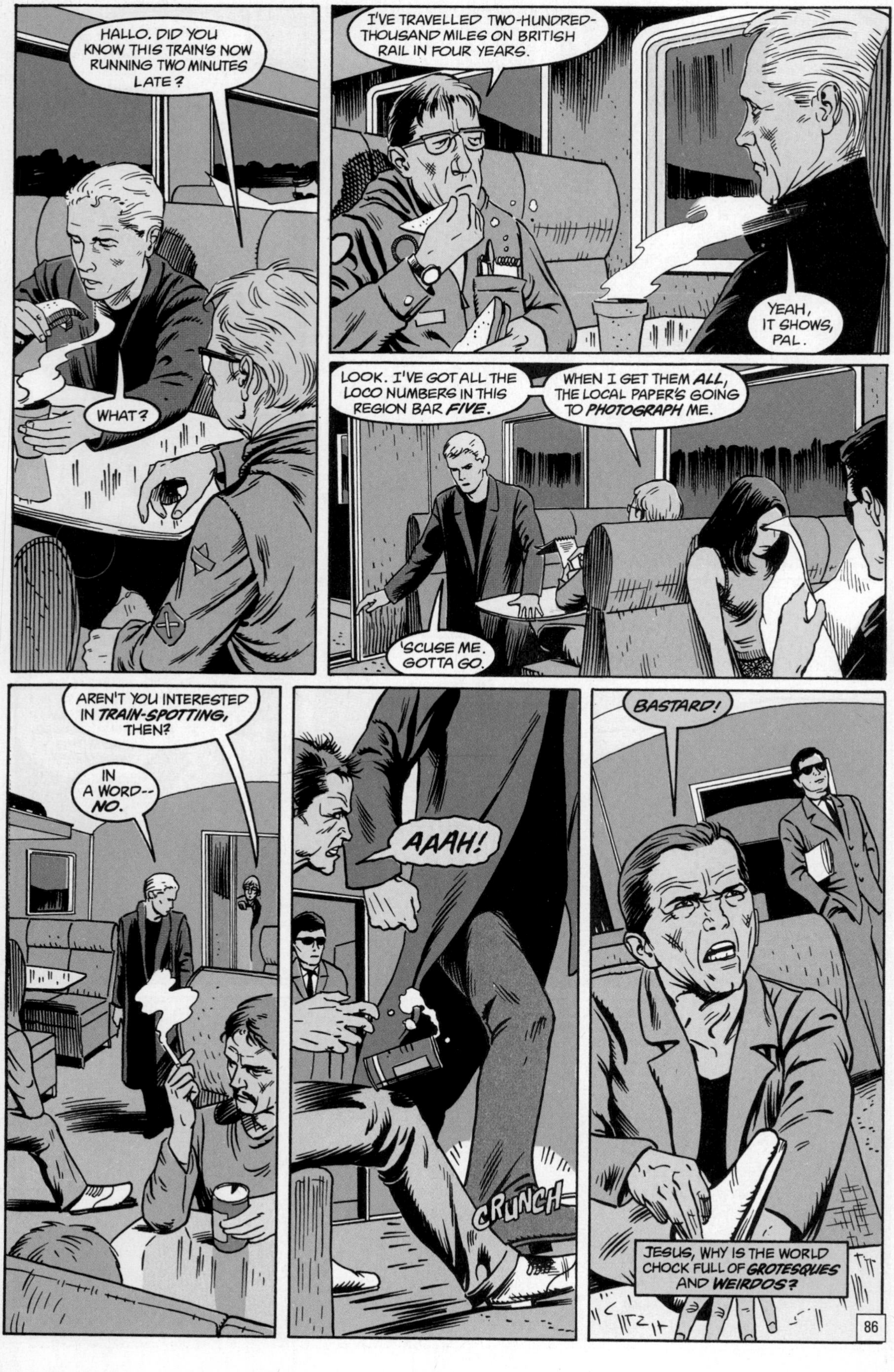
HALLO. DID YOU KNOW THIS TRAIN'S NOW RUNNING TWO MINUTES LATE?
WHAT?
I'VE TRAVELLED TWO-HUNDRED-THOUSAND MILES ON BRITISH RAIL IN FOUR YEARS.
YEAH, IT SHOWS, PAL.
LOOK. I'VE GOT ALL THE LOCO NUMBERS IN THIS REGION BAR FIVE.
WHEN I GET THEM ALL, THE LOCAL PAPER'S GOING TO PHOTOGRAPH ME.
'SCUSE ME. GOTTA GO.
AREN'T YOU INTERESTED IN TRAIN-SPOTTING, THEN?
IN A WORD-- NO.
AAAH!
CRUNCH
BASTARD!
JESUS, WHY IS THE WORLD CHOCK FULL OF GROTESQUES AND WEIRDOS?

SO, DOCTOR FULTON, YOUR *FEAR MACHINE* ACTUALLY WORKS.

IT'S NOT *PERFECT*, MISTER WEBSTER--BUT OUR *IMPROVEMENTS* ON THE *MEGALITHIC* LEY SYSTEM GIVE US A LOT MORE *CONTROL*.

"WE STILL NEED THE PSYCHICS TO ACT AS *ACCUMULATORS*--TO *INTENSIFY* AND *FOCUS* THE EMOTIONAL CHARGE BEFORE WE RELEASE IT INTO THE *GEO-TECHNICAL WEB*."

"BUT YOU CAN *SCARE* PEOPLE TO *DEATH*?"

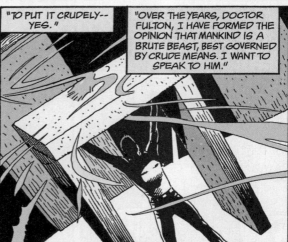

"TO PUT IT CRUDELY-- YES."

"OVER THE YEARS, DOCTOR FULTON, I HAVE FORMED THE OPINION THAT MANKIND IS A BRUTE BEAST, BEST GOVERNED BY CRUDE MEANS. I WANT TO SPEAK TO HIM."

CORPORAL MORGAN. I WILL NEED IMMEDIATE CONFIRMATION OF SUCCESS. WHEN THE CHARGE IS DELIVERED TO THE TARGET, *YOU* WILL REMAIN *WITH* IT AND REPORT THE *RESULTS*.

BUT...

IS THAT *UNDERSTOOD*, CORPORAL?

'SSIR.

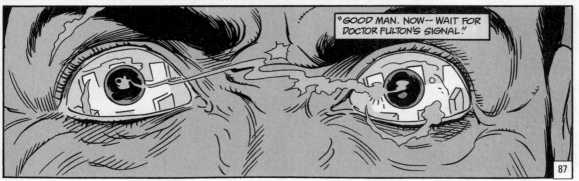

"GOOD MAN. NOW-- WAIT FOR DOCTOR FULTON'S SIGNAL!"

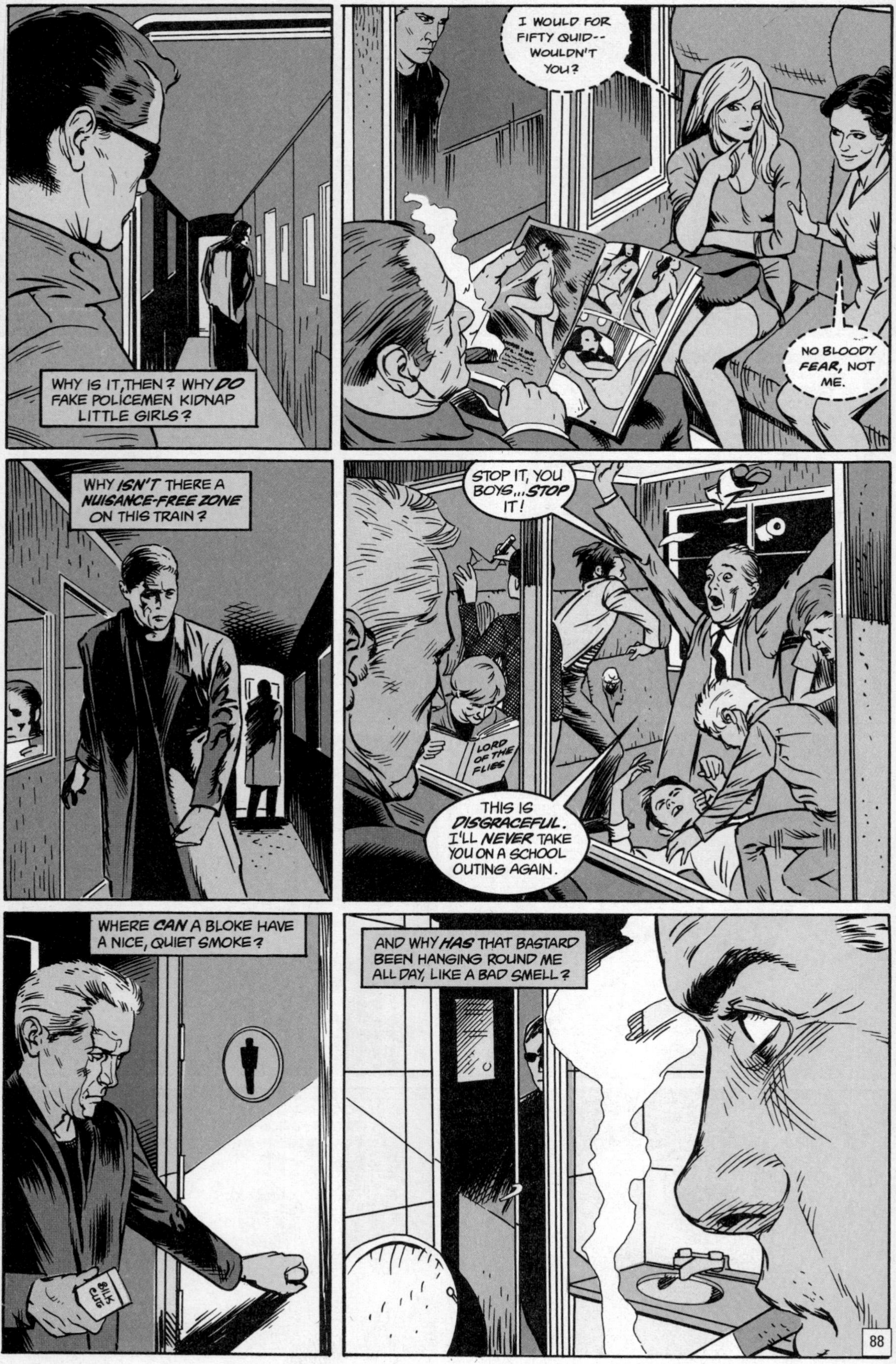
WHY IS IT, THEN? WHY DO FAKE POLICEMEN KIDNAP LITTLE GIRLS?
I WOULD FOR FIFTY QUID-- WOULDN'T YOU?
NO BLOODY FEAR, NOT ME.
WHY ISN'T THERE A NUISANCE-FREE ZONE ON THIS TRAIN?
STOP IT, YOU BOYS... STOP IT!
LORD OF THE FLIES
THIS IS DISGRACEFUL. I'LL NEVER TAKE YOU ON A SCHOOL OUTING AGAIN.
WHERE CAN A BLOKE HAVE A NICE, QUIET SMOKE?
AND WHY HAS THAT BASTARD BEEN HANGING ROUND ME ALL DAY, LIKE A BAD SMELL?

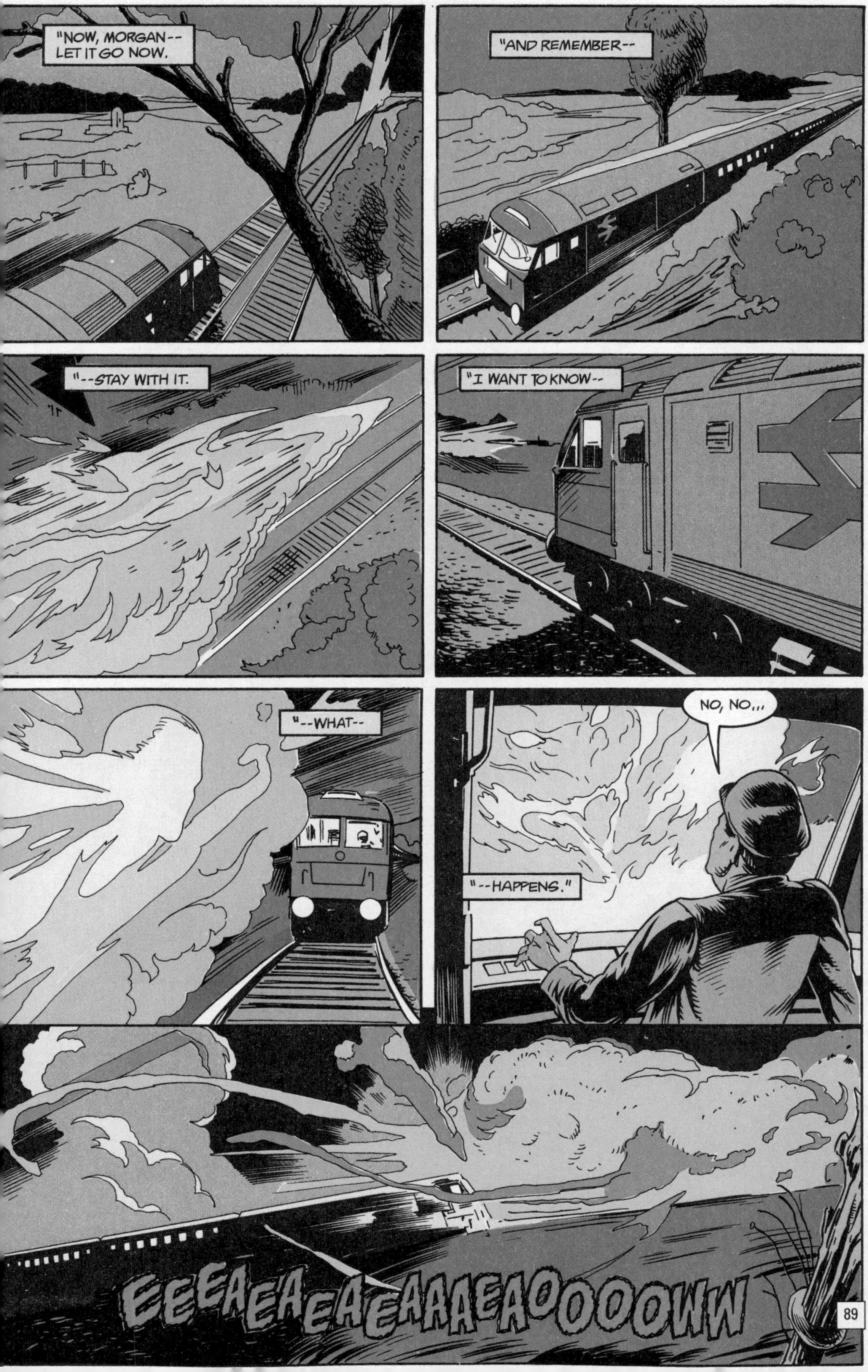
"NOW, MORGAN--
LET IT GO NOW.
"AND REMEMBER--
"--STAY WITH IT.
"I WANT TO KNOW--
"--WHAT--
NO, NO,,,
"--HAPPENS."
EEEAEAEAEAAAAEAOOOOWW

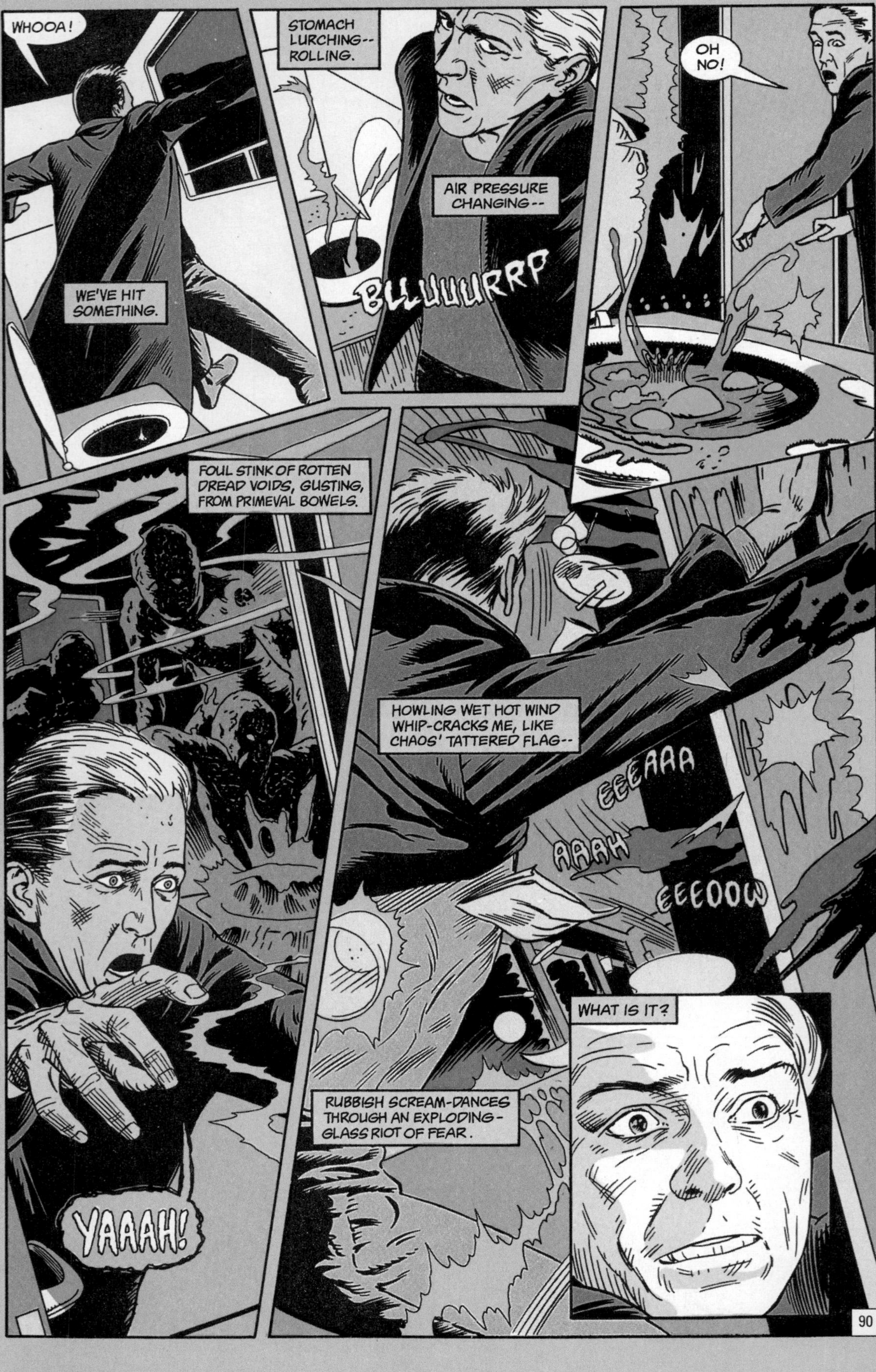
WHOOA!
WE'VE HIT SOMETHING.
STOMACH LURCHING-- ROLLING.
AIR PRESSURE CHANGING--
BLLUUUURRP
OH NO!
FOUL STINK OF ROTTEN DREAD VOIDS, GUSTING, FROM PRIMEVAL BOWELS.
YAAAH!
HOWLING WET HOT WIND WHIP-CRACKS ME, LIKE CHAOS' TATTERED FLAG--
EEEAAA
AAAH
EEEOOW
RUBBISH SCREAM-DANCES THROUGH AN EXPLODING-GLASS RIOT OF FEAR.
WHAT IS IT?

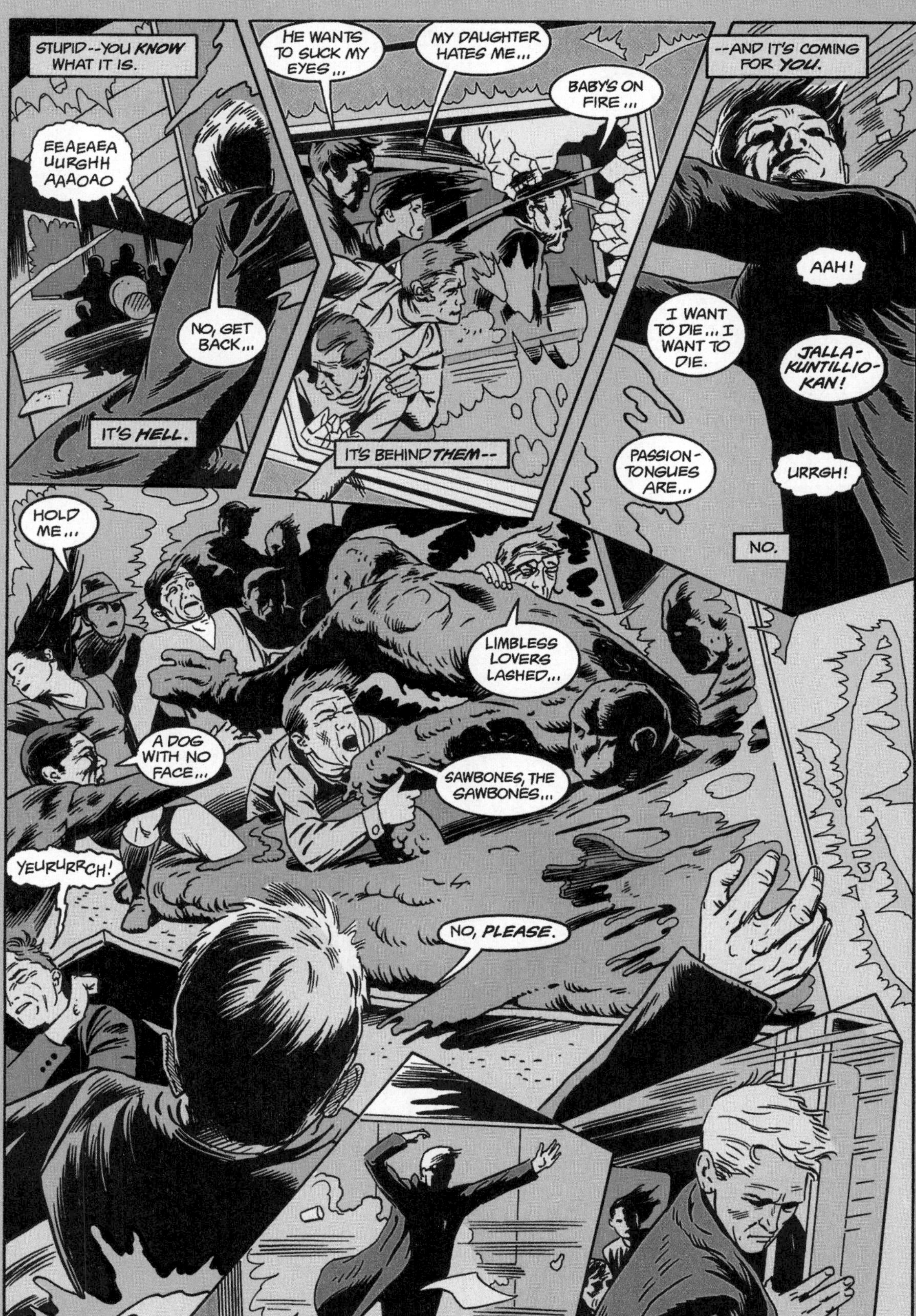

STUPID--YOU KNOW WHAT IT IS.
EEAEAEA UURGHH AAAOAO
NO, GET BACK...
IT'S HELL.
HE WANTS TO SUCK MY EYES...
MY DAUGHTER HATES ME...
BABY'S ON FIRE...
IT'S BEHIND THEM--
--AND IT'S COMING FOR YOU.
I WANT TO DIE... I WANT TO DIE.
AAH!
JALLA-KUNTILLIO-KAN!
PASSION-TONGUES ARE...
URRGH!
NO.
HOLD ME...
LIMBLESS LOVERS LASHED...
A DOG WITH NO FACE...
SAWBONES, THE SAWBONES...
YEURURRCH!
NO, PLEASE.
NOT YET--
I CAN'T GO YET--

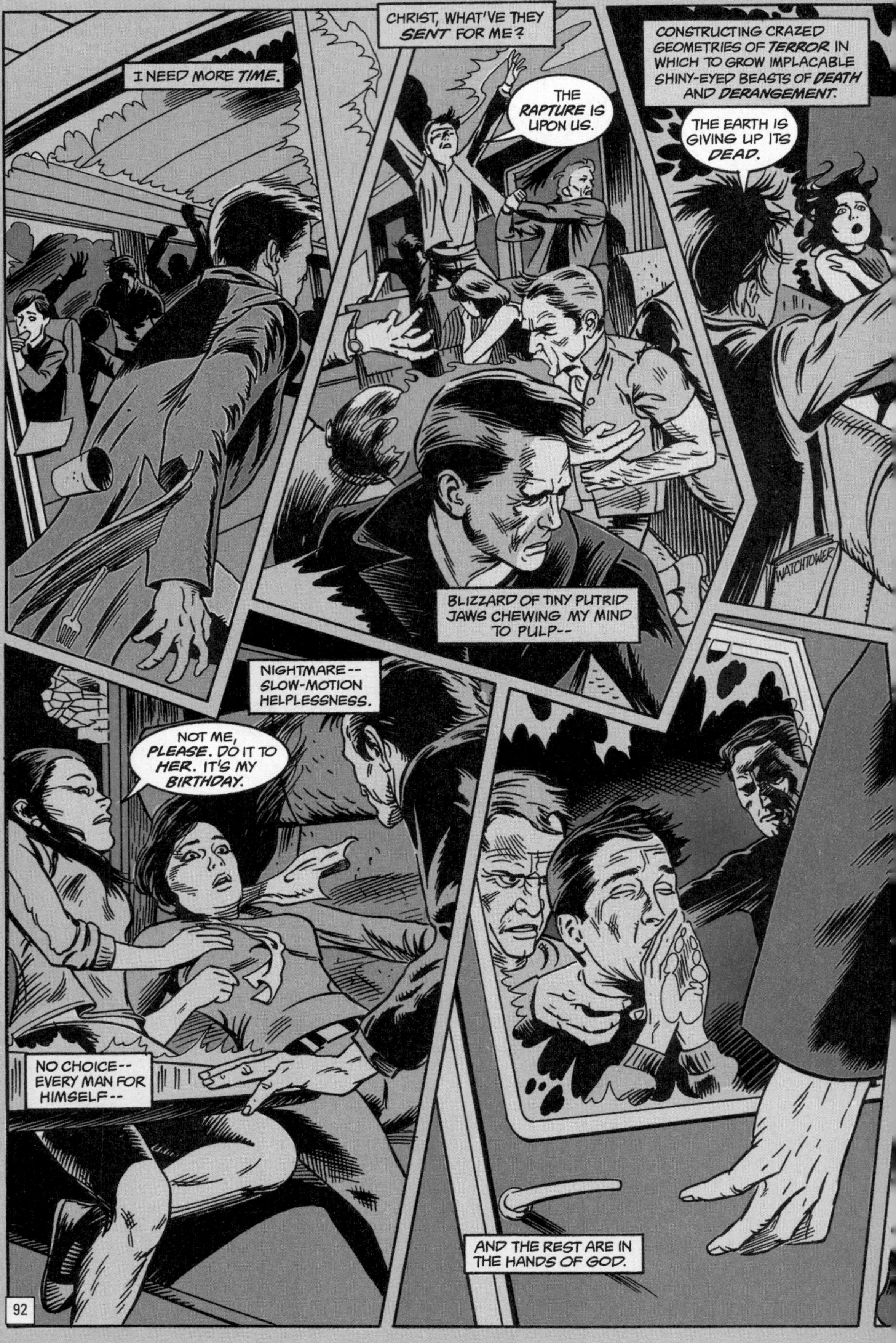
I NEED MORE *TIME*.
CHRIST, WHAT'VE THEY *SENT* FOR ME?
THE *RAPTURE* IS UPON US.
CONSTRUCTING CRAZED GEOMETRIES OF *TERROR* IN WHICH TO GROW IMPLACABLE SHINY-EYED BEASTS OF *DEATH* AND *DERANGEMENT*.
THE EARTH IS GIVING UP ITS *DEAD*.
WATCHTOWER
BLIZZARD OF TINY PUTRID JAWS CHEWING MY MIND TO PULP--
NIGHTMARE-- SLOW-MOTION HELPLESSNESS.
NOT ME, *PLEASE*. DO IT TO *HER*. IT'S MY *BIRTHDAY*.
NO CHOICE-- EVERY MAN FOR HIMSELF--
AND THE REST ARE IN THE HANDS OF GOD.

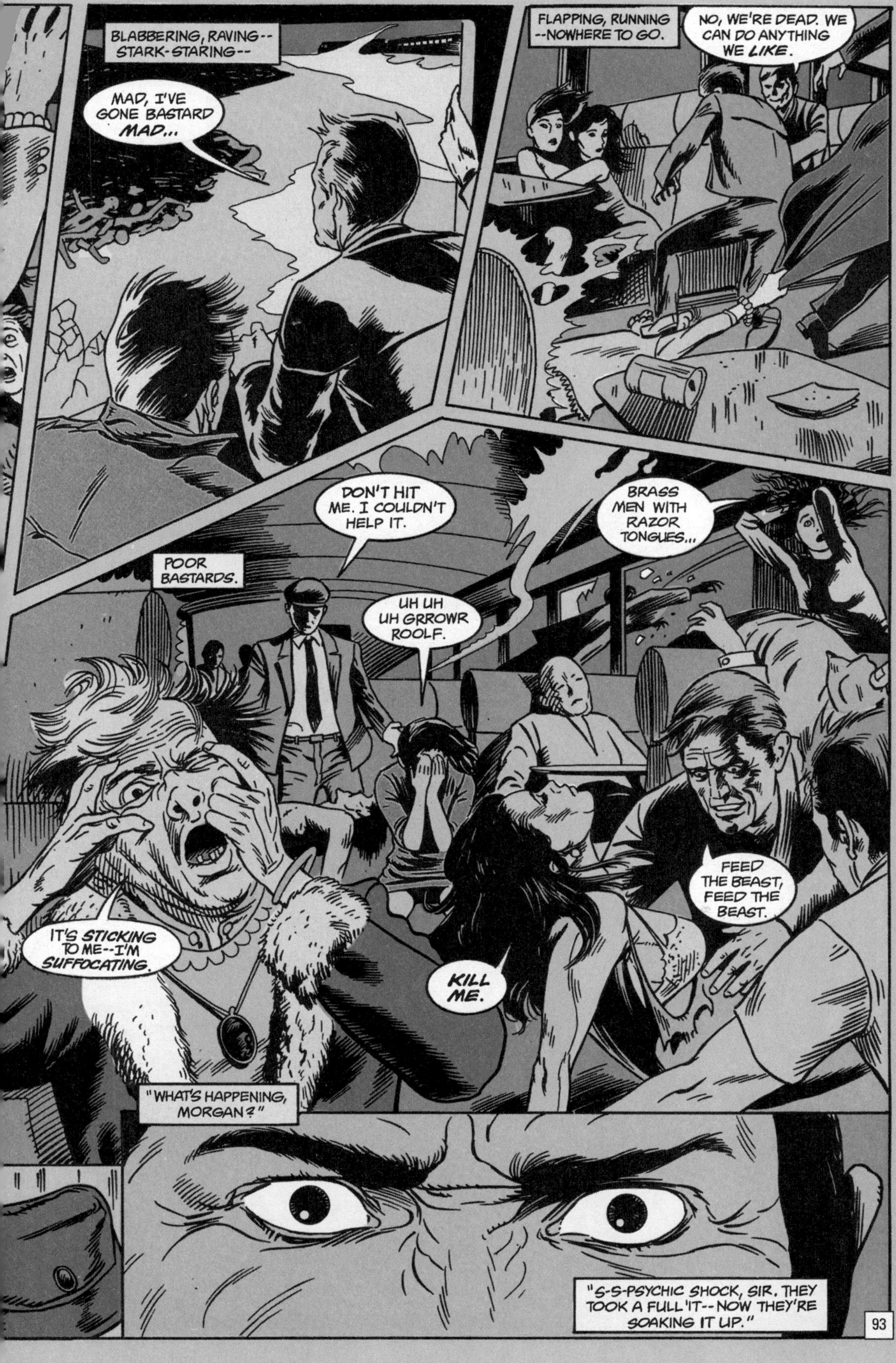
BLABBERING, RAVING-- STARK-STARING--
MAD, I'VE GONE BASTARD MAD...
FLAPPING, RUNNING --NOWHERE TO GO.
NO, WE'RE DEAD. WE CAN DO ANYTHING WE LIKE.
DON'T HIT ME. I COULDN'T HELP IT.
BRASS MEN WITH RAZOR TONGUES...
POOR BASTARDS.
UH UH UH GRROWR ROOLF.
FEED THE BEAST, FEED THE BEAST.
IT'S STICKING TO ME--I'M SUFFOCATING.
KILL ME.
"WHAT'S HAPPENING, MORGAN?"
"S-S-PSYCHIC SHOCK, SIR. THEY TOOK A FULL 'IT'--NOW THEY'RE SOAKING IT UP."

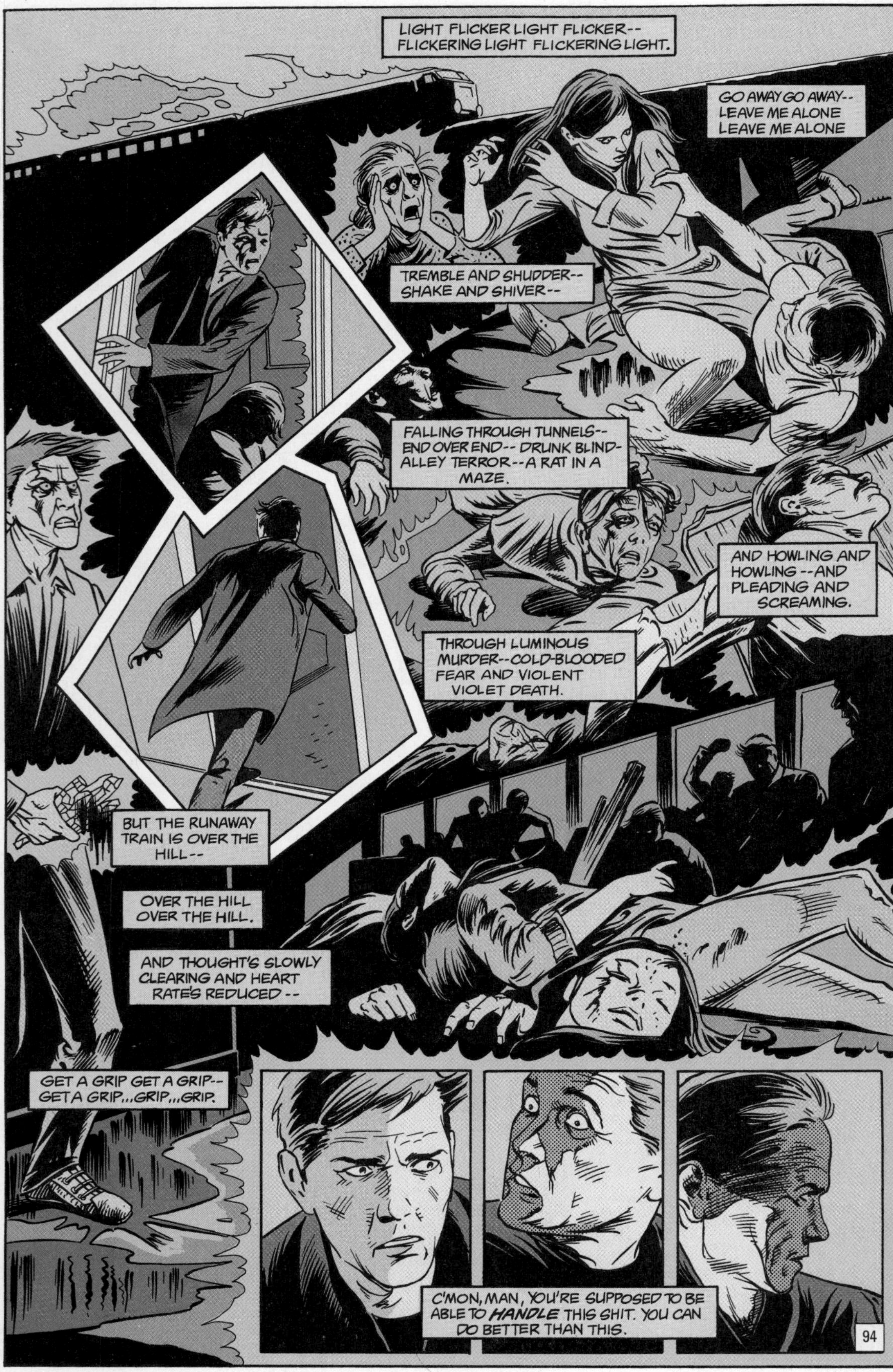
LIGHT FLICKER LIGHT FLICKER-- FLICKERING LIGHT FLICKERING LIGHT.
GO AWAY GO AWAY-- LEAVE ME ALONE LEAVE ME ALONE
TREMBLE AND SHUDDER-- SHAKE AND SHIVER--
FALLING THROUGH TUNNELS-- END OVER END-- DRUNK BLIND-ALLEY TERROR--A RAT IN A MAZE.
AND HOWLING AND HOWLING --AND PLEADING AND SCREAMING.
THROUGH LUMINOUS MURDER--COLD-BLOODED FEAR AND VIOLENT VIOLET DEATH.
BUT THE RUNAWAY TRAIN IS OVER THE HILL--
OVER THE HILL OVER THE HILL.
AND THOUGHT'S SLOWLY CLEARING AND HEART RATE'S REDUCED --
GET A GRIP GET A GRIP-- GET A GRIP,,,GRIP,,,GRIP.
C'MON, MAN, YOU'RE SUPPOSED TO BE ABLE TO HANDLE THIS SHIT. YOU CAN DO BETTER THAN THIS.

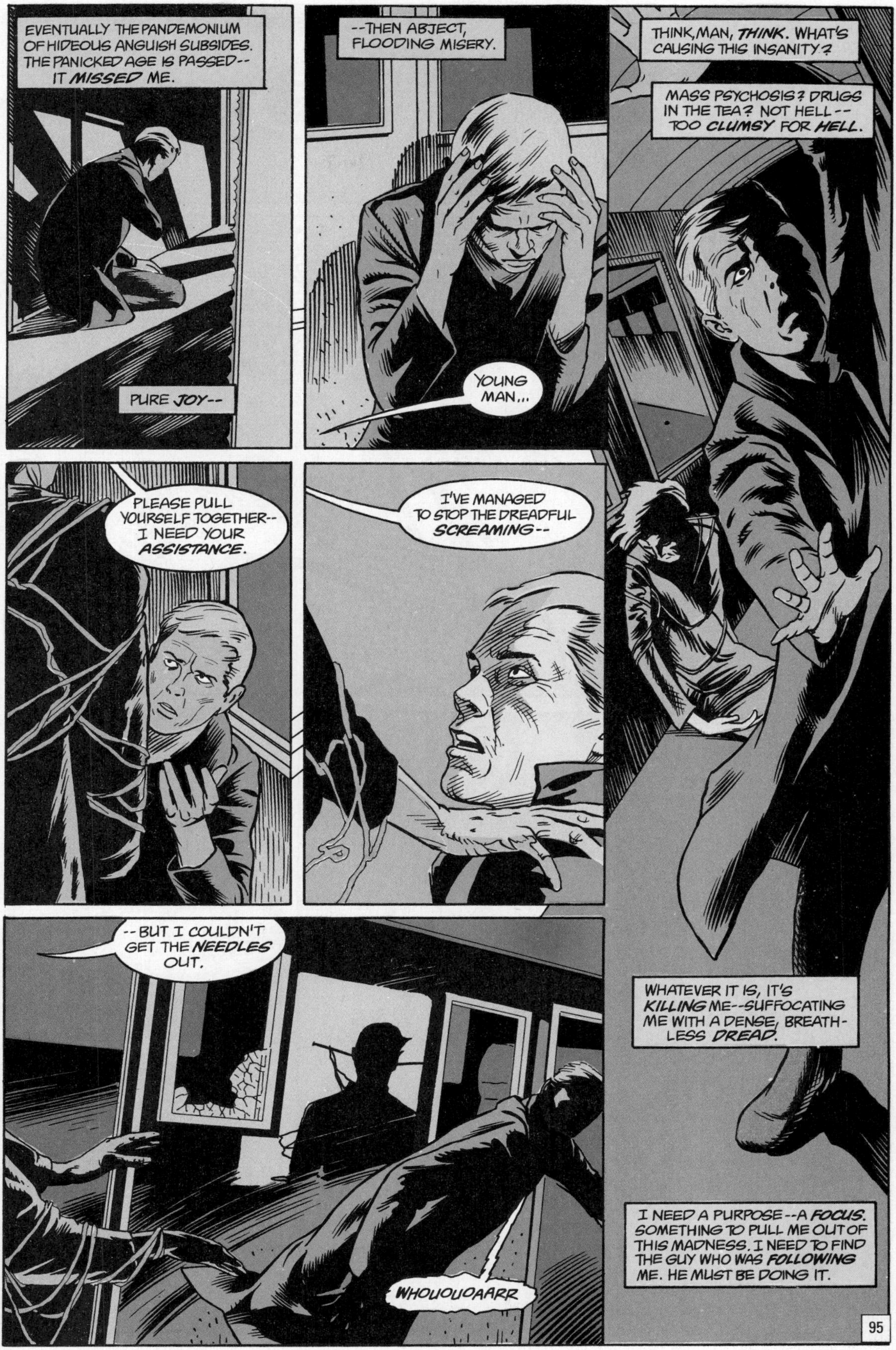
EVENTUALLY THE PANDEMONIUM OF HIDEOUS ANGUISH SUBSIDES. THE PANICKED AGE IS PASSED-- IT MISSED ME.
PURE JOY--
--THEN ABJECT, FLOODING MISERY.
YOUNG MAN...
THINK, MAN, THINK. WHAT'S CAUSING THIS INSANITY?
MASS PSYCHOSIS? DRUGS IN THE TEA? NOT HELL -- TOO CLUMSY FOR HELL.
PLEASE PULL YOURSELF TOGETHER-- I NEED YOUR ASSISTANCE.
I'VE MANAGED TO STOP THE DREADFUL SCREAMING--
--BUT I COULDN'T GET THE NEEDLES OUT.
WHOUOUOAARR
WHATEVER IT IS, IT'S KILLING ME--SUFFOCATING ME WITH A DENSE, BREATHLESS DREAD.
I NEED A PURPOSE --A FOCUS. SOMETHING TO PULL ME OUT OF THIS MADNESS. I NEED TO FIND THE GUY WHO WAS FOLLOWING ME. HE MUST BE DOING IT.

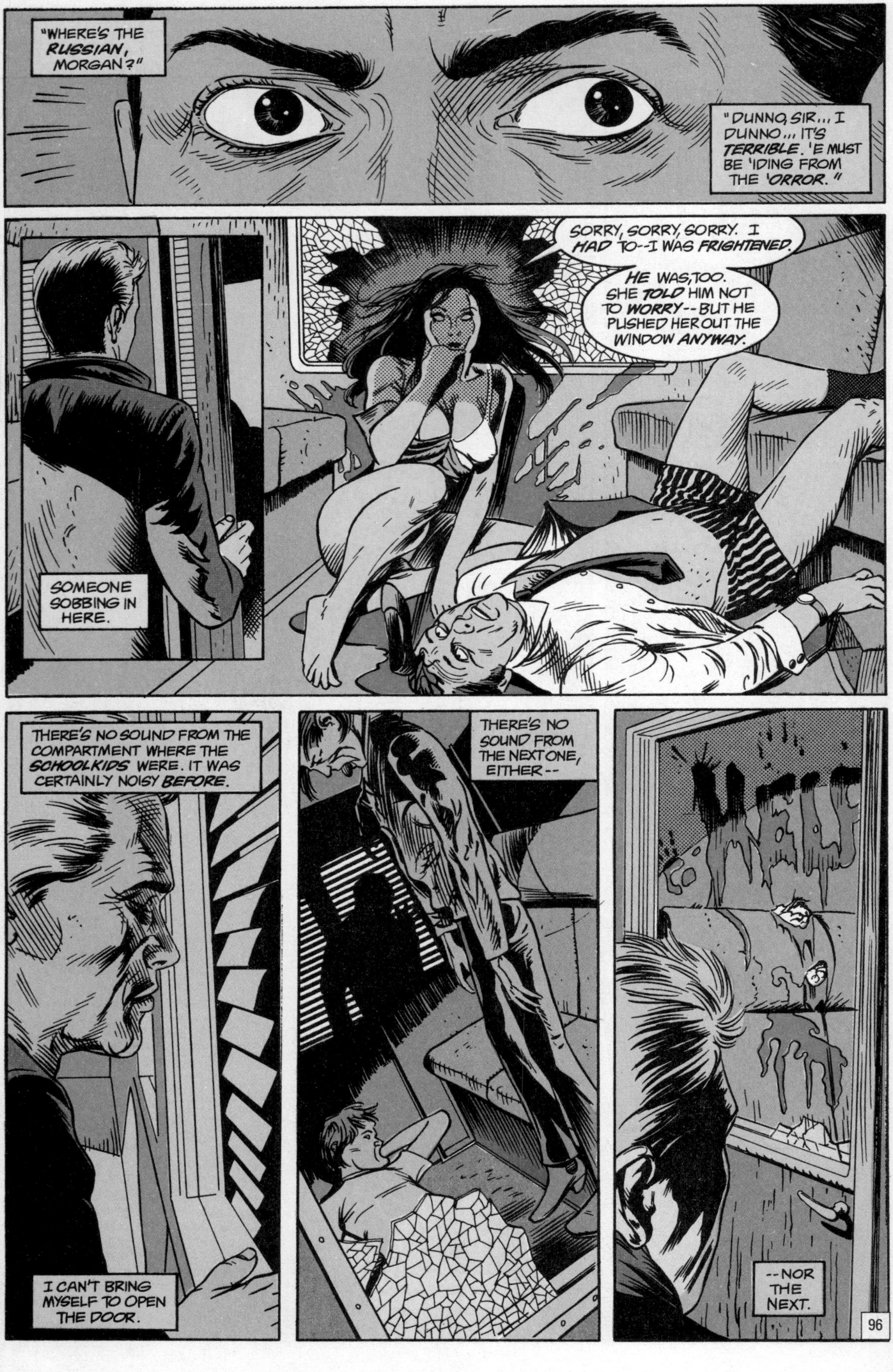
"WHERE'S THE RUSSIAN, MORGAN?"
"DUNNO, SIR... I DUNNO... IT'S TERRIBLE. 'E MUST BE 'IDING FROM THE 'ORROR."
SORRY, SORRY, SORRY. I HAD TO--I WAS FRIGHTENED.
HE WAS, TOO. SHE TOLD HIM NOT TO WORRY--BUT HE PUSHED HER OUT THE WINDOW ANYWAY.
SOMEONE SOBBING IN HERE.
THERE'S NO SOUND FROM THE COMPARTMENT WHERE THE SCHOOLKIDS WERE. IT WAS CERTAINLY NOISY BEFORE.
I CAN'T BRING MYSELF TO OPEN THE DOOR.
THERE'S NO SOUND FROM THE NEXT ONE, EITHER--
--NOR THE NEXT.

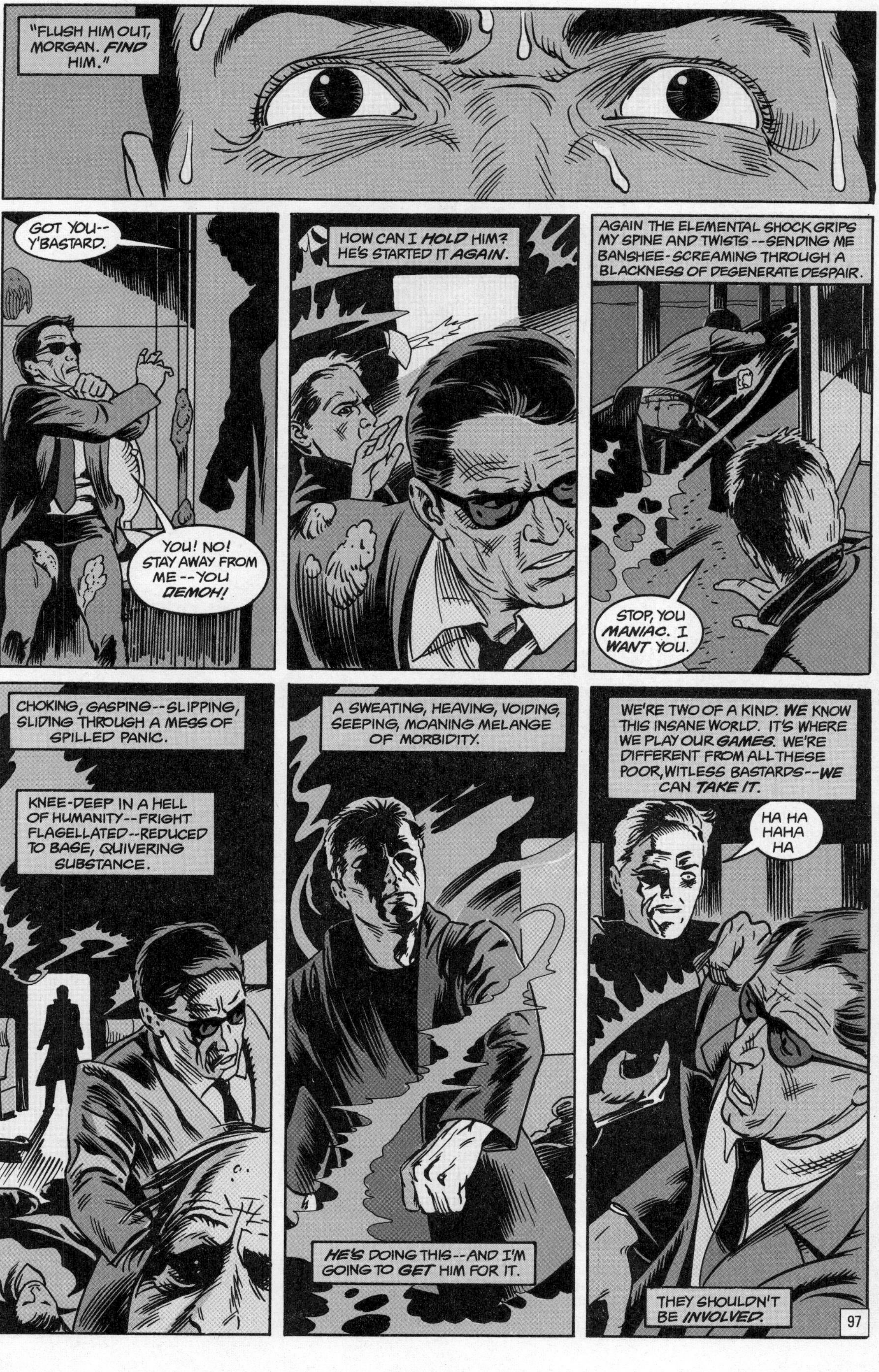
"FLUSH HIM OUT, MORGAN. FIND HIM."
GOT YOU--Y'BASTARD.
YOU! NO! STAY AWAY FROM ME--YOU DEMON!
HOW CAN I HOLD HIM? HE'S STARTED IT AGAIN.
AGAIN THE ELEMENTAL SHOCK GRIPS MY SPINE AND TWISTS--SENDING ME BANSHEE-SCREAMING THROUGH A BLACKNESS OF DEGENERATE DESPAIR.
STOP, YOU MANIAC. I WANT YOU.
CHOKING, GASPING--SLIPPING, SLIDING THROUGH A MESS OF SPILLED PANIC.
KNEE-DEEP IN A HELL OF HUMANITY--FRIGHT FLAGELLATED--REDUCED TO BASE, QUIVERING SUBSTANCE.
A SWEATING, HEAVING, VOIDING, SEEPING, MOANING MELANGE OF MORBIDITY.
HE'S DOING THIS--AND I'M GOING TO GET HIM FOR IT.
WE'RE TWO OF A KIND. WE KNOW THIS INSANE WORLD. IT'S WHERE WE PLAY OUR GAMES. WE'RE DIFFERENT FROM ALL THESE POOR, WITLESS BASTARDS--WE CAN TAKE IT.
HA HA HAHA HA
THEY SHOULDN'T BE INVOLVED.

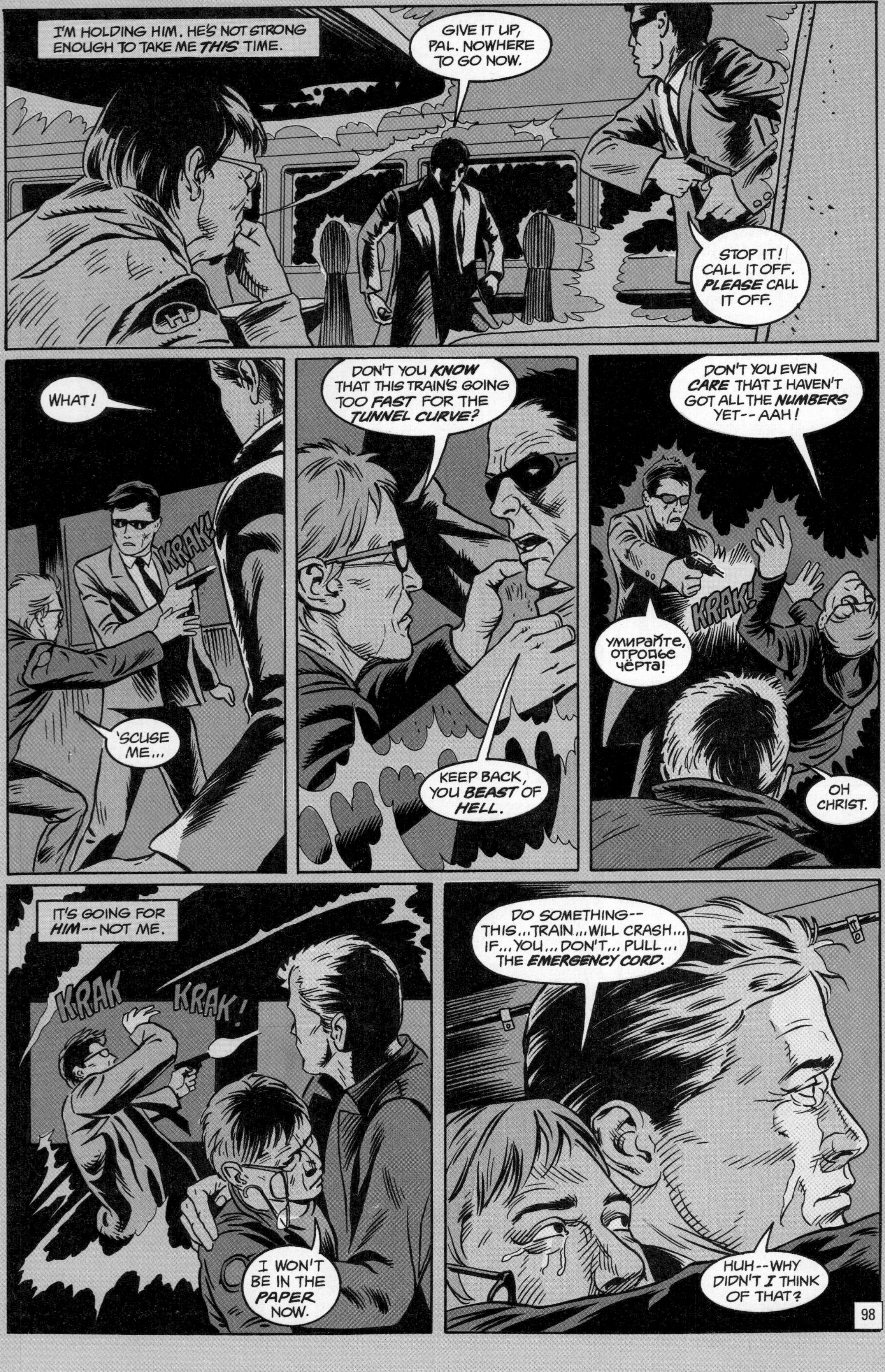
I'M HOLDING HIM. HE'S NOT STRONG ENOUGH TO TAKE ME THIS TIME.
GIVE IT UP, PAL. NOWHERE TO GO NOW.
STOP IT! CALL IT OFF. PLEASE CALL IT OFF.
WHAT!
KRAK!
'SCUSE ME...
DON'T YOU KNOW THAT THIS TRAIN'S GOING TOO FAST FOR THE TUNNEL CURVE?
KEEP BACK, YOU BEAST OF HELL.
DON'T YOU EVEN CARE THAT I HAVEN'T GOT ALL THE NUMBERS YET-- AAH!
умирайте, отродье чёрта!
KRAK!
OH CHRIST.
IT'S GOING FOR HIM-- NOT ME.
KRAK
KRAK!
I WON'T BE IN THE PAPER NOW.
DO SOMETHING-- THIS... TRAIN... WILL CRASH... IF... YOU... DON'T... PULL... THE EMERGENCY CORD.
HUH-- WHY DIDN'T I THINK OF THAT?

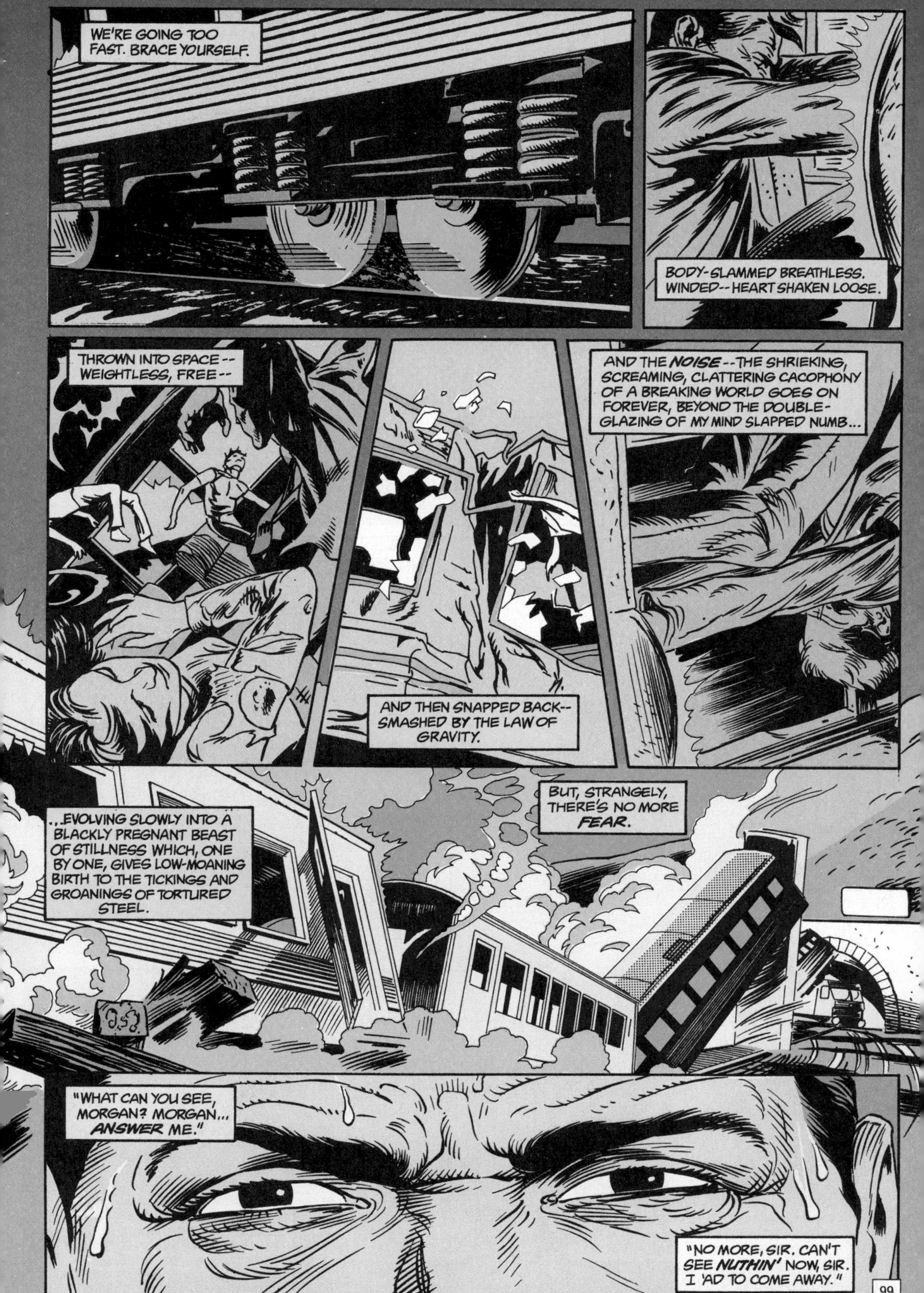
WE'RE GOING TOO FAST. BRACE YOURSELF.
BODY-SLAMMED BREATHLESS. WINDED--HEART SHAKEN LOOSE.
THROWN INTO SPACE--WEIGHTLESS, FREE--
AND THEN SNAPPED BACK--SMASHED BY THE LAW OF GRAVITY.
AND THE NOISE--THE SHRIEKING, SCREAMING, CLATTERING CACOPHONY OF A BREAKING WORLD GOES ON FOREVER, BEYOND THE DOUBLE-GLAZING OF MY MIND SLAPPED NUMB...
...EVOLVING SLOWLY INTO A BLACKLY PREGNANT BEAST OF STILLNESS WHICH, ONE BY ONE, GIVES LOW-MOANING BIRTH TO THE TICKINGS AND GROANINGS OF TORTURED STEEL.
BUT, STRANGELY, THERE'S NO MORE FEAR.
"WHAT CAN YOU SEE, MORGAN? MORGAN... ANSWER ME."
"NO MORE, SIR. CAN'T SEE NUTHIN' NOW, SIR. I 'AD TO COME AWAY."

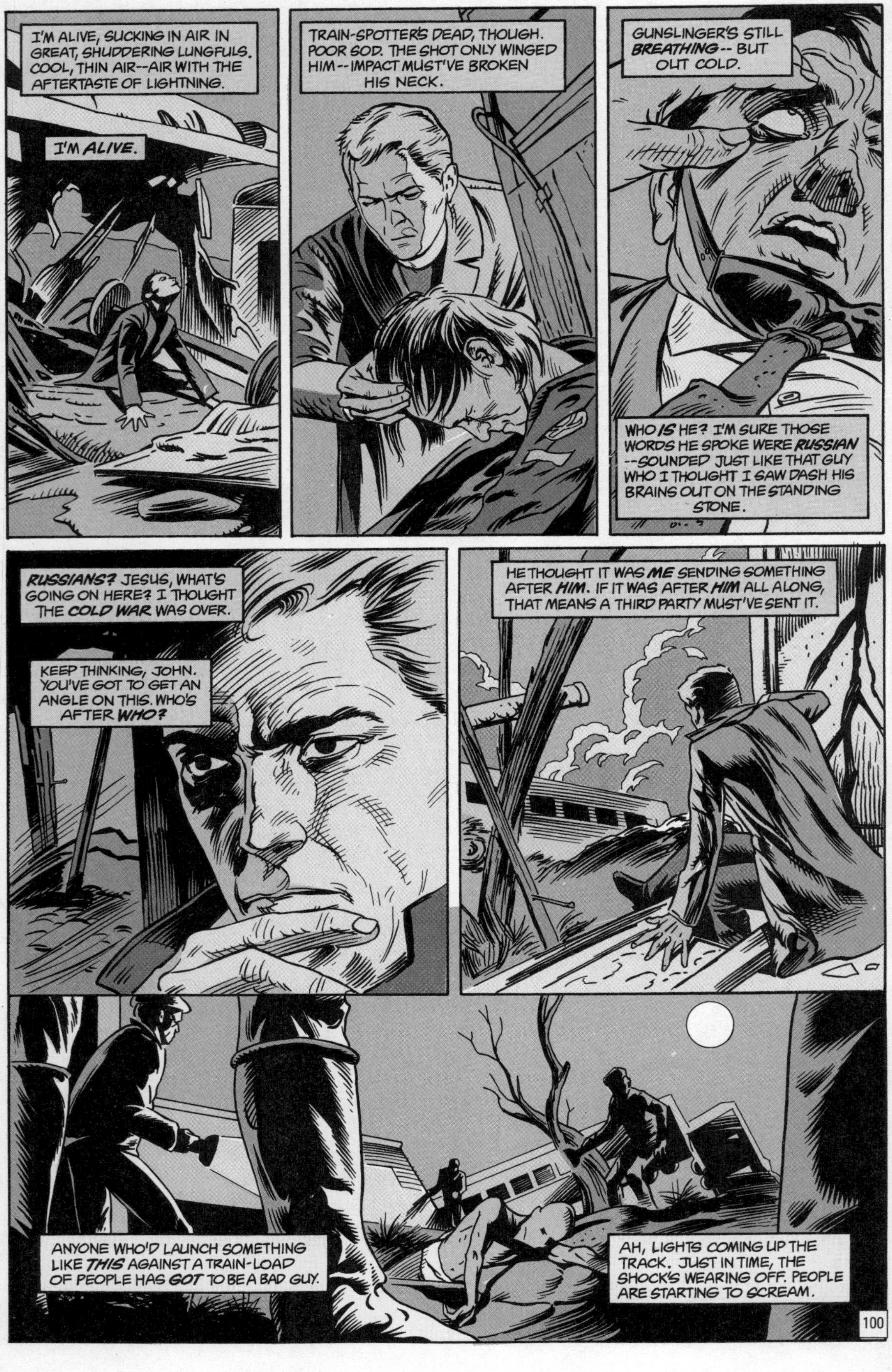

I'M ALIVE, SUCKING IN AIR IN GREAT, SHUDDERING LUNGFULS. COOL, THIN AIR--AIR WITH THE AFTERTASTE OF LIGHTNING.
I'M ALIVE.
TRAIN-SPOTTER'S DEAD, THOUGH. POOR SOD. THE SHOT ONLY WINGED HIM--IMPACT MUST'VE BROKEN HIS NECK.
GUNSLINGER'S STILL BREATHING-- BUT OUT COLD.
WHO IS HE? I'M SURE THOSE WORDS HE SPOKE WERE RUSSIAN --SOUNDED JUST LIKE THAT GUY WHO I THOUGHT I SAW DASH HIS BRAINS OUT ON THE STANDING STONE.
RUSSIANS? JESUS, WHAT'S GOING ON HERE? I THOUGHT THE COLD WAR WAS OVER.
KEEP THINKING, JOHN. YOU'VE GOT TO GET AN ANGLE ON THIS. WHO'S AFTER WHO?
HE THOUGHT IT WAS ME SENDING SOMETHING AFTER HIM. IF IT WAS AFTER HIM ALL ALONG, THAT MEANS A THIRD PARTY MUST'VE SENT IT.
ANYONE WHO'D LAUNCH SOMETHING LIKE THIS AGAINST A TRAIN-LOAD OF PEOPLE HAS GOT TO BE A BAD GUY.
AH, LIGHTS COMING UP THE TRACK. JUST IN TIME, THE SHOCK'S WEARING OFF. PEOPLE ARE STARTING TO SCREAM.

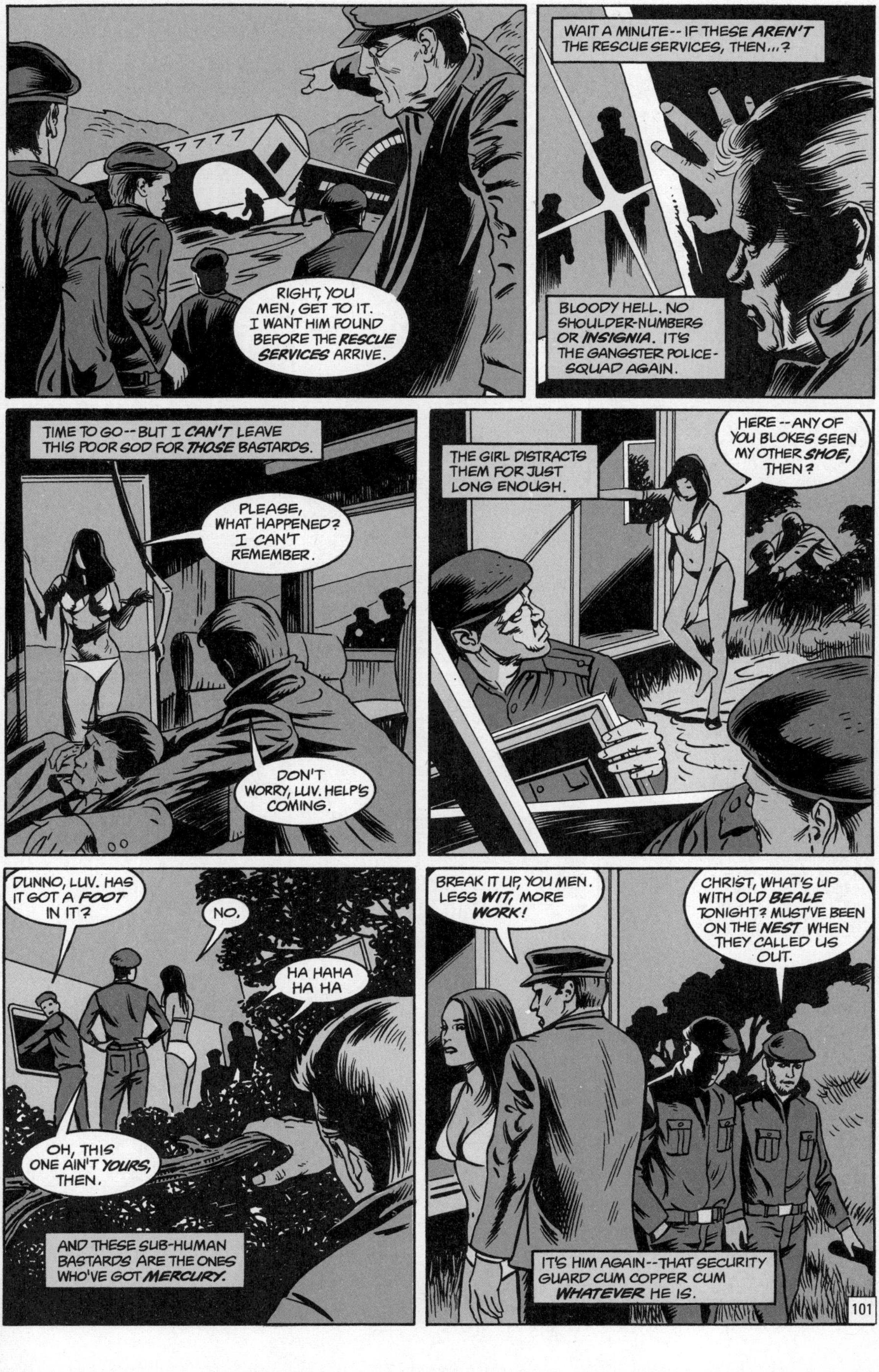
RIGHT, YOU MEN, GET TO IT. I WANT HIM FOUND BEFORE THE RESCUE SERVICES ARRIVE.
WAIT A MINUTE-- IF THESE AREN'T THE RESCUE SERVICES, THEN...?
BLOODY HELL. NO SHOULDER-NUMBERS OR INSIGNIA. IT'S THE GANGSTER POLICE-SQUAD AGAIN.
TIME TO GO-- BUT I CAN'T LEAVE THIS POOR SOD FOR THOSE BASTARDS.
PLEASE, WHAT HAPPENED? I CAN'T REMEMBER.
DON'T WORRY, LUV. HELP'S COMING.
THE GIRL DISTRACTS THEM FOR JUST LONG ENOUGH.
HERE -- ANY OF YOU BLOKES SEEN MY OTHER SHOE, THEN?
DUNNO, LUV. HAS IT GOT A FOOT IN IT?
NO.
HA HAHA HA HA
OH, THIS ONE AIN'T YOURS, THEN.
AND THESE SUB-HUMAN BASTARDS ARE THE ONES WHO'VE GOT MERCURY.
BREAK IT UP, YOU MEN. LESS WIT, MORE WORK!
CHRIST, WHAT'S UP WITH OLD BEALE TONIGHT? MUST'VE BEEN ON THE NEST WHEN THEY CALLED US OUT.
IT'S HIM AGAIN--THAT SECURITY GUARD CUM COPPER CUM WHATEVER HE IS.

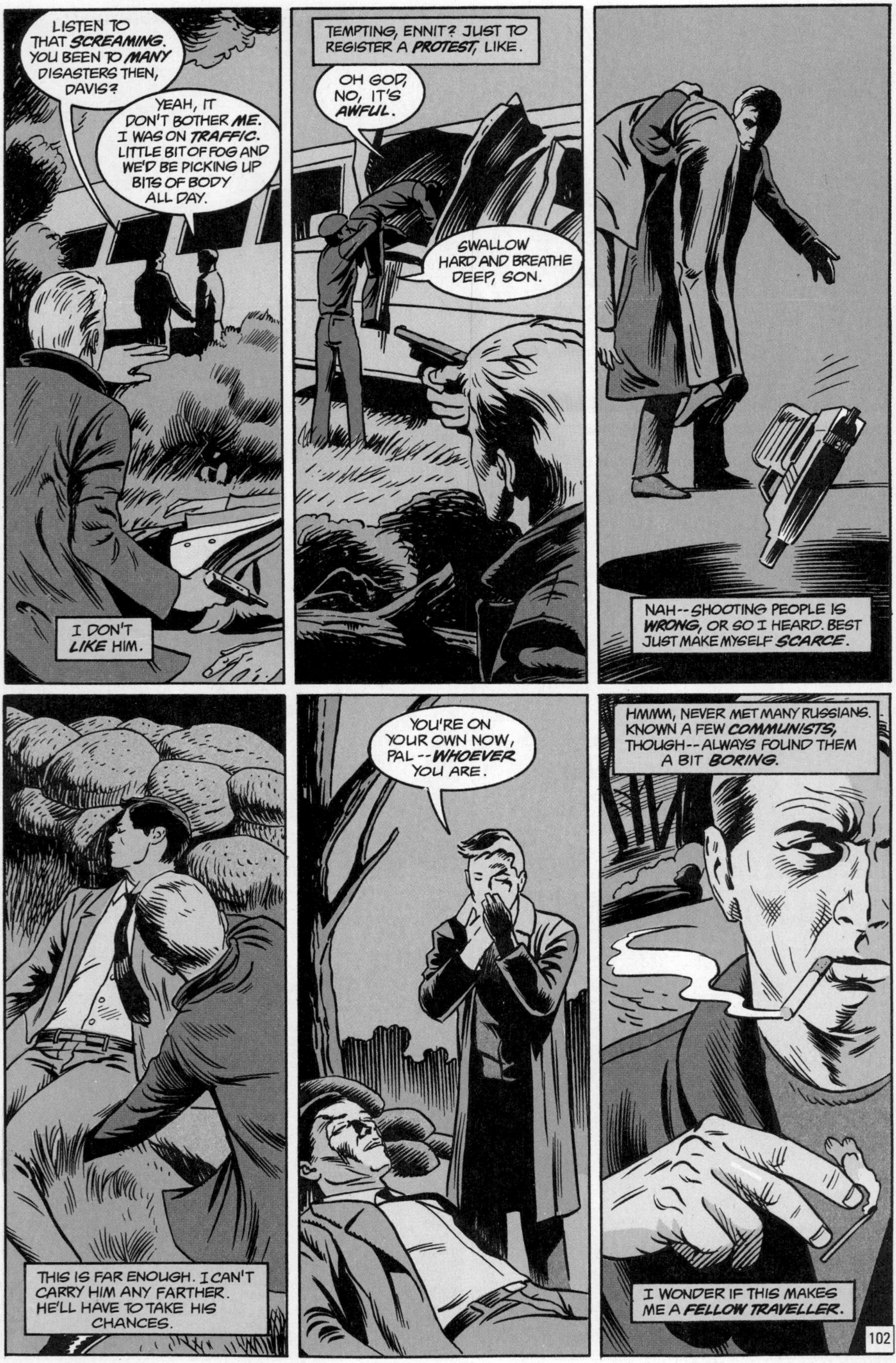
LISTEN TO THAT SCREAMING. YOU BEEN TO MANY DISASTERS THEN, DAVIS?
YEAH, IT DON'T BOTHER ME. I WAS ON TRAFFIC. LITTLE BIT OF FOG AND WE'D BE PICKING UP BITS OF BODY ALL DAY.
I DON'T LIKE HIM.
TEMPTING, ENNIT? JUST TO REGISTER A PROTEST, LIKE.
OH GOD, NO, IT'S AWFUL.
SWALLOW HARD AND BREATHE DEEP, SON.
NAH--SHOOTING PEOPLE IS WRONG, OR SO I HEARD. BEST JUST MAKE MYSELF SCARCE.
THIS IS FAR ENOUGH. I CAN'T CARRY HIM ANY FARTHER. HE'LL HAVE TO TAKE HIS CHANCES.
YOU'RE ON YOUR OWN NOW, PAL--WHOEVER YOU ARE.
HMMM, NEVER MET MANY RUSSIANS. KNOWN A FEW COMMUNISTS, THOUGH--ALWAYS FOUND THEM A BIT BORING.
I WONDER IF THIS MAKES ME A FELLOW TRAVELLER.

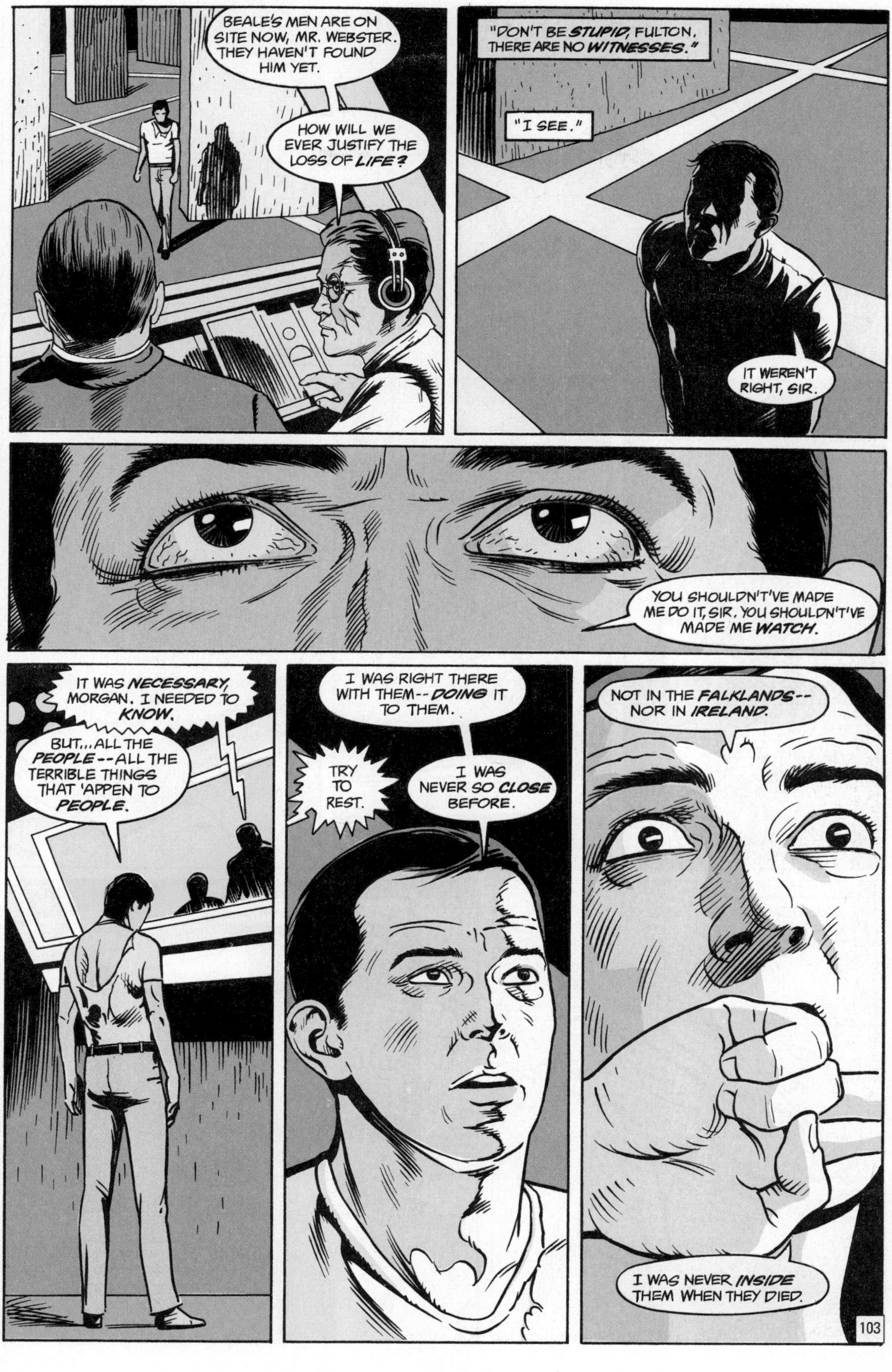

BEALE'S MEN ARE ON SITE NOW, MR. WEBSTER. THEY HAVEN'T FOUND HIM YET.
HOW WILL WE EVER JUSTIFY THE LOSS OF *LIFE?*
"DON'T BE *STUPID,* FULTON. THERE ARE NO *WITNESSES.*"
"I SEE."
IT WEREN'T RIGHT, SIR.
YOU SHOULDN'T'VE MADE ME DO IT, SIR. YOU SHOULDN'T'VE MADE ME *WATCH.*
IT WAS *NECESSARY,* MORGAN. I NEEDED TO *KNOW.*
BUT... ALL THE *PEOPLE*-- ALL THE TERRIBLE THINGS THAT 'APPEN TO *PEOPLE.*
I WAS RIGHT THERE WITH THEM-- *DOING* IT TO THEM.
TRY TO REST.
I WAS NEVER SO *CLOSE* BEFORE.
NOT IN THE *FALKLANDS*-- NOR IN *IRELAND.*
I WAS NEVER *INSIDE* THEM WHEN THEY DIED.

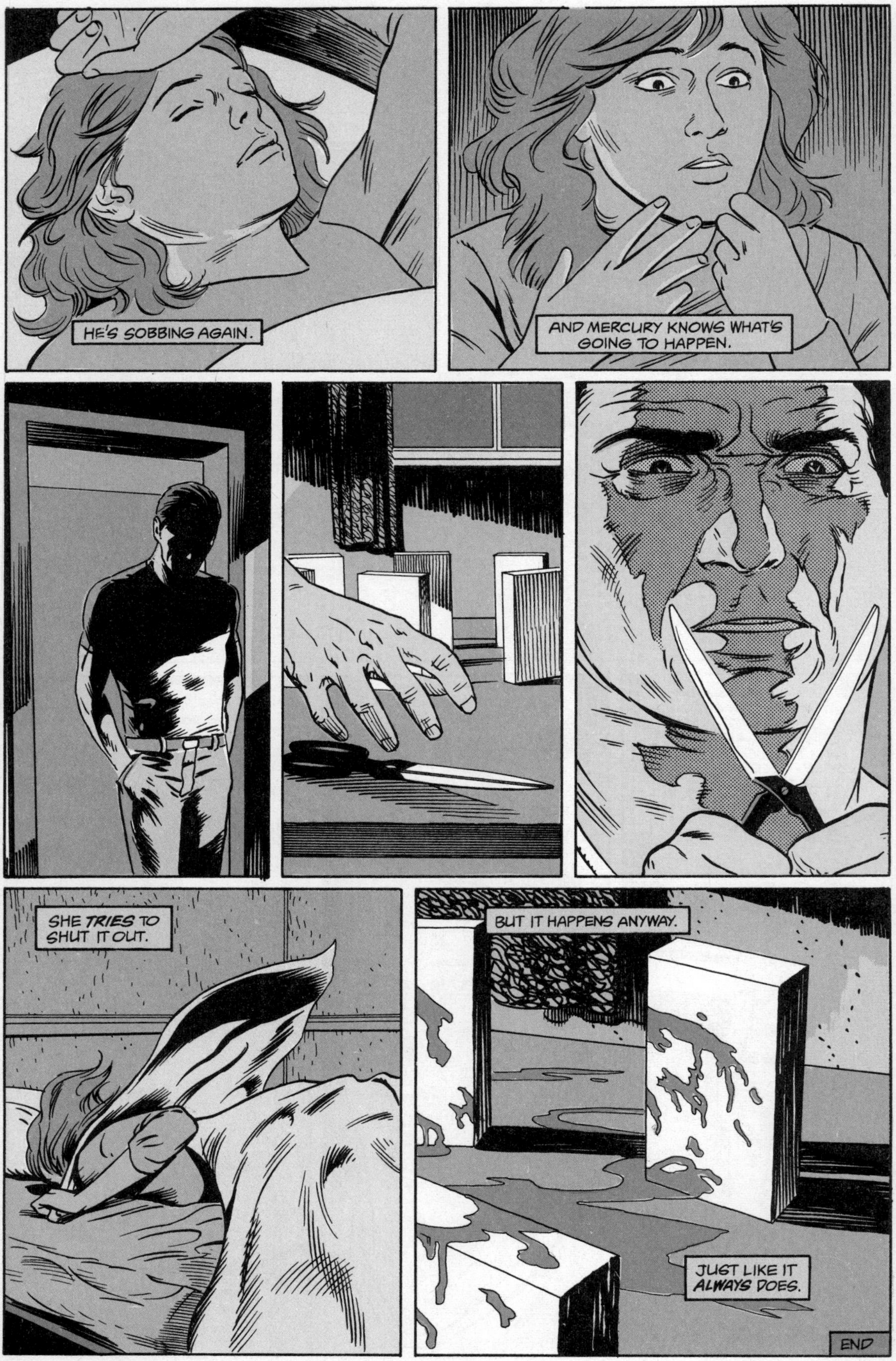
HE'S SOBBING AGAIN.
AND MERCURY KNOWS WHAT'S GOING TO HAPPEN.
SHE *TRIES* TO SHUT IT OUT.
BUT IT HAPPENS ANYWAY.
JUST LIKE IT *ALWAYS* DOES.
END

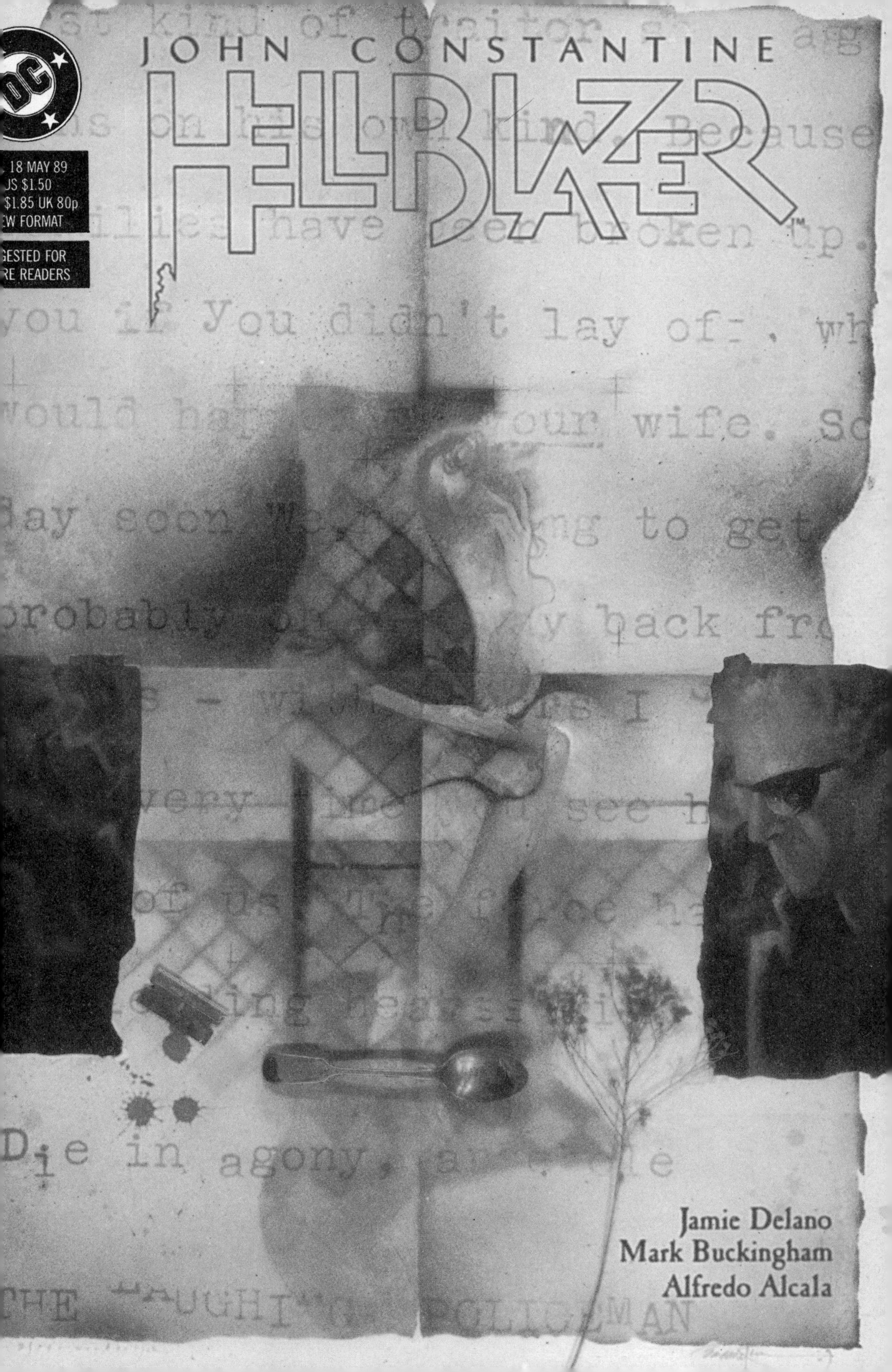
JOHN CONSTANTINE
HELLBLAZER
18 MAY 89
JS $1.50
$1.85 UK 80p
EW FORMAT
GESTED FOR
RE READERS
Jamie Delano
Mark Buckingham
Alfredo Alcala

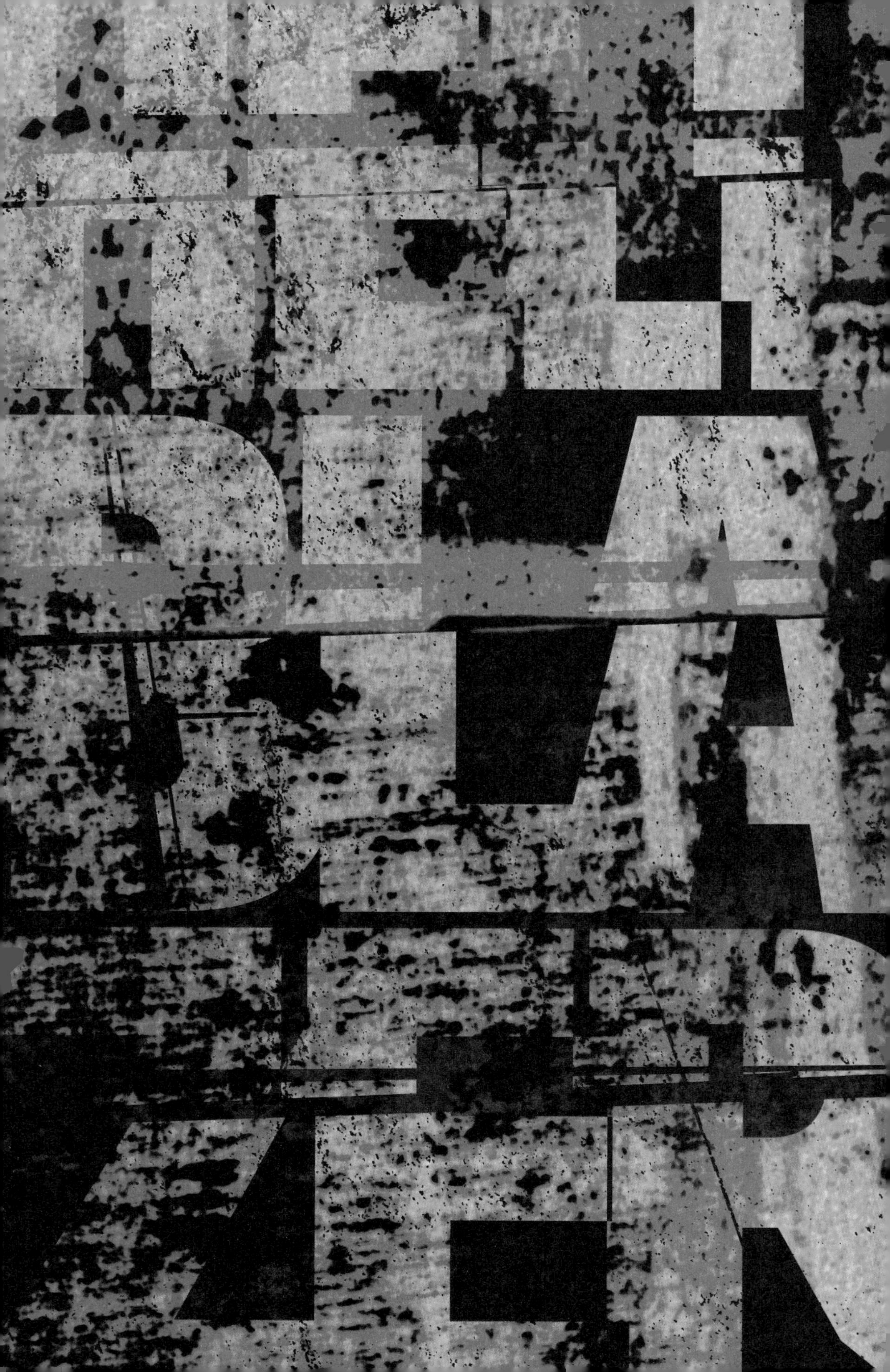

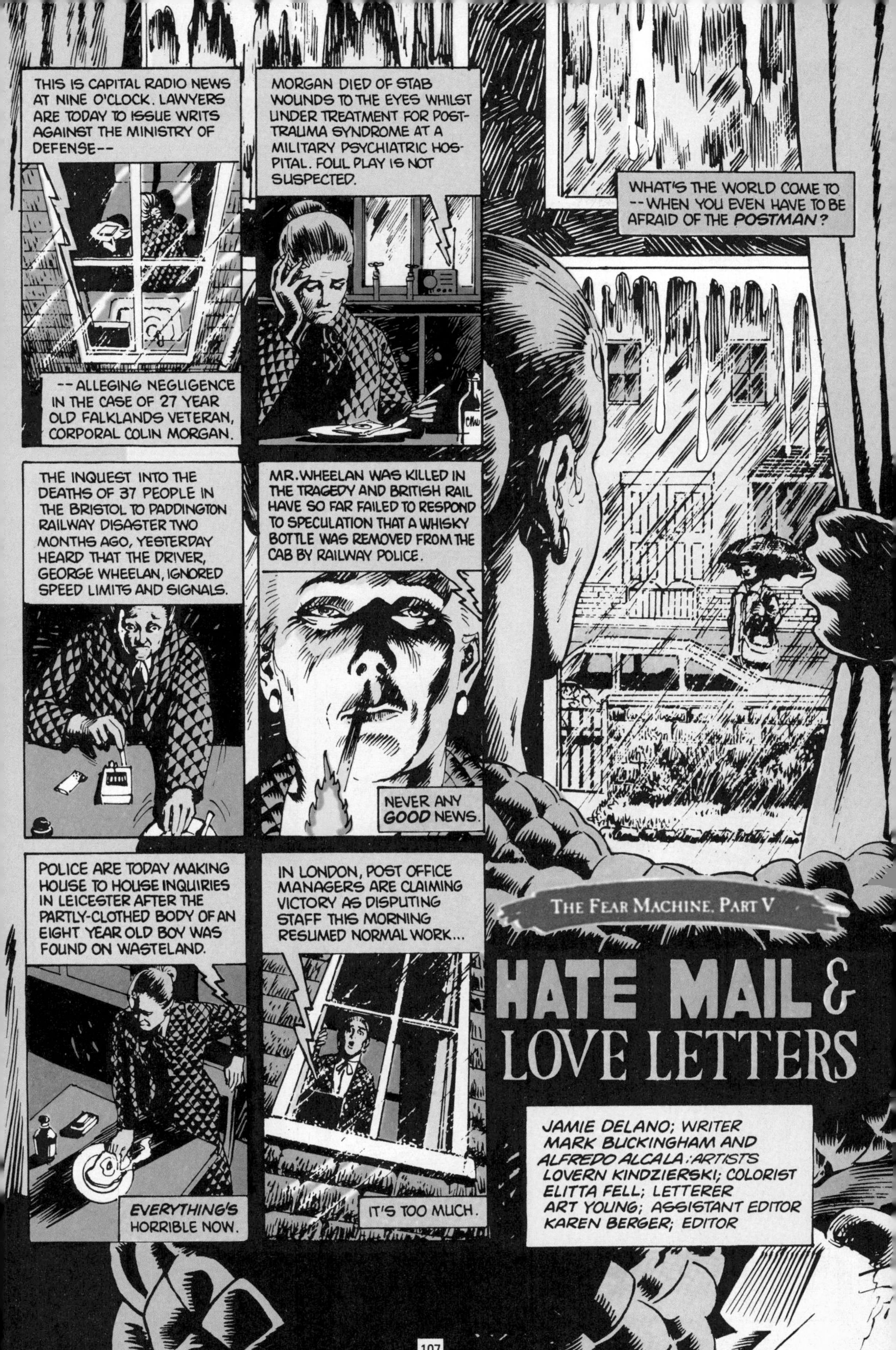

THIS IS CAPITAL RADIO NEWS AT NINE O'CLOCK. LAWYERS ARE TODAY TO ISSUE WRITS AGAINST THE MINISTRY OF DEFENSE--
--ALLEGING NEGLIGENCE IN THE CASE OF 27 YEAR OLD FALKLANDS VETERAN, CORPORAL COLIN MORGAN.
MORGAN DIED OF STAB WOUNDS TO THE EYES WHILST UNDER TREATMENT FOR POST-TRAUMA SYNDROME AT A MILITARY PSYCHIATRIC HOSPITAL. FOUL PLAY IS NOT SUSPECTED.
WHAT'S THE WORLD COME TO --WHEN YOU EVEN HAVE TO BE AFRAID OF THE *POSTMAN*?
THE INQUEST INTO THE DEATHS OF 37 PEOPLE IN THE BRISTOL TO PADDINGTON RAILWAY DISASTER TWO MONTHS AGO, YESTERDAY HEARD THAT THE DRIVER, GEORGE WHEELAN, IGNORED SPEED LIMITS AND SIGNALS.
MR. WHEELAN WAS KILLED IN THE TRAGEDY AND BRITISH RAIL HAVE SO FAR FAILED TO RESPOND TO SPECULATION THAT A WHISKY BOTTLE WAS REMOVED FROM THE CAB BY RAILWAY POLICE.
NEVER ANY *GOOD* NEWS.
POLICE ARE TODAY MAKING HOUSE TO HOUSE INQUIRIES IN LEICESTER AFTER THE PARTLY-CLOTHED BODY OF AN EIGHT YEAR OLD BOY WAS FOUND ON WASTELAND.
EVERYTHING'S HORRIBLE NOW.
IN LONDON, POST OFFICE MANAGERS ARE CLAIMING VICTORY AS DISPUTING STAFF THIS MORNING RESUMED NORMAL WORK...
IT'S TOO MUCH.
THE FEAR MACHINE, PART V
HATE MAIL & LOVE LETTERS
JAMIE DELANO; WRITER
MARK BUCKINGHAM AND ALFREDO ALCALA: ARTISTS
LOVERN KINDZIERSKI; COLORIST
ELITTA FELL; LETTERER
ART YOUNG; ASSISTANT EDITOR
KAREN BERGER; EDITOR

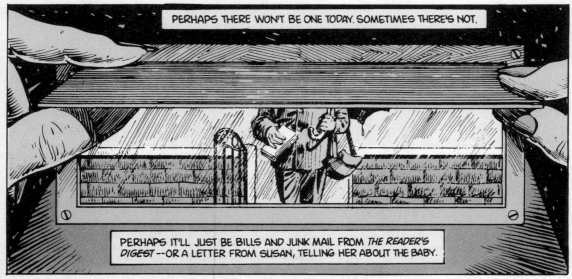

PERHAPS THERE WON'T BE ONE TODAY. SOMETIMES THERE'S NOT.

PERHAPS IT'LL JUST BE BILLS AND JUNK MAIL FROM *THE READER'S DIGEST* --OR A LETTER FROM SUSAN, TELLING HER ABOUT THE BABY.

SHE USED TO *LIKE* GETTING LETTERS. NOT ANYMORE, THOUGH --PEOPLE DON'T WRITE *NICE* LETTERS ANYMORE.

THAT WOULD BE *LOVELY.*

Mr. CLEAN BASTARD TALBOT
4-2 CUMFER ll
WIMBLEDON.
LONDON

...f you families ...
...n broken up, we warned ...
...f you didn't lay off, what ...
...ould happen to your wife
So one day soon we're
going to get her - probably
...n her way back from the doctors-
...with razors, I should think. Then
every time you see her face
you'll think of us. The force has
got room for bleeding
hearts like you.
Die in agony, Arsehole.
The Laughing Policeman

JUST FILTHY, FILTHY, VILE HATEFUL, *EVIL* LETTERS.

HOW COULD ANYONE HATE SO *MUCH.*

GEOFFREY ALWAYS SAID THAT THERE WERE TRULY EVIL PEOPLE IN THE WORLD.

SHE KNEW HE WAS RIGHT--BUT SOMEHOW, SHE COULD ONLY EVER THINK OF THEIR *MOTHERS.*

HENDON   1958

GEOFFREY, SO HONEST, SO SURE OF HIMSELF. IF *HE* KNEW THERE WERE *POLICEMEN* WHO HATED HIM LIKE THIS, IT WOULD *DESTROY* HIM.

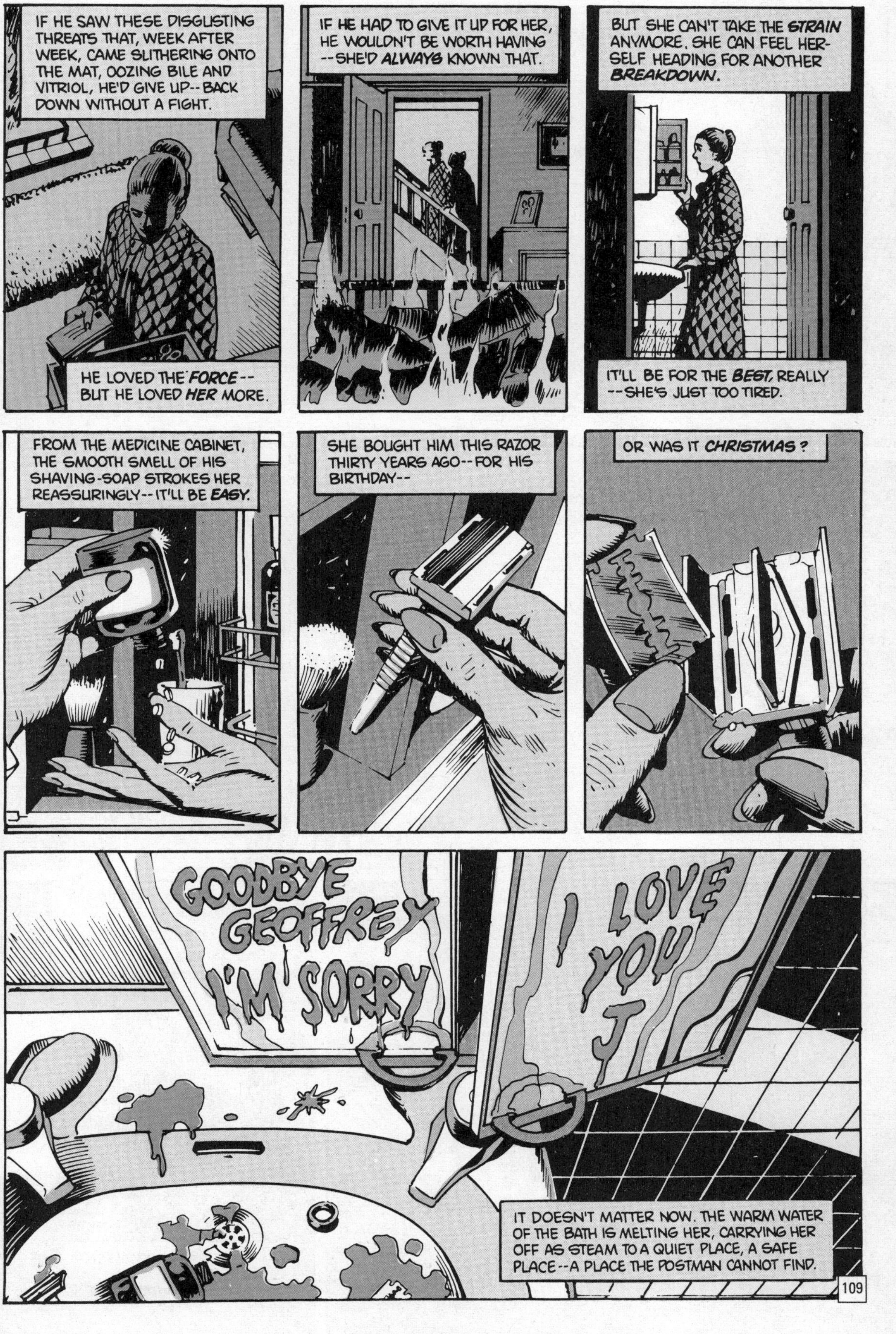
IF HE SAW THESE DISGUSTING THREATS THAT, WEEK AFTER WEEK, CAME SLITHERING ONTO THE MAT, OOZING BILE AND VITRIOL, HE'D GIVE UP-- BACK DOWN WITHOUT A FIGHT.
HE LOVED THE FORCE-- BUT HE LOVED HER MORE.
IF HE HAD TO GIVE IT UP FOR HER, HE WOULDN'T BE WORTH HAVING --SHE'D ALWAYS KNOWN THAT.
BUT SHE CAN'T TAKE THE STRAIN ANYMORE. SHE CAN FEEL HER-SELF HEADING FOR ANOTHER BREAKDOWN.
IT'LL BE FOR THE BEST, REALLY --SHE'S JUST TOO TIRED.
FROM THE MEDICINE CABINET, THE SMOOTH SMELL OF HIS SHAVING-SOAP STROKES HER REASSURINGLY-- IT'LL BE EASY.
SHE BOUGHT HIM THIS RAZOR THIRTY YEARS AGO-- FOR HIS BIRTHDAY--
OR WAS IT CHRISTMAS?
GOODBYE GEOFFREY I'M SORRY
I LOVE YOU J
IT DOESN'T MATTER NOW. THE WARM WATER OF THE BATH IS MELTING HER, CARRYING HER OFF AS STEAM TO A QUIET PLACE, A SAFE PLACE--A PLACE THE POSTMAN CANNOT FIND.

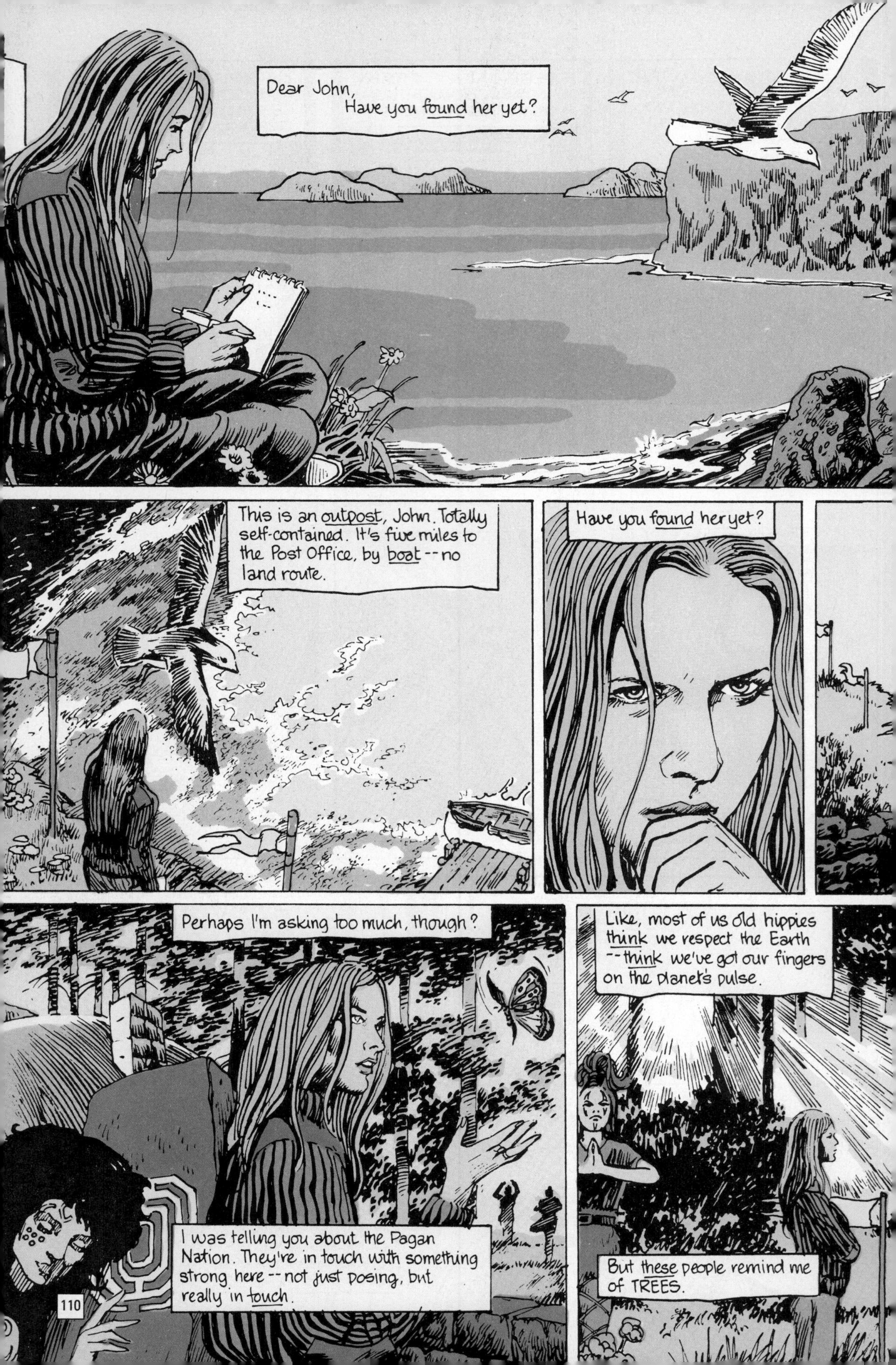
Dear John,
Have you found her yet?
This is an outpost, John. Totally self-contained. It's five miles to the Post Office, by boat -- no land route.
Have you found her yet?
Perhaps I'm asking too much, though?
I was telling you about the Pagan Nation. They're in touch with something strong here -- not just posing, but really in touch.
Like, most of us old hippies think we respect the Earth -- think we've got our fingers on the planet's pulse.
But these people remind me of TREES.

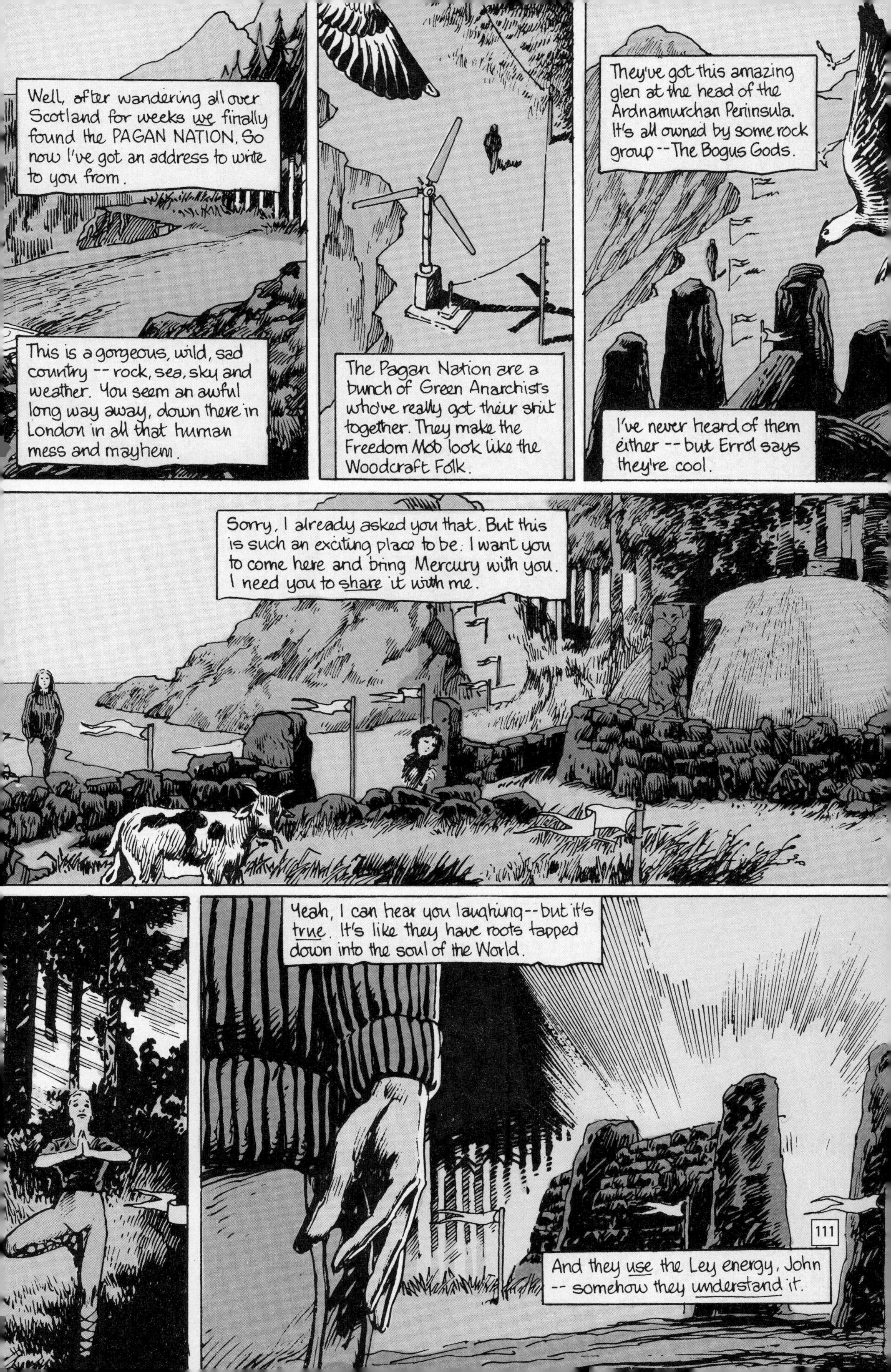
Well, after wandering all over Scotland for weeks we finally found the PAGAN NATION. So now I've got an address to write to you from.
This is a gorgeous, wild, sad country -- rock, sea, sky and weather. You seem an awful long way away, down there in London in all that human mess and mayhem.
The Pagan Nation are a bunch of Green Anarchists who've really got their shit together. They make the Freedom Mob look like the Woodcraft Folk.
They've got this amazing glen at the head of the Ardnamurchan Peninsula. It's all owned by some rock group -- The Bogus Gods.
I've never heard of them either -- but Errol says they're cool.
Sorry, I already asked you that. But this is such an exciting place to be. I want you to come here and bring Mercury with you. I need you to share it with me.
Yeah, I can hear you laughing -- but it's true. It's like they have roots tapped down into the soul of the World.
111
And they use the Ley energy, John -- somehow they understand it.

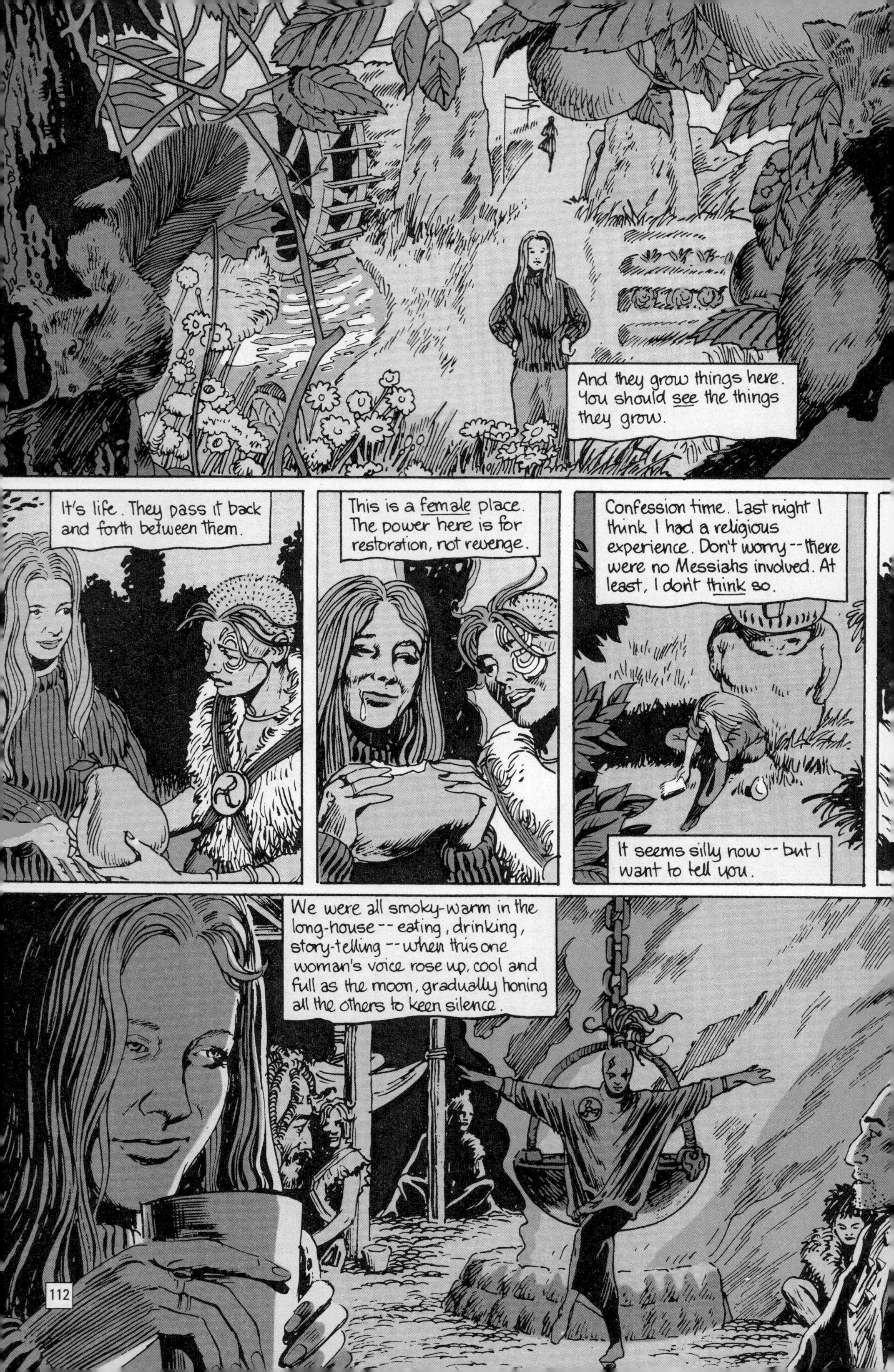
And they grow things here. You should see the things they grow.
It's life. They pass it back and forth between them.
This is a female place. The power here is for restoration, not revenge.
Confession time. Last night I think I had a religious experience. Don't worry -- there were no Messiahs involved. At least, I don't think so.
It seems silly now -- but I want to tell you.
We were all smoky-warm in the long-house -- eating, drinking, story-telling -- when this one woman's voice rose up, cool and full as the moon, gradually honing all the others to keen silence.

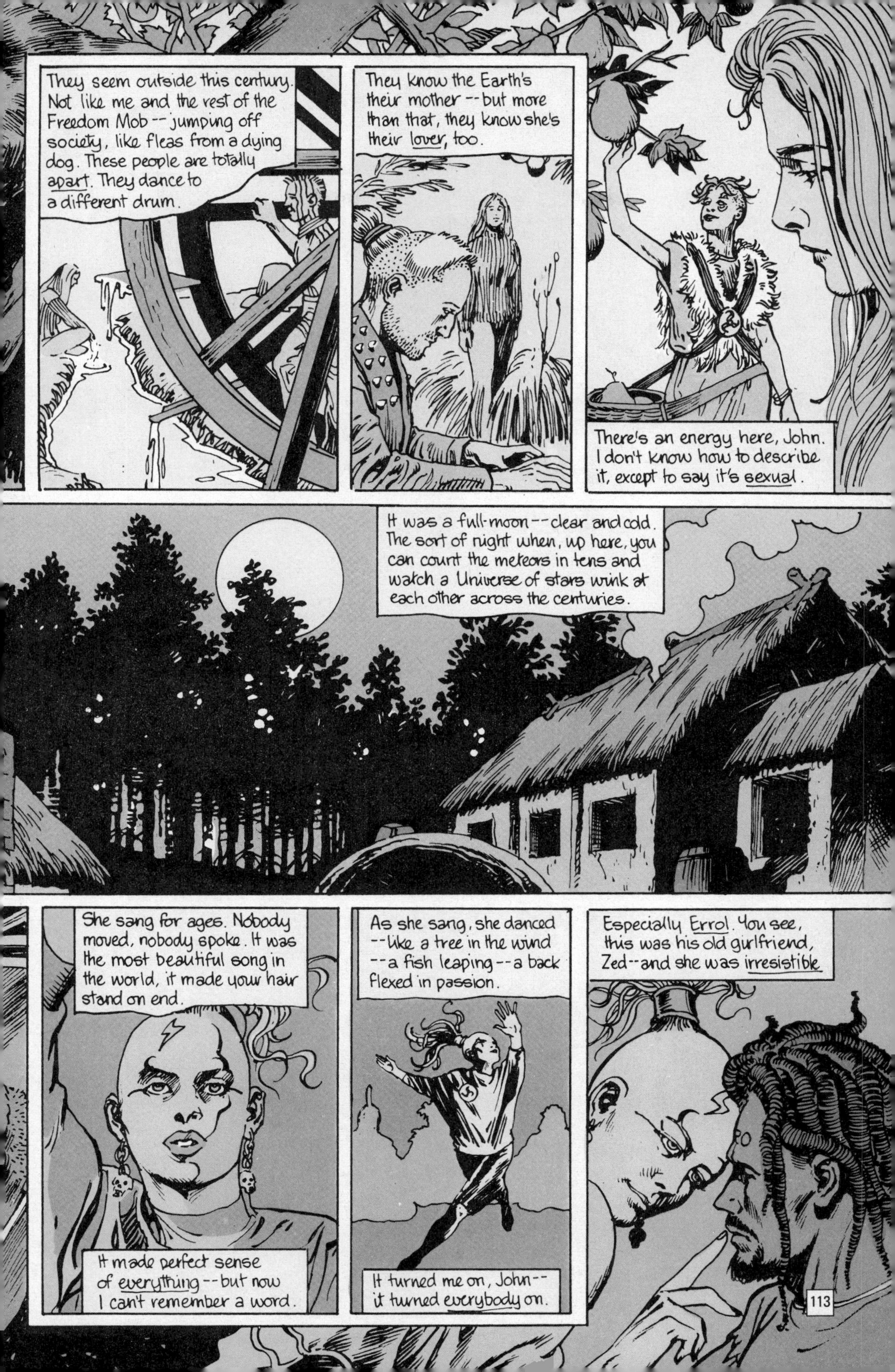

They seem outside this century. Not like me and the rest of the Freedom Mob -- jumping off society, like fleas from a dying dog. These people are totally apart. They dance to a different drum.
They know the Earth's their mother -- but more than that, they know she's their lover, too.
There's an energy here, John. I don't know how to describe it, except to say it's sexual.
It was a full-moon -- clear and cold. The sort of night when, up here, you can count the meteors in tens and watch a Universe of stars wink at each other across the centuries.
She sang for ages. Nobody moved, nobody spoke. It was the most beautiful song in the world, it made your hair stand on end.
It made perfect sense of everything -- but now I can't remember a word.
As she sang, she danced -- like a tree in the wind -- a fish leaping -- a back flexed in passion.
It turned me on, John -- it turned everybody on.
Especially Errol. You see, this was his old girlfriend, Zed -- and she was irresistible

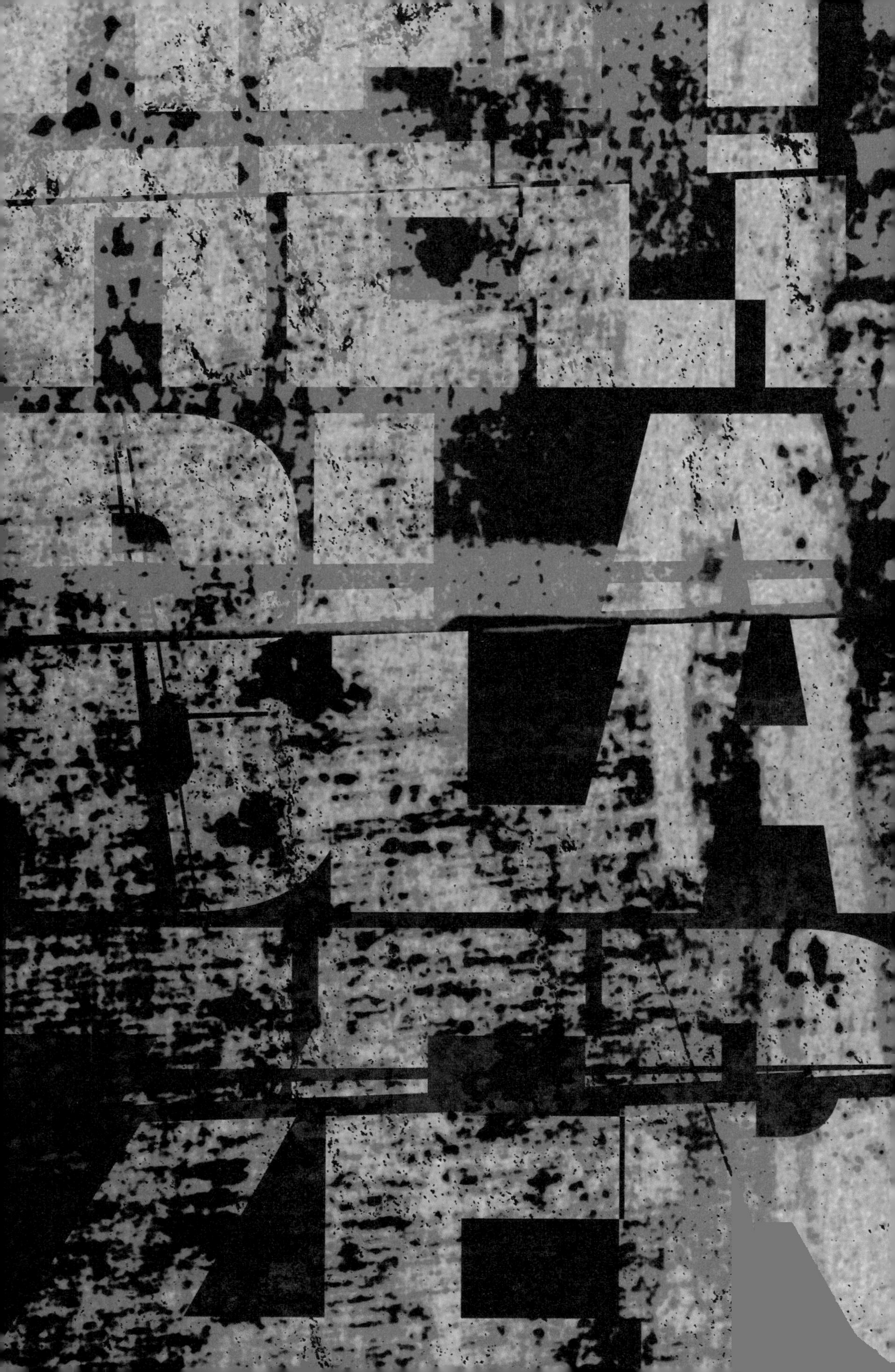

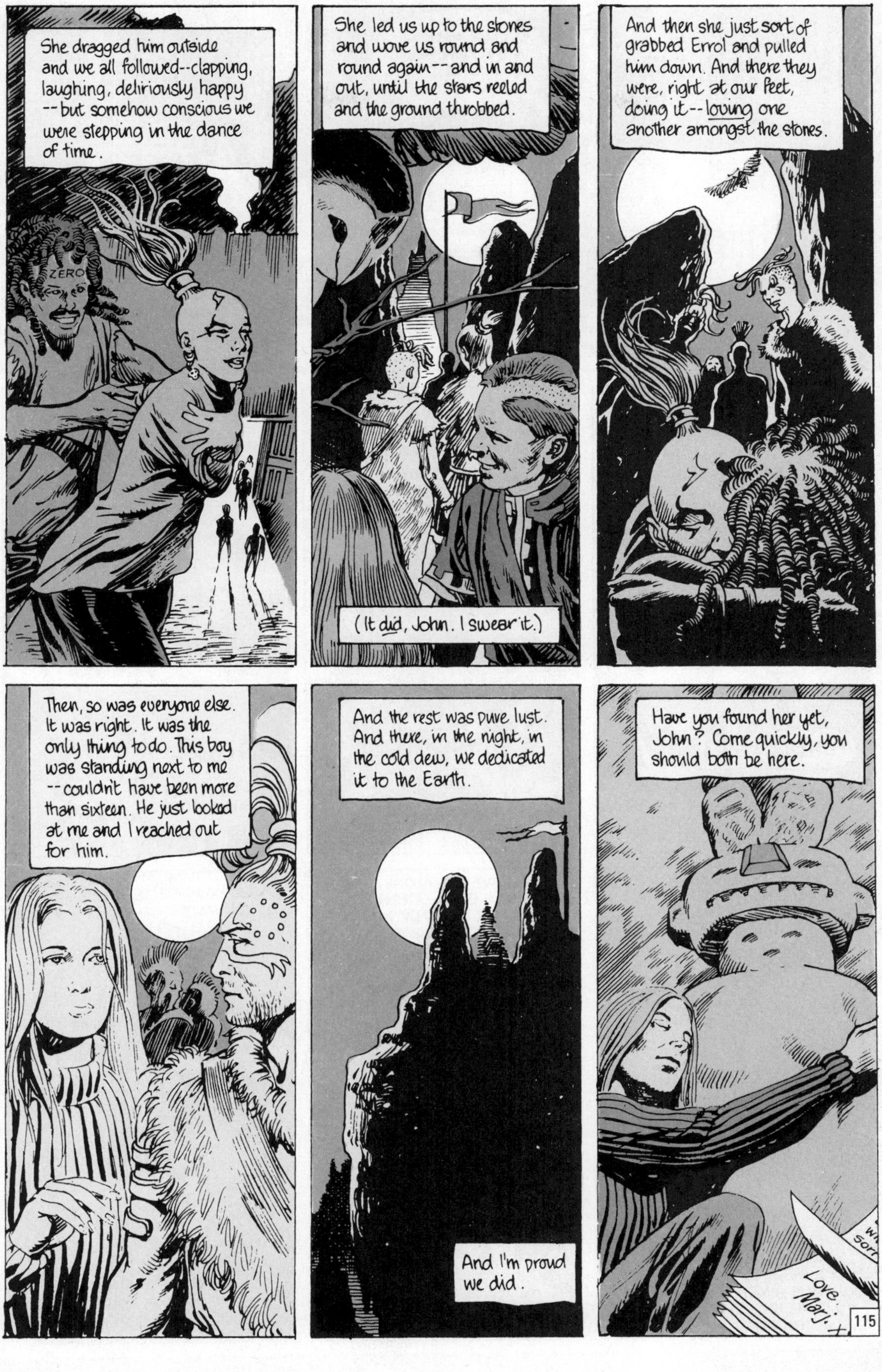
She dragged him outside and we all followed--clapping, laughing, deliriously happy --but somehow conscious we were stepping in the dance of time.
ZERO
She led us up to the stones and wove us round and round again--and in and out, until the stars reeled and the ground throbbed.
(It did, John. I swear it.)
And then she just sort of grabbed Errol and pulled him down. And there they were, right at our feet, doing it--loving one another amongst the stones.
Then, so was everyone else. It was right. It was the only thing to do. This boy was standing next to me --couldn't have been more than sixteen. He just looked at me and I reached out for him.
And the rest was pure lust. And there, in the night, in the cold dew, we dedicated it to the Earth.
And I'm proud we did.
Have you found her yet, John? Come quickly, you should both be here.
Love. Marj. x

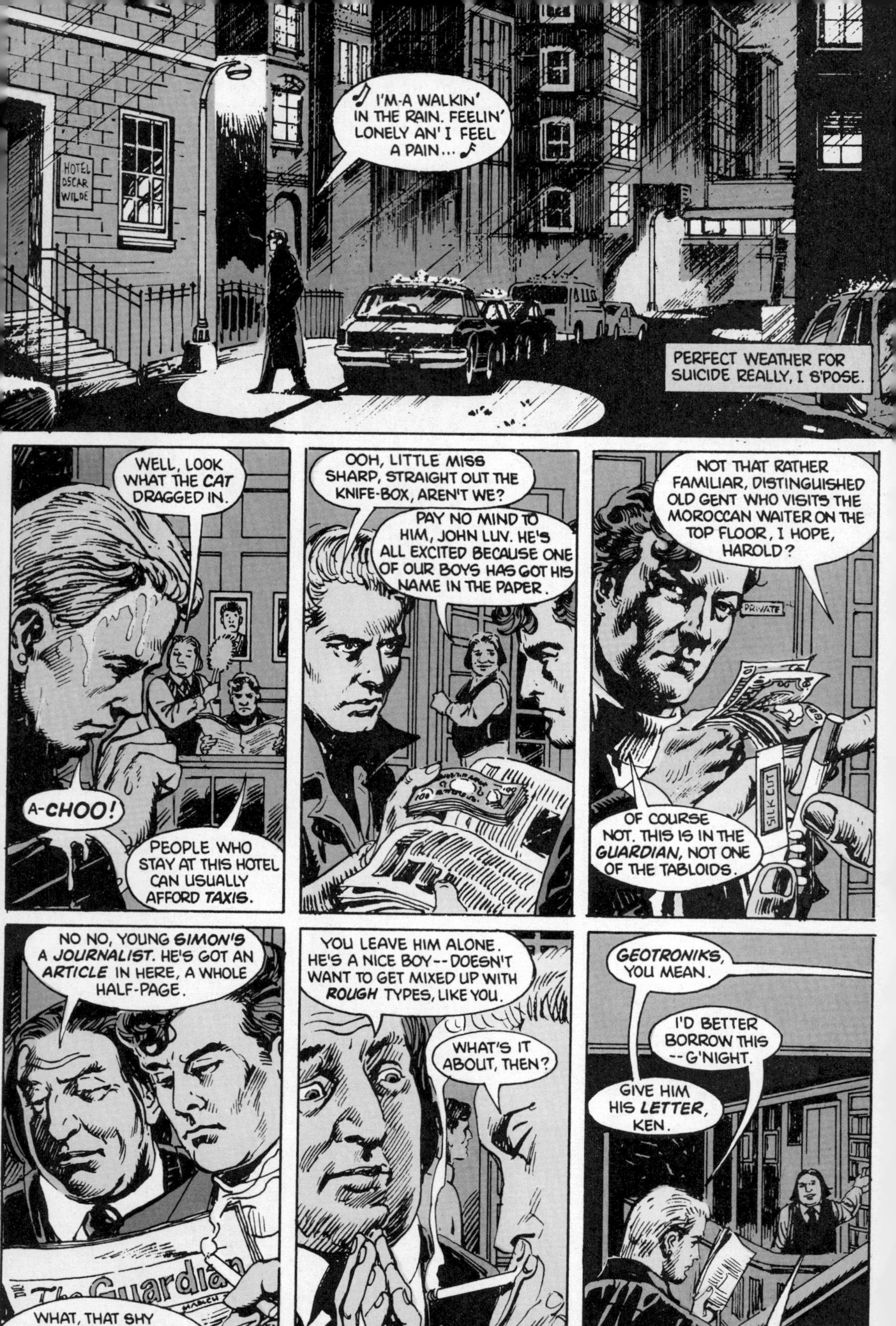
HOTEL OSCAR WILDE
I'M-A WALKIN' IN THE RAIN. FEELIN' LONELY AN' I FEEL A PAIN...
PERFECT WEATHER FOR SUICIDE REALLY, I S'POSE.
WELL, LOOK WHAT THE CAT DRAGGED IN.
A-CHOO!
PEOPLE WHO STAY AT THIS HOTEL CAN USUALLY AFFORD TAXIS.
OOH, LITTLE MISS SHARP, STRAIGHT OUT THE KNIFE-BOX, AREN'T WE?
PAY NO MIND TO HIM, JOHN LUV. HE'S ALL EXCITED BECAUSE ONE OF OUR BOYS HAS GOT HIS NAME IN THE PAPER.
NOT THAT RATHER FAMILIAR, DISTINGUISHED OLD GENT WHO VISITS THE MOROCCAN WAITER ON THE TOP FLOOR, I HOPE, HAROLD?
PRIVATE
SILK CUT
OF COURSE NOT. THIS IS IN THE GUARDIAN, NOT ONE OF THE TABLOIDS.
NO NO, YOUNG SIMON'S A JOURNALIST. HE'S GOT AN ARTICLE IN HERE, A WHOLE HALF-PAGE.
The Guardian
WHAT, THAT SHY BLOKE IN THE ROOM NEXT TO MINE IS SIMON HUGHES? I'LL HAVE TO GET HIS AUTOGRAPH.
YOU LEAVE HIM ALONE. HE'S A NICE BOY--DOESN'T WANT TO GET MIXED UP WITH ROUGH TYPES, LIKE YOU.
WHAT'S IT ABOUT, THEN?
ALL THESE GHASTLY SUICIDES CONNECTED WITH THIS COMPANY CALLED GEOTECHNIKS...
GEOTRONIKS, YOU MEAN.
I'D BETTER BORROW THIS --G'NIGHT.
GIVE HIM HIS LETTER, KEN.
OH YES, THIS CAME FOR YOU--FROM SCOTLAND.

'STREWTH, EVERYTHING HAPPENS AT ONCE, DUNNIT --TA...

A-*CHOO!*

IF I WERE YOU, YOUNG JOHN, I'D GET BY THE FIRE WITH A RUM TODDY--BEFORE YOU CATCH YOUR *DEATH.*

NAH, US *ROUGH* TYPES DON'T DIE OF COLDS.

PERHAPS I'LL TIPTOE UP LATER WITH SOME WARM TOWELS AND A HOTTY-BOTTLE.

'SALRIGHT, THANKS --YOU SAVE YOUR OLD PINS, ME DUCK.

HUH, I'LL HAVE YOU KNOW THAT THESE LEGS CAN STILL HIGH-STEP WITH THE *FINEST,* LUV--KICK YOUR HAT RIGHT INTO YOUR LAP.

Dear Marj -- sorry darlin', but no, I haven't found her yet. Things are starting to move in the right direction, though.

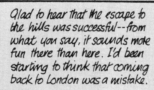

Glad to hear that the escape to the hills was successful -- from what you say, it sounds more fun there than here. I'd been starting to think that coming back to London was a mistake.

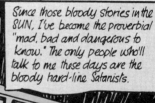

Since those bloody stories in the SUN, I've become the proverbial "mad, bad and dangerous to know." The only people who'll talk to me these days are the bloody hard-line Satanists.

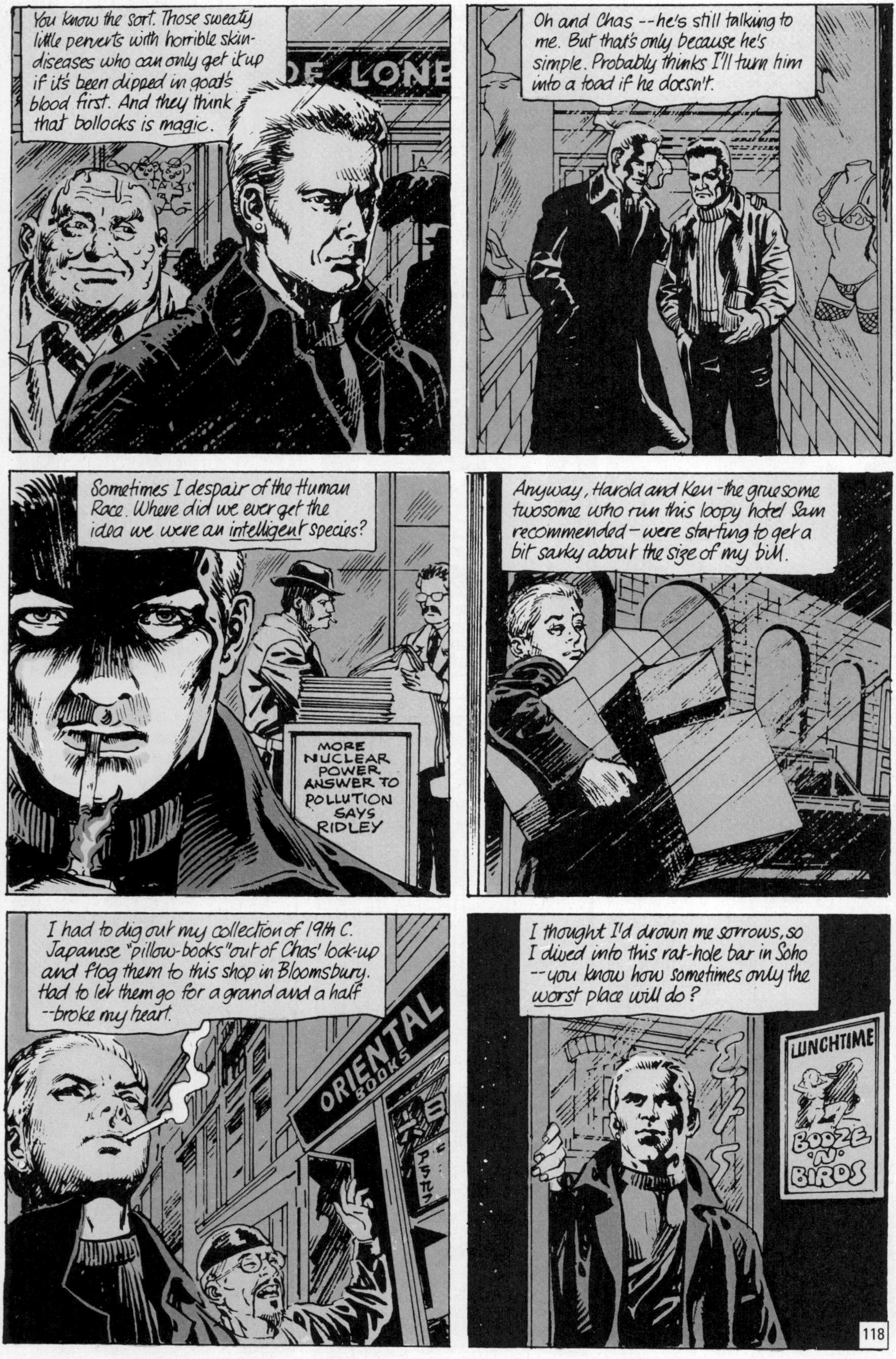
You know the sort. Those sweaty little perverts with horrible skin-diseases who can only get it up if it's been dipped in goat's blood first. And they think that bollocks is magic.
Oh and Chas --he's still talking to me. But that's only because he's simple. Probably thinks I'll turn him into a toad if he doesn't.
Sometimes I despair of the Human Race. Where did we ever get the idea we were an intelligent species?
MORE NUCLEAR POWER ANSWER TO POLLUTION SAYS RIDLEY
Anyway, Harold and Ken-the gruesome twosome who run this loopy hotel Sam recommended-were starting to get a bit sarky about the size of my bill.
I had to dig out my collection of 19th C. Japanese "pillow-books" out of Chas' lock-up and flog them to this shop in Bloomsbury. Had to let them go for a grand and a half --broke my heart.
ORIENTAL BOOKS
I thought I'd drown me sorrows, so I dived into this rat-hole bar in Soho --you know how sometimes only the worst place will do?
LUNCHTIME
BOOZE N BIRDS

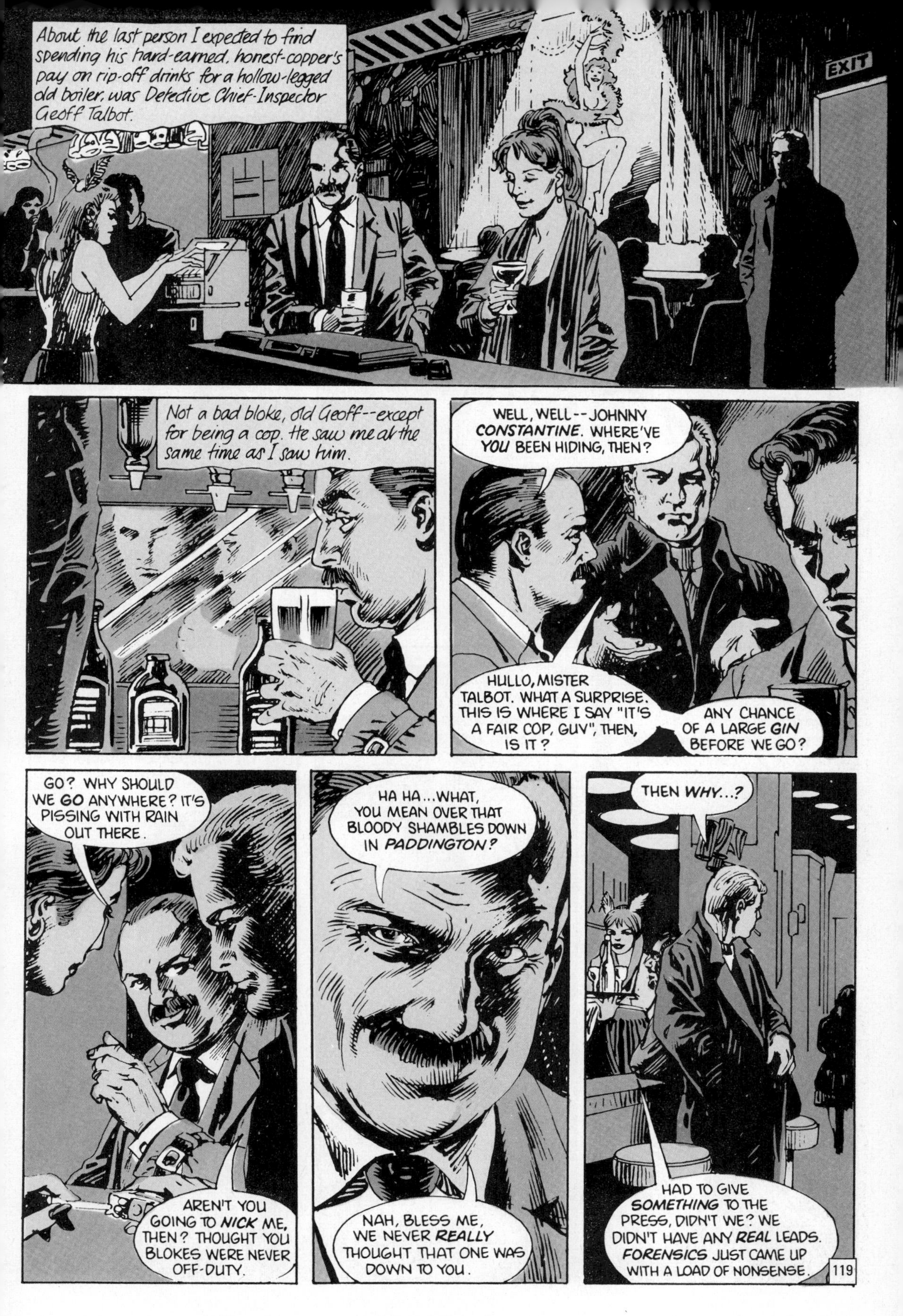
About the last person I expected to find spending his hard-earned, honest-copper's pay on rip-off drinks for a hollow-legged old boiler, was Detective Chief-Inspector Geoff Talbot.
EXIT
Not a bad bloke, old Geoff--except for being a cop. He saw me at the same time as I saw him.
WELL, WELL--JOHNNY CONSTANTINE. WHERE'VE YOU BEEN HIDING, THEN?
HULLO, MISTER TALBOT. WHAT A SURPRISE. THIS IS WHERE I SAY "IT'S A FAIR COP, GUV", THEN, IS IT?
ANY CHANCE OF A LARGE GIN BEFORE WE GO?
GO? WHY SHOULD WE GO ANYWHERE? IT'S PISSING WITH RAIN OUT THERE.
AREN'T YOU GOING TO NICK ME, THEN? THOUGHT YOU BLOKES WERE NEVER OFF-DUTY.
HA HA...WHAT, YOU MEAN OVER THAT BLOODY SHAMBLES DOWN IN PADDINGTON?
NAH, BLESS ME, WE NEVER REALLY THOUGHT THAT ONE WAS DOWN TO YOU.
THEN WHY...?
HAD TO GIVE SOMETHING TO THE PRESS, DIDN'T WE? WE DIDN'T HAVE ANY REAL LEADS. FORENSICS JUST CAME UP WITH A LOAD OF NONSENSE.

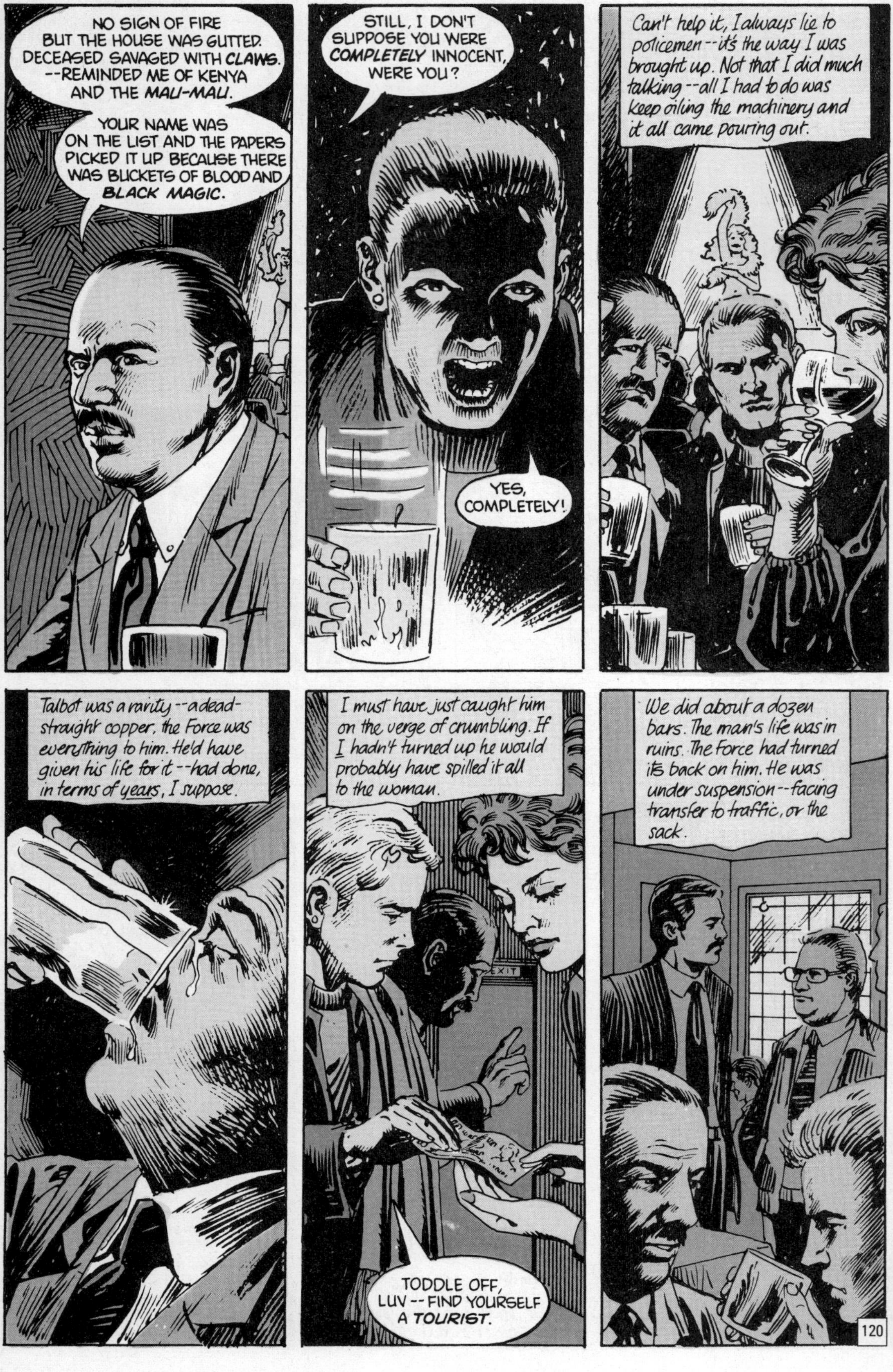
NO SIGN OF FIRE BUT THE HOUSE WAS GUTTED. DECEASED SAVAGED WITH CLAWS. --REMINDED ME OF KENYA AND THE MAU-MAU.
YOUR NAME WAS ON THE LIST AND THE PAPERS PICKED IT UP BECAUSE THERE WAS BUCKETS OF BLOOD AND BLACK MAGIC.
STILL, I DON'T SUPPOSE YOU WERE COMPLETELY INNOCENT, WERE YOU?
YES, COMPLETELY!
Can't help it, I always lie to policemen--it's the way I was brought up. Not that I did much talking--all I had to do was keep oiling the machinery and it all came pouring out.
Talbot was a rarity--a dead-straight copper, the Force was everything to him. He'd have given his life for it--had done, in terms of years, I suppose.
I must have just caught him on the verge of crumbling. If I hadn't turned up he would probably have spilled it all to the woman.
EXIT
TODDLE OFF, LUV--FIND YOURSELF A TOURIST.
We did about a dozen bars. The man's life was in ruins. The Force had turned its back on him. He was under suspension--facing transfer to traffic, or the sack.

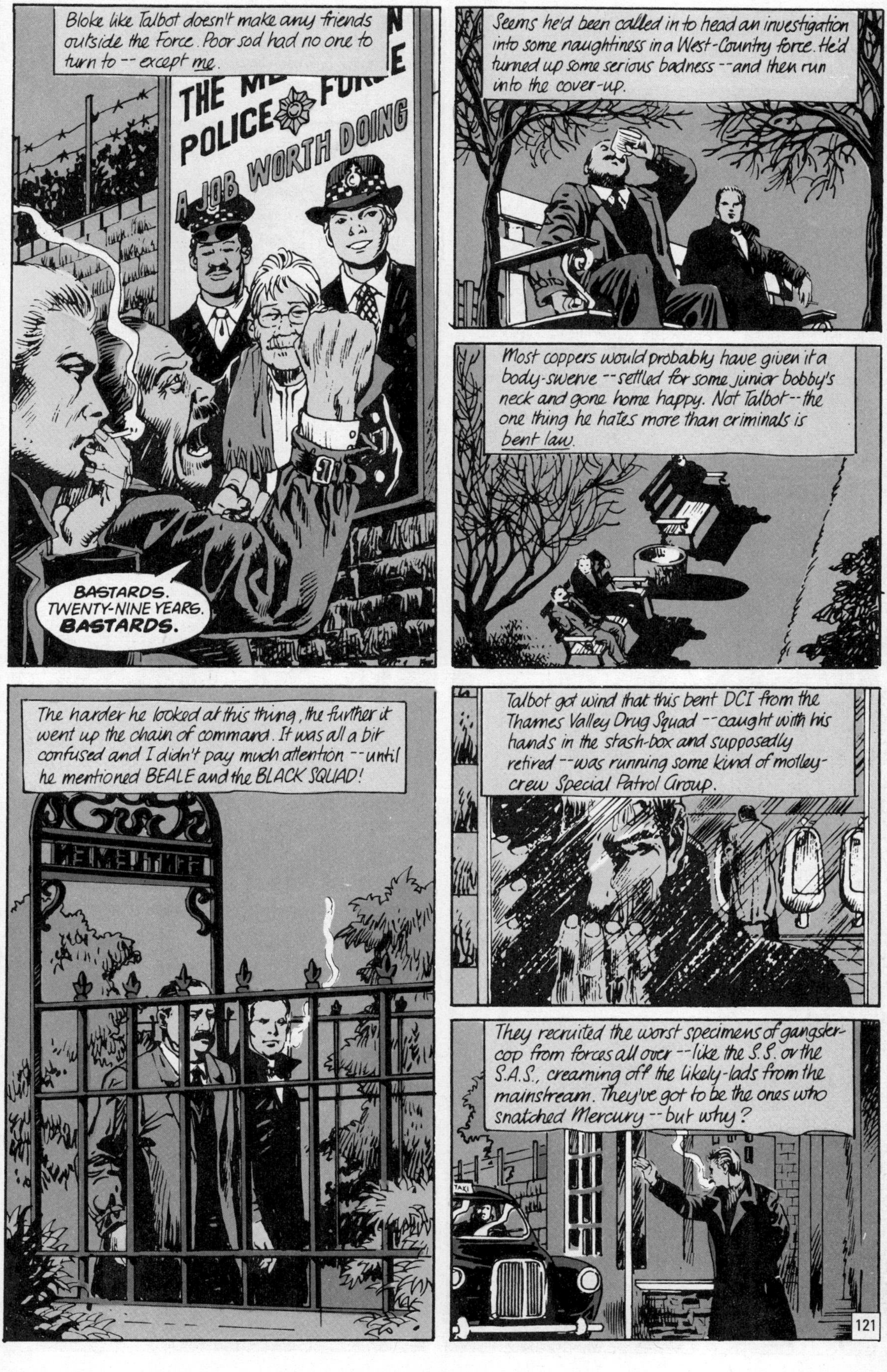
Bloke like Talbot doesn't make any friends outside the Force. Poor sod had no one to turn to -- except me.
THE ME
POLICE FORCE
A JOB WORTH DOING
BASTARDS. TWENTY-NINE YEARS. BASTARDS.
Seems he'd been called in to head an investigation into some naughtiness in a West-Country force. He'd turned up some serious badness -- and then run into the cover-up.
Most coppers would probably have given it a body-swerve -- settled for some junior bobby's neck and gone home happy. Not Talbot -- the one thing he hates more than criminals is bent law.
The harder he looked at this thing, the further it went up the chain of command. It was all a bit confused and I didn't pay much attention -- until he mentioned BEALE and the BLACK SQUAD!
Talbot got wind that this bent DCI from the Thames Valley Drug Squad -- caught with his hands in the stash-box and supposedly retired -- was running some kind of motley-crew Special Patrol Group.
They recruited the worst specimens of gangster-cop from forces all over -- like the S.S. or the S.A.S., creaming off the likely-lads from the mainstream. They've got to be the ones who snatched Mercury -- but why?
TAXI

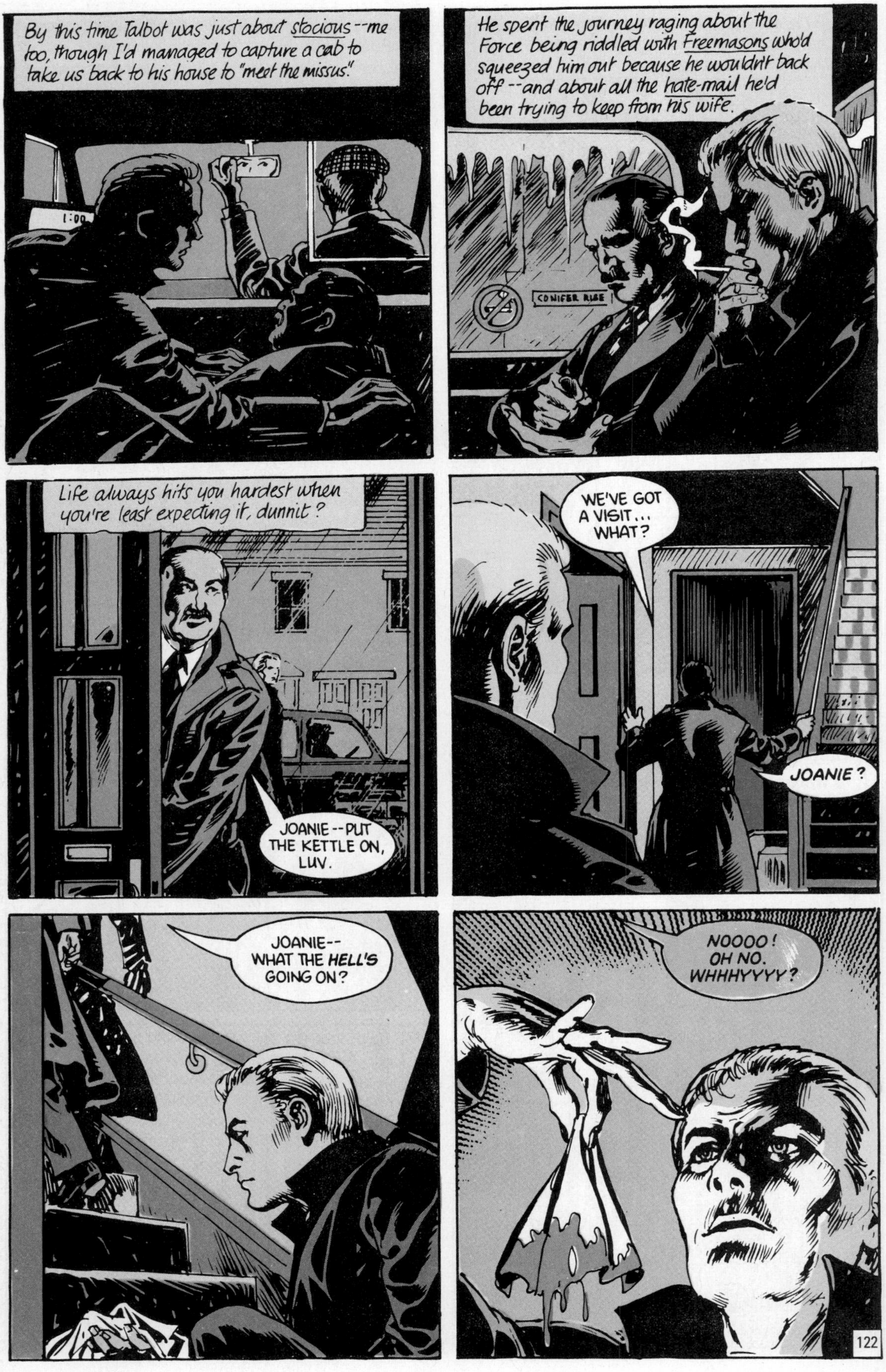

By this time Talbot was just about stocious--me too, though I'd managed to capture a cab to take us back to his house to "meet the missus."
1:00
He spent the journey raging about the Force being riddled with Freemasons who'd squeezed him out because he wouldn't back off--and about all the hate-mail he'd been trying to keep from his wife.
CONIFER RISE
Life always hits you hardest when you're least expecting it, dunnit?
JOANIE--PUT THE KETTLE ON, LUV.
WE'VE GOT A VISIT... WHAT?
JOANIE?
JOANIE-- WHAT THE HELL'S GOING ON?
NOOOO! OH NO. WHHHYYYY?

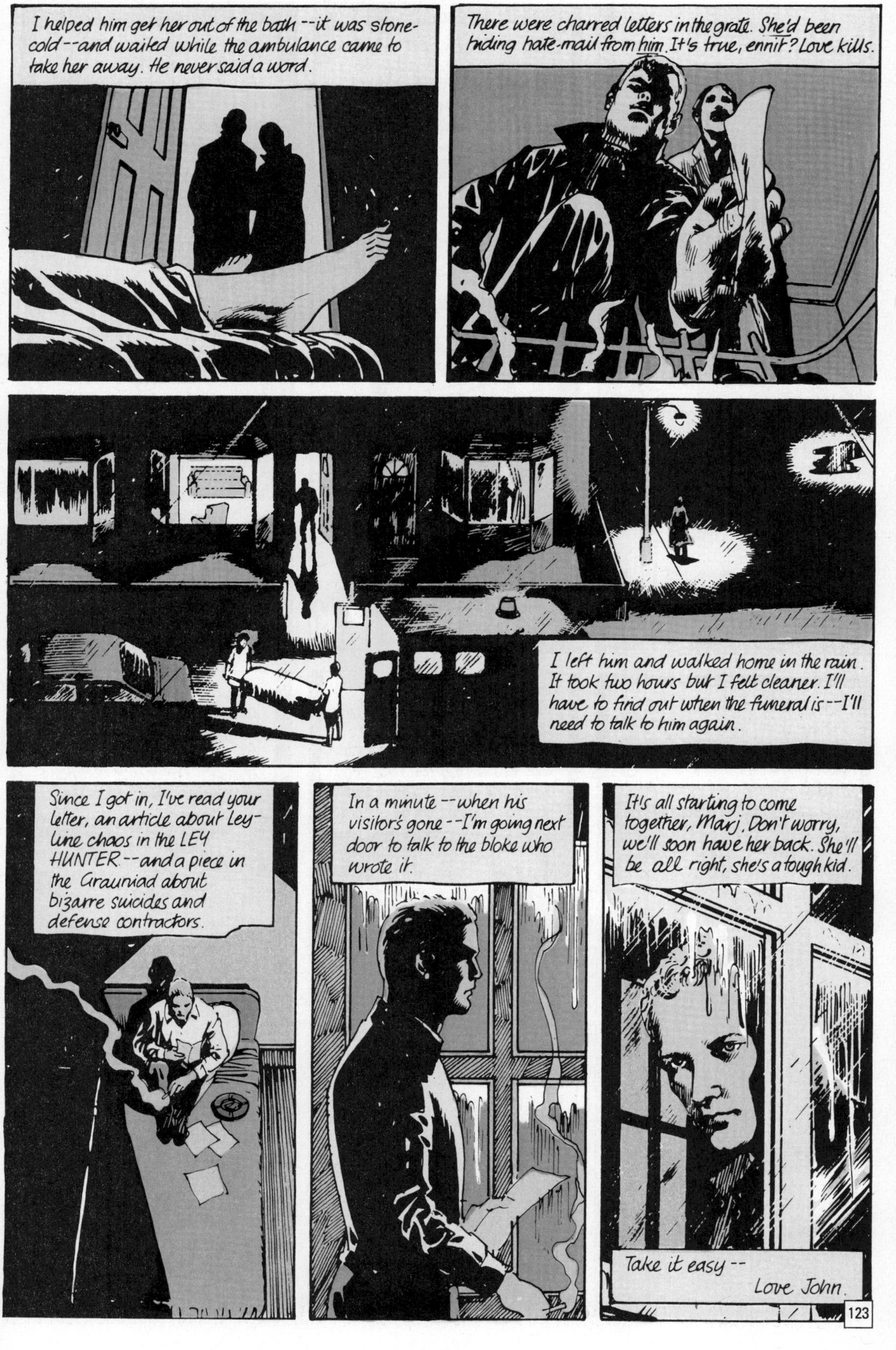
I helped him get her out of the bath --it was stone-cold--and waited while the ambulance came to take her away. He never said a word.
There were charred letters in the grate. She'd been hiding hate-mail from him. It's true, ennit? Love kills.
I left him and walked home in the rain. It took two hours but I felt cleaner. I'll have to find out when the funeral is--I'll need to talk to him again.
Since I got in, I've read your letter, an article about Ley-line chaos in the LEY HUNTER--and a piece in the Grauniad about bizarre suicides and defense contractors.
In a minute--when his visitor's gone--I'm going next door to talk to the bloke who wrote it.
It's all starting to come together, Marj. Don't worry, we'll soon have her back. She'll be all right, she's a tough kid.
Take it easy --
Love John.

Dear Nosey Parker:
This is a private diary which I'm keeping because there's no one else to talk to here.

GEOTRONIKS
AUTHORIZED
PERSONNEL ONLY

They still won't tell me where I am. But I don't suppose that matters. Sometimes it's frightening here, but other times it's really exciting.

That creepy Dr. Fulton is teaching me how to use the stuff I can do with my mind to help people. This is good because they have people here who need help bad.

We started off on easy-peasy guessing games. But then he showed me how to get inside people's heads, I right inside. It's spooky.

Sometimes I do it to Dr. Fulton, for a joke. He hates it. He gets all hot and bothered and tries to hide all his thoughts. Like Pete with the dope -- when the police would come.

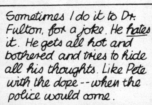

I think he likes me. He's always watching me. Imagine him kissing you. UGH! It doesn't bother me, though. I'm much stronger --I can get him anytime.

124

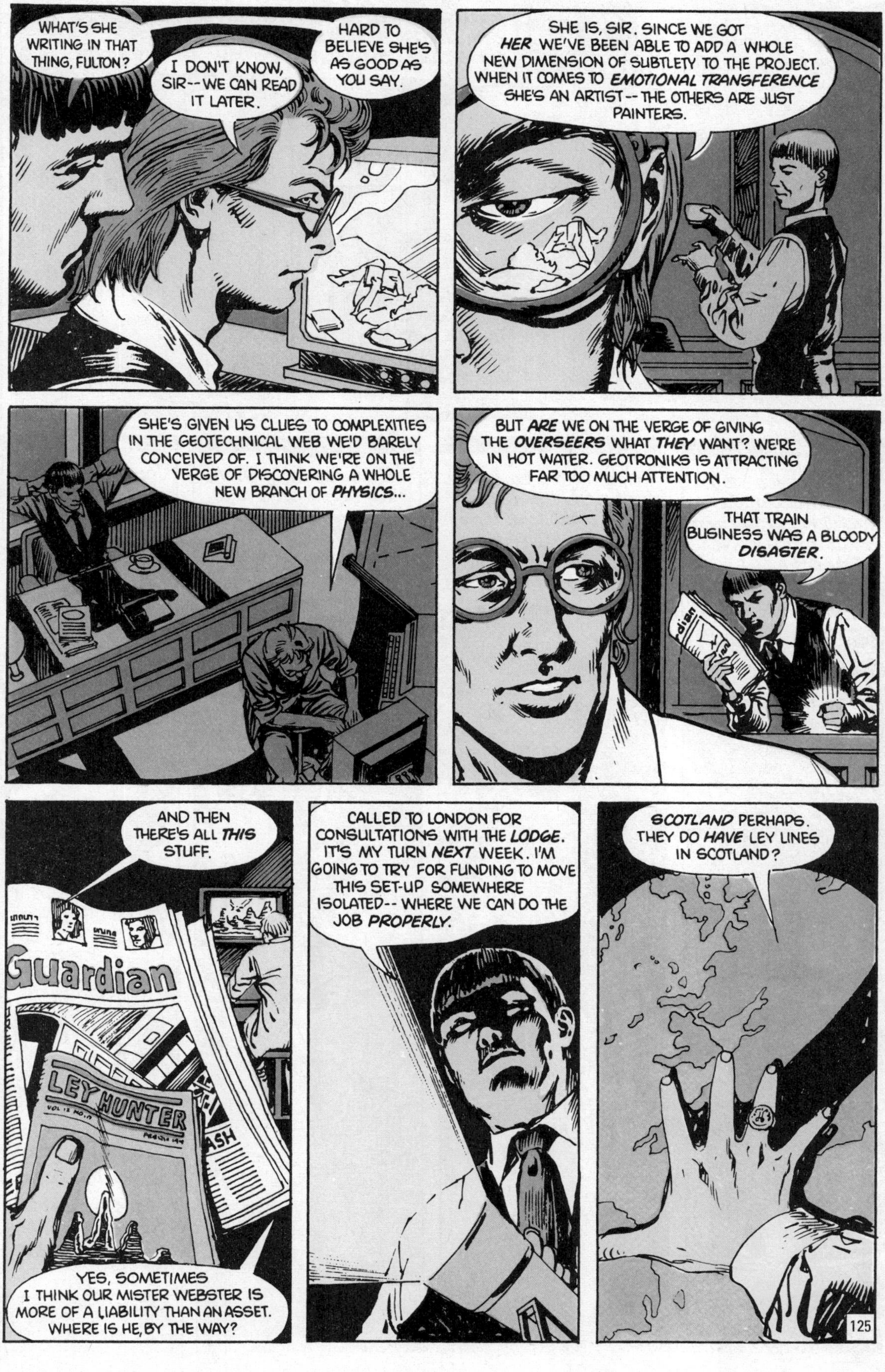

WHAT'S SHE WRITING IN THAT THING, FULTON?
I DON'T KNOW, SIR-- WE CAN READ IT LATER.
HARD TO BELIEVE SHE'S AS GOOD AS YOU SAY.
SHE IS, SIR. SINCE WE GOT HER WE'VE BEEN ABLE TO ADD A WHOLE NEW DIMENSION OF SUBTLETY TO THE PROJECT. WHEN IT COMES TO EMOTIONAL TRANSFERENCE SHE'S AN ARTIST-- THE OTHERS ARE JUST PAINTERS.
SHE'S GIVEN US CLUES TO COMPLEXITIES IN THE GEOTECHNICAL WEB WE'D BARELY CONCEIVED OF. I THINK WE'RE ON THE VERGE OF DISCOVERING A WHOLE NEW BRANCH OF PHYSICS...
BUT ARE WE ON THE VERGE OF GIVING THE OVERSEERS WHAT THEY WANT? WE'RE IN HOT WATER. GEOTRONIKS IS ATTRACTING FAR TOO MUCH ATTENTION.
THAT TRAIN BUSINESS WAS A BLOODY DISASTER.
AND THEN THERE'S ALL THIS STUFF.
Guardian
LEY HUNTER
YES, SOMETIMES I THINK OUR MISTER WEBSTER IS MORE OF A LIABILITY THAN AN ASSET. WHERE IS HE, BY THE WAY?
CALLED TO LONDON FOR CONSULTATIONS WITH THE LODGE. IT'S MY TURN NEXT WEEK. I'M GOING TO TRY FOR FUNDING TO MOVE THIS SET-UP SOMEWHERE ISOLATED-- WHERE WE CAN DO THE JOB PROPERLY.
SCOTLAND PERHAPS. THEY DO HAVE LEY LINES IN SCOTLAND?

Where are you, Marj? Where are you, John? I miss you.

The other good thing here is that they know about Ley-Lines. More than Eddy, even. They use them as a sort of machine for focusing thoughts and feelings.

That's my job -- to get the Fear out of the frightened people and put it in the trap. It's not as easy as it sounds. You need to be really talented to do it.

I only did one "scaredy" today, Old Mrs. Corbett. (That's what I call them, Scaredies. It's a bit unkind -- but it helps me be strong to make jokes.)

I leave my body in the main stone-circle and send my mind-self down a short line to where they keep the Scaredies. Then I have to slip inside their Headworlds.

They're usually too busy worrying about the Terrors to notice.

I have to chase the Terrors out of their Headworlds and into the trap.

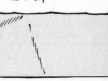

When you're part of the machine, it's like having roots instead of legs -- roots you can _see_ and _feel_ with.

They've got two indoor stone-circles here. The other one is scary. It's like a _trap_, for the Fear.

In Mrs. Corbett's Headworld, she's a little girl running through the streets of this burning city. I think it might be London.

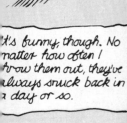

It's funny, though. No matter how often I throw them out, they've always snuck back in a day or so.

127

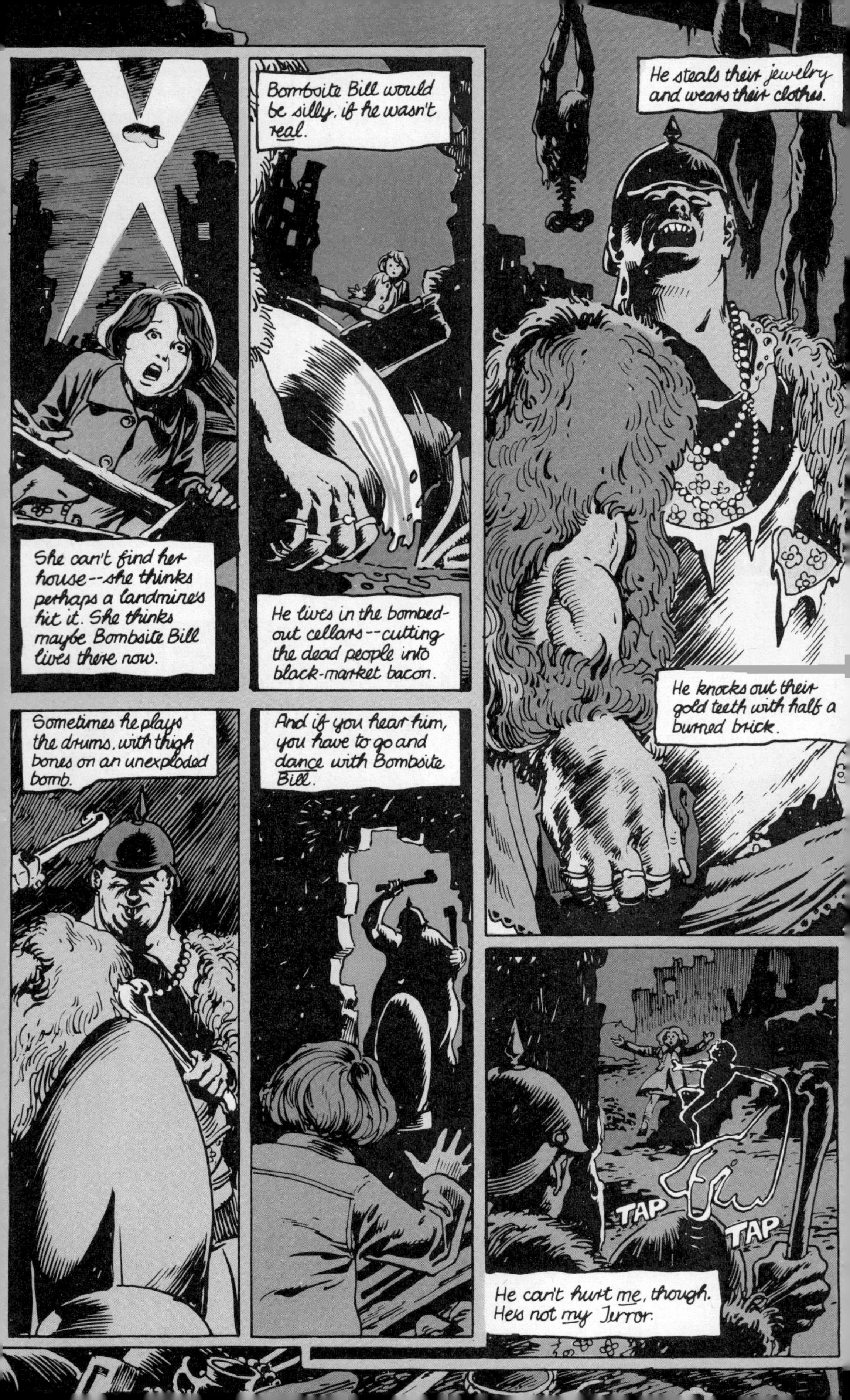

She can't find her house--she thinks perhaps a landmine's hit it. She thinks maybe Bombsite Bill lives there now.
Bombsite Bill would be silly, if he wasn't real.
He lives in the bombed-out cellars--cutting the dead people into black-market bacon.
He steals their jewelry and wears their clothes.
He knocks out their gold teeth with half a burned brick.
Sometimes he plays the drums, with thigh bones on an unexploded bomb.
And if you hear him, you have to go and dance with Bombsite Bill.
TAP
TAP
He can't hurt me, though. He's not my Terror.

To me he's just a bag of rags, tied up *ugly*.

If you don't keep your eye on him, he can surprise you and give you a bit of a fright -- but some of the others are a lot worse.

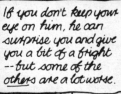

Mrs. Corbett always sleeps for at least two days after I've done her. That makes me feel really good.

Sometimes, when I throw the Terrors in the trap, I get a glimpse of something growing in there, that's when I get scared. Perhaps it's *my* Terror

People all have different Terrors. But right now, I'm too tired to tell you anymore.

So, goodnight, nosey-parker.

129

BLOKE LOOKS LIKE A *DOCTOR*. CRAZY SHOES.

ABOUT TIME HE WENT THROUGH. THOUGHT IT WAS GOING TO BE AN ALL-NIGHTER.

IT'S A BIT LATE--BUT THIS CAN'T WAIT FOR MORNING. I'VE GOT TO FIND OUT WHAT ELSE THIS BLOKE KNOWS ABOUT *GEOTRONIKS*.

AMAZING, ENNIT? BEEN LIVING ACROSS THE HALL FROM HIM FOR SIX WEEKS AND HE'S THE ONE I NEEDED ALL ALONG.

NOK! NOK!

HELLO.

'SFUNNY, THERE'S A *NOISE* BUT NO ANSWER.

HELLO... SIMON...

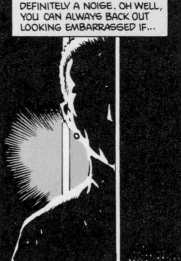

DEFINITELY A NOISE. OH WELL, YOU CAN ALWAYS BACK OUT LOOKING EMBARRASSED IF...

HMMM, MUST BE IN THE KHAZI. UNTIDY SORT--*MOST* GAYS'RE...

HELLO.

BUMP!

HE'S *NOT* IN THE KHAZI--

BUMP! BUMP!

HE'S IN THE BLOODY *WARDROBE*.

130

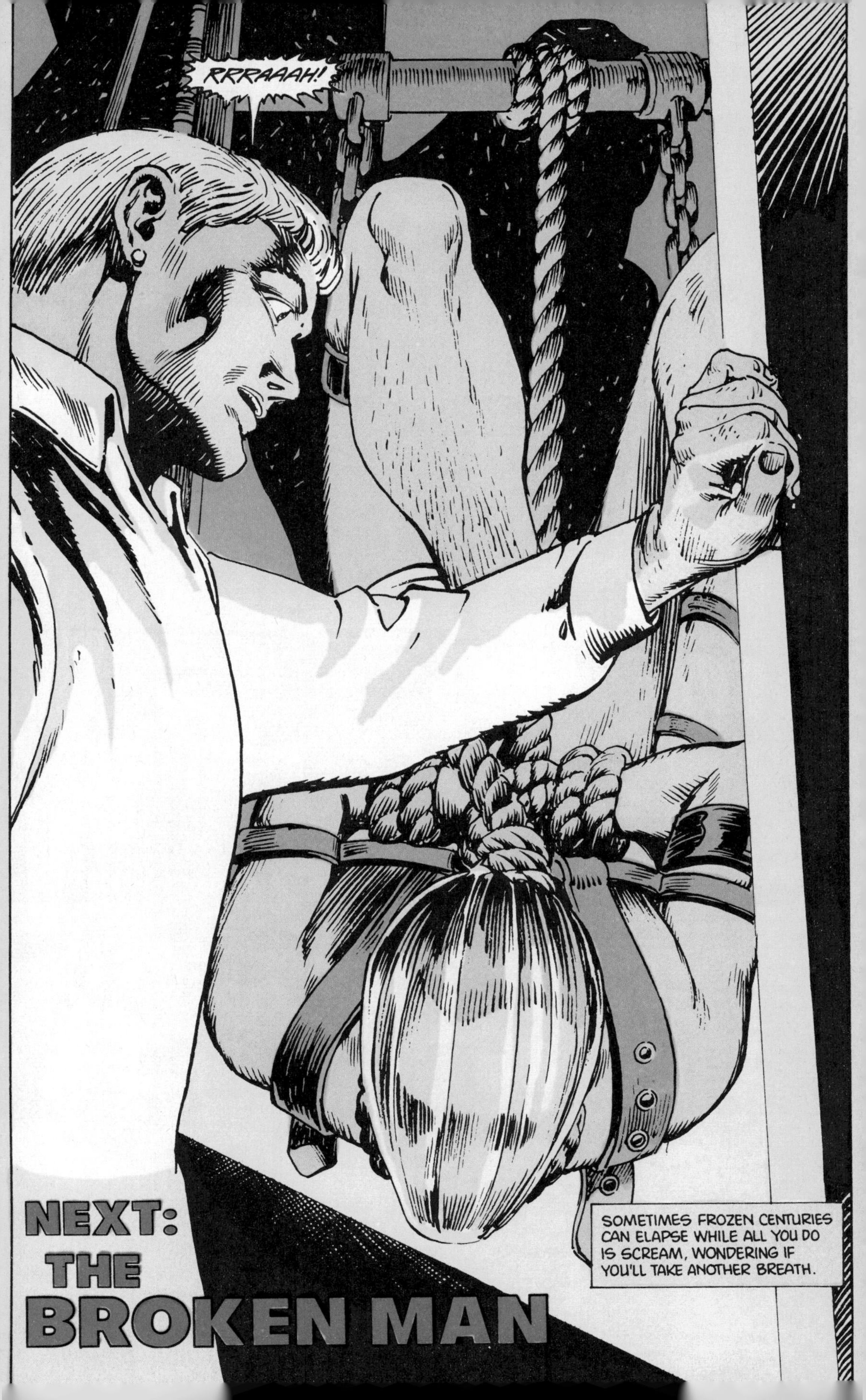
RRRAAAH!
SOMETIMES FROZEN CENTURIES CAN ELAPSE WHILE ALL YOU DO IS SCREAM, WONDERING IF YOU'LL TAKE ANOTHER BREATH.
NEXT: THE BROKEN MAN

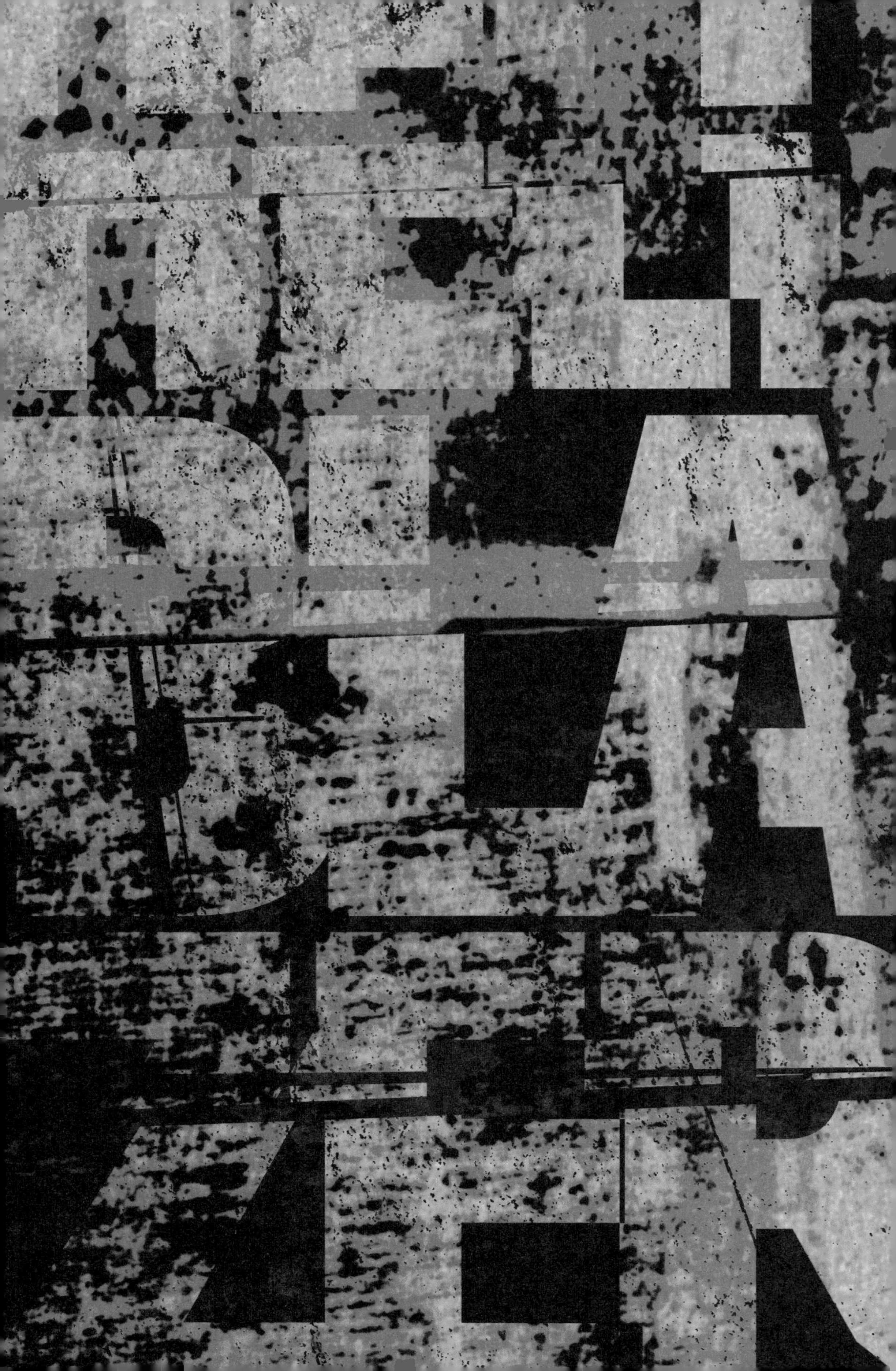

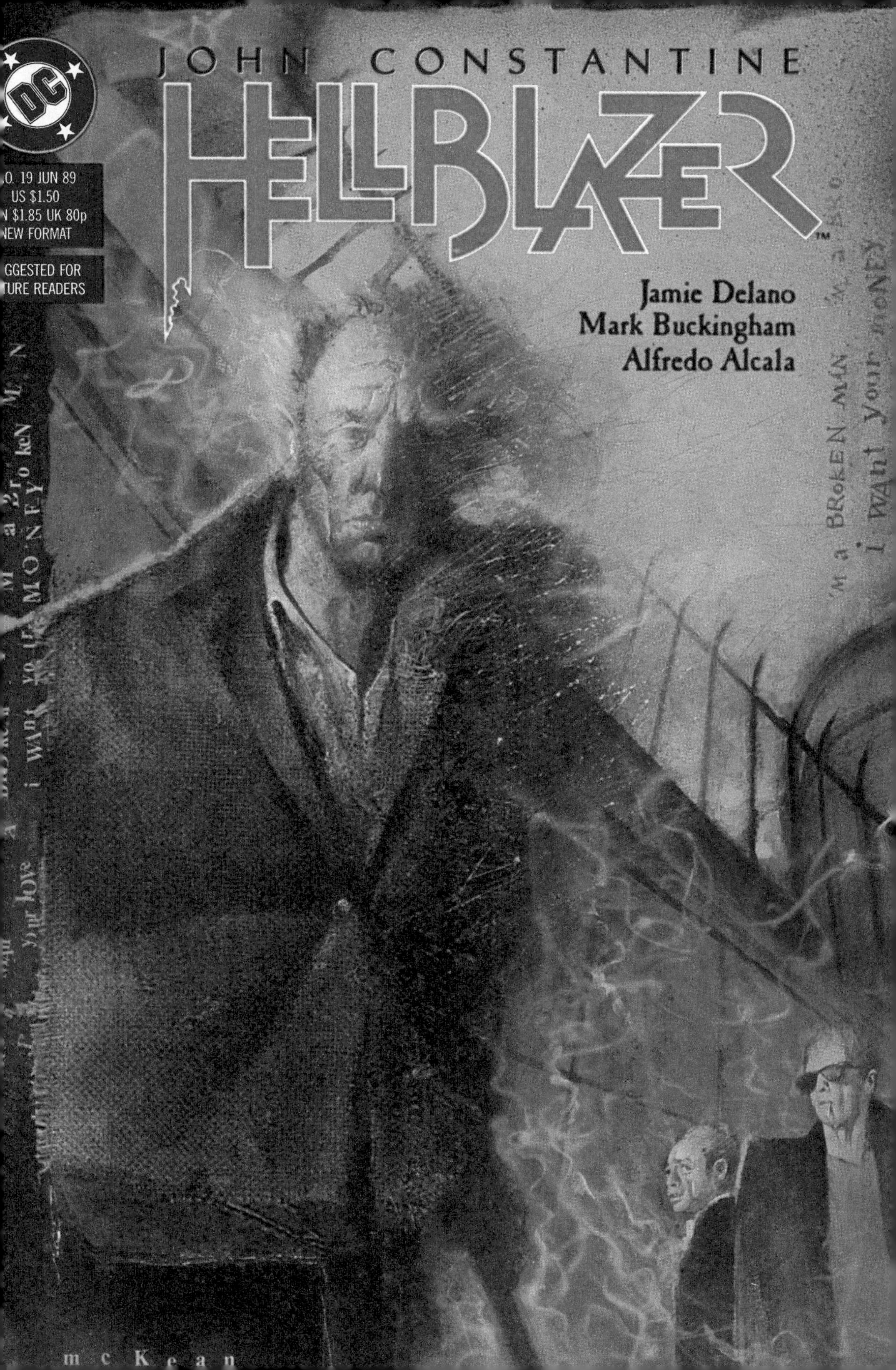

JOHN CONSTANTINE
HELLBLAZER™
O. 19 JUN 89
US $1.50
N $1.85 UK 80p
NEW FORMAT
GGESTED FOR
TURE READERS
Jamie Delano
Mark Buckingham
Alfredo Alcala
'M a BRoKEN MAN
i WANt your MoNEY
mcKean

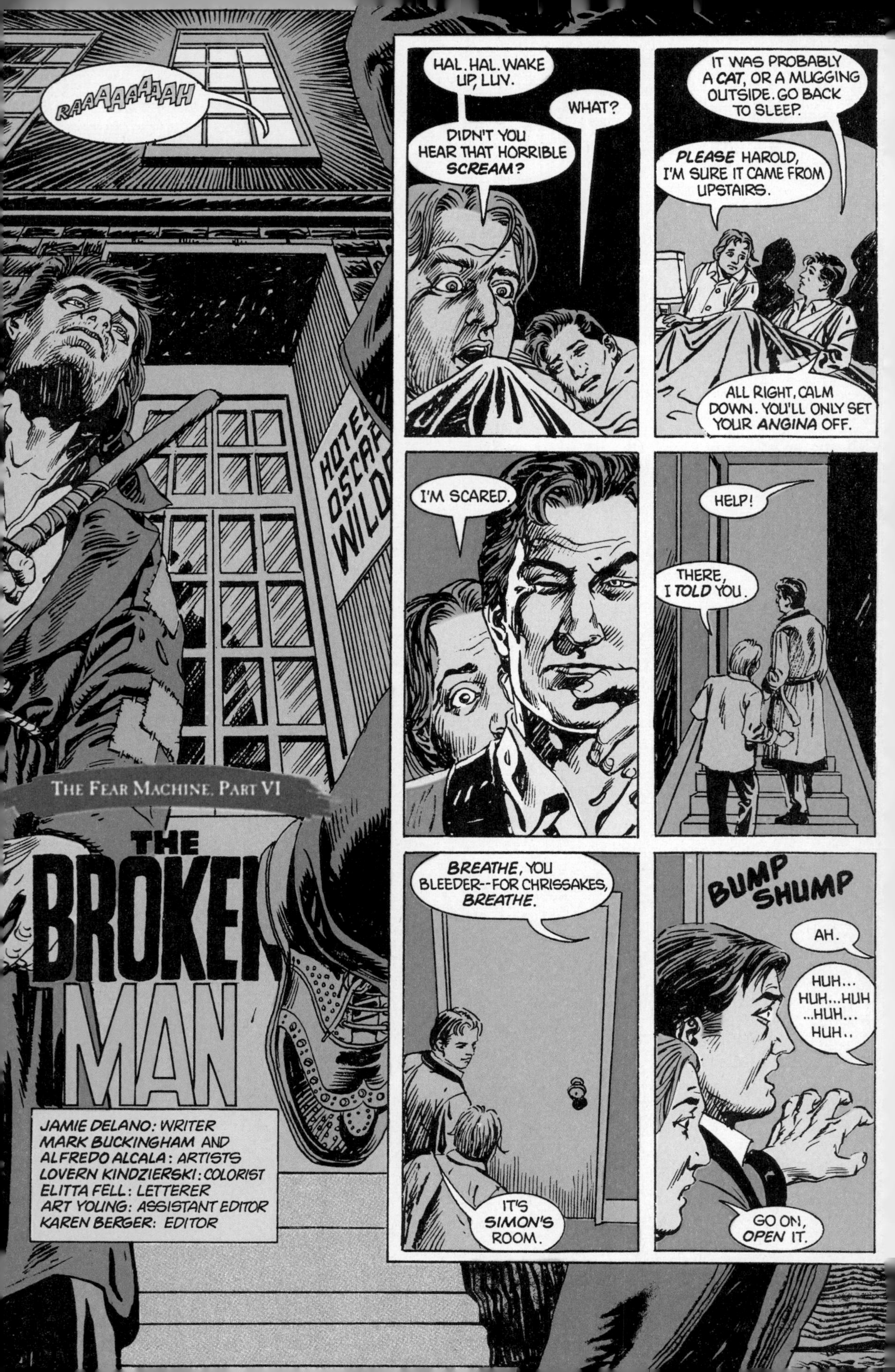
RAAAAAAAAH
HOTEL OSCAR WILDE
THE FEAR MACHINE, PART VI
THE BROKEN MAN
JAMIE DELANO: WRITER
MARK BUCKINGHAM AND
ALFREDO ALCALA: ARTISTS
LOVERN KINDZIERSKI: COLORIST
ELITTA FELL: LETTERER
ART YOUNG: ASSISTANT EDITOR
KAREN BERGER: EDITOR
HAL. HAL. WAKE UP, LUV.
WHAT?
DIDN'T YOU HEAR THAT HORRIBLE SCREAM?
IT WAS PROBABLY A CAT, OR A MUGGING OUTSIDE. GO BACK TO SLEEP.
PLEASE HAROLD, I'M SURE IT CAME FROM UPSTAIRS.
ALL RIGHT, CALM DOWN. YOU'LL ONLY SET YOUR ANGINA OFF.
I'M SCARED.
HELP!
THERE, I TOLD YOU.
BREATHE, YOU BLEEDER--FOR CHRISSAKES, BREATHE.
IT'S SIMON'S ROOM.
BUMP SHUMP
AH.
HUH... HUH...HUH ...HUH... HUH..
GO ON, OPEN IT.

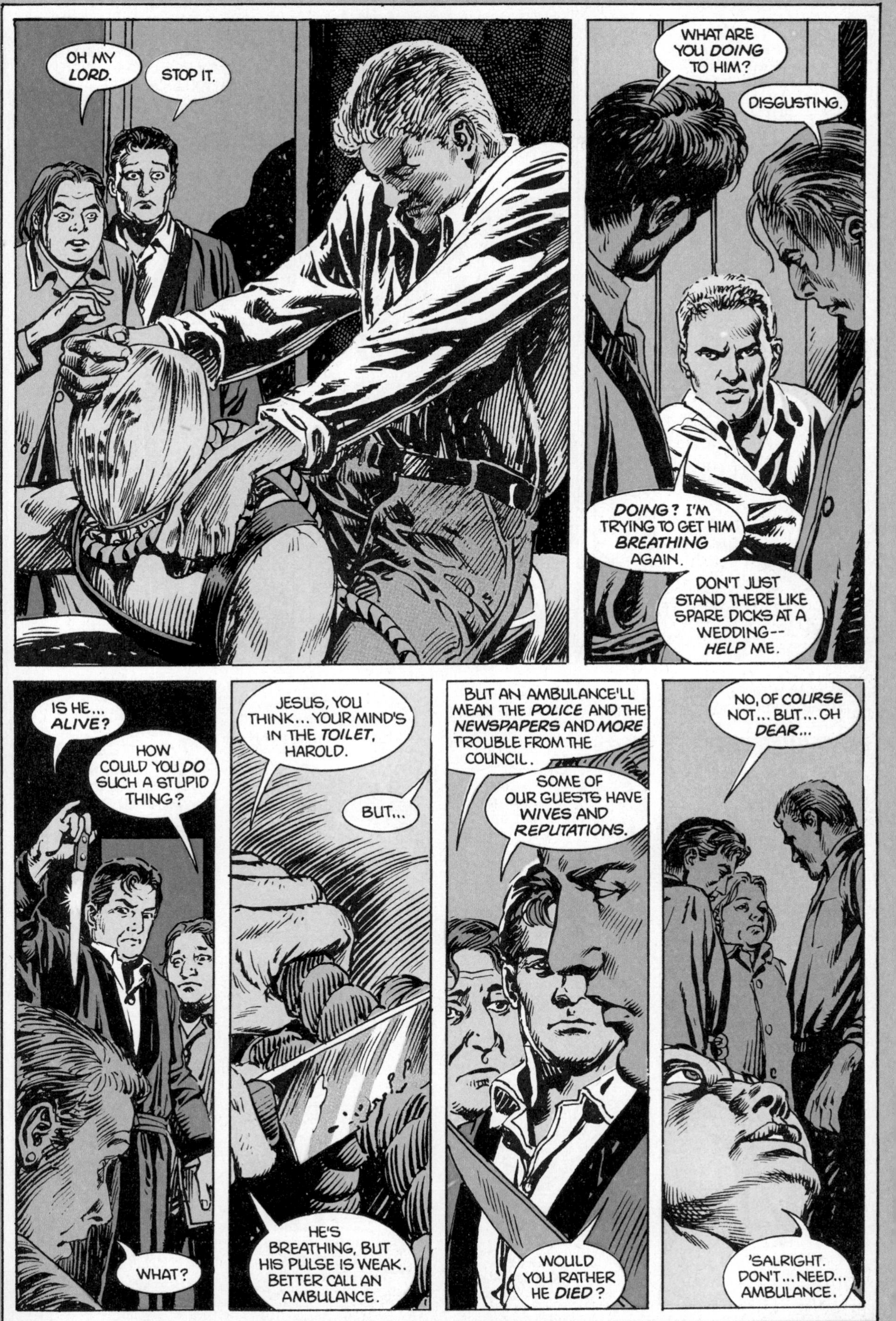
OH MY LORD.
STOP IT.
WHAT ARE YOU DOING TO HIM?
DISGUSTING.
DOING? I'M TRYING TO GET HIM BREATHING AGAIN.
DON'T JUST STAND THERE LIKE SPARE DICKS AT A WEDDING-- HELP ME.
IS HE... ALIVE?
HOW COULD YOU DO SUCH A STUPID THING?
WHAT?
JESUS, YOU THINK... YOUR MIND'S IN THE TOILET, HAROLD.
BUT...
HE'S BREATHING, BUT HIS PULSE IS WEAK. BETTER CALL AN AMBULANCE.
BUT AN AMBULANCE'LL MEAN THE POLICE AND THE NEWSPAPERS AND MORE TROUBLE FROM THE COUNCIL.
SOME OF OUR GUESTS HAVE WIVES AND REPUTATIONS.
WOULD YOU RATHER HE DIED?
NO, OF COURSE NOT... BUT... OH DEAR...
'SALRIGHT. DON'T... NEED... AMBULANCE.

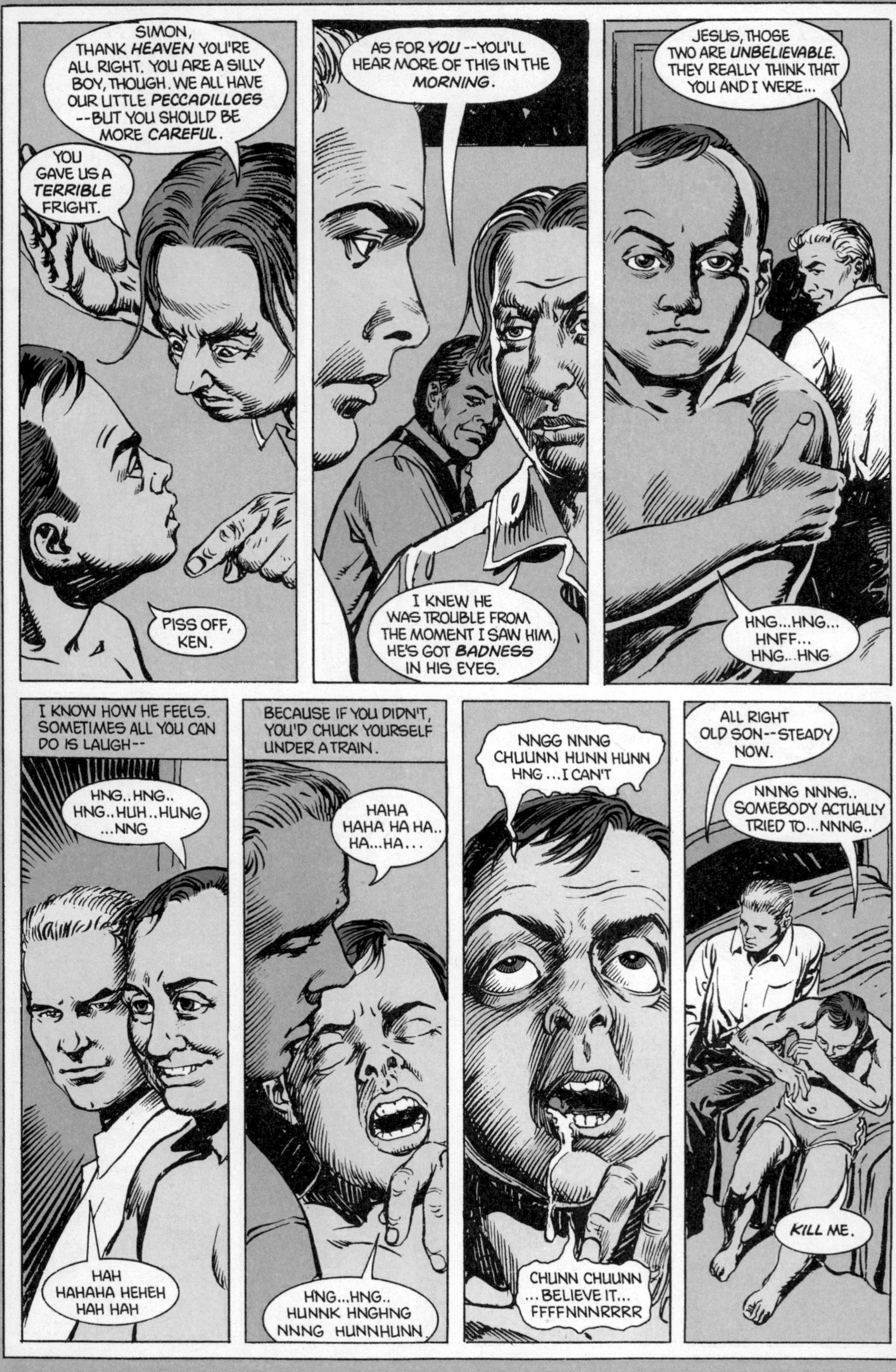
SIMON, THANK HEAVEN YOU'RE ALL RIGHT. YOU ARE A SILLY BOY, THOUGH. WE ALL HAVE OUR LITTLE PECCADILLOES --BUT YOU SHOULD BE MORE CAREFUL.
YOU GAVE US A TERRIBLE FRIGHT.
PISS OFF, KEN.
AS FOR YOU --YOU'LL HEAR MORE OF THIS IN THE MORNING.
I KNEW HE WAS TROUBLE FROM THE MOMENT I SAW HIM, HE'S GOT BADNESS IN HIS EYES.
JESUS, THOSE TWO ARE UNBELIEVABLE. THEY REALLY THINK THAT YOU AND I WERE...
HNG...HNG... HNFF... HNG...HNG
I KNOW HOW HE FEELS. SOMETIMES ALL YOU CAN DO IS LAUGH--
HNG..HNG.. HNG..HUH..HUNG ...NNG
HAH HAHAHA HEHEH HAH HAH
BECAUSE IF YOU DIDN'T, YOU'D CHUCK YOURSELF UNDER A TRAIN.
HAHA HAHA HA HA.. HA...HA...
HNG...HNG.. HUNNK HNGHNG NNNG HUNNHUNN
NNGG NNNG CHUUNN HUNN HUNN HNG ... I CAN'T
CHUNN CHUUNN ... BELIEVE IT... FFFFNNNRRRR
ALL RIGHT OLD SON--STEADY NOW.
NNNG NNNG.. SOMEBODY ACTUALLY TRIED TO...NNNG..
KILL ME.

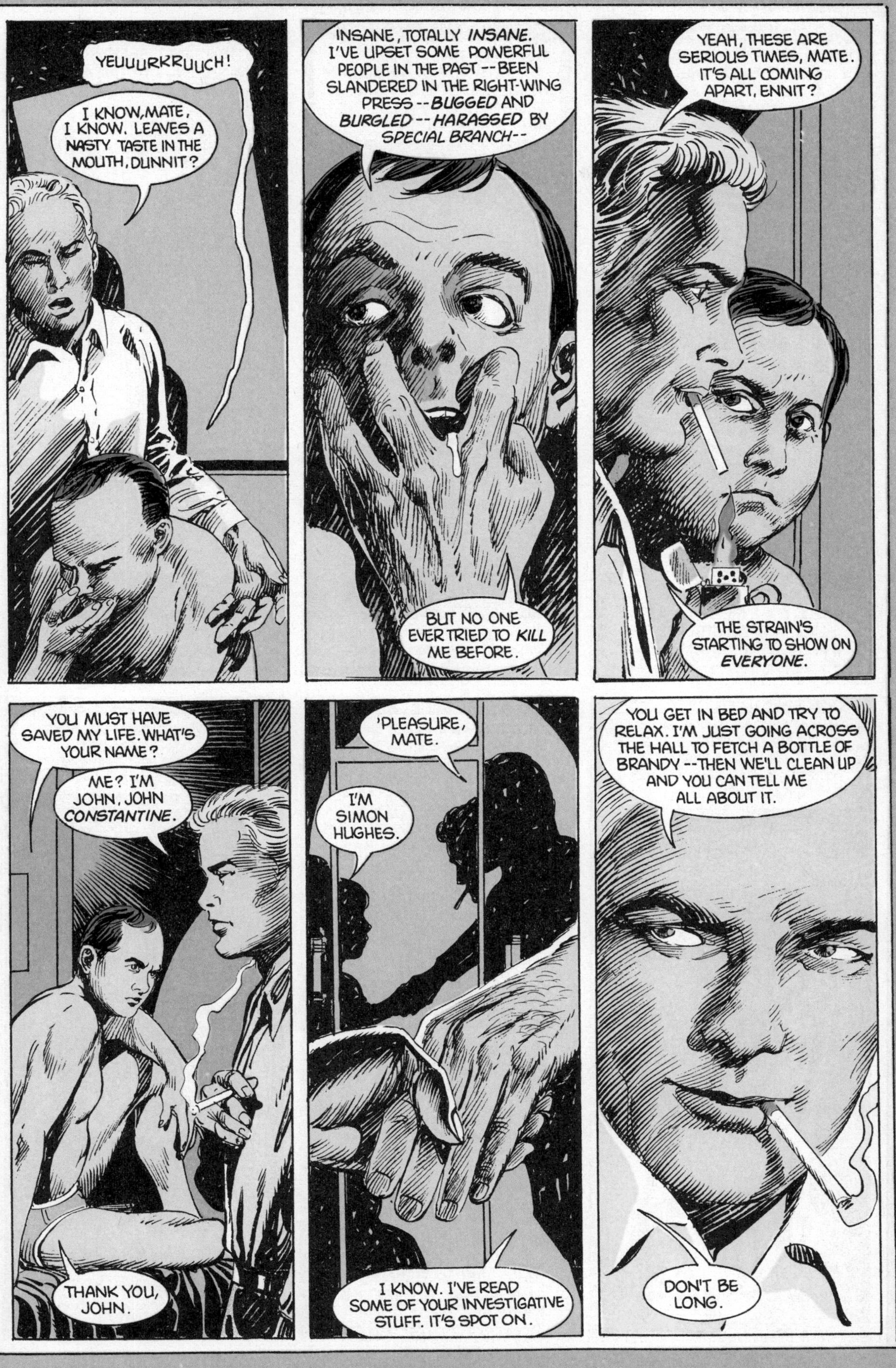
YEUUURKRUUCH!
I KNOW, MATE, I KNOW. LEAVES A NASTY TASTE IN THE MOUTH, DUNNIT?
INSANE, TOTALLY *INSANE*. I'VE UPSET SOME POWERFUL PEOPLE IN THE PAST -- BEEN SLANDERED IN THE RIGHT-WING PRESS -- *BUGGED* AND *BURGLED* -- *HARASSED* BY *SPECIAL BRANCH*--
BUT NO ONE EVER TRIED TO *KILL* ME BEFORE.
YEAH, THESE ARE SERIOUS TIMES, MATE. IT'S ALL COMING APART, ENNIT?
THE STRAIN'S STARTING TO SHOW ON *EVERYONE*.
YOU MUST HAVE SAVED MY LIFE. WHAT'S YOUR NAME?
ME? I'M JOHN, JOHN *CONSTANTINE*.
THANK YOU, JOHN.
'PLEASURE, MATE.
I'M SIMON HUGHES.
I KNOW. I'VE READ SOME OF YOUR INVESTIGATIVE STUFF. IT'S SPOT ON.
YOU GET IN BED AND TRY TO RELAX. I'M JUST GOING ACROSS THE HALL TO FETCH A BOTTLE OF BRANDY --THEN WE'LL CLEAN UP AND YOU CAN TELL ME ALL ABOUT IT.
DON'T BE LONG.

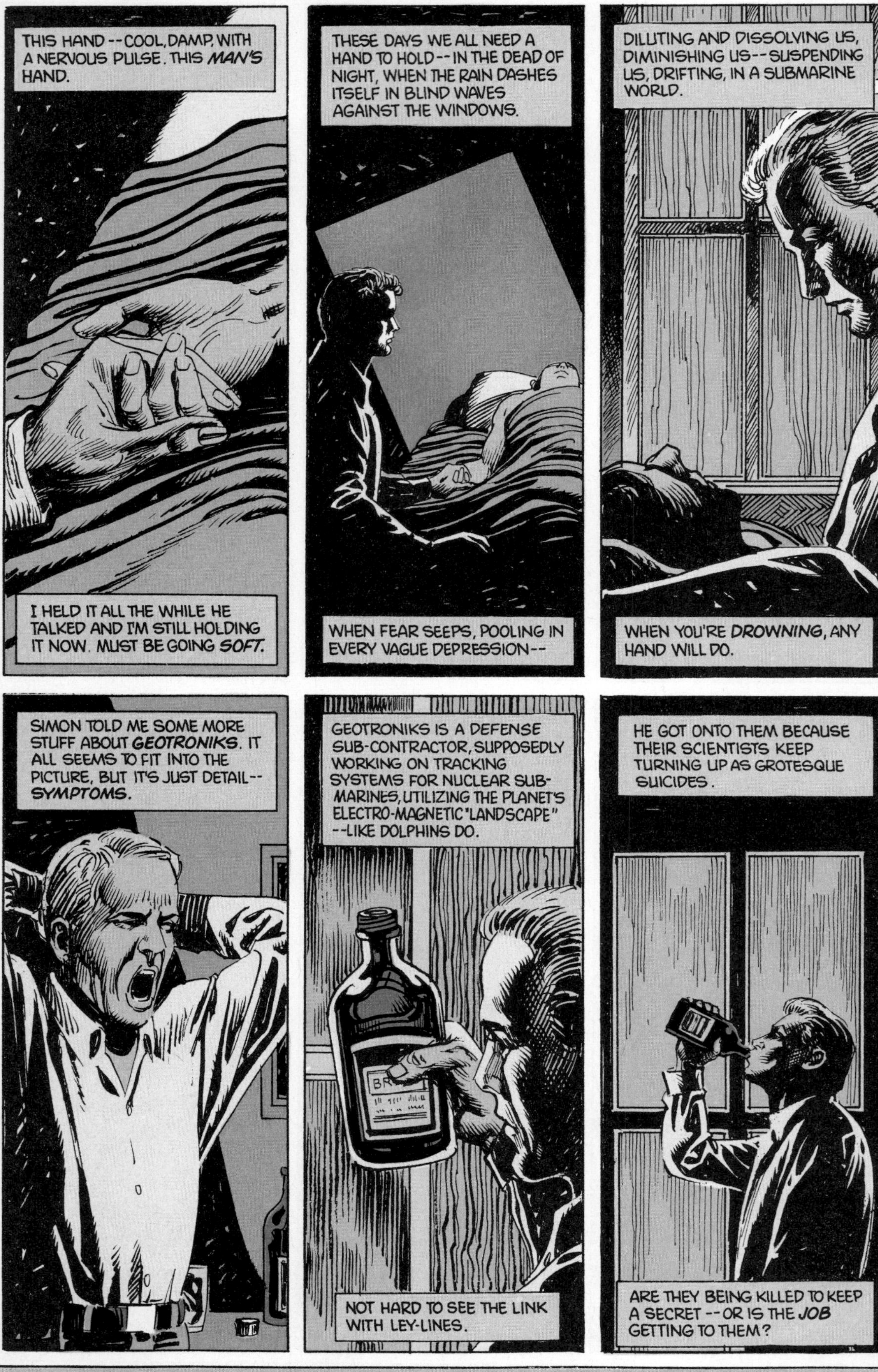
THIS HAND--COOL, DAMP, WITH A NERVOUS PULSE. THIS MAN'S HAND.
I HELD IT ALL THE WHILE HE TALKED AND I'M STILL HOLDING IT NOW. MUST BE GOING SOFT.
THESE DAYS WE ALL NEED A HAND TO HOLD--IN THE DEAD OF NIGHT, WHEN THE RAIN DASHES ITSELF IN BLIND WAVES AGAINST THE WINDOWS.
WHEN FEAR SEEPS, POOLING IN EVERY VAGUE DEPRESSION--
DILUTING AND DISSOLVING US, DIMINISHING US--SUSPENDING US, DRIFTING, IN A SUBMARINE WORLD.
WHEN YOU'RE DROWNING, ANY HAND WILL DO.
SIMON TOLD ME SOME MORE STUFF ABOUT GEOTRONIKS. IT ALL SEEMS TO FIT INTO THE PICTURE, BUT IT'S JUST DETAIL--SYMPTOMS.
GEOTRONIKS IS A DEFENSE SUB-CONTRACTOR, SUPPOSEDLY WORKING ON TRACKING SYSTEMS FOR NUCLEAR SUB-MARINES, UTILIZING THE PLANET'S ELECTRO-MAGNETIC "LANDSCAPE" --LIKE DOLPHINS DO.
NOT HARD TO SEE THE LINK WITH LEY-LINES.
HE GOT ONTO THEM BECAUSE THEIR SCIENTISTS KEEP TURNING UP AS GROTESQUE SUICIDES.
ARE THEY BEING KILLED TO KEEP A SECRET--OR IS THE JOB GETTING TO THEM?

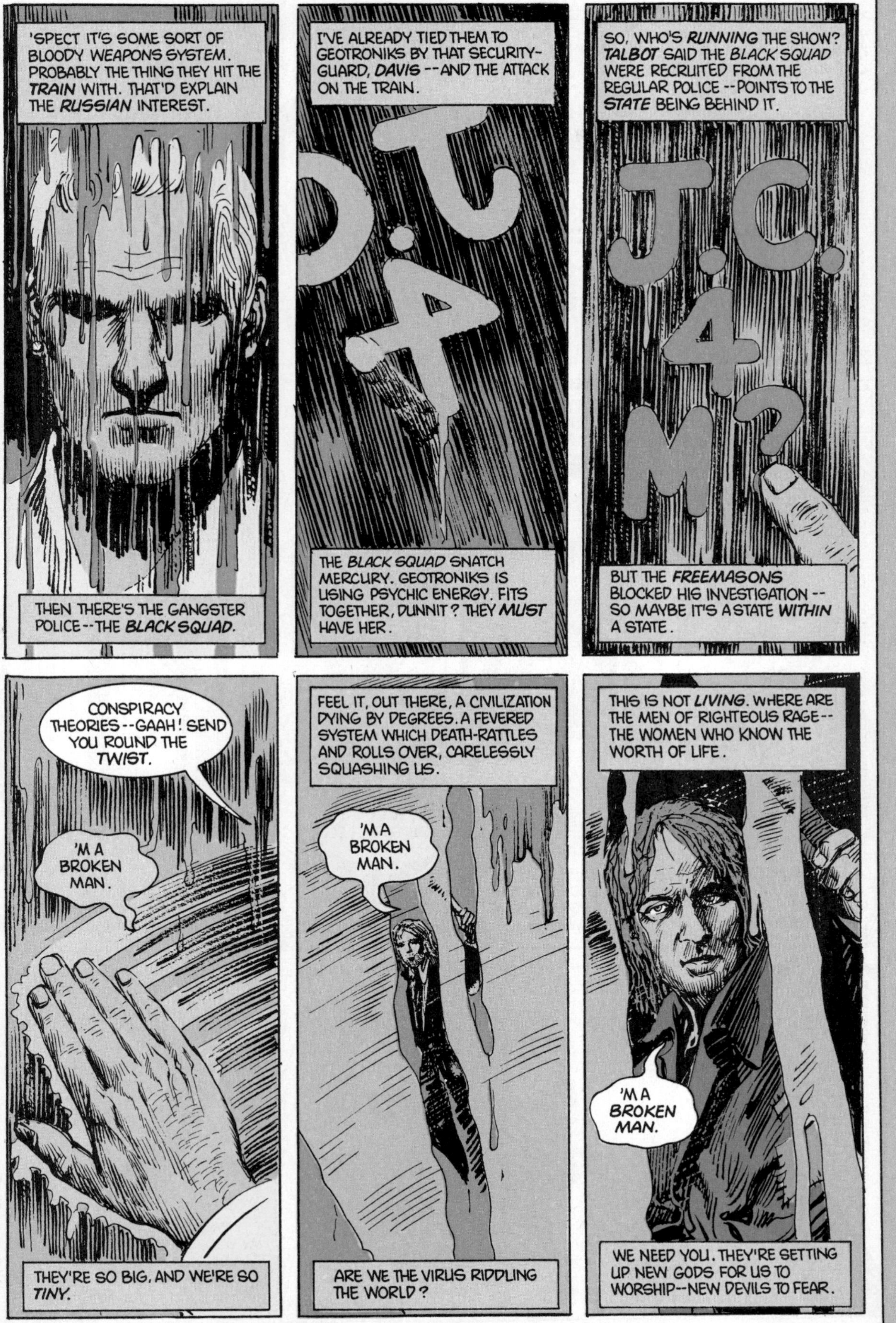
'SPECT IT'S SOME SORT OF BLOODY WEAPONS SYSTEM. PROBABLY THE THING THEY HIT THE TRAIN WITH. THAT'D EXPLAIN THE RUSSIAN INTEREST.
THEN THERE'S THE GANGSTER POLICE--THE BLACK SQUAD.
I'VE ALREADY TIED THEM TO GEOTRONIKS BY THAT SECURITY-GUARD, DAVIS--AND THE ATTACK ON THE TRAIN.
THE BLACK SQUAD SNATCH MERCURY. GEOTRONIKS IS USING PSYCHIC ENERGY. FITS TOGETHER, DUNNIT? THEY MUST HAVE HER.
SO, WHO'S RUNNING THE SHOW? TALBOT SAID THE BLACK SQUAD WERE RECRUITED FROM THE REGULAR POLICE--POINTS TO THE STATE BEING BEHIND IT.
J.C. 4 M?
BUT THE FREEMASONS BLOCKED HIS INVESTIGATION--SO MAYBE IT'S A STATE WITHIN A STATE.
CONSPIRACY THEORIES--GAAH! SEND YOU ROUND THE TWIST.
'M A BROKEN MAN.
THEY'RE SO BIG, AND WE'RE SO TINY.
FEEL IT, OUT THERE, A CIVILIZATION DYING BY DEGREES. A FEVERED SYSTEM WHICH DEATH-RATTLES AND ROLLS OVER, CARELESSLY SQUASHING US.
'M A BROKEN MAN.
ARE WE THE VIRUS RIDDLING THE WORLD?
THIS IS NOT LIVING. WHERE ARE THE MEN OF RIGHTEOUS RAGE--THE WOMEN WHO KNOW THE WORTH OF LIFE.
'M A BROKEN MAN.
WE NEED YOU. THEY'RE SETTING UP NEW GODS FOR US TO WORSHIP--NEW DEVILS TO FEAR.

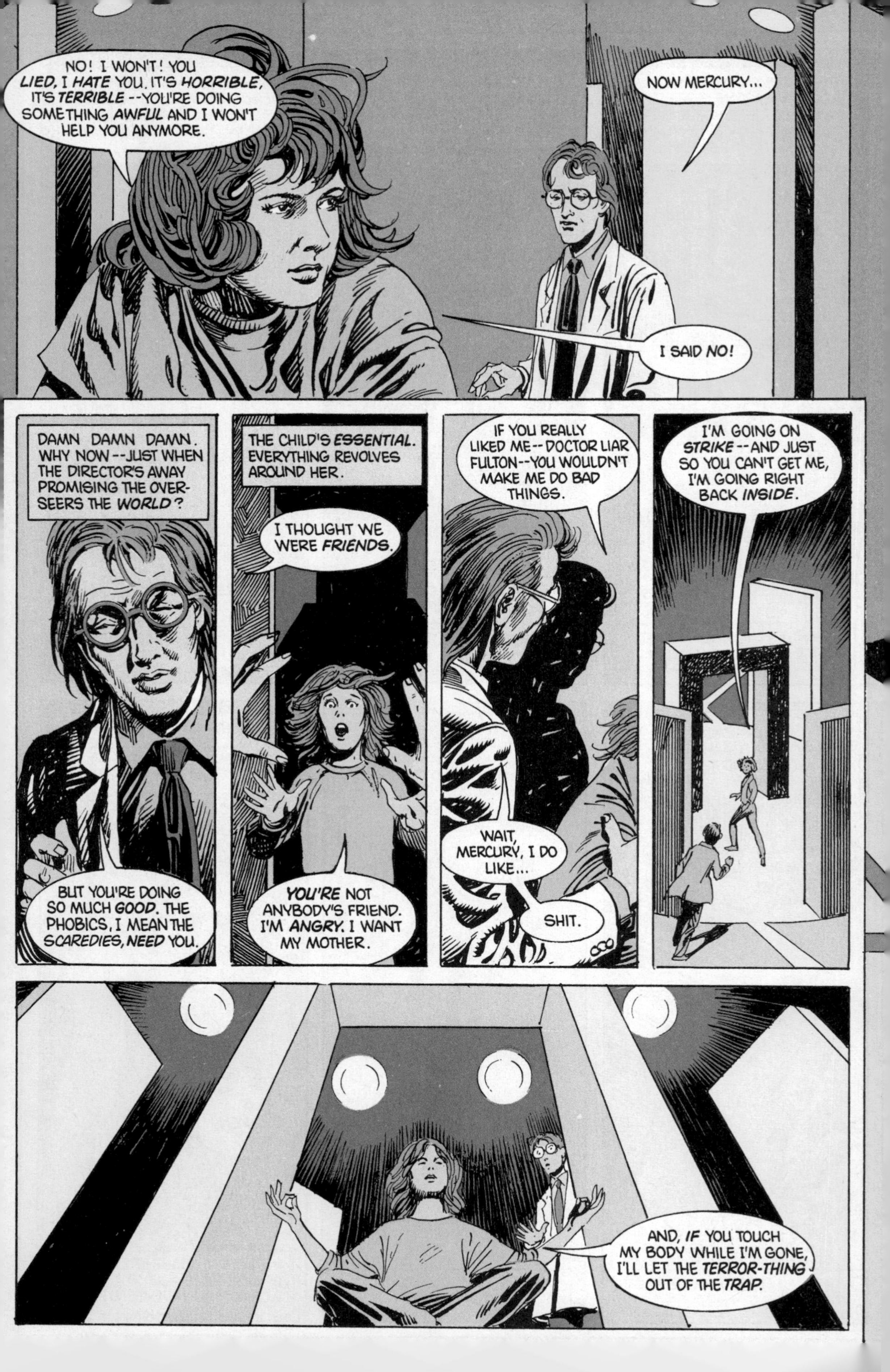
NO! I WON'T! YOU LIED, I HATE YOU. IT'S HORRIBLE, IT'S TERRIBLE--YOU'RE DOING SOMETHING AWFUL AND I WON'T HELP YOU ANYMORE.
NOW MERCURY...
I SAID NO!
DAMN DAMN DAMN. WHY NOW--JUST WHEN THE DIRECTOR'S AWAY PROMISING THE OVERSEERS THE WORLD?
BUT YOU'RE DOING SO MUCH GOOD. THE PHOBICS, I MEAN THE SCAREDIES, NEED YOU.
THE CHILD'S ESSENTIAL. EVERYTHING REVOLVES AROUND HER.
I THOUGHT WE WERE FRIENDS.
YOU'RE NOT ANYBODY'S FRIEND. I'M ANGRY. I WANT MY MOTHER.
IF YOU REALLY LIKED ME--DOCTOR LIAR FULTON--YOU WOULDN'T MAKE ME DO BAD THINGS.
WAIT, MERCURY, I DO LIKE...
SHIT.
I'M GOING ON STRIKE--AND JUST SO YOU CAN'T GET ME, I'M GOING RIGHT BACK INSIDE.
AND, IF YOU TOUCH MY BODY WHILE I'M GONE, I'LL LET THE TERROR-THING OUT OF THE TRAP.

WHY? WHAT'S PROVOKED THIS SUDDEN REBELLION? WITHOUT MERCURY, THE PHASE TWO *FEAR MACHINE* WOULD BE A NON-STARTER.

HE'D THOUGHT THAT ALL HIS CAREFUL WORK HAD PAID OFF --THAT SHE'D BEGUN TO *TRUST* HIM.

LITTLE *COW!*

HER REJECTION IS LIKE A SLAP IN THE FACE. HE *NEEDED* THAT TRUST -- *WANTED* IT. UNTIL NOW HE HADN'T UNDERSTOOD HOW *MUCH.*

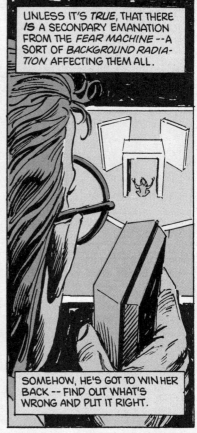

UNLESS IT'S *TRUE,* THAT THERE *IS* A SECONDARY EMANATION FROM THE *FEAR MACHINE* --A SORT OF *BACKGROUND RADIATION* AFFECTING THEM ALL.

SOMEHOW, HE'S GOT TO WIN HER BACK -- FIND OUT WHAT'S WRONG AND PUT IT RIGHT.

IN THE MEANTIME, *BEALE'S* MEN COULD BE TRYING TO FIND HER MOTHER.

TRANSFERENCE OPS

T.O/1988/9

SHE'D BEEN FINE WHEN SHE'D STARTED THIS MORNING'S PROGRAM. SOMETHING HAD HAPPENED WHILE SHE WAS OUT OF HER BODY IN THE SYSTEM. HE'LL HAVE TO REVIEW THE TAPES.

TRANQUILIZER

BUT BEFORE HE CAN PRESS THE BUTTONS, HE NEEDS ANOTHER TRANQ TO STOP HIS HANDS FROM SHAKING.

MUST BE WORKING TOO HARD.

THAT'S WHAT *SISKIN* HAD SAID.

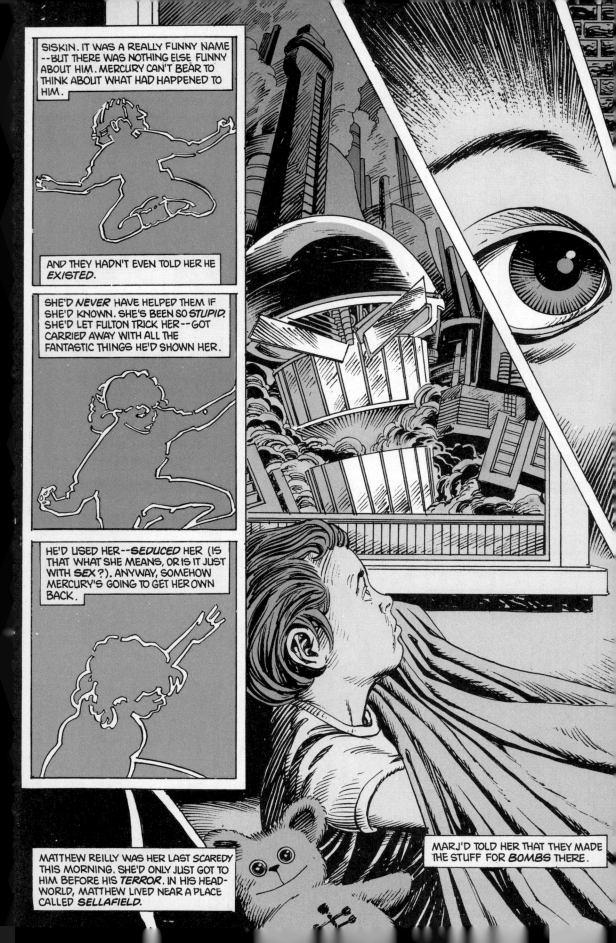

SISKIN. IT WAS A REALLY FUNNY NAME --BUT THERE WAS NOTHING ELSE FUNNY ABOUT HIM. MERCURY CAN'T BEAR TO THINK ABOUT WHAT HAD HAPPENED TO HIM.

AND THEY HADN'T EVEN TOLD HER HE *EXISTED*.

SHE'D *NEVER* HAVE HELPED THEM IF SHE'D KNOWN. SHE'S BEEN SO *STUPID*. SHE'D LET FULTON TRICK HER--GOT CARRIED AWAY WITH ALL THE FANTASTIC THINGS HE'D SHOWN HER.

HE'D USED HER--*SEDUCED* HER (IS THAT WHAT SHE MEANS, OR IS IT JUST WITH *SEX*?). ANYWAY, SOMEHOW MERCURY'S GOING TO GET HER OWN BACK.

MATTHEW REILLY WAS HER LAST *SCAREDY* THIS MORNING. SHE'D ONLY JUST GOT TO HIM BEFORE HIS *TERROR*. IN HIS HEAD-WORLD, MATTHEW LIVED NEAR A PLACE CALLED *SELLAFIELD*.

MARJ'D TOLD HER THAT THEY MADE THE STUFF FOR *BOMBS* THERE.

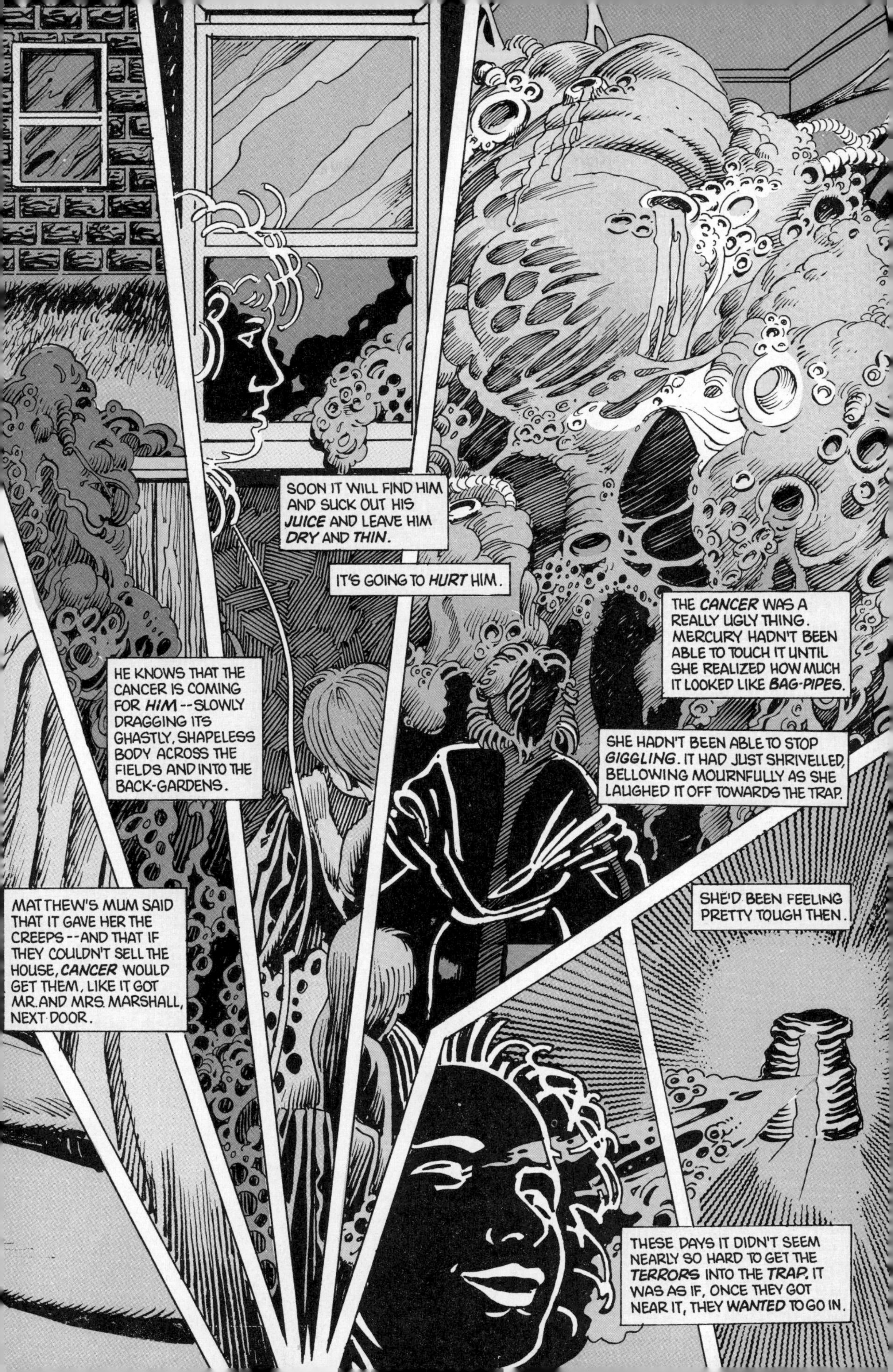
MATTHEW'S MUM SAID THAT IT GAVE HER THE CREEPS--AND THAT IF THEY COULDN'T SELL THE HOUSE, CANCER WOULD GET THEM, LIKE IT GOT MR. AND MRS. MARSHALL, NEXT DOOR.
HE KNOWS THAT THE CANCER IS COMING FOR HIM--SLOWLY DRAGGING ITS GHASTLY, SHAPELESS BODY ACROSS THE FIELDS AND INTO THE BACK-GARDENS.
SOON IT WILL FIND HIM AND SUCK OUT HIS JUICE AND LEAVE HIM DRY AND THIN.
IT'S GOING TO HURT HIM.
THE CANCER WAS A REALLY UGLY THING. MERCURY HADN'T BEEN ABLE TO TOUCH IT UNTIL SHE REALIZED HOW MUCH IT LOOKED LIKE BAG-PIPES.
SHE HADN'T BEEN ABLE TO STOP GIGGLING. IT HAD JUST SHRIVELLED, BELLOWING MOURNFULLY AS SHE LAUGHED IT OFF TOWARDS THE TRAP.
SHE'D BEEN FEELING PRETTY TOUGH THEN.
THESE DAYS IT DIDN'T SEEM NEARLY SO HARD TO GET THE TERRORS INTO THE TRAP. IT WAS AS IF, ONCE THEY GOT NEAR IT, THEY WANTED TO GO IN.

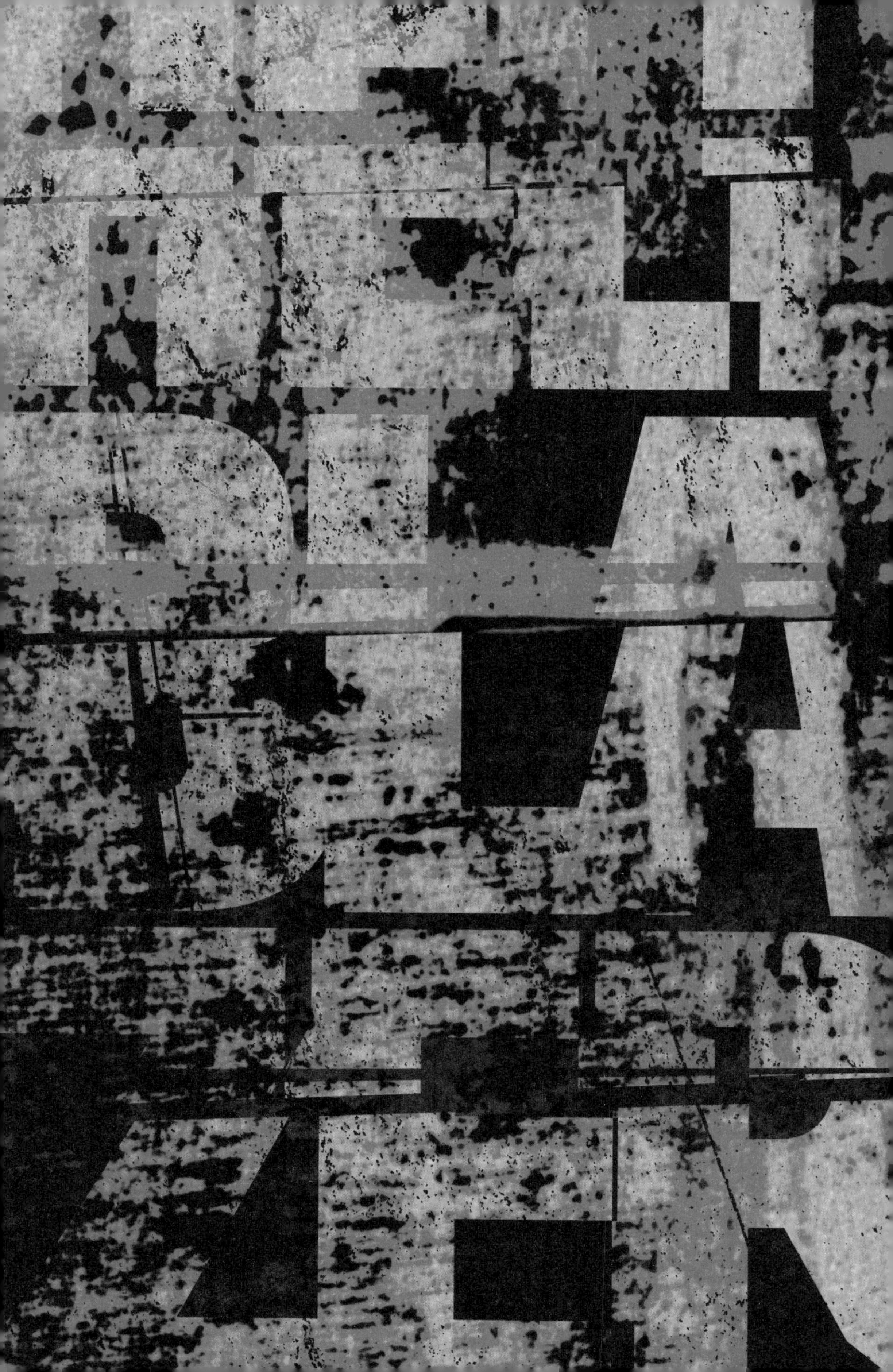

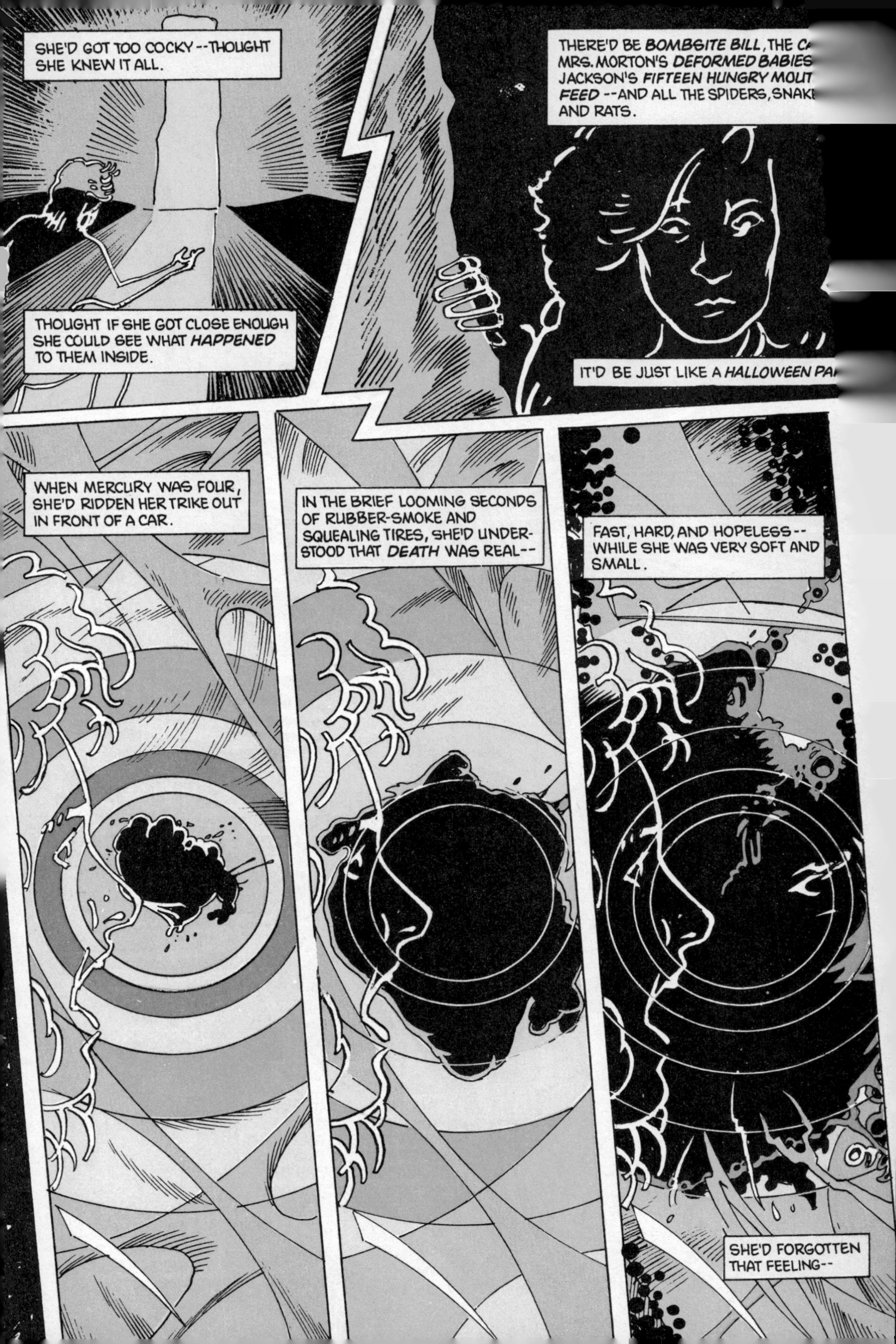
SHE'D GOT TOO COCKY --THOUGHT SHE KNEW IT ALL.
THOUGHT IF SHE GOT CLOSE ENOUGH SHE COULD SEE WHAT HAPPENED TO THEM INSIDE.
THERE'D BE BOMBSITE BILL, THE CA MRS. MORTON'S DEFORMED BABIES JACKSON'S FIFTEEN HUNGRY MOUT FEED --AND ALL THE SPIDERS, SNAKE AND RATS.
IT'D BE JUST LIKE A HALLOWEEN PA
WHEN MERCURY WAS FOUR, SHE'D RIDDEN HER TRIKE OUT IN FRONT OF A CAR.
IN THE BRIEF LOOMING SECONDS OF RUBBER-SMOKE AND SQUEALING TIRES, SHE'D UNDERSTOOD THAT DEATH WAS REAL--
FAST, HARD, AND HOPELESS-- WHILE SHE WAS VERY SOFT AND SMALL.
SHE'D FORGOTTEN THAT FEELING--

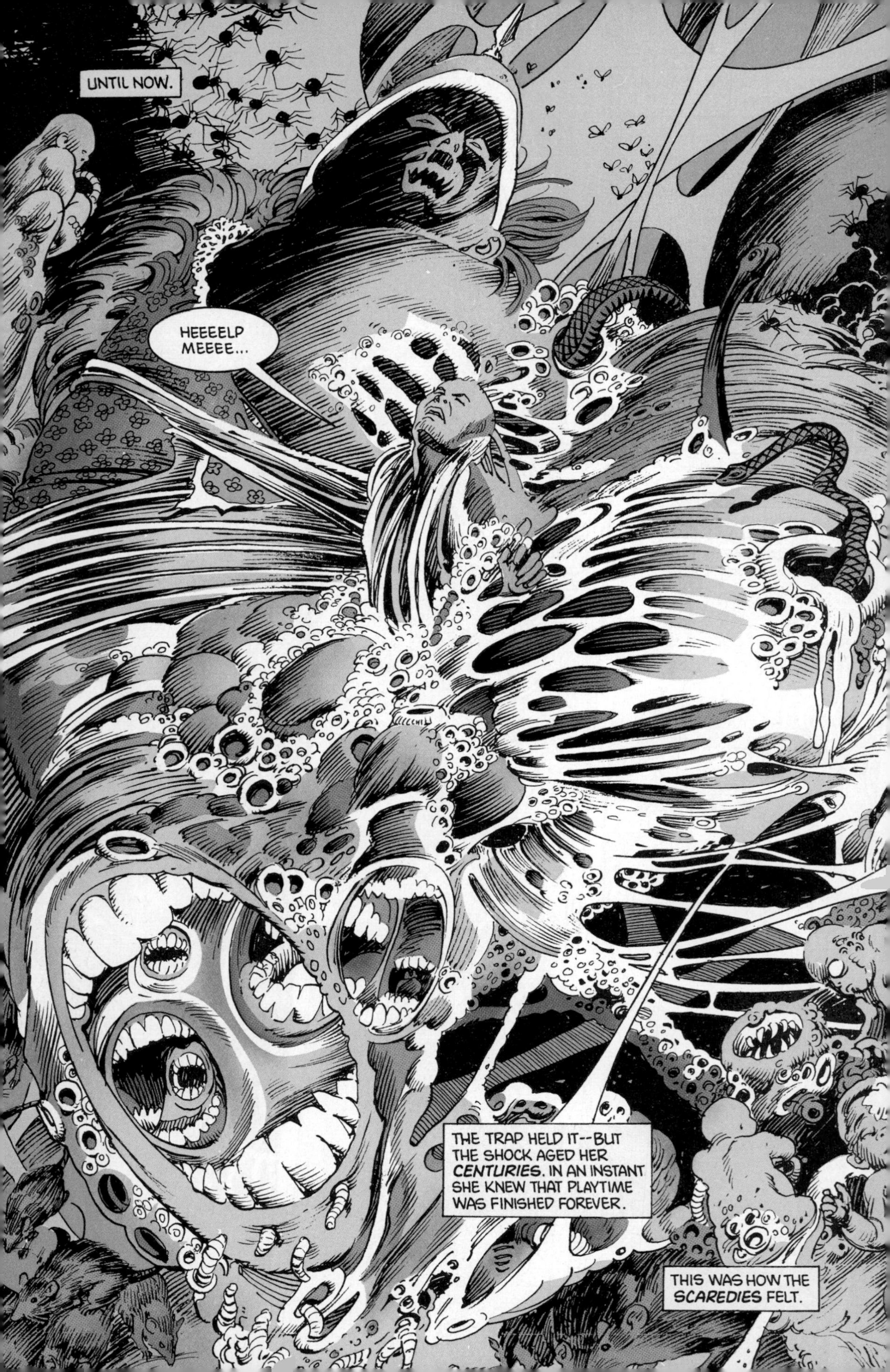
UNTIL NOW.
HEEEELP MEEEE...
THE TRAP HELD IT--BUT THE SHOCK AGED HER CENTURIES. IN AN INSTANT SHE KNEW THAT PLAYTIME WAS FINISHED FOREVER.
THIS WAS HOW THE SCAREDIES FELT.

THE RECORDINGS ALL LOOK NORMAL --SHOWING HIGH ALPHA-WAVE ACTIVITY ON BOTH THE PHOBICS THAT MERCURY *MILKED"THIS MORNING.

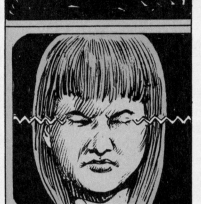

FIRST, THE PHANTOM PREGNANCY WOMAN, MORTON.

THEN THE BOY, REILLY--NOTHING STRANGE THERE, EITHER.

BUT WAIT, HERE'S THE ANOMALY. VIOLENT BRAIN ACTIVITY FROM *SISKIN.*

AMAZING, HE'S BEEN CATATONIC SINCE THEY BURNED HIM OUT ON THE WYKES VALLEY TEST.

SOMEHOW THE GIRL MUST HAVE *ACCESSED* HIM. WHAT DOES IT MEAN? CAN SHE *TALK* WITH THEM IN THERE?

WHAT WOULD HE HAVE TOLD HER IF SHE HAD?

THEY KNOW SO LITTLE. THEY'RE GOING TOO FAST. IT'S LIKE THE EARLY DAYS OF NUCLEAR PHYSICS. THEY'RE TRYING TO USE SOME-THING THEY DON'T UNDERSTAND --AND IT'S RUNNING AWAY WITH THEM.

NOW MERCURY'S RUN AWAY AS WELL. THEY SHOULD SHUT IT ALL DOWN, MOVE THE LOT AND START AGAIN--LIKE THE DIRECTOR SAID.

BUT THEY CAN'T EVEN DO THAT UNTIL THE GIRL COMES OUT OF HIDING.

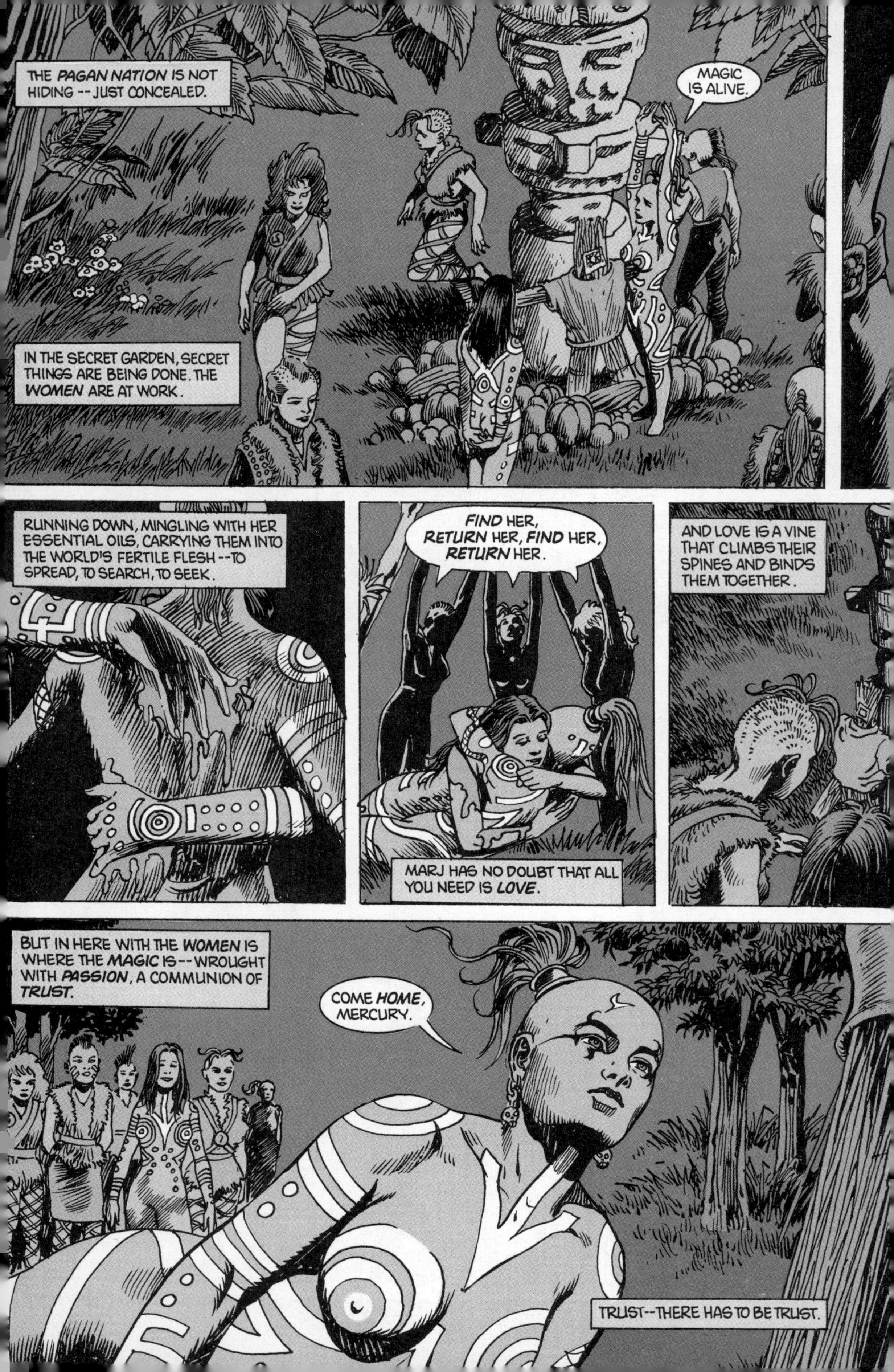

THE *PAGAN NATION* IS NOT HIDING -- JUST CONCEALED.
MAGIC IS ALIVE.
IN THE SECRET GARDEN, SECRET THINGS ARE BEING DONE. THE *WOMEN* ARE AT WORK.
RUNNING DOWN, MINGLING WITH HER ESSENTIAL OILS, CARRYING THEM INTO THE WORLD'S FERTILE FLESH -- TO SPREAD, TO SEARCH, TO SEEK.
FIND HER, *RETURN* HER, *FIND* HER, *RETURN* HER.
MARJ HAS NO DOUBT THAT ALL YOU NEED IS *LOVE*.
AND LOVE IS A VINE THAT CLIMBS THEIR SPINES AND BINDS THEM TOGETHER.
BUT IN HERE WITH THE *WOMEN* IS WHERE THE *MAGIC* IS -- WROUGHT WITH *PASSION*, A COMMUNION OF *TRUST*.
COME *HOME*, MERCURY.
TRUST -- THERE HAS TO BE TRUST.

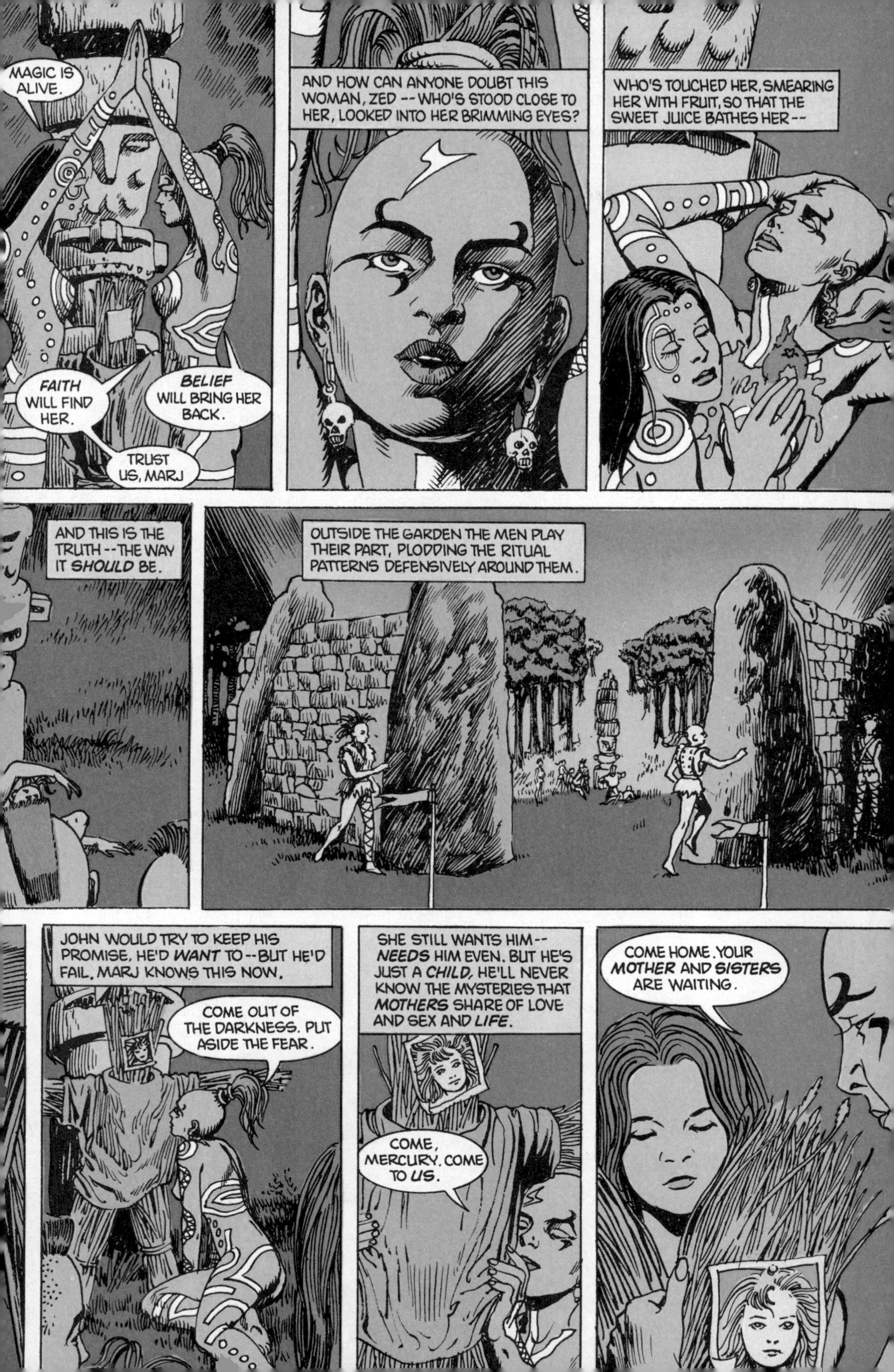
MAGIC IS ALIVE.
FAITH WILL FIND HER.
BELIEF WILL BRING HER BACK.
TRUST US, MARJ
AND HOW CAN ANYONE DOUBT THIS WOMAN, ZED -- WHO'S STOOD CLOSE TO HER, LOOKED INTO HER BRIMMING EYES?
WHO'S TOUCHED HER, SMEARING HER WITH FRUIT, SO THAT THE SWEET JUICE BATHES HER --
AND THIS IS THE TRUTH -- THE WAY IT SHOULD BE.
OUTSIDE THE GARDEN THE MEN PLAY THEIR PART, PLODDING THE RITUAL PATTERNS DEFENSIVELY AROUND THEM.
JOHN WOULD TRY TO KEEP HIS PROMISE. HE'D WANT TO -- BUT HE'D FAIL. MARJ KNOWS THIS NOW.
COME OUT OF THE DARKNESS. PUT ASIDE THE FEAR.
SHE STILL WANTS HIM -- NEEDS HIM EVEN. BUT HE'S JUST A CHILD, HE'LL NEVER KNOW THE MYSTERIES THAT MOTHERS SHARE OF LOVE AND SEX AND LIFE.
COME, MERCURY. COME TO US.
COME HOME. YOUR MOTHER AND SISTERS ARE WAITING.

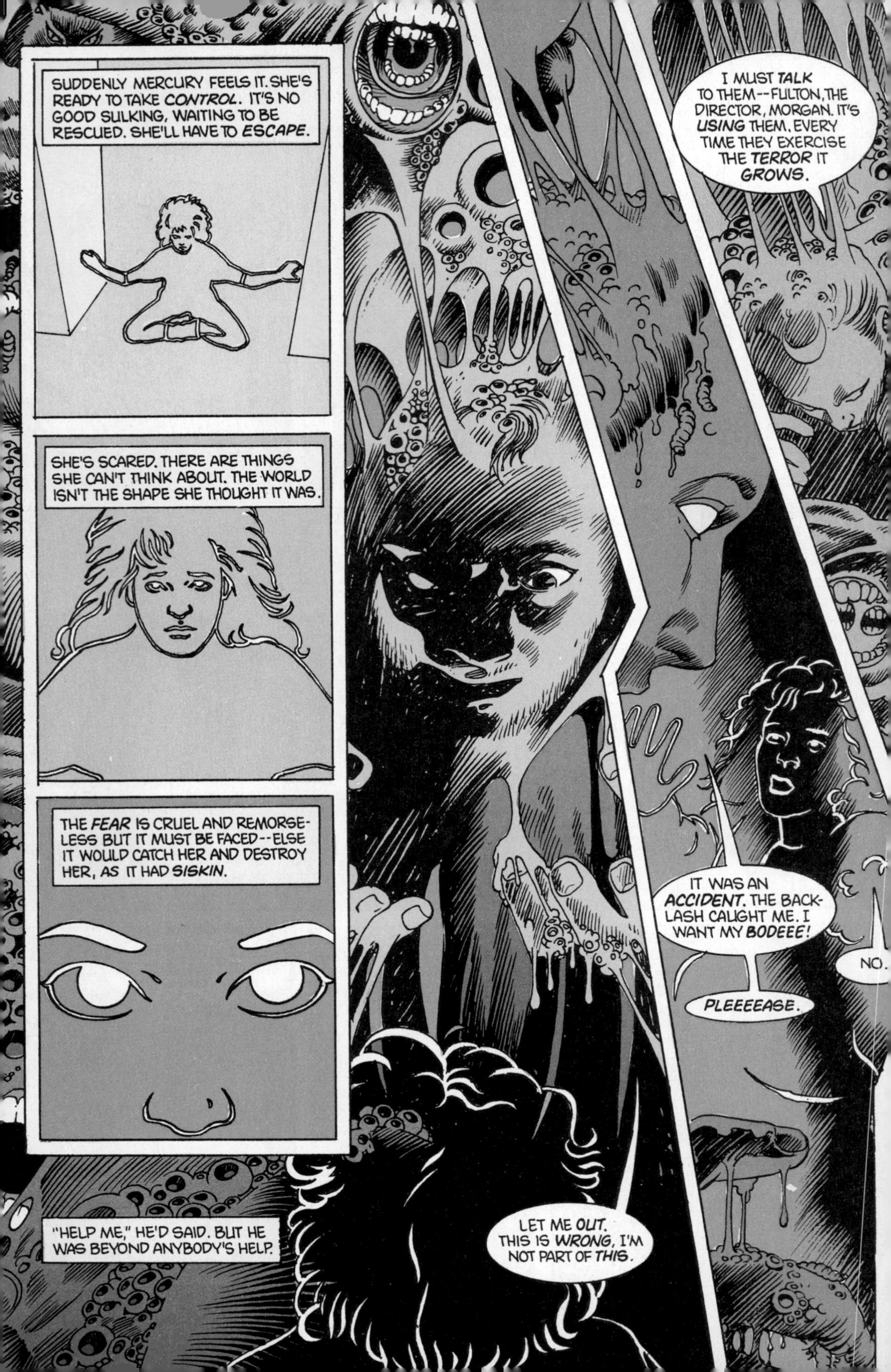
SUDDENLY MERCURY FEELS IT. SHE'S READY TO TAKE *CONTROL*. IT'S NO GOOD SULKING, WAITING TO BE RESCUED. SHE'LL HAVE TO *ESCAPE*.
SHE'S SCARED. THERE ARE THINGS SHE CAN'T THINK ABOUT. THE WORLD ISN'T THE SHAPE SHE THOUGHT IT WAS.
THE *FEAR* IS CRUEL AND REMORSELESS BUT IT MUST BE FACED--ELSE IT WOULD CATCH HER AND DESTROY HER, AS IT HAD *SISKIN*.
"HELP ME," HE'D SAID. BUT HE WAS BEYOND ANYBODY'S HELP.
I MUST *TALK* TO THEM--FULTON, THE DIRECTOR, MORGAN. IT'S *USING* THEM. EVERY TIME THEY EXERCISE THE *TERROR* IT *GROWS*.
IT WAS AN *ACCIDENT*. THE BACKLASH CAUGHT ME. I WANT MY *BODEEE*!
PLEEEEASE.
NO.
LET ME *OUT*. THIS IS *WRONG*, I'M NOT PART OF *THIS*.

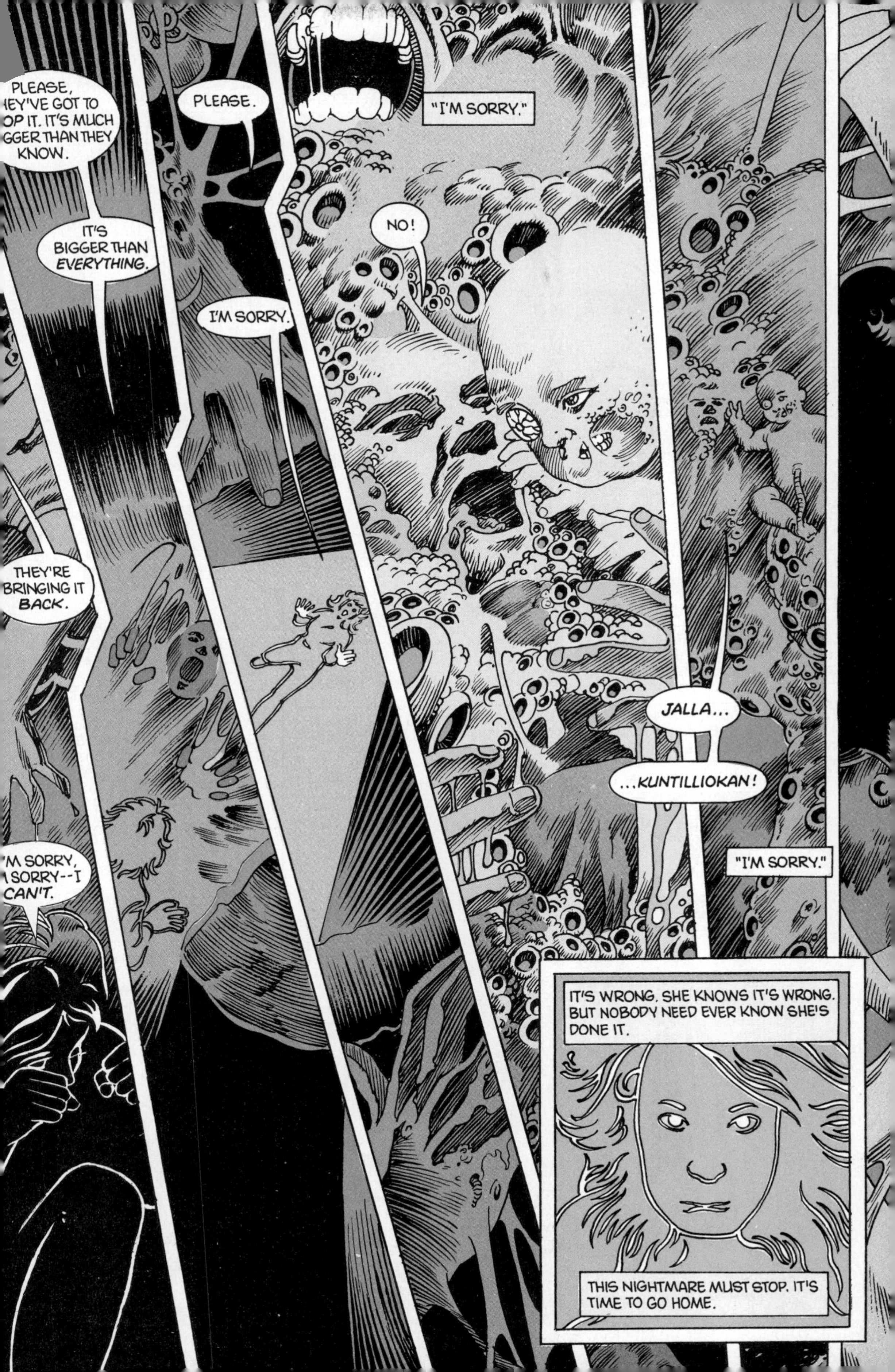

PLEASE, HEY'VE GOT TO OP IT. IT'S MUCH GGER THAN THEY KNOW.
IT'S BIGGER THAN EVERYTHING.
THEY'RE BRINGING IT BACK.
'M SORRY, SORRY--I CAN'T.
PLEASE.
I'M SORRY.
"I'M SORRY."
NO!
JALLA...
...KUNTILLIOKAN!
"I'M SORRY."
IT'S WRONG. SHE KNOWS IT'S WRONG. BUT NOBODY NEED EVER KNOW SHE'S DONE IT.
THIS NIGHTMARE MUST STOP. IT'S TIME TO GO HOME.

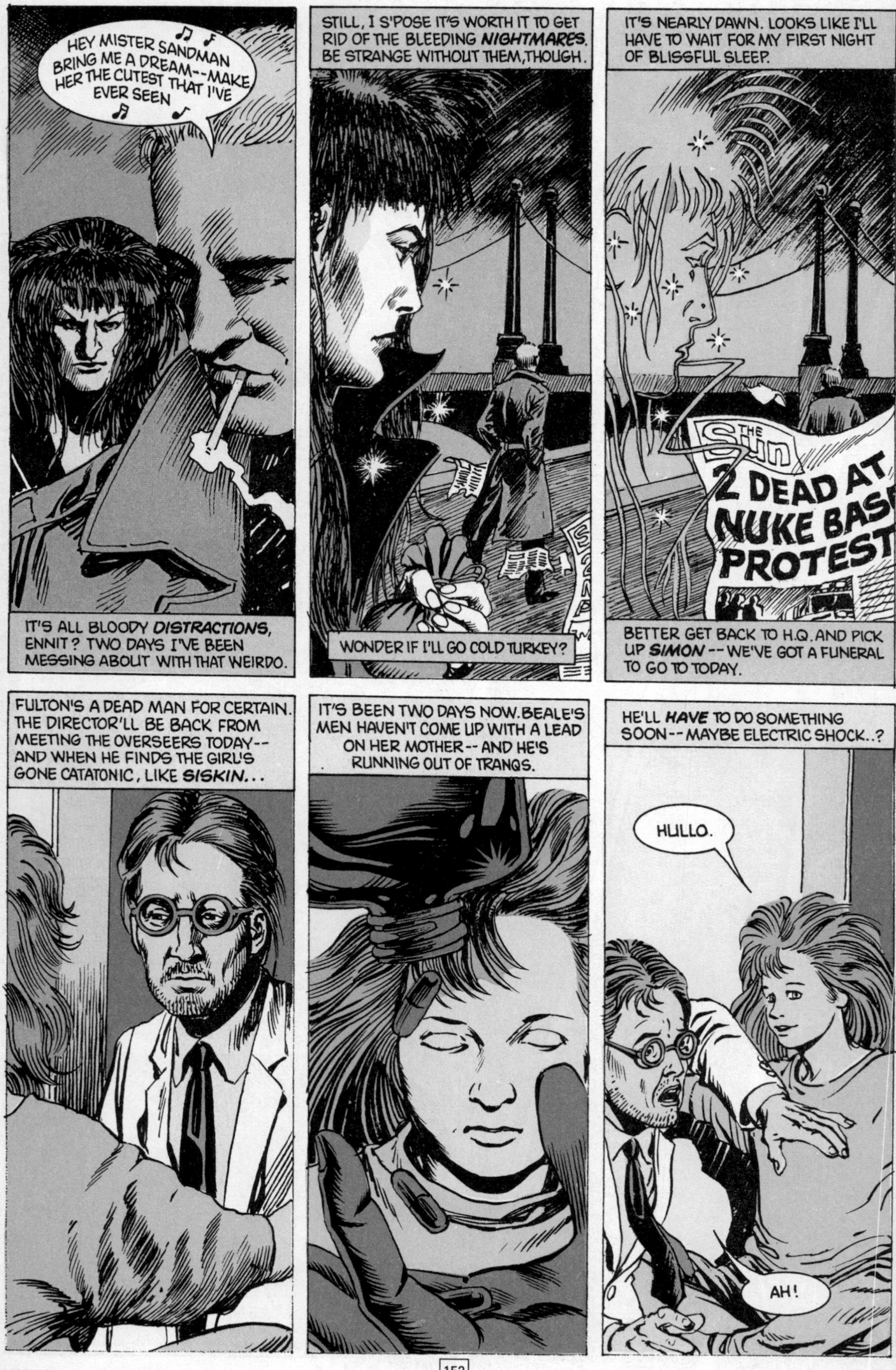
HEY MISTER SANDMAN BRING ME A DREAM--MAKE HER THE CUTEST THAT I'VE EVER SEEN
IT'S ALL BLOODY DISTRACTIONS, ENNIT? TWO DAYS I'VE BEEN MESSING ABOUT WITH THAT WEIRDO.
STILL, I S'POSE IT'S WORTH IT TO GET RID OF THE BLEEDING NIGHTMARES. BE STRANGE WITHOUT THEM, THOUGH.
WONDER IF I'LL GO COLD TURKEY?
IT'S NEARLY DAWN. LOOKS LIKE I'LL HAVE TO WAIT FOR MY FIRST NIGHT OF BLISSFUL SLEEP.
THE Sun
2 DEAD AT NUKE BAS
PROTEST
BETTER GET BACK TO H.Q. AND PICK UP SIMON -- WE'VE GOT A FUNERAL TO GO TO TODAY.
FULTON'S A DEAD MAN FOR CERTAIN. THE DIRECTOR'LL BE BACK FROM MEETING THE OVERSEERS TODAY-- AND WHEN HE FINDS THE GIRL'S GONE CATATONIC, LIKE SISKIN...
IT'S BEEN TWO DAYS NOW. BEALE'S MEN HAVEN'T COME UP WITH A LEAD ON HER MOTHER -- AND HE'S RUNNING OUT OF TRANQS.
HE'LL HAVE TO DO SOMETHING SOON--MAYBE ELECTRIC SHOCK..?
HULLO.
AH!

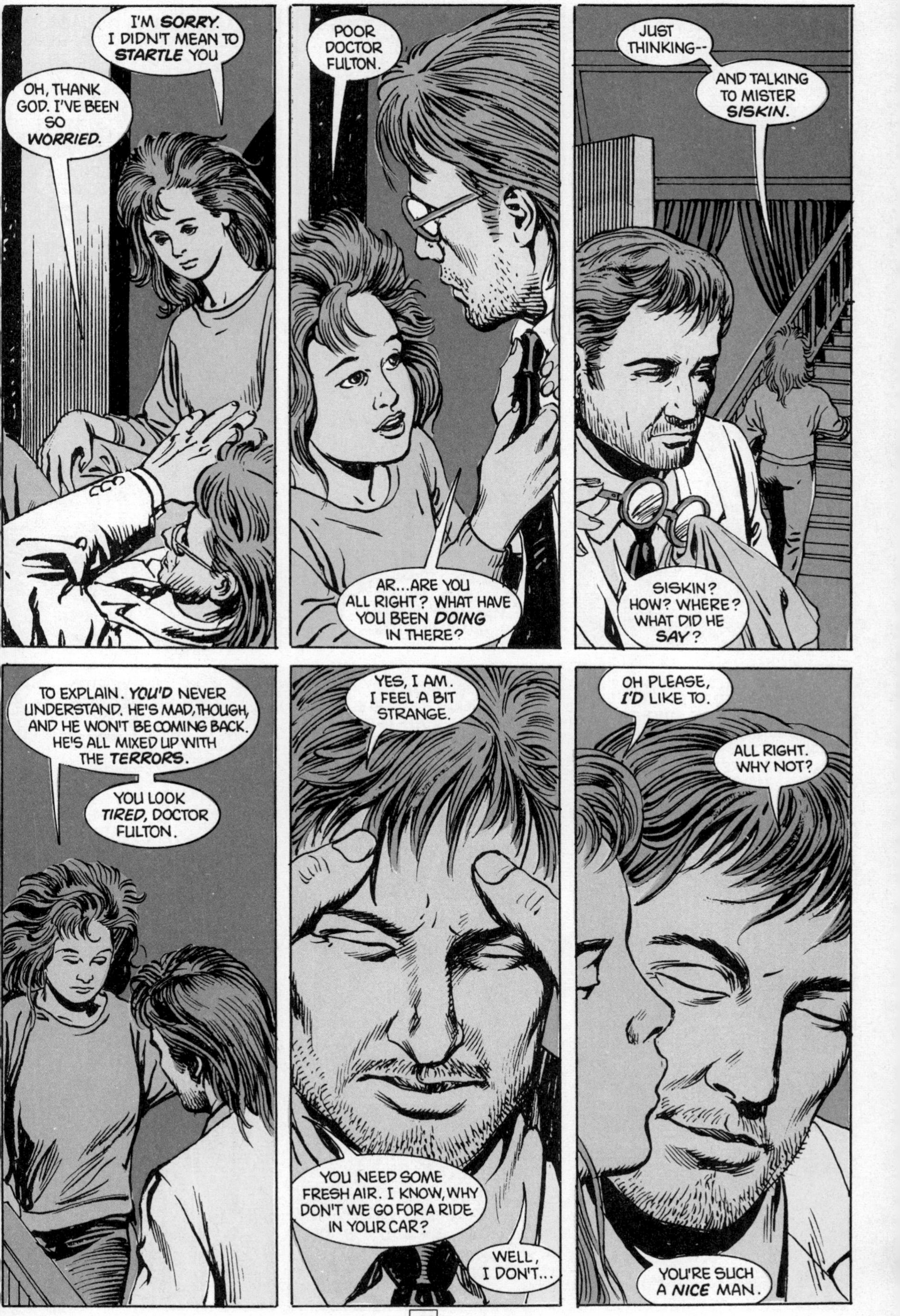
I'M SORRY. I DIDN'T MEAN TO STARTLE YOU
OH, THANK GOD. I'VE BEEN SO WORRIED.
POOR DOCTOR FULTON.
AR...ARE YOU ALL RIGHT? WHAT HAVE YOU BEEN DOING IN THERE?
JUST THINKING--
AND TALKING TO MISTER SISKIN.
SISKIN? HOW? WHERE? WHAT DID HE SAY?
TO EXPLAIN. YOU'D NEVER UNDERSTAND. HE'S MAD, THOUGH, AND HE WON'T BE COMING BACK. HE'S ALL MIXED UP WITH THE TERRORS.
YOU LOOK TIRED, DOCTOR FULTON.
YES, I AM. I FEEL A BIT STRANGE.
YOU NEED SOME FRESH AIR. I KNOW, WHY DON'T WE GO FOR A RIDE IN YOUR CAR?
WELL, I DON'T...
OH PLEASE, I'D LIKE TO.
ALL RIGHT. WHY NOT?
YOU'RE SUCH A NICE MAN.

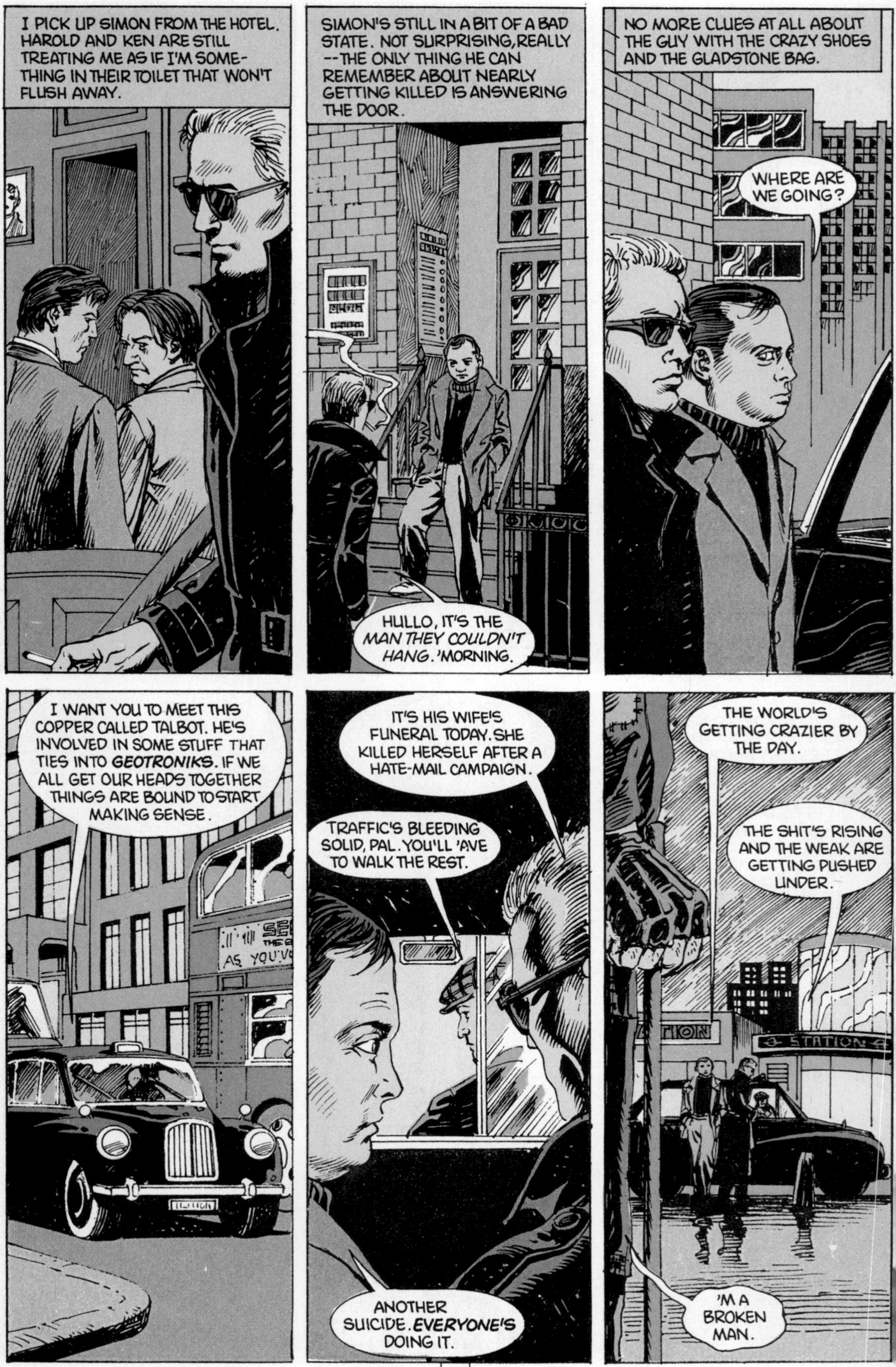
I PICK UP SIMON FROM THE HOTEL. HAROLD AND KEN ARE STILL TREATING ME AS IF I'M SOMETHING IN THEIR TOILET THAT WON'T FLUSH AWAY.
SIMON'S STILL IN A BIT OF A BAD STATE. NOT SURPRISING, REALLY --THE ONLY THING HE CAN REMEMBER ABOUT NEARLY GETTING KILLED IS ANSWERING THE DOOR.
HULLO, IT'S THE *MAN THEY COULDN'T HANG*. 'MORNING.
NO MORE CLUES AT ALL ABOUT THE GUY WITH THE CRAZY SHOES AND THE GLADSTONE BAG.
WHERE ARE WE GOING?
I WANT YOU TO MEET THIS COPPER CALLED TALBOT. HE'S INVOLVED IN SOME STUFF THAT TIES INTO **GEOTRONIKS**. IF WE ALL GET OUR HEADS TOGETHER THINGS ARE BOUND TO START MAKING SENSE.
IT'S HIS WIFE'S FUNERAL TODAY. SHE KILLED HERSELF AFTER A HATE-MAIL CAMPAIGN.
TRAFFIC'S BLEEDING SOLID, PAL. YOU'LL 'AVE TO WALK THE REST.
ANOTHER SUICIDE. **EVERYONE'S** DOING IT.
THE WORLD'S GETTING CRAZIER BY THE DAY.
THE SHIT'S RISING AND THE WEAK ARE GETTING PUSHED UNDER.
'M A BROKEN MAN.

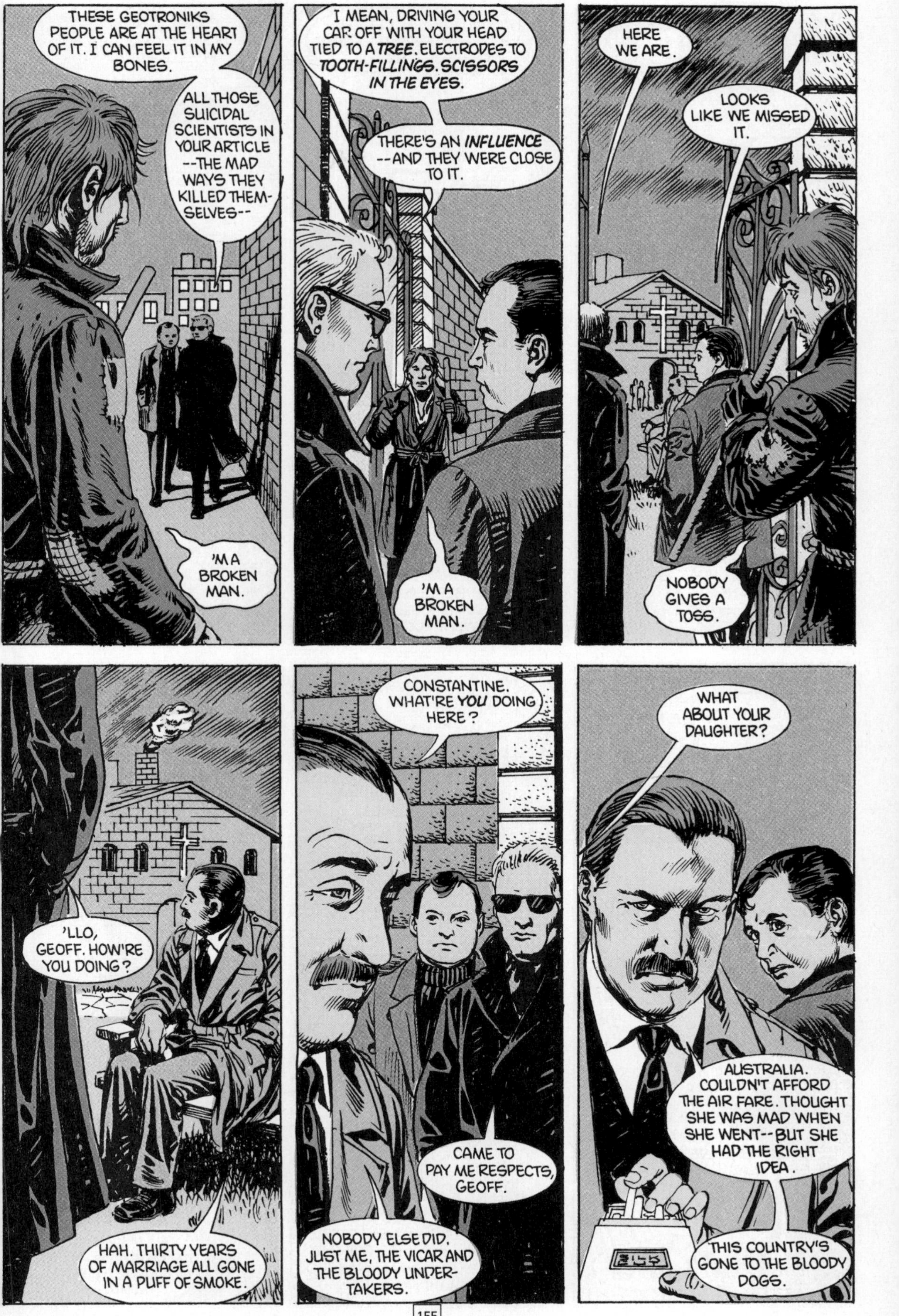
THESE GEOTRONIKS PEOPLE ARE AT THE HEART OF IT. I CAN FEEL IT IN MY BONES.
ALL THOSE SUICIDAL SCIENTISTS IN YOUR ARTICLE --THE MAD WAYS THEY KILLED THEM-SELVES--
'M A BROKEN MAN.
I MEAN, DRIVING YOUR CAR OFF WITH YOUR HEAD TIED TO A TREE. ELECTRODES TO TOOTH-FILLINGS. SCISSORS IN THE EYES.
THERE'S AN INFLUENCE --AND THEY WERE CLOSE TO IT.
'M A BROKEN MAN.
HERE WE ARE.
LOOKS LIKE WE MISSED IT.
NOBODY GIVES A TOSS.
'LLO, GEOFF. HOW'RE YOU DOING?
HAH. THIRTY YEARS OF MARRIAGE ALL GONE IN A PUFF OF SMOKE.
CONSTANTINE. WHAT'RE YOU DOING HERE?
CAME TO PAY ME RESPECTS, GEOFF.
NOBODY ELSE DID. JUST ME, THE VICAR AND THE BLOODY UNDER-TAKERS.
WHAT ABOUT YOUR DAUGHTER?
AUSTRALIA. COULDN'T AFFORD THE AIR FARE. THOUGHT SHE WAS MAD WHEN SHE WENT--BUT SHE HAD THE RIGHT IDEA.
THIS COUNTRY'S GONE TO THE BLOODY DOGS.

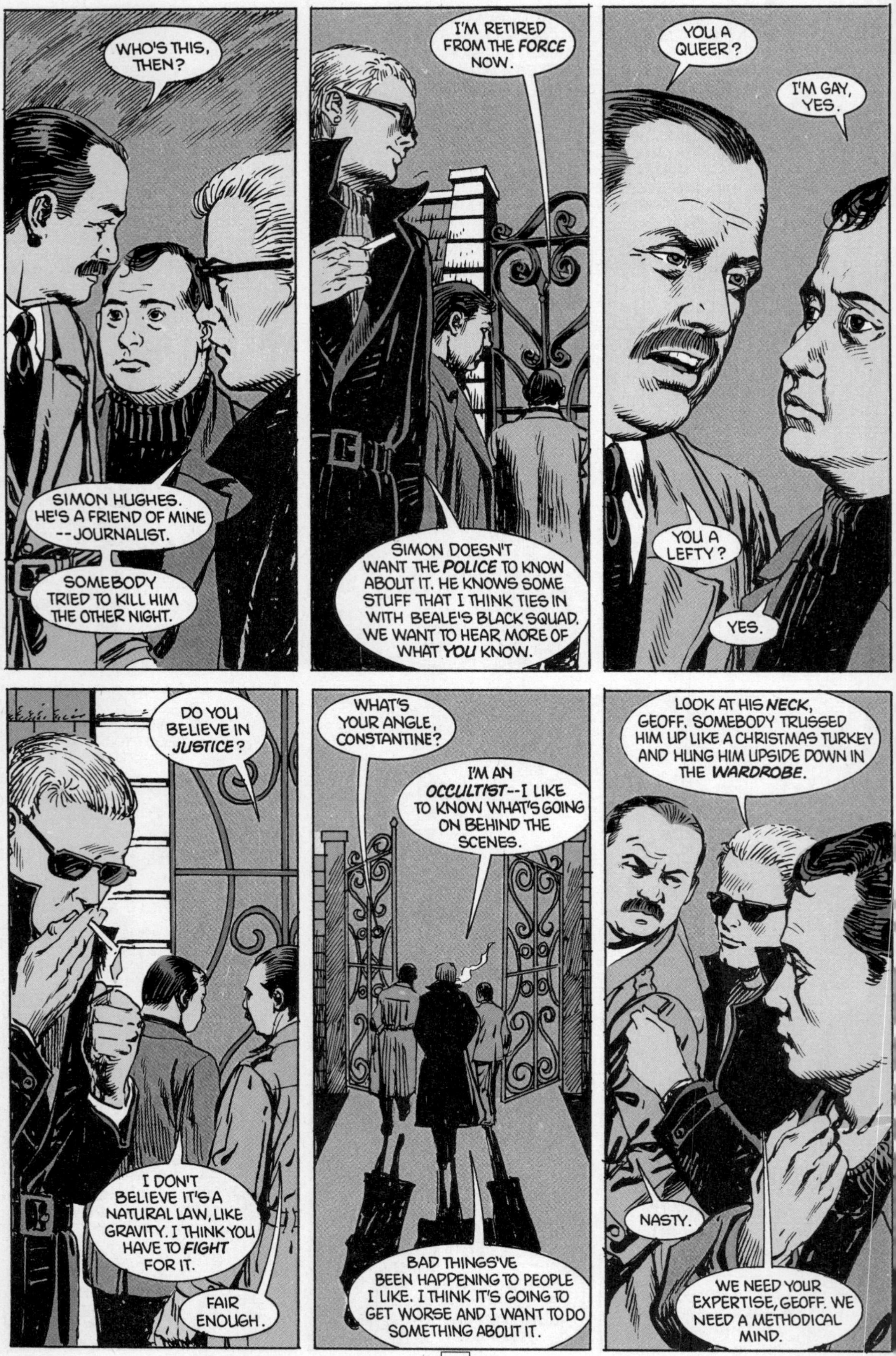
WHO'S THIS, THEN?
SIMON HUGHES. HE'S A FRIEND OF MINE --JOURNALIST.
SOMEBODY TRIED TO KILL HIM THE OTHER NIGHT.
I'M RETIRED FROM THE FORCE NOW.
SIMON DOESN'T WANT THE POLICE TO KNOW ABOUT IT. HE KNOWS SOME STUFF THAT I THINK TIES IN WITH BEALE'S BLACK SQUAD. WE WANT TO HEAR MORE OF WHAT YOU KNOW.
YOU A QUEER?
I'M GAY, YES.
YOU A LEFTY?
YES.
DO YOU BELIEVE IN JUSTICE?
I DON'T BELIEVE IT'S A NATURAL LAW, LIKE GRAVITY. I THINK YOU HAVE TO FIGHT FOR IT.
FAIR ENOUGH.
WHAT'S YOUR ANGLE, CONSTANTINE?
I'M AN OCCULTIST--I LIKE TO KNOW WHAT'S GOING ON BEHIND THE SCENES.
BAD THINGS'VE BEEN HAPPENING TO PEOPLE I LIKE. I THINK IT'S GOING TO GET WORSE AND I WANT TO DO SOMETHING ABOUT IT.
LOOK AT HIS NECK, GEOFF. SOMEBODY TRUSSED HIM UP LIKE A CHRISTMAS TURKEY AND HUNG HIM UPSIDE DOWN IN THE WARDROBE.
NASTY.
WE NEED YOUR EXPERTISE, GEOFF. WE NEED A METHODICAL MIND.

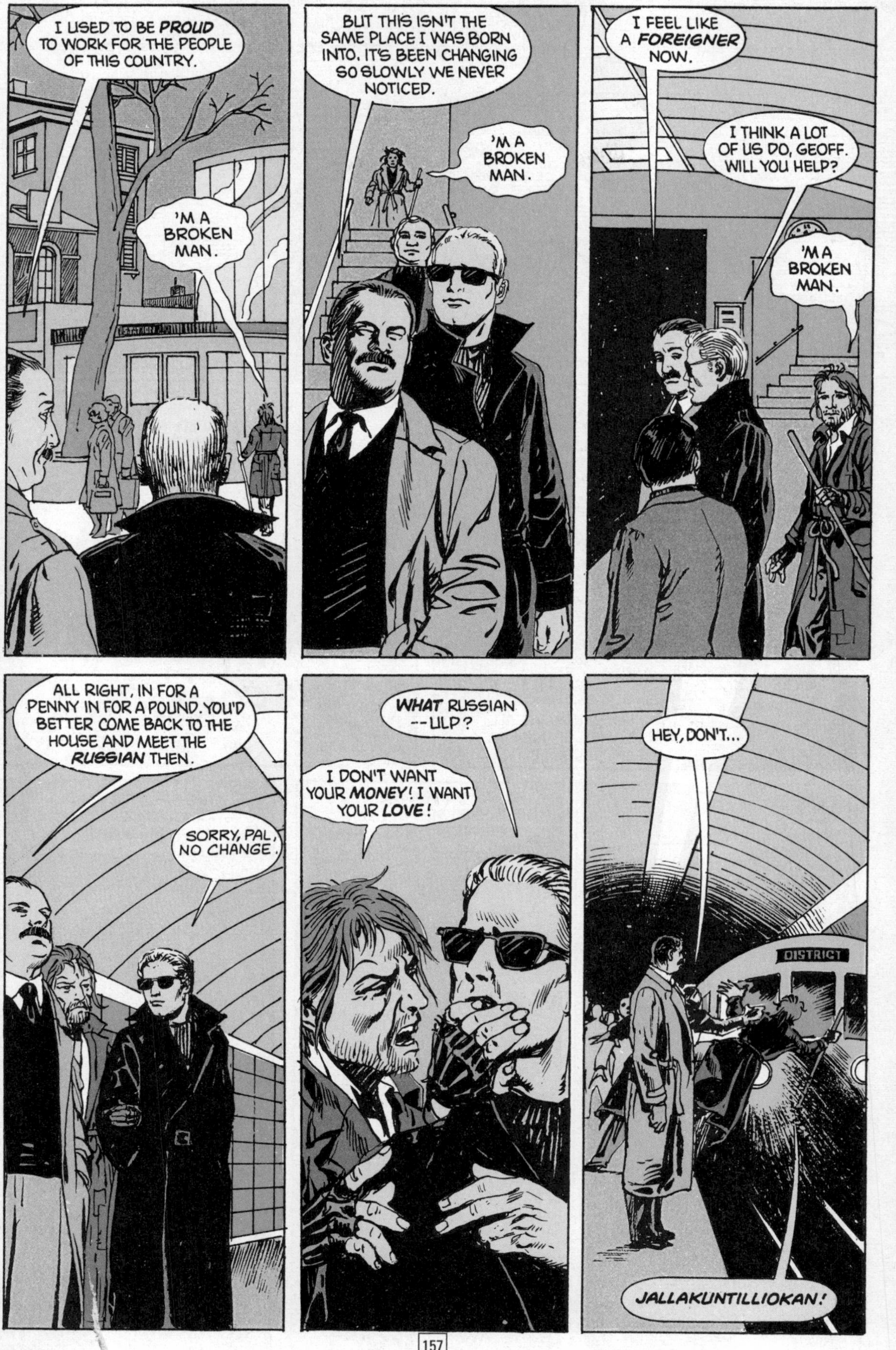
I USED TO BE PROUD TO WORK FOR THE PEOPLE OF THIS COUNTRY.
'M A BROKEN MAN.
BUT THIS ISN'T THE SAME PLACE I WAS BORN INTO. IT'S BEEN CHANGING SO SLOWLY WE NEVER NOTICED.
'M A BROKEN MAN.
STATION
I FEEL LIKE A FOREIGNER NOW.
I THINK A LOT OF US DO, GEOFF. WILL YOU HELP?
'M A BROKEN MAN.
ALL RIGHT, IN FOR A PENNY IN FOR A POUND. YOU'D BETTER COME BACK TO THE HOUSE AND MEET THE RUSSIAN THEN.
SORRY, PAL, NO CHANGE.
WHAT RUSSIAN --ULP?
I DON'T WANT YOUR MONEY! I WANT YOUR LOVE!
HEY, DON'T...
DISTRICT
JALLAKUNTILLIOKAN!

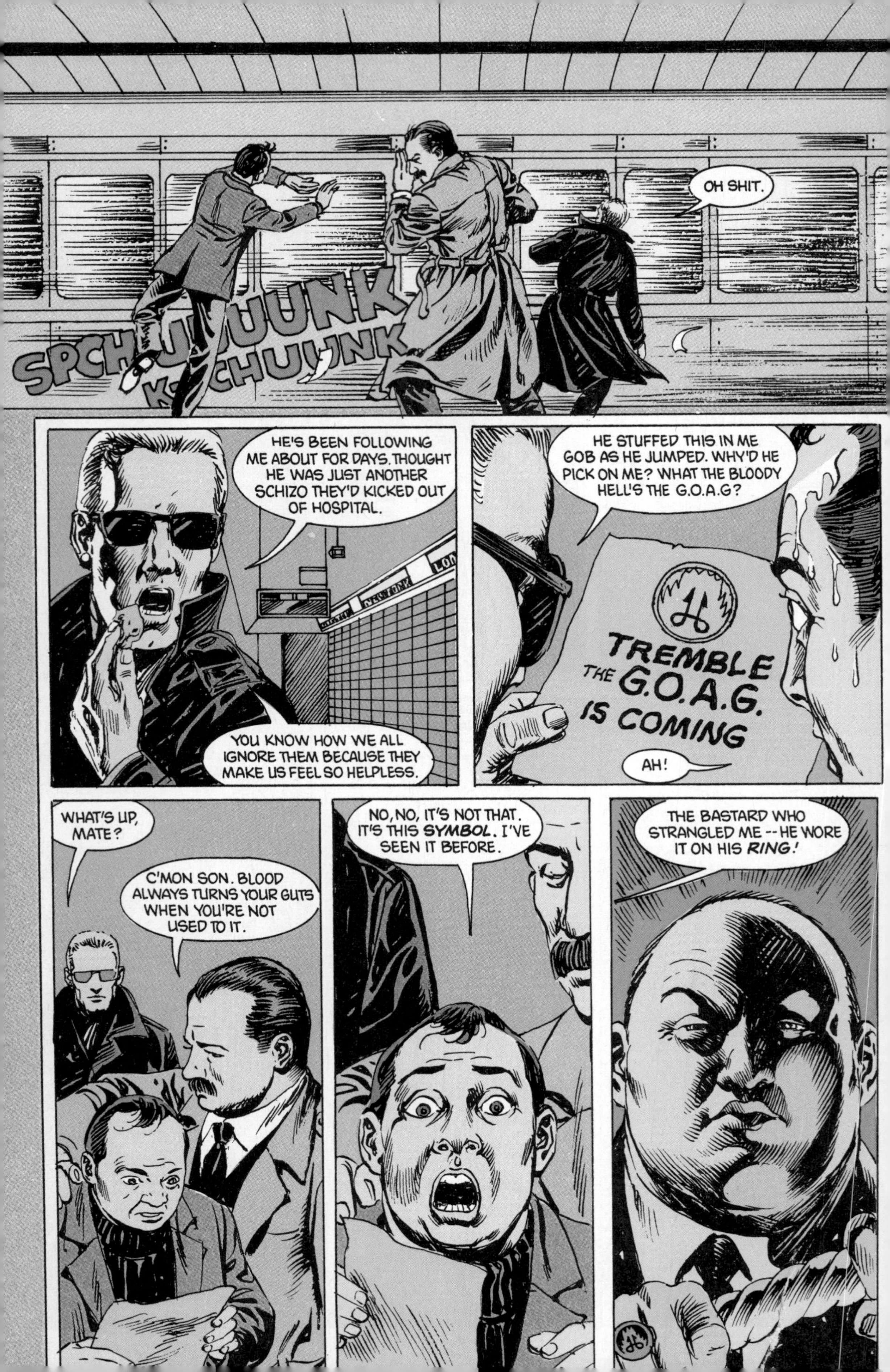

OH SHIT.
SPCHUUUUNK
K-CHUUUNK
HE'S BEEN FOLLOWING ME ABOUT FOR DAYS. THOUGHT HE WAS JUST ANOTHER SCHIZO THEY'D KICKED OUT OF HOSPITAL.
YOU KNOW HOW WE ALL IGNORE THEM BECAUSE THEY MAKE US FEEL SO HELPLESS.
HE STUFFED THIS IN ME GOB AS HE JUMPED. WHY'D HE PICK ON ME? WHAT THE BLOODY HELL'S THE G.O.A.G?
TREMBLE THE G.O.A.G. IS COMING
AH!
WHAT'S UP, MATE?
C'MON SON. BLOOD ALWAYS TURNS YOUR GUTS WHEN YOU'RE NOT USED TO IT.
NO, NO, IT'S NOT THAT. IT'S THIS SYMBOL. I'VE SEEN IT BEFORE.
THE BASTARD WHO STRANGLED ME -- HE WORE IT ON HIS RING!

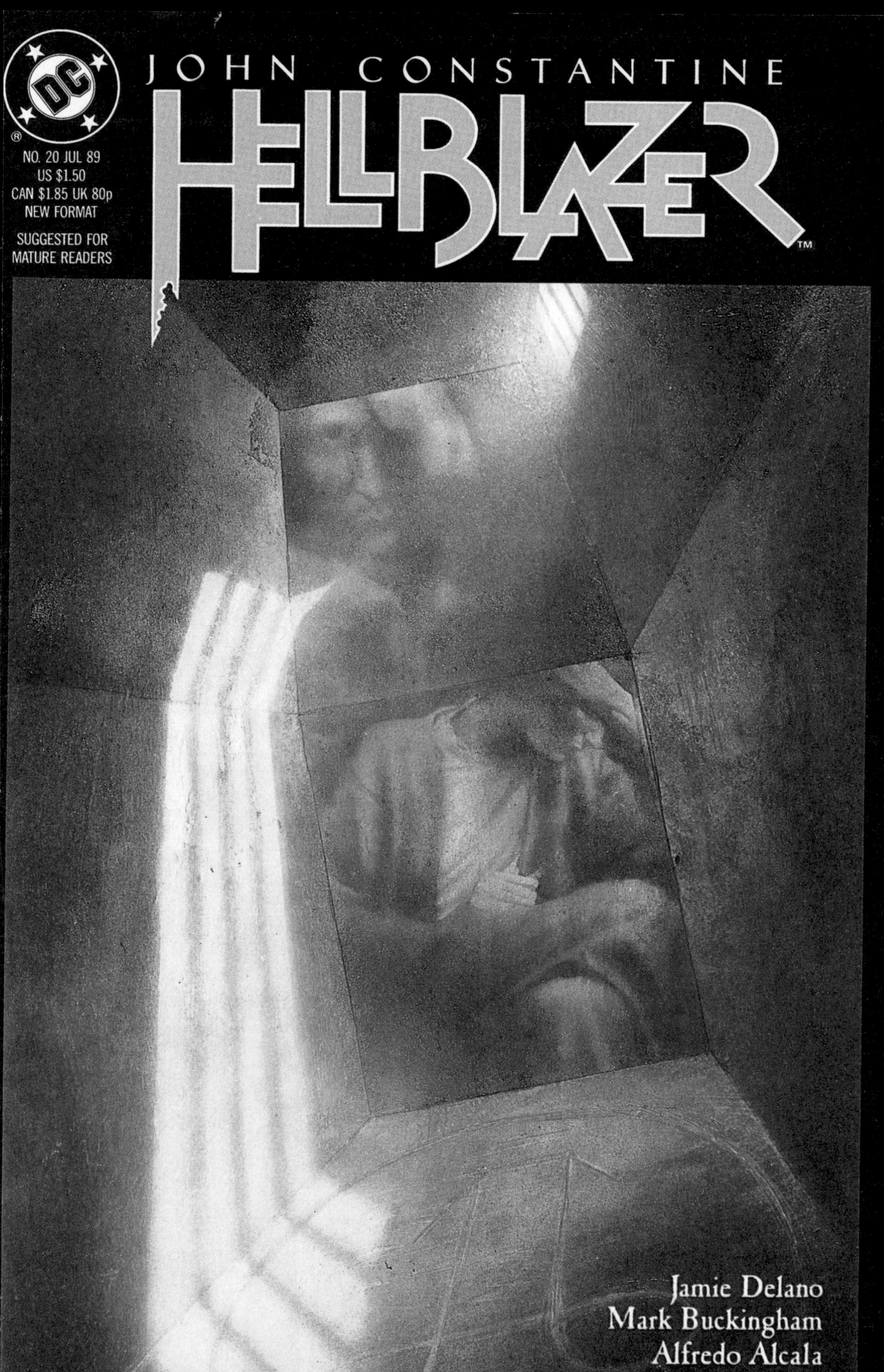
JOHN CONSTANTINE
HELLBLAZER™
NO. 20 JUL 89
US $1.50
CAN $1.85 UK 80p
NEW FORMAT
SUGGESTED FOR
MATURE READERS
Jamie Delano
Mark Buckingham
Alfredo Alcala

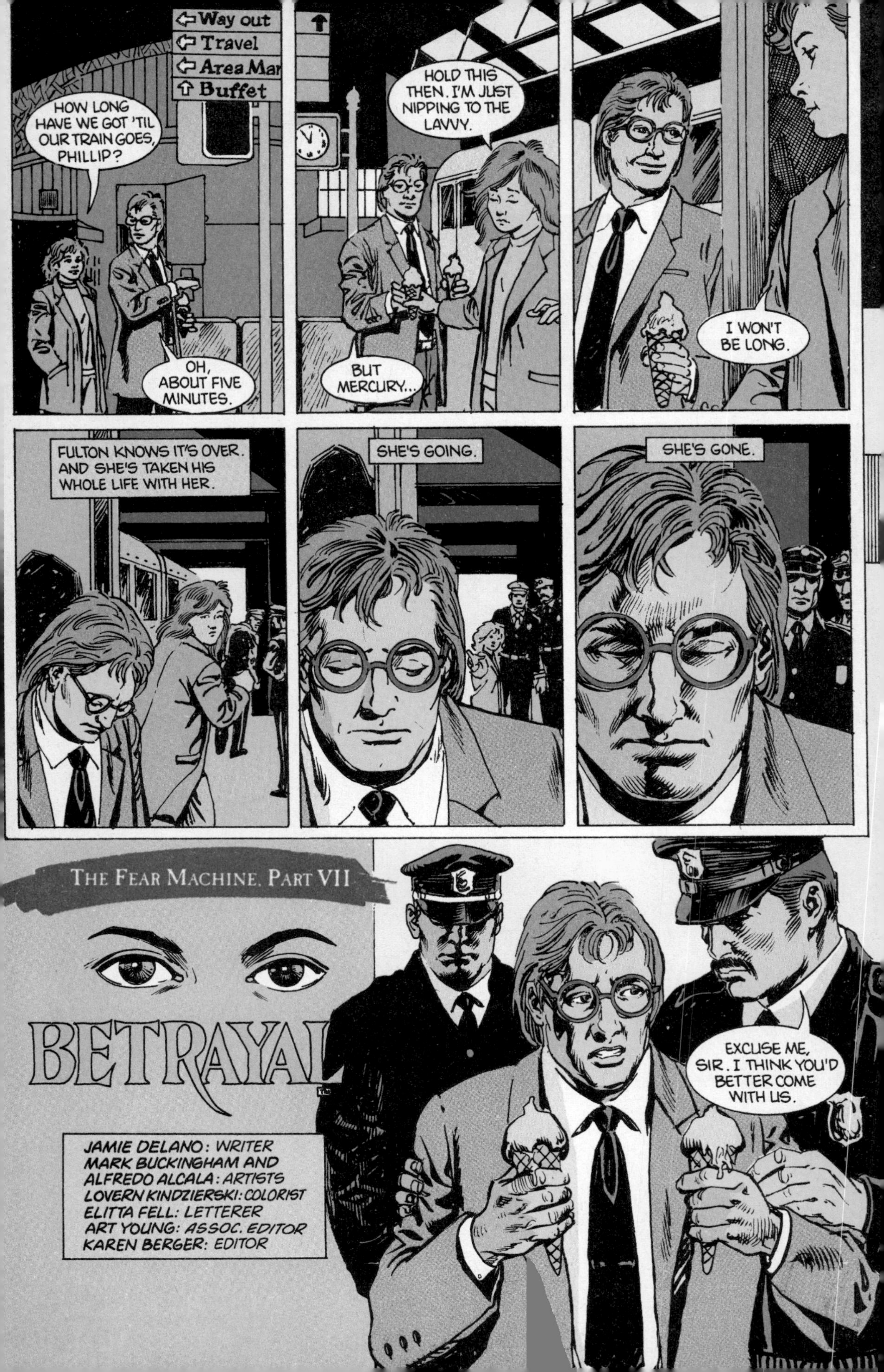

Way out
Travel
Area Ma
Buffet
HOW LONG HAVE WE GOT 'TIL OUR TRAIN GOES, PHILLIP?
OH, ABOUT FIVE MINUTES.
HOLD THIS THEN. I'M JUST NIPPING TO THE LAVVY.
BUT MERCURY...
I WON'T BE LONG.
FULTON KNOWS IT'S OVER. AND SHE'S TAKEN HIS WHOLE LIFE WITH HER.
SHE'S GOING.
SHE'S GONE.
THE FEAR MACHINE, PART VII
BETRAYAL
EXCUSE ME, SIR. I THINK YOU'D BETTER COME WITH US.
JAMIE DELANO: WRITER
MARK BUCKINGHAM AND ALFREDO ALCALA: ARTISTS
LOVERN KINDZIERSKI: COLORIST
ELITTA FELL: LETTERER
ART YOUNG: ASSOC. EDITOR
KAREN BERGER: EDITOR

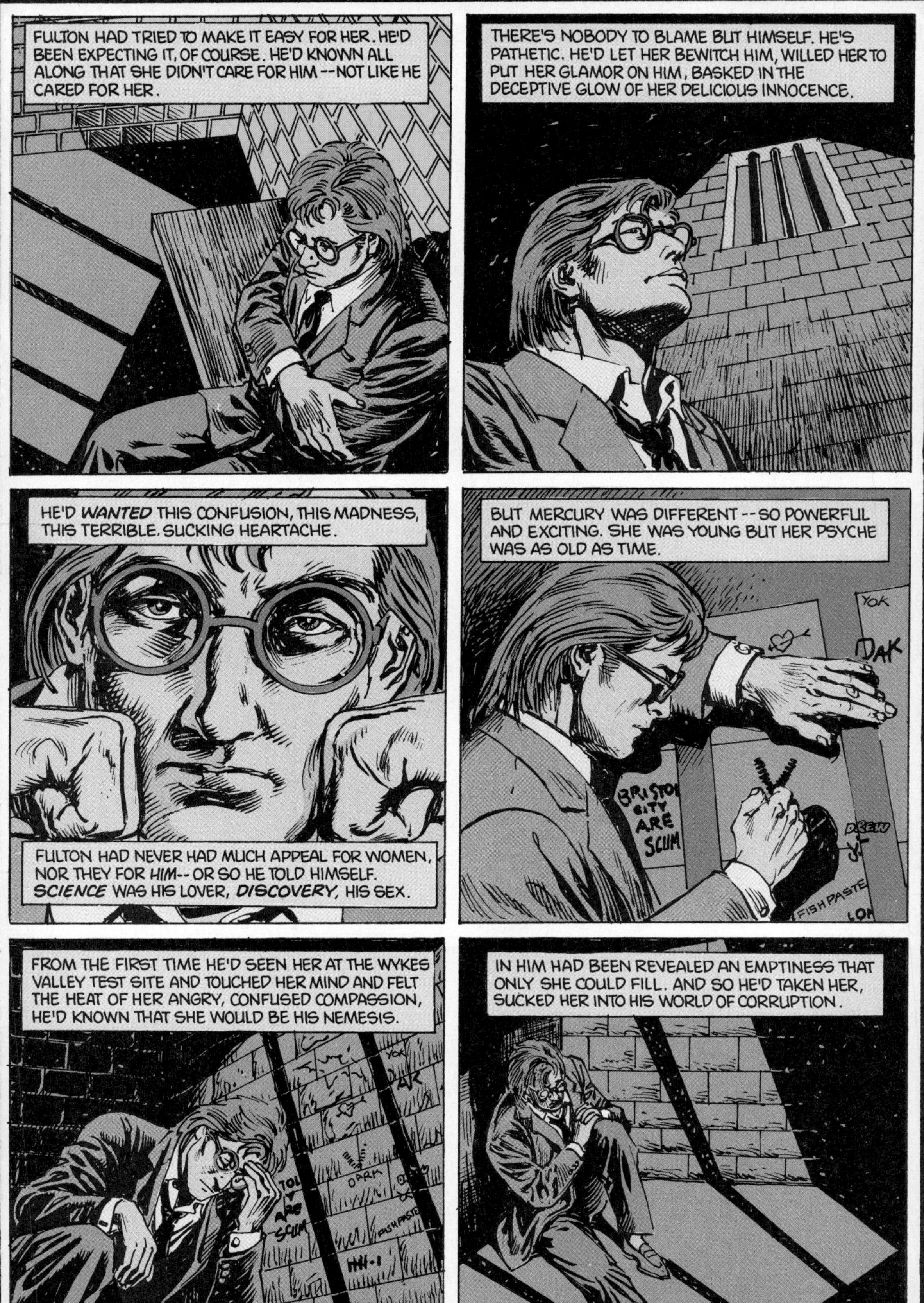
FULTON HAD TRIED TO MAKE IT EASY FOR HER. HE'D BEEN EXPECTING IT, OF COURSE. HE'D KNOWN ALL ALONG THAT SHE DIDN'T CARE FOR HIM -- NOT LIKE HE CARED FOR HER.
THERE'S NOBODY TO BLAME BUT HIMSELF. HE'S PATHETIC. HE'D LET HER BEWITCH HIM, WILLED HER TO PUT HER GLAMOR ON HIM, BASKED IN THE DECEPTIVE GLOW OF HER DELICIOUS INNOCENCE.
HE'D *WANTED* THIS CONFUSION, THIS MADNESS, THIS TERRIBLE, SUCKING HEARTACHE.
FULTON HAD NEVER HAD MUCH APPEAL FOR WOMEN, NOR THEY FOR *HIM*-- OR SO HE TOLD HIMSELF. *SCIENCE* WAS HIS LOVER, *DISCOVERY*, HIS SEX.
BUT MERCURY WAS DIFFERENT -- SO POWERFUL AND EXCITING. SHE WAS YOUNG BUT HER PSYCHE WAS AS OLD AS TIME.
YOK
DAK
CITY ARE SCUM
DREW
FISH PASTE
FROM THE FIRST TIME HE'D SEEN HER AT THE WYKES VALLEY TEST SITE AND TOUCHED HER MIND AND FELT THE HEAT OF HER ANGRY, CONFUSED COMPASSION, HE'D KNOWN THAT SHE WOULD BE HIS NEMESIS.
IN HIM HAD BEEN REVEALED AN EMPTINESS THAT ONLY SHE COULD FILL. AND SO HE'D TAKEN HER, SUCKED HER INTO HIS WORLD OF CORRUPTION.
HE'D WRONGED HER.

HE'D IMPRISONED HER BODY AND KEPT HER MIND ENTHRALLED WITH THE PROMISE OF KNOWLEDGE. ALL THE WHILE CRAVING HER FORGIVENESS, NEEDING THE ABSOLUTION OF HER SMILE, HER TOUCH--

YESTERDAY THEY'D RUN AWAY TOGETHER AND, FINALLY, HE'D BEEN HAPPY. DRIVING IN HIS CAR, AT THE FAIR, THE CINEMA--HE'D BEEN *PROUD* WITH HER, LIKE A FATHER. NO, LIKE A *MAN*. SHE WAS NOT A CHILD TO *HIM*.

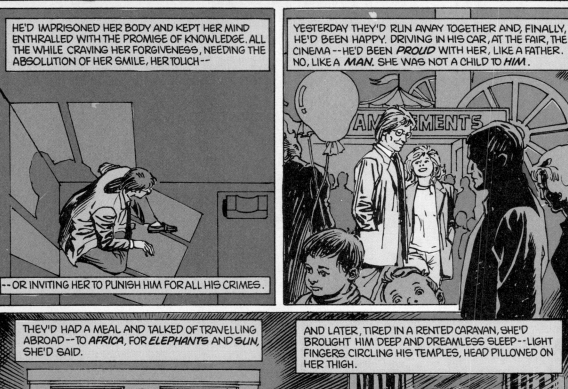

--OR INVITING HER TO PUNISH HIM FOR ALL HIS CRIMES.

THEY'D HAD A MEAL AND TALKED OF TRAVELLING ABROAD--TO *AFRICA*, FOR *ELEPHANTS* AND *SUN*, SHE'D SAID.

AND LATER, TIRED IN A RENTED CARAVAN, SHE'D BROUGHT HIM DEEP AND DREAMLESS SLEEP--LIGHT FINGERS CIRCLING HIS TEMPLES, HEAD PILLOWED ON HER THIGH.

AND HE'D NEVER WANTED MORE THAN THAT SWEET PEACE.

THIS MORNING THEY'D WOKEN AND SHE COULD NOT MEET HIS EYE. HE KNEW THAT SHE WOULD LEAVE-- AND THAT HE WOULD NOT STOP HER.

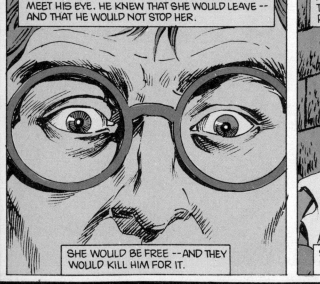

SHE WOULD BE FREE--AND THEY WOULD KILL HIM FOR IT.

A TRAITOR TO A CAUSE CAN STILL BE LOYAL TO *LOVE*. TREACHERY HAS ITS PRICE BUT LOVE IS ITS OWN REWARD.

SOON THERE WILL BE *WEBSTER* AND HIS ROPE-- BUT THEN SILENCE, LONG, DARK, SILENCE.

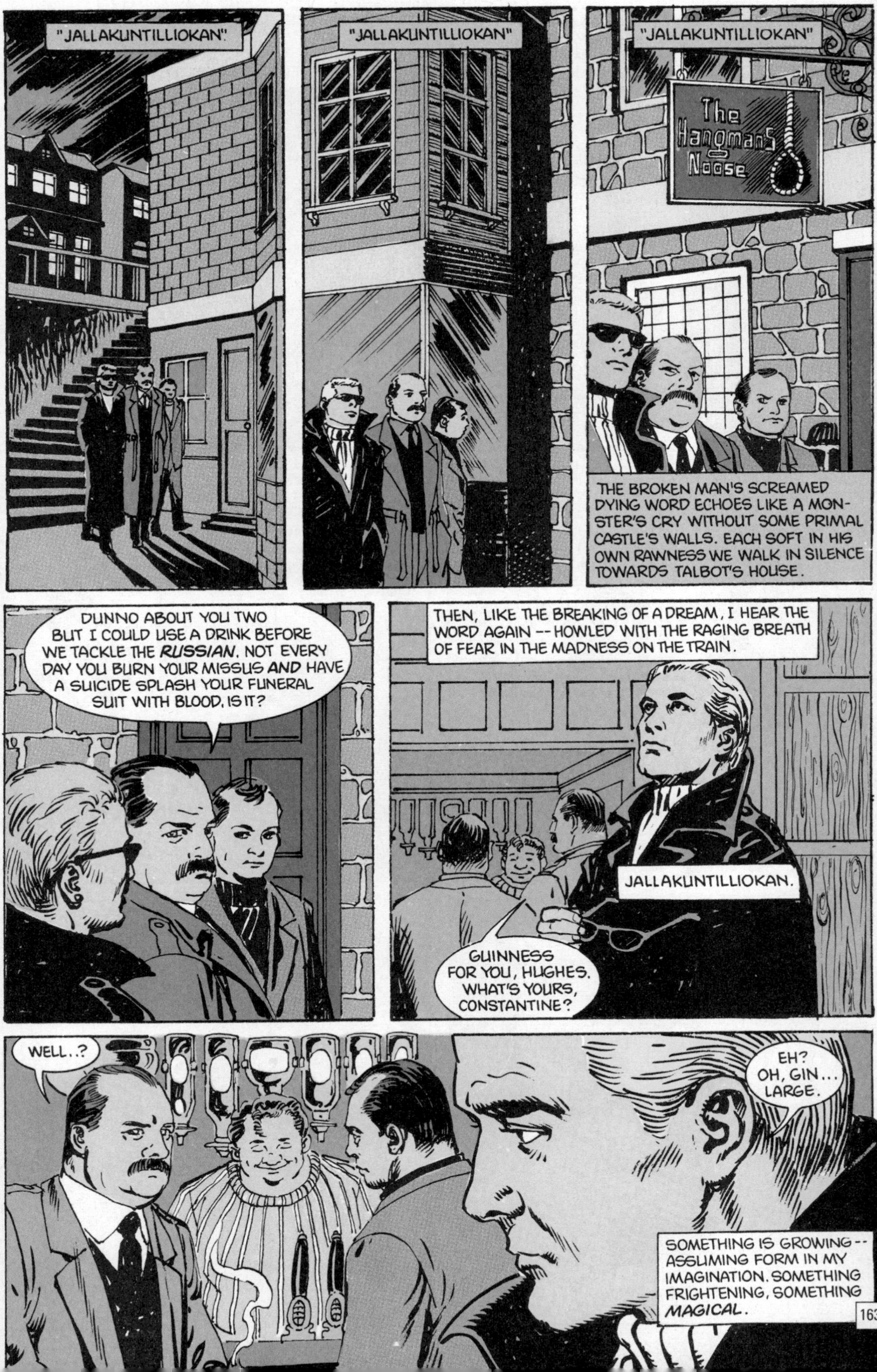
"JALLAKUNTILLIOKAN".
"JALLAKUNTILLIOKAN"
"JALLAKUNTILLIOKAN"
The Hangman's Noose
THE BROKEN MAN'S SCREAMED DYING WORD ECHOES LIKE A MONSTER'S CRY WITHOUT SOME PRIMAL CASTLE'S WALLS. EACH SOFT IN HIS OWN RAWNESS WE WALK IN SILENCE TOWARDS TALBOT'S HOUSE.
DUNNO ABOUT YOU TWO BUT I COULD USE A DRINK BEFORE WE TACKLE THE RUSSIAN. NOT EVERY DAY YOU BURN YOUR MISSUS AND HAVE A SUICIDE SPLASH YOUR FUNERAL SUIT WITH BLOOD, IS IT?
THEN, LIKE THE BREAKING OF A DREAM, I HEAR THE WORD AGAIN -- HOWLED WITH THE RAGING BREATH OF FEAR IN THE MADNESS ON THE TRAIN.
JALLAKUNTILLIOKAN.
GUINNESS FOR YOU, HUGHES. WHAT'S YOURS, CONSTANTINE?
WELL..?
EH? OH, GIN... LARGE.
SOMETHING IS GROWING -- ASSUMING FORM IN MY IMAGINATION. SOMETHING FRIGHTENING, SOMETHING MAGICAL.

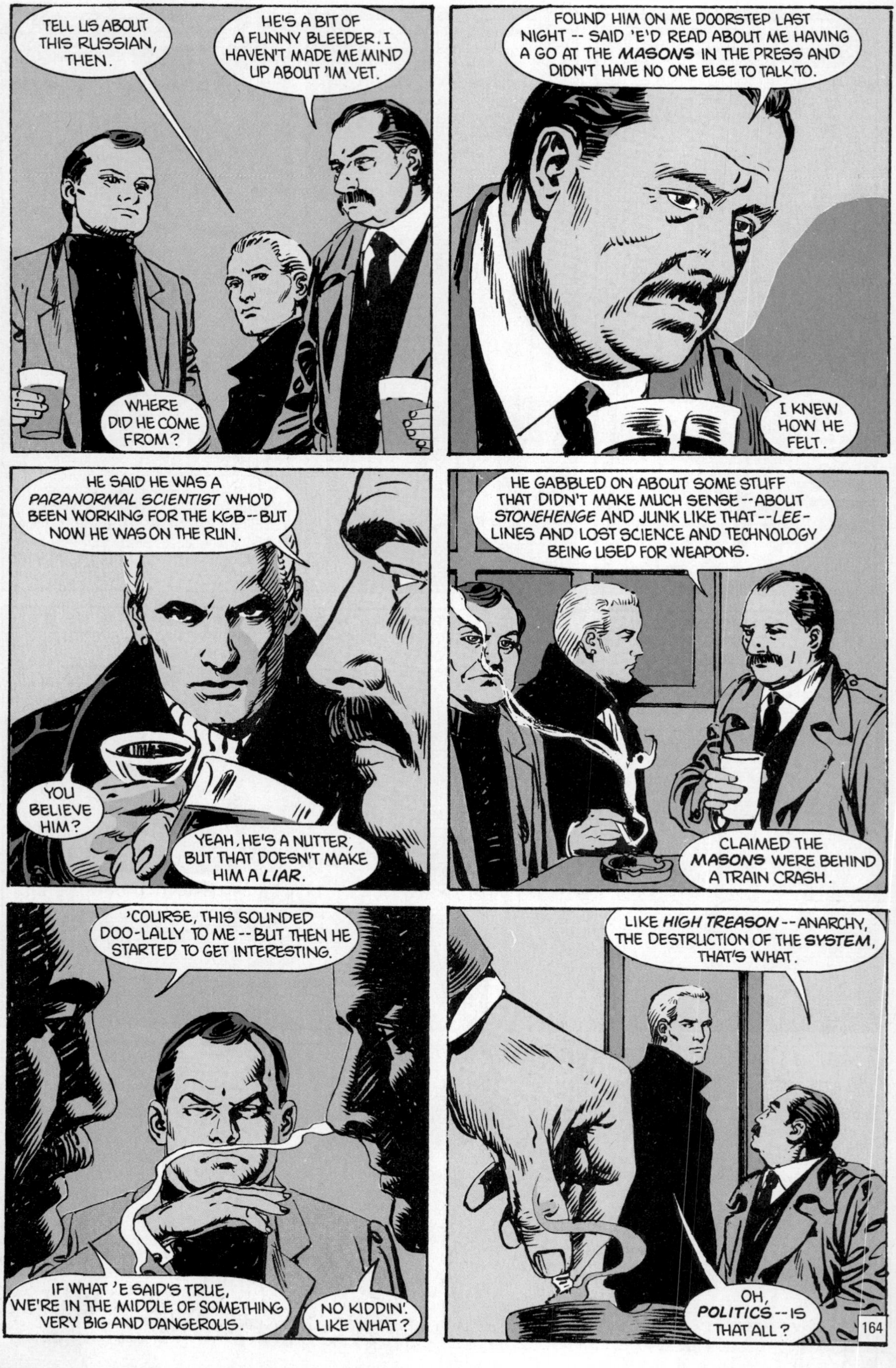
TELL US ABOUT THIS RUSSIAN, THEN.
HE'S A BIT OF A FUNNY BLEEDER. I HAVEN'T MADE ME MIND UP ABOUT 'IM YET.
WHERE DID HE COME FROM?
FOUND HIM ON ME DOORSTEP LAST NIGHT -- SAID 'E'D READ ABOUT ME HAVING A GO AT THE MASONS IN THE PRESS AND DIDN'T HAVE NO ONE ELSE TO TALK TO.
I KNEW HOW HE FELT.
HE SAID HE WAS A PARANORMAL SCIENTIST WHO'D BEEN WORKING FOR THE KGB--BUT NOW HE WAS ON THE RUN.
YOU BELIEVE HIM?
YEAH, HE'S A NUTTER, BUT THAT DOESN'T MAKE HIM A LIAR.
HE GABBLED ON ABOUT SOME STUFF THAT DIDN'T MAKE MUCH SENSE--ABOUT STONEHENGE AND JUNK LIKE THAT--LEE-LINES AND LOST SCIENCE AND TECHNOLOGY BEING USED FOR WEAPONS.
CLAIMED THE MASONS WERE BEHIND A TRAIN CRASH.
'COURSE, THIS SOUNDED DOO-LALLY TO ME--BUT THEN HE STARTED TO GET INTERESTING.
IF WHAT 'E SAID'S TRUE, WE'RE IN THE MIDDLE OF SOMETHING VERY BIG AND DANGEROUS.
NO KIDDIN'. LIKE WHAT?
LIKE HIGH TREASON--ANARCHY, THE DESTRUCTION OF THE SYSTEM, THAT'S WHAT.
OH, POLITICS--IS THAT ALL?

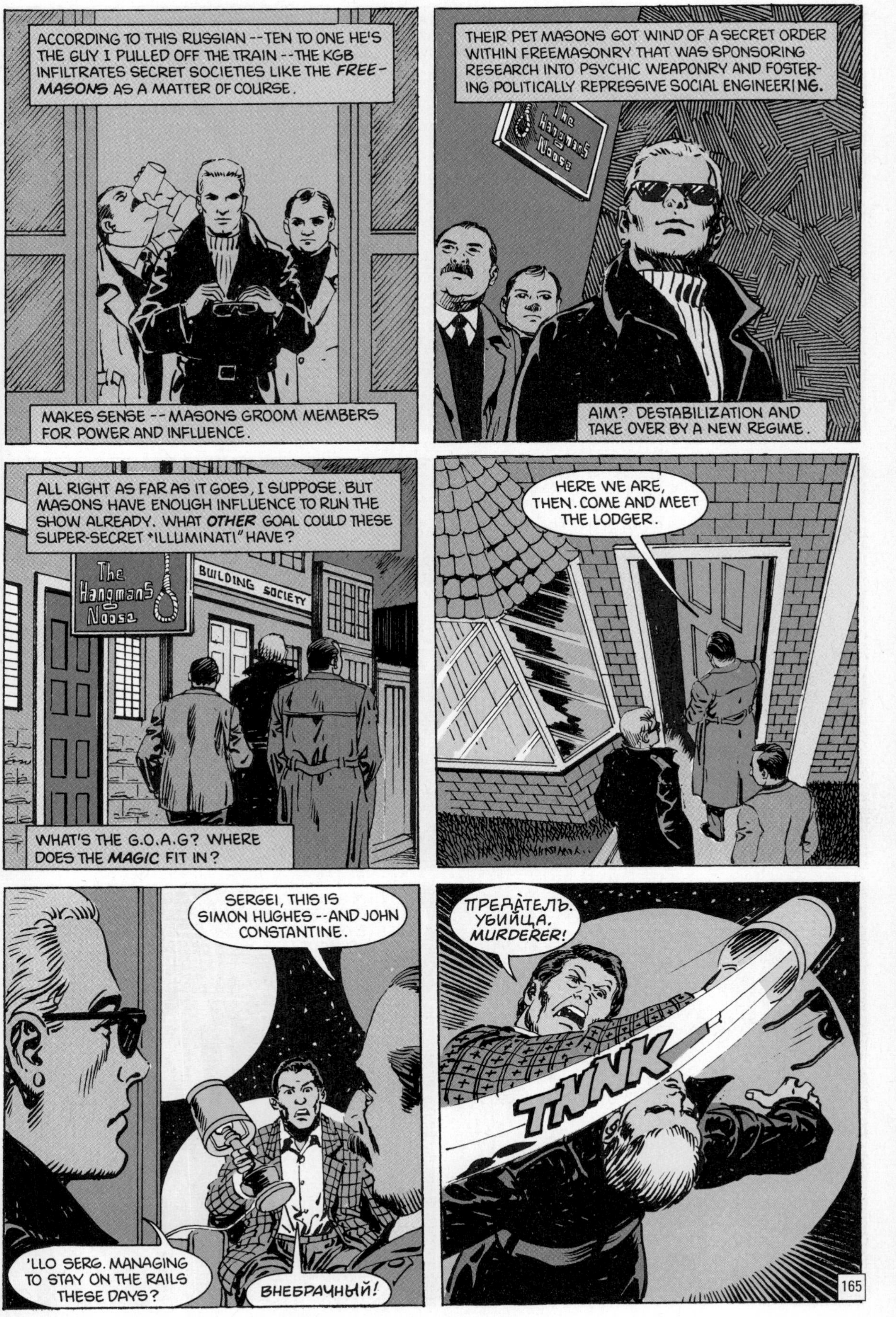
ACCORDING TO THIS RUSSIAN --TEN TO ONE HE'S THE GUY I PULLED OFF THE TRAIN --THE KGB INFILTRATES SECRET SOCIETIES LIKE THE FREE-MASONS AS A MATTER OF COURSE.
MAKES SENSE -- MASONS GROOM MEMBERS FOR POWER AND INFLUENCE.
THEIR PET MASONS GOT WIND OF A SECRET ORDER WITHIN FREEMASONRY THAT WAS SPONSORING RESEARCH INTO PSYCHIC WEAPONRY AND FOSTERING POLITICALLY REPRESSIVE SOCIAL ENGINEERING.
The HangmanS Noose
AIM? DESTABILIZATION AND TAKE OVER BY A NEW REGIME.
ALL RIGHT AS FAR AS IT GOES, I SUPPOSE. BUT MASONS HAVE ENOUGH INFLUENCE TO RUN THE SHOW ALREADY. WHAT OTHER GOAL COULD THESE SUPER-SECRET "ILLUMINATI" HAVE?
The HangmanS Noose
BUILDING SOCIETY
WHAT'S THE G.O.A.G? WHERE DOES THE MAGIC FIT IN?
HERE WE ARE, THEN. COME AND MEET THE LODGER.
SERGEI, THIS IS SIMON HUGHES --AND JOHN CONSTANTINE.
'LLO SERG. MANAGING TO STAY ON THE RAILS THESE DAYS?
ВНЕБРАЧНЫЙ!
ПРЕДАТЕЛЬ. УБИЙЦА. MURDERER!
TNNK

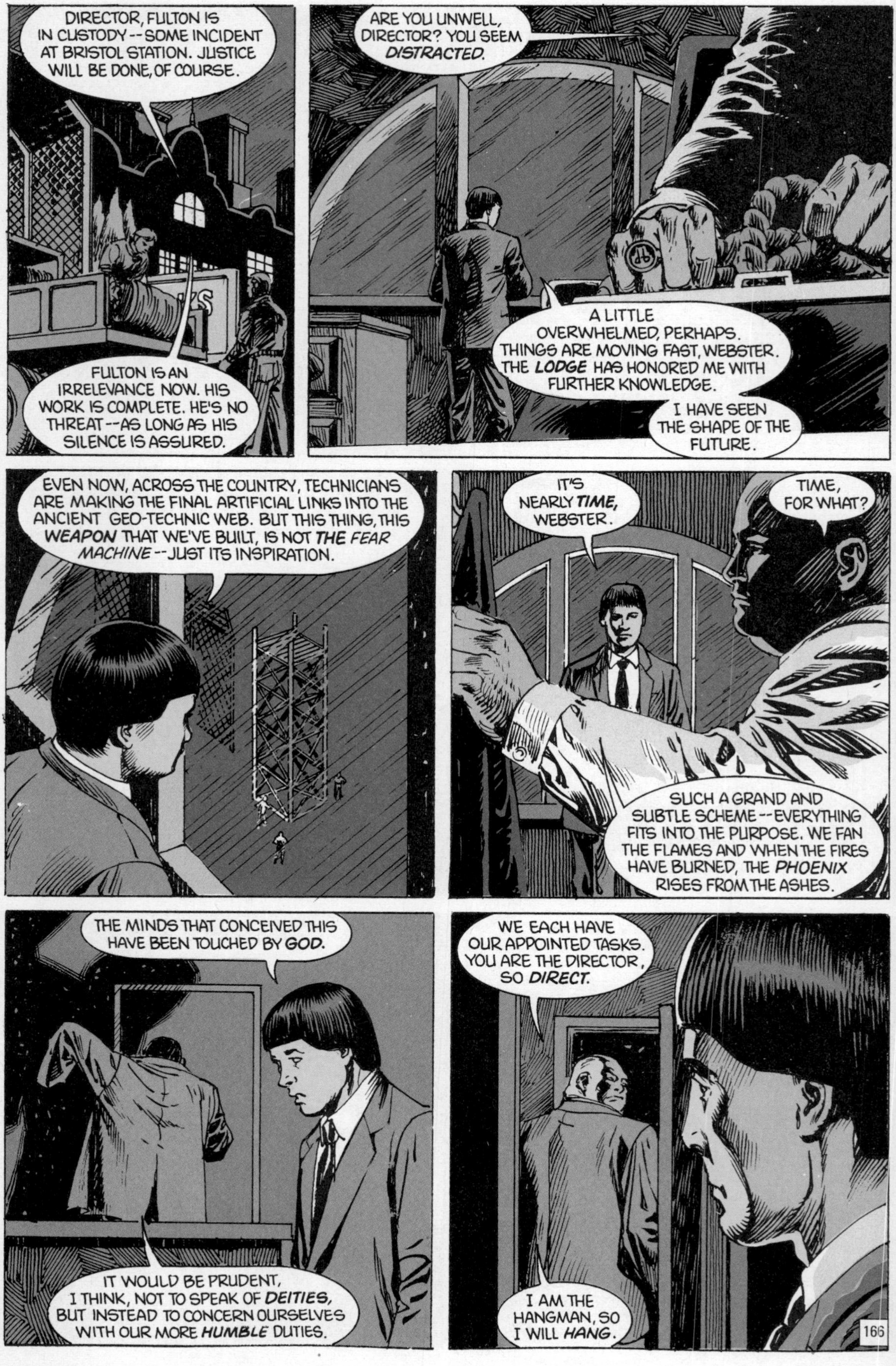
DIRECTOR, FULTON IS IN CUSTODY -- SOME INCIDENT AT BRISTOL STATION. JUSTICE WILL BE DONE, OF COURSE.
FULTON IS AN IRRELEVANCE NOW. HIS WORK IS COMPLETE. HE'S NO THREAT -- AS LONG AS HIS SILENCE IS ASSURED.
ARE YOU UNWELL, DIRECTOR? YOU SEEM DISTRACTED.
A LITTLE OVERWHELMED, PERHAPS. THINGS ARE MOVING FAST, WEBSTER. THE LODGE HAS HONORED ME WITH FURTHER KNOWLEDGE.
I HAVE SEEN THE SHAPE OF THE FUTURE.
EVEN NOW, ACROSS THE COUNTRY, TECHNICIANS ARE MAKING THE FINAL ARTIFICIAL LINKS INTO THE ANCIENT GEO-TECHNIC WEB. BUT THIS THING, THIS WEAPON THAT WE'VE BUILT, IS NOT THE FEAR MACHINE -- JUST ITS INSPIRATION.
IT'S NEARLY TIME, WEBSTER.
TIME, FOR WHAT?
SUCH A GRAND AND SUBTLE SCHEME -- EVERYTHING FITS INTO THE PURPOSE. WE FAN THE FLAMES AND WHEN THE FIRES HAVE BURNED, THE PHOENIX RISES FROM THE ASHES.
THE MINDS THAT CONCEIVED THIS HAVE BEEN TOUCHED BY GOD.
IT WOULD BE PRUDENT, I THINK, NOT TO SPEAK OF DEITIES, BUT INSTEAD TO CONCERN OURSELVES WITH OUR MORE HUMBLE DUTIES.
WE EACH HAVE OUR APPOINTED TASKS. YOU ARE THE DIRECTOR, SO DIRECT.
I AM THE HANGMAN, SO I WILL HANG.

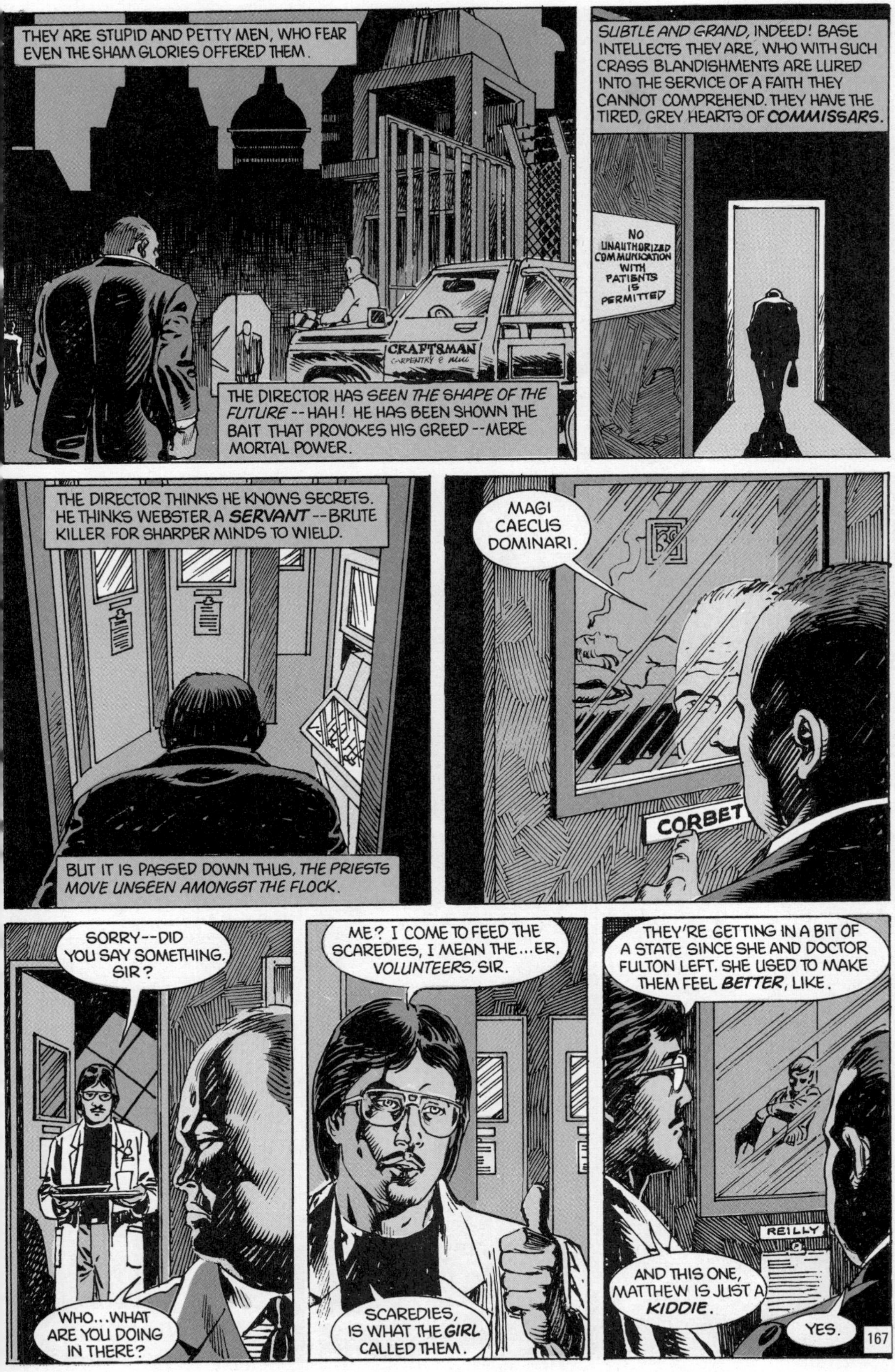
THEY ARE STUPID AND PETTY MEN, WHO FEAR EVEN THE SHAM GLORIES OFFERED THEM.
CRAFTSMAN CARPENTRY & MILL
THE DIRECTOR HAS SEEN THE SHAPE OF THE FUTURE --HAH! HE HAS BEEN SHOWN THE BAIT THAT PROVOKES HIS GREED --MERE MORTAL POWER.
SUBTLE AND GRAND, INDEED! BASE INTELLECTS THEY ARE, WHO WITH SUCH CRASS BLANDISHMENTS ARE LURED INTO THE SERVICE OF A FAITH THEY CANNOT COMPREHEND. THEY HAVE THE TIRED, GREY HEARTS OF COMMISSARS.
NO UNAUTHORIZED COMMUNICATION WITH PATIENTS IS PERMITTED
THE DIRECTOR THINKS HE KNOWS SECRETS. HE THINKS WEBSTER A SERVANT --BRUTE KILLER FOR SHARPER MINDS TO WIELD.
BUT IT IS PASSED DOWN THUS, THE PRIESTS MOVE UNSEEN AMONGST THE FLOCK.
MAGI CAECUS DOMINARI.
CORBET
SORRY--DID YOU SAY SOMETHING, SIR?
WHO...WHAT ARE YOU DOING IN THERE?
ME? I COME TO FEED THE SCAREDIES, I MEAN THE...ER, VOLUNTEERS, SIR.
SCAREDIES, IS WHAT THE GIRL CALLED THEM.
THEY'RE GETTING IN A BIT OF A STATE SINCE SHE AND DOCTOR FULTON LEFT. SHE USED TO MAKE THEM FEEL BETTER, LIKE.
REILLY
AND THIS ONE, MATTHEW IS JUST A KIDDIE.
YES.

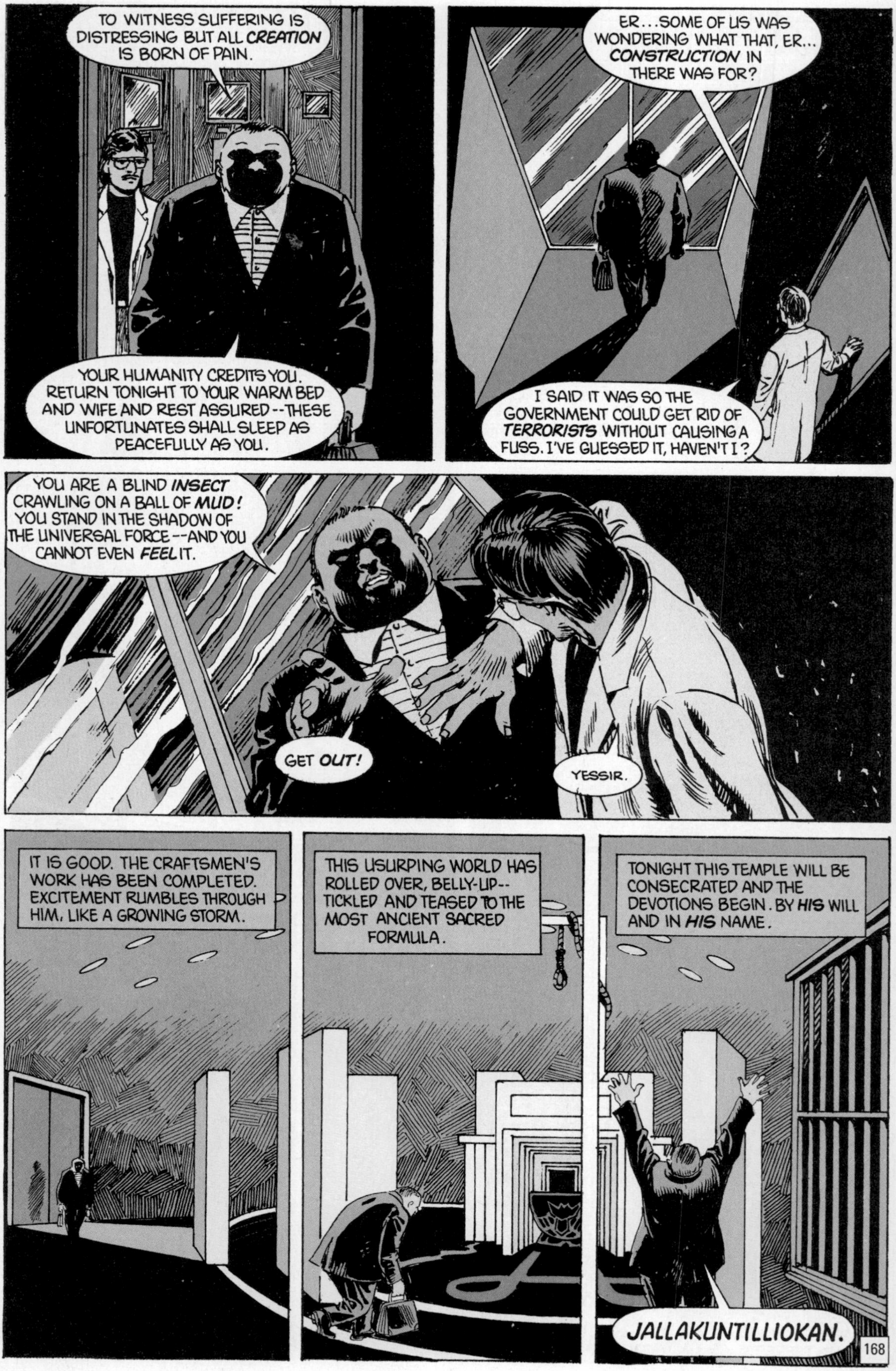
TO WITNESS SUFFERING IS DISTRESSING BUT ALL CREATION IS BORN OF PAIN.
YOUR HUMANITY CREDITS YOU. RETURN TONIGHT TO YOUR WARM BED AND WIFE AND REST ASSURED--THESE UNFORTUNATES SHALL SLEEP AS PEACEFULLY AS YOU.
ER...SOME OF US WAS WONDERING WHAT THAT, ER... CONSTRUCTION IN THERE WAS FOR?
I SAID IT WAS SO THE GOVERNMENT COULD GET RID OF TERRORISTS WITHOUT CAUSING A FUSS. I'VE GUESSED IT, HAVEN'T I?
YOU ARE A BLIND INSECT CRAWLING ON A BALL OF MUD! YOU STAND IN THE SHADOW OF THE UNIVERSAL FORCE--AND YOU CANNOT EVEN FEEL IT.
GET OUT!
YESSIR.
IT IS GOOD. THE CRAFTSMEN'S WORK HAS BEEN COMPLETED. EXCITEMENT RUMBLES THROUGH HIM, LIKE A GROWING STORM.
THIS USURPING WORLD HAS ROLLED OVER, BELLY-UP--TICKLED AND TEASED TO THE MOST ANCIENT SACRED FORMULA.
TONIGHT THIS TEMPLE WILL BE CONSECRATED AND THE DEVOTIONS BEGIN. BY HIS WILL AND IN HIS NAME.
JALLAKUNTILLIOKAN.

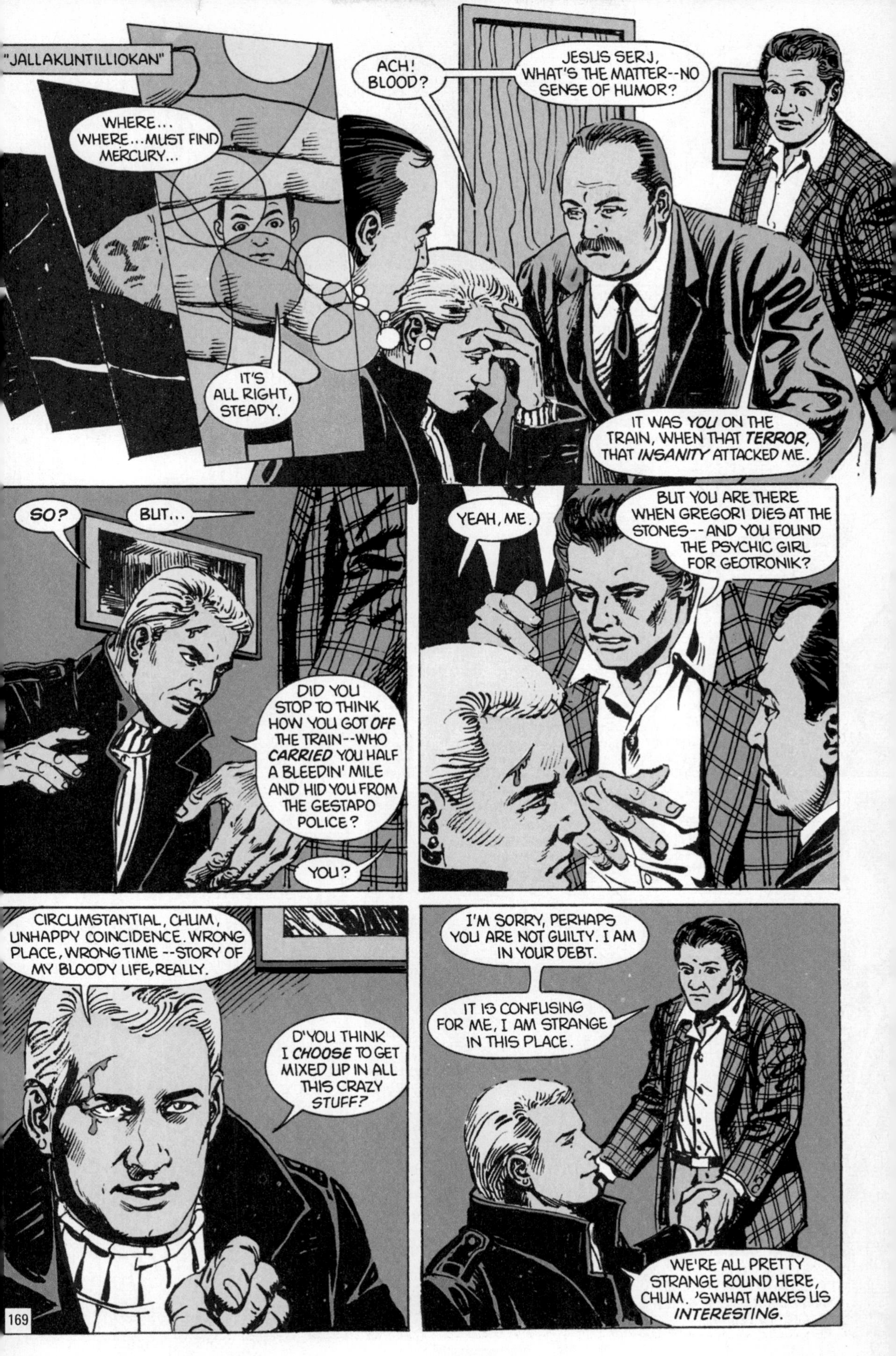
"JALLAKUNTILLIOKAN"
WHERE... WHERE...MUST FIND MERCURY...
ACH! BLOOD?
JESUS SERJ, WHAT'S THE MATTER--NO SENSE OF HUMOR?
IT'S ALL RIGHT, STEADY.
IT WAS *YOU* ON THE TRAIN, WHEN THAT *TERROR*, THAT *INSANITY* ATTACKED ME.
SO?
BUT...
DID YOU STOP TO THINK HOW YOU GOT *OFF* THE TRAIN--WHO *CARRIED* YOU HALF A BLEEDIN' MILE AND HID YOU FROM THE GESTAPO POLICE?
YOU?
YEAH, ME.
BUT YOU ARE THERE WHEN GREGORI DIES AT THE STONES--AND YOU FOUND THE PSYCHIC GIRL FOR GEOTRONIK?
CIRCUMSTANTIAL, CHUM, UNHAPPY COINCIDENCE. WRONG PLACE, WRONG TIME --STORY OF MY BLOODY LIFE, REALLY.
D'YOU THINK I *CHOOSE* TO GET MIXED UP IN ALL THIS CRAZY *STUFF?*
I'M SORRY, PERHAPS YOU ARE NOT GUILTY. I AM IN YOUR DEBT.
IT IS CONFUSING FOR ME, I AM STRANGE IN THIS PLACE.
WE'RE ALL PRETTY STRANGE ROUND HERE, CHUM. 'SWHAT MAKES US *INTERESTING*.

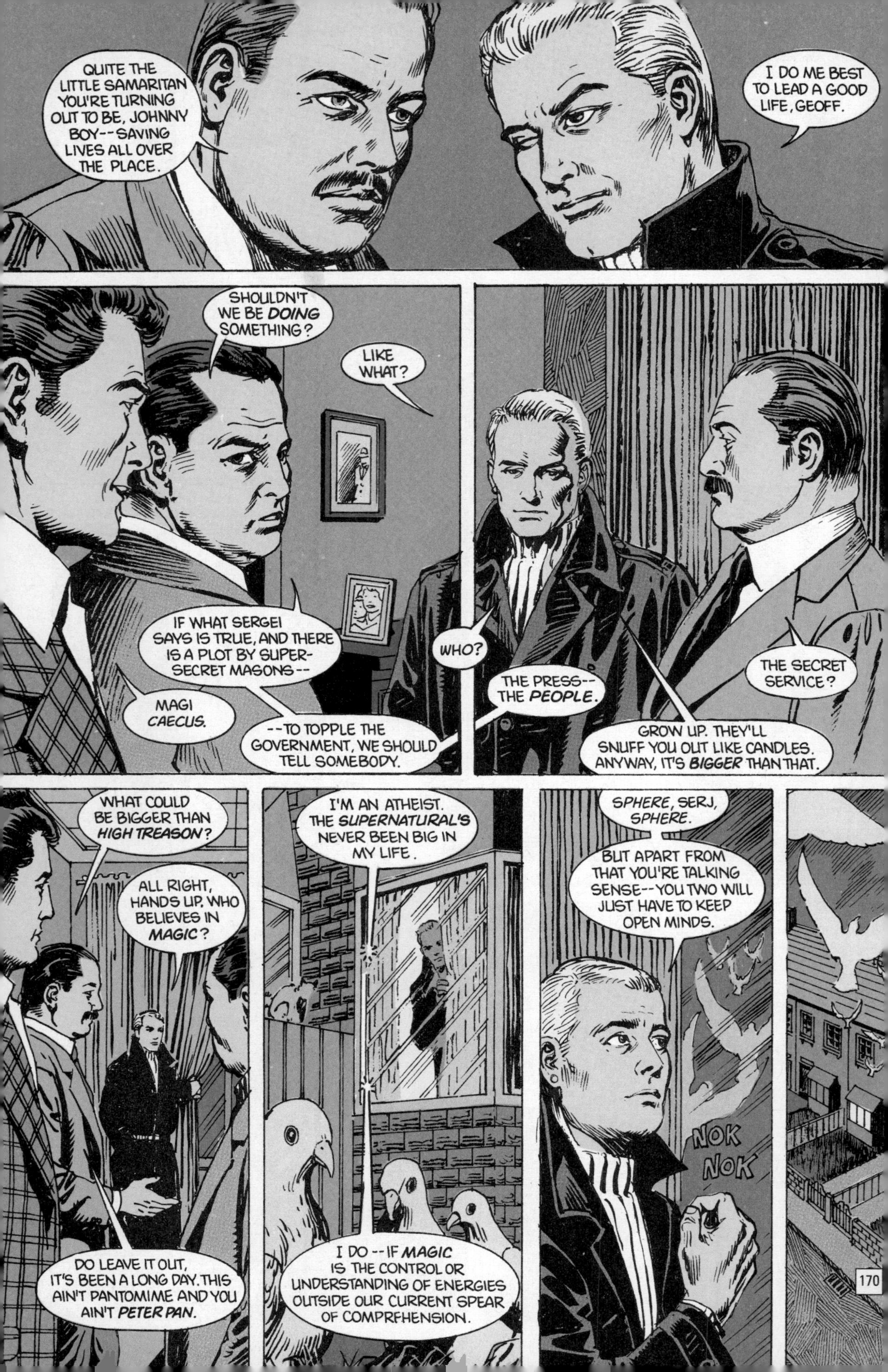
QUITE THE LITTLE SAMARITAN YOU'RE TURNING OUT TO BE, JOHNNY BOY--SAVING LIVES ALL OVER THE PLACE.
I DO ME BEST TO LEAD A GOOD LIFE, GEOFF.
SHOULDN'T WE BE *DOING* SOMETHING?
LIKE WHAT?
IF WHAT SERGEI SAYS IS TRUE, AND THERE IS A PLOT BY SUPER-SECRET MASONS--
MAGI *CAECUS.*
--TO TOPPLE THE GOVERNMENT, WE SHOULD TELL SOMEBODY.
WHO?
THE PRESS--THE *PEOPLE*.
THE SECRET SERVICE?
GROW UP. THEY'LL SNUFF YOU OUT LIKE CANDLES. ANYWAY, IT'S *BIGGER* THAN THAT.
WHAT COULD BE BIGGER THAN *HIGH TREASON*?
ALL RIGHT, HANDS UP. WHO BELIEVES IN *MAGIC*?
DO LEAVE IT OUT, IT'S BEEN A LONG DAY. THIS AIN'T PANTOMIME AND YOU AIN'T *PETER PAN*.
I'M AN ATHEIST. THE *SUPERNATURAL'S* NEVER BEEN BIG IN MY LIFE.
I DO--IF *MAGIC* IS THE CONTROL OR UNDERSTANDING OF ENERGIES OUTSIDE OUR CURRENT SPEAR OF COMPRFHENSION.
SPHERE, SERJ, *SPHERE*.
BUT APART FROM THAT YOU'RE TALKING SENSE--YOU TWO WILL JUST HAVE TO KEEP OPEN MINDS.
NOK NOK

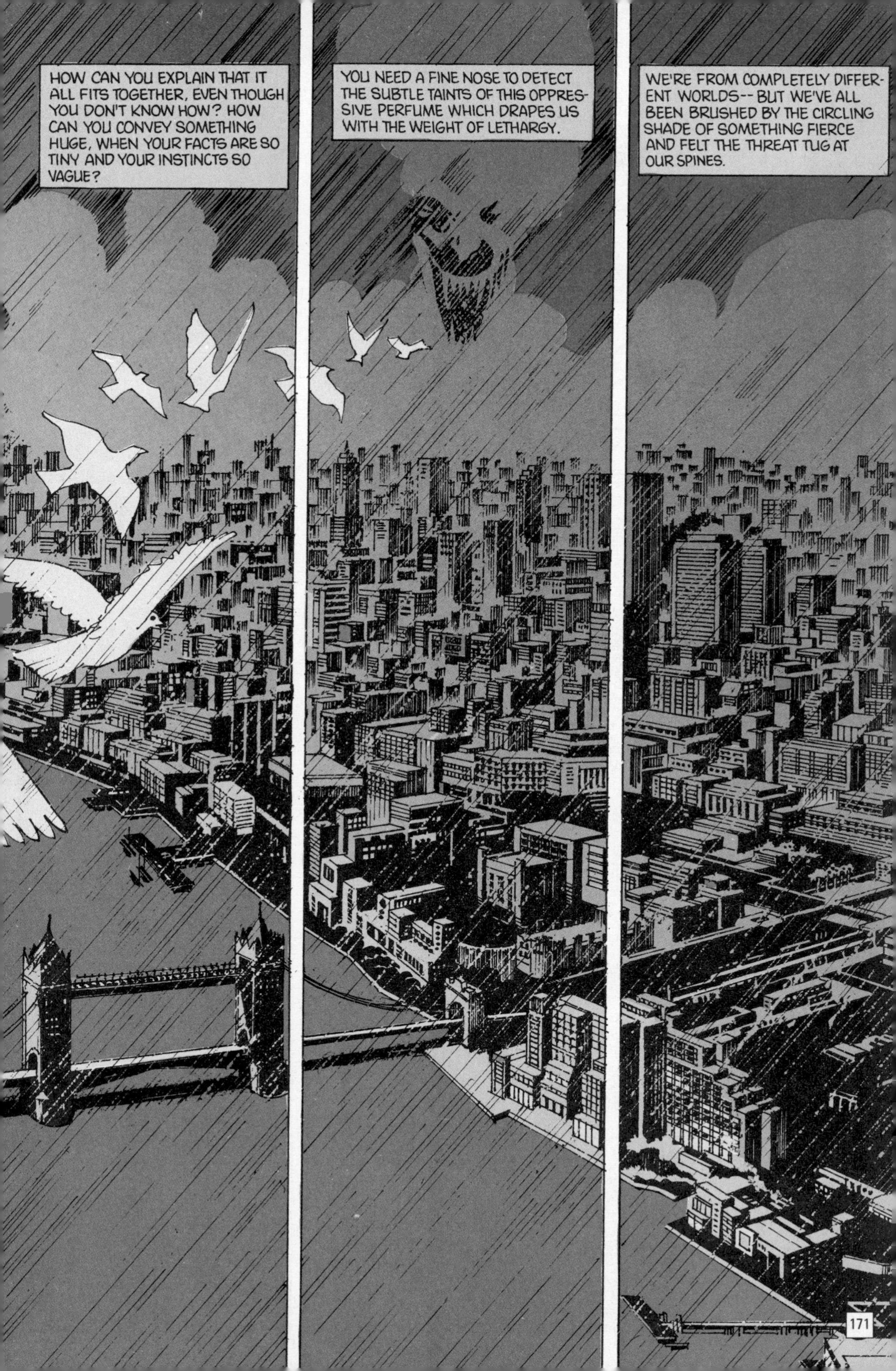
HOW CAN YOU EXPLAIN THAT IT ALL FITS TOGETHER, EVEN THOUGH YOU DON'T KNOW HOW? HOW CAN YOU CONVEY SOMETHING HUGE, WHEN YOUR FACTS ARE SO TINY AND YOUR INSTINCTS SO VAGUE?
YOU NEED A FINE NOSE TO DETECT THE SUBTLE TAINTS OF THIS OPPRESSIVE PERFUME WHICH DRAPES US WITH THE WEIGHT OF LETHARGY.
WE'RE FROM COMPLETELY DIFFERENT WORLDS-- BUT WE'VE ALL BEEN BRUSHED BY THE CIRCLING SHADE OF SOMETHING FIERCE AND FELT THE THREAT TUG AT OUR SPINES.

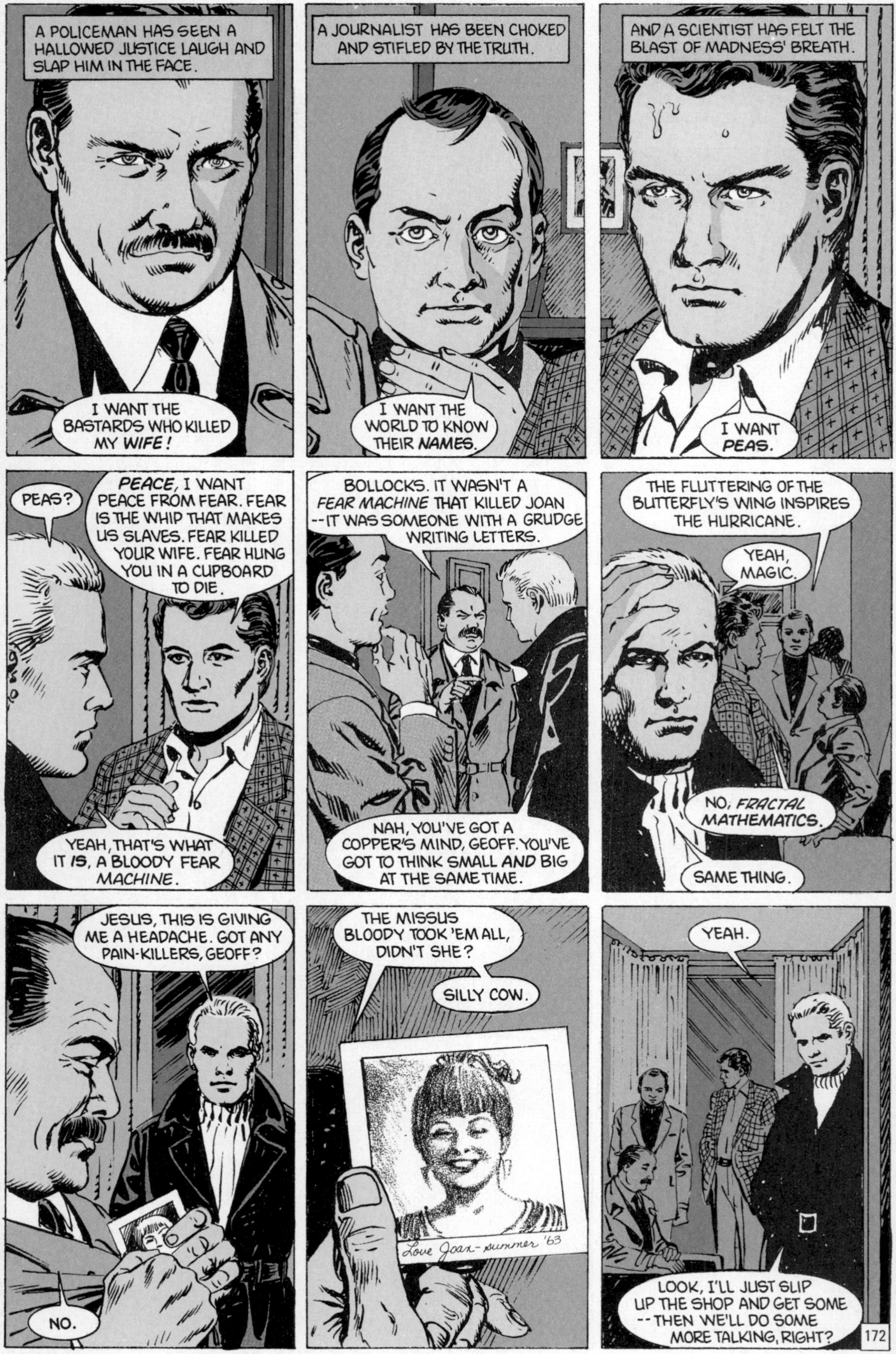
A POLICEMAN HAS SEEN A HALLOWED JUSTICE LAUGH AND SLAP HIM IN THE FACE.
I WANT THE BASTARDS WHO KILLED MY *WIFE*!
A JOURNALIST HAS BEEN CHOKED AND STIFLED BY THE TRUTH.
I WANT THE WORLD TO KNOW THEIR *NAMES*.
AND A SCIENTIST HAS FELT THE BLAST OF MADNESS' BREATH.
I WANT *PEAS*.
PEAS?
PEACE, I WANT PEACE FROM FEAR. FEAR IS THE WHIP THAT MAKES US SLAVES. FEAR KILLED YOUR WIFE. FEAR HUNG YOU IN A CUPBOARD TO DIE.
YEAH, THAT'S WHAT IT *IS*, A BLOODY FEAR *MACHINE*.
BOLLOCKS. IT WASN'T A *FEAR MACHINE* THAT KILLED JOAN --IT WAS SOMEONE WITH A GRUDGE WRITING LETTERS.
NAH, YOU'VE GOT A COPPER'S MIND, GEOFF. YOU'VE GOT TO THINK SMALL *AND* BIG AT THE SAME TIME.
THE FLUTTERING OF THE BUTTERFLY'S WING INSPIRES THE HURRICANE.
YEAH, MAGIC.
NO, *FRACTAL MATHEMATICS*.
SAME THING.
JESUS, THIS IS GIVING ME A HEADACHE. GOT ANY PAIN-KILLERS, GEOFF?
NO.
THE MISSUS BLOODY TOOK 'EM ALL, DIDN'T SHE?
SILLY COW.
Love Joan - summer '63
YEAH.
LOOK, I'LL JUST SLIP UP THE SHOP AND GET SOME --THEN WE'LL DO SOME MORE TALKING, RIGHT?

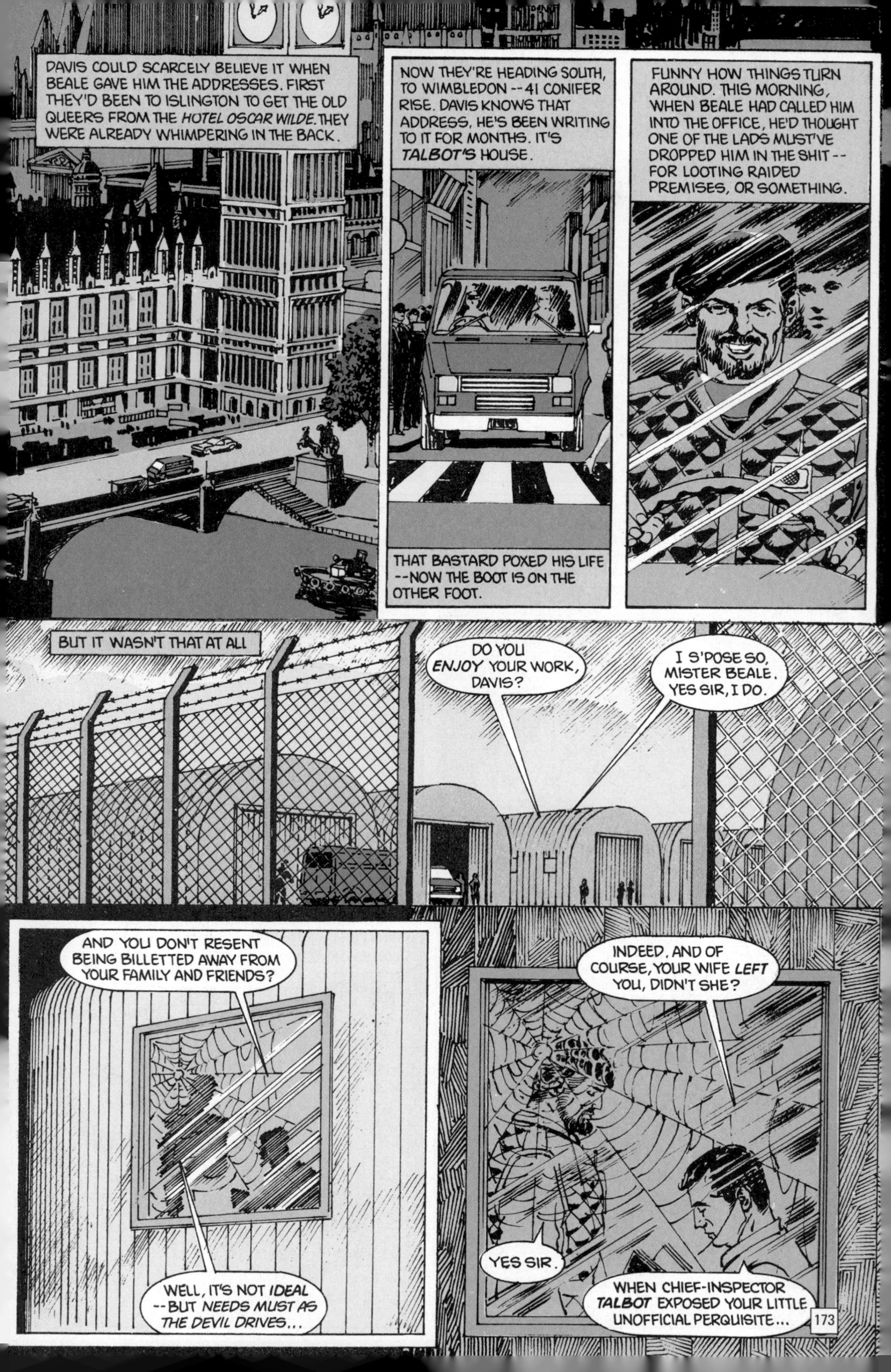

DAVIS COULD SCARCELY BELIEVE IT WHEN BEALE GAVE HIM THE ADDRESSES. FIRST THEY'D BEEN TO ISLINGTON TO GET THE OLD QUEERS FROM THE *HOTEL OSCAR WILDE*. THEY WERE ALREADY WHIMPERING IN THE BACK.
NOW THEY'RE HEADING SOUTH, TO WIMBLEDON --41 CONIFER RISE. DAVIS KNOWS THAT ADDRESS, HE'S BEEN WRITING TO IT FOR MONTHS. IT'S *TALBOT'S* HOUSE.
THAT BASTARD POXED HIS LIFE --NOW THE BOOT IS ON THE OTHER FOOT.
FUNNY HOW THINGS TURN AROUND. THIS MORNING, WHEN BEALE HAD CALLED HIM INTO THE OFFICE, HE'D THOUGHT ONE OF THE LADS MUST'VE DROPPED HIM IN THE SHIT-- FOR LOOTING RAIDED PREMISES, OR SOMETHING.
BUT IT WASN'T THAT AT ALL
DO YOU *ENJOY* YOUR WORK, DAVIS?
I S'POSE SO, MISTER BEALE. YES SIR, I DO.
AND YOU DON'T RESENT BEING BILLETTED AWAY FROM YOUR FAMILY AND FRIENDS?
WELL, IT'S NOT *IDEAL* --BUT *NEEDS MUST AS THE DEVIL DRIVES*...
INDEED. AND OF COURSE, YOUR WIFE *LEFT* YOU, DIDN'T SHE?
YES SIR.
WHEN CHIEF-INSPECTOR *TALBOT* EXPOSED YOUR LITTLE UNOFFICIAL PERQUISITE...

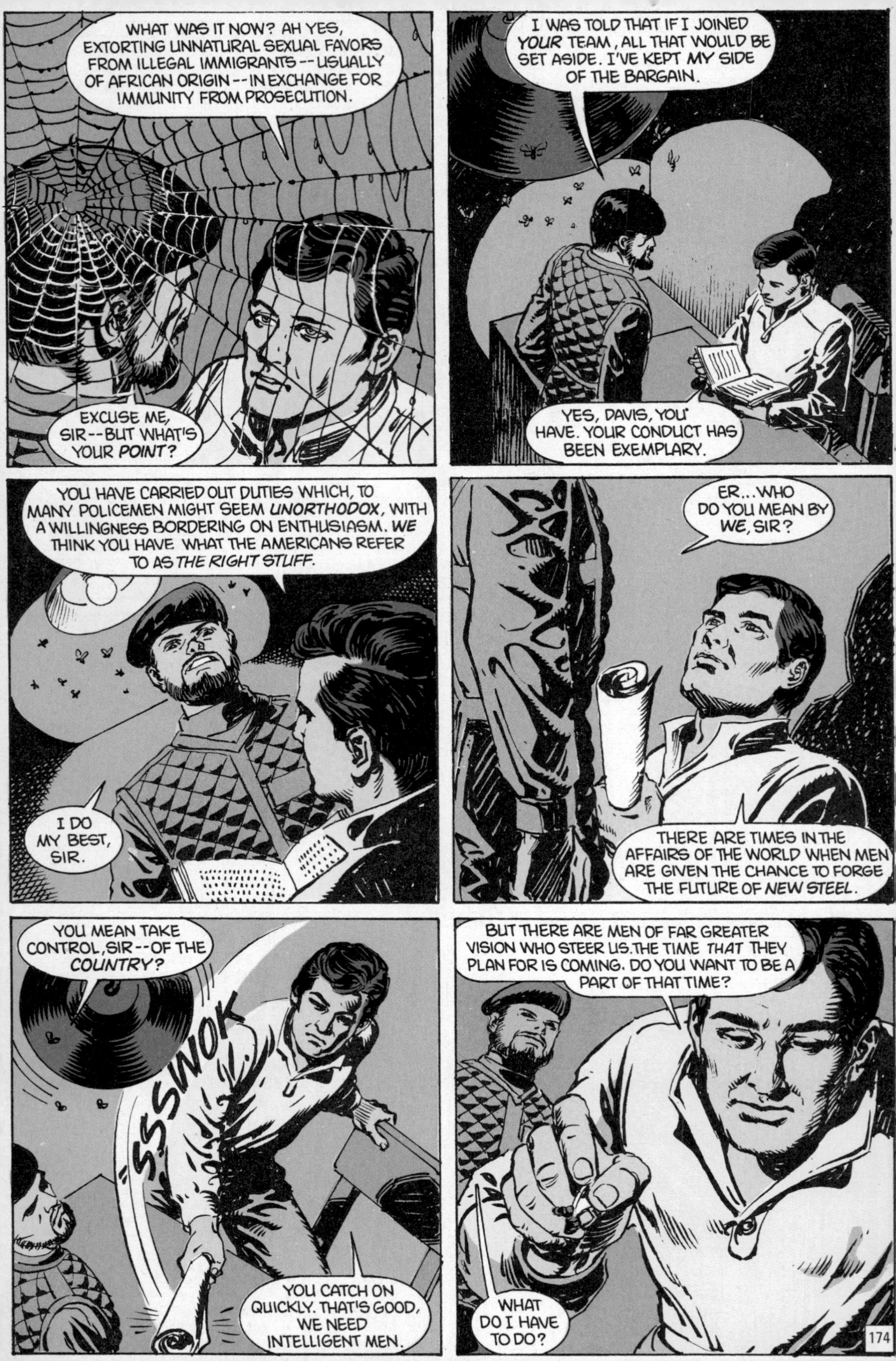
WHAT WAS IT NOW? AH YES, EXTORTING UNNATURAL SEXUAL FAVORS FROM ILLEGAL IMMIGRANTS--USUALLY OF AFRICAN ORIGIN--IN EXCHANGE FOR IMMUNITY FROM PROSECUTION.
EXCUSE ME, SIR--BUT WHAT'S YOUR *POINT*?
I WAS TOLD THAT IF I JOINED *YOUR* TEAM, ALL THAT WOULD BE SET ASIDE. I'VE KEPT *MY* SIDE OF THE BARGAIN.
YES, DAVIS, YOU HAVE. YOUR CONDUCT HAS BEEN EXEMPLARY.
YOU HAVE CARRIED OUT DUTIES WHICH, TO MANY POLICEMEN MIGHT SEEM *UNORTHODOX*, WITH A WILLINGNESS BORDERING ON ENTHUSIASM. *WE* THINK YOU HAVE WHAT THE AMERICANS REFER TO AS *THE RIGHT STUFF*.
I DO MY BEST, SIR.
ER... WHO DO YOU MEAN BY *WE*, SIR?
THERE ARE TIMES IN THE AFFAIRS OF THE WORLD WHEN MEN ARE GIVEN THE CHANCE TO FORGE THE FUTURE OF *NEW STEEL*.
YOU MEAN TAKE CONTROL, SIR--OF THE *COUNTRY*?
SSSWOK
YOU CATCH ON QUICKLY. THAT'S GOOD, WE NEED INTELLIGENT MEN.
BUT THERE ARE MEN OF FAR GREATER VISION WHO STEER US. THE TIME *THAT* THEY PLAN FOR IS COMING. DO YOU WANT TO BE A PART OF THAT TIME?
WHAT DO I HAVE TO DO?

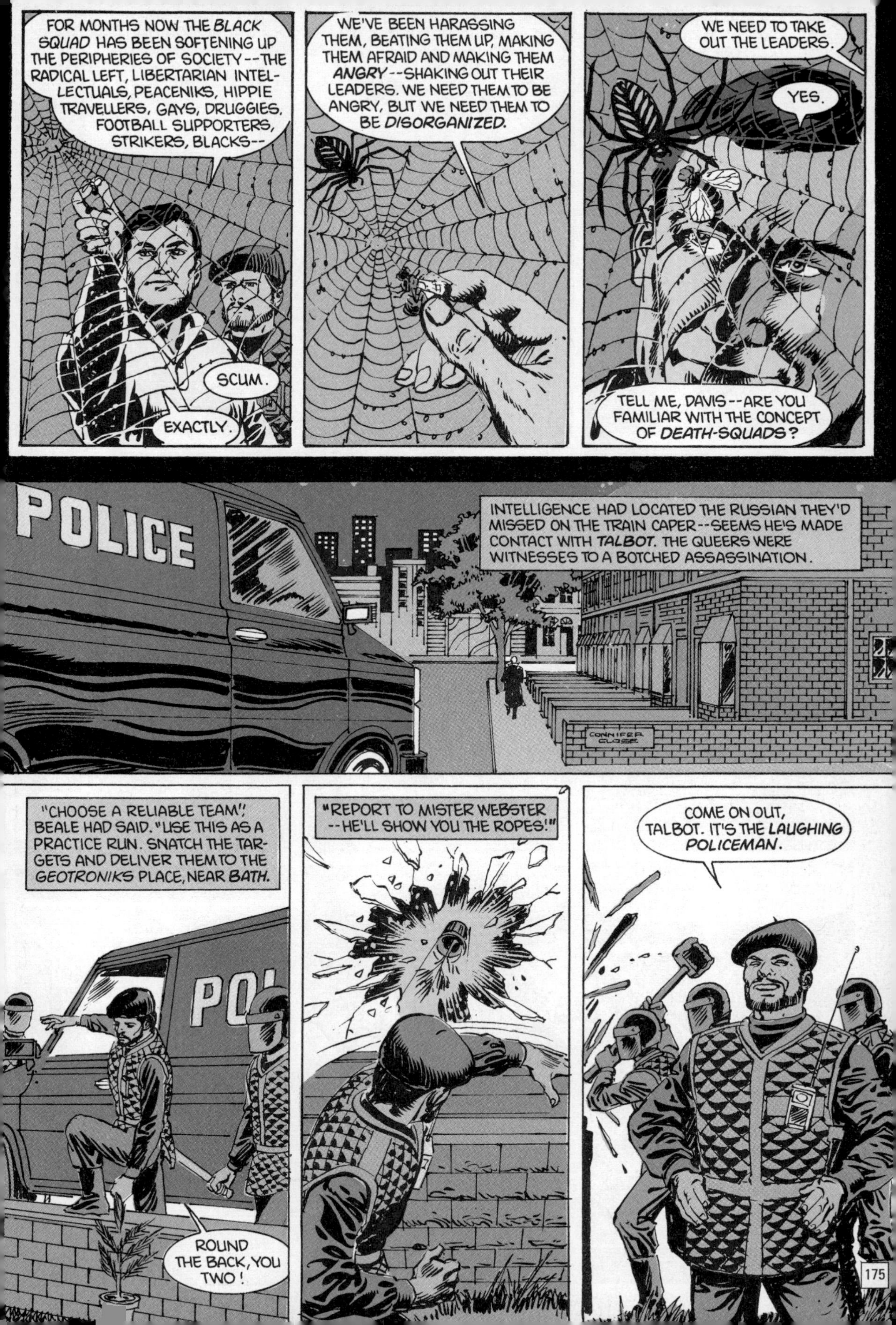
FOR MONTHS NOW THE BLACK SQUAD HAS BEEN SOFTENING UP THE PERIPHERIES OF SOCIETY--THE RADICAL LEFT, LIBERTARIAN INTELLECTUALS, PEACENIKS, HIPPIE TRAVELLERS, GAYS, DRUGGIES, FOOTBALL SUPPORTERS, STRIKERS, BLACKS--
SCUM.
EXACTLY.
WE'VE BEEN HARASSING THEM, BEATING THEM UP, MAKING THEM AFRAID AND MAKING THEM ANGRY--SHAKING OUT THEIR LEADERS. WE NEED THEM TO BE ANGRY, BUT WE NEED THEM TO BE DISORGANIZED.
WE NEED TO TAKE OUT THE LEADERS.
YES.
TELL ME, DAVIS--ARE YOU FAMILIAR WITH THE CONCEPT OF DEATH-SQUADS?
POLICE
INTELLIGENCE HAD LOCATED THE RUSSIAN THEY'D MISSED ON THE TRAIN CAPER--SEEMS HE'S MADE CONTACT WITH TALBOT. THE QUEERS WERE WITNESSES TO A BOTCHED ASSASSINATION.
CONNIFER CLOSE
"CHOOSE A RELIABLE TEAM," BEALE HAD SAID. "USE THIS AS A PRACTICE RUN. SNATCH THE TARGETS AND DELIVER THEM TO THE GEOTRONIKS PLACE, NEAR BATH.
POL
ROUND THE BACK, YOU TWO!
"REPORT TO MISTER WEBSTER --HE'LL SHOW YOU THE ROPES!"
COME ON OUT, TALBOT. IT'S THE LAUGHING POLICEMAN.

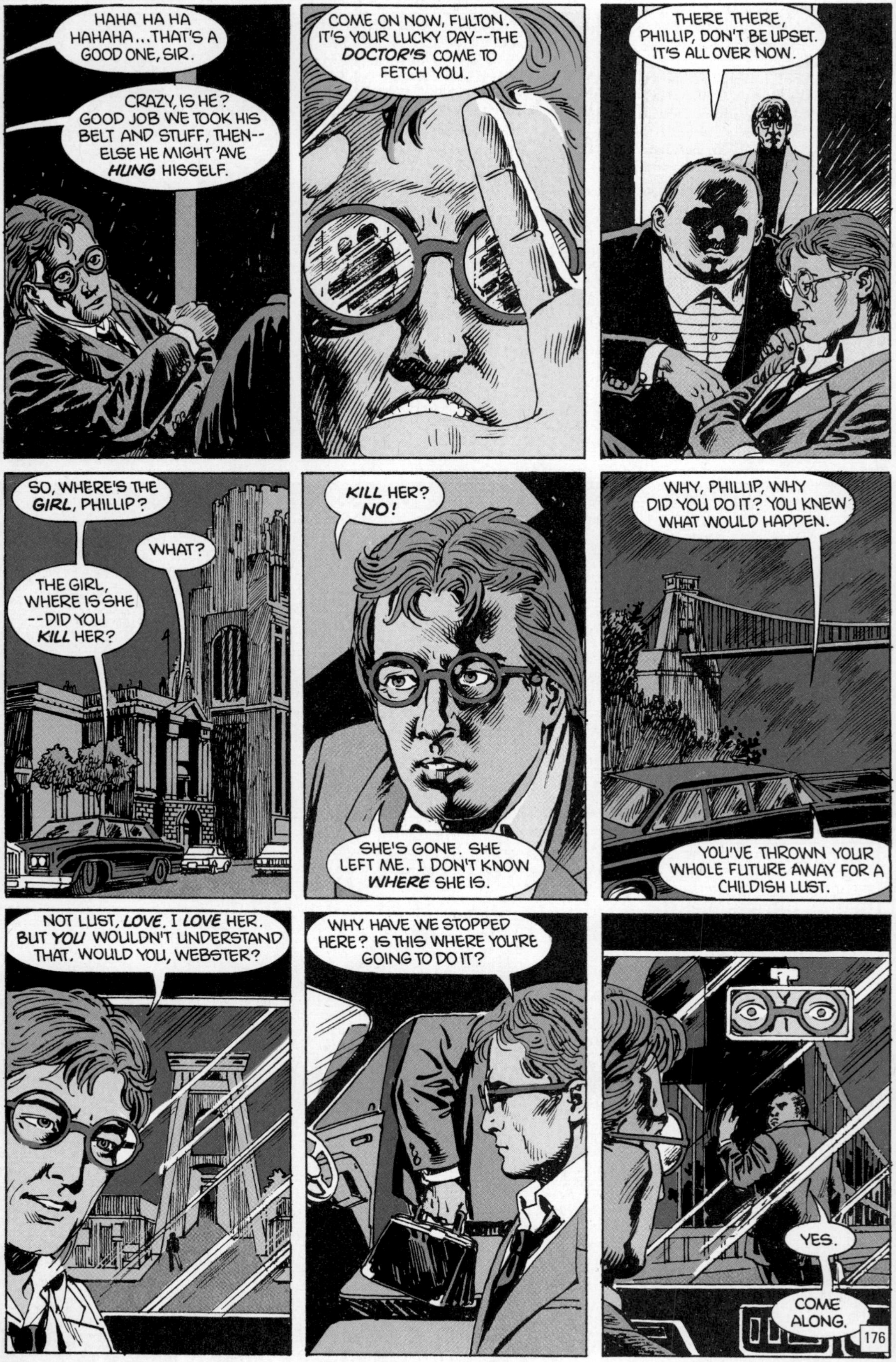
HAHA HA HA HAHAHA...THAT'S A GOOD ONE, SIR.
CRAZY, IS HE? GOOD JOB WE TOOK HIS BELT AND STUFF, THEN-- ELSE HE MIGHT 'AVE HUNG HISSELF.
COME ON NOW, FULTON. IT'S YOUR LUCKY DAY--THE DOCTOR'S COME TO FETCH YOU.
THERE THERE, PHILLIP, DON'T BE UPSET. IT'S ALL OVER NOW.
SO, WHERE'S THE GIRL, PHILLIP?
WHAT?
THE GIRL, WHERE IS SHE --DID YOU KILL HER?
KILL HER? NO!
SHE'S GONE. SHE LEFT ME. I DON'T KNOW WHERE SHE IS.
WHY, PHILLIP, WHY DID YOU DO IT? YOU KNEW WHAT WOULD HAPPEN.
YOU'VE THROWN YOUR WHOLE FUTURE AWAY FOR A CHILDISH LUST.
NOT LUST, LOVE. I LOVE HER. BUT YOU WOULDN'T UNDERSTAND THAT, WOULD YOU, WEBSTER?
WHY HAVE WE STOPPED HERE? IS THIS WHERE YOU'RE GOING TO DO IT?
YES.
COME ALONG.

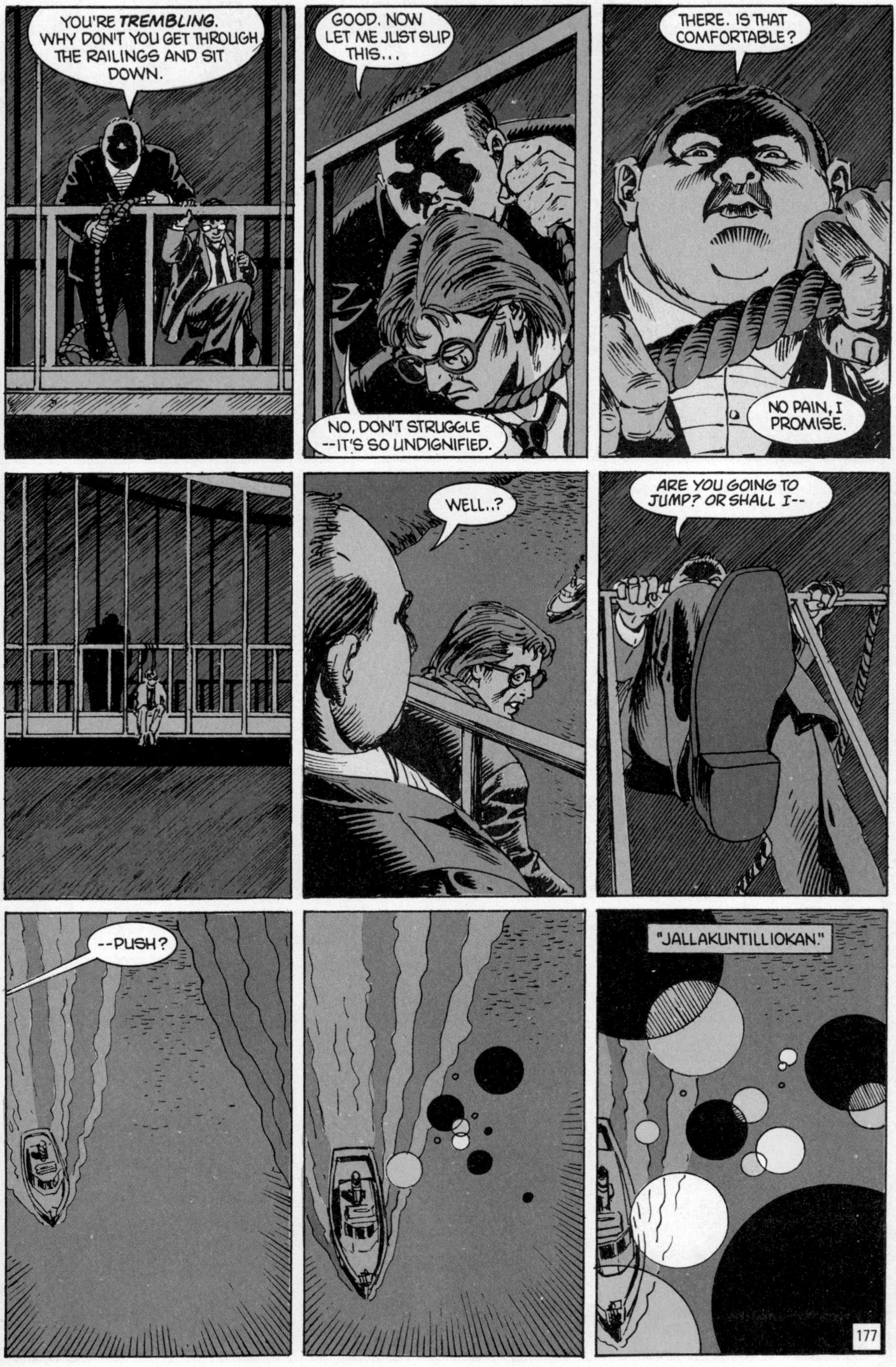
YOU'RE TREMBLING. WHY DON'T YOU GET THROUGH THE RAILINGS AND SIT DOWN.
GOOD. NOW LET ME JUST SLIP THIS...
NO, DON'T STRUGGLE --IT'S SO UNDIGNIFIED.
THERE. IS THAT COMFORTABLE?
NO PAIN, I PROMISE.
WELL..?
ARE YOU GOING TO JUMP? OR SHALL I--
--PUSH?
"JALLAKUNTILLIOKAN."

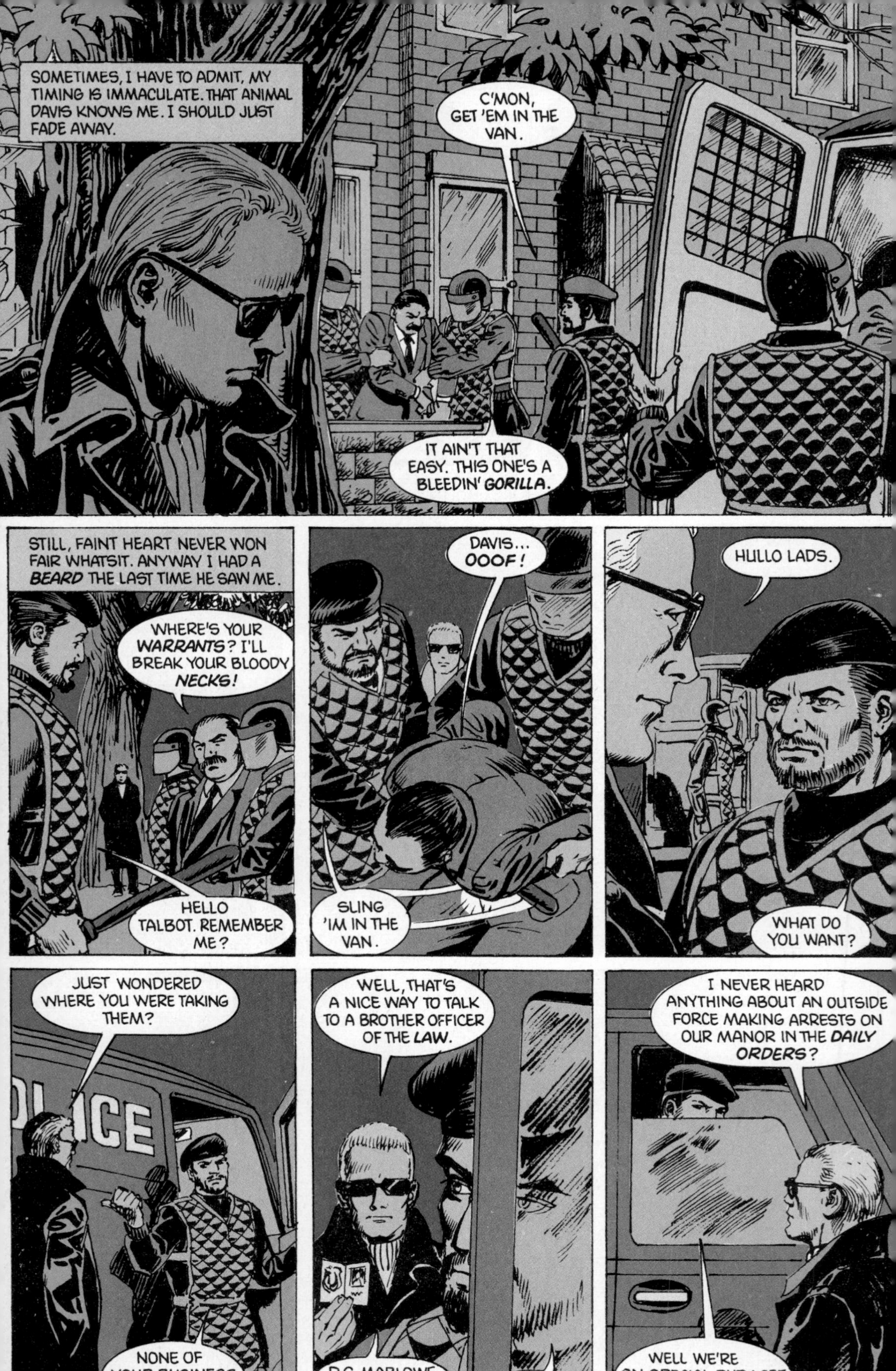

SOMETIMES, I HAVE TO ADMIT, MY TIMING IS IMMACULATE. THAT ANIMAL DAVIS KNOWS ME. I SHOULD JUST FADE AWAY.
C'MON, GET 'EM IN THE VAN.
IT AIN'T THAT EASY. THIS ONE'S A BLEEDIN' GORILLA.
STILL, FAINT HEART NEVER WON FAIR WHATSIT. ANYWAY I HAD A BEARD THE LAST TIME HE SAW ME.
WHERE'S YOUR WARRANTS? I'LL BREAK YOUR BLOODY NECKS!
HELLO TALBOT. REMEMBER ME?
DAVIS... OOOF!
SLING 'IM IN THE VAN.
HULLO LADS.
WHAT DO YOU WANT?
JUST WONDERED WHERE YOU WERE TAKING THEM?
OLICE
NONE OF YOUR BUSINESS, PAL. SLING YOUR HOOK!
WELL, THAT'S A NICE WAY TO TALK TO A BROTHER OFFICER OF THE LAW.
D.C. MARLOWE --LOCAL C.I.D.
OH, THE PLOD, EH?
I NEVER HEARD ANYTHING ABOUT AN OUTSIDE FORCE MAKING ARRESTS ON OUR MANOR IN THE DAILY ORDERS?
WELL WE'RE ON SPECIAL DUTY, SEE --COUNTER-ESPIONAGE.

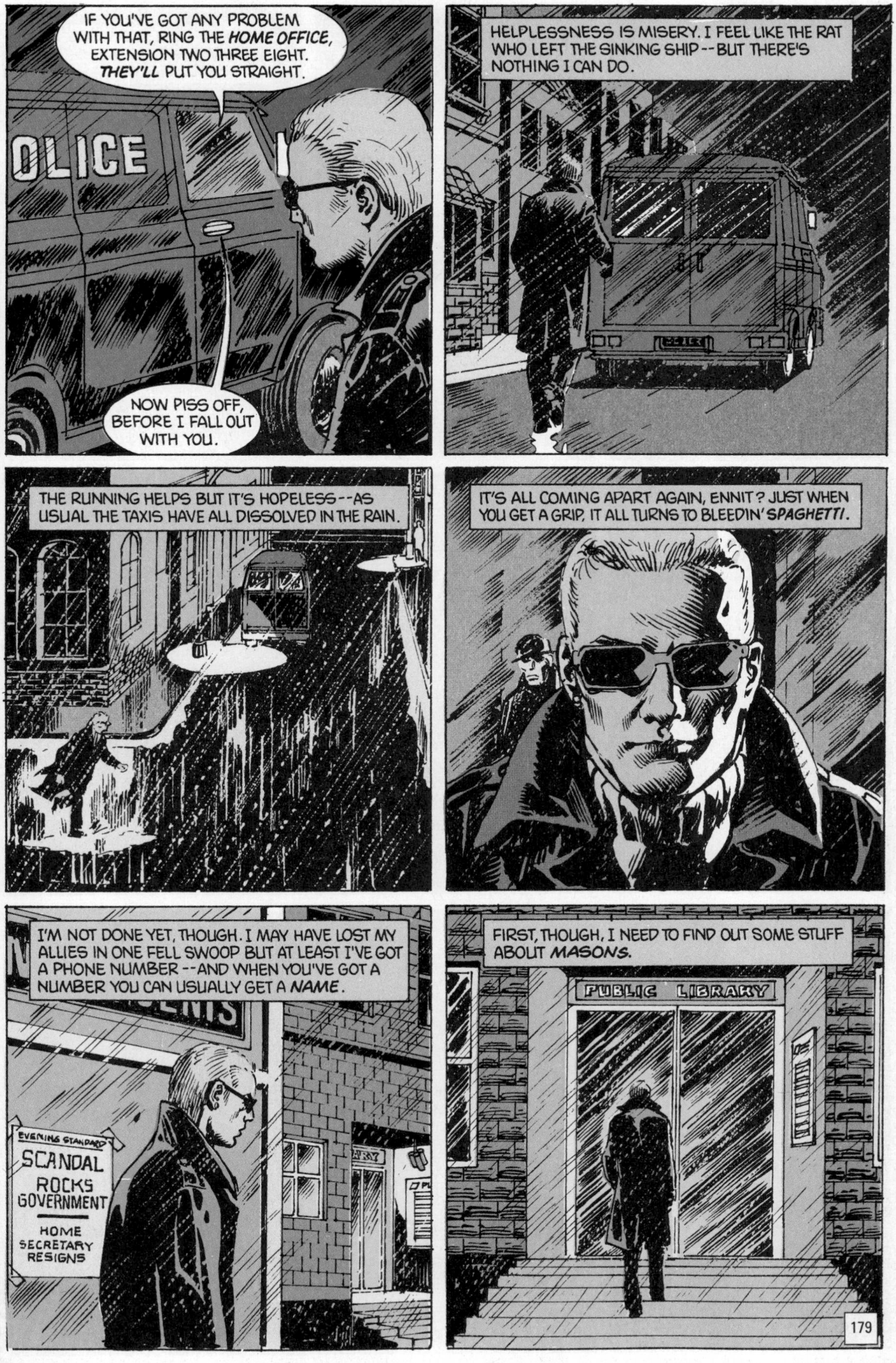

IF YOU'VE GOT ANY PROBLEM WITH THAT, RING THE *HOME OFFICE*, EXTENSION TWO THREE EIGHT. *THEY'LL* PUT YOU STRAIGHT.
OLICE
NOW PISS OFF, BEFORE I FALL OUT WITH YOU.
HELPLESSNESS IS MISERY. I FEEL LIKE THE RAT WHO LEFT THE SINKING SHIP--BUT THERE'S NOTHING I CAN DO.
THE RUNNING HELPS BUT IT'S HOPELESS--AS USUAL THE TAXIS HAVE ALL DISSOLVED IN THE RAIN.
IT'S ALL COMING APART AGAIN, ENNIT? JUST WHEN YOU GET A GRIP, IT ALL TURNS TO BLEEDIN' *SPAGHETTI*.
I'M NOT DONE YET, THOUGH. I MAY HAVE LOST MY ALLIES IN ONE FELL SWOOP BUT AT LEAST I'VE GOT A PHONE NUMBER--AND WHEN YOU'VE GOT A NUMBER YOU CAN USUALLY GET A *NAME*.
EVENING STANDARD
SCANDAL ROCKS GOVERNMENT
HOME SECRETARY RESIGNS
FIRST, THOUGH, I NEED TO FIND OUT SOME STUFF ABOUT *MASONS*.
PUBLIC LIBRARY

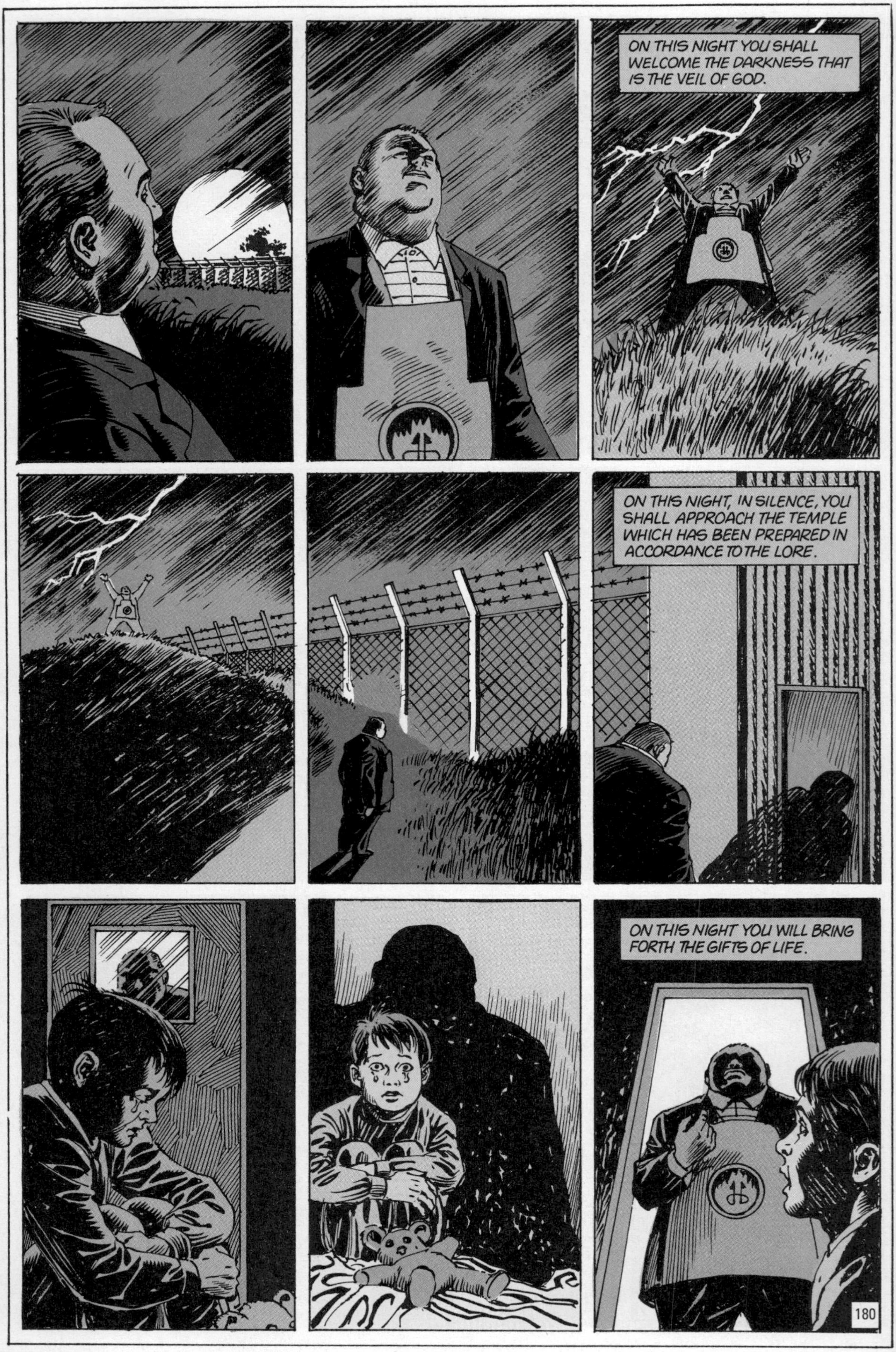
ON THIS NIGHT YOU SHALL WELCOME THE DARKNESS THAT IS THE VEIL OF GOD.
ON THIS NIGHT, IN SILENCE, YOU SHALL APPROACH THE TEMPLE WHICH HAS BEEN PREPARED IN ACCORDANCE TO THE LORE.
ON THIS NIGHT YOU WILL BRING FORTH THE GIFTS OF LIFE.

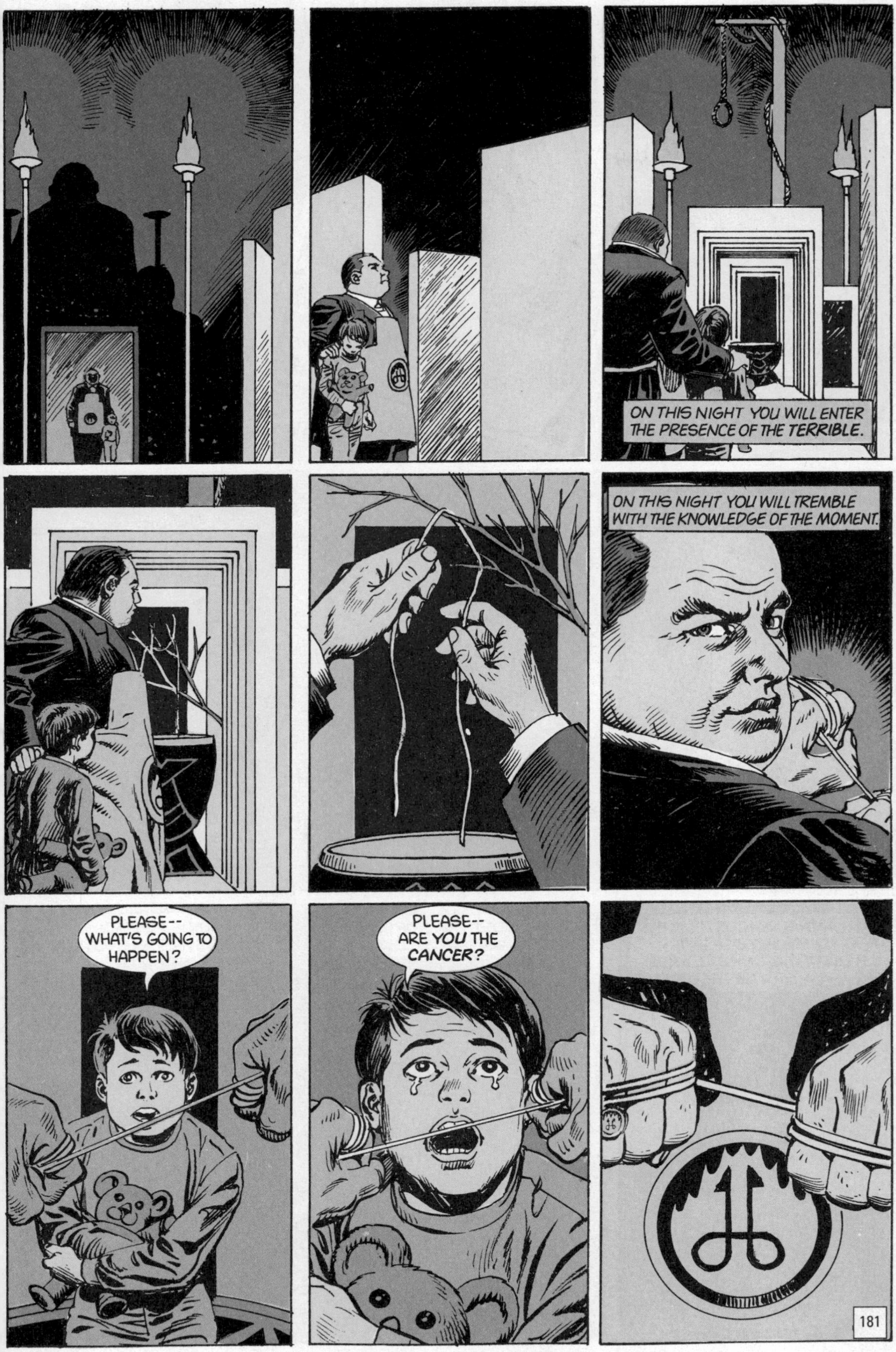
ON THIS NIGHT YOU WILL ENTER THE PRESENCE OF THE TERRIBLE.
ON THIS NIGHT YOU WILL TREMBLE WITH THE KNOWLEDGE OF THE MOMENT.
PLEASE-- WHAT'S GOING TO HAPPEN?
PLEASE-- ARE YOU THE CANCER?

ON THIS NIGHT THE EARTH IS MADE READY FOR THE PLOUGH.

ON THIS NIGHT SHALL THE SEED BE WATERED.

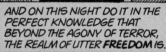

AND ON THIS NIGHT DO IT IN THE PERFECT KNOWLEDGE THAT BEYOND THE AGONY OF TERROR, THE REALM OF UTTER **FREEDOM** IS.

MARK OUT THE NAME OF LIBERTY AND MAKE HIM WELCOME.

THUS IT IS PASSED DOWN. BY HIS WILL DO IT. ON THIS NIGHT DO IT.

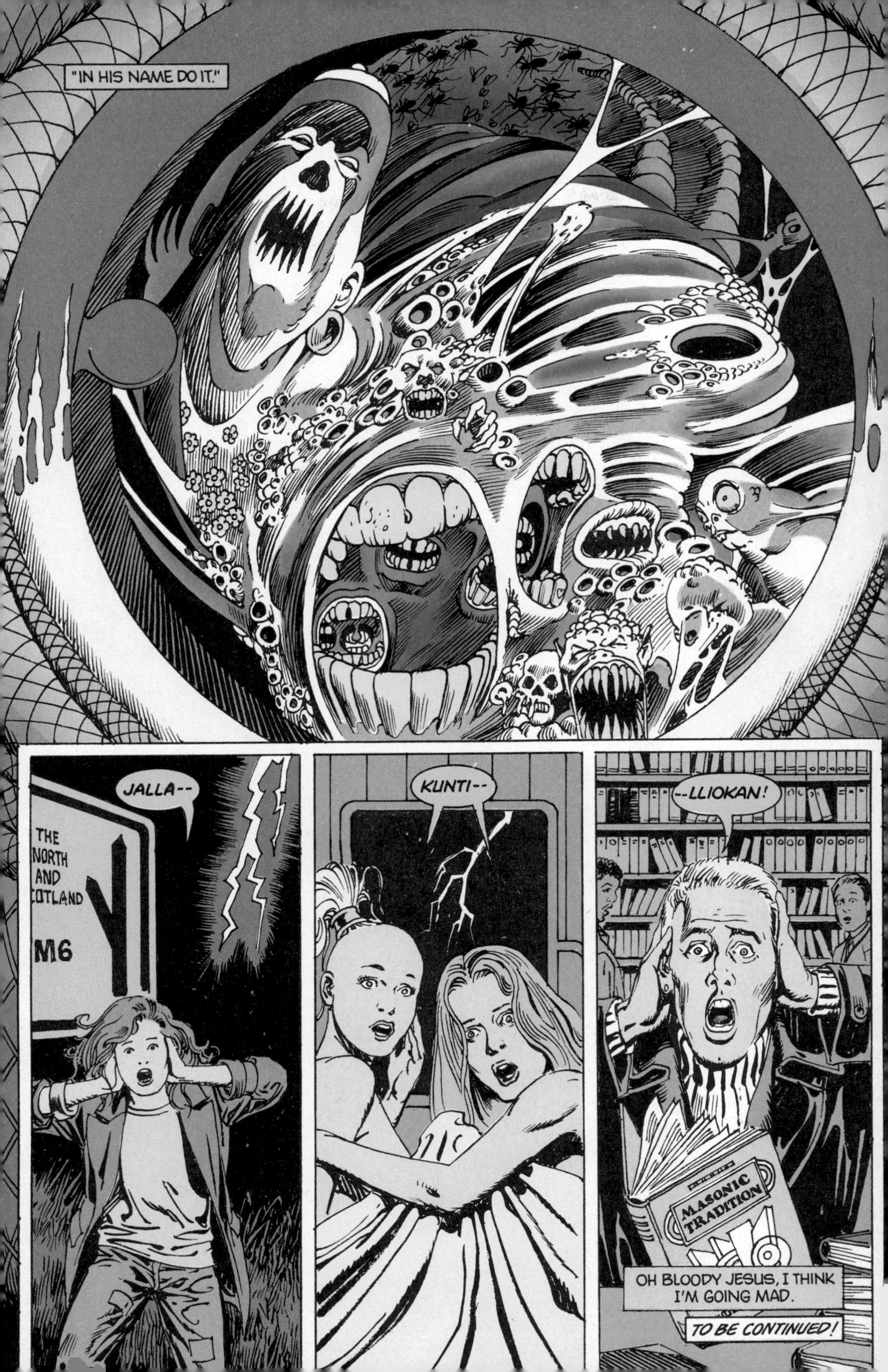
"IN HIS NAME DO IT."
JALLA--
THE NORTH AND COTLAND
M6
KUNTI--
--LLIOKAN!
MASONIC TRADITION
OH BLOODY JESUS, I THINK I'M GOING MAD.
TO BE CONTINUED!

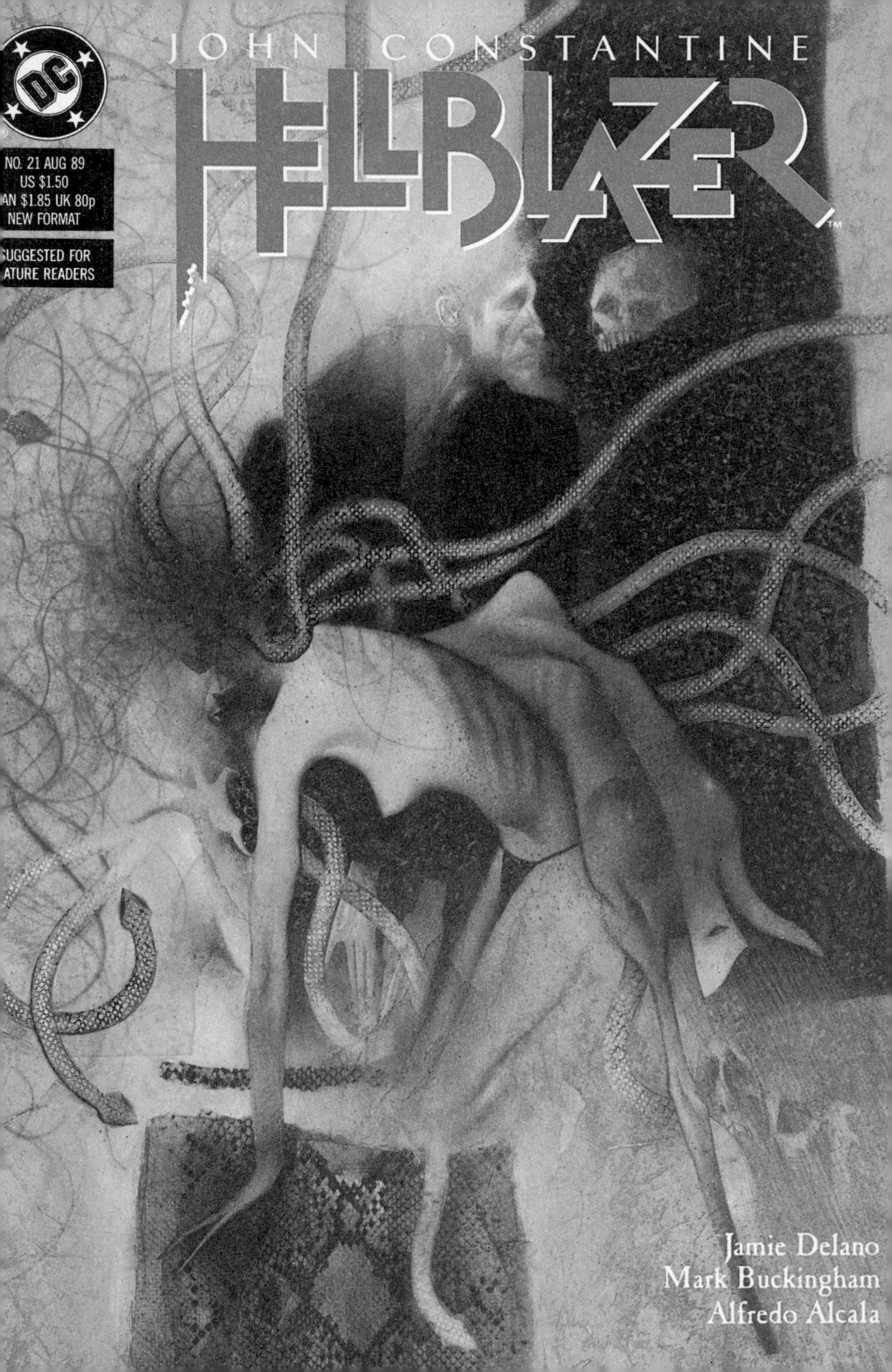
JOHN CONSTANTINE
HELLBLAZER
NO. 21 AUG 89
US $1.50
AN $1.85 UK 80p
NEW FORMAT
UGGESTED FOR
ATURE READERS
Jamie Delano
Mark Buckingham
Alfredo Alcala

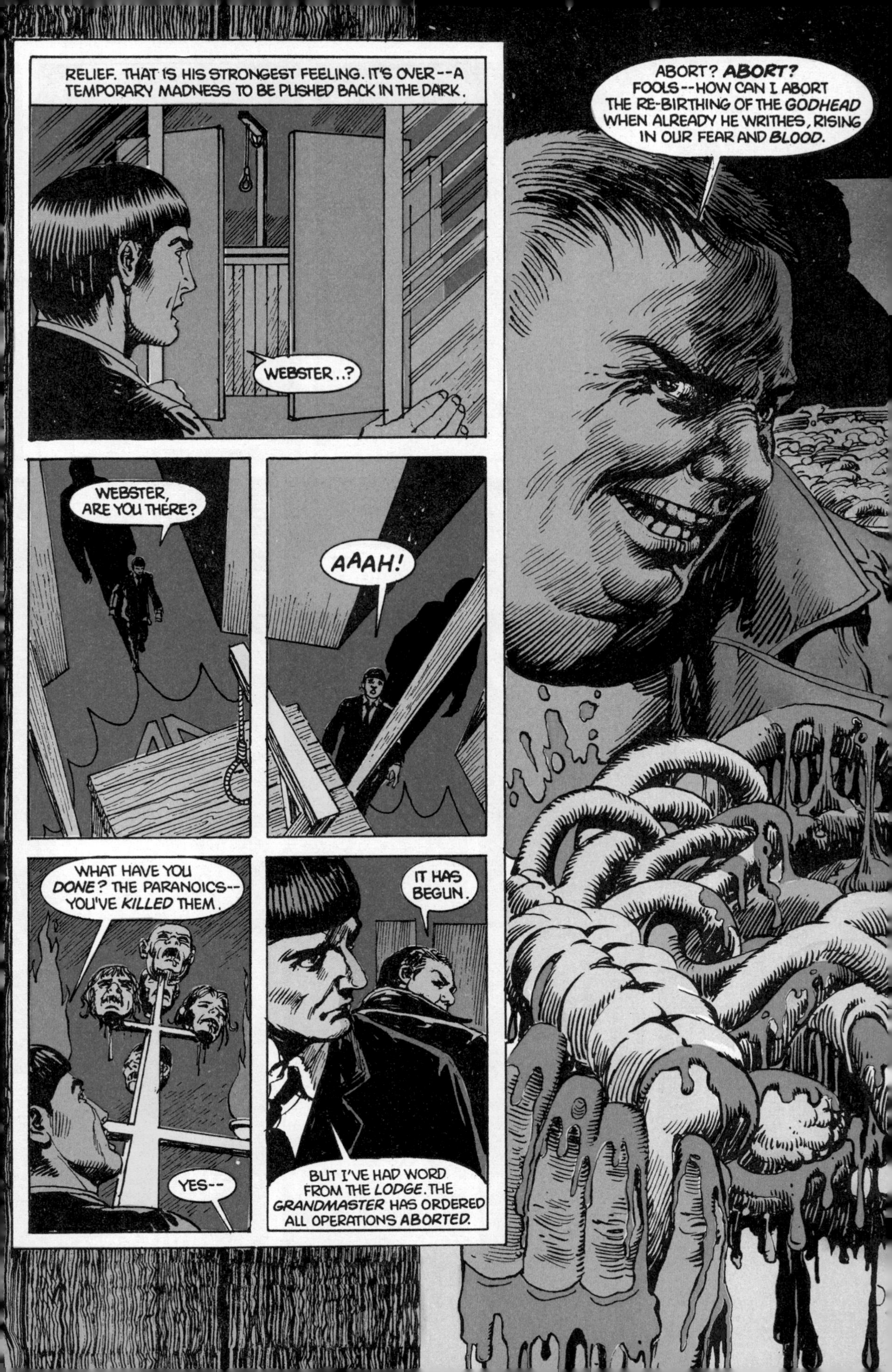
RELIEF. THAT IS HIS STRONGEST FEELING. IT'S OVER--A TEMPORARY MADNESS TO BE PUSHED BACK IN THE DARK.
WEBSTER..?
WEBSTER, ARE YOU THERE?
AAAH!
WHAT HAVE YOU *DONE*? THE PARANOICS-- YOU'VE *KILLED* THEM.
YES--
IT HAS BEGUN.
BUT I'VE HAD WORD FROM THE *LODGE*. THE *GRANDMASTER* HAS ORDERED ALL OPERATIONS **ABORTED**.
ABORT? ***ABORT?*** FOOLS--HOW CAN I ABORT THE RE-BIRTHING OF THE *GODHEAD* WHEN ALREADY HE WRITHES, RISING IN OUR FEAR AND *BLOOD*.

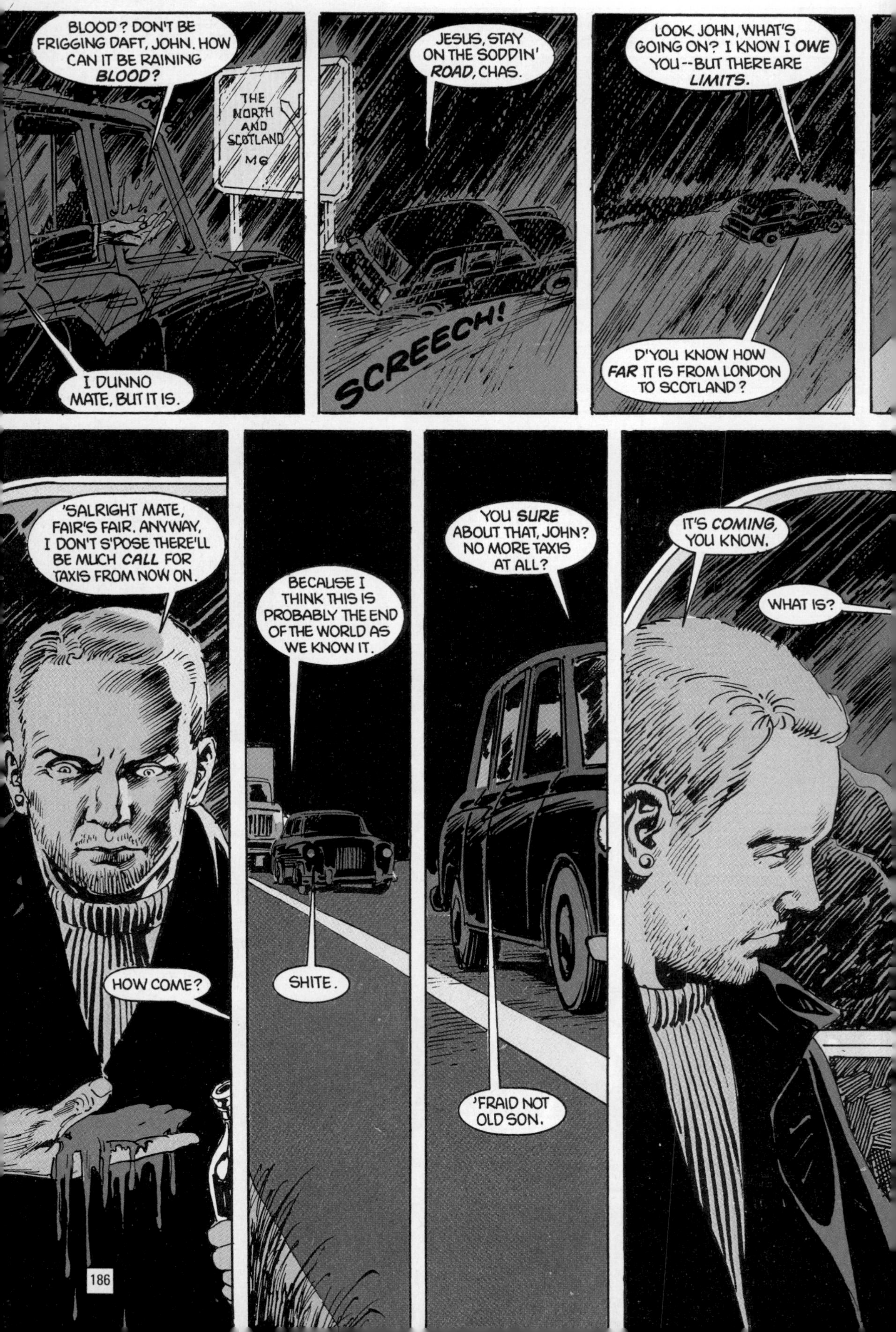
BLOOD? DON'T BE FRIGGING DAFT, JOHN. HOW CAN IT BE RAINING BLOOD?
THE NORTH AND SCOTLAND M6
I DUNNO MATE, BUT IT IS.
JESUS, STAY ON THE SODDIN' ROAD, CHAS.
SCREECH!
LOOK JOHN, WHAT'S GOING ON? I KNOW I OWE YOU--BUT THERE ARE LIMITS.
D'YOU KNOW HOW FAR IT IS FROM LONDON TO SCOTLAND?
'SALRIGHT MATE, FAIR'S FAIR. ANYWAY, I DON'T S'POSE THERE'LL BE MUCH CALL FOR TAXIS FROM NOW ON.
HOW COME?
BECAUSE I THINK THIS IS PROBABLY THE END OF THE WORLD AS WE KNOW IT.
SHITE.
YOU SURE ABOUT THAT, JOHN? NO MORE TAXIS AT ALL?
'FRAID NOT OLD SON.
IT'S COMING, YOU KNOW.
WHAT IS?

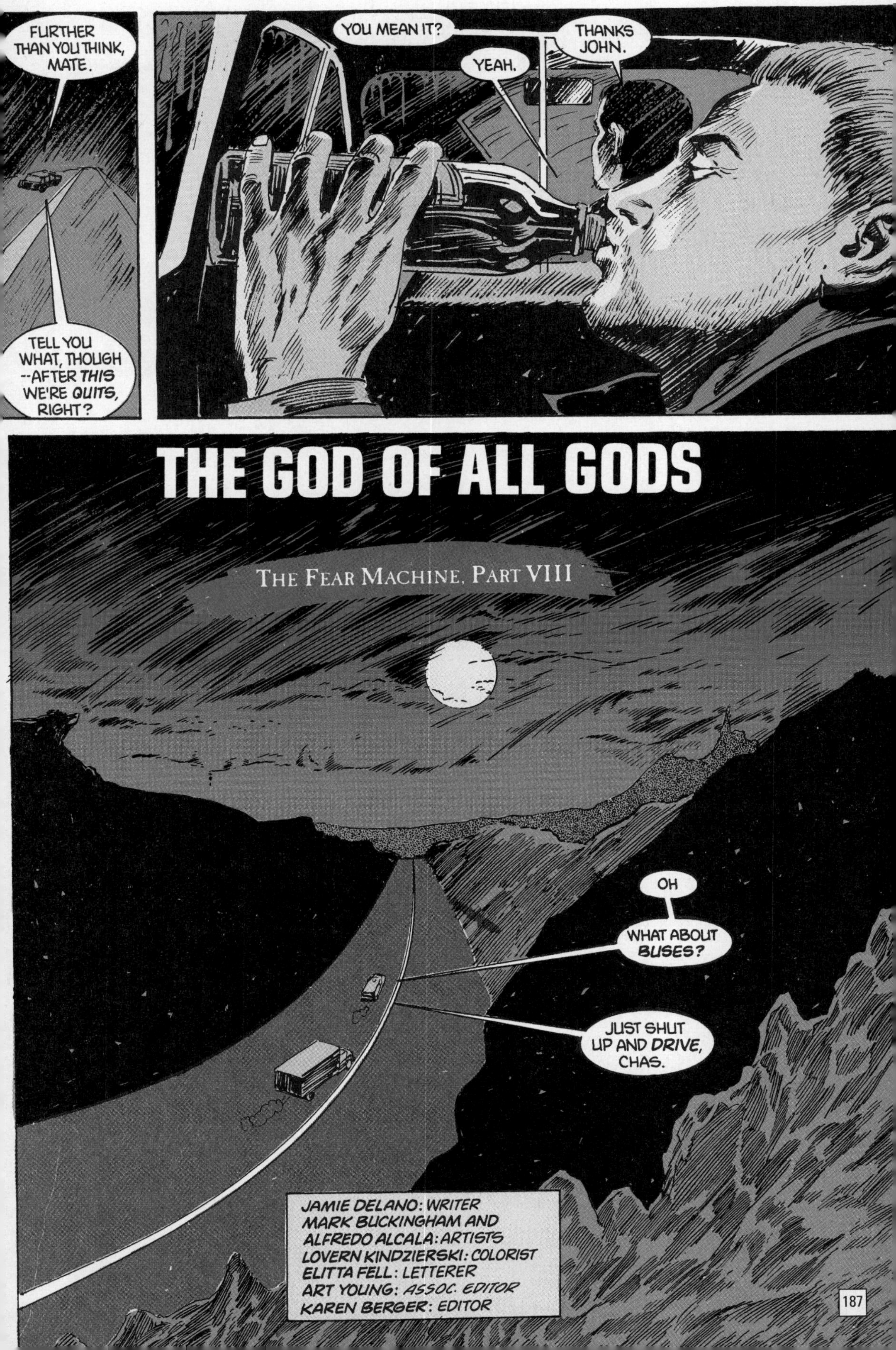
FURTHER THAN YOU THINK, MATE.
TELL YOU WHAT, THOUGH --AFTER *THIS* WE'RE *QUITS*, RIGHT?
YOU MEAN IT?
YEAH.
THANKS JOHN.
THE GOD OF ALL GODS
THE FEAR MACHINE, PART VIII
OH
WHAT ABOUT *BUSES?*
JUST SHUT UP AND *DRIVE*, CHAS.
JAMIE DELANO: WRITER
MARK BUCKINGHAM AND ALFREDO ALCALA: ARTISTS
LOVERN KINDZIERSKI: COLORIST
ELITTA FELL: LETTERER
ART YOUNG: ASSOC. EDITOR
KAREN BERGER: EDITOR

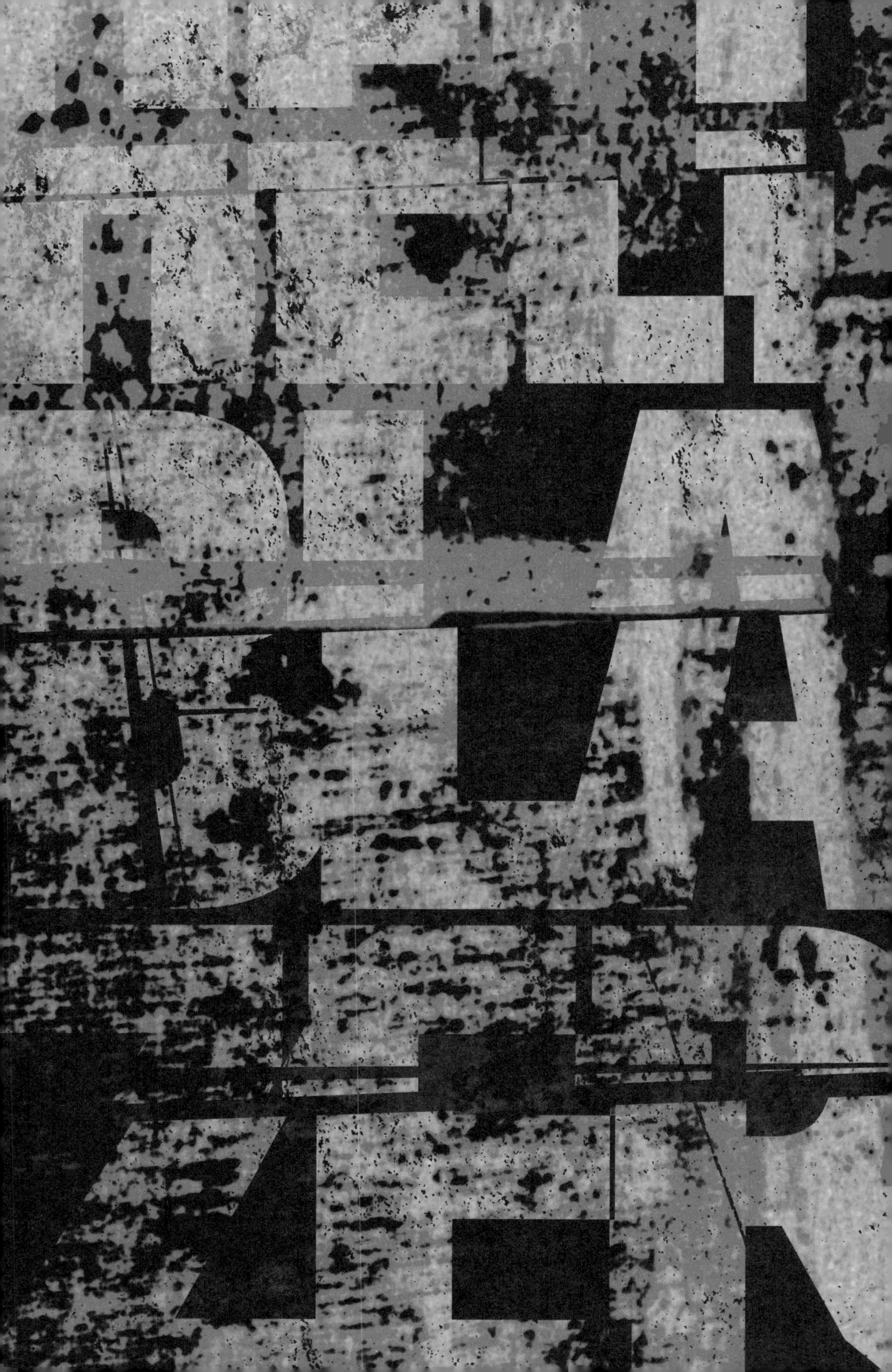

AMAZING, ENNIT--HOW YOU CAN WAIT YOUR WHOLE LIFE FOR SOMETHING TO HAPPEN AND THEN NOT RECOGNIZE IT WHEN IT DOES?

MASONIC TRADITION

IT CAME OVER ME IN THE LIBRARY--A SUB-SONIC INTESTINAL GROWL, A PRIMAL QUAKING IN THE BOWELS OF MY BEING.

EXIT

MASONO

I WOULD'VE LAUGHED IF I WASN'T SO *SCARED*. AT LAST THE SUBVERSIVE WORM HAS TURNED-- IT'S TIME FOR US ALL TO CHANGE OUR MINDS.

LIBRARY

WHEN I REALIZED, I JUST WANTED TO RUN NORTH TO SCOTLAND, TO FIND MARJ AND ZED AND THE FREEDOM MOB--TO BE WITH FRIENDS AND LOVERS IN THE FACE OF THE BREAKING WAVE.

Midland Bank

BUT I PROMISED I'D FIND *MERCURY*--AND MY ONLY CHANCE WAS UNRAVELLING THIS MAD CON SPIRACY.

HELLO...HOME OFFICE? EXTENSION TWO-THREE-EIGHT PLEASE.

TELEPHONE

OH, I SEE, THE *PARLIAMENTARY UNDER-SECRETARY'S* LEFT FOR HIS CLUB, HAS HE?

NO, NO MESSAGE.

HAH--PISSING INTO THE WIND, REALLY. *EVERY-THING'S* A BLOODY CONSPIRACY. MIGHT AS WELL TRY TO UNRAVEL THE *WORLD*.

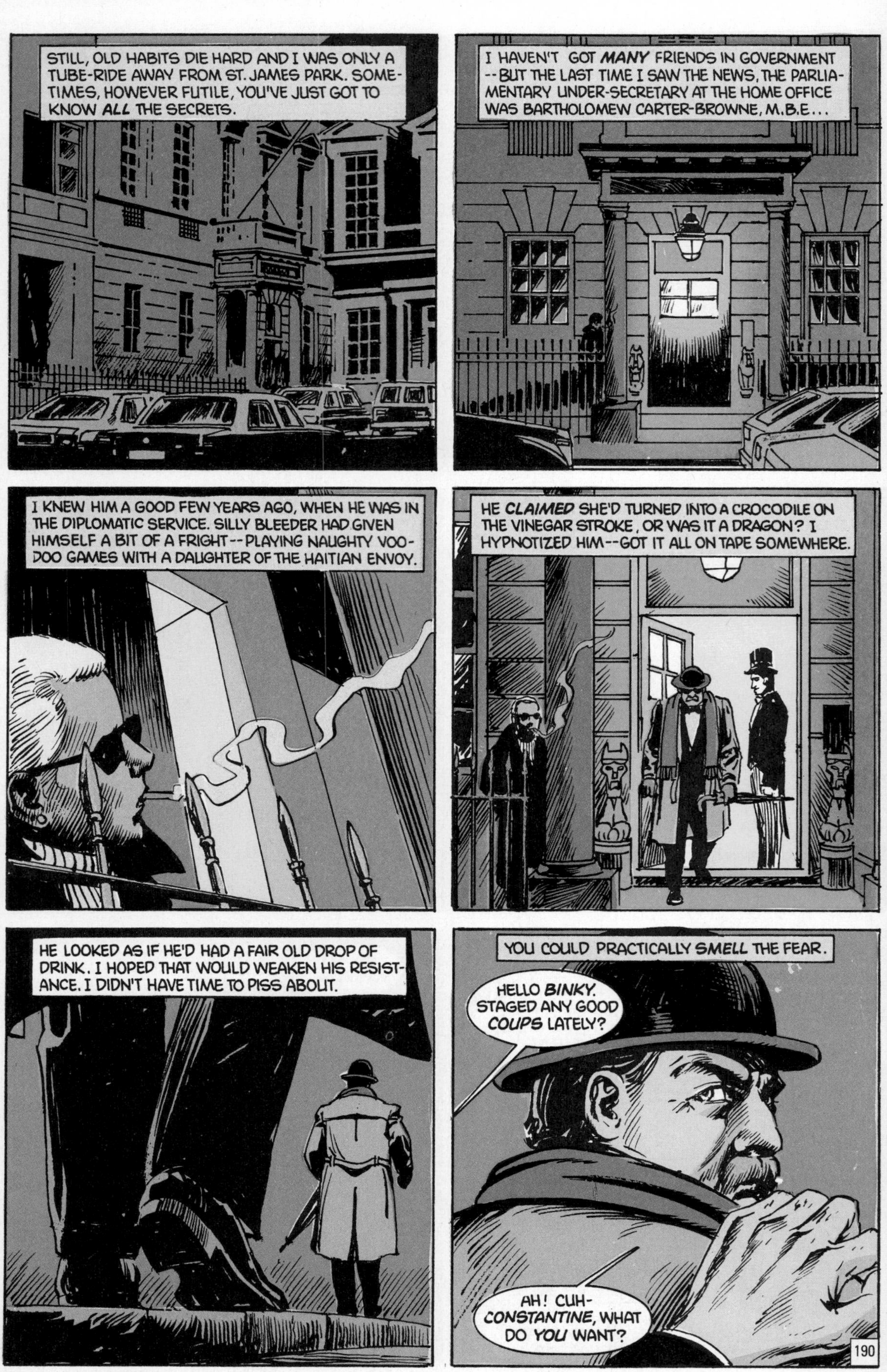

STILL, OLD HABITS DIE HARD AND I WAS ONLY A TUBE-RIDE AWAY FROM ST. JAMES PARK. SOMETIMES, HOWEVER FUTILE, YOU'VE JUST GOT TO KNOW ALL THE SECRETS.
I HAVEN'T GOT MANY FRIENDS IN GOVERNMENT -- BUT THE LAST TIME I SAW THE NEWS, THE PARLIAMENTARY UNDER-SECRETARY AT THE HOME OFFICE WAS BARTHOLOMEW CARTER-BROWNE, M.B.E...
I KNEW HIM A GOOD FEW YEARS AGO, WHEN HE WAS IN THE DIPLOMATIC SERVICE. SILLY BLEEDER HAD GIVEN HIMSELF A BIT OF A FRIGHT -- PLAYING NAUGHTY VOODOO GAMES WITH A DAUGHTER OF THE HAITIAN ENVOY.
HE CLAIMED SHE'D TURNED INTO A CROCODILE ON THE VINEGAR STROKE, OR WAS IT A DRAGON? I HYPNOTIZED HIM -- GOT IT ALL ON TAPE SOMEWHERE.
HE LOOKED AS IF HE'D HAD A FAIR OLD DROP OF DRINK. I HOPED THAT WOULD WEAKEN HIS RESISTANCE. I DIDN'T HAVE TIME TO PISS ABOUT.
YOU COULD PRACTICALLY SMELL THE FEAR.
HELLO BINKY. STAGED ANY GOOD COUPS LATELY?
AH! CUH-CONSTANTINE, WHAT DO YOU WANT?

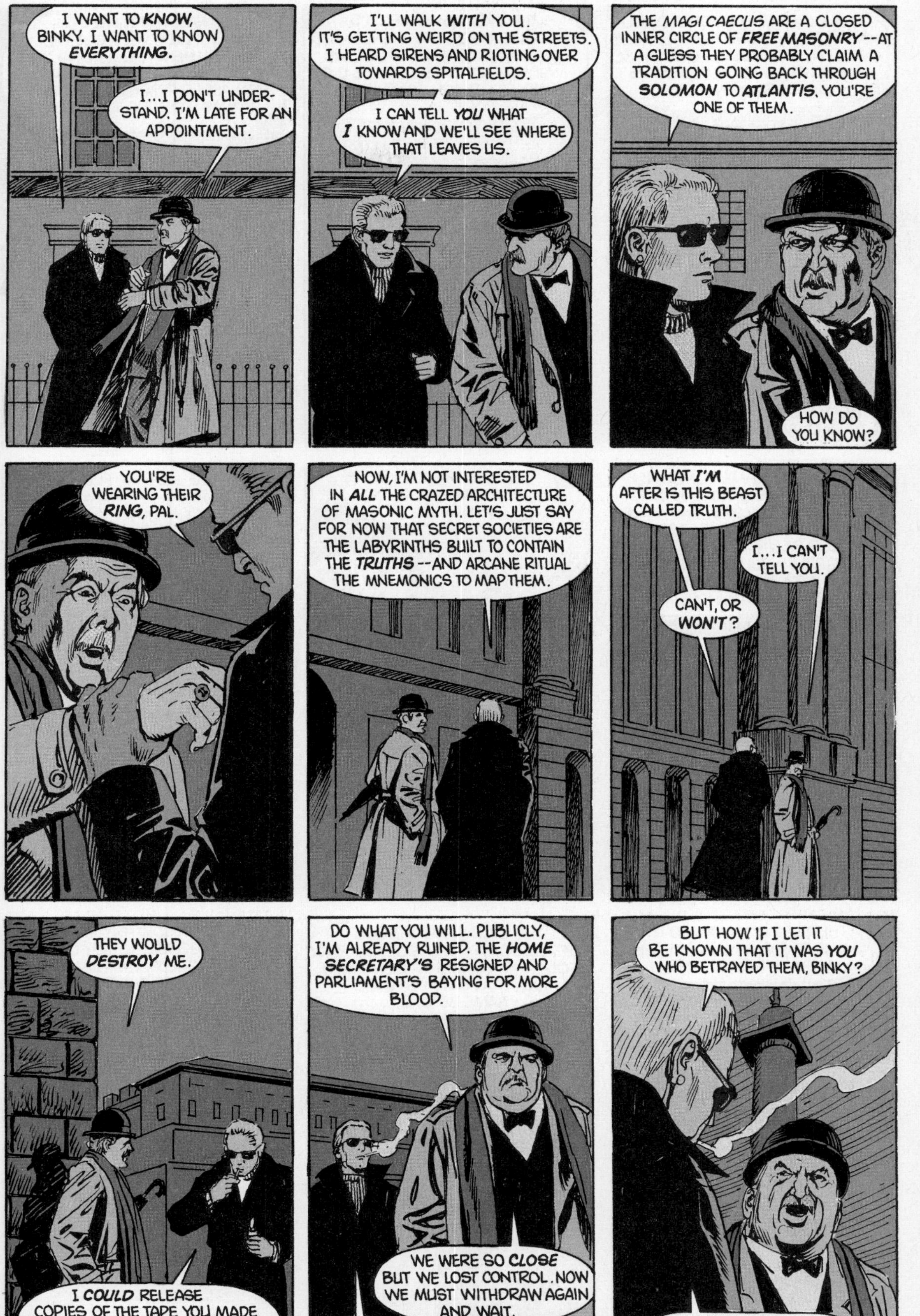
I WANT TO KNOW, BINKY. I WANT TO KNOW EVERYTHING.
I...I DON'T UNDER-STAND. I'M LATE FOR AN APPOINTMENT.
I'LL WALK WITH YOU. IT'S GETTING WEIRD ON THE STREETS. I HEARD SIRENS AND RIOTING OVER TOWARDS SPITALFIELDS.
I CAN TELL YOU WHAT I KNOW AND WE'LL SEE WHERE THAT LEAVES US.
THE MAGI CAECUS ARE A CLOSED INNER CIRCLE OF FREE MASONRY--AT A GUESS THEY PROBABLY CLAIM A TRADITION GOING BACK THROUGH SOLOMON TO ATLANTIS. YOU'RE ONE OF THEM.
HOW DO YOU KNOW?
YOU'RE WEARING THEIR RING, PAL.
NOW, I'M NOT INTERESTED IN ALL THE CRAZED ARCHITECTURE OF MASONIC MYTH. LET'S JUST SAY FOR NOW THAT SECRET SOCIETIES ARE THE LABYRINTHS BUILT TO CONTAIN THE TRUTHS--AND ARCANE RITUAL THE MNEMONICS TO MAP THEM.
WHAT I'M AFTER IS THIS BEAST CALLED TRUTH.
I...I CAN'T TELL YOU.
CAN'T, OR WON'T?
THEY WOULD DESTROY ME.
I COULD RELEASE COPIES OF THE TAPE YOU MADE RECOUNTING YOUR EXPLOITS WITH THE CROCODILE LADY...
DO WHAT YOU WILL. PUBLICLY, I'M ALREADY RUINED. THE HOME SECRETARY'S RESIGNED AND PARLIAMENT'S BAYING FOR MORE BLOOD.
WE WERE SO CLOSE BUT WE LOST CONTROL. NOW WE MUST WITHDRAW AGAIN AND WAIT.
HMMMM
BUT HOW IF I LET IT BE KNOWN THAT IT WAS YOU WHO BETRAYED THEM, BINKY?
YOU WHO TOLD ME ABOUT JALLAKUNTILLIOKAN.

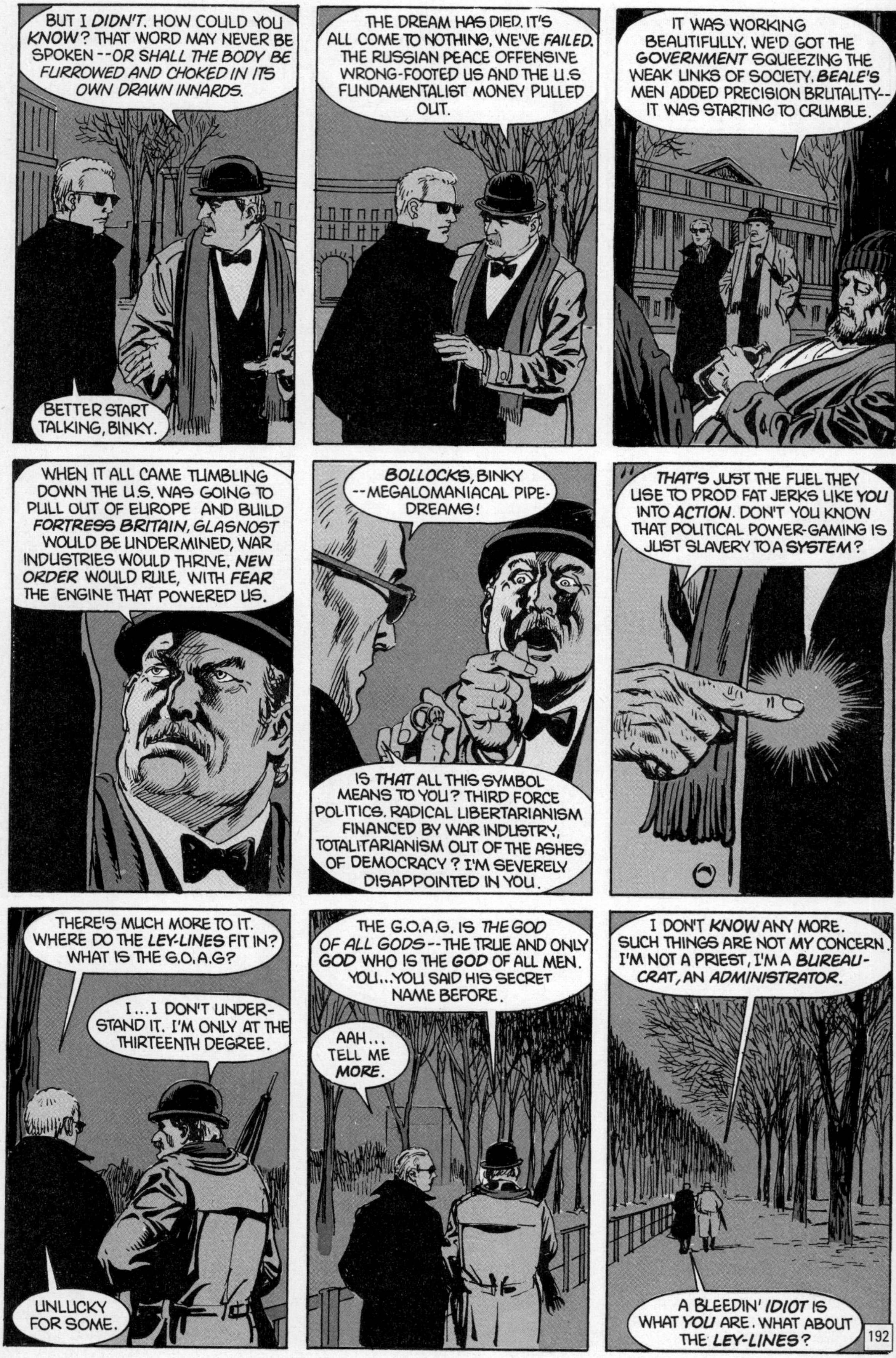
BUT I DIDN'T. HOW COULD YOU KNOW? THAT WORD MAY NEVER BE SPOKEN --OR SHALL THE BODY BE FURROWED AND CHOKED IN ITS OWN DRAWN INNARDS.
BETTER START TALKING, BINKY.
THE DREAM HAS DIED. IT'S ALL COME TO NOTHING, WE'VE FAILED. THE RUSSIAN PEACE OFFENSIVE WRONG-FOOTED US AND THE U.S FUNDAMENTALIST MONEY PULLED OUT.
IT WAS WORKING BEAUTIFULLY. WE'D GOT THE GOVERNMENT SQUEEZING THE WEAK LINKS OF SOCIETY. BEALE'S MEN ADDED PRECISION BRUTALITY-- IT WAS STARTING TO CRUMBLE.
WHEN IT ALL CAME TUMBLING DOWN THE U.S. WAS GOING TO PULL OUT OF EUROPE AND BUILD FORTRESS BRITAIN, GLASNOST WOULD BE UNDERMINED, WAR INDUSTRIES WOULD THRIVE. NEW ORDER WOULD RULE, WITH FEAR THE ENGINE THAT POWERED US.
BOLLOCKS, BINKY --MEGALOMANIACAL PIPE-DREAMS!
IS THAT ALL THIS SYMBOL MEANS TO YOU? THIRD FORCE POLITICS. RADICAL LIBERTARIANISM FINANCED BY WAR INDUSTRY, TOTALITARIANISM OUT OF THE ASHES OF DEMOCRACY? I'M SEVERELY DISAPPOINTED IN YOU.
THAT'S JUST THE FUEL THEY USE TO PROD FAT JERKS LIKE YOU INTO ACTION. DON'T YOU KNOW THAT POLITICAL POWER-GAMING IS JUST SLAVERY TO A SYSTEM?
THERE'S MUCH MORE TO IT. WHERE DO THE LEY-LINES FIT IN? WHAT IS THE G.O.A.G?
I...I DON'T UNDERSTAND IT. I'M ONLY AT THE THIRTEENTH DEGREE.
UNLUCKY FOR SOME.
THE G.O.A.G. IS THE GOD OF ALL GODS--THE TRUE AND ONLY GOD WHO IS THE GOD OF ALL MEN. YOU...YOU SAID HIS SECRET NAME BEFORE.
AAH... TELL ME MORE.
I DON'T KNOW ANY MORE. SUCH THINGS ARE NOT MY CONCERN. I'M NOT A PRIEST, I'M A BUREAUCRAT, AN ADMINISTRATOR.
A BLEEDIN' IDIOT IS WHAT YOU ARE. WHAT ABOUT THE LEY-LINES?

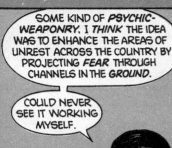

SOME KIND OF *PSYCHIC-WEAPONRY.* I *THINK* THE IDEA WAS TO ENHANCE THE AREAS OF UNREST ACROSS THE COUNTRY BY PROJECTING *FEAR* THROUGH CHANNELS IN THE *GROUND.*

COULD NEVER SEE IT WORKING MYSELF.

LAST REPORTS WERE THAT GEOTRONIKS HAD ACQUIRED SOME PSYCHIC GIRL AND WERE MAKING DRAMATIC PROGRESS -- THEN THE FOOLS LET HER ESCAPE.

ESCAPE?

SO THAT'S IT? END OF STORY -- JUST LIKE THAT? YOU CAN'T JUST SHRUG OFF SOMETHING AS BIG AS *THIS,* YOU KNOW.

WHAT ABOUT ALL THE *PEOPLE* YOU'VE SUCKED IN?

IMMATERIAL NOW -- *THEY'LL* HAVE BEEN SHUT DOWN WITH EVERYONE ELSE.

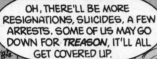

OH, THERE'LL BE MORE RESIGNATIONS, SUICIDES, A FEW ARRESTS. SOME OF US MAY GO DOWN FOR *TREASON,* IT'LL ALL GET COVERED UP.

I HAVE TO LEAVE YOU HERE AND SEE WHAT COURSE THE *LODGE* HAS CHARTED FOR ME.

AND WHAT ABOUT THE BLOODY *INVISIBLE MAGI,* THEN?

MAGI CAECUS DOMINARI --

THE INVISIBLE MAGI DOMINATE. THEY WILL SURVIVE, THEY HAVE FRIENDS IN THE *HIGHEST* PLACES. GOODBYE.

HEY! YOU CAN'T GO IN...

...THERE.

BINKY WASN'T JOKING. IT WENT *RIGHT* TO THE TOP. LIKE I SAID, THOUGH, YOU CAN'T ISOLATE CONSPIRACIES. WHEN IT COMES DOWN TO IT A BLOKE MIGHT AS WELL JUST HEAD FOR THE HILLS.

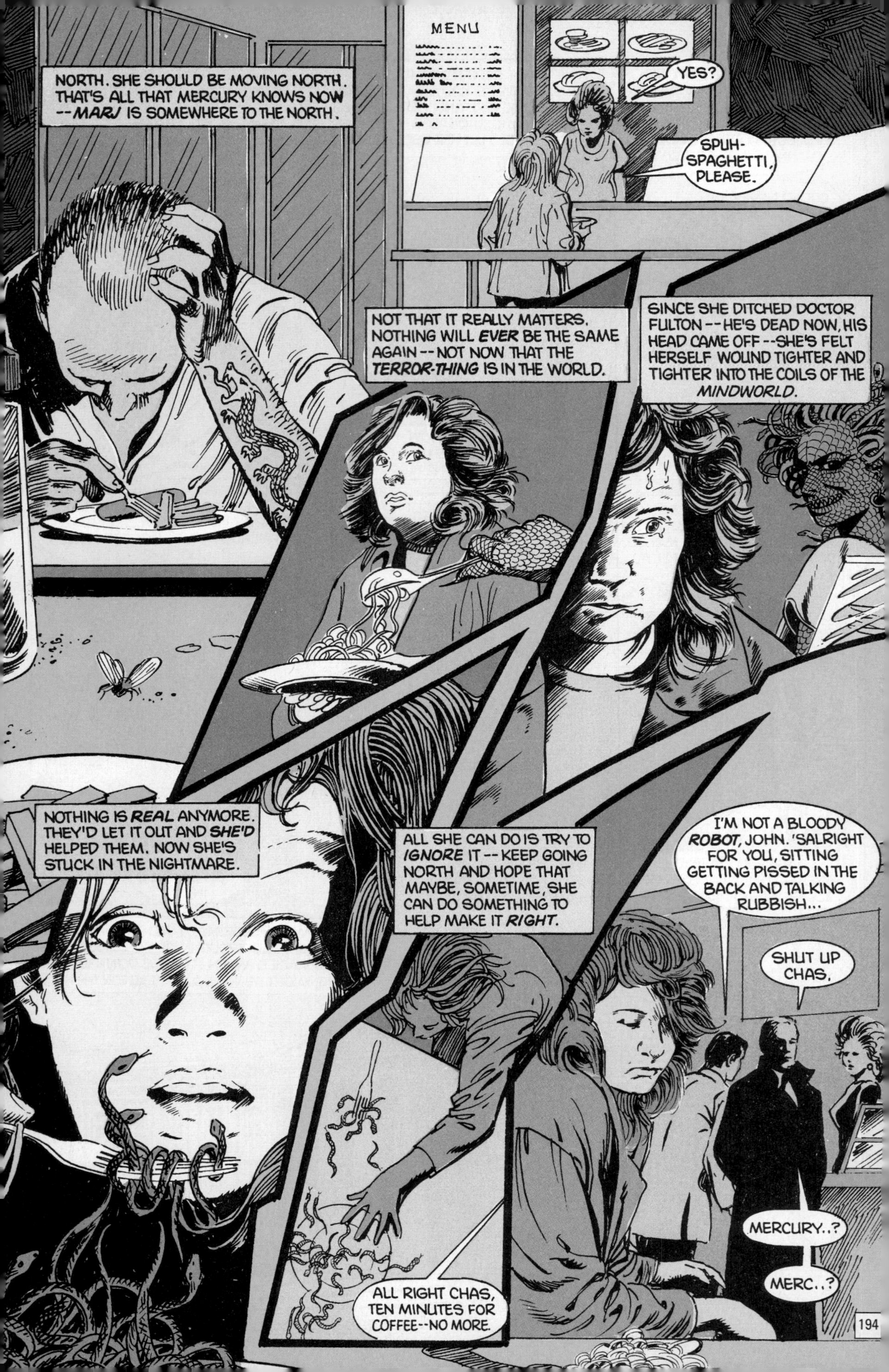
MENU
NORTH. SHE SHOULD BE MOVING NORTH. THAT'S ALL THAT MERCURY KNOWS NOW --MARJ IS SOMEWHERE TO THE NORTH.
YES?
SPUH-SPAGHETTI, PLEASE.
NOT THAT IT REALLY MATTERS. NOTHING WILL EVER BE THE SAME AGAIN -- NOT NOW THAT THE TERROR-THING IS IN THE WORLD.
SINCE SHE DITCHED DOCTOR FULTON -- HE'S DEAD NOW, HIS HEAD CAME OFF -- SHE'S FELT HERSELF WOUND TIGHTER AND TIGHTER INTO THE COILS OF THE MINDWORLD.
NOTHING IS REAL ANYMORE. THEY'D LET IT OUT AND SHE'D HELPED THEM. NOW SHE'S STUCK IN THE NIGHTMARE.
ALL SHE CAN DO IS TRY TO IGNORE IT -- KEEP GOING NORTH AND HOPE THAT MAYBE, SOMETIME, SHE CAN DO SOMETHING TO HELP MAKE IT RIGHT.
I'M NOT A BLOODY ROBOT, JOHN. 'SALRIGHT FOR YOU, SITTING GETTING PISSED IN THE BACK AND TALKING RUBBISH...
SHUT UP CHAS.
ALL RIGHT CHAS, TEN MINUTES FOR COFFEE--NO MORE.
MERCURY..?
MERC..?

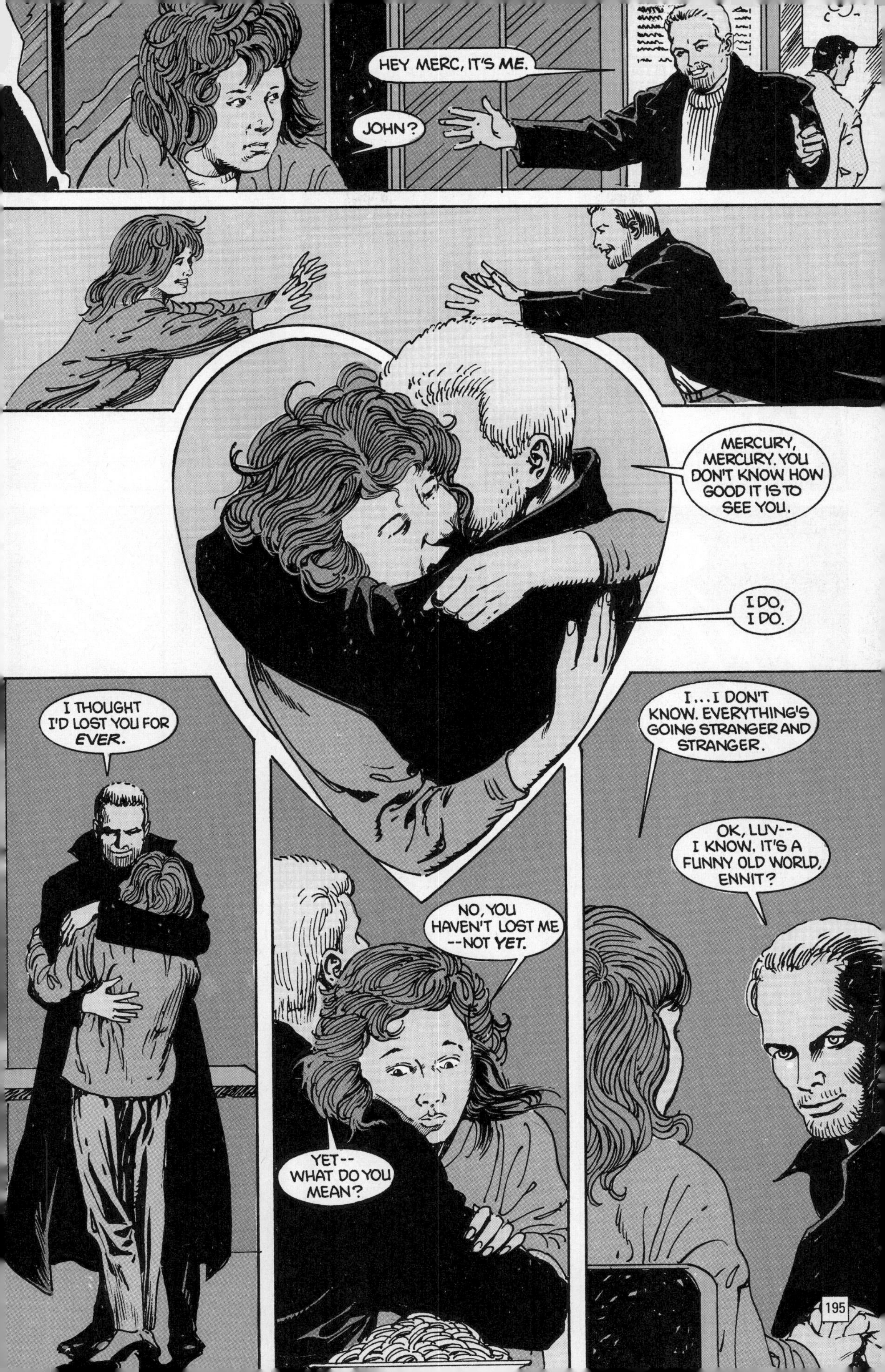

HEY MERC, IT'S ME.
JOHN?
MERCURY, MERCURY. YOU DON'T KNOW HOW GOOD IT IS TO SEE YOU.
I DO, I DO.
I THOUGHT I'D LOST YOU FOR EVER.
NO, YOU HAVEN'T LOST ME --NOT YET.
YET-- WHAT DO YOU MEAN?
I... I DON'T KNOW. EVERYTHING'S GOING STRANGER AND STRANGER.
OK, LUV-- I KNOW. IT'S A FUNNY OLD WORLD, ENNIT?

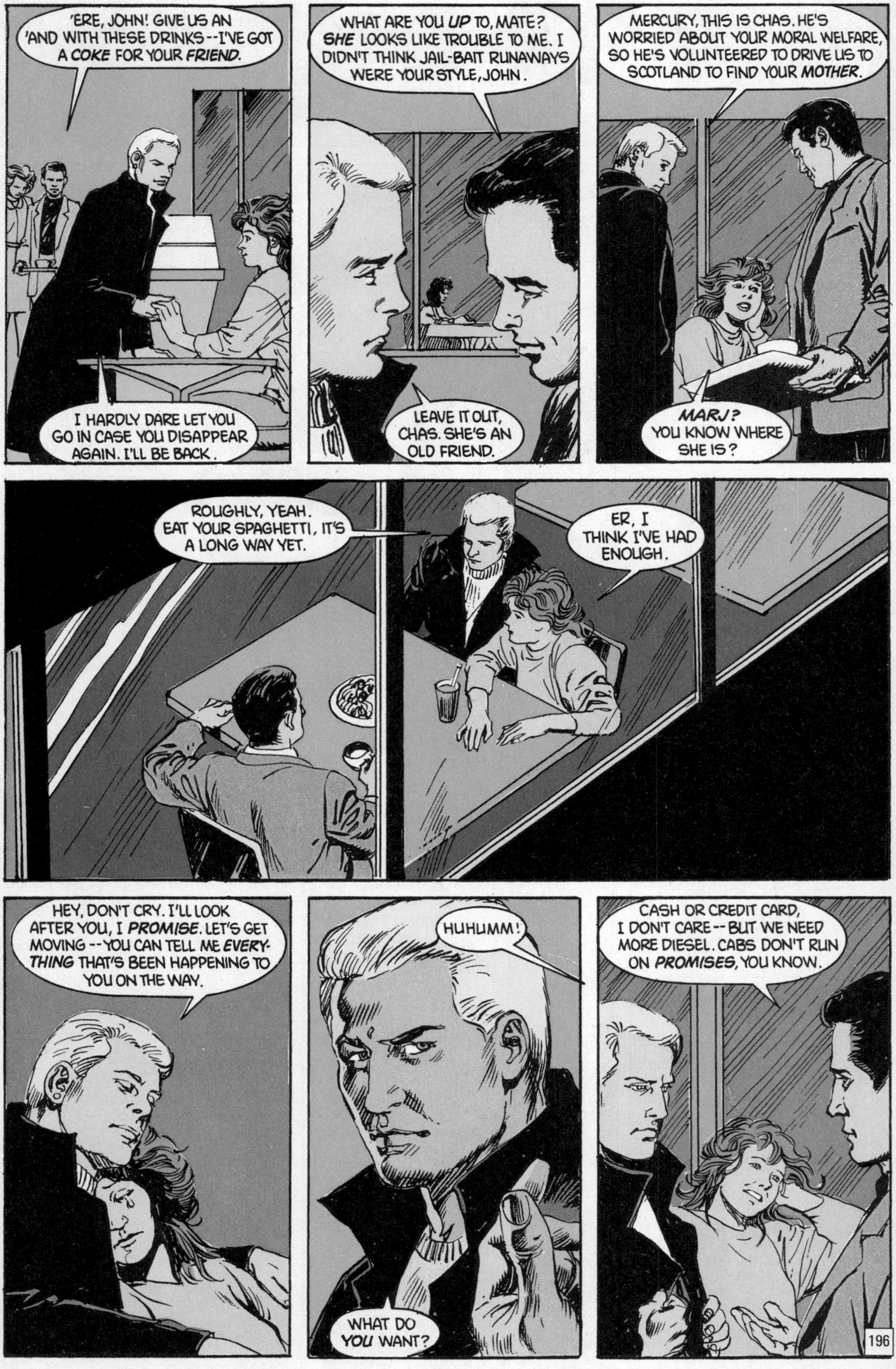
'ERE, JOHN! GIVE US AN 'AND WITH THESE DRINKS--I'VE GOT A COKE FOR YOUR FRIEND.
I HARDLY DARE LET YOU GO IN CASE YOU DISAPPEAR AGAIN. I'LL BE BACK.
WHAT ARE YOU UP TO, MATE? SHE LOOKS LIKE TROUBLE TO ME. I DIDN'T THINK JAIL-BAIT RUNAWAYS WERE YOUR STYLE, JOHN.
LEAVE IT OUT, CHAS. SHE'S AN OLD FRIEND.
MERCURY, THIS IS CHAS. HE'S WORRIED ABOUT YOUR MORAL WELFARE, SO HE'S VOLUNTEERED TO DRIVE US TO SCOTLAND TO FIND YOUR MOTHER.
MARJ? YOU KNOW WHERE SHE IS?
ROUGHLY, YEAH. EAT YOUR SPAGHETTI, IT'S A LONG WAY YET.
ER, I THINK I'VE HAD ENOUGH.
HEY, DON'T CRY. I'LL LOOK AFTER YOU, I PROMISE. LET'S GET MOVING--YOU CAN TELL ME EVERYTHING THAT'S BEEN HAPPENING TO YOU ON THE WAY.
HUHUMM!
WHAT DO YOU WANT?
CASH OR CREDIT CARD, I DON'T CARE--BUT WE NEED MORE DIESEL. CABS DON'T RUN ON PROMISES, YOU KNOW.

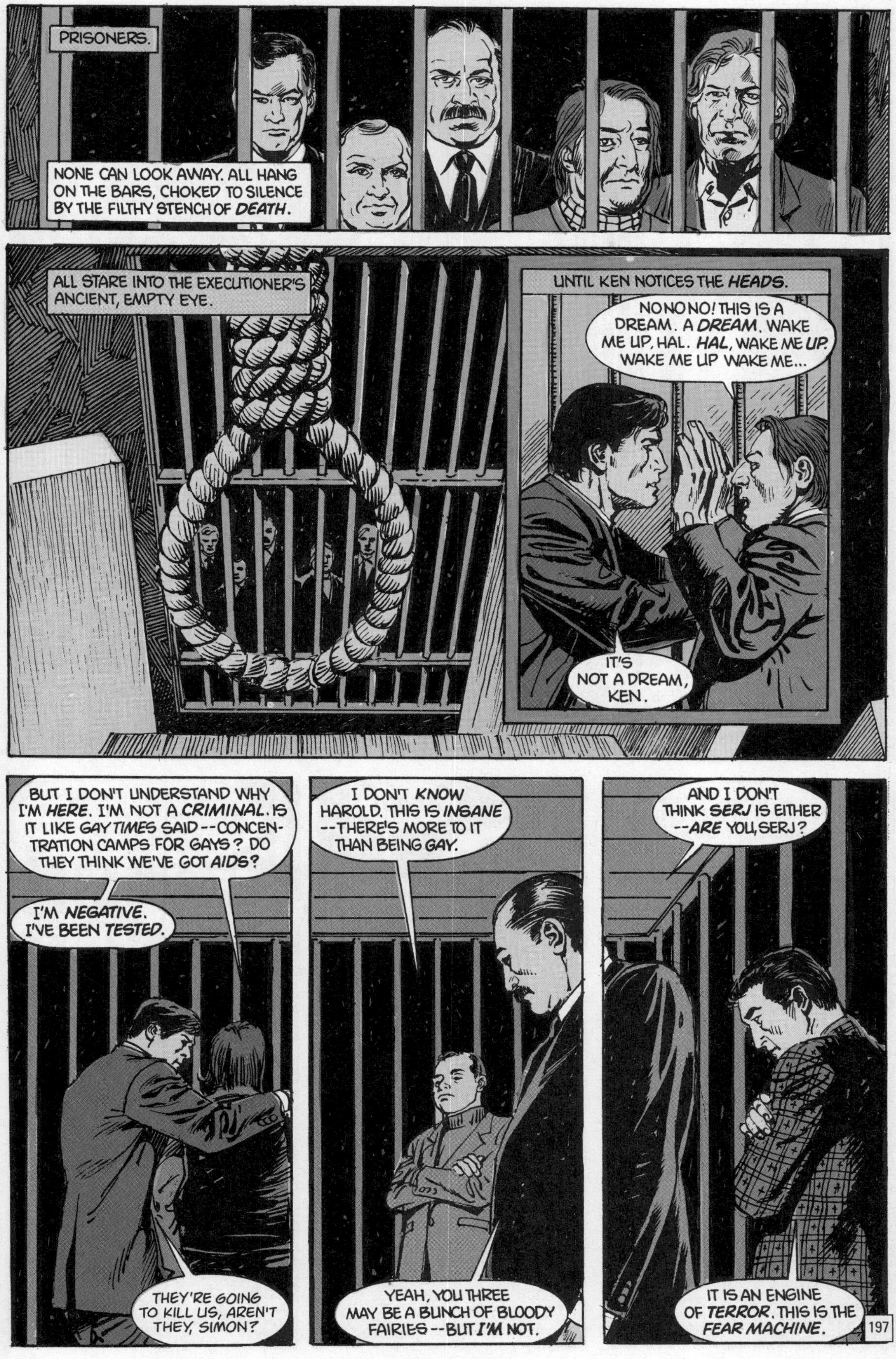

PRISONERS.
NONE CAN LOOK AWAY. ALL HANG ON THE BARS, CHOKED TO SILENCE BY THE FILTHY STENCH OF *DEATH*.
ALL STARE INTO THE EXECUTIONER'S ANCIENT, EMPTY EYE.
UNTIL KEN NOTICES THE *HEADS*.
NONONO! THIS IS A DREAM. A *DREAM*. WAKE ME UP, HAL. *HAL*, WAKE ME *UP*. WAKE ME UP WAKE ME...
IT'S NOT A DREAM, KEN.
BUT I DON'T UNDERSTAND WHY I'M *HERE*. I'M NOT A *CRIMINAL*. IS IT LIKE GAY *TIMES* SAID--CONCENTRATION CAMPS FOR GAYS? DO THEY THINK WE'VE GOT *AIDS*?
I'M *NEGATIVE*. I'VE BEEN *TESTED*.
THEY'RE GOING TO KILL US, AREN'T THEY, SIMON?
I DON'T *KNOW* HAROLD. THIS IS *INSANE* --THERE'S MORE TO IT THAN BEING *GAY*.
YEAH, YOU THREE MAY BE A BUNCH OF BLOODY FAIRIES--BUT *I'M* NOT.
AND I DON'T THINK *SERJ* IS EITHER --*ARE* YOU, SERJ?
IT IS AN ENGINE OF *TERROR*. THIS IS THE *FEAR MACHINE*.

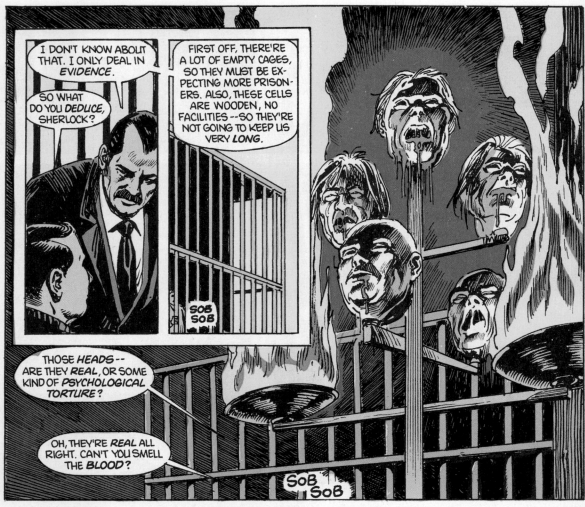

I DON'T KNOW ABOUT THAT. I ONLY DEAL IN *EVIDENCE.*

SO WHAT DO YOU *DEDUCE,* SHERLOCK?

FIRST OFF, THERE'RE A LOT OF EMPTY CAGES, SO THEY MUST BE EXPECTING MORE PRISONERS. ALSO, THESE CELLS ARE WOODEN, NO FACILITIES -- SO THEY'RE NOT GOING TO KEEP US VERY *LONG.*

SOB SOB

THOSE *HEADS* -- ARE THEY *REAL,* OR SOME KIND OF *PSYCHOLOGICAL TORTURE?*

OH, THEY'RE *REAL* ALL RIGHT. CAN'T YOU SMELL THE *BLOOD?*

SOB SOB

KEN, FOR GOD'S SAKE STOP THAT BLOODY AWFUL *NOISE,* OR, SO HELP ME, I'LL SWING FOR YOU!

AAAH!

THERE *IS* SOMEONE ELSE IN HERE.

LOOK AT THE *RING.* IT'S HIM -- THE ONE WHO *DID* IT TO ME.

YEAH? WELL, HE MUST'VE HAD A FALLING OUT WITH HIS MATES, THEN. THIS BASTARD'S THREE-PARTS DEAD.

THEN *I'LL* BE ONLY A *QUARTER-MURDERER,* WON'T I?

198

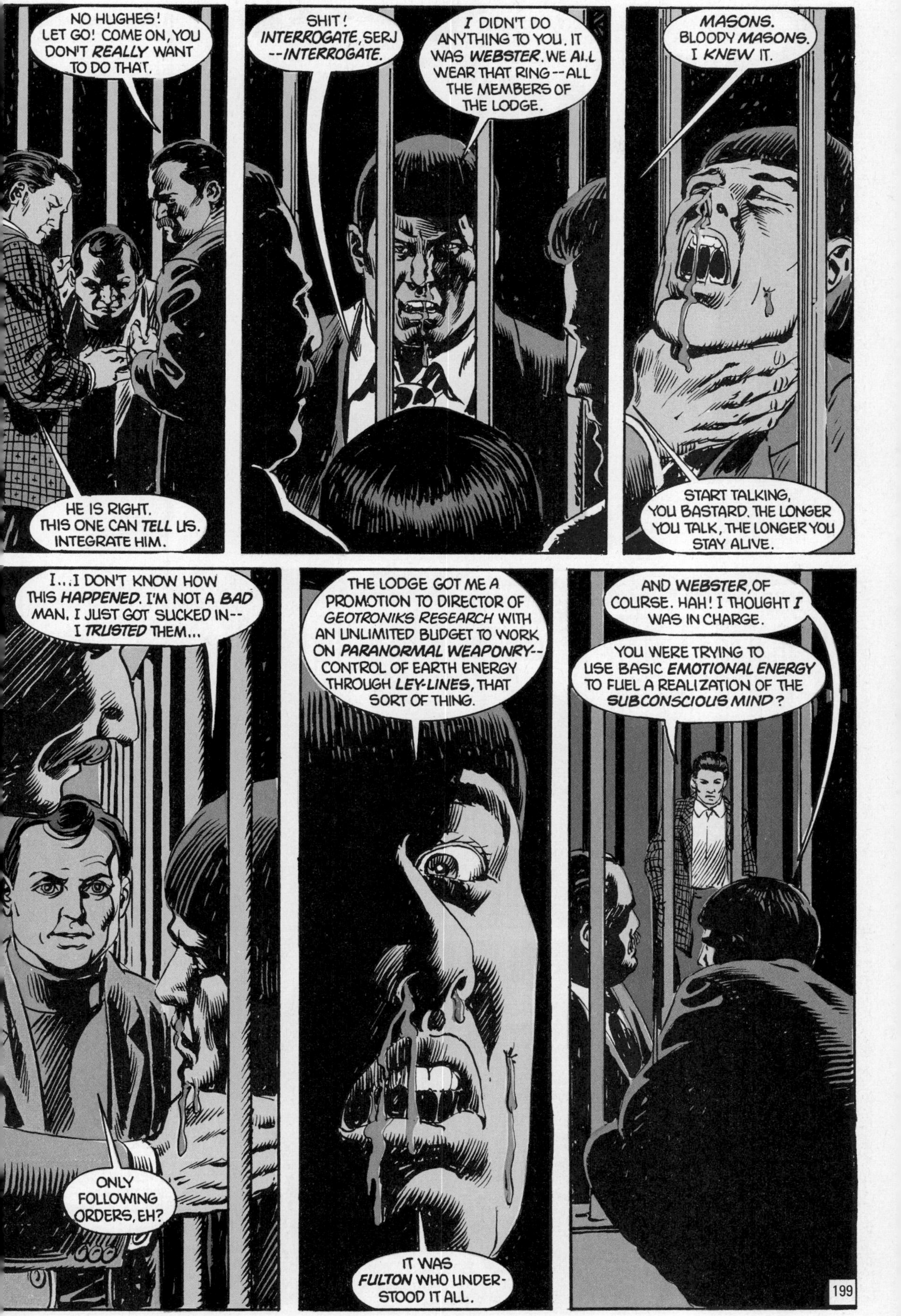
NO HUGHES! LET GO! COME ON, YOU DON'T REALLY WANT TO DO THAT.
HE IS RIGHT. THIS ONE CAN TELL US. INTEGRATE HIM.
SHIT! INTERROGATE, SERJ --INTERROGATE.
I DIDN'T DO ANYTHING TO YOU. IT WAS WEBSTER. WE ALL WEAR THAT RING--ALL THE MEMBERS OF THE LODGE.
MASONS. BLOODY MASONS. I KNEW IT.
START TALKING, YOU BASTARD. THE LONGER YOU TALK, THE LONGER YOU STAY ALIVE.
I...I DON'T KNOW HOW THIS HAPPENED. I'M NOT A BAD MAN. I JUST GOT SUCKED IN-- I TRUSTED THEM...
ONLY FOLLOWING ORDERS, EH?
THE LODGE GOT ME A PROMOTION TO DIRECTOR OF GEOTRONIKS RESEARCH WITH AN UNLIMITED BUDGET TO WORK ON PARANORMAL WEAPONRY-- CONTROL OF EARTH ENERGY THROUGH LEY-LINES, THAT SORT OF THING.
IT WAS FULTON WHO UNDER-STOOD IT ALL.
AND WEBSTER, OF COURSE. HAH! I THOUGHT I WAS IN CHARGE.
YOU WERE TRYING TO USE BASIC EMOTIONAL ENERGY TO FUEL A REALIZATION OF THE SUBCONSCIOUS MIND?

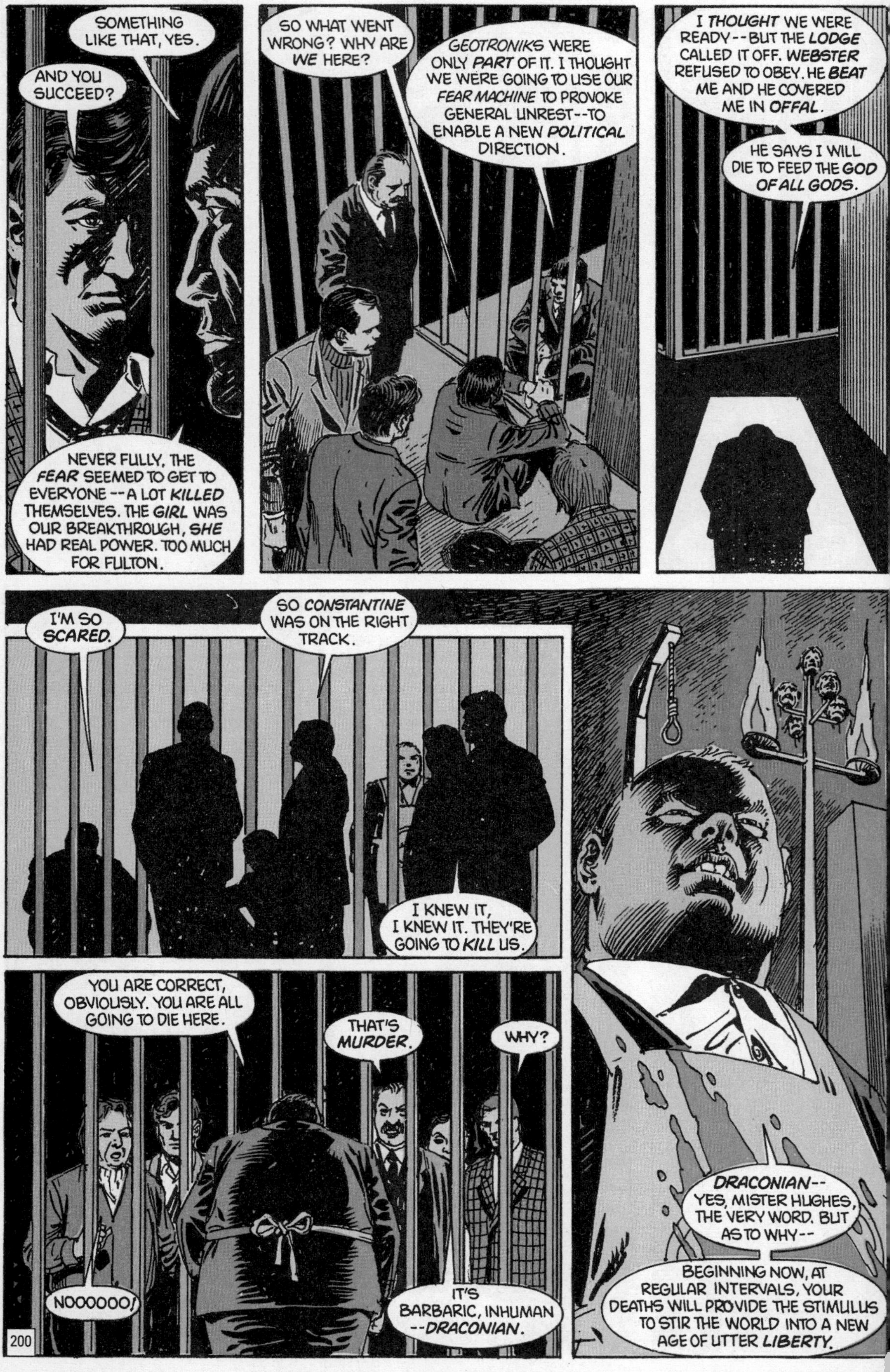

SOMETHING LIKE THAT, YES.
AND YOU SUCCEED?
NEVER FULLY, THE FEAR SEEMED TO GET TO EVERYONE--A LOT KILLED THEMSELVES. THE GIRL WAS OUR BREAKTHROUGH, SHE HAD REAL POWER. TOO MUCH FOR FULTON.
SO WHAT WENT WRONG? WHY ARE WE HERE?
GEOTRONIKS WERE ONLY PART OF IT. I THOUGHT WE WERE GOING TO USE OUR FEAR MACHINE TO PROVOKE GENERAL UNREST--TO ENABLE A NEW POLITICAL DIRECTION.
I THOUGHT WE WERE READY--BUT THE LODGE CALLED IT OFF. WEBSTER REFUSED TO OBEY. HE BEAT ME AND HE COVERED ME IN OFFAL.
HE SAYS I WILL DIE TO FEED THE GOD OF ALL GODS.
I'M SO SCARED.
SO CONSTANTINE WAS ON THE RIGHT TRACK.
I KNEW IT, I KNEW IT. THEY'RE GOING TO KILL US.
YOU ARE CORRECT, OBVIOUSLY. YOU ARE ALL GOING TO DIE HERE.
NOOOOOO!
THAT'S MURDER.
IT'S BARBARIC, INHUMAN --DRACONIAN.
WHY?
DRACONIAN--YES, MISTER HUGHES, THE VERY WORD. BUT AS TO WHY--
BEGINNING NOW, AT REGULAR INTERVALS, YOUR DEATHS WILL PROVIDE THE STIMULUS TO STIR THE WORLD INTO A NEW AGE OF UTTER LIBERTY.

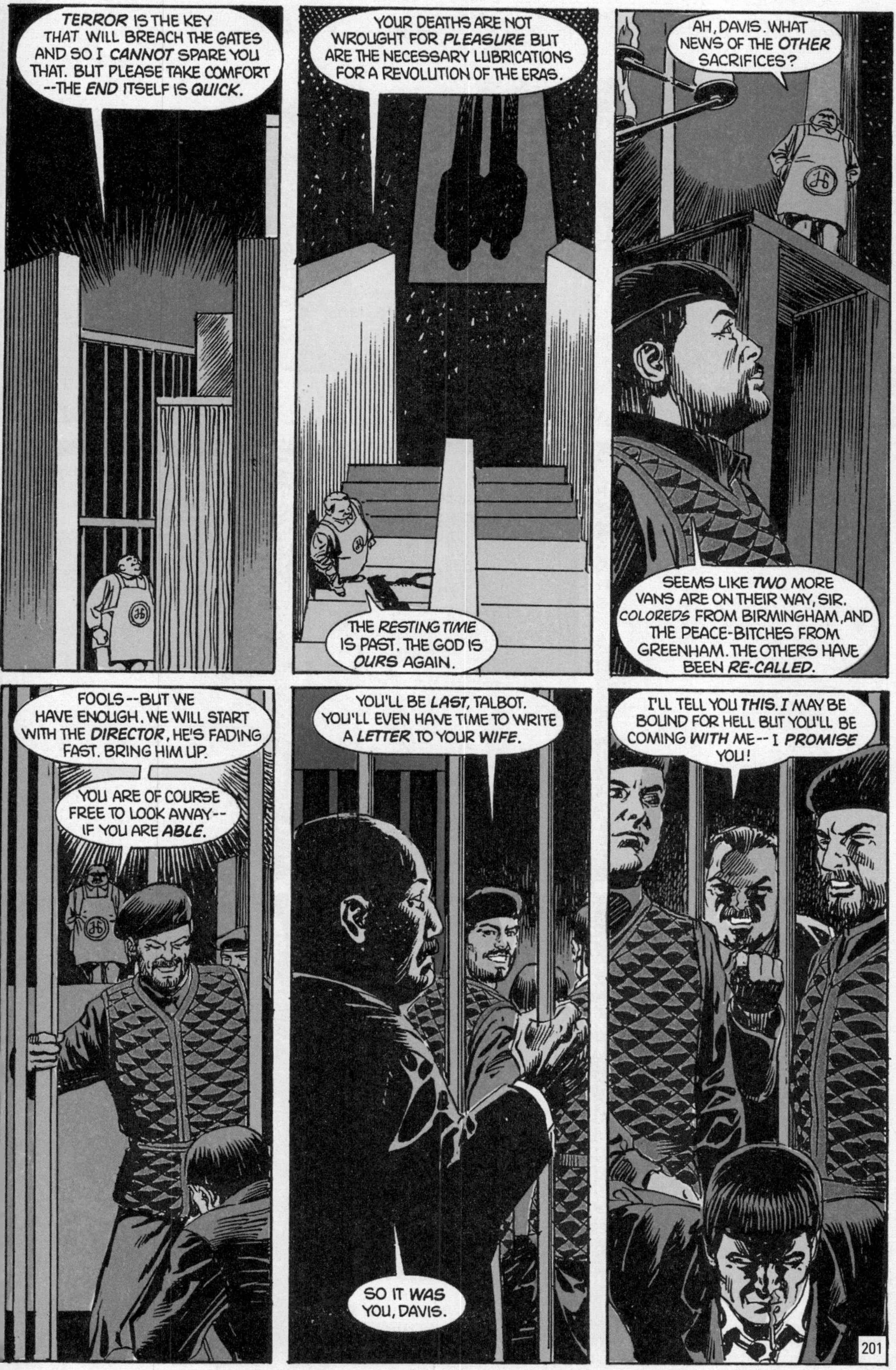
TERROR IS THE KEY THAT WILL BREACH THE GATES AND SO I CANNOT SPARE YOU THAT. BUT PLEASE TAKE COMFORT --THE END ITSELF IS QUICK.
YOUR DEATHS ARE NOT WROUGHT FOR PLEASURE BUT ARE THE NECESSARY LUBRICATIONS FOR A REVOLUTION OF THE ERAS.
THE RESTING TIME IS PAST. THE GOD IS OURS AGAIN.
AH, DAVIS. WHAT NEWS OF THE OTHER SACRIFICES?
SEEMS LIKE TWO MORE VANS ARE ON THEIR WAY, SIR. COLOREDS FROM BIRMINGHAM, AND THE PEACE-BITCHES FROM GREENHAM. THE OTHERS HAVE BEEN RE-CALLED.
FOOLS--BUT WE HAVE ENOUGH. WE WILL START WITH THE DIRECTOR, HE'S FADING FAST. BRING HIM UP.
YOU ARE OF COURSE FREE TO LOOK AWAY-- IF YOU ARE ABLE.
YOU'LL BE LAST, TALBOT. YOU'LL EVEN HAVE TIME TO WRITE A LETTER TO YOUR WIFE.
SO IT WAS YOU, DAVIS.
I'LL TELL YOU THIS. I MAY BE BOUND FOR HELL BUT YOU'LL BE COMING WITH ME-- I PROMISE YOU!

SO, I'M HERE. THIS IS THE PAGAN NATION *PARADISE* MARJ TALKED ABOUT IN HER LETTER. AS USUAL THOUGH, *I'M* TOO LATE TO GET THE BENEFIT. IT WASN'T QUITE THE REUNION I MIGHT'VE HOPED FOR.

THANKS, ERROL.

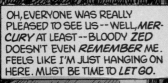

OH, EVERYONE WAS REALLY PLEASED TO SEE US--WELL, *MERCURY* AT LEAST--BLOODY *ZED* DOESN'T EVEN *REMEMBER* ME. FEELS LIKE I'M JUST HANGING ON HERE. MUST BE TIME TO *LET GO.*

IT MUST'VE BEEN PRETTY COOL HERE.

IT WAS THE *BOLLOCKS*, JOHN. IT HAD EVERYTHING--REALLY FELT LIKE *HOME.*

THE *FREEDOM MOB* AND THE *PAGAN NATION* WENT TOGETHER GREAT--BEFORE THE *BAD WEIRDNESS* STARTED.

AND THE *WOMEN* WERE GETTING THEIR SHIT TOGETHER, TOO. IT WAS *EXCITING* HERE --*IMPORTANT.*

BUT IT'S ALWAYS THE SAME, WHENEVER I GET TO FEELING HAPPY--*DISASTER.*

YEAH, IT'S USUALLY THE WAY, ERROL.

AND IT *HAPPENED* LAST NIGHT, YOU SAY?

YEAH, THERE WAS A *STORM.* WE THOUGHT *LIGHTNING* HAD STARTED A FIRE IN THE *GARDEN.* SOME OF THE BOYS RAN TO PUT IT OUT.

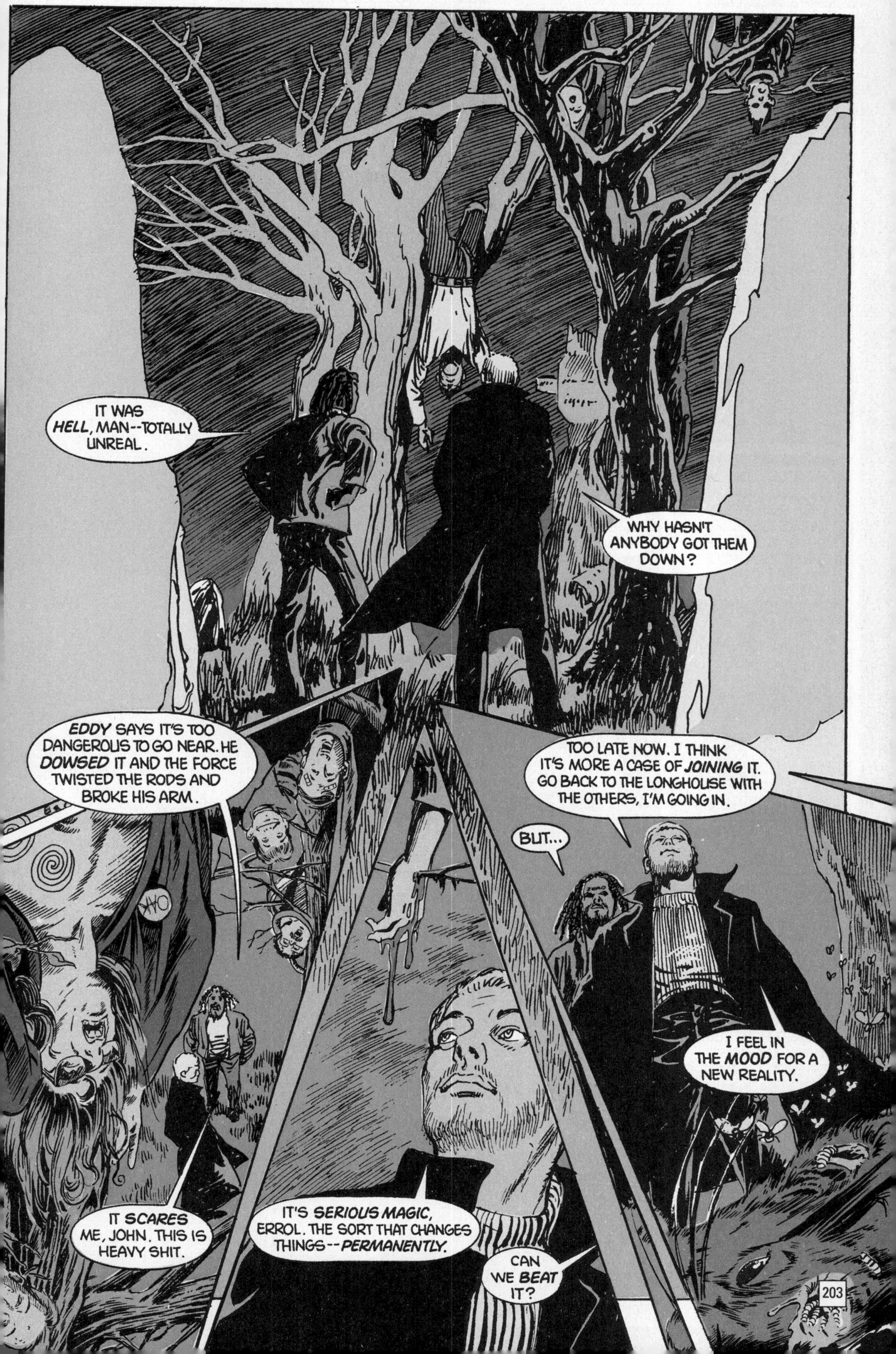
IT WAS HELL, MAN--TOTALLY UNREAL.
WHY HASN'T ANYBODY GOT THEM DOWN?
EDDY SAYS IT'S TOO DANGEROUS TO GO NEAR. HE DOWSED IT AND THE FORCE TWISTED THE RODS AND BROKE HIS ARM.
TOO LATE NOW. I THINK IT'S MORE A CASE OF JOINING IT. GO BACK TO THE LONGHOUSE WITH THE OTHERS, I'M GOING IN.
BUT...
I FEEL IN THE MOOD FOR A NEW REALITY.
IT SCARES ME, JOHN. THIS IS HEAVY SHIT.
IT'S SERIOUS MAGIC, ERROL. THE SORT THAT CHANGES THINGS--PERMANENTLY.
CAN WE BEAT IT?

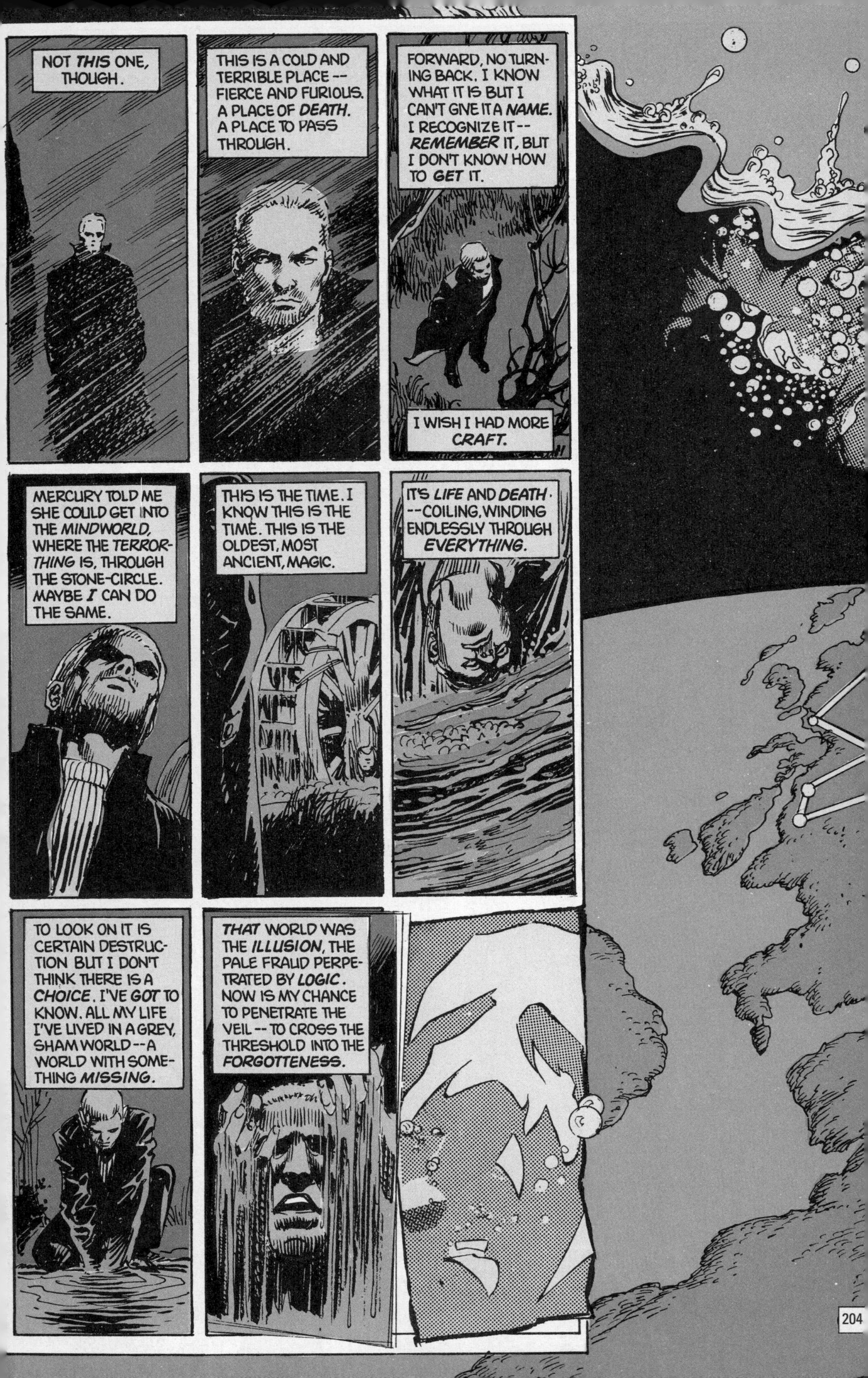
NOT THIS ONE, THOUGH.
THIS IS A COLD AND TERRIBLE PLACE -- FIERCE AND FURIOUS. A PLACE OF DEATH. A PLACE TO PASS THROUGH.
FORWARD, NO TURNING BACK. I KNOW WHAT IT IS BUT I CAN'T GIVE IT A NAME. I RECOGNIZE IT -- REMEMBER IT, BUT I DON'T KNOW HOW TO GET IT.
I WISH I HAD MORE CRAFT.
MERCURY TOLD ME SHE COULD GET INTO THE MINDWORLD, WHERE THE TERROR-THING IS, THROUGH THE STONE-CIRCLE. MAYBE I CAN DO THE SAME.
THIS IS THE TIME. I KNOW THIS IS THE TIME. THIS IS THE OLDEST, MOST ANCIENT, MAGIC.
IT'S LIFE AND DEATH. --COILING, WINDING ENDLESSLY THROUGH EVERYTHING.
TO LOOK ON IT IS CERTAIN DESTRUCTION BUT I DON'T THINK THERE IS A CHOICE. I'VE GOT TO KNOW. ALL MY LIFE I'VE LIVED IN A GREY, SHAM WORLD--A WORLD WITH SOMETHING MISSING.
THAT WORLD WAS THE ILLUSION, THE PALE FRAUD PERPETRATED BY LOGIC. NOW IS MY CHANCE TO PENETRATE THE VEIL -- TO CROSS THE THRESHOLD INTO THE FORGOTTENESS.

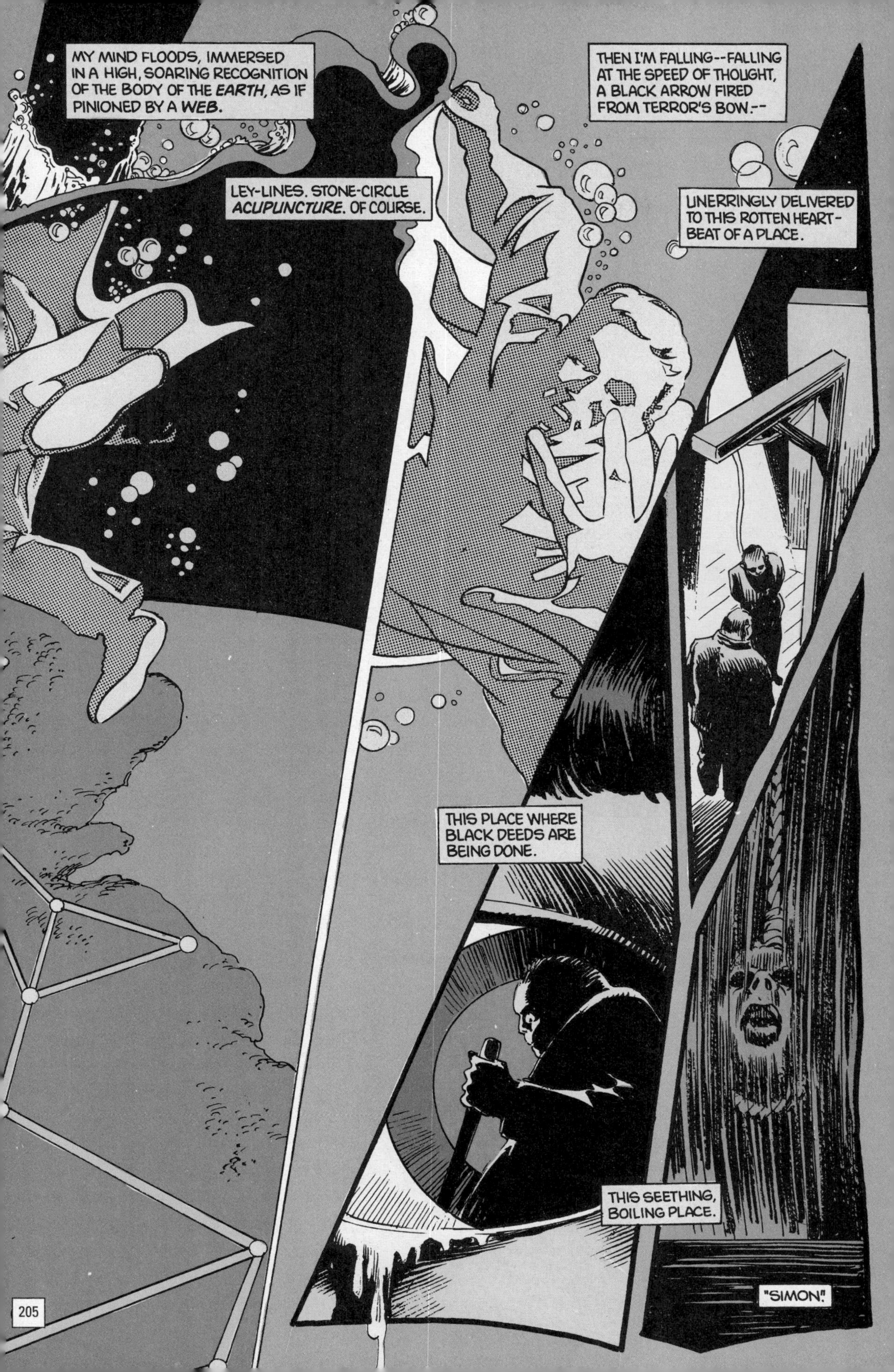
MY MIND FLOODS, IMMERSED IN A HIGH, SOARING RECOGNITION OF THE BODY OF THE *EARTH*, AS IF PINIONED BY A *WEB*.
LEY-LINES. STONE-CIRCLE *ACUPUNCTURE*. OF COURSE.
THEN I'M FALLING--FALLING AT THE SPEED OF THOUGHT, A BLACK ARROW FIRED FROM TERROR'S BOW.--
UNERRINGLY DELIVERED TO THIS ROTTEN HEART-BEAT OF A PLACE.
THIS PLACE WHERE BLACK DEEDS ARE BEING DONE.
THIS SEETHING, BOILING PLACE.
"SIMON."

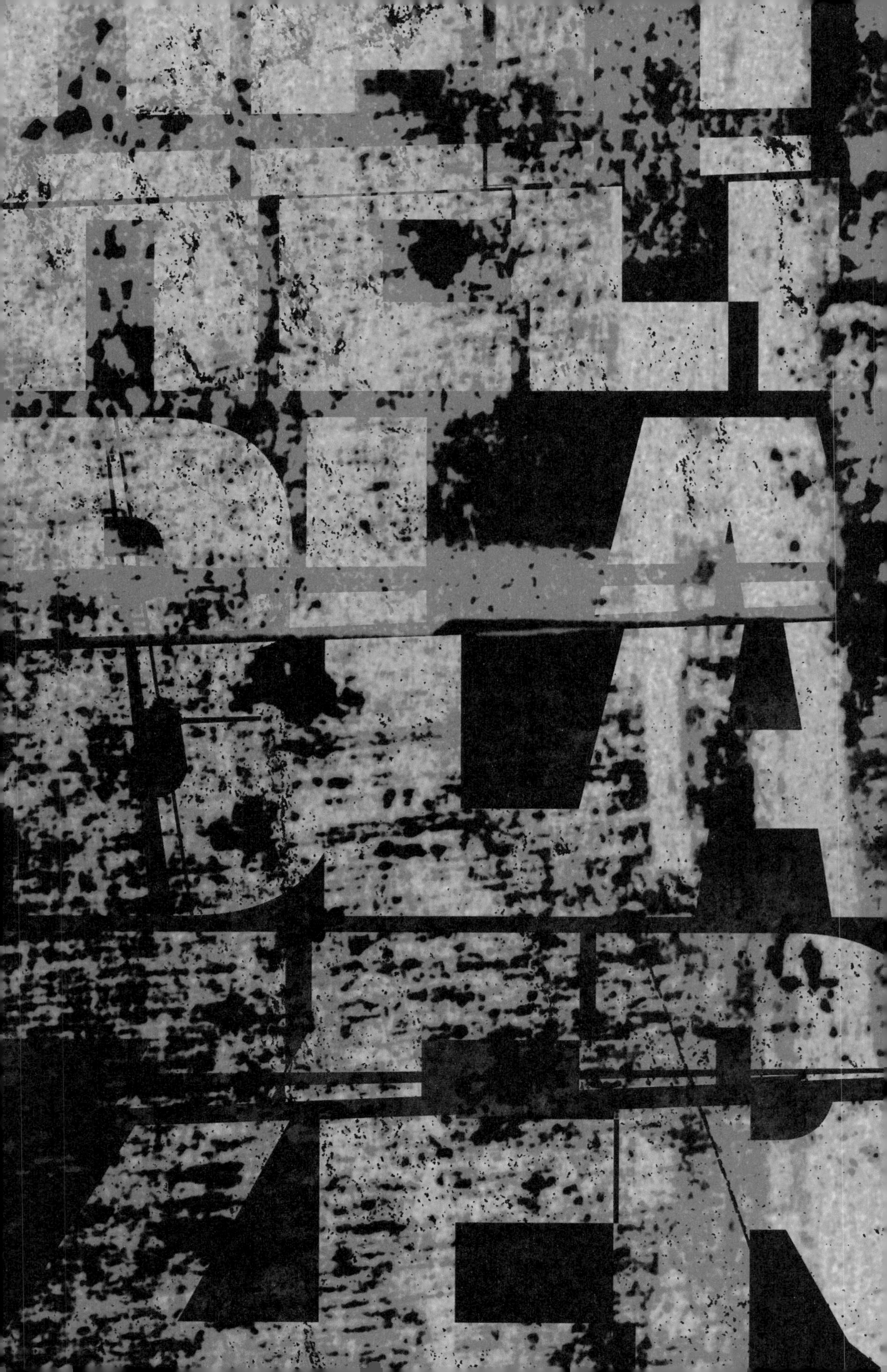

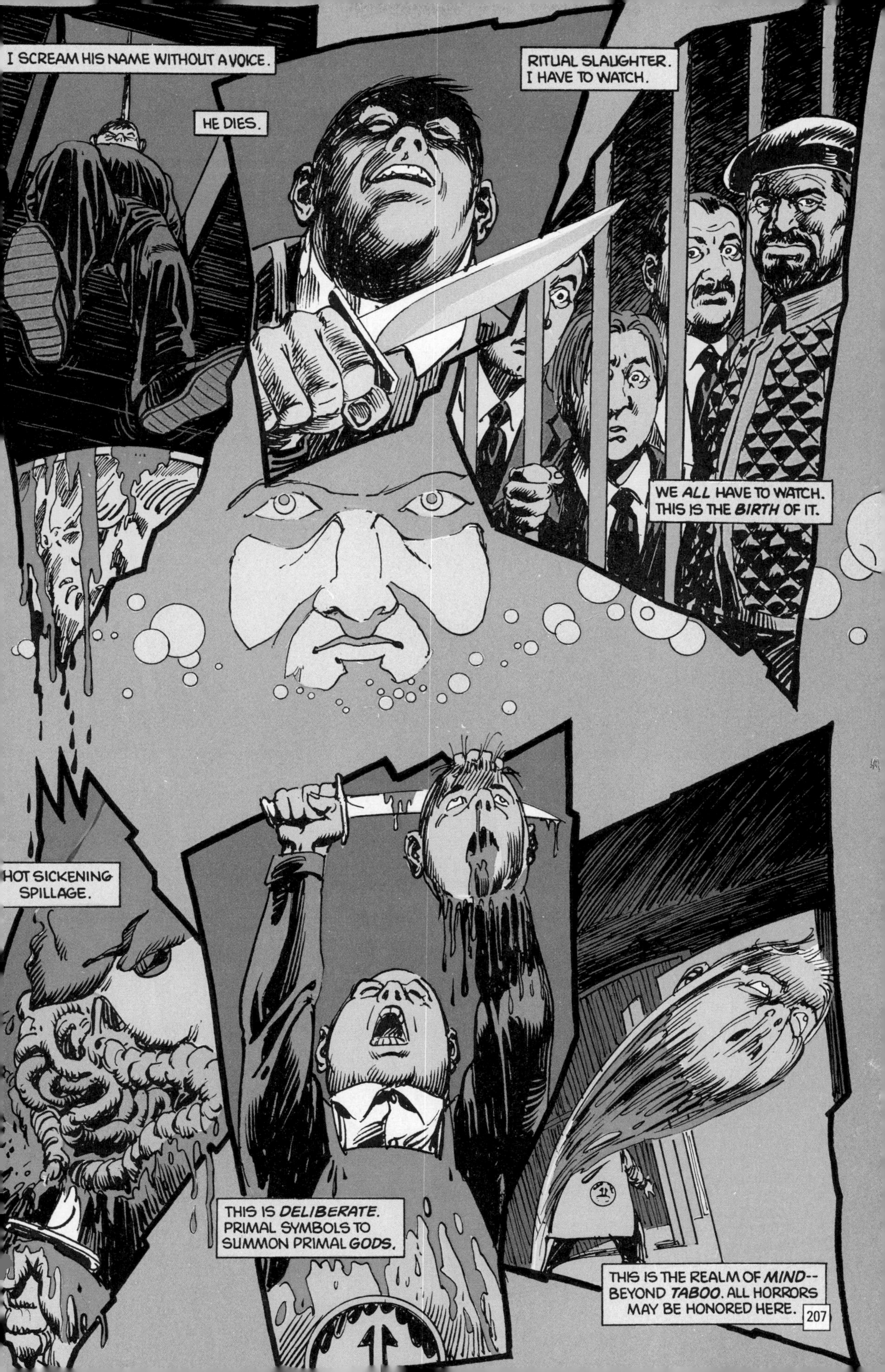
I SCREAM HIS NAME WITHOUT A VOICE.
HE DIES.
RITUAL SLAUGHTER. I HAVE TO WATCH.
WE *ALL* HAVE TO WATCH. THIS IS THE *BIRTH* OF IT.
HOT SICKENING SPILLAGE.
THIS IS *DELIBERATE*. PRIMAL SYMBOLS TO SUMMON PRIMAL *GODS*.
THIS IS THE REALM OF *MIND*-- BEYOND *TABOO*. ALL HORRORS MAY BE HONORED HERE.

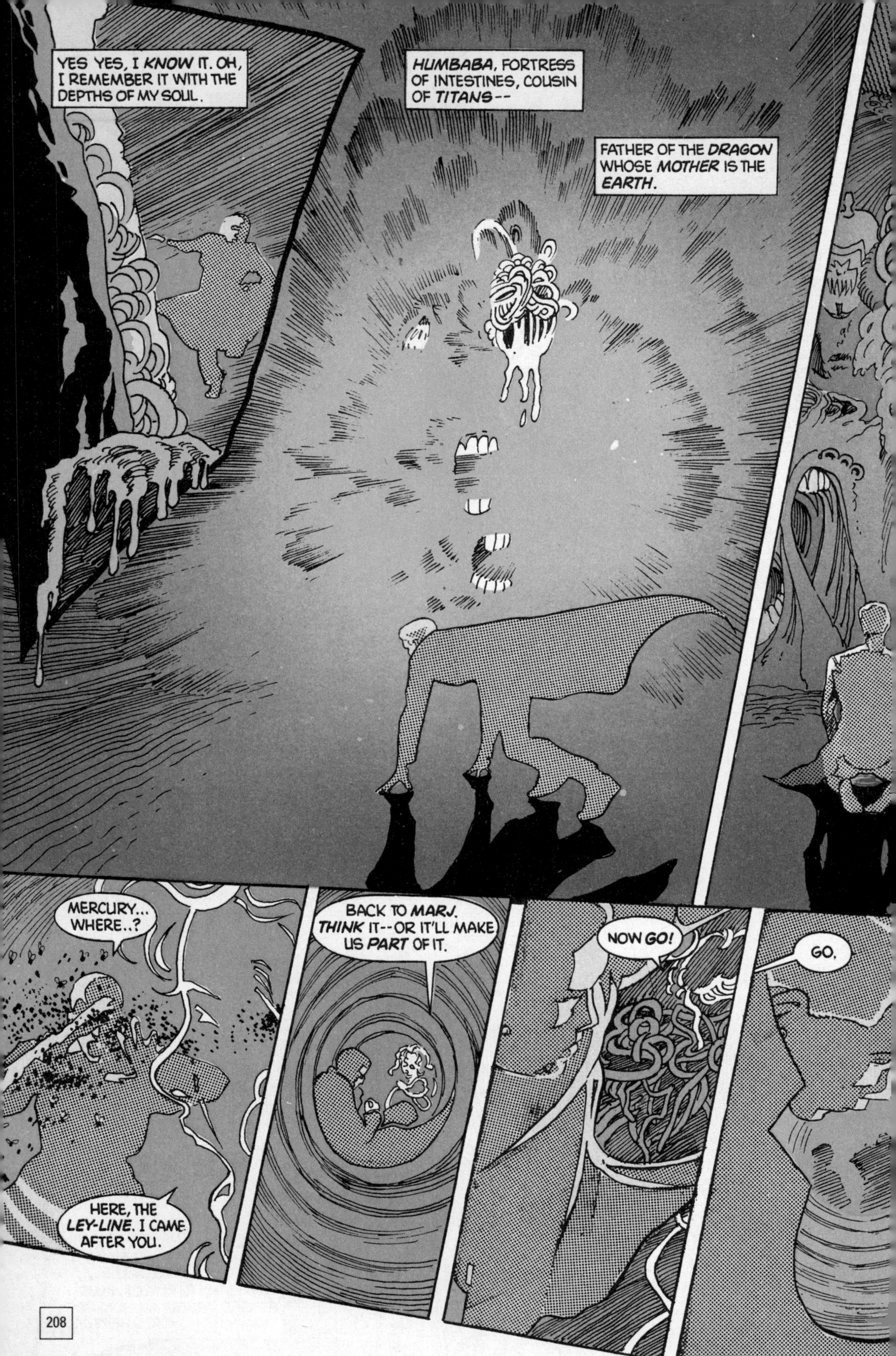
YES YES, I KNOW IT. OH, I REMEMBER IT WITH THE DEPTHS OF MY SOUL.
HUMBABA, FORTRESS OF INTESTINES, COUSIN OF TITANS--
FATHER OF THE DRAGON WHOSE MOTHER IS THE EARTH.
MERCURY... WHERE..?
HERE, THE LEY-LINE. I CAME AFTER YOU.
BACK TO MARJ. THINK IT--OR IT'LL MAKE US PART OF IT.
NOW GO!
GO.

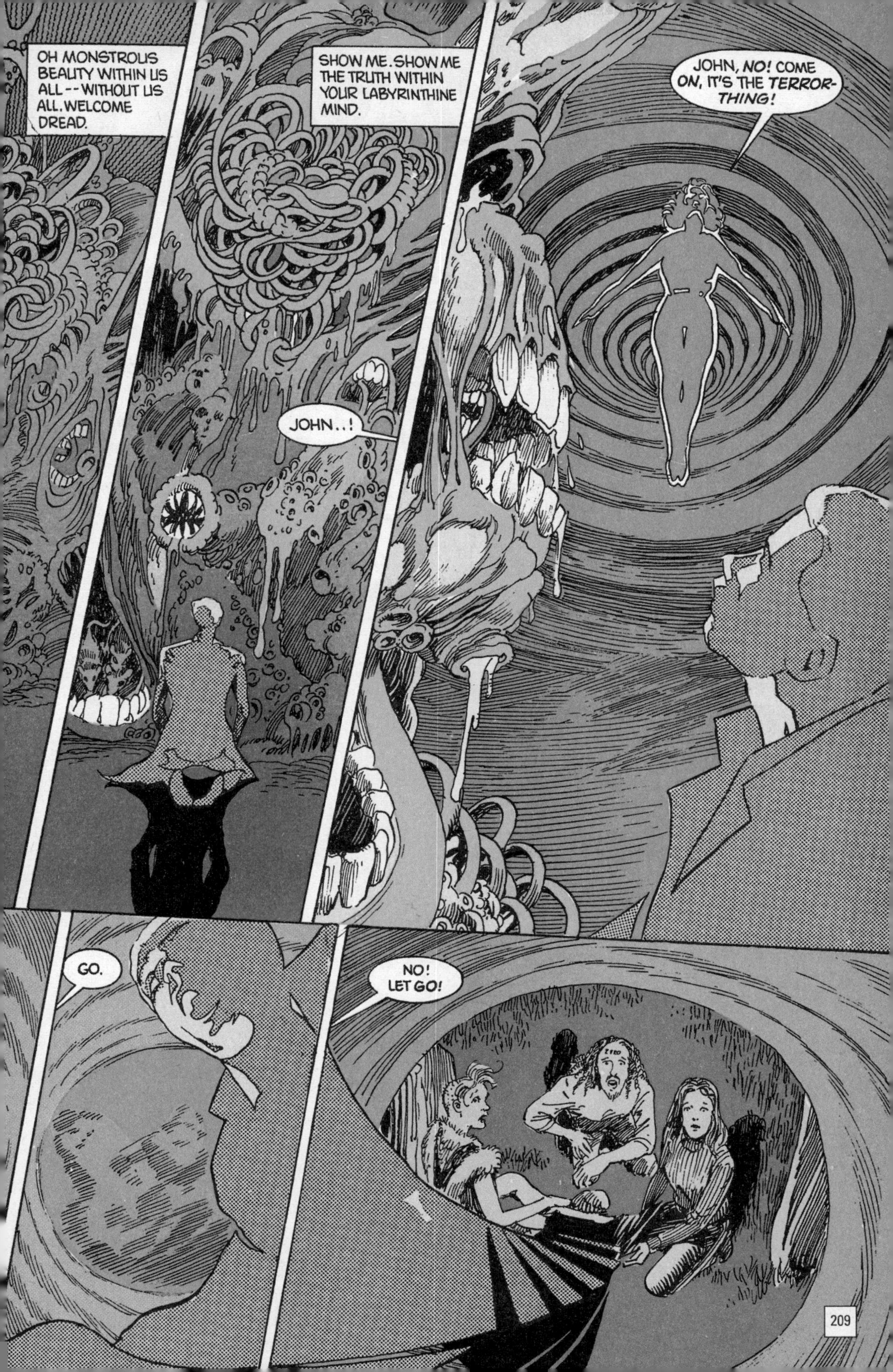
OH MONSTROUS BEAUTY WITHIN US ALL--WITHOUT US ALL. WELCOME DREAD.
SHOW ME. SHOW ME THE TRUTH WITHIN YOUR LABYRINTHINE MIND.
JOHN..!
JOHN, NO! COME ON, IT'S THE TERROR-THING!
GO.
NO! LET GO!

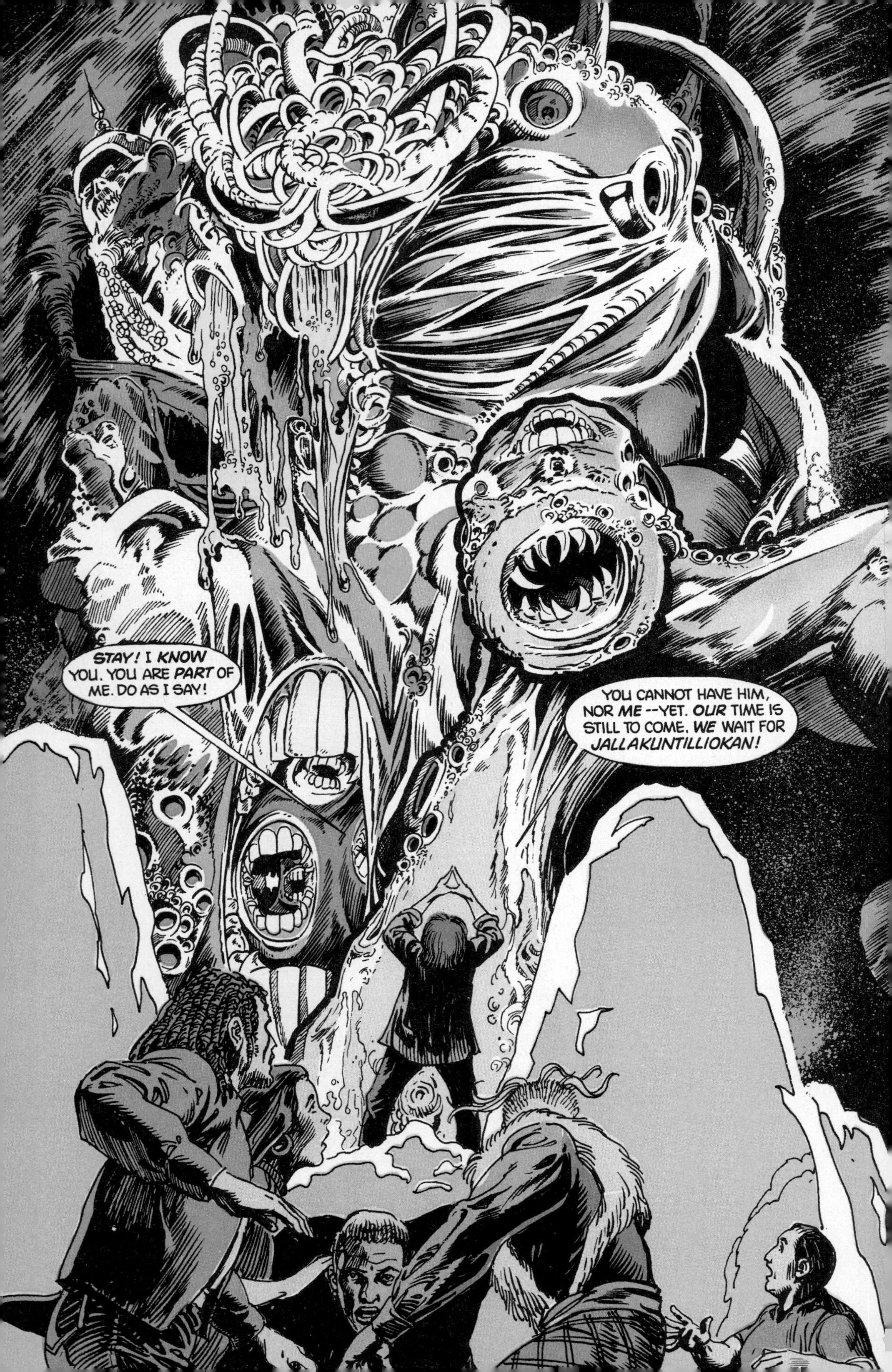
STAY! I KNOW YOU. YOU ARE PART OF ME. DO AS I SAY!
YOU CANNOT HAVE HIM, NOR ME--YET. OUR TIME IS STILL TO COME. WE WAIT FOR JALLAKUNTILLIOKAN!

22 SEP 89
US $1.50
$1.85 UK 80p
W FORMAT

GESTED FOR
RE READERS

JOHN CONSTANTINE

HELLBLAZER ™

Jamie Delano ● Mark Buckingham ● Alfredo Alcala

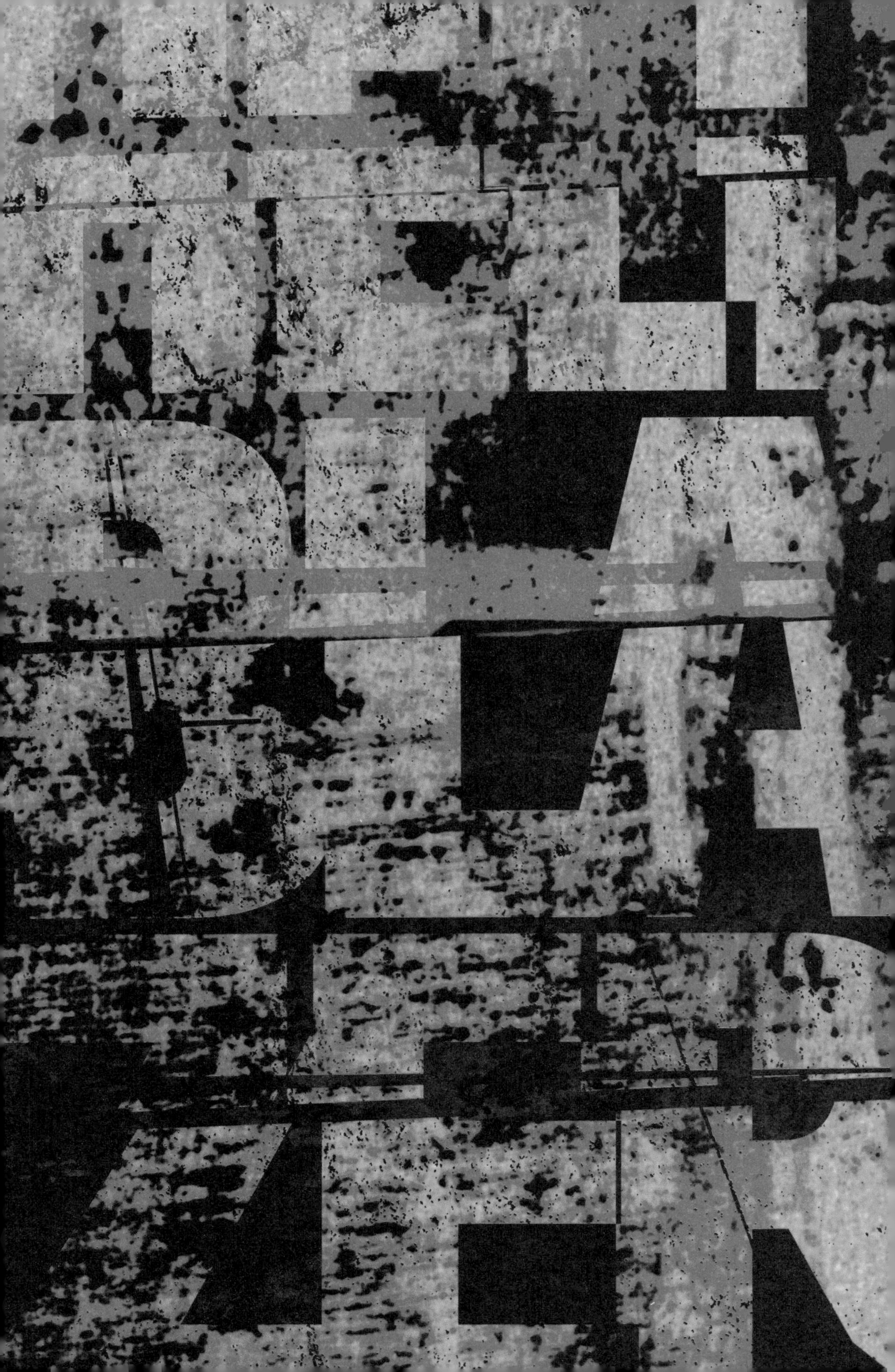

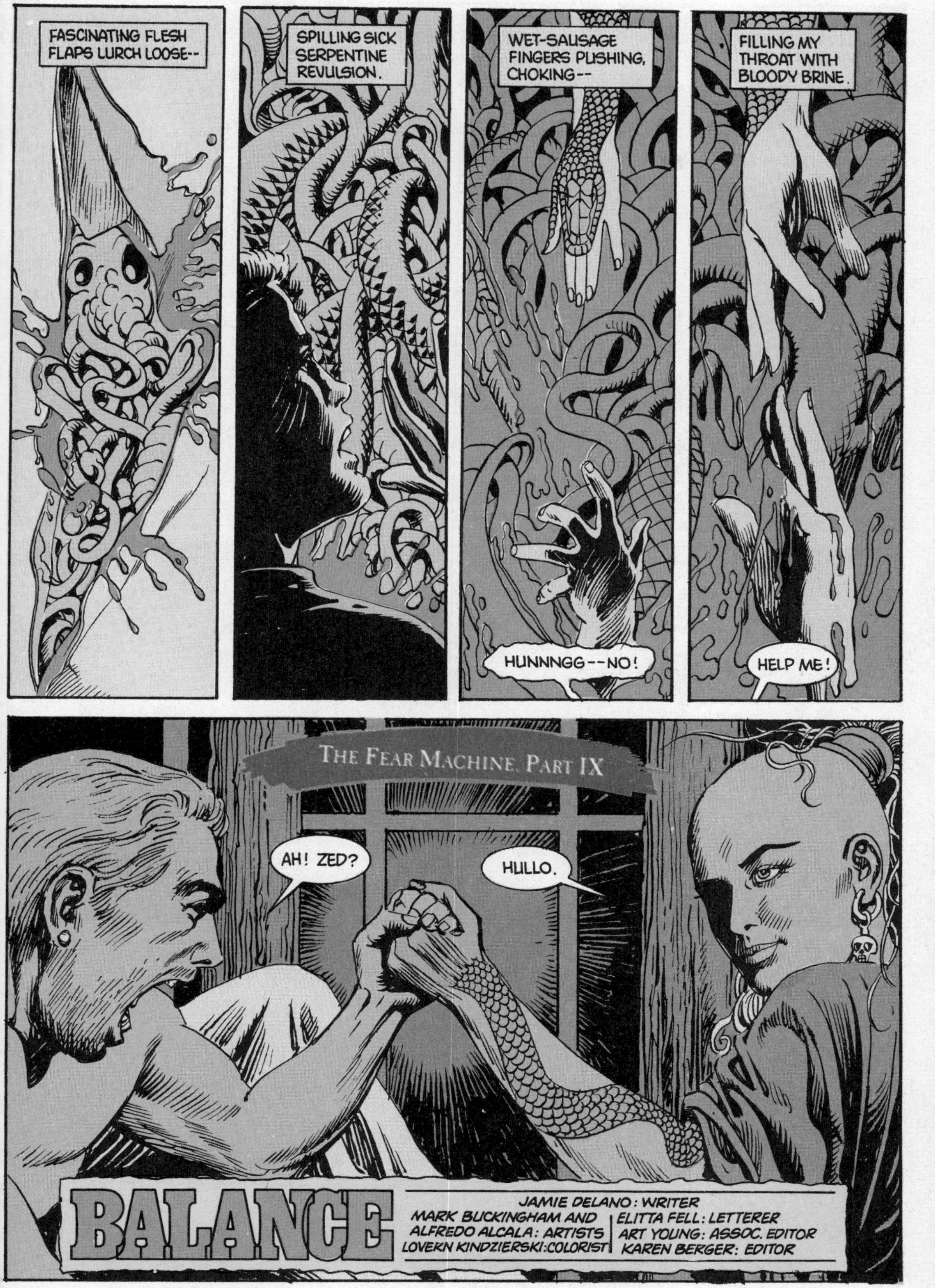
FASCINATING FLESH FLAPS LURCH LOOSE--
SPILLING SICK SERPENTINE REVULSION.
WET-SAUSAGE FINGERS PUSHING, CHOKING--
HUNNNGG--NO!
FILLING MY THROAT WITH BLOODY BRINE.
HELP ME!
THE FEAR MACHINE, PART IX
AH! ZED?
HULLO.
BALANCE
JAMIE DELANO: WRITER
MARK BUCKINGHAM AND ALFREDO ALCALA: ARTISTS
LOVERN KINDZIERSKI: COLORIST
ELITTA FELL: LETTERER
ART YOUNG: ASSOC. EDITOR
KAREN BERGER: EDITOR

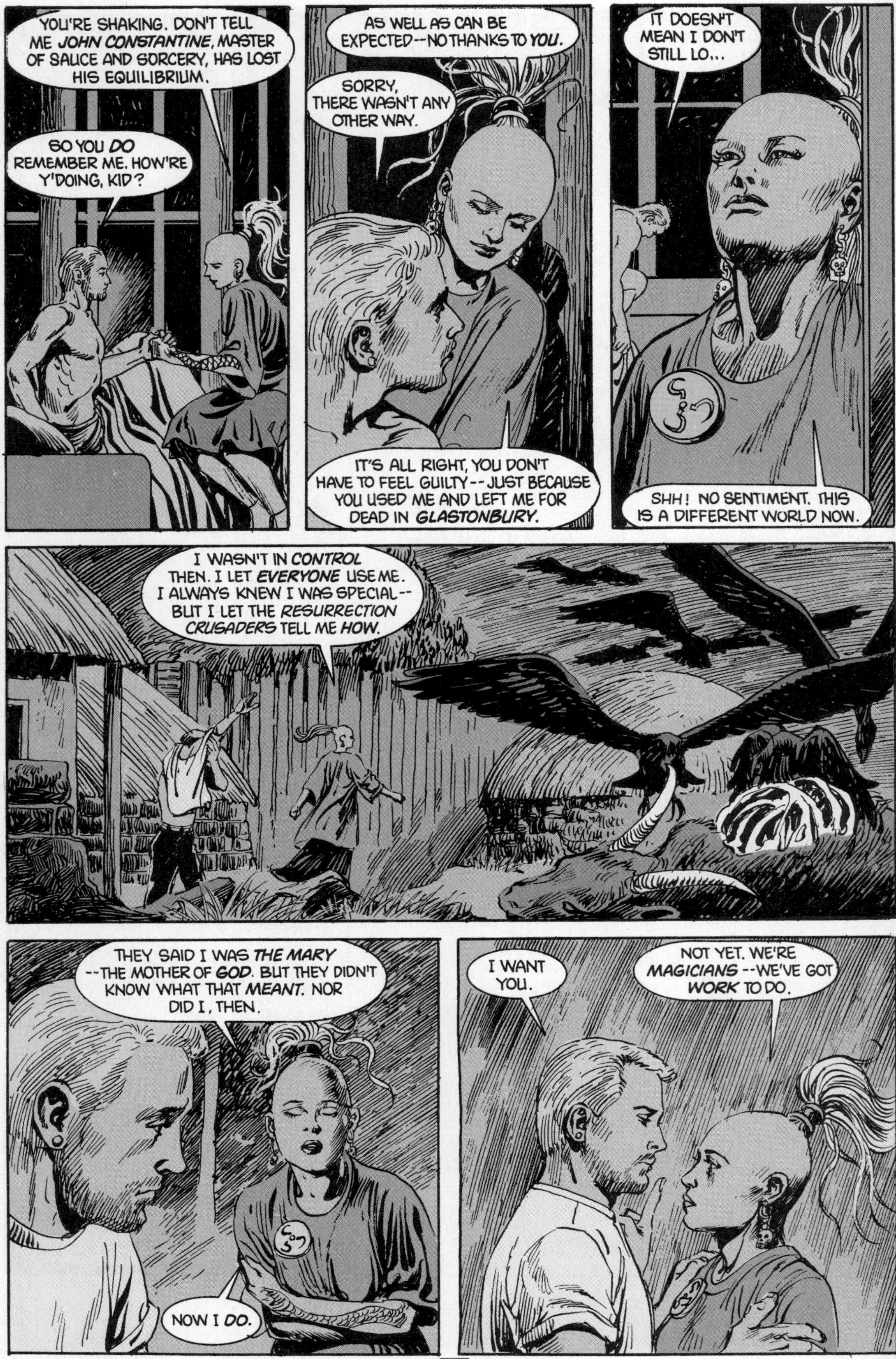
YOU'RE SHAKING. DON'T TELL ME JOHN CONSTANTINE, MASTER OF SAUCE AND SORCERY, HAS LOST HIS EQUILIBRIUM.
SO YOU DO REMEMBER ME. HOW'RE Y'DOING, KID?
AS WELL AS CAN BE EXPECTED--NO THANKS TO YOU.
SORRY, THERE WASN'T ANY OTHER WAY.
IT'S ALL RIGHT, YOU DON'T HAVE TO FEEL GUILTY--JUST BECAUSE YOU USED ME AND LEFT ME FOR DEAD IN GLASTONBURY.
IT DOESN'T MEAN I DON'T STILL LO...
SHH! NO SENTIMENT. THIS IS A DIFFERENT WORLD NOW.
I WASN'T IN CONTROL THEN. I LET EVERYONE USE ME. I ALWAYS KNEW I WAS SPECIAL--BUT I LET THE RESURRECTION CRUSADERS TELL ME HOW.
THEY SAID I WAS THE MARY --THE MOTHER OF GOD. BUT THEY DIDN'T KNOW WHAT THAT MEANT. NOR DID I, THEN.
NOW I DO.
I WANT YOU.
NOT YET. WE'RE MAGICIANS--WE'VE GOT WORK TO DO.

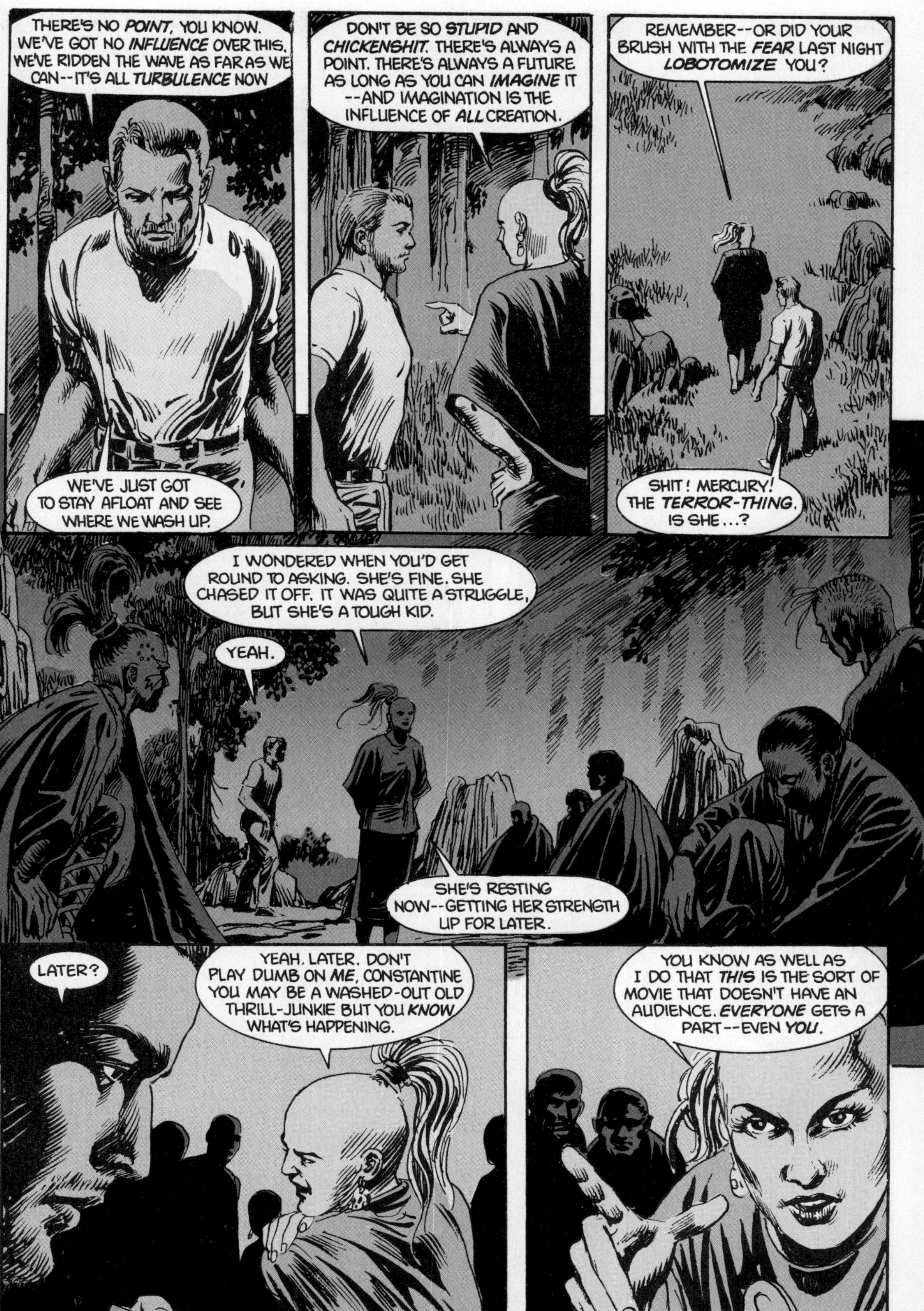

THERE'S NO *POINT*, YOU KNOW. WE'VE GOT NO *INFLUENCE* OVER THIS. WE'VE RIDDEN THE WAVE AS FAR AS WE CAN--IT'S ALL *TURBULENCE* NOW
WE'VE JUST GOT TO STAY AFLOAT AND SEE WHERE WE WASH UP.
DON'T BE SO *STUPID* AND *CHICKENSHIT*. THERE'S ALWAYS A POINT. THERE'S ALWAYS A FUTURE AS LONG AS YOU CAN *IMAGINE* IT --AND IMAGINATION IS THE INFLUENCE OF *ALL* CREATION.
REMEMBER--OR DID YOUR BRUSH WITH THE *FEAR* LAST NIGHT *LOBOTOMIZE* YOU?
SHIT! MERCURY! THE *TERROR-THING*. IS SHE...?
I WONDERED WHEN YOU'D GET ROUND TO ASKING. SHE'S FINE. SHE CHASED IT OFF. IT WAS QUITE A STRUGGLE, BUT SHE'S A TOUGH KID.
YEAH.
SHE'S RESTING NOW--GETTING HER STRENGTH UP FOR LATER.
LATER?
YEAH. LATER. DON'T PLAY DUMB ON *ME*, CONSTANTINE YOU MAY BE A WASHED-OUT OLD THRILL-JUNKIE BUT YOU *KNOW* WHAT'S HAPPENING.
YOU KNOW AS WELL AS I DO THAT *THIS* IS THE SORT OF MOVIE THAT DOESN'T HAVE AN AUDIENCE. *EVERYONE* GETS A PART--EVEN *YOU*.

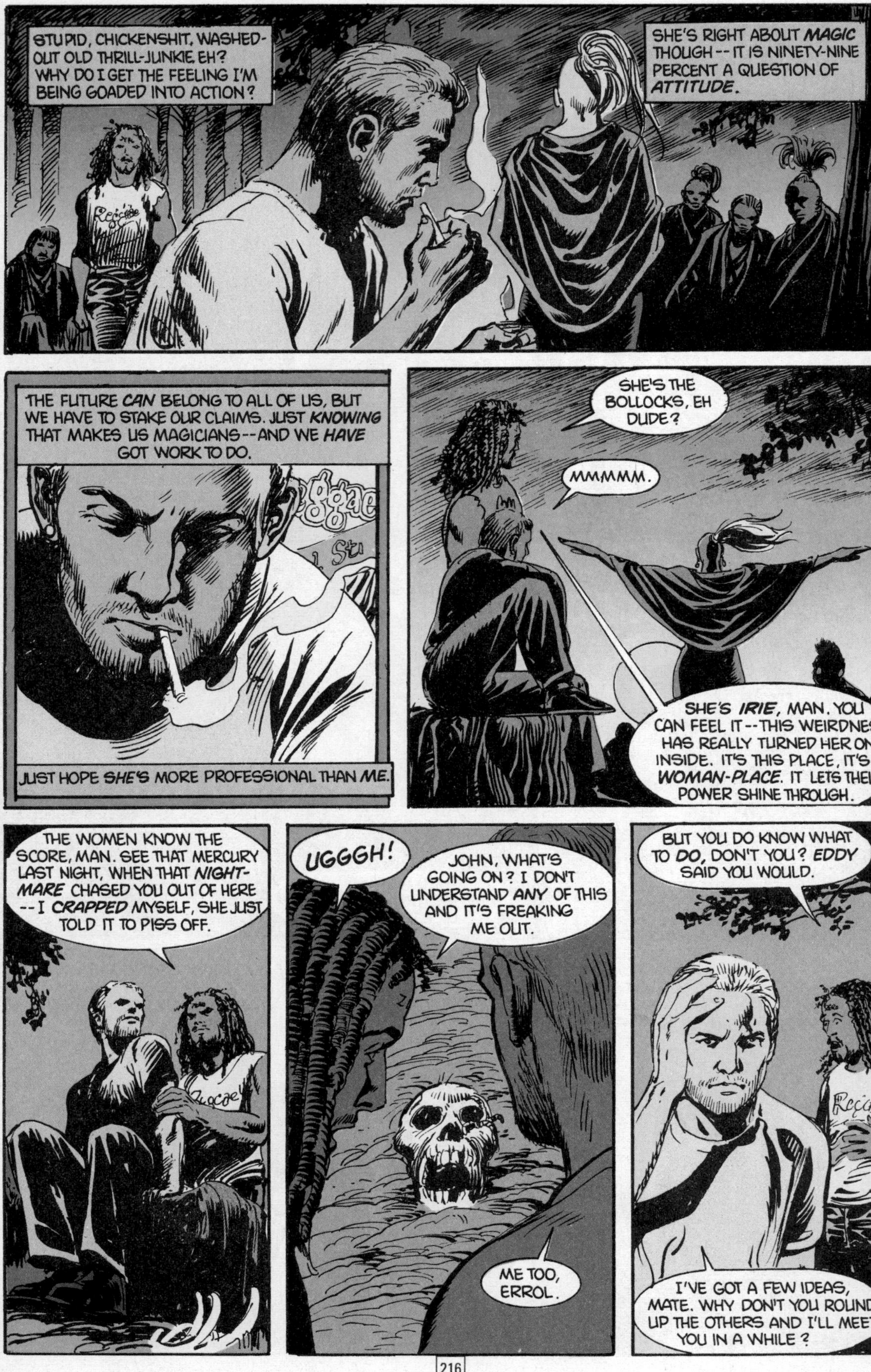
STUPID, CHICKENSHIT, WASHED-OUT OLD THRILL-JUNKIE, EH? WHY DO I GET THE FEELING I'M BEING GOADED INTO ACTION?
SHE'S RIGHT ABOUT MAGIC THOUGH -- IT IS NINETY-NINE PERCENT A QUESTION OF ATTITUDE.
THE FUTURE CAN BELONG TO ALL OF US, BUT WE HAVE TO STAKE OUR CLAIMS. JUST KNOWING THAT MAKES US MAGICIANS--AND WE HAVE GOT WORK TO DO.
JUST HOPE SHE'S MORE PROFESSIONAL THAN ME.
SHE'S THE BOLLOCKS, EH DUDE?
MMMMM.
SHE'S IRIE, MAN. YOU CAN FEEL IT--THIS WEIRDNESS HAS REALLY TURNED HER ON INSIDE. IT'S THIS PLACE, IT'S A WOMAN-PLACE. IT LETS THEIR POWER SHINE THROUGH.
THE WOMEN KNOW THE SCORE, MAN. SEE THAT MERCURY LAST NIGHT, WHEN THAT NIGHT-MARE CHASED YOU OUT OF HERE --I CRAPPED MYSELF, SHE JUST TOLD IT TO PISS OFF.
UGGGH!
JOHN, WHAT'S GOING ON? I DON'T UNDERSTAND ANY OF THIS AND IT'S FREAKING ME OUT.
ME TOO, ERROL.
BUT YOU DO KNOW WHAT TO DO, DON'T YOU? EDDY SAID YOU WOULD.
I'VE GOT A FEW IDEAS, MATE. WHY DON'T YOU ROUND UP THE OTHERS AND I'LL MEET YOU IN A WHILE?

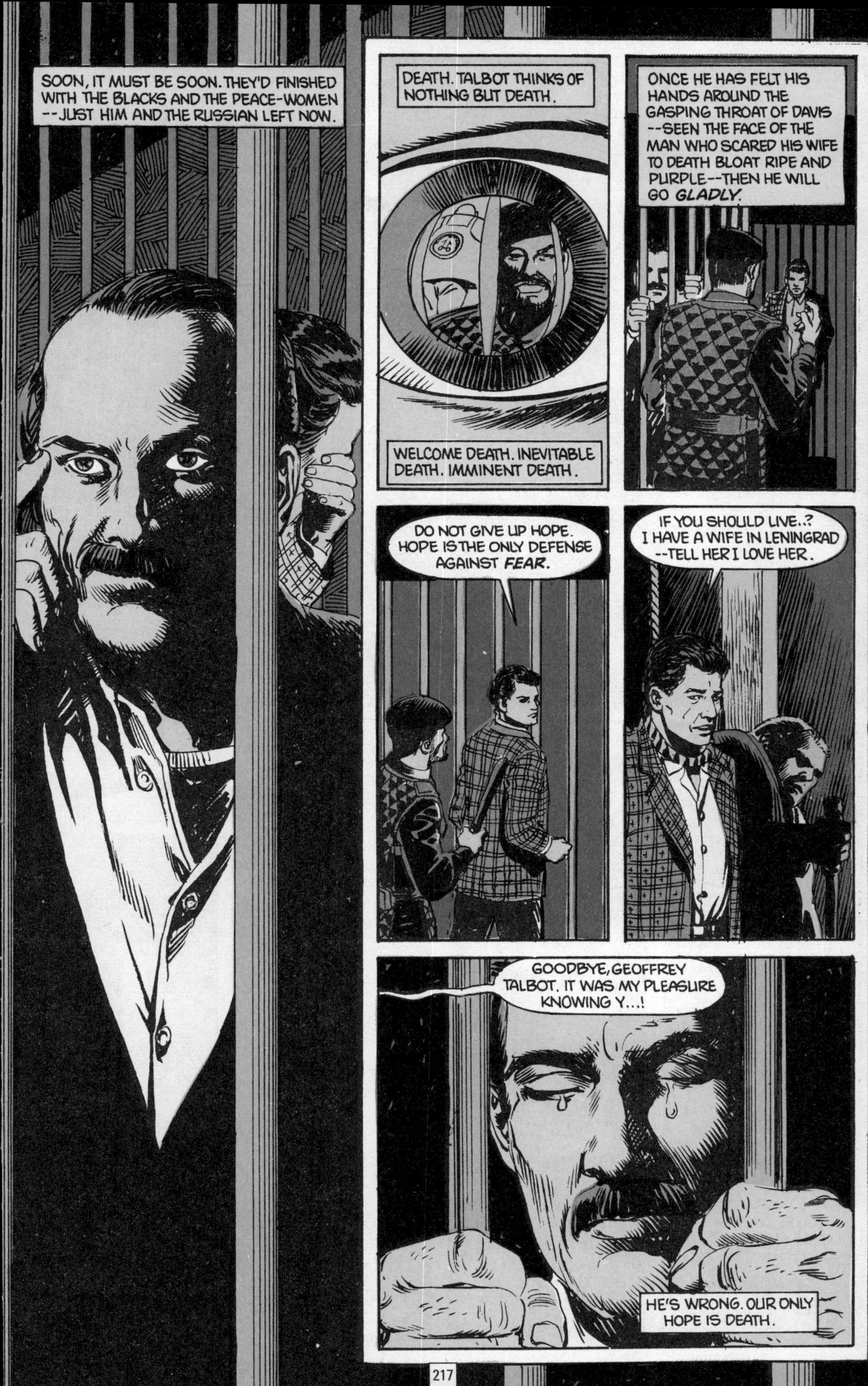
SOON, IT MUST BE SOON. THEY'D FINISHED WITH THE BLACKS AND THE PEACE-WOMEN --JUST HIM AND THE RUSSIAN LEFT NOW.
DEATH. TALBOT THINKS OF NOTHING BUT DEATH.
WELCOME DEATH. INEVITABLE DEATH. IMMINENT DEATH.
ONCE HE HAS FELT HIS HANDS AROUND THE GASPING THROAT OF DAVIS --SEEN THE FACE OF THE MAN WHO SCARED HIS WIFE TO DEATH BLOAT RIPE AND PURPLE--THEN HE WILL GO *GLADLY*.
DO NOT GIVE UP HOPE. HOPE IS THE ONLY DEFENSE AGAINST *FEAR*.
IF YOU SHOULD LIVE..? I HAVE A WIFE IN LENINGRAD --TELL HER I LOVE HER.
GOODBYE, GEOFFREY TALBOT. IT WAS MY PLEASURE KNOWING Y...!
HE'S WRONG. OUR ONLY HOPE IS DEATH.

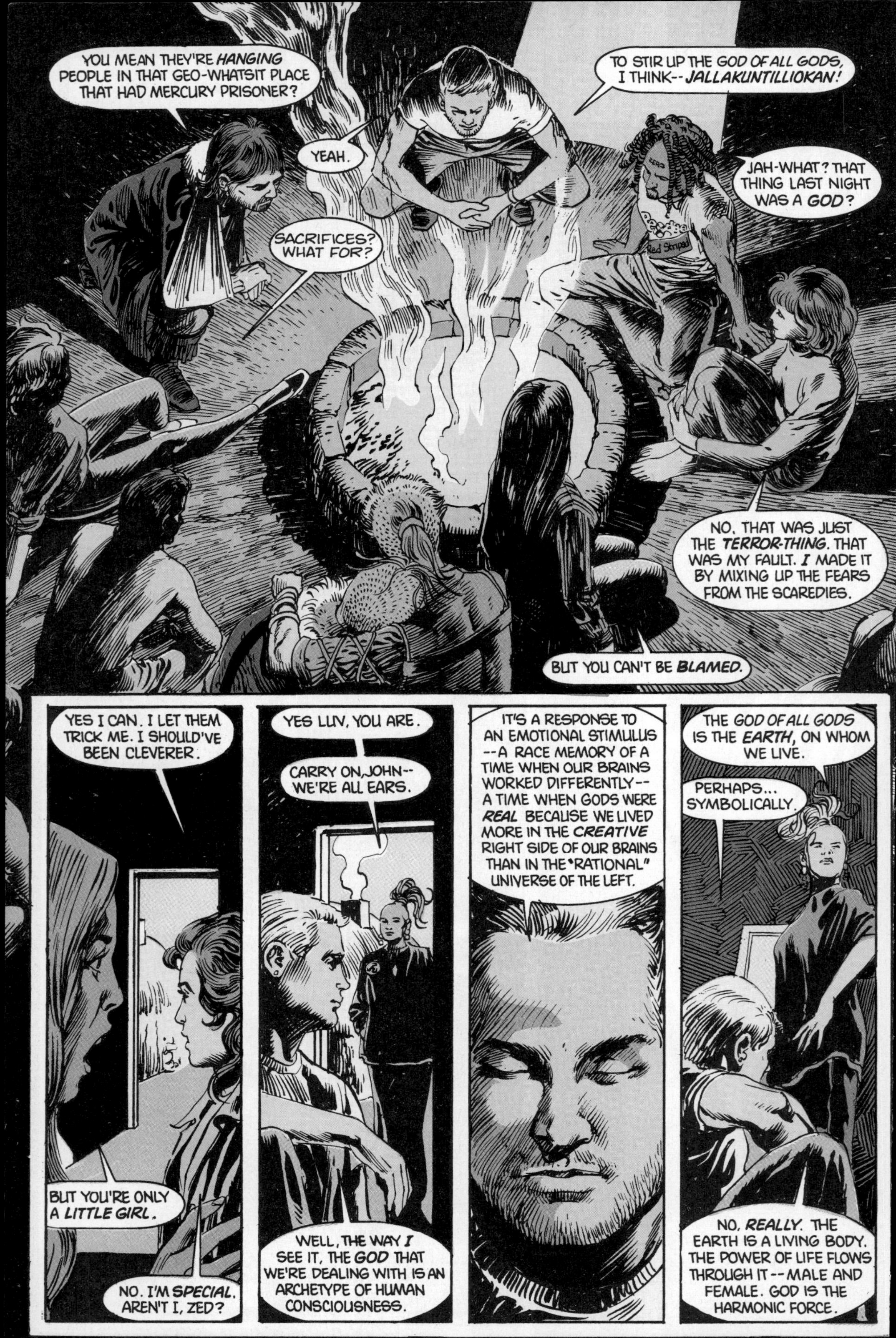
YOU MEAN THEY'RE HANGING PEOPLE IN THAT GEO-WHATSIT PLACE THAT HAD MERCURY PRISONER?
YEAH.
SACRIFICES? WHAT FOR?
TO STIR UP THE GOD OF ALL GODS, I THINK-- JALLAKUNTILLIOKAN!
JAH-WHAT? THAT THING LAST NIGHT WAS A GOD?
NO, THAT WAS JUST THE TERROR-THING. THAT WAS MY FAULT. I MADE IT BY MIXING UP THE FEARS FROM THE SCAREDIES.
BUT YOU CAN'T BE BLAMED.
YES I CAN. I LET THEM TRICK ME. I SHOULD'VE BEEN CLEVERER.
BUT YOU'RE ONLY A LITTLE GIRL.
NO. I'M SPECIAL. AREN'T I, ZED?
YES LUV, YOU ARE.
CARRY ON, JOHN-- WE'RE ALL EARS.
WELL, THE WAY I SEE IT, THE GOD THAT WE'RE DEALING WITH IS AN ARCHETYPE OF HUMAN CONSCIOUSNESS.
IT'S A RESPONSE TO AN EMOTIONAL STIMULUS --A RACE MEMORY OF A TIME WHEN OUR BRAINS WORKED DIFFERENTLY-- A TIME WHEN GODS WERE REAL BECAUSE WE LIVED MORE IN THE CREATIVE RIGHT SIDE OF OUR BRAINS THAN IN THE "RATIONAL" UNIVERSE OF THE LEFT.
THE GOD OF ALL GODS IS THE EARTH, ON WHOM WE LIVE.
PERHAPS... SYMBOLICALLY.
NO, REALLY. THE EARTH IS A LIVING BODY. THE POWER OF LIFE FLOWS THROUGH IT -- MALE AND FEMALE. GOD IS THE HARMONIC FORCE.

YEAH, THE *LEY-LINES* --THE POSITIVE AND NEGATIVE ENERGY FLOWS.

NO, EDDY, YOU'RE WRONG. THE LEY-LINES ARE JUST AN EARLY ATTEMPT BY A MALE PRIESTHOOD TO DOMINATE THE FEMALE PRINCIPLE AND UNBALANCE THE NATURE OF GOD.

OF COURSE, EVERYONE *ASSUMES* THE LEY-LINES ARE BENEFICIAL JUST BECAUSE THEY'RE OLD AND ESOTERIC.

BUT THEY CARRY *GOOD* ENERGY.

NO, IT'S THE *DRAGON* LINES THAT'RE IMPORTANT.

THE *FENG SHUI?*

YES, THE *ORIENTAL* TRADITION OF GEOMANCY PLOTS THE EARTH'S ENERGY IN NATURAL, FLOWING PATTERNS.

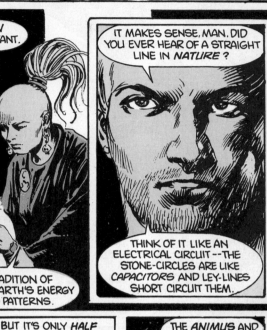

IT MAKES SENSE, MAN. DID YOU EVER HEAR OF A STRAIGHT LINE IN *NATURE?*

THINK OF IT LIKE AN ELECTRICAL CIRCUIT --THE STONE-CIRCLES ARE LIKE *CAPACITORS* AND LEY-LINES SHORT CIRCUIT THEM.

BUT WHY WOULD THEY *DO* IT?

TO CAPTURE POWER, OF COURSE. WHY ELSE DO *MEN* DO ANYTHING? THEY TIED DOWN THE *EARTH* SPIRIT --BOUND THE *DRAGON.*

AND NOW THEY'RE LETTING IT OUT AGAIN. WHAT'S WRONG WITH THAT? A BIT OF DRAGON ENERGY IS PROBABLY JUST WHAT THE WORLD *NEEDS.*

BUT IT'S ONLY *HALF* OF IT THAT THEY'RE LETTING GO. THE *DRAGON* IS A *TWIN* GOD -- OF LIFE AND DEATH, YIN AND YANG, POSITIVE AND NEGATIVE, MALE AND FEMALE--

THE *ANIMUS* AND THE *ANIMA.*

EXACTLY.

THESE *MAGI CAECUS* ARE THE GUARDIANS OF A MAGICAL TRADITION OF MALE SUPREMACY HANDED DOWN FROM THE BUILDERS OF THE STONE-CIRCLES -- THE MASONS OF ATLANTIS, PROBABLY.

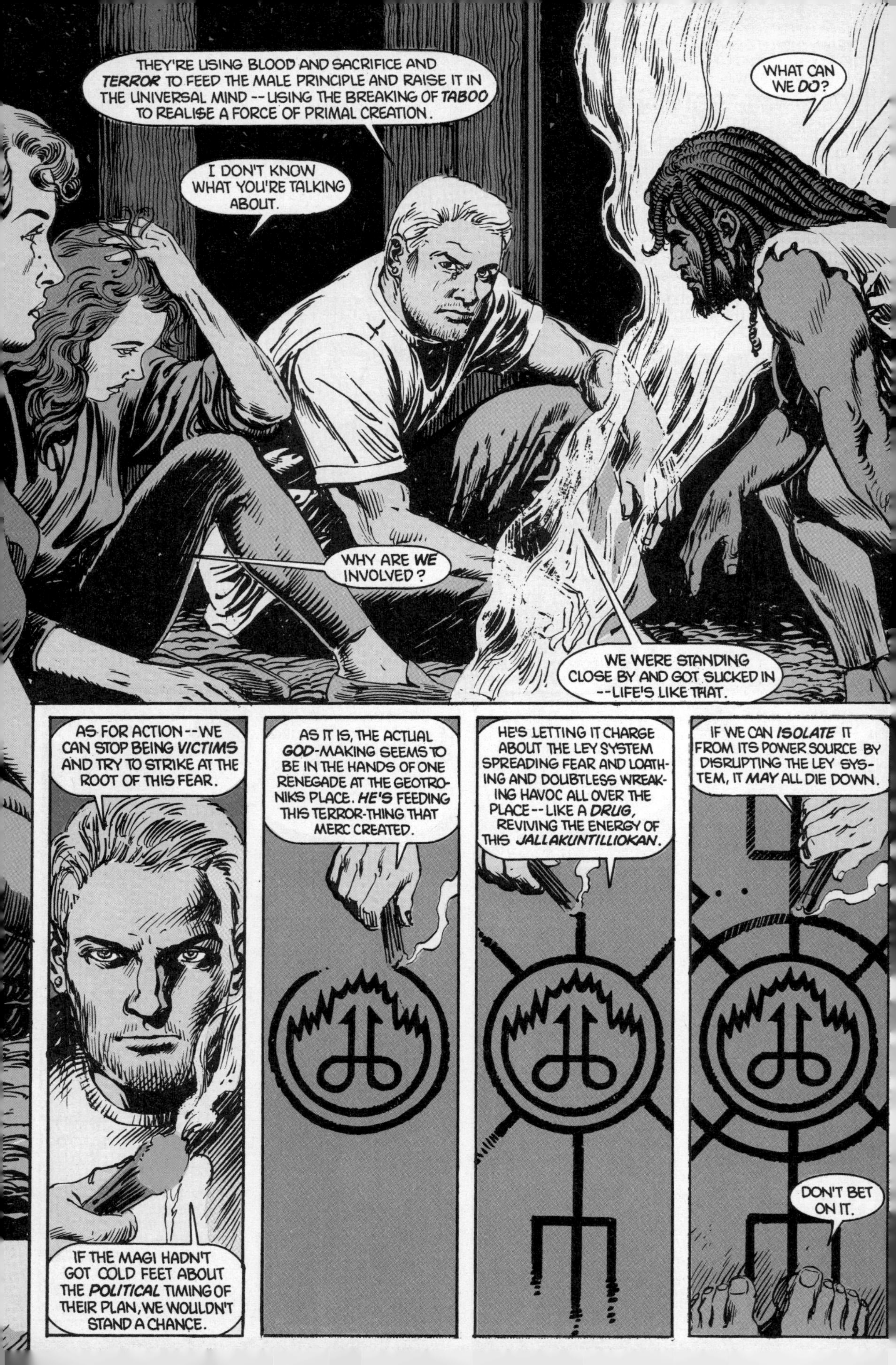
THEY'RE USING BLOOD AND SACRIFICE AND TERROR TO FEED THE MALE PRINCIPLE AND RAISE IT IN THE UNIVERSAL MIND -- USING THE BREAKING OF TABOO TO REALISE A FORCE OF PRIMAL CREATION.
I DON'T KNOW WHAT YOU'RE TALKING ABOUT.
WHAT CAN WE DO?
WHY ARE WE INVOLVED?
WE WERE STANDING CLOSE BY AND GOT SUCKED IN --LIFE'S LIKE THAT.
AS FOR ACTION -- WE CAN STOP BEING VICTIMS AND TRY TO STRIKE AT THE ROOT OF THIS FEAR.
IF THE MAGI HADN'T GOT COLD FEET ABOUT THE POLITICAL TIMING OF THEIR PLAN, WE WOULDN'T STAND A CHANCE.
AS IT IS, THE ACTUAL GOD-MAKING SEEMS TO BE IN THE HANDS OF ONE RENEGADE AT THE GEOTRONIKS PLACE. HE'S FEEDING THIS TERROR-THING THAT MERC CREATED.
HE'S LETTING IT CHARGE ABOUT THE LEY SYSTEM SPREADING FEAR AND LOATHING AND DOUBTLESS WREAKING HAVOC ALL OVER THE PLACE -- LIKE A DRUG, REVIVING THE ENERGY OF THIS JALLAKUNTILLIOKAN.
IF WE CAN ISOLATE IT FROM ITS POWER SOURCE BY DISRUPTING THE LEY SYSTEM, IT MAY ALL DIE DOWN.
DON'T BET ON IT.

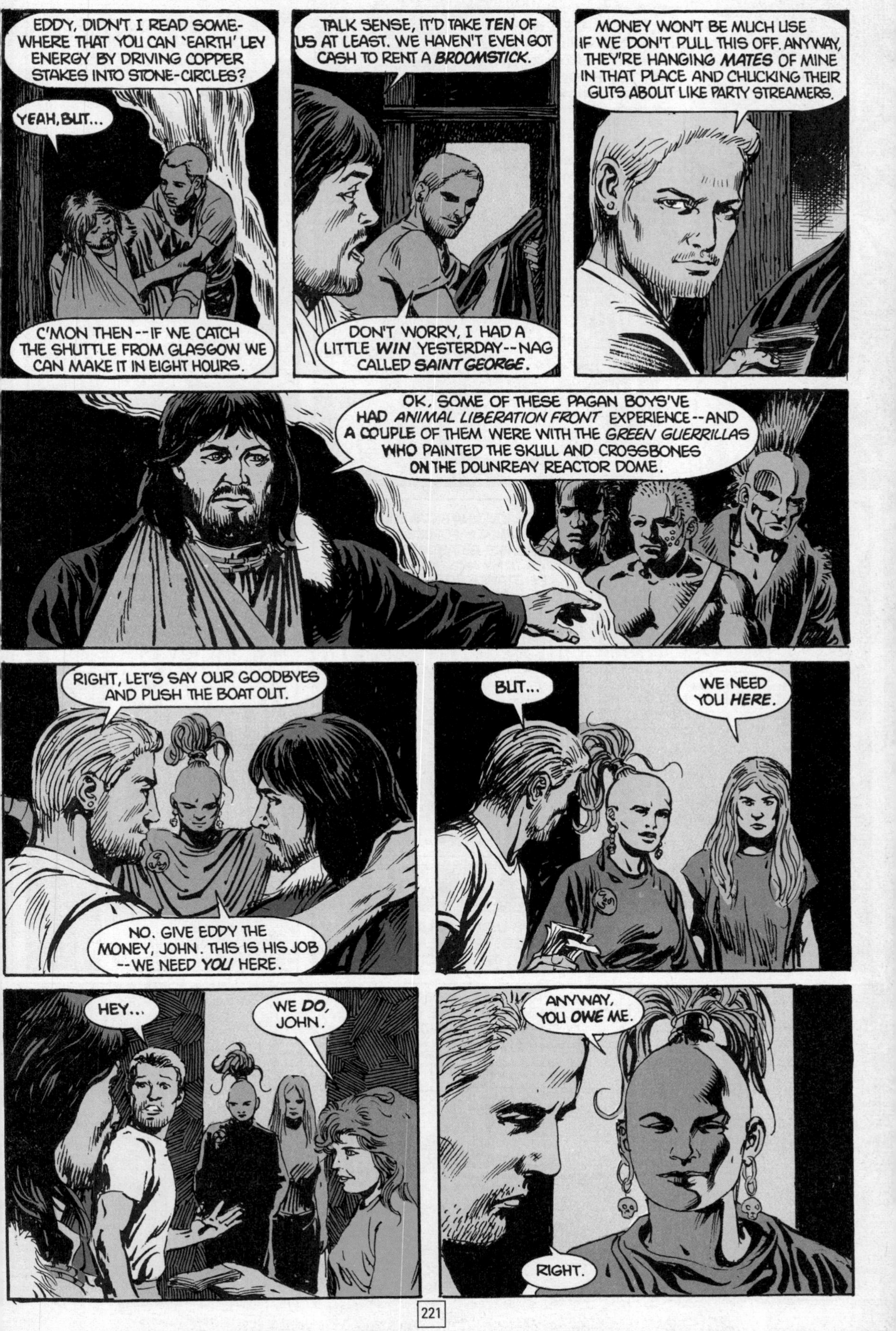
EDDY, DIDN'T I READ SOMEWHERE THAT YOU CAN 'EARTH' LEY ENERGY BY DRIVING COPPER STAKES INTO STONE-CIRCLES?
YEAH, BUT...
C'MON THEN--IF WE CATCH THE SHUTTLE FROM GLASGOW WE CAN MAKE IT IN EIGHT HOURS.
TALK SENSE, IT'D TAKE TEN OF US AT LEAST. WE HAVEN'T EVEN GOT CASH TO RENT A BROOMSTICK.
DON'T WORRY, I HAD A LITTLE WIN YESTERDAY--NAG CALLED SAINT GEORGE.
MONEY WON'T BE MUCH USE IF WE DON'T PULL THIS OFF. ANYWAY, THEY'RE HANGING MATES OF MINE IN THAT PLACE AND CHUCKING THEIR GUTS ABOUT LIKE PARTY STREAMERS.
OK, SOME OF THESE PAGAN BOYS'VE HAD ANIMAL LIBERATION FRONT EXPERIENCE--AND A COUPLE OF THEM WERE WITH THE GREEN GUERRILLAS WHO PAINTED THE SKULL AND CROSSBONES ON THE DOUNREAY REACTOR DOME.
RIGHT, LET'S SAY OUR GOODBYES AND PUSH THE BOAT OUT.
NO. GIVE EDDY THE MONEY, JOHN. THIS IS HIS JOB --WE NEED YOU HERE.
BUT...
WE NEED YOU HERE.
HEY...
WE DO, JOHN.
ANYWAY, YOU OWE ME.
RIGHT.

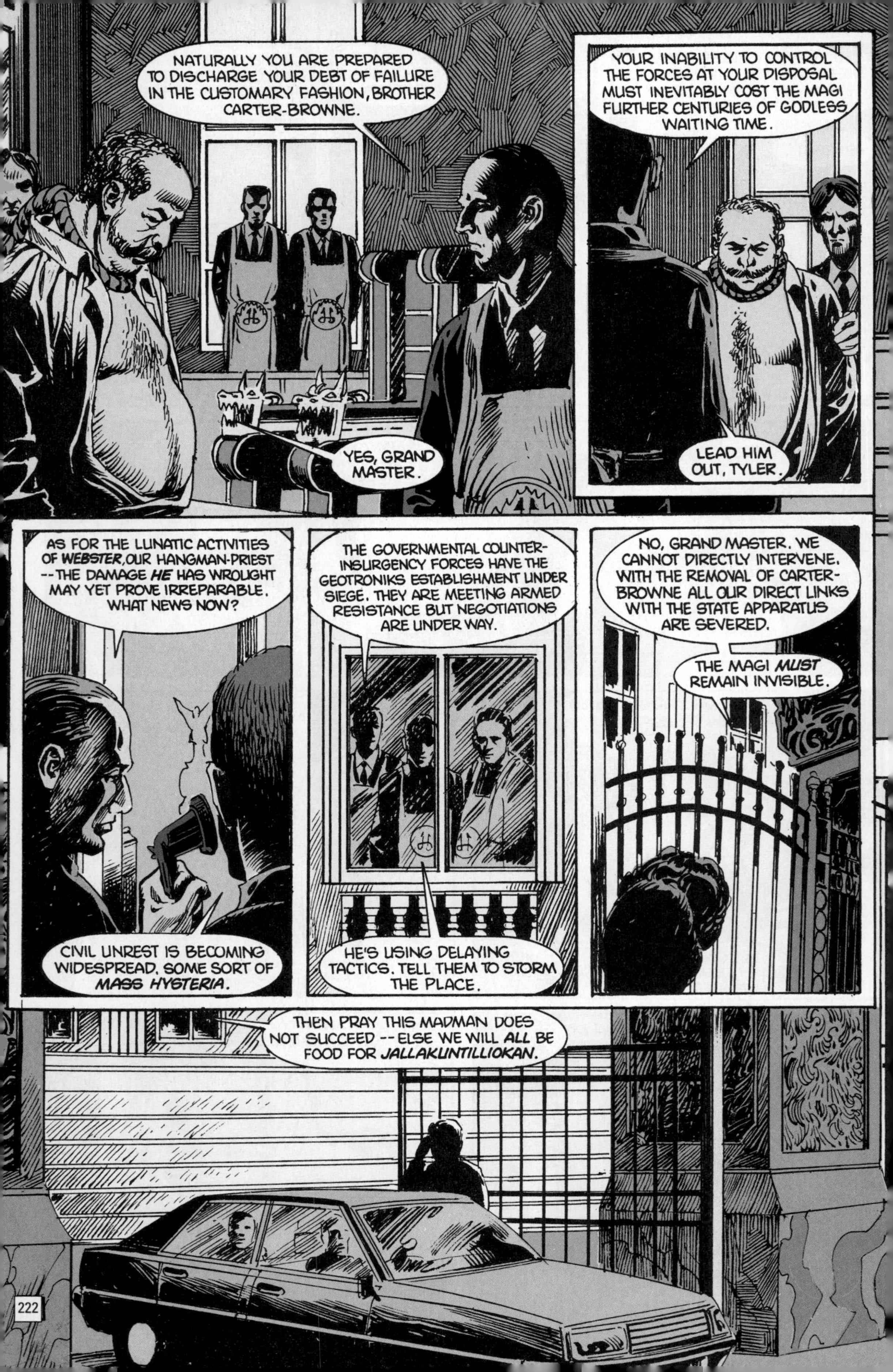
NATURALLY YOU ARE PREPARED TO DISCHARGE YOUR DEBT OF FAILURE IN THE CUSTOMARY FASHION, BROTHER CARTER-BROWNE.
YES, GRAND MASTER.
YOUR INABILITY TO CONTROL THE FORCES AT YOUR DISPOSAL MUST INEVITABLY COST THE MAGI FURTHER CENTURIES OF GODLESS WAITING TIME.
LEAD HIM OUT, TYLER.
AS FOR THE LUNATIC ACTIVITIES OF WEBSTER, OUR HANGMAN-PRIEST --THE DAMAGE HE HAS WROUGHT MAY YET PROVE IRREPARABLE. WHAT NEWS NOW?
CIVIL UNREST IS BECOMING WIDESPREAD. SOME SORT OF MASS HYSTERIA.
THE GOVERNMENTAL COUNTER-INSURGENCY FORCES HAVE THE GEOTRONIKS ESTABLISHMENT UNDER SIEGE. THEY ARE MEETING ARMED RESISTANCE BUT NEGOTIATIONS ARE UNDER WAY.
HE'S USING DELAYING TACTICS. TELL THEM TO STORM THE PLACE.
NO, GRAND MASTER. WE CANNOT DIRECTLY INTERVENE. WITH THE REMOVAL OF CARTER-BROWNE ALL OUR DIRECT LINKS WITH THE STATE APPARATUS ARE SEVERED.
THE MAGI MUST REMAIN INVISIBLE.
THEN PRAY THIS MADMAN DOES NOT SUCCEED --ELSE WE WILL ALL BE FOOD FOR JALLAKUNTILLIOKAN.

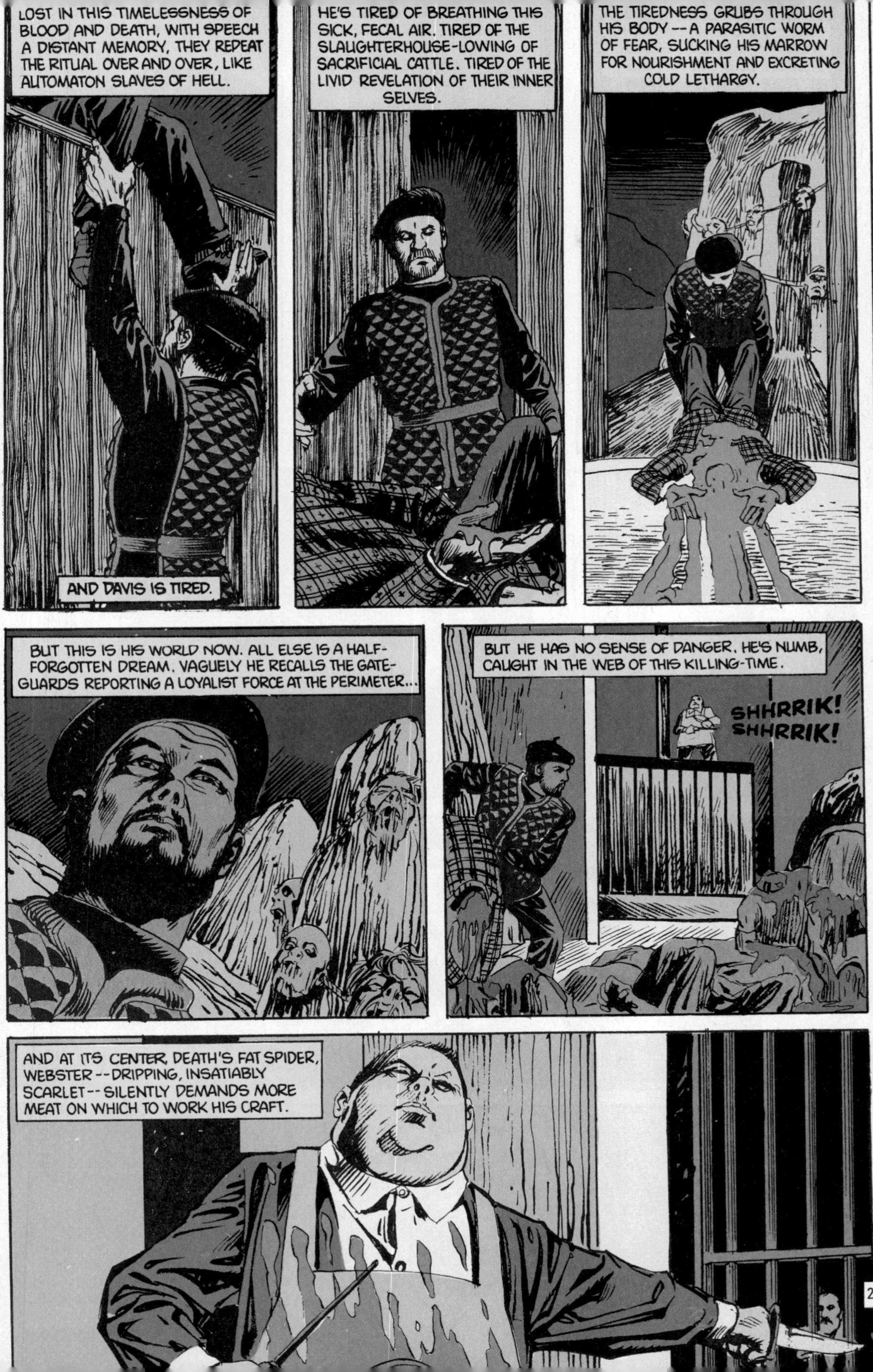
LOST IN THIS TIMELESSNESS OF BLOOD AND DEATH, WITH SPEECH A DISTANT MEMORY, THEY REPEAT THE RITUAL OVER AND OVER, LIKE AUTOMATON SLAVES OF HELL.
AND DAVIS IS TIRED.
HE'S TIRED OF BREATHING THIS SICK, FECAL AIR. TIRED OF THE SLAUGHTERHOUSE-LOWING OF SACRIFICIAL CATTLE. TIRED OF THE LIVID REVELATION OF THEIR INNER SELVES.
THE TIREDNESS GRUBS THROUGH HIS BODY -- A PARASITIC WORM OF FEAR, SUCKING HIS MARROW FOR NOURISHMENT AND EXCRETING COLD LETHARGY.
BUT THIS IS HIS WORLD NOW. ALL ELSE IS A HALF-FORGOTTEN DREAM. VAGUELY HE RECALLS THE GATE-GUARDS REPORTING A LOYALIST FORCE AT THE PERIMETER...
BUT HE HAS NO SENSE OF DANGER. HE'S NUMB, CAUGHT IN THE WEB OF THIS KILLING-TIME.
SHHRRIK! SHHRRIK!
AND AT ITS CENTER, DEATH'S FAT SPIDER, WEBSTER -- DRIPPING, INSATIABLY SCARLET -- SILENTLY DEMANDS MORE MEAT ON WHICH TO WORK HIS CRAFT.

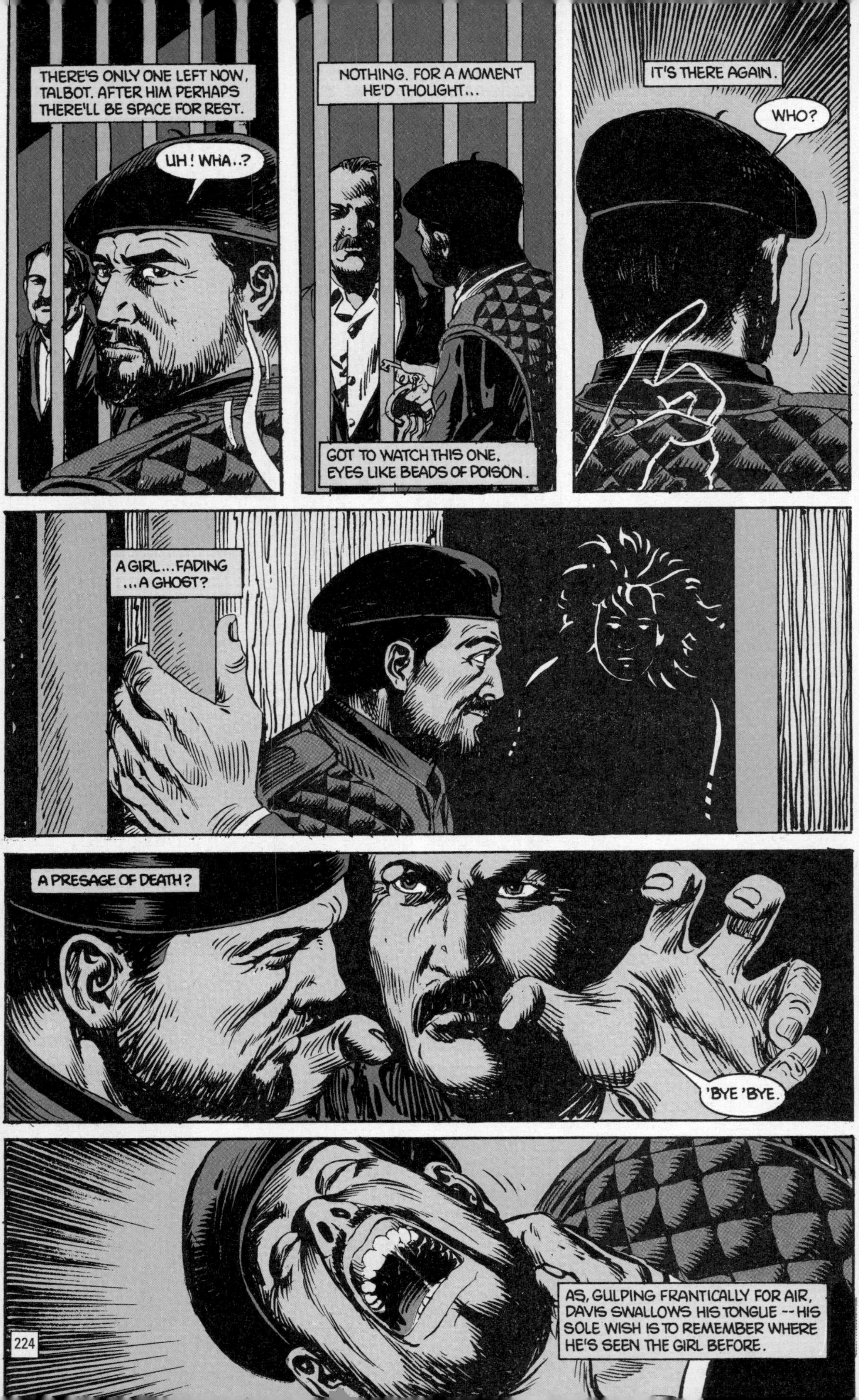

THERE'S ONLY ONE LEFT NOW, TALBOT. AFTER HIM PERHAPS THERE'LL BE SPACE FOR REST.
UH! WHA..?
NOTHING. FOR A MOMENT HE'D THOUGHT...
GOT TO WATCH THIS ONE. EYES LIKE BEADS OF POISON.
IT'S THERE AGAIN.
WHO?
A GIRL...FADING ...A GHOST?
A PRESAGE OF DEATH?
'BYE 'BYE.
AS, GULPING FRANTICALLY FOR AIR, DAVIS SWALLOWS HIS TONGUE -- HIS SOLE WISH IS TO REMEMBER WHERE HE'S SEEN THE GIRL BEFORE.

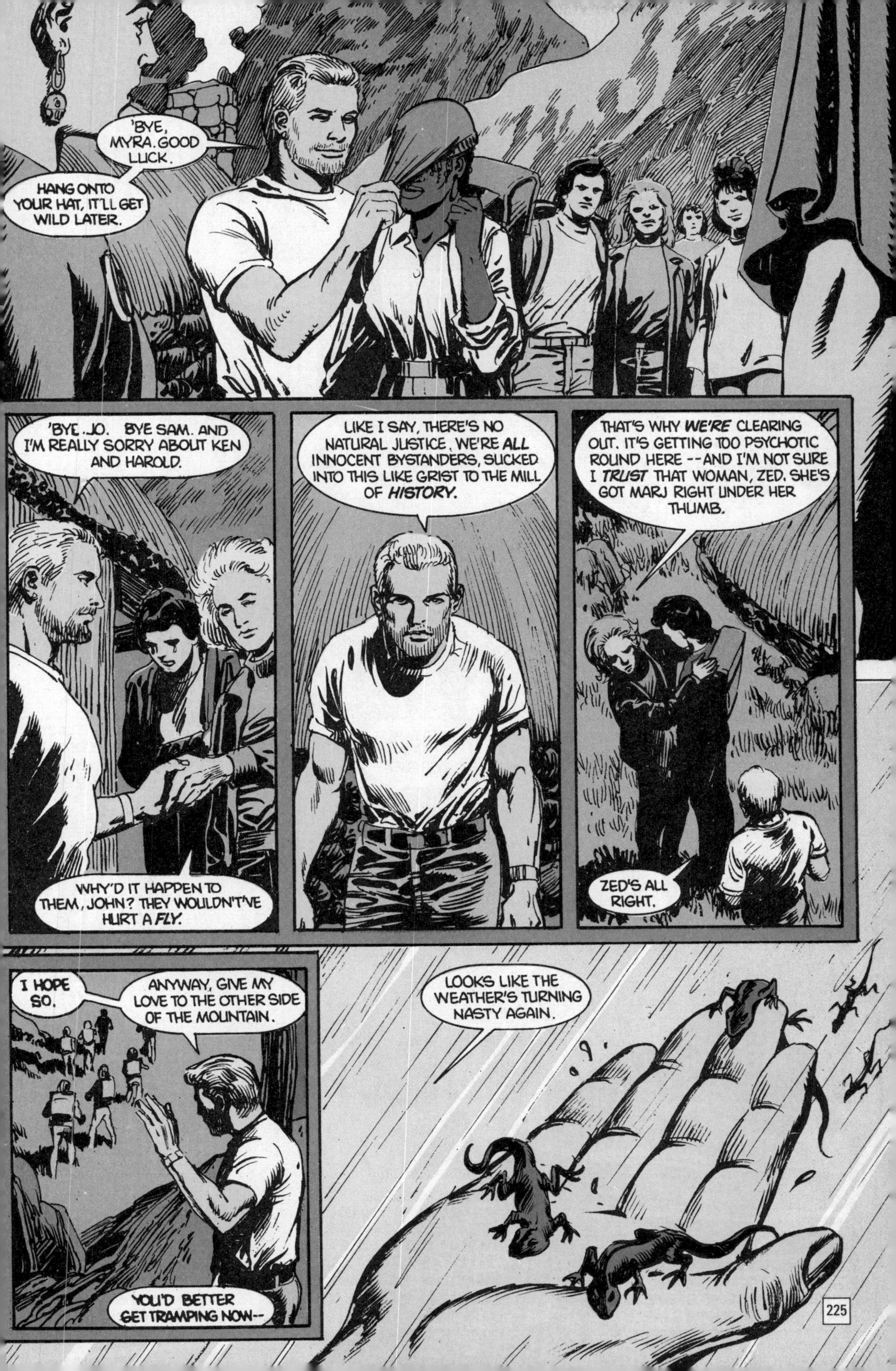
'BYE, MYRA. GOOD LUCK.
HANG ONTO YOUR HAT, IT'LL GET WILD LATER.
'BYE..JO. BYE SAM. AND I'M REALLY SORRY ABOUT KEN AND HAROLD.
WHY'D IT HAPPEN TO THEM, JOHN? THEY WOULDN'T'VE HURT A FLY.
LIKE I SAY, THERE'S NO NATURAL JUSTICE, WE'RE ALL INNOCENT BYSTANDERS, SUCKED INTO THIS LIKE GRIST TO THE MILL OF HISTORY.
THAT'S WHY WE'RE CLEARING OUT. IT'S GETTING TOO PSYCHOTIC ROUND HERE --AND I'M NOT SURE I TRUST THAT WOMAN, ZED. SHE'S GOT MARJ RIGHT UNDER HER THUMB.
ZED'S ALL RIGHT.
I HOPE SO.
ANYWAY, GIVE MY LOVE TO THE OTHER SIDE OF THE MOUNTAIN.
YOU'D BETTER GET TRAMPING NOW--
LOOKS LIKE THE WEATHER'S TURNING NASTY AGAIN.

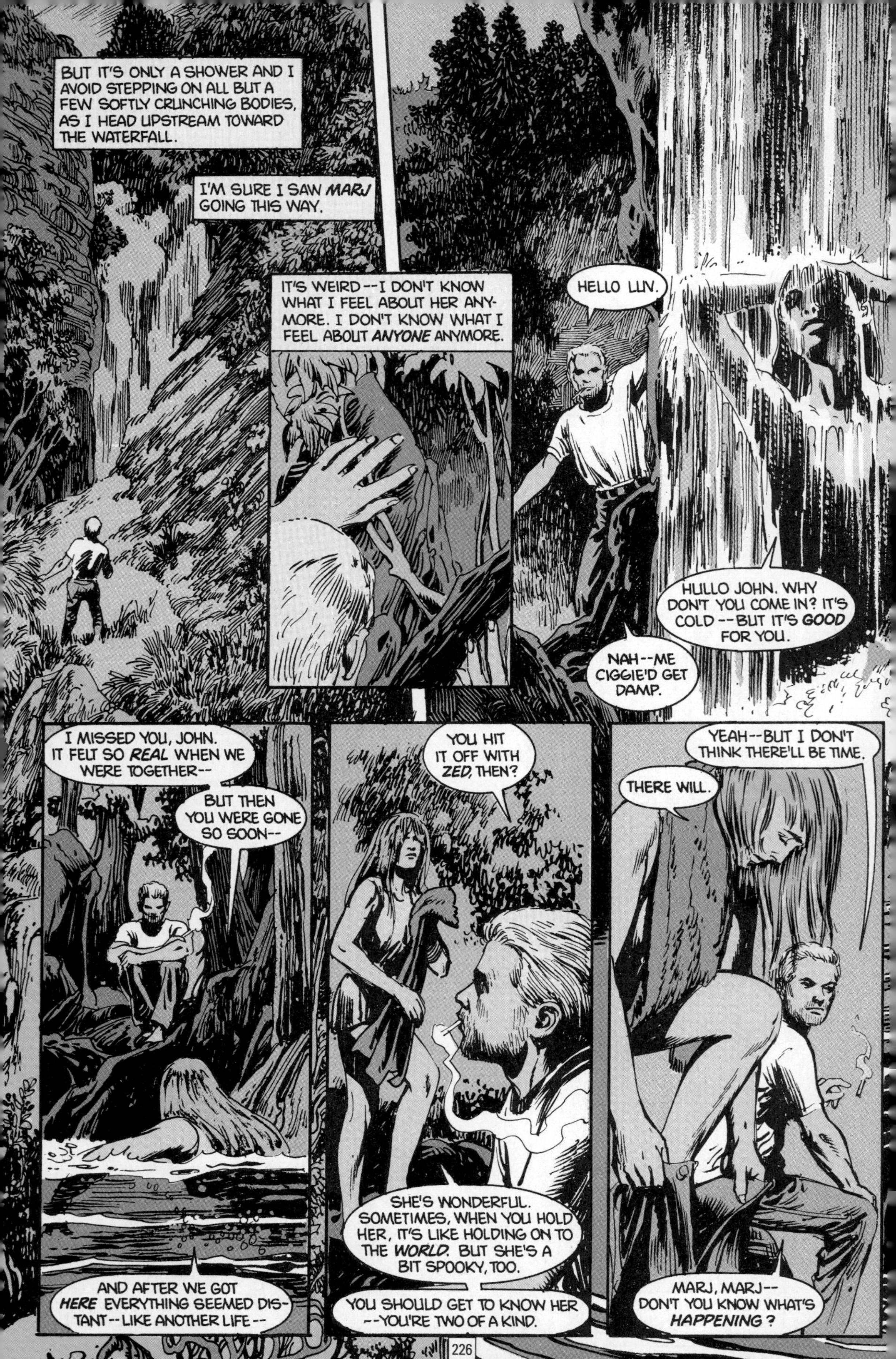
BUT IT'S ONLY A SHOWER AND I AVOID STEPPING ON ALL BUT A FEW SOFTLY CRUNCHING BODIES, AS I HEAD UPSTREAM TOWARD THE WATERFALL.
I'M SURE I SAW MARJ GOING THIS WAY.
IT'S WEIRD--I DON'T KNOW WHAT I FEEL ABOUT HER ANY-MORE. I DON'T KNOW WHAT I FEEL ABOUT ANYONE ANYMORE.
HELLO LUV.
HULLO JOHN. WHY DON'T YOU COME IN? IT'S COLD--BUT IT'S GOOD FOR YOU.
NAH--ME CIGGIE'D GET DAMP.
I MISSED YOU, JOHN. IT FELT SO REAL WHEN WE WERE TOGETHER--
BUT THEN YOU WERE GONE SO SOON--
AND AFTER WE GOT HERE EVERYTHING SEEMED DIS-TANT--LIKE ANOTHER LIFE--
YOU HIT IT OFF WITH ZED, THEN?
SHE'S WONDERFUL. SOMETIMES, WHEN YOU HOLD HER, IT'S LIKE HOLDING ON TO THE WORLD. BUT SHE'S A BIT SPOOKY, TOO.
YOU SHOULD GET TO KNOW HER--YOU'RE TWO OF A KIND.
YEAH--BUT I DON'T THINK THERE'LL BE TIME.
THERE WILL.
MARJ, MARJ--DON'T YOU KNOW WHAT'S HAPPENING?

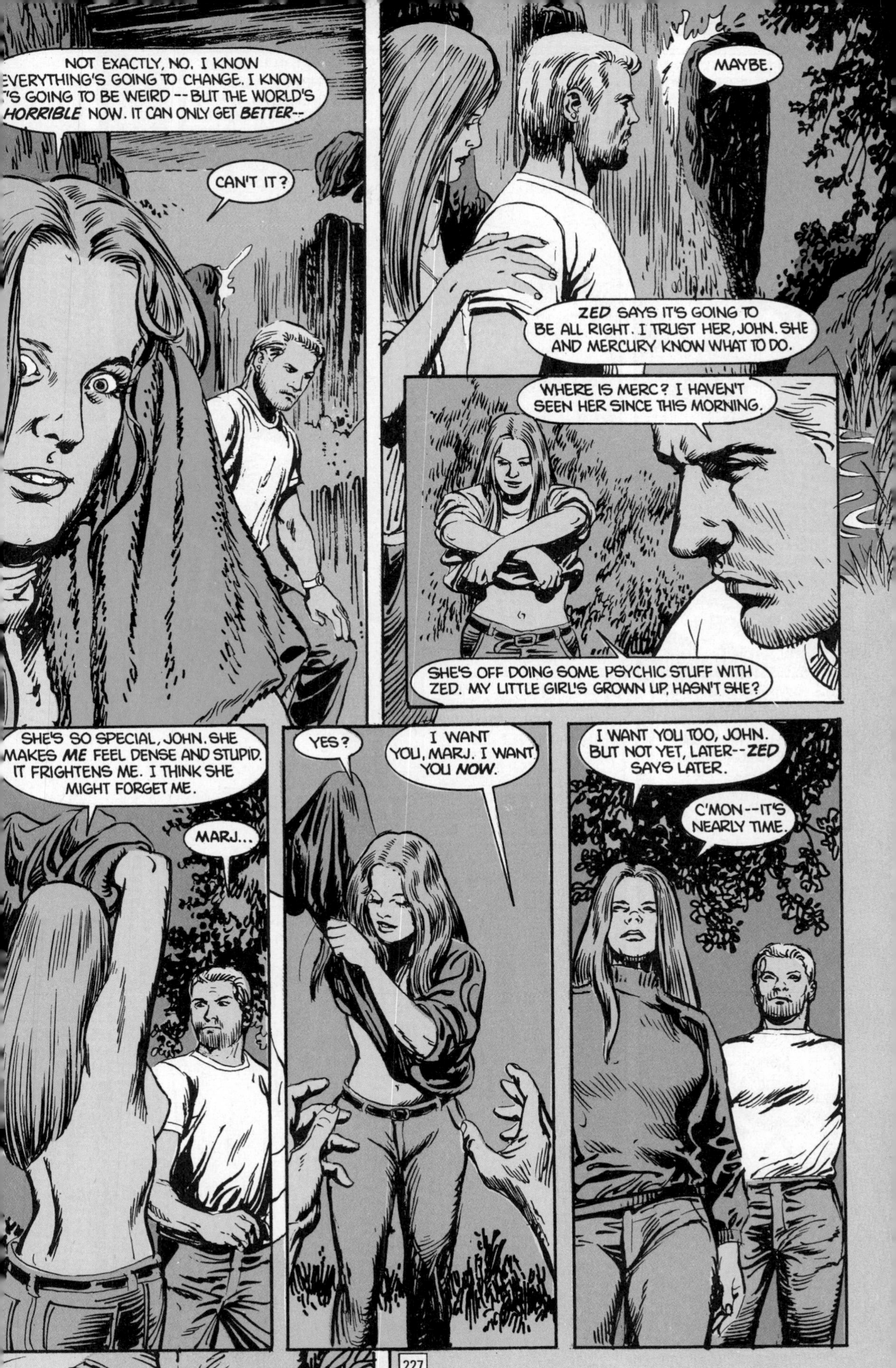

NOT EXACTLY, NO. I KNOW EVERYTHING'S GOING TO CHANGE. I KNOW IT'S GOING TO BE WEIRD -- BUT THE WORLD'S HORRIBLE NOW. IT CAN ONLY GET BETTER--
CAN'T IT?
MAYBE.
ZED SAYS IT'S GOING TO BE ALL RIGHT. I TRUST HER, JOHN. SHE AND MERCURY KNOW WHAT TO DO.
WHERE IS MERC? I HAVEN'T SEEN HER SINCE THIS MORNING.
SHE'S OFF DOING SOME PSYCHIC STUFF WITH ZED. MY LITTLE GIRL'S GROWN UP, HASN'T SHE?
SHE'S SO SPECIAL, JOHN. SHE MAKES ME FEEL DENSE AND STUPID. IT FRIGHTENS ME. I THINK SHE MIGHT FORGET ME.
MARJ...
YES?
I WANT YOU, MARJ. I WANT YOU NOW.
I WANT YOU TOO, JOHN. BUT NOT YET, LATER--ZED SAYS LATER.
C'MON--IT'S NEARLY TIME.

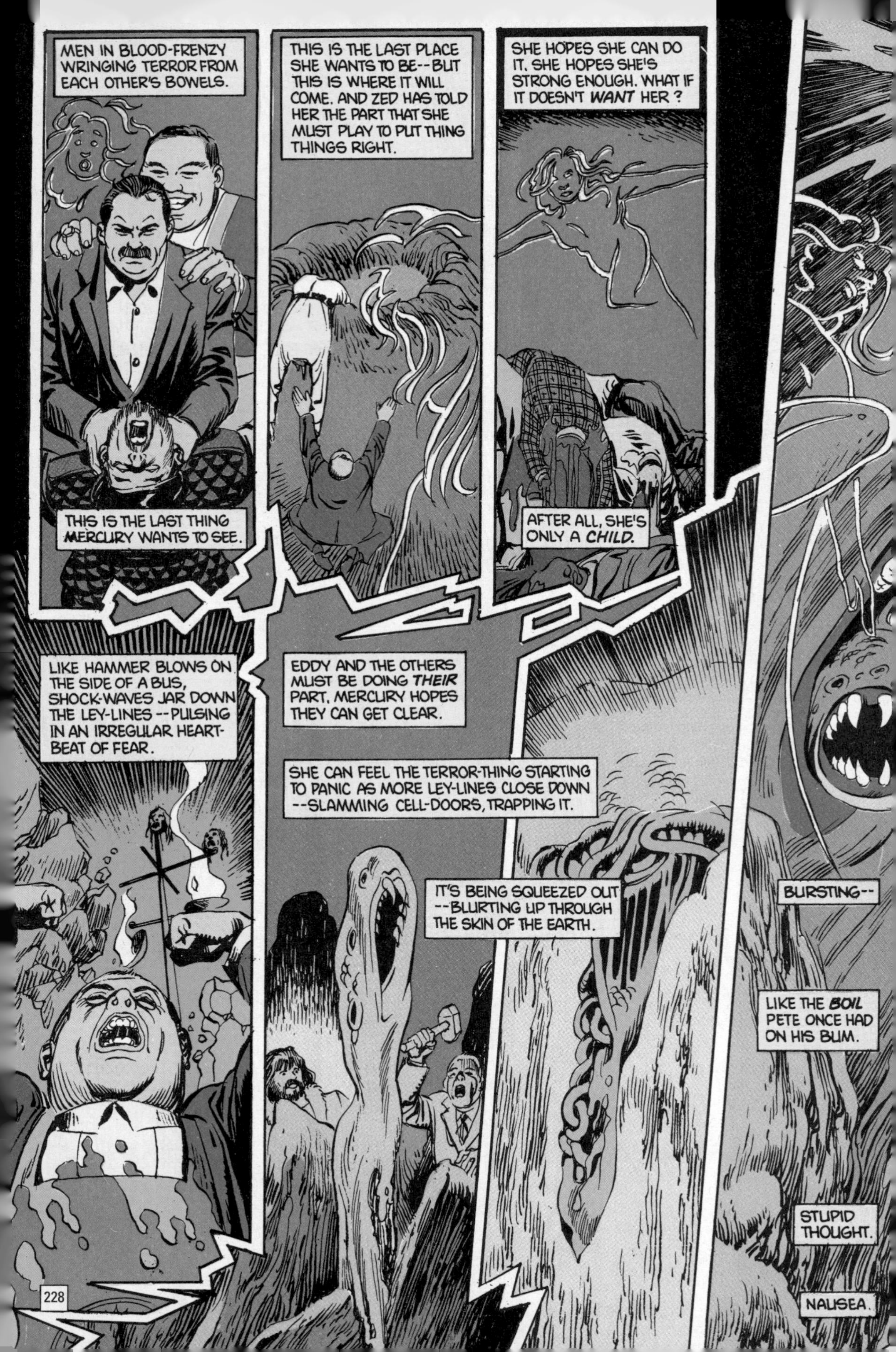
MEN IN BLOOD-FRENZY WRINGING TERROR FROM EACH OTHER'S BOWELS.
THIS IS THE LAST THING MERCURY WANTS TO SEE.
THIS IS THE LAST PLACE SHE WANTS TO BE-- BUT THIS IS WHERE IT WILL COME. AND ZED HAS TOLD HER THE PART THAT SHE MUST PLAY TO PUT THING THINGS RIGHT.
SHE HOPES SHE CAN DO IT. SHE HOPES SHE'S STRONG ENOUGH. WHAT IF IT DOESN'T WANT HER ?
AFTER ALL, SHE'S ONLY A CHILD.
LIKE HAMMER BLOWS ON THE SIDE OF A BUS, SHOCK-WAVES JAR DOWN THE LEY-LINES --PULSING IN AN IRREGULAR HEART-BEAT OF FEAR.
EDDY AND THE OTHERS MUST BE DOING THEIR PART. MERCURY HOPES THEY CAN GET CLEAR.
SHE CAN FEEL THE TERROR-THING STARTING TO PANIC AS MORE LEY-LINES CLOSE DOWN --SLAMMING CELL-DOORS, TRAPPING IT.
IT'S BEING SQUEEZED OUT --BLURTING UP THROUGH THE SKIN OF THE EARTH.
BURSTING--
LIKE THE BOIL PETE ONCE HAD ON HIS BUM.
STUPID THOUGHT.
NAUSEA.

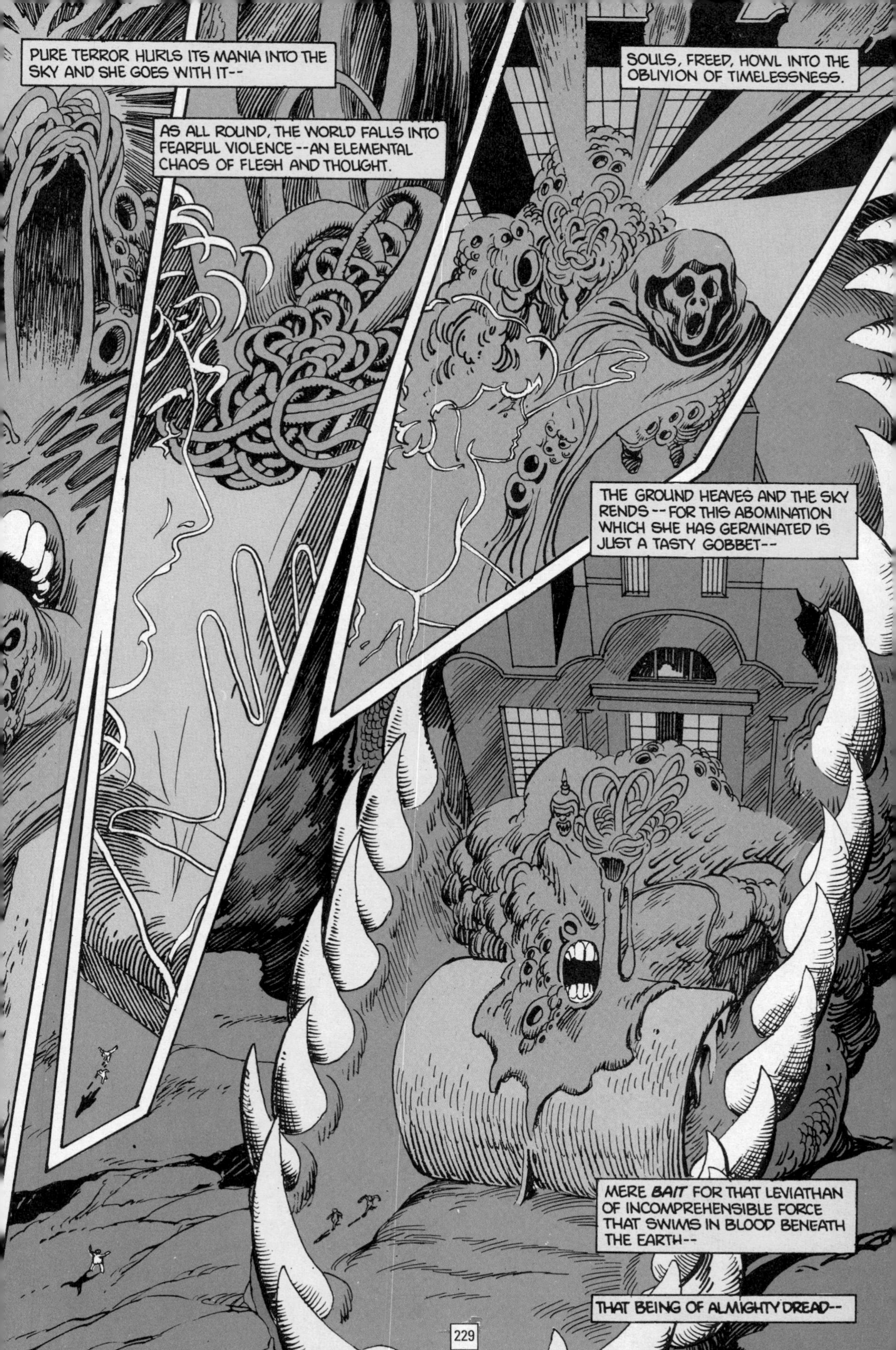
PURE TERROR HURLS ITS MANIA INTO THE SKY AND SHE GOES WITH IT--
AS ALL ROUND, THE WORLD FALLS INTO FEARFUL VIOLENCE--AN ELEMENTAL CHAOS OF FLESH AND THOUGHT.
SOULS, FREED, HOWL INTO THE OBLIVION OF TIMELESSNESS.
THE GROUND HEAVES AND THE SKY RENDS--FOR THIS ABOMINATION WHICH SHE HAS GERMINATED IS JUST A TASTY GOBBET--
MERE *BAIT* FOR THAT LEVIATHAN OF INCOMPREHENSIBLE FORCE THAT SWIMS IN BLOOD BENEATH THE EARTH--
THAT BEING OF ALMIGHTY DREAD--

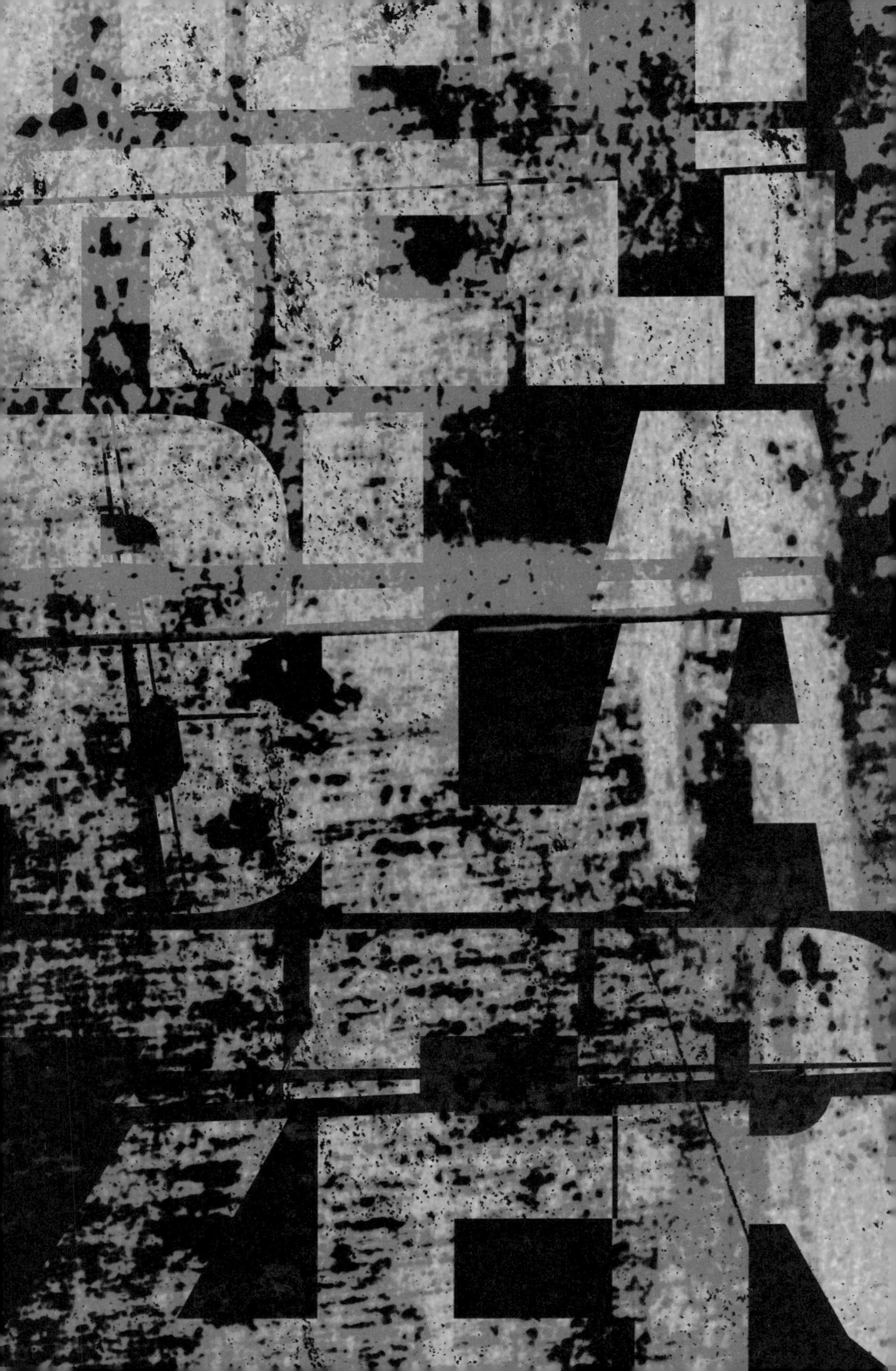

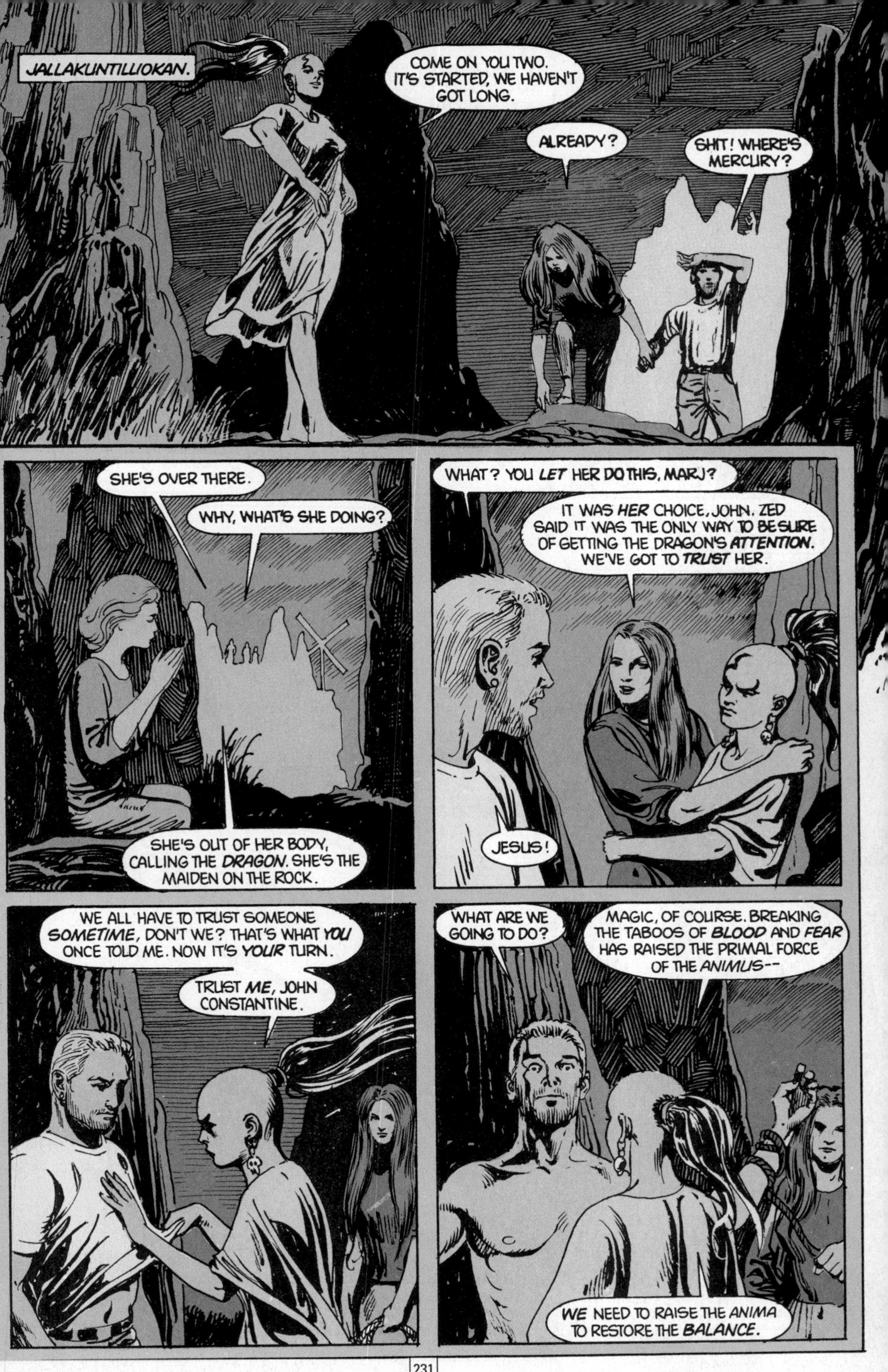
JALLAKUNTILLIOKAN.
COME ON YOU TWO. IT'S STARTED, WE HAVEN'T GOT LONG.
ALREADY?
SHIT! WHERE'S MERCURY?
SHE'S OVER THERE.
WHY, WHAT'S SHE DOING?
SHE'S OUT OF HER BODY, CALLING THE *DRAGON*. SHE'S THE MAIDEN ON THE ROCK.
WHAT? YOU *LET* HER DO THIS, MARJ?
IT WAS *HER* CHOICE, JOHN. ZED SAID IT WAS THE ONLY WAY TO BE SURE OF GETTING THE DRAGON'S *ATTENTION*. WE'VE GOT TO *TRUST* HER.
JESUS!
WE ALL HAVE TO TRUST SOMEONE *SOMETIME*, DON'T WE? THAT'S WHAT *YOU* ONCE TOLD ME. NOW IT'S *YOUR* TURN.
TRUST *ME*, JOHN CONSTANTINE.
WHAT ARE WE GOING TO DO?
MAGIC, OF COURSE. BREAKING THE TABOOS OF *BLOOD* AND *FEAR* HAS RAISED THE PRIMAL FORCE OF THE *ANIMUS*--
WE NEED TO RAISE THE *ANIMA* TO RESTORE THE *BALANCE*.

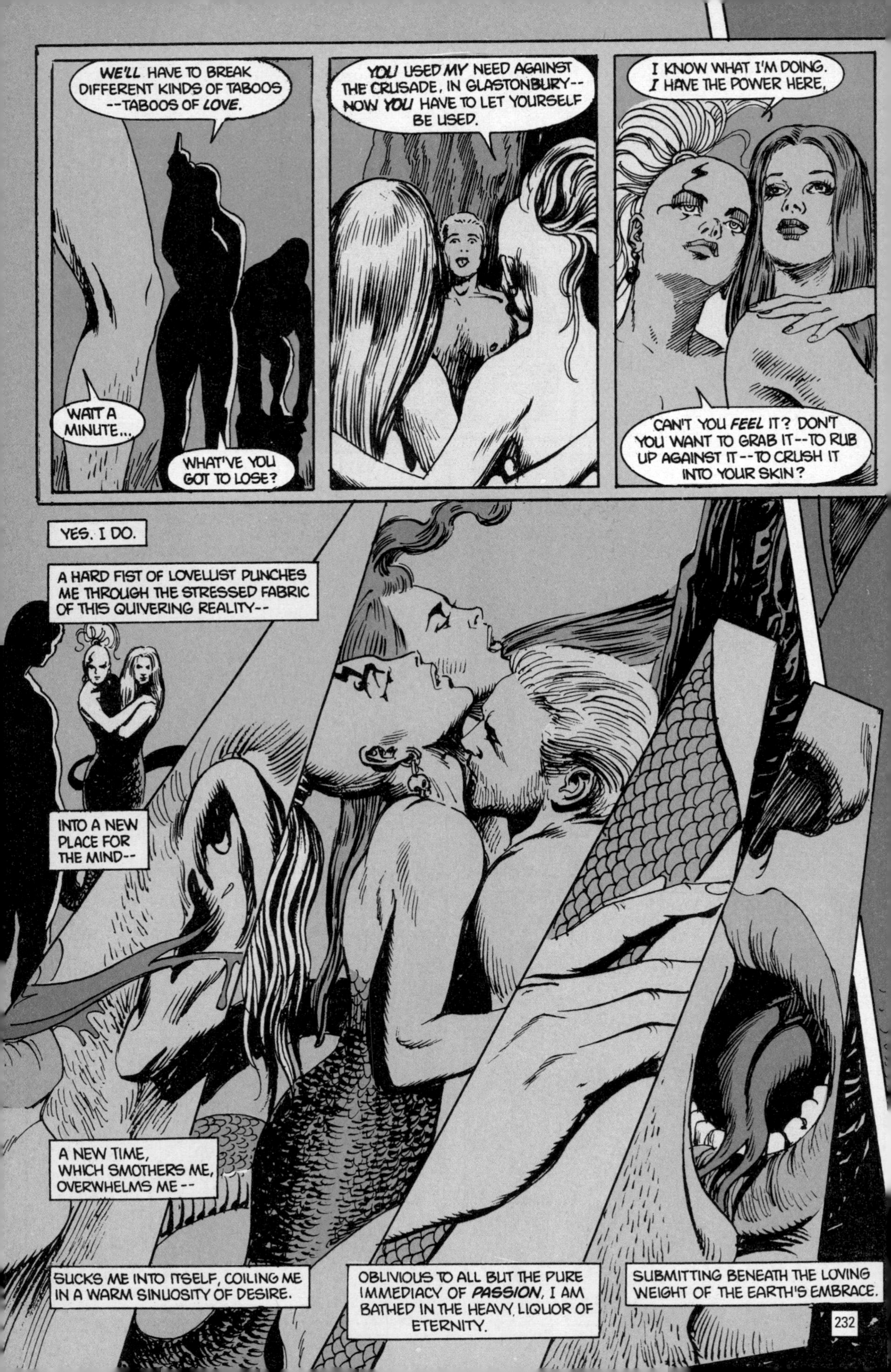
WE'LL HAVE TO BREAK DIFFERENT KINDS OF TABOOS --TABOOS OF LOVE.
WAIT A MINUTE...
WHAT'VE YOU GOT TO LOSE?
YOU USED MY NEED AGAINST THE CRUSADE, IN GLASTONBURY-- NOW YOU HAVE TO LET YOURSELF BE USED.
I KNOW WHAT I'M DOING. I HAVE THE POWER HERE,
CAN'T YOU FEEL IT? DON'T YOU WANT TO GRAB IT--TO RUB UP AGAINST IT--TO CRUSH IT INTO YOUR SKIN?
YES. I DO.
A HARD FIST OF LOVELUST PUNCHES ME THROUGH THE STRESSED FABRIC OF THIS QUIVERING REALITY--
INTO A NEW PLACE FOR THE MIND--
A NEW TIME, WHICH SMOTHERS ME, OVERWHELMS ME--
SUCKS ME INTO ITSELF, COILING ME IN A WARM SINUOSITY OF DESIRE.
OBLIVIOUS TO ALL BUT THE PURE IMMEDIACY OF PASSION, I AM BATHED IN THE HEAVY, LIQUOR OF ETERNITY.
SUBMITTING BENEATH THE LOVING WEIGHT OF THE EARTH'S EMBRACE.

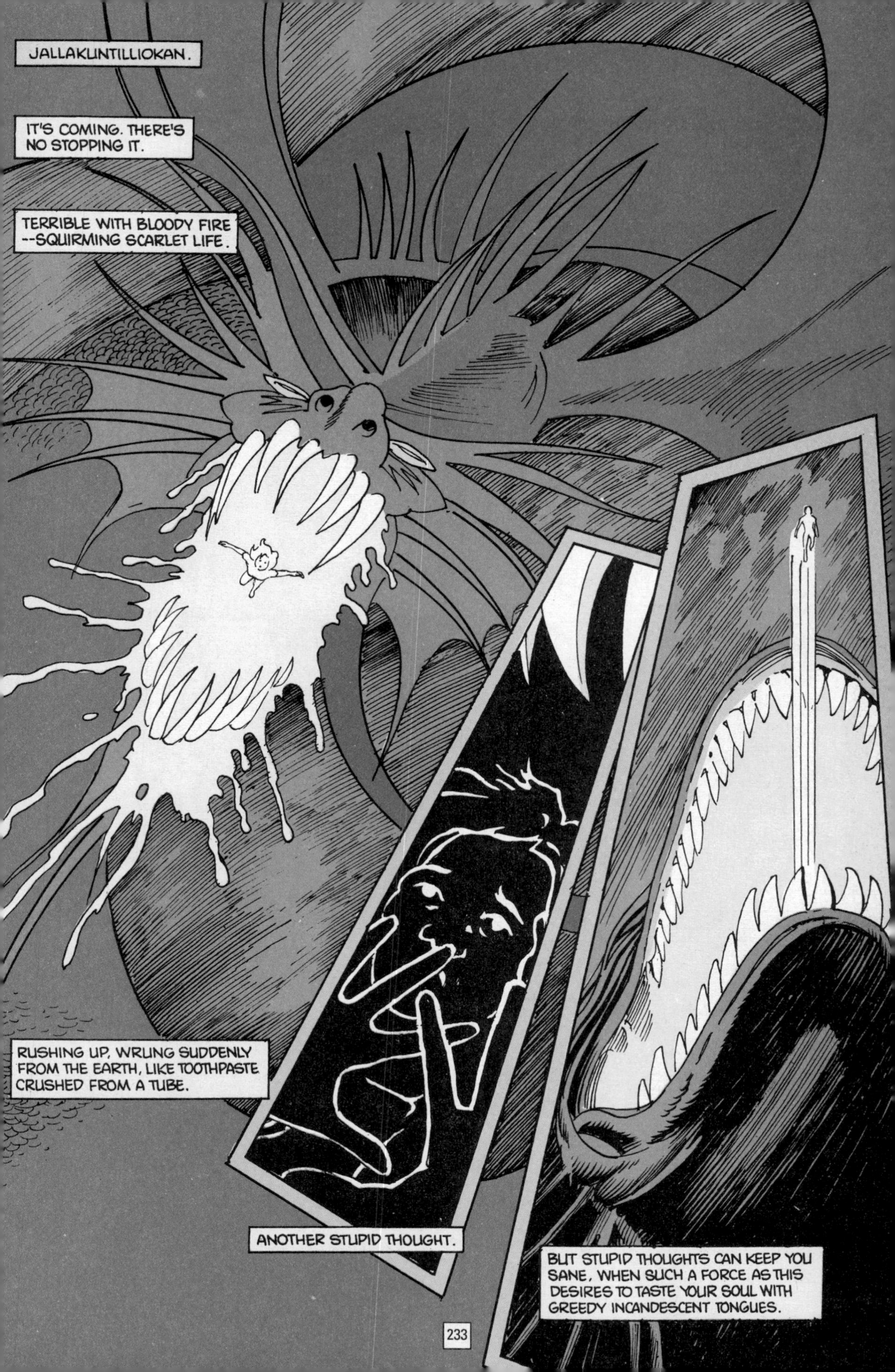
JALLAKUNTILLIOKAN.
IT'S COMING. THERE'S NO STOPPING IT.
TERRIBLE WITH BLOODY FIRE --SQUIRMING SCARLET LIFE.
RUSHING UP, WRUNG SUDDENLY FROM THE EARTH, LIKE TOOTHPASTE CRUSHED FROM A TUBE.
ANOTHER STUPID THOUGHT.
BUT STUPID THOUGHTS CAN KEEP YOU SANE, WHEN SUCH A FORCE AS THIS DESIRES TO TASTE YOUR SOUL WITH GREEDY INCANDESCENT TONGUES.

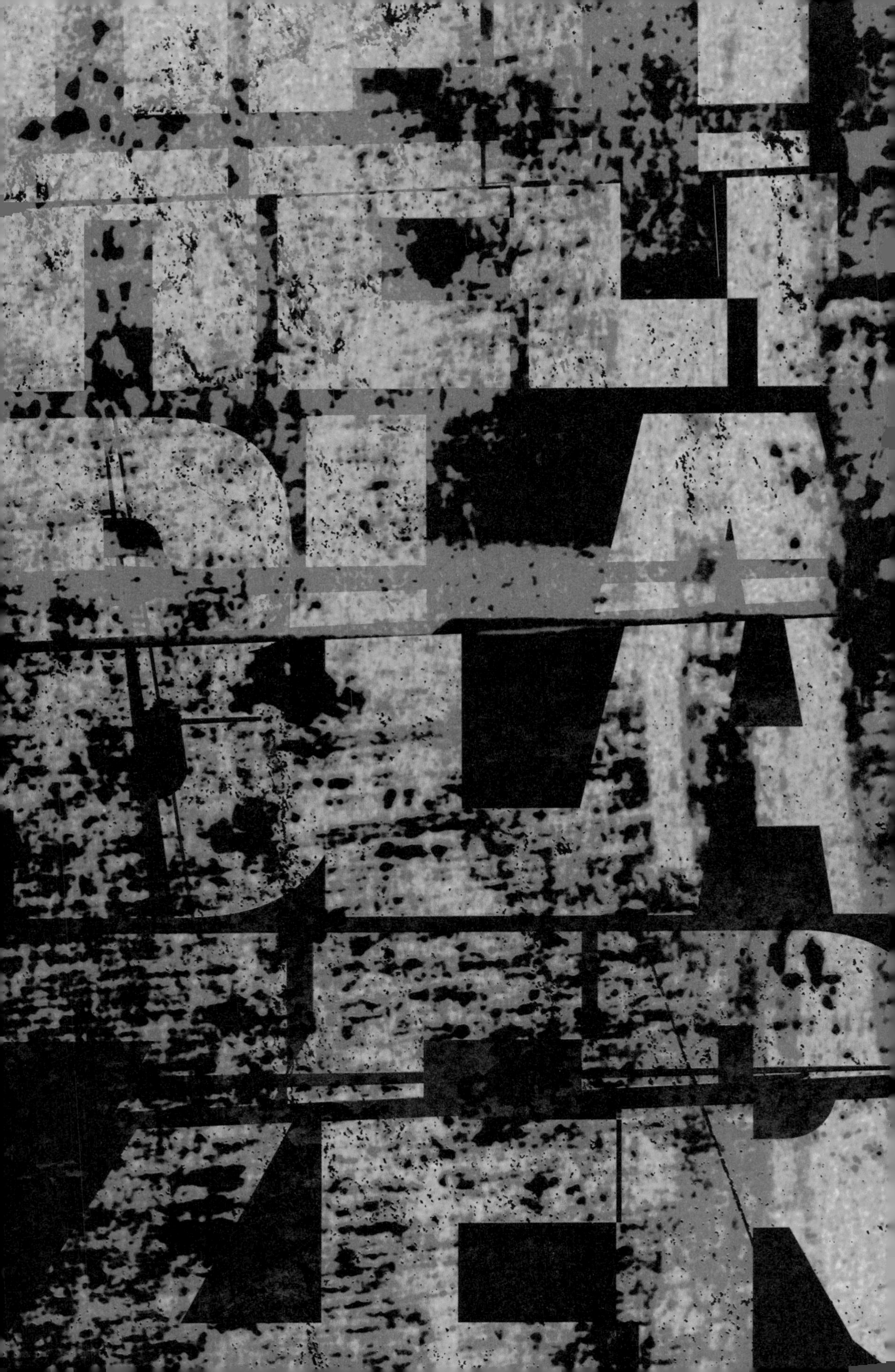

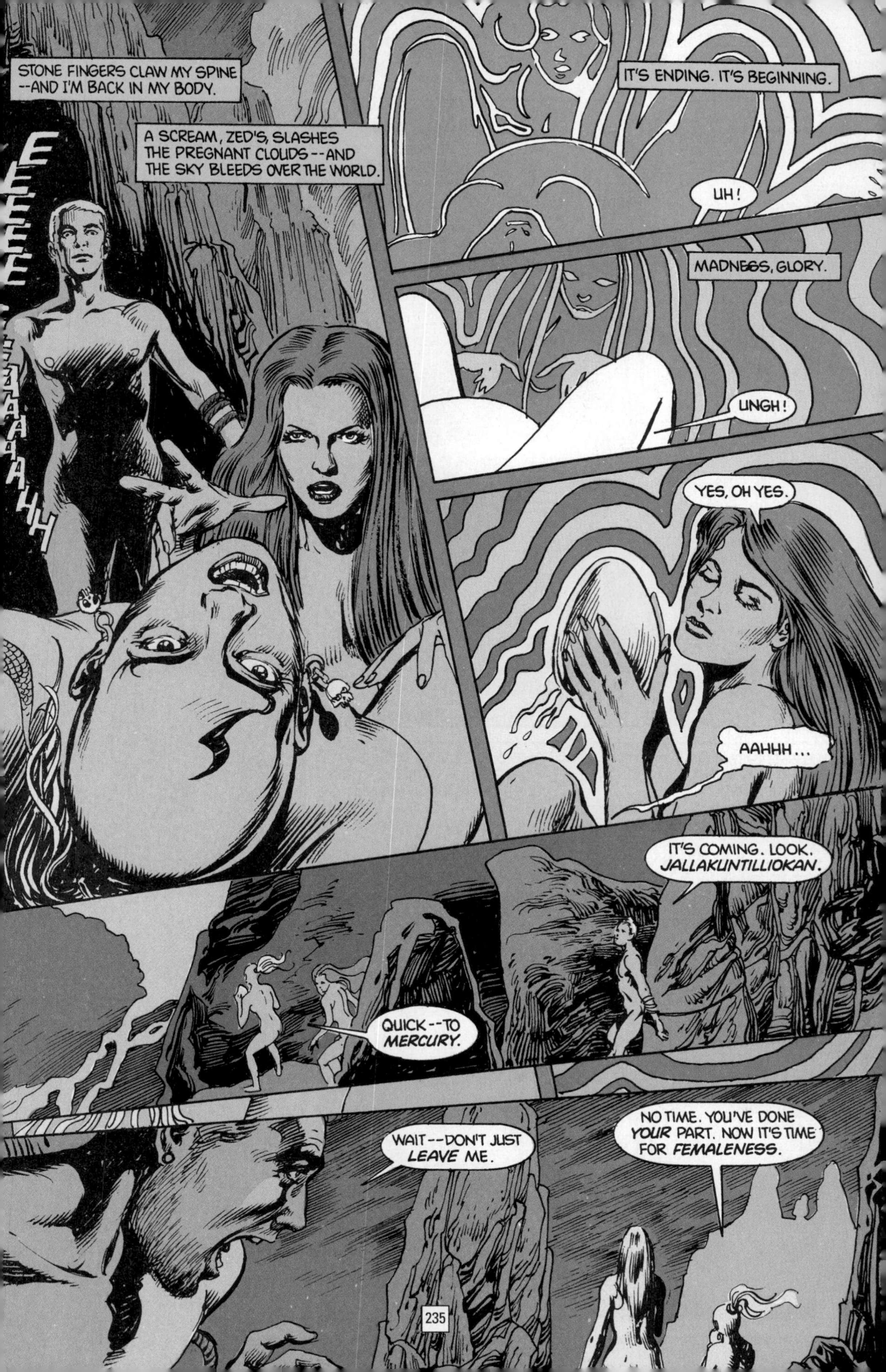
STONE FINGERS CLAW MY SPINE --AND I'M BACK IN MY BODY.
A SCREAM, ZED'S, SLASHES THE PREGNANT CLOUDS--AND THE SKY BLEEDS OVER THE WORLD.
IT'S ENDING. IT'S BEGINNING.
UH!
MADNESS, GLORY.
UNGH!
YES, OH YES.
AAHHH...
IT'S COMING. LOOK. JALLAKUNTILLIOKAN.
QUICK--TO MERCURY.
WAIT--DON'T JUST LEAVE ME.
NO TIME. YOU'VE DONE YOUR PART. NOW IT'S TIME FOR FEMALENESS.

BUT I DON'T WANT TO BE ALONE IN THE FACE OF *THIS*.

WAIT!

PLEASE WAIT. JUST ONE MORE MOMENT -- I'M NEARLY THERE.

DON'T START WITHOUT--

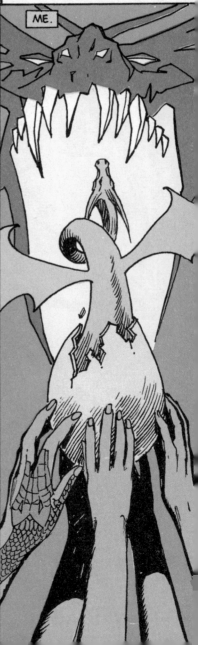

ME.

THE EGG, THEY MUSN'T DROP THE EGG. IT'S MY EGG TOO AND I WANT TO SEE IT HATCH.

BLOOD SUCKS THE ROCK. THE WORLD TURNS WITH THE FLOOD TIDES OF MEETING PAST AND FUTURE.

SHE'S DONE IT. SHE'S WORKED A *REAL* MAGIC.

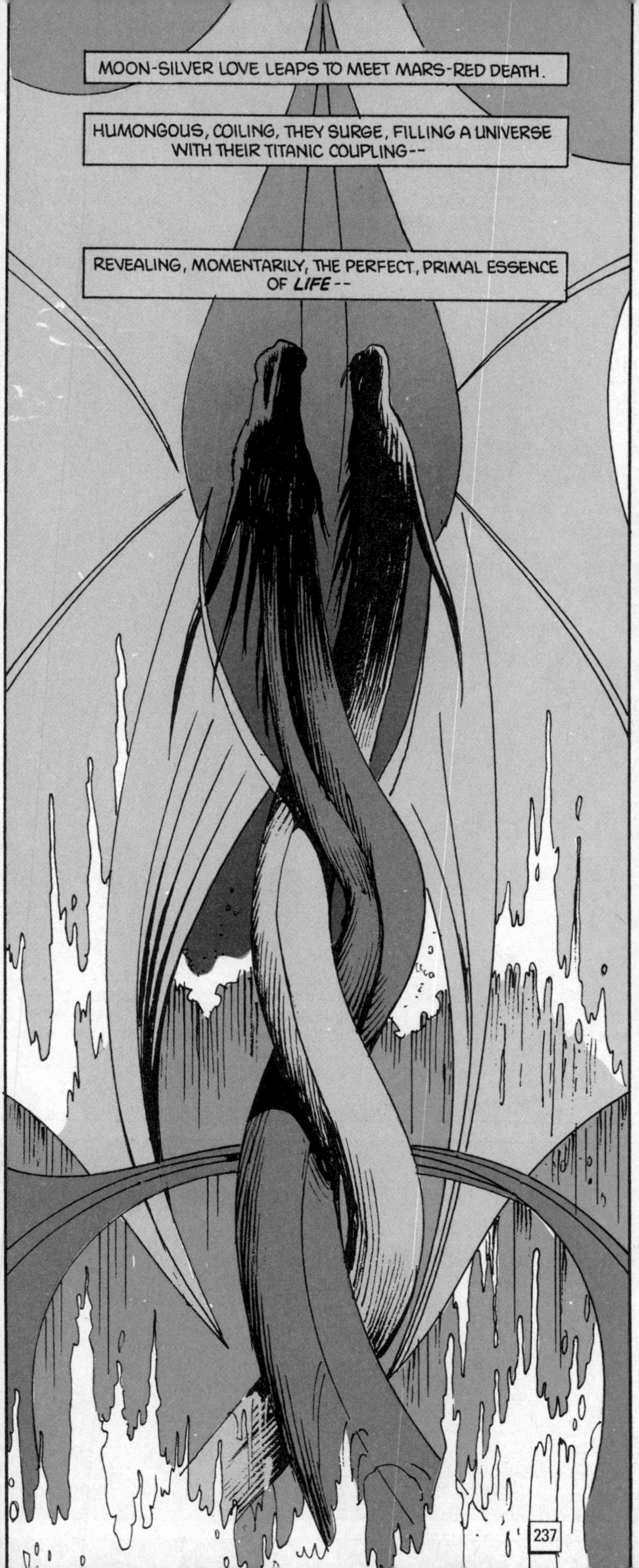

MOON-SILVER LOVE LEAPS TO MEET MARS-RED DEATH.
HUMONGOUS, COILING, THEY SURGE, FILLING A UNIVERSE WITH THEIR TITANIC COUPLING--
REVEALING, MOMENTARILY, THE PERFECT, PRIMAL ESSENCE OF *LIFE*--

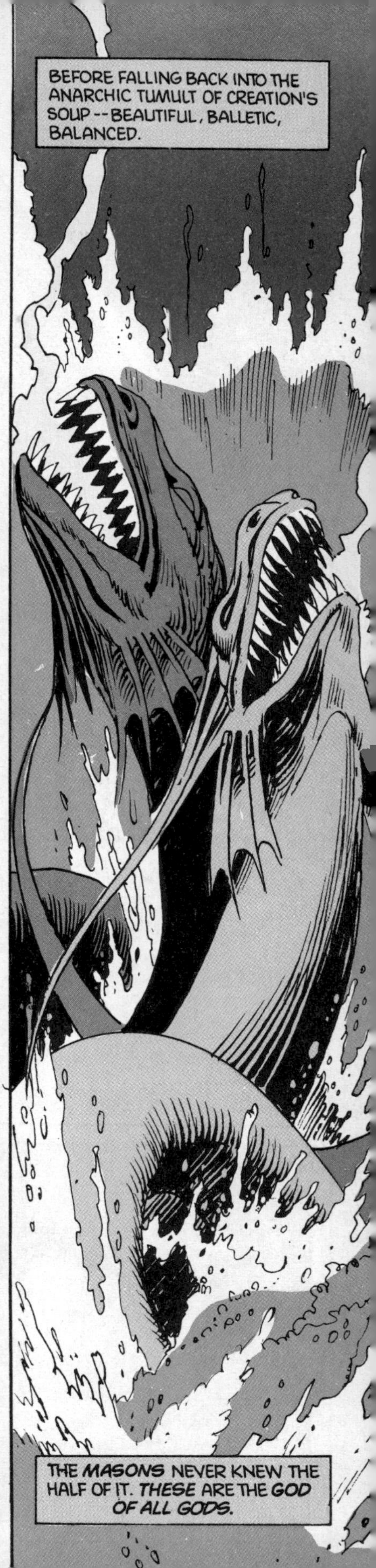

BEFORE FALLING BACK INTO THE ANARCHIC TUMULT OF CREATION'S SOUP--BEAUTIFUL, BALLETIC, BALANCED.
THE *MASONS* NEVER KNEW THE HALF OF IT. *THESE* ARE THE *GOD OF ALL GODS*.

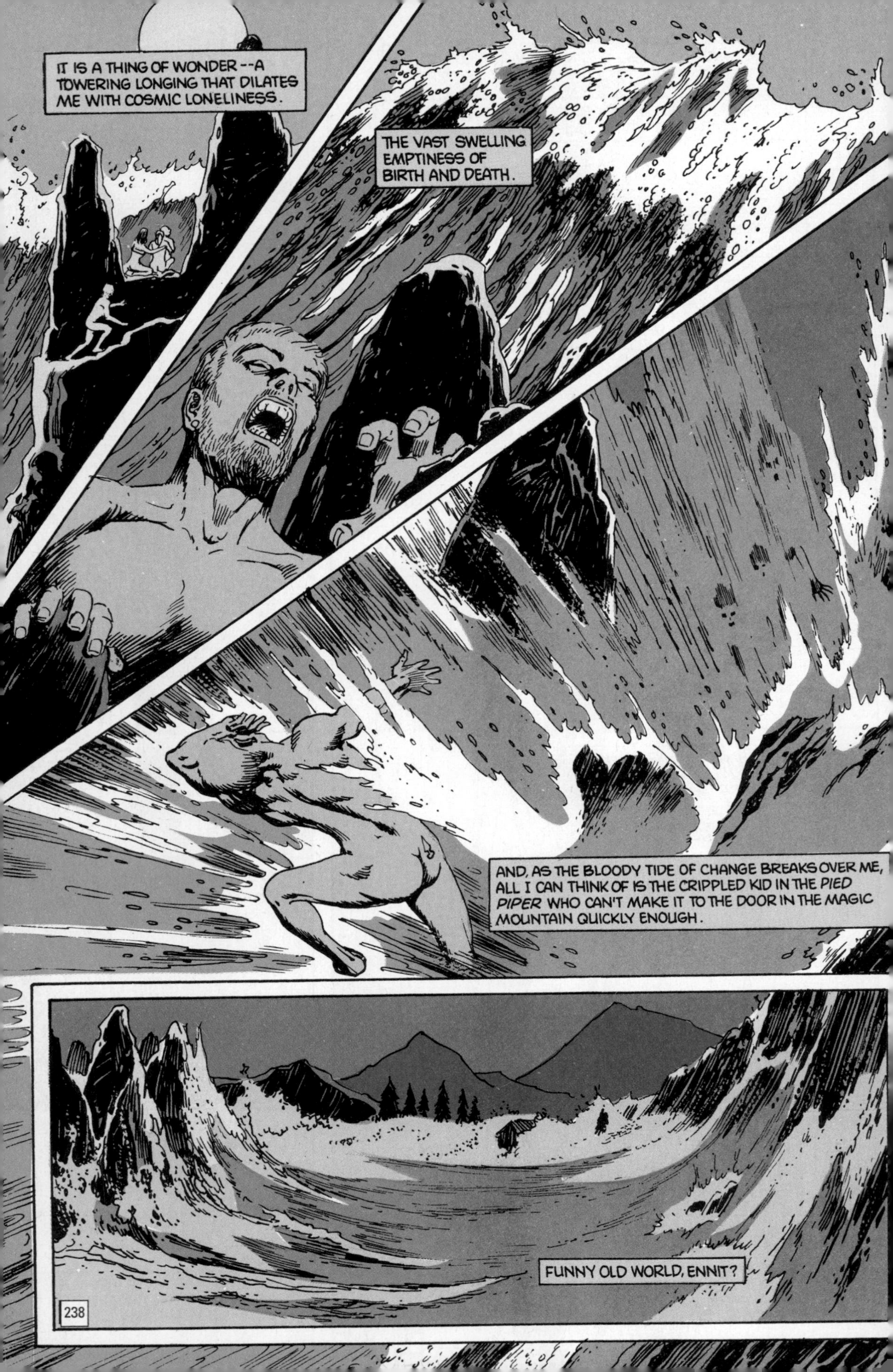
IT IS A THING OF WONDER--A TOWERING LONGING THAT DILATES ME WITH COSMIC LONELINESS.
THE VAST SWELLING EMPTINESS OF BIRTH AND DEATH.
AND, AS THE BLOODY TIDE OF CHANGE BREAKS OVER ME, ALL I CAN THINK OF IS THE CRIPPLED KID IN THE PIED PIPER WHO CAN'T MAKE IT TO THE DOOR IN THE MAGIC MOUNTAIN QUICKLY ENOUGH.
FUNNY OLD WORLD, ENNIT?

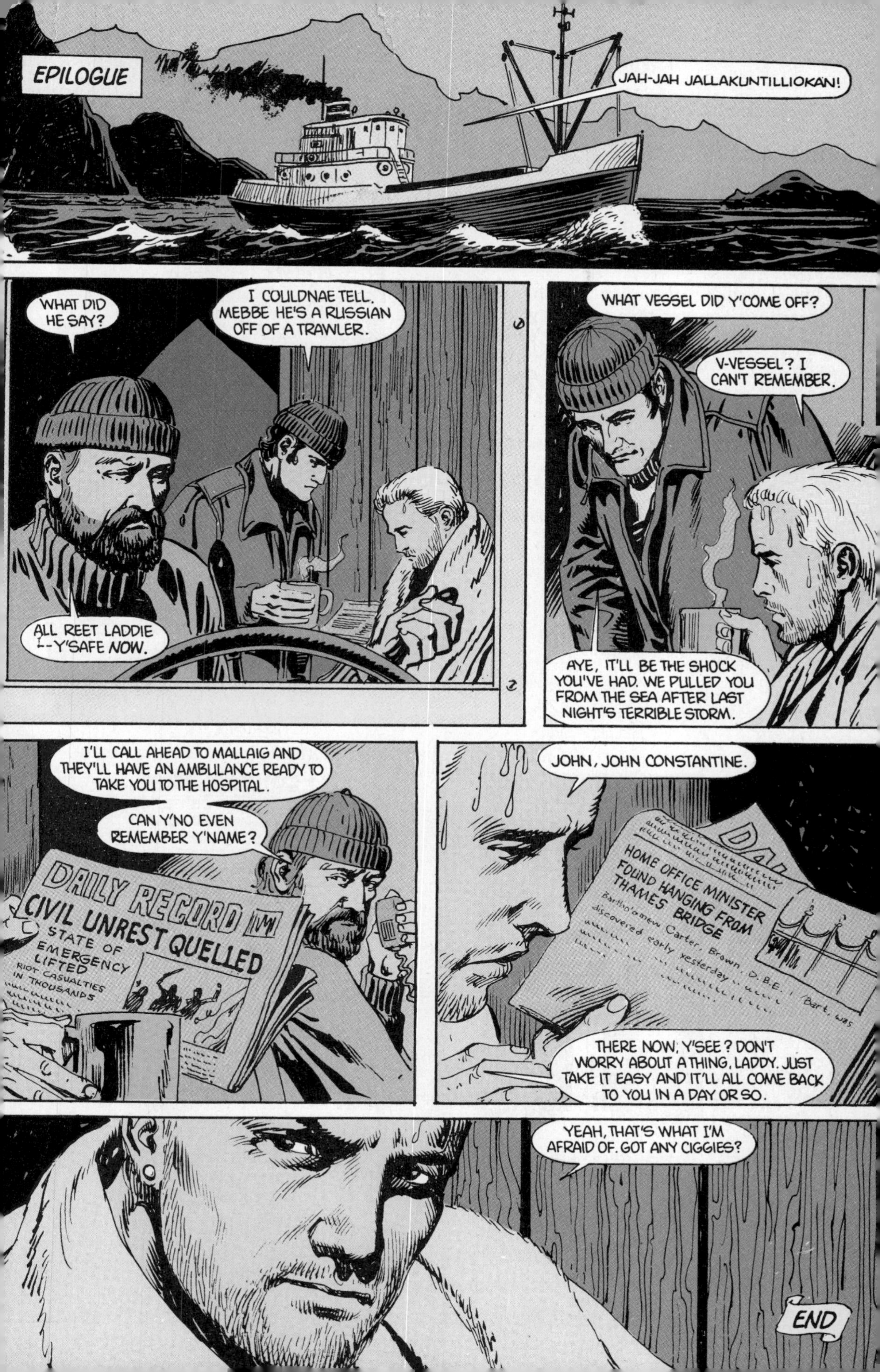
EPILOGUE
JAH-JAH JALLAKUNTILLIOKAN!
WHAT DID HE SAY?
I COULDNAE TELL. MEBBE HE'S A RUSSIAN OFF OF A TRAWLER.
ALL REET LADDIE --Y'SAFE NOW.
WHAT VESSEL DID Y'COME OFF?
V-VESSEL? I CAN'T REMEMBER.
AYE, IT'LL BE THE SHOCK YOU'VE HAD. WE PULLED YOU FROM THE SEA AFTER LAST NIGHT'S TERRIBLE STORM.
I'LL CALL AHEAD TO MALLAIG AND THEY'LL HAVE AN AMBULANCE READY TO TAKE YOU TO THE HOSPITAL.
CAN Y'NO EVEN REMEMBER Y'NAME?
DAILY RECORD
CIVIL UNREST QUELLED
STATE OF EMERGENCY LIFTED
RIOT CASUALTIES IN THOUSANDS
JOHN, JOHN CONSTANTINE.
HOME OFFICE MINISTER FOUND HANGING FROM THAMES BRIDGE
Bartholomew Carter, Brown, D.B.E., /Bart, was discovered early yesterday
THERE NOW; Y'SEE? DON'T WORRY ABOUT A THING, LADDY. JUST TAKE IT EASY AND IT'LL ALL COME BACK TO YOU IN A DAY OR SO.
YEAH, THAT'S WHAT I'M AFRAID OF. GOT ANY CIGGIES?
END

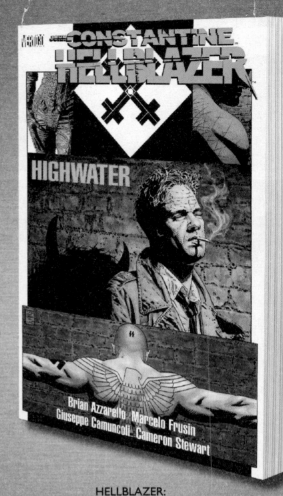